CONTROLLED DRUGS:
STATUTES AND CASES

CONTROLLED DRUGS: STATUTES AND CASES

Robert S. Shiels, M.A., LL.B., LL.M., Ph.D.
Solicitor in the Supreme Courts of Scotland

W. GREEN/Sweet & Maxwell
EDINBURGH
1997

First edition, 1991
Second edition, 1997

© 1997
ROBERT S. SHIELS

ISBN 0 414 01122 8

A CIP catalogue record of this book is available from the British Library

Typeset by Trinity Typesetting, Edinburgh
Printed and bound in Great Britain by Redwood Books, Trowbridge, Wiltshire

For Margaret

PREFACE TO SECOND EDITION

It is still hoped that the practising criminal lawyer will find this collection of case law to be of some assistance. The aggregate of case law reflects the universal application of the Misuse of Drugs Act 1971 throughout the United Kingdom. The same cannot be said of confiscation which is now dealt with by the Proceeds of Crime (Scotland) Act 1995. The complexity of the law of confiscation has been left for others to deal with.

Robert Shiels
Edinburgh
June 1997

PREFACE TO FIRST EDITION

The aim of this book is to provide the practising criminal lawyer with a convenient collection of important cases on controlled drugs. In addition, it is hoped that it will be of assistance to those coming to the subject for the first time.

It follows that this book does not contain any protracted jurisprudential or academic discussion of the many legal issues raised by the cases. Nor is there any attempt to propose what the law ought to be. Medical matters are barely mentioned. The Misuse of Drugs Act 1971 and the principal subordinate legislation are reproduced here along with extracts from other relevant statutes, in so far as they apply to Scotland.

Each of the existing textbooks on controlled drugs contributes something to the literature on the law of controlled drugs. The failure or major omission of them all, it is submitted, is not to consider all relevant cases on the substantive law and sentencing policy. Moreover, English lawyers frequently overlook Scottish case law on a statute common to all of the United Kingdom jurisdictions.

Ordinarily, this state of affairs would not be a matter to dwell on for long, but the Misuse of Drugs Act 1971 is one of the few criminal statutes to apply universally throughout the United Kingdom so that the decisions in one jurisdiction ought, at the very least, to be highly persuasive in the others. There are some Scottish decisions where a conclusion has been reached by a court without, apparently, regard to English decisions in point. In *Cording v. Halse* [1955] 1 Q.B. 63, dealing with road traffic legislation, Lord Goddard, L.C.J. said (at p. 70): "It is very desirable that with statutes of this nature [*viz.* the Road Traffic Act 1930] the same interpretation should be given on either side of the Border. It would be very unfortunate to have, on a similar set of facts, a conviction of England and no conviction in Scotland or vice versa. In this class of case dealing with this class of subject-matter this court always tries to follow the decisions of the Scottish courts if they can, and I think that Scottish courts always pay the same respect to decisions in this country so that one may get uniformity, which is certainly very desirable."

But what of sentencing? The English legal system has developed a detailed and wide-ranging set of principles for sentencing along with a tariff of actual sentences. Sentencing cases are said not to be binding (see *R. v. de Havilland* [1983] Crim.L.R. 490) although in practice this seems to mean a little less binding than the more strictly legal precedents.

The Scottish legal system does not have such a hierarchy of sentencing decisions and deliberately so. That is not to say that there are no rules at all, but only that the rules are broader and relate more to approach than to the actual sentence to be passed. In *Strawhorn v. McLeod*, 1987 S.C.C.R. 413, for example, a practice of allowing a discount on sentence for an early plea of guilty was expressly disapproved by the High Court of Justiciary sitting in its appellate capacity. Such a rule allowing a discount, it was said, necessarily disabled a sheriff from exercising his discretion fully and freely in a particular case.

There is no tariff in Scotland so that the table of sentences as set out in Richard Lord's book *Controlled Drugs: Law and Practice* (Appendix 5 at p. 208) is irrelevant here. In practice, such comparisons as that author attempts cannot succeed as every case is easily distinguishable from others on the basis of its own facts and circumstances, the varying local conditions and the accused's personal background. The English decisions are included in this work as a means of discerning general approaches rather than seeking binding precedents.

I am most grateful to Daniel Kelly, Advocate, who read and commented on a draft of this work, although I alone am responsible for the final work. Where I have expressed a view on any aspect of the law then it is a view that is entirely my own and is not to be taken as binding on any Government department or other body.

Robert Shiels,
Glasgow.
July 1991

CONTENTS

Contents   xiii

TABLE OF CASES

[Reference is to paragraph numbers only.]

XXX *Controlled Drugs*

TABLE OF STATUTES

TABLE OF ACKNOWLEDGMENTS

We reproduce with kind permission of Butterworth & Co. Publishers Ltd extracts from:

R. v. Ardalan [1972] 2 All E.R. 258
Byron v. Low [1972] 3 All E.R. 586
R. v. Neal [1984] 3 All E.R. 156
R. v. Taaffe [1984] 1 All E.R. 747
Garrett v. Arthur Churchill (Glass) Ltd [1969] 2 All E.R. 1141
D.P.P. v. Doot [1973] 1 All E.R. 940
Haggard v. Mason [1976] 1 All E.R. 337
R. v. Chatwood [1980] 1 All E.R. 467
Hambleton v. Callinan [1968] 2 All E.R. 943
R. v. Delgado [1984] 1 All E.R. 449
R. v. Fraser [1967] 3 All E.R. 544
R. v. Johnston [1989] 1 All E.R. 121
R. v. Tao [1976] 3 All E.R. 65
R. v. Vickers [1975] 2 All E.R. 945
R. v. Young [1984] 2 All E.R. 164
R. v. Ashton-Rickardt [1978] 1 All E.R. 173
R. v. Menocal [1979] 2 All E.R. 510
R. v. Cuthbertson [1980] 2 All E.R. 401
R. v. Greensmith [1983] 3 All E.R. 444
R. v. Watt [1984] 2 All E.R. 380
Rao v. Wyles [1949] 2 All E.R. 685

We reproduce with kind permission of the Incorporated Council of Law Reporting for England and Wales extracts from:

John Calder (Publications) Ltd v. Powell [1965] 1 Q.B. 509
R. v. Beard [1974] 1 W.L.R. 1549
R. v. Boyesen [1982] 2 W.L.R. 882
R. v. Hunt [1986] 3 W.L.R. 1115
R. v. Maginnis [1987] 2 W.L.R. 765
R. v. Martindale [1986] 1 W.L.R. 1042
R. v. Panayi and Karte [1989] 1 W.L.R. 187
R. v. Russell [1972] 1 W.L.R. 64
R. v. Shupuri [1986] 2 W.L.R. 988

We reproduce with kind permission of the Incorporated Council of Law Reporting for Ireland extracts from:

Morrison's Application [1991] N.I. 70
R. v. McCay [1991] N.I. 5

We reproduce with kind permission of Justice of the Peace Ltd extracts from:

R. v. McNamara (1988) 152 J.P. 390
R. v. Scott (1921) 86 J.P. 69

We reproduce with kind permission by the Law Society of Scotland extracts from:

Montes v. H.M. Advocate, 1990 S.C.C.R. 645
Howarth v. H.M. Advocate, 1992 S.C.C.R. 364
McCadden v. H.M. Advocate, 1986 S.C.C.R. 16
Kerr v. H.M. Advocate, 1986 S.C.C.R. 81
McDowall v. H.M. Advocate, 1991 S.C.C.R. 197
Rodden v. H.M. Advocate, 1994 S.C.C.R. 841
Carlin v. H.M. Advocate, 1994 S.C.C.R. 763
H.M. Advocate v. McPhee, 1994 S.C.C.R. 830
H.M. Advocate v. Lee, 1996 S.C.C.R. 205
Hughes v. Guild, 1990 S.C.C.R. 257
Davidson v. H.M. Advocate, 1990 S.C.C.R. 699
Campbell v. H.M. Advocate, 1992 S.C.C.R. 35
Sim v. H.M. Advocate, 1996 S.C.C.R. 77
Morrison v. Smith, 1983 S.C.C.R. 171
Donnelly v. H.M. Advocate, 1984 S.C.C.R. 419
McDowall v. H.M. Advocate, 1991 S.C.C.R. 197
Mattison v. H.M. Advocate, 1991 S.C.C.R. 211
Martin v. H.M. Advocate, 1992 S.C.C.R. 356
Lockhart v. Hardie, 1994 S.C.C.R. 722
Hoy v. McLeod, 1983 S.C.C.R. 149
Ramsay v. H.M. Advocate, 1984 S.C.C.R. 409
Donnelly v. H.M. Advocate, 1984 S.C.C.R. 93
Money v. H.M. Advocate, 1988 S.C.C.R. 127
Meighan v. Jessop, 1989 S.C.C.R. 208
Munro v. H.M. Advocate, 1994 S.C.C.R. 220
Grundison v. Brown, 1987 S.C.C.R. 186
McCleary v. Walkingshaw, 1996 S.C.C.R. 13
Cunningham v. H.M. Advocate, 1988 S.C.C.R. 514
Walker v. H.M. Advocate, 1987 S.C.C.R. 379
Mullady v. H.M. Advocate, 1988 S.C.C.R. 113
Varley v. H.M. Advocate, 1985 S.C.C.R. 55
Wright v. Houghton, 1987 S.C.C.R. 674
McQueen v. Hingston, 1992 S.C.C.R. 92
Lucas v. Lockhart, 1980 S.C.C.R. 256
Johns v. Hamilton, 1988 S.C.C.R. 282
Weir v. Jessop, 1991 S.C.C.R. 242
Cooper v. Buchanan, 1996 S.C.C.R. 448
H.M. Advocate v. Cumming, 1983 S.C.C.R. 15
Allan v. Tant, 1986 S.C.C.R. 175
Bell v. H.M. Advocate, 1988 S.C.C.R. 292
Guthrie v. Hamilton, 1988 S.C.C.R. 330
Baird v. H.M. Advocate, 1989 S.C.C.R. 55
H.M. Advocate v. Rae, 1992 S.C.C.R. 1
Carmichael v. Brannan, 1985 S.C.C.R. 234
Annan v. McIntosh, 1993 S.C.C.R. 938
Tudhope v. McKee, 1987 S.C.C.R. 663
Heywood v. Macrae, 1987 S.C.C.R. 627
White v. H.M. Advocate, 1986 S.C.C.R. 224
Haq v. H.M. Advocate, 1987 S.C.C.R. 433
Wilson v. H.M. Advocate, 1988 S.C.C.R. 384
Bauros and Ferns v. H.M. Advocate, 1991 S.C.C.R. 768
H.M. Advocate v. Harper, 1989 S.C.C.R. 472
Kerr v. H.M. Advocate, 1991 S.C.C.R. 774

Normand v. Wotherspoon, 1993 S.C.C.R. 912
Isdale v. Scott, 1991 S.C.C.R. 491
Cormack v. H.M. Advocate, 1996 S.C.C.R. 53
H.M. Advocate v. Riganti, 1992 S.C.C.R. 891

We reproduce with kind permission of Newspaper Publishing plc and The Independent Law Reports extracts from:

Hodder v. D.P.P., December 14, 1989

Extracts derived from original reports by Times Newspapers Limited:

R v. Dye and Williamson, December 19, 1991
R v. Inglesias, November 15, 1982
R v. Kempley, April 15, 1994
R v. Klug, November 23, 1977
R v. McConkey, September 23, 1982
R v. Marchon, February 23, 1993
R v. Strong; R v. Berry, January 26, 1989

PART A

STATUTES

CHAPTER ONE

Introduction   **1.1**

Misuse of Drugs Act 1971 and the principal subordinate legislation are reproduced here along with extracts from other relevant statutes in so far as they apply to Scotland.

Misuse of Drugs Act 1971   **1.2**

CHAPTER 38

ARRANGEMENT OF SECTIONS

The Advisory Council on the Misuse of Drugs

SCHEDULES

1971 CHAPTER 38

An Act to make new provision with respect to dangerous or otherwise harmful drugs and related matters, and for purposes connected therewith.   [27th May 1971]

BE IT ENACTED by the Queen's most Excellent Majesty, by and with the advice and consent of the Lords Spiritual and Temporal, and Commons, in this present Parliament assembled, and by the authority of the same, as follows:—

The Advisory Council on the Misuse of Drugs

The Advisory Council on the Misuse of Drugs

1.—(1) There shall be constituted in accordance with Schedule 1 to **1.2.1** this Act an Advisory Council on the Misuse of Drugs (in this Act referred to as "the Advisory Council"); and the supplementary provisions contained in that Schedule shall have effect in relation to the Council.

(2) It shall be the duty of the Advisory Council to keep under review the situation in the United Kingdom with respect to drugs which are being or appear to them likely to be misused and of which the misuse is having or appears to them capable of having harmful effects sufficient to constitute a social problem, and to give to any one or more of the Ministers, where either the Council consider it expedient to do so or they are consulted by the Minister or Ministers in question, advice on measures (whether or not involving alteration of the law) which in the opinion of the Council ought to be taken for preventing the misuse of such drugs or dealing with social problems connected with their misuse, and in particular on measures which in the opinion of the Council, ought to be taken—

   (*a*)   for restricting the availability of such drugs or supervising the arrangements for their supply;

   (*b*)   for enabling persons affected by the misuse of such drugs to obtain proper advice, and for securing the provision of proper facilities and services for the treatment, rehabilitation and after-care of such persons;

   (*c*)   for promoting co-operation between the various professional and community services which in the opinion of the Council have a part to play in dealing with social problems connected with the misuse of such drugs;

   (*d*)   for educating the public (and in particular the young) in the dangers of misusing such drugs, and for giving publicity to those dangers; and

   (*e*)   for promoting research into, or otherwise obtaining information about, any matter which in the opinion of the Council is of relevance for the purpose of preventing the misuse of such drugs or dealing with any social problem connected with their misuse.

(3) It shall also be the duty of the Advisory Council to consider any matter relating to drug dependence or the misuse of drugs which may be referred to them by any one or more of the Ministers and to advise the Minister or Ministers in question thereon, and in particular to consider and advise the Secretary of State with respect to any communication referred by him to the Council, being a communication relating to the control of any dangerous or otherwise harmful drug made to Her Majesty's Government in the United Kingdom by any organisation or authority established by or under any treaty, convention or other agreement or arrangement to which that Government is for the time being a party.

(4) In this section "the Ministers" means the Secretary of State for the Home Department, the Secretaries of State respectively concerned with health in England, Wales and Scotland, the Secretaries of State respectively concerned with education in England, Wales and Scotland, the Minister of Home Affairs for Northern Ireland, the Minister of Health and Social Services for Northern Ireland and the Minister of Education for Northern Ireland.

Controlled drugs and their classification

Controlled drugs and their classification for purposes of this Act

1.2.2   **2.**—(1) In this Act—

(*a*)   the expression "controlled drug" means any substance or product for the time being specified in Part I, II, or III of Schedule 2 to this Act; and

(*b*)   the expressions "Class A drug", "Class B drug" and "Class C drug" mean any of the substances and products for the time being specified respectively in Part I, Part II and Part III of that Schedule;

and the provisions of Part IV of that Schedule shall have effect with respect to the meanings of expressions used in that Schedule.

(2) Her Majesty may by Order in Council make such amendments in Schedule 2 to this Act as may be requisite for the purpose of adding any substance or product to, or removing any substance or product from, any of Parts I to III of that Schedule, including amendments for securing that no substance or product is for the time being specified in a particular one of those Parts or for inserting any substance or product into any of those Parts in which no substance or product is for the time being specified.

(3) An Order in Council under this section may amend Part IV of Schedule 2 to this Act, and may do so whether or not it amends any other Part of that Schedule.

(4) An Order in Council under this section may be varied or revoked by a subsequent Order in Council thereunder.

(5) No recommendation shall be made to Her Majesty in Council to make an Order under this section unless a draft of the Order has been laid before Parliament and approved by a resolution of each House of Parliament; and the Secretary of State shall not lay a draft of such an Order before Parliament except after consultation with or on the recommendation of the Advisory Council.

Restrictions relating to controlled drugs etc.

Restriction of importation and exportation of controlled drugs

3.—(1) Subject to subsection (2) below—   **1.2.3**

(a)   the importation of a controlled drug; and
(b)   the exportation of a controlled drug,

are hereby prohibited.

(2) Subsection (1) above does not apply—

(a)   to the importation or exportation of a controlled drug which is for the time being excepted from paragraph (a) or, as the case may be, paragraph (b) of subsection (1) above by regulations under section 7 of this Act; or
(b)   to the importation or exportation of a controlled drug under and in accordance with the terms of a licence issued by the Secretary of State and in compliance with any conditions attached thereto.[1]

NOTE
[1] For an extension of this provision see s. 19 of the Criminal Justice (International Co-operation) Act 1990.

Restriction of production and supply of controlled drugs   **1.2.4**

4.—(1) Subject to any regulations under section 7 of this Act for the time being in force, it shall not be lawful for a person—

(a)   to produce a controlled drug; or
(b)   to supply or offer to supply a controlled drug to another.

(2) Subject to section 28 of this Act, it is an offence for a person—

(a)   to produce a controlled drug in contravention of subsection (1) above; or
(b)   to be concerned in the production of such a drug in contravention of that subsection by another.

(3) Subject to section 28 of this Act, it is an offence for a person—

8   *Controlled Drugs*

(*a*)   to supply or offer to supply a controlled drug to another in contravention of subsection (1) above; or

(*b*)   to be concerned in the supplying of such a drug to another in contravention of that subsection; or

(*c*)   to be concerned in the making to another in contravention of that subsection of an offer to supply such a drug.

Restriction of possession of controlled drugs

1.2.5   **5.**—(1) Subject to any regulations under section 7 of this Act for the time being in force, it shall not be lawful for a person to have a controlled drug in his possession.

(2) Subject to section 28 of this Act and to subsection (4) below, it is an offence for a person to have a controlled drug in his possession in contravention of subsection (1) above.

(3) Subject to section 28 of this Act, it is an offence for a person to have a controlled drug in his possession, whether lawfully or not, with intent to supply it to another in contravention of section 4(1) of this Act.

(4) In any proceedings for an offence under subsection (2) above in which it is proved that the accused had a controlled drug in his possession, it shall be a defence for him to prove—

(*a*)   that, knowing or suspecting it to be a controlled drug, he took possession of it for the purpose of preventing another from committing or continuing to commit an offence in connection with that drug and that as soon as possible after taking possession of it he took all steps as were reasonably open to him to destroy the drug or to deliver it into the custody of a person lawfully entitled to take custody of it; or

(*b*)   that, knowing or suspecting it to be a controlled drug, he took possession of it for the purpose of delivering it into the custody of a person lawfully entitled to take custody of it and that as soon as possible after taking possession of it he took all such steps as were reasonably open to him to deliver it into the custody of such a person.

(5) Subsection (4) above shall apply in the case of proceedings for an offence under section 19(1) of this Act consisting of an attempt to commit an offence under subsection (2) above as it applies in the case of proceedings for an offence under subsection (2), subject to the following modifications, that is to say—

(*a*)   for the references to the accused having in his possession, and to his taking possession of, a controlled drug there shall be substituted respectively references to his attempting to get, and to his attempting to take, possession of such a drug; and

(b)   in paragraphs (a) and (b) the words from "and that as soon as possible" onwards shall be omitted.[1]

(6) Nothing in subsection (4) [or (5)][2] above shall prejudice any defence which it is open to a person charged with an offence under this section to raise apart from that subsection.

NOTES

[1] s. 5(5) omitted for England and Wales by Criminal Attempts Act 1981, s. 10.

[2] Words in brackets repealed for England and Wales by Criminal Attempts Act 1981, s. 10.

Restriction of cultivation of cannabis plant

6.—(1) Subject to any regulations under section 7 of this Act for the time being in force, it shall not be lawful for a person to cultivate any plant of the genus *Cannabis*.   **1.2.6**

(2) Subject to section 28 of this Act, it is an offence to cultivate any such plant in contravention of subsection (1) above.

Authorisation of activities otherwise unlawful under foregoing provisions

7.—(1) The Secretary of State may by regulations—   **1.2.7**

(a)   except from section 3(1)(a) or (b), 4(1)(a) or (b) or 5(1) of this Act such controlled drugs as may be specified in the regulations; and

(b)   make such other provision as he thinks fit for the purpose of making it lawful for persons to do things which under any of the following provisions of this Act, that is to say sections 4(1), 5(1) and 6(1), it would otherwise be unlawful for them to do.

(2) Without prejudice to the generality of paragraph (b) of subsection (1) above, regulations under that subsection authorising the doing of any such thing as is mentioned in that paragraph may in particular provide for the doing of that thing to be lawful—

(a)   if it is done under and in accordance with the terms of a licence or other authority issued by the Secretary of State and in compliance with any conditions attached thereto; or

(b)   if it is done in compliance with such conditions as may be prescribed.

(3) Subject to subsection (4) below, the Secretary of State shall so exercise his power to make regulations under subsection (1) above as to secure—

(*a*)   that it is not unlawful under section 4(1) of this Act for a doctor, dentist, veterinary practitioner or veterinary surgeon, acting in his capacity as such, to prescribe, administer, manufacture, compound or supply a controlled drug, or for a pharmacist or a person lawfully conducting a retail pharmacy business, acting in either case in his capacity as such, to manufacture, compound or supply a controlled drug; and

(*b*)   that it is not unlawful under section 5(1) of this Act for a doctor, dentist, veterinary practitioner, veterinary surgeon, pharmacist or person lawfully conducting a retail pharmacy business to have a controlled drug in his possession for the purpose of acting in his capacity as such.

(4) If in the case of any controlled drug the Secretary of State is of the opinion that it is in the public interest—

(*a*)   for production, supply and possession of that drug to be either wholly unlawful or unlawful except for purposes of research or other special purposes; or

(*b*)   for it to be unlawful for practitioners, pharmacists and persons lawfully conducting retail pharmacy businesses to do in relation to that drug any of the things mentioned in subsection (3) above except under a licence or other authority issues by the Secretary of State,

he may by order designate that drug as a drug to which this subsection applies; and while there is in force an order under this subsection designating a controlled drug as one to which this subsection applies, subsection (3) above shall not apply as regards that drug.

(5) Any order under subsection (4) above may be varied or revoked by a subsequent order thereunder.

(6) The power to make orders under subsection (4) above shall be exercisable by statutory instrument, which shall be subject to annulment in pursuance of a resolution of either House of Parliament.

(7) The Secretary of State shall not make any order under subsection (4) above except after consultation with or on the recommendation of the Advisory Council.

(8) References in this section to a person's "doing" things include references to his having things in his possession.

(9) In its application to Northern Ireland this section shall have effect as if for references to the Secretary of State there were substituted references to the Ministry of Home Affairs for Northern Ireland and as if for subsection (6) there were substituted—

      "(6) Any order made under subsection (4) above by the Ministry of Home Affairs for Northern Ireland shall be subject to negative resolution within the meaning of section 41(6) of the

Interpretation Act (Northern Ireland) 1954 [c. 33 (N.I.)] as if it
were a statutory instrument within the meaning of that Act."

Miscellaneous offences involving controlled drugs etc.

**Occupiers etc. of premises to be punishable for permitting certain
activities to take place there**

8. A person commits an offence if, being the occupier or concerned in   **1.2.8**
the management of any premises, he knowingly permits or suffers any of
the following activities to take place on those premises, that is to say—

(a)   producing or attempting to produce a controlled drug in
      contravention of section 4(1) of this Act;
(b)   supplying or attempting to supply a controlled drug to another
      in contravention of section 4(1) of this Act, or offering to supply
      a controlled drug to another in contravention of section 4(1);
(c)   preparing opium for smoking;
(d)   smoking cannabis, cannabis resin or prepared opium.

Prohibition of certain activities etc. relating to opium

9. Subject to section 28 of this Act, it is an offence for a person—   **1.2.9**

(a)   to smoke or otherwise use prepared opium; or
(b)   to frequent a place used for the purpose of opium smoking; or
(c)   to have in his possession—
      (i)   any pipes or other utensils made or adapted for use in
            connection with the smoking of opium, being pipes or
            utensils which have been used by him or with his knowledge
            and permission in that connection or which he intends to
            use or permit others to use in that connection; or
      (ii) any utensils which have been used by him or with his
            knowledge and permission in connection with the
            preparation of opium for smoking.

**Prohibition of supply etc. of articles for administering or preparing
controlled drugs**

9A.—(1) A person who supplies or offers to supply any article   **1.2.9A**
which may be used or adapted to be used (whether by itself or in
combination with another article or other articles) in the
administration by any person of a controlled drug to himself or
another, believing that the article (or the article as adapted) is to be
so used in circumstances where the administration is unlawful, is
guilty of an offence.

(2) It is not an offence under subsection (1) above to supply or offer to supply a hypodermic syringe, or any part of one.

(3) A person who supplies or offers to supply any article which may be used to prepare a controlled drug for administration by any person to himself or another believing that the article is to be so used in circumstances where the administration is unlawful is guilty of an offence.

(4) For the purposes of this section, any administration of a controlled drug is unlawful except—

(*a*) the administration by any person of a controlled drug to another in circumstances where the administration of the drug is not unlawful under section 4(1) of this Act, or

(*b*) the administration by any person of a controlled drug to himself in circumstances where having the controlled drug in his possession is not unlawful under section 5(1) of this Act.

(5) In this section, references to administration by any person of a controlled drug to himself include a reference to his administering it to himself with the assistance of another.[1]

NOTE
[1] Inserted by s. 34 of the Drug Trafficking Offences Act 1986.

Powers of Secretary of State for preventing misuse of controlled drugs

Power to make regulations for preventing misuse of controlled drugs

1.2.10   **10.**—(1) Subject to the provisions of this Act, the Secretary of State may by regulations make such provision as appears to him necessary or expedient for preventing the misuse of controlled drugs.

(2) Without prejudice to the generality of subsection (1) above, regulations under this section may in particular make provision—

(*a*) for requiring precautions to be taken for the safe custody of controlled drugs;

(*b*) for imposing requirements as to the documentation of transactions involving controlled drugs, and for requiring copies of documents relating to such transactions to be furnished to the prescribed authority;

(*c*) for requiring the keeping of records and the furnishing of information with respect to controlled drugs in such circumstances and in such manner as may be prescribed;

(*d*) for the inspection of any precautions taken or records kept in pursuance of regulations under this section;

(*e*) as to the packaging and labelling of controlled drugs;

(*f*)   for regulating the transport of controlled drugs and the methods used for destroying or otherwise disposing of such drugs when no longer required;

(*g*)   for regulating the issue of prescriptions containing controlled drugs and the supply of controlled drugs on prescriptions, and for requiring persons issuing or dispensing prescriptions containing such drugs to furnish to the prescribed authority such information relating to those prescriptions as may be prescribed;

(*h*)   for requiring any doctor who attends a person who he considers, or has reasonable grounds to suspect, is addicted (within the meaning of the regulations) to controlled drugs of any description to furnish to the prescribed authority such particulars with respect to that person as may be prescribed;

(*i*)   for prohibiting any doctor from administering, supplying and authorising the administration and supply to persons so addicted, and from prescribing for such persons, such controlled drugs as may be prescribed, except under and in accordance with the terms of a licence issued by the Secretary of State in pursuance of the regulations.

Power to direct special precautions for safe custody of controlled drugs to be taken at certain premises

11.—(1) Without prejudice to any requirement imposed by regulations **1.2.11** made in pursuance of section 10(2)(*a*) of this Act, the Secretary of State by notice in writing served on the occupier of any premises on which controlled drugs are or are proposed to be kept give directions as to the taking of precautions or further precautions for the safe custody of any controlled drugs of a description specified in the notice which are kept on those premises.

(2) It is an offence to contravene any directions given under subsection (1) above.

Directions prohibiting prescribing, supply etc. of controlled drugs by practitioners' etc. convicted of certain offences

12.—(1) Where a person who is a practitioner or pharmacist has after **1.2.12** the coming into operation of this subsection been convicted—

(*a*)   of an offence under this Act or under the Dangerous Drugs Act 1965 [c. 15] or any enactment repealed by that Act; or

(*b*)   of an offence under section 45, 56 or 304 of the Customs and Excise Act 1952 [c. 44] in [or under sections 50, 68 or 170 of the Customs and Excise Management Act 1979][1] connection with a prohibition of or restriction on importation or exportation of a controlled drug having effect by virtue of section 3 of this Act or which had effect by virtue of any provision contained in or repealed by the Dangerous Drugs Act 1965.

²(*c*) of an offence under section 12 or 13 of the Criminal Justice (International Co-operation) Act 1990 [c. 5];

the Secretary of State may give a direction under subsection (2) below in respect of that person.

(2) A direction under this subsection in respect of a person shall–

(*a*) if that person is a practitioner, be a direction prohibiting him from having in his possession, prescribing, administering, manufacturing, compounding and supplying and from authorising the administration and supply of such controlled drugs as may be specified in the direction;

(*b*) if that person is a pharmacist, be a direction prohibiting him from having in his possession, manufacturing, compounding and supplying and from supervising and controlling the manufacture, compounding and supply of such controlled drugs as may be specified in the direction.

(3) The Secretary of State may at any time give a direction cancelling or suspending any direction given by him under subsection (2) above, or cancelling any direction of his under this subsection by which a direction so given is suspended.

(4) The Secretary of State shall cause a copy of any direction given by him under this section to be served on the person to whom it applies, and shall cause notice of any such direction to be published in the London, Edinburgh and Belfast Gazettes.

(5) A direction under this section shall take effect when a copy of it is served on the person to whom it applies.

(6) It is an offence to contravene a direction given under subsection (2) above.

(7) In section 80 of the Medicines Act 1968 [c. 67] (under which a body corporate carrying on a retail pharmacy business may be disqualified for the purposes of Part IV of that Act and have its premises removed from the register kept under section 75 of that Act, where that body or any member of the board of that body or any officer of any employee of that body is convicted of an offence under any of the relevant Acts as defined in subsection (5)), for the words "and this Act" in subsection (5) there shall be substituted the words "this Act and the Misuse of Drugs Act 1971".

NOTES

¹ Words in brackets inserted by Customs and Excise Management Act 1979, s. 177(1); Sched. 4, para. 8.

² Inserted by s. 23(2) of the Criminal Justice (International Co-operation) Act 1990 (c. 5).

Directions prohibiting prescribing, supplying, supply etc. of controlled drugs by practitioners in other cases.

13.—(1) In the event of a contravention by a doctor of regulations **1.2.13** made in pursuance of paragraph (*h*) or (*i*) of section 10(2) of this Act, or of the terms of a licence issued under regulations made in pursuance of the said paragraph (*i*), the Secretary of State may, subject to and in accordance with section 14 of this Act, give a direction in respect of the doctor concerned prohibiting him from prescribing, administering and supplying and from authorising the administration and supply of such controlled drugs as may be specified in the direction.

(2) If the Secretary of State is of the opinion that a practitioner is or has after the coming into operation of this subsection been prescribing, administering or supplying or authorising the administration or supply of any controlled drugs in an irresponsible manner, the Secretary of State may, subject to and in accordance with section 14 or 15 of this Act, give a direction in respect of the practitioner concerned prohibiting him from prescribing, administering and supplying and from authorising the administration and supply of such controlled drugs as may be specified in the direction.

(3) A contravention such as is mentioned in subsection (1) above does not as such constitute an offence, but it is an offence to contravene a direction given under subsection (1) or (2) above.

Investigation where grounds for a direction under s. 13 are considered to exist

14.—(1) If the Secretary of State considers that there are grounds for **1.2.14** giving a direction under subsection (1) of section 13 of this Act on account of such a contravention by a doctor as is there mentioned, or for giving a direction under subsection (2) of that section on account of such conduct by a practitioner as is mentioned in the said subsection (2), he may refer the case to a tribunal for the purpose in accordance with the following provisions of this Act; and it shall be the duty of the tribunal to consider the case and report on it to the Secretary of State.

(2) In this Act "the respondent", in relation to a reference under this section, means the doctor or other practitioner in respect of whom the reference is made.

(3) Where—

(*a*)   in the case of a reference relating to the giving of a direction under the said subsection (1), the tribunal finds that there has been no such contravention as aforesaid by the respondent or finds that there has been such a contravention but does not recommend the giving of a direction under that subsection in respect of the respondent; or (*b*) in the case of a reference relating to the giving of a direction under the said subsection (2), the tribunal finds that there has been no such conduct as aforesaid by the respondent or finds that there has been such conduct by the respondent but does not recommend the giving of a direction under the said subsection (2) in respect of him,

the Secretary of State shall cause notice to that effect to be served on the respondent.

(4) Where the tribunal finds—

(*a*) in the case of a reference relating to the giving of a direction under the said subsection (1), that there has been such a contravention as aforesaid by the respondent; or

(*b*) in the case of a reference relating to the giving of a direction under the said subsection (2), that there has been such conduct as aforesaid by the respondent,

and considers that a direction under the subsection in question should be given in respect of him, the tribunal shall include in its report a recommendation to that effect indicating the controlled drugs which it considers should be specified in the direction or indicating that the direction should specify all controlled drugs.

(5) Where the tribunal makes such a recommendation as aforesaid, the Secretary of State shall cause a notice to be served on the respondent stating whether or not he proposes to give a direction pursuant thereto, and where he does so propose the notice shall—

(*a*) set out the terms of the proposed direction; and

(*b*) inform the respondent that considerations will be given to any representations relating to the case which are made by him in writing to the Secretary of State within the period of 28 days beginning with the date of service of the notice.

(6) If any such representations are received by the Secretary of State within the period aforesaid, he shall refer the case to an advisory body constituted for the purpose in accordance with the following provisions of this Act; and it shall be the duty of the advisory body to consider the case and to advise the Secretary of State as to the exercise of his powers under subsection (7) below.

(7) After the expiration of the said period of 28 days and, in the case of a reference to an advisory body under subsection (6) above, after considering the advice of that body, the Secretary of State may either—

(*a*) give in respect of the respondent a direction under subsection (1) or, as in the case may be, subsection (2) of section 13 of this Act specifying all or any of the controlled drugs indicated in the recommendation of the tribunal; or (*b*)   order that the case be referred back to the tribunal, or referred to another tribunal constituted as aforesaid; or

(*c*)   order that no further proceedings under this section shall be taken in the case.

(8) Where a case is referred or referred back to a tribunal in pursuance of subsection (7) above, the provisions of subsections (2) to (7) above shall apply as if the case had been referred to the tribunal in pursuance of subsection (1) above, and any finding, recommendation or advice previously made or given in respect of the case in pursuance of those provisions shall be disregarded.

Temporary directions under s. 13(2)

15.—(1) If the Secretary of State considers that there are grounds for giving a direction under subsection (2) of section 13 of this Act in respect of a practitioner on account of such conduct by him as is mentioned in that subsection and that the circumstances of the case require such a direction to be given with the minimum of delay, he may, subject to the following provisions of this section, give such a direction in respect of him by virtue of this section; and a direction under section 13(2) given by virtue of this section may specify such controlled drugs as the Secretary of State things fit. **1.2.15**

(2) Where the Secretary of State proposes to give such a direction as aforesaid by virtue of this section, he shall refer the case to a professional panel constituted for the purpose in accordance with the following provisions of this Act; and

(*a*)   it shall be the duty of the panel, after affording the respondent an opportunity of appearing before and being heard by the panel, to consider the circumstances of the case, so far as known to it, and to report to the Secretary of State whether the information before the panel appears to it to afford reasonable grounds for thinking that there has been such conduct by the respondent as is mentioned in section 13(2) of this Act; and

(*b*)   the Secretary of State shall not by virtue of this section give such a direction as aforesaid in respect of the respondent unless the panel reports that the information before it appears to it to afford reasonable grounds for so thinking.

(3) In this Act "the respondent", in relation to a reference under subsection (2) above, means the practitioner in respect of whom the reference is made.

(4) Where the Secretary of State gives such a direction as aforesaid by virtue of this section he shall, if he has not already done so, forthwith refer the case to a tribunal in accordance with section 14(1) of this Act.

(5) Subject to subsection (6) below, the period of operation of a direction under section 13(2) of this Act given by virtue of this section shall be a period of six weeks beginning with the date on which the direction takes effect.

(6) Where a direction under section 13(2) of this Act had been given in respect of a person by virtue of this section and the case has been referred to a tribunal in accordance with section 14(1), the Secretary of State may from time to time, by notice in writing served on the person to whom the direction applies, extend or further extend the period of operation of the direction for a further 28 days from the time when that period would otherwise expire, but shall not so extend or further extend that period without the consent of that tribunal, or, if the case has been referred to another tribunal in pursuance of section 14(7) of this Act, of that other tribunal.

(7) A direction under section 13(2) of this Act given in respect of a person by virtue of this section shall (unless previously cancelled under section 16(3) of this Act) cease to have effect on the occurrence of any of the following events, that is to say—

(*a*)   the service on that person of a notice under section 14(3) of this Act relating to his case;

(*b*)   the service on that person of a notice under section 14(5) of this Act relating to his case stating that the Secretary of State does not propose to give a direction under section 13(2) of this Act pursuant to a recommendation of the tribunal that such a direction should be given;

(*c*)   the service on that person of a copy of such a direction given in respect of him in pursuance of section 14(7) of this Act;

(*d*)   the making of an order by the Secretary of State in pursuance of section 14(7) that no further proceedings under section 14 shall be taken in the case;

(*e*)   the expiration of the period of operation of the direction under section 13(2) given by virtue of this section.

Provisions supplementary to ss. 14 and 15

1.2.16   **16.**—(1) The provisions of Schedule 3 to this Act shall have effect with respect to the constitution and procedure of any tribunal, advisory body or professional panel appointed for the purpose of section 14 or 15 of this Act, and with respect to the other matters there mentioned.

(2) The Secretary of State shall cause a copy of any order or direction made or given by him in pursuance of section 14(7) of this Act or any direction given by him by virtue of the said section 15 to be served on the person to whom it applies and shall cause notice of any such direction, and a copy of any notice served under section 15(6) of this Act, to be published in the London, Edinburgh and Belfast Gazettes.

(3) The Secretary of State may at any time give a direction—

(a)   cancelling or suspending any direction given by him in pursuance of section 14(7) of this Act or cancelling any directions of his under this subsection by which a direction so given is suspended; or

(b)   cancelling any direction given by him by virtue of section 15 of this Act,

and shall cause a copy of any direction of his under this subsection to be served on the person to whom it applies and notice of it to be published as aforesaid.

(4) A direction given under section 13(1) or (2) of this Act or under subsection (3) above shall take effect when a copy of it is served on the person to whom it applies.

Power to obtain information from doctors, pharmacists etc. in certain circumstances

17.—(1) If it appears to the Secretary of State that there exists in any **1.2.17** area in Great Britain a social problem caused by the extensive misuse of dangerous or otherwise harmful drugs in that area, he may by notice in writing served on any doctor or pharmacist practising in or in the vicinity of that area, or on any person carrying on a retail pharmacy business within the meaning of the Medicines Act 1968 [c. 67] at any premises situated in or in the vicinity of that area, require him to furnish to the Secretary of State, with respect to any such drugs specified in the notice and as regards any period so specified, such particulars as may be so specified relating to the quantities in which and the number and frequency of the occasions on which those drugs—

(a)   in the case of a doctor, were prescribed, administered or supplied by him;

(b)   in the case of a pharmacist, were supplied by him; or

(c)   in the case of a person carrying on a retail pharmacy business, were supplied in the course of that business at any premises so situated which may be specified in the notice.

(2) A notice under this section may require any such particulars to be furnished in such manner and within such time as may be specified in the notice and, if served on a pharmacist or person carrying on a retail pharmacy business, may require him to furnish the names and addresses of doctors on whose prescriptions any dangerous or otherwise harmful drugs to which the notice relates were supplied, but shall not require any person to furnish any particulars relating to the identity of any person for or to whom any such drug has been prescribed, administered or supplied.

(3) A person commits an offence if without reasonable excuse (proof of which shall lie on him) he fails to comply with any requirement to which he is subject by virtue of subsection (1) above.

(4) A person commits an offence if in purported compliance with a requirement imposed under this section he gives any information which he knows to be false in a material particular or recklessly gives any information which is so false.

(5) In its application to Northern Ireland this section shall have effect as if for the references to Great Britain and the Secretary of State there were substituted respectively references to Northern Ireland and the Ministry of Home Affairs for Northern Ireland.

Miscellaneous offences and powers

Miscellaneous offences

1.2.18   **18.**—(1) It is an offence for a person to contravene any regulations made under this Act other than regulations made in pursuance in section 10(2)(*h*) or (*i*).

(2) It is an offence for a person to contravene a condition or other term of a licence issued under section 3 of this Act or of a licence or other authority issued under regulations made under this Act, not being a licence issued under regulations made in pursuance of section 19(2)(*i*).

(3) A person commits an offence if, in purported compliance with any obligation to give information to which he is subject under or by virtue of regulations made under this Act, he gives any information which he knows to be false in a material particular or recklessly gives any information which is so false.

(4) A person commits an offence if, for the purpose of obtaining, whether for himself or another, the issue or renewal of a licence or other authority under this Act or under any regulations made under this Act, he—

    (*a*)   makes any statement or gives any information which he knows to be false in a material particular or recklessly gives any information which is so false; or

    (*b*)   produces or otherwise makes use of any book, record or other document which to his knowledge contains any statement or information which he knows to be false in a material particular.

Attempts etc. to commit offences

1.2.19   **19.** It is an offence for a person [to attempt to commit an offence under any other provision of this Act or to incite or attempt][1] to incite another to commit such an offence.

NOTE
[1]Omitted for England and Wales by s. 10 of the Criminal Attempts Act 1981.

Assisting in or inducing commission outside United Kingdom of offence punishable under a corresponding law

20. A person commits an offence if in the United Kingdom he assists in or induces the commission in any place outside the United Kingdom of an offence punishable under the provision of a corresponding law in force in that place.   **1.2.20**

Offences by corporations

21. Where an offence under this Act [or Part II of the Criminal Justice (International Co-operation) Act 1990][1] committed by a body corporate is proved to have been committed with the consent or connivance of, or to be attributable to any neglect on the part of, any director, manager, secretary or other similar officer of the body corporate, or any person purporting to act in any such capacity, he as well as the body corporate shall be guilty of that offence and shall be liable to be proceeded against accordingly.   **1.2.21**

NOTE
[1]Inserted by s. 23(3) of the Criminal Justice (International Co-operation) Act 1990, (c. 5).

Further powers to make regulations

22. The Secretary of State may by regulations make provision—   **1.2.22**

(*a*) for exceeding in such cases as may be prescribed—
  (i) the application of any provision of this Act which creates an offence; or
  (ii) the application of any of the following provisions of the Customs and Excise Management Act 1979 [c. 2], that is to say sections 50(1) to (4), 68(2) and (3) and 170, in so far as they apply in relation to a prohibition or restriction on importation or exportation having effect by virtue of section 3 of this Act;[1]

(*b*) for applying any of the provisions of sections 14 to 16 of this Act and Schedule 3 thereto, with such modifications (if any) as may be prescribed—
  (i) in relation to any proposal by the Secretary of State to give a direction under section 12(2) of this Act; or
  (ii) for such purposes of regulations under this Act as may be prescribed;

(*c*)   for the application of any of the provisions of this Act or
        regulations or order thereunder to servants or agent of the Crown,
        subject to such exceptions, adaptations and modifications as may
        be prescribed.

NOTE
[1]Amended by the Customs and Excise Management Act 1979, s. 177(1);
Sched. 4, para. 12.

Law enforcement and punishment of offences

Powers to search and obtain evidence

1.2.23   **23.**—(1) A constable or other person authorised in that behalf by a
general or special order of the Secretary of State (or in Northern Ireland
either of the Secretary of State or the Ministry of Home Affairs for Northern
Ireland) shall, for the purposes of the execution of this Act, have power to
enter the premises of a person carrying on business as a producer or
supplier of any controlled drugs and to demand the production of, and to
inspect, any books or documents relating to dealings in any such drugs
and to inspect any stocks of any such drugs.
    (2) If a constable has reasonable grounds to suspect that any person is
in possession of a controlled drug in contravention of this Act or of any
regulations made thereunder, the constable may—

(*a*)   search that person, and detain him for the purpose of searching
        him;
(*b*)   search any vehicle or vessel in which the constable suspects that
        the drug may be found, and for that purpose require the person
        in control of the vehicle or vessel to stop it;
(*c*)   seize and detain, for the purposes of proceedings under this Act,
        anything found in the course of the search which appears to the
        constable to the evidence of an offence under this Act.

    In this subsection "vessel" includes a hovercraft within the meaning of
the Hovercraft Act 1968 [c. 59]; and nothing in this subsection shall
prejudice any power of search or any power to seize or detain property
which is exercisable by a constable apart from this subsection.
    (3) If a justice of the peace (or in Scotland a justice of the peace, a
magistrate or a sheriff) is satisfied by information on oath that there is
reasonable ground for suspecting—

(*a*)   that any controlled drugs are, in contravention of this Act or of
        any regulations made thereunder, in the possession of a person
        on any premises; or
(*b*)   that a document directly or indirectly relating to, or connected
        with, a transaction or dealing which was, or an intended

transaction or dealing which would if carried out be, an offence under this Act, or in the case of a transaction or dealing carried out or intended to be carried out in a place outside the United Kingdom, an offence against the provisions of a corresponding law in force in that place, is in the possession of a person on any premises,

he may grant a warrant authorising any constable acting for the police area in which the premises are situated at any time or times within one month from the date of the warrant, to enter, if need be by force, the premises named in the warrant, and to search the premises and any persons found therein and, if there is reasonable ground for suspecting that an offence under this Act has been committed in relation to any controlled drugs found on the premises or in the possession of any such persons, or that a document so found is such a document as is mentioned in paragraph (*b*) above, to seize and detain those drugs or that document, as the case may be.

[1](3A) The powers conferred by subsection (1) above shall be exercisable also for the purposes of the execution of Part II of the Criminal Justice (International Co-operation) Act 1990 [c. 5] and subsection (3) above (excluding paragraph (*a*) shall apply also to offences under section 12 or 13 of that Act, taking references in those provisions to controlled drugs as references to scheduled substances within the meaning of that Part.

(4) A person commits an offence if he—

(*a*)   intentionally obstructs a person in the exercise of his powers under this section; or

(*b*)   conceals from a person acting in the exercise of his powers under subsection (1) above any such books, documents, stocks or drugs as are mentioned in that subsection; or

(*c*)   without reasonable excuse (proof of which shall lie on him) fails to produce any such books or documents as are so mentioned where their production is demanded by a person in the exercise of his powers under that subsection.

(5) In its application to Northern Ireland subsection (3) above shall have effect as if the words "acting for the police area in which the premises are situated" were omitted.

NOTE
[1]Inserted by s. 23(4) of the Criminal Justice (International Co-operation) Act 1990.

Power of arrest

[1]**24.**—(1) A constable may arrest without warrant a person who has **1.2.24** committed, or whom the constable, with reasonable cause, suspects to have committed, an offence under this Act, if—

(*a*)   he, with reasonable cause, believes that that person will abscond unless arrested; or

(*b*)   the name and address of that person are unknown to, and cannot be ascertained by, him; or

(*c*)   he is not satisfied that a name and address furnished by that person as his name and address are true.

(2) This section shall not prejudice any power of arrest conferred by law apart from this section.

NOTE

[1]Repealed for England and Wales by s. 119 of and Sched. 7 to the Police and Criminal Evidence Act 1984.

Prosecution and punishment of offences

1.2.25   **25.**—(1) Schedule 4 to this Act shall have effect, in accordance with subsection (2) below, with respect to the way in which offences under this Act are punishable on conviction.

(2) In relation to an offence under a provision of this Act specified in the first column of the Schedule (the general nature of the offence being described in the second column)—

(*a*)   the third column shows whether the offence is punishable on summary conviction or on indictment or in either way;

(*b*)   the fourth, fifth and sixth columns show respectively the punishments which may be imposed on a person convicted of the offence in the way specified in relation thereto in the third column (that is to say, summarily or on indictment) according to whether the controlled drug in relation to which the offence was committed was a Class A drug, a Class B drug or a Class C drug; and

(*c*)   the seventh column shows the punishments which may be imposed on a person convicted of the offence in the way specified in relation thereto in the third column (that is to say, summarily or on indictment), whether or not the offence was committed in relation to a controlled drug and, if it was so committed, irrespective of whether the drug was a Class A drug, a Class B drug or a Class C drug;

and in the fourth, fifth, sixth and seventh columns a reference to a period gives the maximum term of imprisonment and a reference to a sum of money the maximum fine.

(3) An offence under section 19 of this Act shall be punishable on summary conviction, on indictment or in either way according to whether, under Schedule 4 to this Act, the substantive offence is punishable on summary conviction, on indictment or in either way; and

the punishments which may be imposed on a person convicted of an offence under that section are the same as those which, under that Schedule, may be imposed on a person convicted of the substantive offence.

In this subsection "the substantive offence" means the offence under this Act to which [the attempt or, as the case may be][1] the incitement [or attempted incitement][1] mentioned in section 19 was directed.

(4) Notwithstanding anything in section 127(1) of the Magistrates' Courts Act 1980 [c. 43], a magistrates' court in England and Wales may try an information for an offence under this Act if the information was laid at any time within 12 months from the commission of the offence.[2]

(5) Notwithstanding anything in section 136 of the Criminal Procedure (Scotland) Act 1995 [c. 46] (limitation of time for proceedings in statutory offences) summary proceedings in Scotland for an offence under this Act may be commenced at any time within 12 months from the time when the offence was committed, and subsection (2) of the said section 136 shall apply for the purposes of this subsection as it applies for the purposes of that section.

(6) Notwithstanding anything in Article 19(1) of the Magistrates Courts (Northern Ireland) Order 1981,[3] a magistrates' court in Northern Ireland may hear and determine a complaint for an offence under this Act if the complaint was made at any time within 12 months from the commission of the offence.

NOTES

[1]Omitted for England and Wales by s. 10 of the Criminal Attempts Act 1981.

[2]Amended for England and Wales by the Magistrates Court Act 1980, s. 154; Sched. 7, para. 102.

[3]Amended for Northern Ireland by S.I. 1981 No. 1675; Sched. 6.

26. [Repealed by s. 177(3) and Schedule 6 of the Customs and Excise **1.2.26** Management Act 1979 and see Schedule 1 to that Act for variations of punishment.]

Forfeiture

27.—(1) Subject to subsection (2) below, the court by or before which **1.2.27** a person is convicted of an offence under this Act [or a drug trafficking offence, as defined in section 38(1) of the Drug Trafficking Offences Act 1986][1] [or an offence to which section 1 of the Criminal Justice (Scotland) Act 1987 relates][2] may order anything shown to the satisfaction of the court to relate to the offence, to be forfeited and either destroyed or dealt with in such other manner as the court may order.

(2) The court shall not order anything to be forfeited under this section, where a person claiming to be the owner of or otherwise interested in it

applied to be heard by the court, unless an opportunity has been given to him to show cause why the order should not be made.[3]

NOTES
[1] Inserted by s. 70 of the Criminal Justice Act 1988.
[2] Inserted by s. 31(1) of and Sched. 4 to the Criminal Justice (International Co-operation) Act 1990.
[3] For England and Wales see also s. 1(5)(b)(iii) of the Drug Trafficking Offences Act 1986 which requires in certain circumstances a forfeiture order to be taken into account. The provision does not apply to Scotland: see s. 40(4) of the 1986 Act.

Miscellaneous and supplementary provisions

Proof of lack of knowledge etc. to be a defence in proceedings for certain offences

1.2.28 **28.**—(1) This section applies to offences under any of the following provisions of this Act, that is to say section 4(2) and (3), section 5(2) and (3), section 6(2) and section 9.

(2) Subject to subsection (3) below, in any proceedings for an offence to which this section applies it shall be a defence for the accused to prove that he neither knew of nor suspected nor had reason to suspect the existence of some fact alleged by the prosecution which it is necessary for the prosecution to prove if he is to be convicted of the offence charged.

(3) Where in any proceedings for an offence to which this section applies it is necessary, if the accused is to be convicted of the offence charged, for the prosecution to prove that some substance or product involved in the alleged offence was the controlled drug which the prosecution alleges it to have been, and it is proved that the substance or product in question was that controlled drug, the accused—

(a) shall not be acquitted of the offence charged by reason only of proving that he neither knew nor suspected nor had reason to suspect that substance or product in question was the particular controlled drug alleged; but

(b) shall be acquitted thereof—
(i) if he proves that he neither believed nor suspected nor had reason to suspect that the substance or product in question was a controlled drug; or
(ii) if he proves that he believed the substance or product in question to be a controlled drug, or a controlled drug of a description, such that, if it had in fact been that controlled drug or a controlled drug of that description, he would not at the material time have been committing any offence to which this section applies.

(4) Nothing in this section shall prejudice any defence which it is open to a person charged with an offence to which this section applies to raise apart from this section.

Service of documents

29.—(1) Any notice or other document required or authorised by any provision of this Act to be served on any person may be served on him either by delivering it to him or by leaving it at his proper address or by sending it by post. **1.2.29**

(2) Any notice or other document so required or authorised to be served on a body corporate shall be duly served if it is served on the secretary or clerk of that body.

(3) For the purposes of this section, and of section 26 of the Interpretation Act 1889 [c. 63] in its application to this section, the proper address of any person shall, in the case of the secretary or clerk of a body corporate, be that of the registered or principal office of that body, and in any other case shall be the last address of the person to be served which is known to the Secretary of State.

(4) Where any of the following documents, that is to say—

(*a*) a notice under section 11(1) or section 15(6) of this Act; or

(*b*) a copy of direction given under section 12(2), section 13(1) or (2) or section 16(3) of this Act,

is served by sending it by registered post or by the recorded delivery service, service thereof shall be deemed to have been effected at the time when the letter containing it would be delivered in the ordinary course of post; and so much of section 26 of the Interpretation Act 1889 as relates to the time when service by post is deemed to have been effected shall not apply to such a document if it is served by so sending it.

Licences and authorities

30. A licence or other authority issued by the Secretary of State for purposes of this Act or of regulations made under this Act may be, to any degree, general or specific, may be issued on such terms and subject to such conditions (including, in the case of a licence, the payment of a prescribed fee) as the Secretary of State thinks proper, and may be modified or revoked by him at any time. **1.2.30**

General provisions as to regulations

31.—(1) Regulations made by the Secretary of State under any provision of this Act— **1.2.31**

(*a*)   may make different provision in relation to different controlled drugs, different classes of persons, different provisions of this Act or other different cases or circumstances; and

(*b*)   may make the opinion, consent or approval of a prescribed authority or of any person authorised in a prescribed manner material for purposes of any provision of the regulations; and

(*c*)   may contain such supplementary, incidental and transitional provisions as appear expedient to the Secretary of State.

(2) Any power of the Secretary of State to make regulations under this Act shall be exercisable by statutory instrument, which shall be subject to annulment in pursuance of a resolution of either House of Parliament.

(3) The Secretary of State shall not make any regulations under this Act except after consultation with the Advisory Council.

(4) In its application to Northern Ireland this section shall have effect as if for references to the Secretary of State there were substituted references to the Ministry of Home Affairs for Northern Ireland and as if for subsection (2) there were substituted—

"(2) Any regulations made under this Act by the Ministry of Home Affairs for Northern Ireland shall be subject to negative resolution within the meaning of section 41(6) of the Interpretation Act (Northern Ireland) 1954 [c. 33 (N.I.)] as if they were a statutory instrument within the meaning of that Act."

Research

1.2.32   **32.** The Secretary of State may conduct or assist in conducting research into any matter relating to the misuse of dangerous or otherwise harmful drugs.

Amendment of Extradition Act 1870

1.2.33   **33.** The Extradition Act 1870 [c. 52] shall have effect as if conspiring to commit any offence against any enactment for the time being in force relating to dangerous drugs were included in the list of crimes in Schedule 1 to that Act.

1.2.34   **34.** [Repealed by Domestic Proceedings and Magistrates' Courts Act 1978.]

Financial provisions

1.2.35   **35.** There shall be defrayed out of moneys provided by Parliament—

(a) any expenses incurred by the Secretary of State under or in consequence of the provisions of this Act other than section 32; and

(b) any expenses incurred by the Secretary of State with the consent of the Treasury for the purposes of his functions under that section.

Meaning of "corresponding law," and evidence of certain matters by certificate

36.—(1) In this Act the expression "corresponding law" means a **1.2.36** law stated in a certificate purporting to be issued by or on behalf of the government of a country outside the United Kingdom to be a law providing for the control and regulation in that country of the production, supply, use, export and import of drugs and other substances in accordance with the provisions of the Single Convention on Narcotic Drugs signed at New York on March 30, 1961 or a law providing for the control and regulation in that country of the production, supply, use, export and import of dangerous or otherwise harmful drugs in pursuance of any treaty, convention or other agreement or arrangement to which the government of that country and Her Majesty's Government in the United Kingdom are for the time being parties.

(2) A statement in any such certificate as aforesaid to the effect that any facts constitute an offence against the law mentioned in the certificate shall be evidence, and in Scotland sufficient evidence, of the matters stated.

Interpretation

37.—(1) In this Act, except in so far as the context otherwise requires, **1.2.37** the following expressions have the meanings hereby assigned to them respectively, that is to say:—

"the Advisory Council" means the Advisory Council on the Misuse of Drugs established under this Act;

¹"cannabis" (except in the expression "cannabis resin") means any plant of the genus *Cannabis* or any part of any such plant (by whatever name designated) except that it does not include cannabis resin or any of the following products after separation from the rest of the plant, namely—

(a) mature stalk of any such plant,

(b) fibre produced from mature stalk of any such plant, and

(c) seed of any such plant;

"cannabis resin" means the separated resin, whether crude or purified, obtained from any plant of the genus *Cannabis*;

"contravention" includes failure to comply, and "contravene" has a corresponding meaning;

"controlled drug" has the meaning assigned by section 2 of this Act;

"corresponding law" has the meaning assigned by section 36(1) of this Act;

[2]"dentist" means a person registered in the dentist register under the Dentists Act 1984 [c. 24] or entered in the list of visiting EEC practitioners under Schedule 4 to that Act;

[3]"doctor" means a registered medical practitioner within the meaning of Schedule 1 to the Interpretation Act 1978 [c. 30];

"enactment" includes an enactment of the Parliament of Northern Ireland;

"person lawfully conducting a retail pharmacy business", subject to subsection (5) below, means a person lawfully conducting such a business in accordance with section 69 of the Medicines Act 1968 [c. 67];

"pharmacist" means the same meaning as in the Medicines Act 1968;

"practitioner" (except in the expression "veterinary practitioner") means a doctor, dentist, veterinary practitioner or veterinary surgeon;

"prepared opium" means opium prepared for smoking and includes dross and any other residues remaining after opium has been smoked;

"prescribed" means prescribed by regulations made by the Secretary of State under this Act;

"product", where the reference is to producing a controlled drug, means producing it by manufacture, cultivation or any other method, and "production" has a corresponding meaning;

"supplying" includes distributing;

"veterinary practitioner" means a person registered in the supplementary veterinary register kept under section 8 of the Veterinary Surgeons Act 1966;

"veterinary surgeon" means a person registered in the register of veterinary surgeons kept under section 2 of the Veterinary Surgeons Act 1966 [c. 36].

(2) References in this Act to misusing a drug are references to misusing it by taking it; and the reference in the foregoing provision to the taking of a drug is a reference to the taking of it by a human being by way of any form of self-administration, whether or not involving assistance by another.

(3) For the purposes of this Act the things which a person has in his possession shall be taken to include any thing subject to his control which is in the custody of another.

(4) Except in so far as the context otherwise requires, any reference in this Act to an enactment shall be construed as a reference to that enactment as amended or extended by or under any other enactment.

(5) So long as sections 8 to 10 of the Pharmacy and Poisons Act 1933 remain in force, this Act in its application to Great Britain shall have effect as if for the definition of "person lawfully conducting a retail pharmacy business" in subsection (1) above there were substituted—

> "'person lawfully conducting a retail pharmacy business' means an authorised seller of poisons within the meaning of the Pharmacy and Poisons Act 1933;"

and so long as sections 16 to 18 of the Medicines, Pharmacy and Poisons Act (Northern Ireland) 1945 remain in force, this Act in its application to Northern Ireland shall have effect as if for the definition of "person lawfully conducting a retail pharmacy business" in subsection (1) above there were substituted—

> "'person lawfully conducting a retail pharmacy business' means an authorised seller of poisons within the meaning of the Medicines, Pharmacy and Poisons Act (Northern Ireland) 1945;"

NOTES
[1] Inserted by s. 52 of the Criminal Law Act 1977.
[2] Words substituted by the Dentists Act 1984, s. 54(1) and Sched. 5.
[3] Words substituted by the Medical Act 1983, ss. 54, 56(1) and Sched. 5.

Special provisions as to Northern Ireland

38.—(1) In the application of this Act to Northern Ireland, for any **1.2.38** reference to the Secretary of State (except in sections 1, 2, 7, 17, 23(1), 31, 35, 39(3) and 40(3) and Schedules 1 and 3) there shall be substituted a reference to the Ministry of Home Affairs for Northern Ireland.

(2) Nothing in this Act shall authorise any department of the Government of Northern Ireland to incur any expenses attributable to the provisions of this Act until provision has been made by the Parliament of Northern Ireland for those expenses to be defrayed out of moneys provided by that Parliament; and no expenditure shall be incurred by the Ministry of Home Affairs for Northern Ireland for the purposes of its functions under section 32 of this Act except with the consent of the Ministry of Finance for Northern Ireland.

(3) [Repealed by Northern Ireland Constitution Act 1973.]

(4) Without prejudice to section 37(4) of this Act, any reference in this Act to an enactment of the Parliament of Northern Ireland includes a reference to any enactment re-enacting it with or without modifications.

Savings and transitional provisions, repeals, and power to amend local enactments

39.—(1) The savings and transitional provisions contained in Schedule **1.2.39** 5 to this Act shall have effect.

(2) The enactments mentioned in Schedule 6 to this Act are hereby repealed to the extent specified in the third column of that Schedule.

(3) The Secretary of State may by order made by statutory instrument subject to annulment in pursuance of a resolution of either House of Parliament repeal or amend any provision in any local Act, including an Act confirming a provisional order, or in any instrument in the nature of local enactment under any Act, where it appears to him that that provision is inconsistent with, or has become unnecessary or requires modification in consequence of, any provision of this Act.

Short title, extent and commencement

1.2.40 **40.**—(1) This Act may be cited as the Misuse of Drugs Act 1971.

(2) This Act extends to Northern Ireland.

(3) This Act shall come into operation on such day as the Secretary of State may by order made by statutory instrument appoint, and different dates may be appointed under this subsection for different purposes.

Schedules

1.2.41 SCHEDULE 1 **Section 1**

CONSTITUTION ETC. OF ADVISORY COUNCIL ON THE MISUSE OF DRUGS

1.—(1) The members of the Advisory Council, of whom there shall be not less than twenty, shall be appointed by the Secretary of State after consultation with such organisations as he considers appropriate, and shall include—

(a)   in relation to each of the activities specified in sub-paragraph (2) below, at least one person appearing to the Secretary of State to have wide and recent experience of that activity; and

(b)   persons appearing to the Secretary of State to have wide and recent experience of social problems connected with the misuse of drugs.

(2) The activities referred to in sub-paragraph (1)(a) above are—

(a)   the practice of medicine (other than veterinary medicine);
(b)   the practice of dentistry;
(c)   the practice of veterinary medicine;
(d)   the practice of pharmacy;
(e)   the pharmaceutical industry;
(f)   chemistry other than pharmaceutical chemistry.

(3) The Secretary of State shall appoint one of the members of the Advisory Council to be chairman of the Council.

2. The Advisory Council may appointed committees, which may consist in part of persons who are not members of the Council, to consider and report to the Council on any matter referred to them by the Council.

3. At meetings of the Advisory Council the quorum shall be seven, and subject to that the Council may determine their own procedure.

4. The Secretary of State may pay to the members of the Advisory Council such remuneration (if any) and such travelling and other allowances as may be determined by him with the consent of the Minister for the Civil Service.

5. Any expenses incurred by the Advisory Council with the approval of the Secretary of State shall be defrayed by the Secretary of State.

SCHEDULE 2   Section 2 **1.2.42**

CONTROLLED DRUGS

PART I

CLASS A DRUGS

1. The following substances and products, namely:

[¹(*a*)] Acetorphine.
[²Alfentanil.]
Allylprodine.
Alphacetylmethadol.
Aphamerprodine.
Alphamethadol.
Alphaprodine.
Anileridine.
Benzethidine.
Benzylmorphine (3-benzylmorphine).
Betacetylmethadol.
Betameprodine.
Betamethadol.
Betaprodine.
Bezitramide.
Bufotenine.
Cannabinol, except where contained in cannabis or cannabis resin.
Cannabinol derivatives, [²⁶not being dronabinol or its stereoisomers]
[³Carfentanil.]
Clonitazene.
Coca leaf.
Cocaine.
Desomorphine.
Dextromoramide.
Diamorphine.
Diampromide.
Diethylthiambutene.
[⁴Difenoxin (1-(3-cynao-3, 3-diphenylpropyl)- 4-phenylpiperidine- 4-carboxylic acid).]
Dihydrocodeinone *O*-carboxymethyloxime.

Dihydromorphine.
Dimenoxadole.
Dimepheptanol.
Dimethylthiambutene.
Dioxaphetyl butyrate.
Diphenoxylate.
Dipipanone.
[⁵Drotebanol (3, 4-dimethoxy-17-methylmorphinan- 6ß, 14-diol).]
Ecgonine, and any derivative of ecgonine which is convertible to ecgonine or to cocaine.
Ethylmethylthiambutene.
[²Eticyclidine.]
Etonitazene.
Etorphine.
Etoxeridine.
Fentanyl.
Furethidine.
Hydrocodone.
Hydromorphinol.
Hydromorphone.
Hydroxypethidine.
Isomethadone.
Ketobemidone.
Levomethorphan.
Levomoramide.
Levophenacylmorphan.
Levorphanol.
[³Lofentanil.]
Lysergamide.
Lysergide and other *N*-alkyl derivatives of lysergamide.
Mescaline.
Metazocine.
Methadone.
Methadyl acetate.
Methyldesorphine.

Methyldihydromorphine (6-
methyldihydromorphine).
Metopon.
Morpheridine.
Morphine.
Morphine methobromide, morphine
N-oxide and other pentavalent
nitrogen morphine derivatives.
Myrophine.
...[16]
Nicomorphine (3, 6-
dinicotinoylmorphine).
Noracymethadol.
Norlevorphanol.
Normethadone.
Normorphine.
Norpipanone.
Opium, whether raw, prepared or
medicinal.
Oxycodone.
Oxymorphone.
Pethidine.
Phenadoxone.
Phenampromide.
Phenazocine.
[19]Phencyclidine.]
Phenomorphan.
Phenoperidine.
Priminodine.
Piritramide.
Poppy-straw and concentrate of
poppy-straw.

Proheptazine.
Properidine (1-methyl- 4-
phenylpiperdine- 4-carboxylic
acid isopropyl ester).
Psilocin.
Racemethorphan.
Racemoramide.
Racemorphan.
[2]Rolicyclidine.]
[20]Sufentanil.]
[2]Tenocylidine.]
Thebacon.
Thebaine.
[20]Tilidate.]
Trimeperidine.
[17]4-Bromo-2, 5-dimethoxy-*a*-
methylphenethylamine].
4-Cyano-2-dimethylamino-4, 4-
diphenylbutane.
4-Cyano-1-methyl-4-
phenylpiperidine.
N,N-Diethyltryptamine.
[20A]N-Hydroxy-tenamphetamine]
1-Methyl-4-phenylpiperidine-4-
carboxylic acid.
2-Methyl-3-morpholino-1, 1-
diphenylpropane-carboxylic acid.
[20B]4-Methyl-aminorex]
4-Phenylpiperidine-4-carboxylic acid
ethyl ester.

[18](*b*)   any compound (not being a compound for the time being specified in sub-
paragraph (*a*) above) structurally derived from tryptamine or from a ring-hydroxy
tryptamine by substitution at the nitrogen atom of the sidechain with one or
more alkyl substituents but no other substituent;

(*c*)   any compound (not being methoxyphenamine or a compound for the time being
specified in sub-paragraph (*a*) above) structurally derived from phenethylamine,
an *N*-alkylphen-ethylamine, *a*-methylphenethylamine, an *N*-alkyl-*a*-methyl-
phenethylamine, *a*-ethylphenethylamine, or an *N*-alkyl-*a*-ethylphenethylamine
by substitution in the ring to any extent with alkyl, alkoxy, alkylenedioxy or
halide substituents, whether or not further substituted in the ring by one or more
other univalent substituents.]

[6](*d*)   any compound (not being a compound for the time being specified in sub-
paragraph (*a*) above) structurally derived from fentanyl by modification in any
of the following ways, that is to say,

(i)   by replacement of the phenyl portion of the phenethyl group by any
heteromonocycle whether or not further substituted in the heterocycle;

(ii)   by substitution in the phenethyl group with alkyl, alkenyl, alkoxy, hydroxy,
halogeno, haloalkyl, amino or nitro groups;

(iii)   by substitution in the piperidine ring with alkyl or alkenyl groups;

(iv)   by substitution in the aniline ring with alkyl, alkoxy, alkylenedioxy,
halogeno or haloalkyl groups;

(v)   by substitution at the 4-position of the piperidine ring with any alkoxycarbonyl or alkoxyalkyl or acyloxy group;

(vi) by replacement of the *N*-propionyl group by another acyl group;

(e)   any compound (not being a compound for the time being specified in sub-paragraph (*a*) above) structurally derived from pethidine by modification in any of the following ways, that is to say,

    (i)   by replacement of the 1-methyl group by an acyl, alkyl whether or not unsaturated, benzyl or phenethyl group, whether or not further substituted;

    (ii) by substitution in the piperdine ring with alkyl or alkenyl groups or with a propano bridge, whether or not further substituted;

    (iii) by substitution in the 4-phenyl ring with alkyl, alkoxy, aryloxy, halogeno or haloalkyl groups;

    (iv) by replacement of the 4-ethoxycarbonyl by and other alkoxycarbonyl or any alkoxyalkyl or acyloxy group;

    (v)   by formation of an *N*-oxide or of a quaternary base.]

2. Any stereoisomeric form of a substance for the time being specified in paragraph 1 above not being dextromethorphan or dextrorphan.

3. Any ester or ether of a substance of the time being specified in paragraph 1 or 2 above [[23]not being a substance for the time being specified in Part II of this Schedule].

4. Any salt of a substance for the time being specified in any of paragraphs 1 to 3 above.

5. Any preparation or other product containing a substance or product for the time being specified in any of paragraphs 1 to 4 above.

6. Any preparation designed for administration by injection which includes a substance or product for the time being specified in any of paragraphs 1 to 3 of Part II of this Schedule.

PART II   **1.2.43**

CLASS B DRUGS

1. Following substances and products, namely:

[[7A](*a*) Acetyldihydrocodeine.	Methylamphetamine.
Amphetamine.	Methylphenidate.
Cannabis and cannabis resin.	[[7]Methylphenobarbitone.]
Codeine.	Nicocodine.
… [8]	[[21]Nicodicodine (6-
Dihydrocodeine.	nicotinoyldihydrocodeine).]
Ethylmorphine	Norcodeine.
(3-ethylmorphine).	[[10]Pentazocine.]
[[9]Glutethimide.]	Phenmetrazine.
[[9]Lefetamine.]	Pholcodine.
[[7]Mecloqualone.]	[[1]Propiram.]
[[7]Methaqualone.]	

[[7B](*b*) any 5,5 disubstituted barbituric acid.]

2. Any stereoisomeric form of a substance for the time being specified in paragraph 1 of this Part of this Schedule.

3. Any salt of a substance for the time being specified in paragraph 1 or 2 of this Part of this Schedule.

4. Any preparation or other product containing a substance or product for the time being specified in any of paragraphs 1 to 3 of this Part of this Schedule, not being a preparation falling within paragraph 6 of Part I of this Schedule.

Class C Drugs

1. (a)[24] The following substances, namely:
[[13]Alprazolam.]
Benzphetamine.
[[13]Bromazepam.]
[[23A]Buprenorphine.]
[[13]Camazepam.]
[[14]Cathine.]
[[14]Cathinone.]
[[13]Chlordiazepoxide.]
Chlorphentermine.
[[13]Clobazam.]
[[13]Clorazepic acid.]
[[13]Clonazepam.]
[[13]Clotiazepam.]
[[13]Cloxazolam.]
[[13]Delorazepam.]
[[20]Dextropropoxyphene.]
[[13]Diazepam.]
[[11]Diethylpropion.]
[[13]Estazolam.]
[[13]Ethchlorvynol.]
[[13]Ethinamate.]
[[13]Ethyl loflazepate.]
[[14]Fencamfamin.]
[[14]Fenethylline.]
[[14]Fenproporex.]
[[13]Fludiazepam.]
[[13]Flunitrazepam.]
[[13]Flurazepam.]
[[13]Halazepam.]
[[13]Haloxazolam.]
[[13]Ketazolam.]
[[13]Loprazolam.]
[[13]Lorazepam.]
[[13]Lormetazepam.]
[[13]Mazindol.]
[[13]Medazepam.]
[[14]Mefenorex.]
...[22]
Mephentermine.
[[13]Meprobamate.]
...[12]
[[13]Methyprylone.]
[[23C]Midazolam.]
[[13]Nimetazepam.]
[[13]Nitrazepam.]
[[13]Nordazepam.]
[[13]Oxazepam.]
[[13]Oxazolam.]
[[23B]Pemoline]
...[22]

Phendimetrazine.
[[13]Phentermine.]
[[13]Pinazepam.]
...[22]
Pipradrol.
[[13]Prazepam.]
...[22]
[[14]Propylhexedrine.]
[[14]Pyrovalerone.]
[[13]Temazepam.]
[[13]Tetrazepam.]
[[13]Triazolam.]
[^{14}N-Ethylamphetamine.]
...[22]

(b)[25] Atamestane.
Bolandiol.
Bolasterone.
Bolazine.
Boldenone.
Bolenol.
Bolmantalate.
Calusterone.
4-Chloromethandienone.
Clostebol.
Drostanolone.
Enestebol.
Epitiostanol.
Ethyloestrenol.
Fluoxymesterone.
Formebolone.
Furazabol.
Mebolazine.
Mepitiostane.
Mesabolone.
Mestanolone.
Mesterolone.
Methandienone.
Methandriol.
Methenolone.
Methyltestosterone.
Metribolone.
Mibolerone.
Nandrolone.
Norboletone.
Norclostebol.
Norethandrolone.
Ovandrotone.
Oxabolone.
Oxandrolone.

Oxymesterone.
Oxymetholone.
Prasterone.
Propetandrol.
Quinbolone.
Roxibolone.
Silandrone.

Stanolone.
Stanozolol.
Stenbolone.
Testosterone.
Thiomesterone.
Trenbolone.

(c)   any compound (not being Trilostone or a compound for the time being specified in sub-paragraph (b) above) structurally derived from 17-hydroxyandrostan-3-one or from 17-hydroxyestran-3-one by modification in any of the following ways, that is to say,

    (i)   by further substitution at position 17 by a methyl or ethyl group;

    (ii)   by substitution to any extent at one or more of positions 1, 2, 4, 6, 7, 9, 11 or 16, but at no other position;

    (iii)   by unsaturation in the carbocyclic ring system to any extent, provided that there are no more than two ethylenic bonds in any one carbocyclic ring;

    (iv)   by fusion of ring A with a heterocyclic system;

(d)   any substance which is an ester or ether (or, where more than one hydroxyl function is available, both an ester and an ether) of a substance specified in sub-paragraph (b) or described in sub-paragraph (c) above;

(e)   Chorionic Gonadotrophin (HCG).
    Glenbuterol.
    Non-human chorionic gonadotrophin.
    Somatotropin.
    Somatrem.
    Somatropin.

2. Any stereoisomeric form of a substance for the time being specified in paragraph 1 of this Part of this Schedule [15not being phenylpropanolamine.]

3. Any salt of a substance for the time being specified in paragraph 1 or 2 of this Part of this Schedule.

4. Any preparation or other product containing a substance for the time being specified in any of paragraphs 1 to 3 of this Part of this Schedule.

PART IV   **1.2.45**

MEANING OF CERTAIN EXPRESSIONS USED IN THIS SCHEDULE

For the purposes of this Schedule the following expressions (which are not among those defined in section 37(1) of this Act) have the meanings hereby assigned to them respectively, that is to say—

"cannabinol derivatives" means the following substances, except where contained in cannabis or cannabis resin, namely tetrahydro derivatives of cannabinol and 3-alkyl homologues of cannabinol or of its tetrahydro derivatives;

"coca leaf" means the leaf of any plant of the genus *Erythroxylon* from whose leaves cocaine can be extracted either directly or by chemical transformation;

"concentrate of poppy-straw" means the material produced when poppy-straw has entered into a process for the concentration of its alkaloids;

"medicinal opium" means raw opium which has undergone the process necessary to adapt it for medicinal use in accordance with the requirements of the British Pharmacopoeia, whether it is in the form of powder or is granulated or is in any other form, and whether it is or is not mixed with neutral substances;

"opium poppy" means the plant of the species *Papaver somniferum* L;

"poppy straw" means all parts, except the seeds, of the opium poppy, after mowing;

"raw opium" includes powdered or granulated opium but does not include medicinal opium.

NOTES

[1]"(*a*)" inserted by S.I. 1977 No. 1243, art. 3(*a*).
[2]Word inserted by S.I. 1984 No. 859, art. 2(2).
[3]Word inserted by S.I. 1986 No. 2230, art. 2(2)(*a*).
[4]Word inserted by S.I. 1975 No. 421, art. 3.
[5]Word inserted by S.I. 1973 No. 771, art. 2.
[6]Sched. 2, para. 1(*d*)(*e*) added at the end of para. 1 by S.I. 1986 No. 2230, art. 2(2)(*b*).
[7]Word inserted by S.I. 1984 No. 859, art. 2(3).
[7A]"(*a*)" inserted by S.I. 1984 No. 859, art. 2(3).
[7B]Sub-para. (*b*) added by S.I. 1984 No. 859, art. 2(3).
[8]Word repealed by S.I. 1985 No. 1995, art. 2(2)(*a*).
[9]Word inserted by S.I. 1985 No. 1995, art. 2(2)(*b*).
[10]Word inserted by S.I. 1985 No. 1995, art. 2(2)(*c*).
[11]Word inserted by S.I. 1984 No. 859, art. 2(4)(*a*).
[12]Word repealed by S.I. 1984 No. 859, art. 2(4)(*a*).
[13]Word inserted by S.I. 1985 No. 1995, art. 2(3).
[14]Word inserted by S.I. 1986 No. 2230, art. 2(3) and deleted by S.I. 1995 No. 1996 art. 2.
[15]Words added at the end of para. 2 by S.I. 1986 No. 2230, art. 2(4).
[16]Words repealed by S.I. 1973 No. 771, art. 2.
[17]Words inserted by S.I. 1975 No. 421, art. 3.
[18]Sched. 2, para. 1(*b*)(*c*) added by S.I. 1977 No. 1243, art. 3(*b*).
[19]Word inserted by S.I. 1979 No. 299, art. 2.
[20]Word inserted by S.I. 1983 No. 765, art. 2(*a*).
[20A]Word inserted by S.I. 1990 No. 2589, art. 2(*a*)(i).
[20B]Word inserted by S.I. 1990 No. 2589, art. 2(*a*)(ii).
[21]Words inserted by S.I. 1973 No. 771, art. 2.
[22]Words repealed by S.I. 1973 No. 771, art. 2.
[23]Words inserted by S.I. 1973 No. 771, art. 2.
[23A]Word inserted by S.I. 1989 No. 1340, art. 2(*a*).
[23B]Word inserted by S.I. 1989 No. 1340, art. 2(*b*).
[23C]Word inserted by S.I. 1990 No. 2589, art. 2(*b*).
[24]Letter inserted by S.I. 1996 No. 1300.
[25]List inserted by S.I. 1996 No. 1300.
[26]Words inserted by S.I. 1995 No. 2047.

SCHEDULE 3 **Section 16**

TRIBUNALS, ADVISORY BODIES AND PROFESSIONAL PANELS

PART I

1.2.46 TRIBUNALS

Membership

1.—(1) A tribunal shall consist of five persons of whom—

(i) a person who has a 7 year general qualification, within the meaning of section 71 of the Courts and Legal Services Act 1990;

(ii) an advocate or solicitor in Scotland of at least 7 years' standing; or

(iii) a member of the Bar of Northern Ireland or solicitor of the Supreme Court of Northern Ireland of at least 7 years' standing,

(*a*) one shall be appointed by the Lord Chancellor to be the chairman of the tribunal; and

(b)   the other four shall be persons appointed by the Secretary of State from among members of the respondent's profession nominated of the purposes of this Schedule by any for the relevant bodies mentioned in sub-paragraph (2) below.

NOTE

¹Substituted by Courts and Legal Services Act 1990: s. 71(2), Sched. 10, para. 33.

(2) The relevant bodies aforesaid are—

(a)   where the respondent is a doctor, the General Medical Council, the Royal Colleges of Physicians of London and Edinburgh, the Royal Colleges of Surgeons of England and Edinburgh, the Royal Colleges of Physicians and Surgeons (Glasgow), the Royal College of Obstetricians and Gynaecologists, the Royal College of General Practitioners, the Royal Medico-Psychological Association and the British Medical Association;

(b)   where the respondent is a dentist, the General Dental Council and the British Dental Association;

(c)   where the respondent is a veterinary practitioner or veterinary surgeon, the Royal College of Veterinary Surgeons and the British Veterinary Association.

(3) Sub-paragraph (1) above shall have the effect in relation to a tribunal in Scotland as if for the reference to the Lord Chancellor there were substituted a reference to the Lord President of the Court of Session.

Procedure

2. The quorum of a tribunal shall be the chairman and two other members of the tribunal.

3. Proceedings before a tribunal shall be held in private unless the respondent requests otherwise and the tribunal accedes to the request.

4.—(1) Subject to paragraph 5 below, the Lord Chancellor may make rules as to the procedure to be followed, and the rules of evidence to be observed, in proceedings before tribunals, and in particular—

(a)   for searching that notice that the proceedings are to be brought shall be given to the respondent at such time and in such manner as may be specified by the rules;

(b)   for determining who, in addition to the respondent, shall be a party to the proceedings;

(c)   for securing that any party to the proceedings shall, if he so requires, be entitled to be heard by the tribunal;

(d)   for enabling any party to the proceedings to be represented by counsel or solicitor.

(2) Sub-paragraph (1) above shall have the effect in relation to a tribunal in Scotland as if for the reference to the Lord Chancellor there were substituted a reference to the Secretary of State.

(3) The power to make rules under this paragraph shall be exercisable by statutory instrument, which shall be subject to annulment in pursuance of a resolution of either House of Parliament.

5.—(1) For the purpose of any proceedings before a tribunal in England or Wales or Northern Ireland the tribunal may administer oaths and any party to the proceedings may sue out writs of subpoena and testificandum and duces tectum, but no person shall be compelled under any such writ to give any evidence or produce any document which he could not be compelled to give or produce on the trial of an action.

¹(2) The provisions of section 36 of the Supreme Court Act 1981 [c. 54], or of the Attendance of Witnesses Act 1854 [c. 34.] which provide special procedures for the issue of such writs so as to be in force throughout the United Kingdom) shall apply in relation to any proceedings before a tribunal in England or Wales or, as the case may be, in Northern Ireland as those provisions apply in relation to causes or matters in the High Court or actions or suits pending in the High Court of Justice in Northern Ireland.

(3) For the purpose of any proceedings before a tribunal in Scotland, the tribunal may administer oaths and the Court of Session shall on the application of any party to the

proceedings have the like power as in any action in that court to grant warrant for the citation of witnesses and havers to give evidence or to produce documents before the tribunal.

6. Subject to the foregoing provisions of this Schedule, a tribunal may regulate its own procedure.

7. The validity of the proceedings of a tribunal shall not be affected by any defect in the appointment of a member of the tribunal or by reason of the fact that a person not entitled to do so took part in the proceedings.

Financial provisions

8. The Secretary of State may pay to any member of a tribunal fees and travelling and other allowances in respect of his services in accordance with such scales and subject to such conditions as the Secretary of State may determine with the approval of the Treasury.

9. The Secretary of State may pay to any person who attends as a witness before the tribunal sums by way of compensation for the loss of his time and travelling and other allowances in accordance with such scales and subject to such conditions as may be determined as aforesaid.

10. If a tribunal recommends to the Secretary of State that the whole or part of the expenses properly incurred by the respondent for the purposes of proceedings before the tribunal should be defrayed out of public funds, the Secretary of State may if he thinks fit make to the respondent such payments in respect of those expenses as the Secretary of State considers appropriate.

11. Any expenses incurred by a tribunal with the approval of the Secretary of State shall be defrayed by the Secretary of State.

Supplemental

12. The Secretary of State shall make available to a tribunal such accommodation, the services of such officers and such other facilities as he considers appropriate for the purpose of enabling the tribunal to perform its functions.

NOTE
[1]Amended by Supreme Court Act 1981, Sched. 5.

PART II

1.2.47

ADVISORY BODIES

Membership

13.—(1) An advisory body shall consist of three persons of whom—

(*a*)   one shall be a person who is of counsel to Her Majesty and is appointed by the Lord Chancellor to be the chairman of the advisory body; and

(*b*)   another shall be a person appointed by the Secretary of State, being a member of the respondent's profession who is an officer of a department of the Government of the United Kingdom; and

(*c*)   the other shall be a person appointed by the Secretary of State from among the members of the respondent's profession nominated as mentioned in paragraph 1 above.

(2) Sub-paragraph (1) above shall have effect in relation to an advisory body in Scotland as if for the reference to the Lord Chancellor there were substituted a reference to the Lord President of the Court of Session.

Procedure

14. The respondent shall be entitled to appear before and be heard by the advisory body either in person or by counsel or solicitor.

15. Subject to the provisions of this Part of this Schedule, an advisory body may regulate its own procedure.

Application of provisions of Part I

16. Paragraphs 3, 7, 8 and 10 to 12 of this Schedule shall apply in relation to an advisory body as they apply in relation to a tribunal.

PART III

PROFESSIONAL PANELS   **1.2.48**

Membership

17. A professional panel shall consist of a chairman and two other persons appointed by the Secretary of State from among the members of the respondent's profession after consultation with such one or more of the relevant bodies mentioned in paragraph 1(2) above as the Secretary of State considers appropriate.

Procedure

18. The respondent shall be entitled to appear before, and be heard by the professional panel either in person or by counsel or solicitor.

19. Subject to the provisions of this Part of this Schedule, a professional panel may regulate its own procedure.

Application of provisions of Part I

20. Paragraphs 3, 7 and 8 of this Schedule shall apply in relation to a professional panel as they apply in relation to a tribunal.

PART IV

APPLICATION OF PARTS I TO III TO NORTHERN IRELAND   **1.2.49**

21. In the application of Parts I to III of this Schedule to Northern Ireland the provisions specified in the first column of the following Table shall have effect subject to the modifications specified in relation thereto in the second column of that Table.

Provision of this Schedule	*Modification*
Paragraph 1	In sub-paragraph (1), for the references to the Lord Chancellor and the Secretary of State there shall be substituted respectively references to the Lord Chief Justice of Northern Ireland and

| | | | the Minister of Home Affairs for Northern Ireland. |

Paragraph 4 ... ... In sub-paragraph (1), for the reference to the Lord Chancellor there shall be substituted a reference to the Ministry of Home Affairs for Northern Ireland.

For sub-paragraph (3) there shall be substituted—
"(3) Any rules made under this paragraph by the Ministry of Home Affairs for Northern Ireland shall be subject to negative resolution within the meaning of section 41(6) of the Interpretation Act (Northern Ireland) 1954 [c. 33 (N.I.)] as if they were a statutory instrument within the meaning of that Act."

Paragraphs 8 to 12 ... For the references to the Secretary of State and the Treasury there shall be substituted respectively references to the Ministry of Home Affairs for Northern Ireland and the Ministry of Finance for Northern Ireland.

Paragraph 13 ... ... In sub-paragraph (1)—
(a) for the references to the Lord Chancellor and Secretary of State there shall be substituted respectively references to the Lord Chief Justice of Northern Ireland and the Minister of Home Affairs for Northern Ireland; and
(b) for the reference to a department of the Government of the United Kingdom there shall be substituted a reference to a department of the Government of Northern Ireland.

Paragraph 16 ... ... The references to paragraphs 8 and 10 to 12 shall be construed as references to those paragraphs as modified by this Part of this Schedule.

Paragraph 17 ... ... For the reference to the Secretary of State there shall be substituted a reference to the Minister of Home Affairs for Northern Ireland.

Paragraph 20 ... ... The reference to paragraph 8 shall be construed as a reference to that paragraph as modified by this Part of this Schedule.

1.2.50

MISUSE OF DRUGS ACT 1971

SCHEDULE 4

PROSECUTION AND PUNISHMENT OF OFFENCES

[SCOTLAND]

Section Creating Offence	General Nature of Offence	Mode of Prosecution	Punishment			
			Class A drug involved	Class B drug involved	Class C drug involved	General
Section 4(2)	Production, or being concerned in the production, of a controlled drug.	(a) Summary … (b) On indictment.	12 months or £5,000, or both. Life or a fine, or both.	12 months or £5,000, or both. 14 years or a fine, or both.	3 months or Level 4, or both. 5 years or a fine, or both.	
Section 4(3)	Supplying or offering to supply a controlled drug or being concerned in the doing of either activity by another.	(a) Summary … (b) On indictment.	12 months or £5,000, or both. Life or a fine, or both.	12 months or £5,000, or both. 14 years or a fine, or both.	3 months or Level 4, or both. 5 years or a fine, or both.	
Section 5(2)	Having possession of a controlled drug.	(a) Summary … (b) On indictment.	6 months or £5,000, or both. 7 years or a fine, or both.	3 months or Level 4, or both. 5 years or a fine, or both.	3 months or Level 4, or both. 2 years or a fine, or both.	
Section 5(3)	Having possession of a controlled drug with intent to supply it to another.	(a) Summary … (b) On indictment.	12 months or £5,000, or both. Life or a fine, or both.	12 months or £5,000, or both. 14 years or a fine, or both.	3 months or Level 4, or both. 5 years or a fine, or both.	

Section Creating Offence	General Nature of Offence	Mode of Prosecution	Punishment			
			Class A drug involved	Class B drug involved	Class C drug involved	General
Section 6(2)	Cultivation of cannabis plant.	(a) Summary ...	—	—	—	6 months or £5,000, or both.
		(b) On indictment.	—	—	—	14 years or a fine, or both.
Section 8	Being the occupier, or concerned in the management, or premises and permitting or suffering certain activities to take place there.	(a) Summary ...	6 months or £5,000, or both.	6 months or £5,000, or both.	3 months or Level 4, or both.	
		(b) On indictment.	14 years or a fine, or both.	14 years or a fine, or both.	5 years or a fine, or both.	
Section 9	Offences relating to opium	(a) Summary ...	—	—	—	6 months or £5,000 or both.
		(b) On indictment	—	—	—	14 years or a fine, or both.
[Section 9A	Supply of articles for administering or preparing controlled drugs.	Summary ...	—	—	—	6 months or £5,000.
Section 11(2)	Contravention of directions relating to safe custody of controlled drugs.	(a) Summary ...	—	—	—	6 months or £5,000, or both.
		(b) On indictment.	—	—	—	2 years or a fine, or both.

Section Creating Offence	General Nature of Offence	Mode of Prosecution	Punishment			
			Class A drug involved	*Class B drug involved*	*Class C drug involved*	*General*
Section 12(6)	Contravention of direction prohibiting practitioner etc. from possessing, supplying etc. controlled drugs.	(a) Summary ...	6 months or £5,000, or both.	6 months or £5,000, or both.	3 months or Level 4, or both.	
		(b) On indictment	14 years or a fine, or both.	14 years or a fine, or both.	5 years or a fine, or both.	
Section 13(3)	Contravention of direction prohibiting practitioner etc. from prescribing, supplying, etc. controlled drugs.	(a) Summary ...	6 months or £5,000, or both.	6 months or £5,000, or both.	3 months or Level 4, or both.	
		(b) On indictment	14 years or a fine, or both.	14 years or a fine, or both.	5 years or a fine, or both.	
Section 17(3)	Failure to comply with notice requiring information relating to prescribing, supplying, etc. of drugs.	Summary ...	—	—	—	£1,000
Section 17(4)	Giving false information in purported compliance with notice requiring information relating to prescribing, supplying, etc. of drugs.	(a) Summary ...	—	—	—	6 months or £5,000, or both.
		(b) On indictment.	—	—	—	2 years or a fine, or both.
Section 18(1)	Contravention of regulations (other than regulations relating to addicts).	(a) Summary ...	—	—	—	6 months or £5,000, or both.
		(b) On indictment.	—	—	—	2 years or a fine, or both.

Section Creating Offence	General Nature of Offence	Mode of Prosecution	Punishment			
			Class A drug involved	Class B drug involved	Class C drug involved	General
Section 18(2)	Contravention of terms of licence or other authority (other than licence issued under regulations relating to addicts).	(a) Summary …	—	—	—	6 months or £5,000, or both.
		(b) On indictment.	—	—	—	2 years or a fine, or both.
Section 18(3)	Giving false information in purported compliance with obligation to give information imposed under or by virtue of regulations	(a) Summary …	—	—	—	6 months or £5,000, or both.
		(b) On indictment.	—	—	—	2 years or a fine, or both.
Section 18(4)	Giving false information, or producing document, etc. containing false statement etc., for purposes of obtaining issue or renewal of a licence or other authority.	(a) Summary …	—	—	—	6 months or £5,000, or both.
		(b) On indictment.	—	—	—	2 years or a fine, or both.
Section 20	Assisting in or inducing commission outside United Kingdom of an offence punishable under a corresponding law.	(a) Summary …	—	—	—	6 months or £5,000, or both.
		(b) On indictment	—	—	—	14 years or a fine, or both.
Section 23(4)	Obstructing exercise of powers of search etc. or concealing books, drugs etc.	(a) Summary …	—	—	—	6 months or £5,000, or both.
		(b) On indictment.	—	—	—	2 years or a fine, or both.

NOTES

¹This version of Sched. 4 represents the present law in Scotland. The original Schedule in the 1971 Act provided for a maximum of 12 months' imprisonment for the following offences *viz.* summary prosecutions for contravening ss. 4(2); 4(3) and 5(3) where Class A or B controlled drugs were involved. These maxima have not been altered for Scotland. However, by reason of the general limitations since imposed on the power of the Magistrates' Court to impose imprisonment these maxima are now six months' imprisonment for England and Wales: see s. 31(1) of the Magistrates' Courts Act 1980 (c. 43). The reason for the competency of 12 months in Scotland lies in the phrase "without prejudice to any wider powers conferred by statute" to be found in the provision that otherwise contains shrieval powers: see s. 5(3) of the Criminal Procedure (Scotland) Act 1995.

²For the standard scale of fines for offences triable only summarily, known as "the standard scale", see s. 225(2) of the Criminal Procedure (Scotland) Act 1995. There the standard scale is as follows:

Level on the scale	Amount of fine
1.	£200
2.	£500
3.	£1,000
4.	£2,500
5.	£5,000

³For "the prescribed sum" see s. 225(8) of the 1995 Act where it means £5,000 or such sum as is for the time being substituted in this definition by an order in force under s. 225(4) of the 1995 Act.

⁴For the various authorities amending the original Sched. 4, see ss. 27, 28 and Sched. 5 of the Criminal Law Act 1977; s. 46(1) of the Criminal Justice Act 1982; the Controlled Drugs (Penalties) Act 1985; and s. 34(2) of the Drug Trafficking Act 1986.

SCHEDULE 5   **Section 39 1.2.51**

Savings and Transitional Provisions

1.—(1) Any addiction regulations which could have been made under this Act shall not be invalidated by any repeal effected by this Act but shall have effect as if made under the provisions of this Act which correspond to the provisions under which the regulations were made; and the validity of any licence issued under any such addiction regulations shall not be affected by any such repeal.

(2) Any order, rule or other instrument or document whatsoever made or issued, any direction given, and any other thing done, under or by virtue of any of the following provisions of the Dangerous Drugs Act 1967 [c. 82], that is to say section 1(2), 2 or 3 or the Schedule, shall be deemed for the purposes of this Act to have been made, issued or done, as the case may be, under the corresponding provision of this Act; and anything begun under any of the said provisions of that Act may be continued under this Act as if begun under this Act.

(3) In this paragraph "addiction regulations" means any regulations made under section 11 of the Dangerous Drugs Act 1965 [c. 15] which include provision for any of the matters for which regulations may be so made by virtue of section 1(1) of the Dangerous Drugs Act 1967.

2. As from the coming into operation of section 3 of this Act any licence granted for the purpose of section 5 of the Drugs (Prevention of Misuse) Act 1964 [c. 64] or sections 2, 3 or 10 of the Dangerous Drugs Act 1965 shall have effect as if granted for the purposes of section 3(2) of this Act.

3.—(1) The Secretary of State may at any time before the coming into operation of section 12 of this Act give a direction under sub-section (2) of that section in respect of any practitioner or pharmacist whose general authority under the Dangerous Drugs Regulations is for the time being withdrawn; but a direction given by virtue of this sub-paragraph shall not take effect until section 12 comes into operation, and shall not take effect at all if the general authority of the person concerned is restored before that section comes into operation.

(2) No direction under section 12(2) of this Act shall be given by virtue of sub-paragraph (1) above in respect of a person while the withdrawal of his general authority under the Dangerous Drugs Regulations is suspended; but where, in the case of any practitioner or pharmacist whose general authority has been withdrawn, the withdrawal is suspended at the time when section 12 comes into operation, the Secretary of State may at any time give a direction under section 12(2) in respect of him by virtue of this sub-paragraph unless the Secretary of State has previously caused to be served on him a notice stating that he is no longer liable to have such a direction given in respect of him by virtue of this sub-paragraph.

(3) In this paragraph "the Dangerous Drugs Regulations" means as regards Great Britain, the Dangerous Drugs (No. 2) Regulations 1964 or, as regards Northern Ireland, the Dangerous Drugs Regulations (Northern Ireland) 1965.

4. Subject to paragraphs 1 to 3 above, and without prejudice to the generality of section 31(1)(c) of this Act, regulations made by the Secretary of State under any provision of this Act may include such provision as the Secretary of State thinks fit for effecting the transition from any provision made by or by virtue of any of the enactments repealed by this Act to any provision made by or by virtue of this Act, and in particular may provide for the continuation in force, with or without modifications, of any licence or other authority issued or having effect as if issued under or by virtue of any of those enactments.

5. For purposes of the enforcement of the enactments repealed by this Act as regards anything done or omitted before their repeal, any powers of search, entry, inspection, seizure or detention conferred by those enactments shall continue to be exercisable as if those enactments were still in force.

6. The mention of particular matters in this Schedule shall not prejudice the general application of section 38(2) of the Interpretation Act 1889 [c. 63] with regard to the effect of repeals.

1.2.52   SCHEDULE 6   **Section 39**

REPEALS

Chapter	Short Title	Extent of Repeal
1964 c. 64.	The Drugs (Prevention of Misuse) Act 1964.	The whole Act.
1965 c. 15.	The Dangerous Drugs Act 1965.	The whole Act.
1967 c. 82.	The Dangerous Drugs Act 1967.	The whole Act.
1968 c. 59.	The Hovercraft Act 1968.	Paragraph 6 of the Schedule.
1968 c. 67.	The Medicines Act 1968.	In Schedule 5, paragraphs 14 and 15.

1973 No. 798

DANGEROUS DRUGS

The Misuse of Drugs (Safe Custody) Regulations 1973   **1.3**

Made - - - -	*19th April* 1973
Laid before Parliament	*7th May* 1973
Coming into Operation—	
Regulations 1, 2, 5 and Schedule 1	*1st July* 1973
Remainder	*1st October* 1974

In pursuance of sections 10(2)(*a*) and 31 of the Misuse of Drugs Act 1971 (c. 38), after consultation with the Advisory Council on the Misuse of Drugs, I hereby make the following Regulations:—

1. These Regulations may be cited as the Misuse of Drugs (Safe **1.3.1** Custody) Regulations 1973 and (with the exception of Regulations 3 and 4 and Schedule 2 which shall come into operation on October 1, 1974) shall come into operation on July 1, 1973.

2.—(1) In these Regulations, unless the context otherwise requires, **1.3.2** the expression—

"the Act" means the Misuse of Drugs Act 1971;

"retail dealer" means a person lawfully conducting a retail pharmacy business or a pharmacist engaged in supplying drugs to the public at a health centre within the meaning of the Medicines Act 1968 (c. 67).

(2) In these Regulations any reference to any enactment shall be construed as a reference to that enactment as amended, and as including a reference thereto as extended or applied, by or under any other enactment.

(3) The Interpretation Act 1889 (c. 63) shall apply for the interpretation of these Regulations as it applies for the interpretation of an Act of Parliament.

3.—(1) This Regulation applies to the following premises, that is to say:— **1.3.3**

(*a*) any premises occupied by a retail dealer for the purposes of his business;

(*b*) any nursing home within the meaning of Part VI of the Public Health Act 1936 (c. 49) or the Nursing Homes Registration (Scotland) Act 1938 (c. 73);

(*c*) any residential or other establishment provided under or by virtue of section 59 of the Social Work (Scotland) Act 1968 (c. 49);

(*d*) any mental nursing home within the meaning of Part III of the Mental Health Act 1959 (c. 72);

(*e*)   any private hospital within the meaning of the Mental Health (Scotland) Act 1960 (c. 61).

(2) Subject to paragraph (4) of this Regulation, the occupier and every person concerned in the management of any premises to which this Regulation applies shall ensure that all controlled drugs (other than those specified in Schedule 1 to these Regulations) on the premises are, so far as circumstances permit, kept in a locked safe, cabinet or room which is so constructed and maintained as to prevent unauthorised access to the drugs.

(3) Subject to Regulation 4 of these Regulations, the relevant requirements of Schedule 2 to these Regulations shall be complied with in relation to every safe, cabinet or room in which controlled drugs are kept in pursuance of paragraph (2) of this Regulation.

(4) It shall not be necessary to comply with the requirements of paragraph (2) of this Regulation in respect of any controlled drug which is for the time being under the direct personal supervision of—

(*a*)   in the case of any premises falling within paragraph (1)(*a*) of this Regulation, a pharmacist in respect of whom no direction under section 12(2) of the Act is for the time being in force; or

(*b*)   in the case of premises falling within paragraph (1)(*b*) to (*e*) of this Regulation, the person in charge of the premises or any member of his staff designated by him for the purpose.

1.3.4   **4.**—(1) Paragraph (3) of Regulation 3 of these Regulations shall not have effect in relation to a safe, cabinet or room situated on any premises occupied for the purposes of his business by a person lawfully conducting a retail pharmacy business (hereafter in this Regulation referred to as "the occupier") if a certificate has been issued in pursuance of paragraph (2) of this Regulation (hereafter in this Regulation referred to as a "certificate") in respect of that safe, cabinet or room and the certificate is for the time being in force.

(2) On receiving written application in that behalf from the occupier, the chief officer of police for the police area in which the premises in question are situated may—

(*a*)   cause the said premises and, in particular, any safe, cabinet or room in which controlled drugs are to be kept, to be inspected; and

(*b*)   if satisfied that, in all the circumstances of the case, the safes, cabinets or rooms in which controlled drugs (other than those specified in Schedule 1 to these Regulations) are to be kept provide an adequate degree of security, issue a certificate in respect of those safes, cabinets or rooms.

(3) Every certificate shall specify—

(*a*)   every safe, cabinet or room to which the certificate relates; and

(*b*)   any conditions necessary to be observed if the safes, cabinets and rooms to which the certificates relates are to provide an adequate degree of security.

(4) Where a certificate is in force in respect of any safe, cabinet or room on any premises, the chief officer of police may cause the premises to be inspected as any reasonable time for the purpose of ascertaining whether any conditions specified in the certificate are being observed and whether as a result of any change of circumstances the safes, cabinets and rooms to which the certificate relates have ceased to provide an adequate degree of security.

(5) A certificate may be cancelled by the chief officer of police if it appears to him that—

(*a*)   there has been a breach of any condition specified in the certificate; or

(*b*)   as a result of any change of circumstances, the safes, cabinets and rooms to which the certificate relates no longer provide an adequate degree of security; or

(*c*)   the occupier has refused entry to any police officer acting in pursuance of paragraph (4) of this Regulation.

(6) A certificate shall, unless previously cancelled in pursuance of paragraph (5) of this Regulation, remain in force for a period of one year from the date of issue thereof, but may from time to time be renewed for a further period of one year.

5.—(1) Where any controlled drug (other than a drug specified in **1.3.5** Schedule 1 to these Regulations) is kept otherwise than in a locked safe, cabinet or room which is so constructed and maintained as to prevent unauthorised access to the drug, any person to whom this Regulation applies having possession of the drug shall ensure that, so far as circumstances permit, it is kept in a locked receptacle which can be opened only by him or by a person authorised by him.

(2) Paragraph (1) of this Regulation applies to any person other than—

(*a*)   a person to whom the drug has been supplied by or on the prescription of a practitioner for his own treatment or that of another person or an animal; or

(*b*)   a person engaged in the business of a carrier when acting in the course of that business; or

(*c*)   a person engaged in the business of the Post Office when acting in the course of that business.

¹SCHEDULE 1   **Regulations 3(2), 4(2)(b) and 5**

EXEMPTED DRUGS   **1.3.6**

1.   Any controlled drug specified in Schedule 4 or 5 to the Misuse of Drugs Regulations 1985.²

2. Any liquid preparation designed for administration otherwise than by injection which contains any of the following substances and products, that is to say:—

(*a*)   Amphetamine
(*b*)   Benzphetamine
(*c*)   Chlorphentermine
(*d*)   Fenethylline
(*e*)   Mephentermine
(*f*)   Methaqualone
(*g*)   Methylamphetamine
(*h*)   Methylphenidate
(*i*)   Phendimetrazine
(*j*)   Phenmetrazine
(*k*)   Pipradrol
(*l*)   Any stereoisomeric form of a substance specified in any of paragraphs (*a*) to (*k*) above.
(*m*)   Any salt of a substance specified in any of paragraphs (*a*) to (*l*) above.

3. Any of the following substances and products, that is to say:—

(*a*)   Any 5, 5 disubstituted barbituric acid
(*b*)   Cathine
(*c*)   Ethchlorvynol
(*d*)   Ethinamate
(*e*)   Mazindol
(*f*)   Meprobamate
(*g*)   Methylphenobarbitone
(*h*)   Methyprylone
(*i*)   Pentazocine
(*j*)   Phentermine
(*k*)   Any stereoisomeric form of a substance specified in any of paragraphs (*a*) to (*j*) above.
(*l*)   Any salt of a substance specified in any of paragraphs (*a*) to (*k*) above.
(*m*)   Any preparation or other product containing a substance or product specified in any of paragraphs (*a*) to (*l*) above.

NOTES

[1]New Schedule inserted by S.I. 1986 No. 2332.
[2]This includes temazepam since April 18, 1996: see S.I. 1995 No. 3244: art. 3.

1.3.7   SCHEDULE 2   **Regulation 3(3)**

STRUCTURAL REQUIREMENTS IN RELATION TO SAFES, CABINETS AND ROOMS USED FOR KEEPING DRUGS

1. In this Schedule, the expression—

"external wall," in relation to any room, means a wall which forms part of the outside of the building in which the room is situated;

"party wall," in relation to any room, means a wall dividing the premises in which the room is situated from other premises under different occupation;

"the Standard of 1963" means the British Standard Specification for Thief Resistant Locks for Hinged Doors B.S. 3621: 1963, as published on May 6, 1963;

"two-leaf door" means a door having two leaves which either close on to each other or on to a central pillar, and the two leaves of any such door shall be treated for the purposes of this Schedule as a single door;

"sheet steel" means mild steel sheet being not lighter than 16 gauge.

Safes and Cabinets

2.—(1) A safe or cabinet shall be constructed of—

(a)   pressed and welded sheet steel; or

(b)   pressed and welded steel mesh; or

(c)   sheet steel or steel mesh welded upon an angle-iron frame of at least 25 millimetres (1 inch) by 25 millimetres (1 inch) section and of at least 5 millimetres ($^3/_{16}$ inch) thickness.

(2) The clearance between the door and jamb or, in the case of a two-leaf door, between the two leaves or each leaf and a central pillar shall not be greater than 3 millimetres ($^1/_8$ inch).

(3) Each door shall be fitted with an effective lock—

(a)   having at least 5 differing levers or, in the case of a pin and tumbler mechanism, at least 6 pins;

(b)   designed to permit at least 1000 effective key-differs independent of wards or any other fixed obstruction to the movement of the key; and

(c)   provided with a dead-bolt which is either of mild steel of at least 19 millimetres ($^3/_4$ inch) by 8 millimetres ($^5/_{16}$ inch) section or incorporates a suitable anti-cutting advice and which has a total throw of at least 12 millimetres ($^1/_2$ inch).

(4) If the length of the vertical closing edge of a door exceeds 914 millimetres (3 feet) and the length of the horizontal edge exceeds 457 millimetres (18 inches) the door shall be fitted with two such locks as are specified in sub-paragraph (3) above, one situated at not more than one third of the length of the vertical closing edge from the top and the other at not more than one third from the bottom, but otherwise the lock required by sub-paragraph (3) above shall be situated in the centre of the vertical closing edge.

(5) If a safe or cabinet is fitted with a two-leaf door, either—

(a)   the lock or locks required by sub-paragraphs (3) and (4) above shall be fitted with an integrated espagnolette bolt which is of at least 19 millimetres ($^3/_4$ inch) by 8 millimetres ($^5/_{16}$ inch) section and which has a total throw, at both the top and bottom, of at least 12 millimetres ($^1/_2$ inch); or

(b)   the second opening leaf shall be secured at the top and bottom by means of internal bolts of mild steel of at least 6 millimetres ($^1/_4$ inch) by 6 millimetres ($^1/_4$ inch) section or 6 millimetres ($^1/_4$ inch) diameter, each of which has a total throw of at least 12 millimetres ($^1/_2$ inch), the bolt handles being returnable into a holding recess.

(6) A safe or cabinet shall be rigidly and securely fixed to a wall or floor by means of at least two rag-bolts each passing through an internal anchor plate of mild steel which is of at least 3 millimetres ($^1/_8$ inch) thickness and which has a surface area of at least 19355 square millimetres (30 square inches).

(7) Nothing shall be displayed outside a safe or cabinet to indicate that drugs are kept inside it.

Rooms

3.—(1) Each wall shall be securely attached to the floor, ceiling and adjacent walls and shall be constructed of—

(a)   bricks laid in cement mortar to at least 229 millimetres (9 inches) thickness or, if the joints are reinforced with metal reinforcing ties, to at least 115 millimetres (4 $^1/_2$ inches) thickness; or

(b)   concrete (being solid concrete, reinforced concrete or dense concrete blocks laid in cement mortar) of at least 152 millimetres (6 inches) thickness, the joints being reinforced with metal reinforcing ties where concrete blocks are used; or

(c)   steel mesh fixed externally by welding upon angle-iron frames of at least 50 millimetres (2 inches) by 50 millimetres (2 inches) section and 6 millimetres ($^1/_4$ inch) thickness, having vertical members not more than 610 millimetres (2 feet) apart and horizontal members not more than 1220 millimetres (4 feet) apart; or

(d)   sheet steel fixed externally by welding, or bolting with steel bolts of not less than 12 millimetres ($^1/_2$ inch) diameter and at intervals of not more than 305 millimetres (1 foot), upon either angle-iron frames as specified in (c) above or timber frames of at least 50 millimetres (2 inches) by 100 millimetres (4 inches) section, having vertical and horizontal members spaced as specified in (c) above.

(2) If a party wall or, in the case of a room of which the floor level is less than 2440 millimetres (8 feet) above the external ground level, an external wall is used to form one of the walls of the room, that wall shall be reinforced internally by means of an additional wall which is constructed in accordance with the requirements of sub-paragraph (1) above.

(3) The floor shall be—

(a)   constructed of solid concrete or reinforced concrete; or
(b)   covered internally with sheet steel or steel mesh, welded at all joints; or
(c)   otherwise so constructed that it cannot be readily penetrated from below.

(4) The ceiling shall be constructed of—

(a)   solid concrete or reinforced concrete as specified in sub-paragraph (1)(b) above; or
(b)   steel mesh fixed externally by welding upon angle-iron frames as specified in sub-paragraph (1)(c) above, the members of which shall not be more than 610 millimetres (2 feet) apart in one direction or more than 1220 millimetres (4 feet) apart in the other; or
(c)   sheet steel fixed externally by welding upon angle-iron frames as specified in sub-paragraph (1)(c) above, the members being spaced as specified in (b) above.

(5) Each door or, in the case of a stable-type door, each half-door shall be constructed of—

(a)   steel mesh fixed externally by welding upon angle-iron frames as specified in sub-paragraph (1)(c) above; or
(b)   sheet steel fixed externally by welding upon angle-iron frames as specified in sub-paragraph (1)(c) above, the members being spaced as specified therein; or
(c)   sheet steel fixed externally by welding upon angle-iron frames as specified in sub-paragraph (1)(c) above, the members being spaced as specified in (b) above.

(5) Each door or, in the case of a stable-type door, each half-door shall be constructed of—

(a)   steel mesh fixed externally by welding upon angle-iron frames as specified in sub-paragraph (1)(c) above; or
(b)   sheet steel fixed externally by welding upon angle-iron frames as specified in sub-paragraph (1)(c) above, the members being spaced as specified therein; or
(c)   sheet steel fixed externally upon a hardwood frame of at least 50 millimetres (2 inches) by 75 millimetres (3 inches) to stiles, rails and braces or muntins by means of coach bolts at intervals of not more than 305 millimetres (1 foot) (the nuts whereof being on the inside of the door) and with non-withdrawable screws between the bolts at intervals not exceeding 100 millimetres (4 inches), the members of the frame being spaced as specified in sub-paragraph (1)(c) above; or
(d)   sheet steel fixed externally upon a solid timber core of at least 50 millimetres (2 inches) thickness.

(6) Each door, or, in the case of a stable-type door, each half-door shall be fitted with an effective lock, being a single-sided dead lock having resistance to manipulation and forcing sufficient to comply with the requirement of the Standard of 1963.

(7) If the room is fitted with a two-leaf door, the second opening leaf shall be secured top and bottom by means of—

(*a*) an espagnolette bolt, operated only from within the room, with vertical fastening rods of mild steel of at least 16 millimetres ($^5/_8$ inch) by 16 millimetres ($^5/_8$ inch) section or 16 millimetres ($^5/_8$ inch) diameter; or

(*b*) at least internal tower bolts of mild steel of at least 16 millimetres ($^5/_8$ inch) diameter, designed to swivel into a secure holding recess when in the thrown position.

and in either case the bolt shall have a total throw at least 25 millimetres (1 inch) greater than the clearance between the door and the floor or lintel, as the case may be, the lower shooting hole being kept at all times free from obstruction.

(8) The closing frame of each doorway shall be constructed of—

(*a*) an angle frame as specified in sub-paragraph (1)(*c*) above; or

(*b*) hardwood of at least 50 millimetres (2 inches) by 100 millimetres (4 inches) section, covered by sheet steel bolted through the timber at intervals not exceeding 457 millimetres (18 inches) by means of coach bolts (the nuts whereof not being accessible from outside the room; or

(*c*) pressed steel not lighter than 10 gauge welded at all joints.

(9) Each section of the closing frame of each doorway shall be fixed to the adjoining wall at intervals not exceeding 457 millimetres (18 inches) by means of—

(*a*) where the wall is constructed of bricks, bent and tanged straps of wrought-iron, screwed or bolted to the frame and built into the brickwork;

(*b*) where the wall is constructed of concrete, rag-bolts; or

(*c*) where the wall is constructed of steel mesh or sheet steel, steel bolts or dowels of at least 12 millimetres ($^1/_2$ inch) diameter or welding to the framework or cladding of the room.

(10) Each glass window shall either be constructed of glass blocks not larger than 190 millimetres (7 $^1/_2$ inches) by 190 millimetres (7 $^1/_2$ inches) and of at least 80 millimetres (3 $^1/_8$ inches) thickness, set in a reinforced concrete frame having a reinforcing bar between every block, or be guarded by a grille consisting of—

(*a*) panels of steel mesh fixed on angle-iron frames as specified in sub-paragraph (1)(*c*) above and fixed—

(i) where the surrounding wall or ceiling is constructed of sheet steel on angle-iron frames, by welding to the sheet steel or framework at intervals not exceeding 305 millimetres (1 foot); or

(ii) where the surrounding walls is constructed of sheet steel on timber frames, by means of steel bolts of at least 12 millimetres ($^1/_2$ inch) diameter, bolted through the timber at intervals not exceeding 457 millimetres (18 inches); or

(iii) where the surrounding wall is constructed of bricks, by means of bent and tanged straps of wrought-iron screwed or bolted to the frame and built into the brickwork at intervals not exceeding 457 millimetres (18 inches); or

(iv) where the surrounding wall or ceiling is constructed of concrete, by means of rag-bolts at intervals not exceeding 457 millimetres (18 inches); or

(*b*) vertical bars of solid mild steel of at least 25 millimetres (1 inch) by 25 millimetres (1 inch) square section, having one of their diagonal axes in a plane parallel to that of the window aperture, spaced not more than 127 millimetres (5 inches) apart centre to centre with the outer bars not more than 75 millimetres (3 inches) from the reveals of the window, and running through and welded to flat mild steel horizontal guard-bars which—

(i) are of at least 62 millimetres (2 $^1/_2$ inches) width and 9 millimetres ($^3/_8$ inch) thickness;

(ii)   are spaced not more than 762 millimetres (2 $1/2$ feet) apart, the upper and lower guard-bars being at a distance not exceeding 100 millimetres (4 inches) from the ends of the vertical bars and not exceeding 75 millimetres (3 inches) from the head and sill of the window;

(iii)   are welded at each end to steel brackets of at least 152 millimetres (6 inches) length, 62 millimetres (2 $1/2$ inches) width and 12 millimetres ($1/2$ inch) thickness fixed to the surrounding wall or ceiling, as the case may be, in the manner required by (*a*) above at a distance of at least 152 millimetres (6 inches) from the reveals of the window;

(iv)   if more than 1830 millimetres (6 feet) in length, have the uppermost and lowermost of them fixed to the head and sill of the window at intervals not exceeding 1830 millimetres (6 feet), by means of angle-iron fixings of at least 50 millimetres (2 inches) section and 6 millimetres ($1/4$ inch) thickness welded to the guard-bars and fixed to the surrounding wall or ceiling, as the case may be, in the manner required by (*a*) above.

(11) Each service-hatch shall be guarded by a grille consisting of—

(i)   panels of steel mesh or sheet steel on angle-iron frames as specified in sub-paragraph (1)(*c*) above; or

(ii)   vertical bars of solid mild steel as specified in sub-paragraph (10((*b*)(i) and (ii) above,

and the grille shall be secured at all times when the hatch is not in use in such a way as to be secure against removal from outside the room.

(12) Each aperture other than a window or service-hatch shall be guarded by a grille which satisfies the requirements of sub-paragraph (10)(*a*) or (*b*) above.

(13) Each shelf in a room shall be so situated as to prevent drugs placed upon it from being extracted from outside through any aperture.

(14) Nothing shall be displayed outside a room to indicate that drugs are kept in the room.

General

4.—(1) Where sheet steel is used in the construction of a safe, cabinet or room, its edges shall be lapped inwards around the margins of apertures and around the edges of doors and service-hatch covers in such manner as to be inaccessible from the outside; and where sheet steel is fixed on a framework, it shall be so fixed as to prevent removal from outside the safe, cabinet or room of which the framework forms part.

(2) Any steel mesh used in the construction of a safe, cabinet or room shall be—

(*a*)   welded steel mesh not lighter than 10 standard wire gauge having rectangular apertures not exceeding 75 millimetres (3 inches) by 12 millimetres ($1/2$ inch); or

(*b*)   expanded steel not lighter than 12 gauge having diamond apertures not exceeding 44 millimetres (1 $3/4$ inches) by 19 millimetres ($3/4$ inch).

(3) Except where otherwise specified in this Schedule, the edges of each panel of sheet steel or steel mesh used in the construction of a safe, cabinet or room shall be arc-welded to a steel frame along their entire length, or, in the absence of a steel frame, continuously arc-welded along the entire length of all joins.

(4) Each hinged door, half-door or leaf of a two-leaf door in a safe, cabinet or room shall be fitted with at least two hinges.

(5) If any part of the hinge of such a door, half-door or leaf of a two-leaf door is on the outside of the door, it shall be fitted—

(*a*)   in the case of a safe or cabinet, with at least two dog-bolts of mild steel of similar gauge and dimensions to the frame of the safe or cabinet or an internal flange or rebate running the entire length of the door and so fitted as to prevent access without unlocking in the event of damage to the hinges;

(*b*)   in the case of a room, with at least two dog-bolts of mild steel which—

(i)   are of similar gauge and dimensions to the jamb and either project at least 16 millimetres ($^5/_8$ inch) into the jamb or are attached to the jamb and project to a similar extent into the frame of the door, where the closing frame of the doorway is constructed of angle-iron; or

(ii)   are of at least 50 millimetres (2 inches) width and 6 millimetres ($^1/_4$ inch) thickness and either project at least 16 millimetres ($^5/_8$ inch) into the jamb or are attached to the jamb and project to a similar extent into the edge of the door, where the closing frame of the doorway is constructed of timber or pressed steel.

(6) Each bar, grille or service-hatch cover and each lock, bolt assembly and other means of securing doors and service-hatch covers in a safe, cabinet or room shall be fitted internally.

(7) The bolt of each lock and each bolt or catch securing the cover of any aperture in a safe, cabinet or room shall be protected against cutting or manipulation from outside.

(8) Each screw, bolt or other fixing device used in the construction of a safe, cabinet or room shall be such as to be incapable of being removed from outside and shall be of a strength at least equal to that of the component part which it fixes.

1973 No. 799

DANGEROUS DRUGS   1.4

The Misuse of Drugs (Notification of and Supply to Addicts) Regulations 1973

Made - - - -	*19th April* 1973
Laid before Parliament	*7th May* 1973
Coming into Operation	*1st July* 1973

In pursuance of sections 10(2)(*h*) and (*i*), 22(*c*) and 31 of the Misuse of Drugs Act 1971 (c. 38), after consultation with the Advisory Council on the Misuse of Drugs, I hereby make the following Regulations:—

1. These Regulations may be cited as the Misuse of Drugs (Notification **1.4.1** of and Supply to Addicts) Regulations 1973 and shall come into operation on July 1, 1973.

2.—(1) In these Regulations, the expression—   **1.4.2**

"drug" means a controlled drug specified in the Schedule to these Regulations;

"hospital"—

(*a*)   as respects England and Wales, has the same meaning as in the National Health Service Act 1946 (c. 81) and includes a nursing home within the meaning of Part VI of the Public Health Act 1936 (c. 49), a mental nursing home within the meaning of Part III of the Mental Health Act 1959 (c. 72) and special hospital within the meaning of that Act;

(*b*)   as respects Scotland, has the same meaning as in the National Health Service (Scotland) Act 1947 (c. 27) and includes a nursing home within the meaning of the Nursing Homes Registration (Scotland) Act 1938 (c. 73), a private hospital within the meaning of the Mental Health (Scotland) Act 1960 (c. 61) and a state hospital within the meaning of that Act.

(2) For the purposes of these Regulations, a person shall be regarded as being addicted to a drug if, and only if, he has as a result of repeated administration become so dependent upon the drug that he has an overpowering desire for the administration of it to be continued.

(3) In these Regulations any reference to any enactment shall be construed as a reference to that enactment as amended, and as including a reference thereto as extended or applied, by or under any other enactment.

(4) The Interpretation Act 1889 (c. 63) shall apply for the interpretation of these Regulations as it applies for the interpretation of an Act of Parliament.

1.4.3   **3.**—(1) Subject to paragraph (2) of this Regulation, any doctor who attends a person who he considers, or has reasonable grounds to suspect, is addicted to any drug shall, within seven days of the attendance, furnish in writing to the Chief Medical Officer at the Home Office such of the following particulars with respect to that person as are known to the doctor, that is to say, the name, address, sex, date of birth and national health service number of that person, the date of the attendance and the name of the drug or drugs concerned.

(2) It shall not be necessary for a doctor who attends a person to comply with the provisions of paragraph (1) of this Regulation in respect of that person if—

(*a*)   the doctor is of the opinion, formed in good faith, that the continued administration of the drug or drugs concerned is required for the purpose of treating organic disease or injury; or

(*b*)   the particulars which, apart from this paragraph, would have been required under those provisions to be furnished have, during the period of 12 months ending with the date of the attendance, been furnished in compliance with those provisions—

(i)   by the doctor; or

(ii)   if the doctor is a partner in or employed by a firm of general practitioners, by a doctor who is a partner in or employed by that firm; or

(iii)   if the attendance is on behalf of another doctor, whether for payment or otherwise, by that doctor; or

(iv)   if the attendance is at a hospital, by a doctor on the staff of that hospital.

1.4.4   **4.**—(1) Subject to paragraph (2) of this Regulation, a doctor shall not administer or supply to a person who he considers, or has reasonable grounds to suspect, is addicted to any drug, or authorise the administration or supply to such a person of, any substance specified in paragraph (3) below, or prescribe for such a person any such substance, except—

   (*a*)   for the purpose of treating organic disease or injury; or
   (*b*)   under and in accordance with the terms of a licence issued by the Secretary of State in pursuance of these Regulations.

(2) Paragraph (1) of this Regulation shall not apply to the administration or supply by a doctor of a substance specified in paragraph (3) below if the administration or supply is authorised by another doctor under and in accordance with the terms of a licence issued to him in pursuance of these Regulations.

(3) The substance referred to in paragraphs (1) and (2) above are—

   (*a*)   cocaine, its salts and any preparation or other product containing cocaine or its salts other than a preparation falling within paragraph 2 of Schedule 1 to the Misuse of Drugs Regulations 1973[1];
   (*b*)   diamorphine, its salts and any preparation or other product containing diamorphine or its salts.
   (*c*)   dipipanone, its salts and any preparation or other product containing dipipanone or its salts.[2]

NOTES
[1]S.I. 1973 No. 797.
[2]Inserted by S.I. 1983 No. 1909.

5. These Regulations and, in relation only to the requirements of these **1.4.5** Regulations, sections 13(1) and (3), 14, 16, 19 and 25 of and Schedule 4 to the Misuse of Drugs Act 1971 (which relate to their enforcement) shall apply to servants and agents of the Crown.

6.—(1) The Dangerous Drugs (Notification of Addicts) Regulations **1.4.6** 1968[1] and the Dangerous Drugs (Supply to Addicts) Regulations 1968[2] are hereby revoked.

(2) For the purposes of paragraph 2(*b*) of Regulation 3 of these Regulations, any particulars furnished, before the coming into operation of these Regulations, in compliance with paragraph (1) Regulation 1 of the Dangerous Drugs (Notification of Addicts) Regulations 1968 shall be deemed to have furnished in compliance with paragraph (1) of Regulation 3 of these Regulations.

(3) Notwithstanding anything in paragraph (1) of this Regulation, any licence issued by the Secretary of State in pursuance of the Dangerous Drugs (Supply to Addicts) Regulations 1968 before the coming into operation of these Regulations shall continue in force for the same time as if these Regulations had not been made and shall be deemed to have been issued in pursuance of these Regulations.

NOTES
[1]S.I. 1968 No. 136.
[2]S.I. 1968 No. 416.

SCHEDULE   **Regulation 2(1)**

1.4.7   CONTROLLED DRUGS TO WHICH THESE REGULATIONS APPLY

1. The following substances and products, namely:—

Cocaine	Hydromorphone	Oxycodone
Dextromoramide	Levorphanol	Pethidine
Diamorphine	Methadone	Phenazocine
Dipipanone	Morphine	Piritramide
Hydrocodone	Opium	

2. Any stereoisomeric form of a substance specified in paragraph 1, above, not being dextrorphan.

3. Any ester or ether of a substance specified in paragraph 1 or 2 above not being a substance for the time being specified in Part II of Schedule 2 to the Misuse of Drugs Act 1971.

4. Any salt of a substance specified in any of paragraphs 1 to 3 above.

5. Any preparation or other product containing a substance or product specified in any of paragraphs 1 to 4 above.

1985 No. 2066

1.5   **DANGEROUS DRUGS**

The Misuse of Drugs Regulations 1985

Made - - -	*19th December* 1985
Laid before Parliament	*15th January* 1986
Coming into Operation	*1st April* 1986

ARRANGEMENT OF REGULATIONS

1. Citation and commencement.
2. Interpretation.
3. Specification of controlled drugs for purposes of Regulations.
4. Exceptions for drugs in Schedules 4 and 5 and poppy-straw.
5. Licences to produce etc. controlled drugs.
6. General authority to supply and possess.
7. Administration of drugs in Schedules 2, 3, 4 and 5.
8. Production and supply of drugs in Schedules 2 and 5.
9. Production and supply of drugs in Schedules 3 and 4.
10. Possession of drugs in Schedules 2, 3 and 4.
11. Exemption for midwives.
12. Cultivation under licence of Cannabis plant.
13. Approval of premises for cannabis smoking for research purposes.
14. Documents to be obtained by supplier of controlled drugs.
15. Form of prescriptions.
16. Provisions as to supply on prescription.

SCHEDULES

NOTE
¹Inserted by S.I. 1996 No. 1597.

In pursuance of sections 7, 10, 22 and 31 of the Misuse of Drugs Act 1971 (c. 38), after consultation with the Advisory Council on the Misuse of Drugs, I hereby make the following Regulations:—

Citation and commencement

1. These Regulations may be cited as the Misuse of Drugs Regulations **1.5.1** 1985 and shall come into operation on April 1, 1986.

Interpretation

2.—(1) In these Regulations, unless the context otherwise requires, **1.5.2** the expression—

"the Act" means the Misuse of Drugs Act 1971[1];

"authorised as a member of a group" means authorised by virtue of being a member of a class as respects which the Secretary of State has granted an authority under and for the purposes of Regulations 8(3), 9(3) or 10(3) which is in force, and "his group authority", in relation to a person who is a member of such a class, means the authority so granted to that class;

"document" has the same meaning as in Part I of the Civil Evidence Act 1968 (c. 64);

"health prescription" means a prescription issued by a doctor or a dentist either under the National Health Service Act 1977 (c. 49), the National Health Service (Scotland) Act 1978 (c. 29), the Health and Personal Social Services (Northern Ireland) Order 1972 (S.I. 1972 No. 1265 (N.I. 14)) or the National Health Service (Isle of Man) Acts 1948 to 1979 (Acts of Tynwald) or upon a form issued by a local authority for use in connection with the health service of that authority;

"installation manager" and "offshore installation" have the same meanings as in the Mineral Workings (Offshore Installations) Act 1971[2];

"master" and "seamen" have the same meaning as in the Merchant Shipping Act 1894 (c. 60);

"medicinal product" has the same meaning as in the Medicines Act 1968 (c. 67);

"the Merchant Shipping Acts" means the Merchant Shipping Acts 1894 to 1984;

"officer of customs and excise" means an officer within the meaning of the Customs and Excise Management Act 1979 (c. 2);

"prescription" means a prescription issued by a doctor for the medical treatment of a single individual, by a dentist for the dental treatment of a single individual or by a veterinary surgeon or veterinary practitioner for the purposes of animal treatment;

"register" means a bound book and does not include any form of loose leaf register or card index;

"registered pharmacy" has the same meaning as in the Medicines Act 1968;

"retail dealer" means a person lawfully conducting a retail pharmacy business or a pharmacist engaged in supplying drugs to the public at a health centre within the meaning of the Medicines Act 1968;

"sister or acting sister" includes any male nurse occupying a similar position;

"wholesale dealer" means a person who carries on the business of selling drugs to persons who buy to sell again.

(2) In these Regulations any reference to a Regulation or Schedule shall be construed as a reference to a Regulation contained in these Regulations or, as the case may be, to a Schedule thereto; and any reference

in a Regulation or Schedule to a paragraph shall be construed as a reference to a paragraph of that Regulation or Schedule.

(3) Nothing in these Regulations shall be construed as derogating from any power or immunity of the Crown, its servants or agents.

NOTES
[1]s. 37(1) (interpretation) of the Act was amended by s. 52 of the Criminal Law Act 1977 (c. 45).
[2]1971 c. 61; s. 1 of the Act was substituted by s. 24 of the Oil and Gas (Enterprise) Act 1982 (c. 23).

Specification of controlled drugs for purposes of Regulations

3. Schedules 1 to 5 shall have effect for the purpose of specifying the **1.5.3** controlled drugs to which certain provisions of these Regulations apply.

Exceptions for drugs in Schedules 4 and 5 and poppy-straw

4.—(1) Section 3(1) of the Act (which prohibits the importation and **1.5.4** exportation of controlled drugs) shall not have effect in relation to the drugs specified in [Part II of][1] Schedule 4 and 5.

[(1A) The application of section 3(1) of the Act in so far as it creates an offence and of sections 50(1) to (4), 68(2) and (3) or 170 of the Customs and Excise Management Act 1979 in so far as they apply in relation to a prohibition or restriction on importation or exportation having effect by virtue of section 3 of the Act, are hereby excluded in the case of importation or exportation by any person for administration to himself of any drug specified in Part I of Schedule 4 which is contained in a medicinal product.][2]

(2) Section 5(1) of the Act (which prohibits the possession of controlled drugs) shall not have effect in relation to—

(*a*)   any drug specified in Schedule 4 which is contained in a medicinal product;
(*b*)   the drugs specified in Schedule 5.

(3) Sections 4(1) (which prohibits the production and supply of controlled drugs) and 5(1) of the Act shall not have effect in relation to poppy-straw.

NOTES
[1]Inserted by S.I. 1996 No. 1597.
[2]Inserted by S.I. 1996 No. 1597.

Licences to produce etc. controlled drugs

5. Where any person is authorised by a licence of the Secretary of **1.5.5** State issued under this Regulation and for the time being in force to produce, supply, offer to supply or have in his possession any controlled drug, it shall not by virtue of section 4(1) or 5(1) of the Act be unlawful for that person to produce, supply, offer to supply or have in his possession that drug in accordance with the terms of the licence and in compliance with any conditions attached to the licence.

General authority to supply and possess

1.5.6   **6.**—(1) Notwithstanding the provisions of section 4(1)(*b*) of the Act, any person who is lawfully in possession of a controlled drug may supply that drug to the person from whom he obtained it.

(2) Notwithstanding the provisions of section 4(1)(*b*) of the Act, any person who has in his possession a drug specified in Schedule 2, 3, 4 or 5 which has been supplied by or on the prescription of a practitioner for the treatment of that person, or of a person whom he represents, may supply that drug to any doctor, dentist or pharmacist for the purpose of destruction.

(3) Notwithstanding the provisions of section 4(1)(*b*) of the Act, any person who is lawfully in possession of a drug specified in Schedule 2, 3, 4 or 5 which has been supplied by or on the prescription of a veterinary practitioner or veterinary surgeon for the treatment of animals may supply that drug to any veterinary practitioner, veterinary surgeon or pharmacist for the purpose of destruction.

(4) It shall not by virtue of section 4(1)(*b*) or 5(1) of the Act be unlawful for any person in respect of whom a licence has been granted and is in force under section 16(1) of the Wildlife and Countryside Act 1981 (c. 69) to supply, offer to supply or have in his possession any drug specified in Schedule [2 or 3][1] for the purposes for which that licence was granted.

(5) Notwithstanding the provisions of section 4(1)(*b*) of the Act, any of the persons specified in paragraph (7) may supply any controlled drug to any person who may lawfully have that drug in his possession.

(6) Notwithstanding the provisions of section 5(1) of the Act, any of the persons so specified may have any controlled drug in his possession.

(7) The persons referred to in paragraphs (5) and (6) are—

(*a*)   a constable when acting in the course of his duty as such;

(*b*)   a person engaged in the business of a carrier when acting in the course of that business;

(*c*)   a person engaged in the business of the Post Office when acting in the course of that business;

(*d*)   an officer of customs and excise when acting in the course of his duty as such;

(*e*)   a person engaged in the work of any laboratory to which the drug has been sent for forensic examination when acting in the course of his duty as a person so engaged;

(*f*)   a person engaged in conveying the drug to a person who may lawfully have that drug in his possession.

NOTE
[1]Inserted by S.I. 1988 No. 916.

Administration of drugs in Schedules 2, 3, 4 and 5

7.—(1) Any person may administer to another any drug specified in **1.5.7**
Schedule 5.

(2) A doctor or dentist may administer to a patient any drug specified
in Schedule 2, 3 or 4.

(3) Any person other than a doctor or dentist may administer to a patient,
in accordance with the directions of a doctor or dentist, any drug specified
in Schedule 2, 3 or 4.

Production and supply of drugs in Schedules 2 and 5

8.—(1) Notwithstanding the provisions of section 4(1)(*a*) of the Act— **1.5.8**

(*a*)   a practitioner or pharmacist, acting in his capacity as such, may
manufacture or compound any drug specified in Schedule 2 or 5.

(*b*)   a person lawfully conducting a retail pharmacy business and
acting in his capacity as such may, at the registered pharmacy at
which he carries on that business, manufacture or compound
any drug specified in Schedule 2 or 5.

(2) Notwithstanding the provisions of section 4(1)(*b*) of the Act, any
of the following persons, that is to say:—

(*a*)   a practitioner;

(*b*)   a pharmacist;

(*c*)   a person lawfully conducting a retail pharmacy business;

(*d*)   the person in charge or acting person in charge of a hospital or
nursing home which is wholly or mainly maintained by a public
authority out of public funds or by a charity or by voluntary
subscriptions;

(*e*)   in the case of such a drug supplied to her by a person responsible
for the dispensing and supply of medicines at the hospital or
nursing home, the sister or acting sister for the time being in
charge of a ward, theatre or other department in such a hospital
or nursing home as aforesaid;

(*f*)   a person who is in charge of a laboratory the recognised activities
of which consist in, or include, the conduct of scientific education
or research and which is attached to a university, university college
or such a hospital as aforesaid or to any other institution approved
for the purpose under this sub-paragraph by the Secretary of State;

(*g*)   a public analyst appointed under section 76 of the Food Act 1984
(c. 30) or section 27 of the Food and Drugs (Scotland) Act 1956
(c. 30).

(*h*) a sampling officer within the meaning of the Food and Drugs (Scotland) Act 1956;

(*i*) a sampling officer within the meaning of Schedule 3 to the Medicines Act 1968;

(*j*) a person employed or engaged in connection with a scheme for testing the quality or amount of the drugs, preparations and appliances supplied under the National Health Service Act 1977 or the National Health Service (Scotland) Act 1978 and the Regulations made thereunder;

(*k*) a person authorised by the Pharmaceutical Society of Great Britain for the purposes of section 108 or 109 of the Medicines Act 1968,

may, when acting in his capacity as such, supply or offer to supply any drug specified in Schedule 2 or 5 to any person who may lawfully have that drug in his possession;

Provided that nothing in this paragraph authorises—

(i) the person in charge or acting person in charge of a hospital or nursing home, having a pharmacist responsible for the dispensing and supply of medicines, to supply or offer to supply any drug;

(ii) a sister or acting sister for the time being in charge of a ward, theatre or other department to supply any drug otherwise than for administration to a patient in that ward, theatre or department in accordance with the directions of a doctor or dentist.

(3) Notwithstanding the provisions of section 4(1)(*b*) of the Act, a person who is authorised as a member of a group may, under and in accordance with the terms of his group authority and in compliance with any conditions attached thereto, supply or offer to supply any drug specified in Schedule 2 or 5 to any person who may lawfully have that drug in his possession.

(4) Notwithstanding the provisions of section 4(1)(*b*) of the Act, a person who is authorised by a written authority issued by the Secretary of State under and for the purposes of this paragraph and for the time being in force may, at the premises specified in that authority and in compliance with any conditions so specified, supply or offer to supply any drug specified in Schedule 5 to any person who may lawfully have that drug in his possession.

(5) Notwithstanding the provisions of section 4(1)(*b*) of the Act—

(*a*) the owner of a ship, or the master of a ship which does not carry a doctor among the seamen employed in it;

(*b*) the installation manager of an offshore installation,

may supply or offer to supply any drug specified in Schedule 2 or 5—

(i) for the purpose of compliance with any of the provisions specified in paragraph (6), to any person on that ship or installation;

(ii) to any person who may lawfully supply that drug to him;
(iii) to any constable for the purpose of the destruction of that drug.

(6) The provisions referred to in paragraph (5) are any provision of, or of any instrument which is in force under—

(a) the Merchant Shipping Acts;
(b) the Mineral Workings (Offshore Installations) Act 1971; or
(c) the Health and Safety at Work etc. Act 1974 (c. 37).

Production and supply of drugs in Schedules 3 and 4

9.—(1) Notwithstanding the provisions of section 4(1)(a) of the Act— **1.5.9**

(a) a practitioner or pharmacist, acting in his capacity as such, may manufacture or compound any drug specified in Schedule 3 or 4;
(b) a person lawfully conducting a retail pharmacy business and acting in his capacity as such may, at the registered pharmacy at which he carried on that business, manufacture or compound any drug specified in Schedule 3 or 4;
(c) a person who is authorised by a written authority issued by the Secretary of State under and for the purposes of this sub-paragraph and for the time being in force may, at the premises specified in that authority and in compliance with any conditions so specified, produce any drug specified in Schedule 3 or 4.

(2) Notwithstanding the provisions of section 4(1)(b) of the Act, any of the following persons, that is to say—

(a) a practitioner;
(b) a pharmacist;
(c) a person lawfully conducting a retail pharmacy business;
(d) a person in charge of a laboratory the recognised activities of which consist in, or include, the conduct of scientific education or research;
(e) a public analyst appointed under section 76 of the Food Act 1984 or section 27 of the Food and Drugs (Scotland) Act 1956;
(f) a sampling officer within the meaning of the Food and Drugs (Scotland) Act 1956;
(g) a sampling officer within the meaning of Schedule 3 to Medicines Act 1968;
(h) a person employed or engaged in connection with a scheme for testing the quality or amount of the drugs, preparations and appliances supplied under the National Health Service Act 1977 or the National Health Service (Scotland) Act 1978 and the Regulations made thereunder;

(*i*)   a person authorised by the Pharmaceutical Society of Great Britain for the purposes of section 108 or 109 of the Medicines Act 1968,

may, when acting in his capacity as such, supply or offer to supply any drug specified in Schedule 3 or 4 to any person who may lawfully have that drug in his possession.

[(3) Notwithstanding the provisions of section 4(1)(*b*) of the Act—

(*a*)   a person who is authorised as a member of a group, under and in accordance with the terms of his group authority and in compliance with any conditions attached thereto;

(*b*)   the person in charge or acting person in charge of a hospital or nursing home;

(*c*)   in the case of such a drug supplied to her by a person responsible for the dispensing and supply of medicines at that hospital or nursing home, the sister or acting sister for the time being in charge of a ward, theatre or other department in a hospital or nursing home, the sister or acting sister for the time being in charge of a ward, theatre or other department in a hospital or nursing home,

may, when acting in his capacity as such, supply or offer to supply any drug specified in Schedule 3, or any drug specified in Schedule 4 which is contained in a medicinal product, to any person who may lawfully have that drug in his possession:

Provided that nothing in this paragraph authorises—

(i)   the person in charge or acting person in charge of a hospital or nursing home, having a pharmacist responsible for the dispensing and supply of medicines, to supply or offer to supply any drug;

(ii)   a sister or acting sister for the time being in charge of a ward, theatre or other department to supply any drug otherwise than for administration to a patient in that ward, theatre or department in accordance with the directions of a doctor or dentist.]¹

NOTE
¹S.I. 1986 No. 2330.

(4) Notwithstanding the provisions of section 4(1)(*b*) of the Act—

(*a*)   a person who is authorised by a written authority issued by the Secretary of State under and for the purposes of this sub-paragraph and for the time being in force may, at the premises specified in that authority and in compliance with any conditions so specified, supply or offer to supply any drug specified in Schedule 3 or 4 to any person who may lawfully have that drug in his possession;

(*b*)   a person who is authorised under paragraph (1)(*c*) may supply or offer to supply any drug which he may, by virtue of being so authorised, lawfully produce to any person who may lawfully have that drug in his possession.

(5) Notwithstanding the provisions of section 4(1)(*b*) of the Act—

(*a*)   the owner of a ship, or the master of a ship which does not carry a doctor among the seamen employed in it;

(*b*)   the installation manager of an offshore installation,

may supply or offer to supply any drug specified in Schedule 3, or any drug specified in Schedule 4 which is contained in a medicinal product—

(i)   for the purpose of compliance with any of the provisions specified in Regulation 8(6), to any person on that ship or installation; or

(ii)   to any person who may lawfully supply that drug to him.

(6) Notwithstanding the provisions of section 4(1)(*b*) of the Act, a person in charge of a laboratory may, when acting in his capacity as such, supply or offer to supply any drug specified in Schedule 3 which is required for use as a buffering agent in chemical analysis to any person who may lawfully have that drug in his possession.

Possession of drugs in Schedules 2, 3 and 4

10.—(1) Notwithstanding the provisions of section 5(1) of the Act—   **1.5.10**

(*a*)   a person specified in one of sub-paragraphs (*a*) to (*k*) of Regulation 8(2) may have in his possession any drug specified in Schedule 2;

(*b*)   a person specified in one of sub-paragraphs (*a*) to (*i*) of Regulation 9(2) may have in his possession any drug specified in Schedule 3 or 4;

(*c*)   a person specified in Regulation 9(3)(*b*) or (*c*) or Regulation 9(6) may have in his possession any drug specified in Schedule 3,

for the purpose of acting in his capacity as such a person:
Provided that nothing in this paragraph authorises—

(i)   a person specified in sub-paragraph (*e*) of Regulation 8(2);

(ii)   a person specified in sub-paragraph (*c*) of Regulation 9(3); or

(iii)   a person specified in Regulation 9(6),

to have in his possession any drug other than such a drug as is mentioned in the paragraph or sub-paragraph in question specifying him.

(2) Notwithstanding the provisions of section 5(1) of the Act, a person may have in his possession any drug specified in Schedule 2 or 3 for

administration for medical, dental or veterinary purposes in accordance with the directions of a practitioner:

Provided that this paragraph shall not have effect in the case of a person to whom the drug has been supplied by or on the prescription of a doctor if—

(a)   that person was then being supplied with any controlled drug by or on the prescription of another doctor and failed to disclose that fact to the first mentioned doctor before the supply by him or on his prescription; or

(b)   that or any other person on his behalf made a declaration or statement, which was false in any particular, for the purpose of obtaining the supply or prescription.

(3) Notwithstanding the provisions of section 5(1) of the Act, a person who is authorised as a member of a group may, under and in accordance with the terms of his group authority and in compliance with any conditions attached thereto, have any drug specified in Schedule 2 or 3 in his possession.

(4) Notwithstanding the provisions of section 5(1) of the Act—

(a)   a person who is authorised by a written authority issued by the Secretary of State under and for the purposes of this sub-paragraph and for the time being in force may, at the premises specified in that authority and in compliance with any conditions so specified, have in his possession any drug specified in Schedule 3 or 4;

(b)   a person who is authorised under Regulation 9(1)(c) may have in his possession any drug which he may, by virtue of being so authorised, lawfully produce;

(c)   a person who is authorised under Regulation 9(4)(a) may have in his possession any drug which he may, by virtue of being so authorised, lawfully supply or offer to supply.

(5) Notwithstanding the provisions of section 5(1) of the Act—

(a)   any person may have in his possession any drug specified in Schedule 2 or 3 for the purpose of compliance with any of the provisions specified in Regulation 8(6);

(b)   the master of a foreign ship which is in a port in Great Britain may have in his possession any drug specified in Schedule 2 or 3 so far as necessary for the equipment of the ship.

(6) The foregoing provisions of this Regulation are without prejudice to the provisions of Regulation 4(2)(a)

Exemption for midwives

1.5.11   **11.**—(1) Notwithstanding the provisions of sections 4(1)(b) and 5(1) of the Act, a registered midwife who has, in accordance with the provisions of rules made under section 15(1)(*b*) of the Act of 1979, notified to the local supervising authority her intention to practise may, subject to the provisions of this Regulation—

(*a*)   so far as necessary to her professional practice, have in her possession;

(*b*)   so far as necessary as aforesaid, administer; and

(*c*)   surrender to the appropriate medical officer such stocks in her possession as are no longer required by her of,

any controlled drug which she may, under and in accordance with the provisions of the Medicines Act 1968 and of any instrument which is in force thereunder, lawfully administer.

(2) Nothing in paragraph (1) authorises a midwife to have in her possession any drug which has been obtained otherwise than on a midwife's supply order signed by the appropriate medical officer.

(3) In this Regulation, the expression—

"the Act of 1979" means the Nurses, Midwives and Health Visitors Act 1979 (c. 36);
"appropriate medical officer" means—

(*a*)   a doctor who is for the time being authorised in writing for the purposes of this Regulation by the local supervising authority for the region or area in which the drug was, or is to be, obtained; or

(*b*)   for the purposes of paragraph (2), a person appointed under and in accordance with section 16 of the Act of 1979 by that authority to exercise supervision over registered midwives within their area, who is for the time being authorised as aforesaid;

"local supervising authority" has the meaning it is given by section 16(1) of the Act of 1979;
"midwife's supply order" means an order in writing specifying the name and occupation of the midwife obtaining the drug, the purpose for which it is required and the total quantity to be obtained.

NOTE
[1]s. 16 of the Act was amended by para. 86 of Sched. 1 to the Health Services Act 1980 (c. 53).

Cultivation under licence of Cannabis plant

12. Where any person is authorised by a licence of the Secretary of State issued under this Regulation and for the time being in force to cultivate plants of the genus *Cannabis*, it shall not by virtue of section 6 of the Act be unlawful for that person to cultivate any such plant in   **1.5.12**

accordance with the terms of the licence and in compliance with any conditions attached to the licence.

Approval of premises for cannabis smoking for research purposes

1.5.13   **13.** Section 8 of the Act (which makes it an offence for the occupier of premises to permit certain activities there) shall not have effect in relation to the smoking of cannabis or cannabis resin for the purposes of research on any premises for the time being approved for the purpose under this Regulation by the Secretary of State.

Documents to be obtained by supplier of controlled drugs

1.5.14   **14.**—(1) Where a person (hereafter in this paragraph referred to as "the supplier"), not being a practitioner, supplies a controlled drug otherwise than on a prescription, the supplier shall not deliver the drug to a person who—

   (*a*)   purports to be sent by or on behalf of the person to whom it is supplied (hereafter in this paragraph referred to as "the recipient"); and

   (*b*)   is not authorised by any provision of these Regulations other than the provisions of Regulations 6(6) and (7)(*f*) to have that drug in his possession,

unless that person produces to the supplier a statement in writing signed by the recipient to the effect that he is empowered by the recipient to receive that drug on behalf of the recipient, and the supplier is reasonably satisfied that the document is a genuine document.

(2) Where a person (hereafter in this paragraph referred to as "the supplier") supplies a controlled drug, otherwise than on a prescription or by way of administration, to any of the persons specified in paragraph (4), the supplier shall not deliver the drug—

   (*a*)   until he has obtained a requisition in writing which—
       (i)   is signed by the person to whom the drug is supplied (hereafter in this paragraph referred to as "the recipient");
       (ii) states the name, address and profession or occupation of the recipient;
       (iii) specifies the purpose for which the drug supplied is required and the total quantity to be supplied; and
       (iv) where appropriate, satisfies the requirements of paragraph (5);

   (*b*)   unless he is reasonably satisfied that the signature is that of the person purporting to have signed the requisition and that that person is engaged in the profession or occupation specified in the requisition:

Provided that where the recipient is a practitioner and he represents that he urgently requires a controlled drug for the purpose of his profession, the supplier may, if he is reasonably satisfied that the recipient so requires the drug and is, by reason of some emergency, unable before delivery to furnish to the supplier a requisition in writing duly signed, deliver the drug to the recipient on an undertaking by the recipient to furnish such a requisition within the 24 hours next following.

(3) A person who has given such an undertaking as aforesaid shall deliver to the person by whom the controlled drug was supplied a signed requisition in accordance with the undertaking.

(4) The persons referred to in paragraph (2) are—

(*a*)   a practitioner;

(*b*)   the person in charge or acting person in charge of a hospital or nursing home;

(*c*)   a person who is in charge of a laboratory;

(*d*)   the owner of a ship, or the master of a ship which does not carry a doctor among the seamen employed in it;

(*e*)   the master of a foreign ship in a port in Great Britain;

(*f*)   the installation manager of an offshore installation.

(5) A requisition furnished for the purposes of paragraph (2) shall—

(*a*)   where furnished by the person in charge or acting person in charge of a hospital or nursing home, be signed by a doctor or dentist employed or engaged in that hospital or nursing home;

(*b*)   where furnished by the master of a foreign ship, contain a statement, signed by the proper officer of the port health authority, or, in Scotland, the medical officer designated under section 14 of the National Health Service (Scotland) Act 1978 by the Health Board, within whose jurisdiction the ship is, that the quantity of the drug to be supplied is the quantity necessary for the equipment of the ship.

(6) Where the person responsible for the dispensing and supply of medicines at any hospital or nursing home supplies a controlled drug to the sister or acting sister for the time being in charge of any ward, theatre or other department in that hospital or nursing home (hereafter in this paragraph referred to as "the recipient") he shall—

(*a*)   obtain a requisition in writing, signed by the recipient, which specifies the total quantity of the drug to be supplied; and

(*b*)   mark the requisition in such manner as to show that it has been complied with,

and any requisition obtained for the purposes of this paragraph shall be retained in the dispensary at which the drug was supplied and a copy of the requisition or a note of it shall be retained or kept by the recipient.

(7) Nothing in this regulation shall have effect in relation to—

(*a*) the drugs specified in Schedules 4 and 5 or poppy-straw;

(*b*) any drug specified in Schedule 3 contained in or comprising a preparation which—

(i) is required for use as a buffering agent in chemical analysis,

(ii) has present in it both a substance specified in paragraph 1 or 2 of that Schedule and a salt of that substance, and

(iii) is premixed in a kit.[1]

NOTE
[1]S.I. 1988 No. 916.

Form of prescriptions

1.5.15 **15.**—(1) Subject to the provisions of this Regulation, a person shall not issue a prescription containing a controlled drug other than a drug specified in Schedule 4 or 5 [or temazepam][1] unless the prescription complies with the following requirements, that is to say, it shall—

(*a*) be in ink or otherwise so as to be indelible and be signed by the person issuing it with his usual signature and dated by him;

(*b*) insofar as it specifies the information required by sub-paragraphs (*e*) and (*f*) below to be specified, be written by the person issuing it in his own handwriting;

(*c*) except in the case of a health prescription, specify the address of the person issuing it;

(*d*) have written thereon, if issued by a dentist, the words "for dental treatment only" and, if issued by a veterinary surgeon or a veterinary practitioner, a declaration that the controlled drug is prescribed for an animal or herd under his care;

(*e*) specify the name and address of the person for whose treatment it is issued or, if it is issued by a veterinary surgeon or veterinary practitioner, of the person to whom the controlled drug prescribed is to be delivered;

(*f*) specify the dose to be taken and—

(i) in the case of a prescription containing a controlled drug which is a preparation, the form and, where appropriate, the strength of the preparation, and either the total quantity (in both words and figures) of the preparation or the number (in both words and figures) of dosage units, as appropriate, to be supplied;

(ii) in any other case, the total quantity (in both words and figures) of the controlled drug to be supplied;

(*g*) in the case of a prescription for a total quantity intended to be supplied by instalments, contain a direction specifying the amount of the instalments of the total amount which may be supplied and the intervals to be observed when supplying.

(2) Paragraph (1)(*b*) shall not have effect in relation to—

(*a*)   a prescription issued by a person approved (whether personally or as a member of a class) for the purposes of this paragraph by the Secretary of State; or

(*b*)   a prescription containing no controlled drug other than—
(i)   phenobarbitone;
(ii) phenobarbitone sodium; or
(iii) a preparation containing a drug specified in paragraph (i) or (ii) above.

(3) In the case of a prescription issued for the treatment of a patient in a hospital or nursing home, it shall be a sufficient compliance with paragraph (1)(*e*) if the prescription is written on the patient's bed card or case sheet.

NOTE
[1]Inserted by S.I. 1995 No. 3244: art. 2(2).

Provisions as to supply on prescription

16.—(1) A person shall not supply a controlled drug other than a drug specified in Schedule 4 or 5 on a prescription—   **1.5.16**

(*a*)   unless the prescription complies with the provisions of Regulation 15;

(*b*)   unless the address specified in the prescription as the address of the person issuing it is an address within the United Kingdom;

(*c*)   unless he either is acquainted with the signature of the person by whom it purports to be issued and has no reason to suppose that it is not genuine, or has taken reasonably sufficient steps to satisfy himself that it is genuine;

(*d*)   before the date specified in the prescription;

(*e*)   subject to paragraph (3), later than 13 weeks after the date specified in the prescription.

(2) Subject to paragraph (3), a person supplying on prescription a controlled drug other than a drug specified in Schedule 4 or 5 shall, at the time of the supply, mark on the prescription the date on which the drug is supplied and, unless it is a health prescription, shall retain the prescription on the premises from which the drug was supplied.

(3) In the case of a prescription containing a controlled drug other than a drug specified in Schedule 4 or 5, which contains a direction that specified instalments of the total amount may be supplied at stated intervals, the person supplying the drug shall not do so otherwise than in accordance with that direction and—

(a)   paragraph (1) shall have effect as if for the requirement contained in sub-paragraph (*e*) thereof there were substituted a requirement that the occasion on which the first instalment is supplied shall not be later than 13 weeks after the date specified in the prescription;

(b)   paragraph (2) shall have effect as if for the words "at the time of the supply" there were substituted the words "on each occasion on which an instalment is supplied."

Exemption for certain prescriptions

1.5.17   **17.** Nothing in Regulations 15 and 16 shall have effect in relation to a prescription issued for the purposes of a scheme for testing the quality or amount of the drugs, preparations and appliances supplied under the National Health Service Act 1977 or the National Health Service (Scotland) Act 1978 and the Regulations made thereunder or to any prescriptions issued for the purposes of the Food and Drugs (Scotland) Act 1956 to a sampling officer within the meaning of that Act or for the purposes of the Medicines Act 1968 to a sampling officer within the meaning of that Act.

Marking of bottles and other containers

1.5.18   **18.**—(1) Subject to paragraph (2), no person shall supply a controlled drug otherwise than in a bottle, package or other container which is plainly marked—

(a)   in the case of a controlled drug other than a preparation, with the amount of the drug contained therein;

(aa)   any drug specified in Schedule 3 contained in or comprising a preparation which—

     (i)   is required for use as a buffering agent in chemical analysis,

     (ii)   has present in it both a substance specified in paragraph 1 or 2 of that Schedule and a salt of that substance, and

     (iii)   is premixed in a kit[1];

NOTE
[1]S.I. 1988 No. 916.

(b)   in the case of a controlled drug which is a preparation—

     (i)   made up into tablets, capsules or other dosage units, with the amount of each component (being a controlled drug) of the preparation in each dosage unit and the number of dosage units in the bottle, package or other container;

     (ii)   not made up as aforesaid, with the total amount of the preparation in the bottle, package or other container and the percentage of each of its components which is a controlled drug.

(2) Nothing in this Regulation shall have effect in relation to—

(*a*)   the drugs specified in Schedules 4 and 5 or poppy-straw;
(*b*)   the supply of a controlled drug by or on the prescription of a practitioner;
(*c*)   the supply of a controlled drug for administration in a clinical trial or a medicinal test on animals.

(3) In this Regulation, the expressions "clinical trial" and "medicinal test on animals" have the same meanings as in the Medicines Act 1968.

Record-keeping requirements in respect of drugs in Schedules 1 and 2

19.—(1) Subject to paragraph (3) and Regulation 21, every person **1.5.19** authorised by or under Regulation 5 or 8 to supply any drug specified in Schedule 1 or 2 shall comply with the following requirements, that is to say—

(*a*)   he shall, in accordance with the provisions of this Regulation and of Regulation 20, keep a register and shall enter therein in chronological sequence in the form specified in Part I or Part II of Schedule 6, as the case may require, particulars of every quantity of a drug specified in Schedule 1 or 2 obtained by him and of every quantity of such a drug supplied (whether by way of administration or otherwise) by him whether to persons within or outside Great Britain;

(*b*)   he shall use a separate register or separate part of the register for entries made in respect of each class of drugs, and each of the drugs specified in paragraphs 1 and 3 of Schedule 1 and paragraphs 1, 3 and 6 of Schedule 2 together with its salts and any preparation or other product containing it or any of its salts shall be treated as a separate class, so however that any stereoisomeric form of a drug or its salts shall be classed with that drug.

(2) Nothing in paragraph (1) shall be taken as preventing the use of a separate section within a register or separate part of a register in respect of different drugs or strengths of drugs comprised within the class of drugs to which that register or separate part relates.

(3) The foregoing provisions of this Regulation shall not have effect in relation to—

(*a*)   in the case of a drug supplied to him for the purpose of destruction in pursuance of Regulation 6(2) or (3), a practitioner or pharmacist;

(*b*)   a person licensed under Regulation 5 to supply any drug, where the licence so directs; or

(*c*)   the sister or acting sister for the time being in charge of a ward, theatre or other department in a hospital or nursing home.

Requirements as to registers

1.5.20   **20.** Any person required to keep a register under Regulation 19 shall comply with the following requirements, that is to say—

(*a*)   the class of drugs to which the entries on any page of any such register relate shall be specified at the head of that page;

(*b*)   every entry required to be made under Regulation 19 in such a register shall be made on the day on which the drug is obtained or, as the case may be, on which the transaction in respect of the supply of the drug by the person required to make the entry takes place or, if that is not reasonably practicable, on the day next following that day;

(*c*)   no cancellation, obliteration or alteration of any such entry shall be made, and a correction of such an entry shall be made only by way of marginal note or footnote which shall specify the date on which the correction is made;

(*d*)   every such entry and every correction of such an entry shall be made in ink or otherwise so as to be indelible;

(*e*)   such a register shall not be used for any purpose other than the purposes of these Regulations;

(*f*)   a separate register shall be kept in respect of each premises at which the person required to keep the register carries on his business or occupation, but subject to that not more than one register shall be kept at one time in respect of each class of drugs in respect of which he is required to keep a separate register, so, however, that a separate register may, with the approval of the Secretary of State, be kept in respect of each department of the business carried on by him;

(*g*)   every such register in which entries are currently being made shall be kept at the premises to which it relates.

Record-keeping requirements in respect of drugs in Schedule 2 in
particular cases

1.5.21   **21.**—(1) Where a drug specified in Schedule 2 is supplied in accordance with Regulation 8(5)(*a*)(i) to any person on a ship, an entry in the official log book required to be kept under the Merchant Shipping Acts or, in the case of a ship which is not required to carry such an official logbook, a report signed by the master of the ship, shall, notwithstanding anything in these Regulations, be a sufficient record of the supply if the entry or report specifies the drug supplied and, in the case of a report, it is delivered as soon as may be to a superintendent at a Marine Office established and maintained under the Merchant Shipping Acts.

(2) Where a drug specified in Schedule 2 is supplied in accordance with Regulation 8(5)(*b*)(i) to a person on an offshore installation, an entry in the installation logbook required to be maintained under the Offshore Installations (Logbooks and Registration of Death) Regulations 1972 (S.I. 1972 No. 1542) which specifies the drug supplied shall, notwithstanding anything in these Regulations, be a sufficient record of the supply.

(3) A midwife authorised by Regulation 11(1) to have any drug specified in Schedule 2 in her possession shall—

(*a*)   on each occasion on which she obtains a supply of such a drug, enter in a book kept by her and used solely for the purposes of this paragraph the date, the name and address of the person from whom the drug was obtained, the amount obtained and the form in which it was obtained; and

(*b*)   on administering such a drug to a patient, enter in the said book as soon as practicable the name and address of the patient, the amount administered and the form in which it was administered.

Record-keeping requirements in respect of drugs in Schedule 3 and 4

22.—(1) Every person who is authorised under Regulation 5 or 9(1)(*c*)   **1.5.22** to produce any drug specified in Schedule 3 or 4 shall make a record of each quantity of such a drug produced by him.

(2) Every person who is authorised by or under any provision of the Act to import or export any drug specified in Schedule 3 shall make a record of each quantity of such a drug imported or exported by him.

(3) Every person who is authorised under Regulation 9(4) to supply any drug specified in Schedule 4 shall make a record of each quantity of such a drug imported or exported by him.

(4) Paragraph (2) shall not have effect in relation to a person licensed under the Act to import or export any drug where the licence so directs.

Preservation of registers, books and other documents

23.—(1) All registers and books kept in pursuance of Regulation 19 or   **1.5.23** 21(3) shall be preserved for a period of two years from the date on which the last entry therein is made.

(2) Every record made in pursuance of Regulation 22 shall be preserved for a period of two years from the date on which the record was made.

(3) Every requisition, order or prescription (other than a health prescription) on which a controlled drug is supplied in pursuance of these

Regulations shall be preserved for a period of two years from the date on which the last delivery under it was made.

Preservation of records relating to drugs in Schedules 3 and 5

1.5.24   **24.**—(1) A producer of any drug specified in Schedule 3 or 5 and a wholesale dealer in any such drug shall keep every invoice or other like record issued in respect of each quantity of such a drug obtained by him and in respect of each quantity of such a drug supplied by him.

(2) A person who is authorised under Regulation 9(4)(*a*) to supply any drug specified in Schedule 3 shall keep every invoice or other like record issued in respect of each quantity of such a drug obtained by him and in respect of each quantity of such a drug supplied by him.

(3) A retail dealer in any drug specified in Schedule 3, a person in charge or acting person in charge of a hospital or nursing home and a person in charge of a laboratory shall keep every invoice or other like record issued in respect of each quantity of such a drug obtained by him and in respect of each quantity of such a drug supplied by him.

(4) A retail dealer in any drug specified in Schedule 5 shall keep every invoice or other like record issued in respect of each quantity of such a drug obtained by him.

(5) Every invoice or other record which is required by this Regulation to be kept in respect of a drug specified in Schedule 3 shall contain information sufficient to identify the date of the transaction and the person by whom or to whom the drug was supplied.

(6) Every document kept in pursuance of this Regulation (other than a health prescription) shall be preserved for a period of two years from the date on which it is issued:

Provided that the keeping of a copy of the document made at any time during the said period of two years shall be treated for the purposes of this paragraph as if it were the keeping of the original document.

Furnishing of information with respect to controlled drugs

1.5.25   **25.**—(1) The persons specified in paragraph (2) shall on demand made by the Secretary of State or by any person authorised in writing by the Secretary of State in that behalf—

(*a*)   furnish such particulars as may be requested in respect of the producing, obtaining or supplying by him of any controlled drug or in respect of any stock of such drugs in his possession;

(*b*)   for the purpose of confirming any such particulars, produce any stock of such drugs in his possession;

(*c*)   produce any register, book or document required to be kept under these Regulations relating to any dealings in controlled drugs which is in his possession.

(2) The persons referred to in paragraph (1) are—

(*a*)   any person authorised by or under these Regulations to produce any controlled drug;

(*b*)   any person authorised by or under any provision of the Act to import or export any controlled drug;

(*c*)   a wholesale dealer;

(*d*)   a retail dealer;

(*e*)   a practitioner;

(*f*)   the person in charge or acting person in charge of a hospital or nursing home;

(*g*)   a person who is in charge of a laboratory;

(*h*)   a person who is authorised under Regulation 9(4)(*a*) to supply any controlled drug.

(3) Nothing in this Regulation shall require the furnishing of personal records which a person has acquired or created in the course of his profession or occupation and which he holds in confidence; and in this paragraph "personal records" means documentary and other records concerning an individual (whether living or dead) who can be identified from them and relating to his physical or mental health.

Destruction of controlled drugs

26.—(1) No person who is required by any provision of, or by any **1.5.26** term or condition of a licence having effect under, these Regulations to keep records with respect to a drug specified in Schedule 1, 2, 3 or 4 shall destroy such a drug or cause such a drug to be destroyed except in the presence of and in accordance with any directions given by a person authorised (whether personally or as a member of a class) for the purposes of this paragraph by the Secretary of State (hereafter in this Regulation referred to as an "authorised person").

(2) An authorised person may, for the purposes of analysis, take a sample of a drug specified in Schedule 1, 2, 3 or 4 which is to be destroyed.

(3) Where a drug specified in Schedule 1, 2, 3 or 4 is destroyed in pursuance of paragraph (1) by or at the instance of a person who is required by any provision of, or by any term or condition of a licence having effect under, these Regulations to keep a record in respect of the obtaining or supply of that drug, that record shall include particulars of the date of destruction and the quantity destroyed and shall be signed by the authorised person in whose presence the drug is destroyed.

(4) Where the master or owner of a ship or installation manager of an offshore installation has in his possession a drug specified in Schedule 2 which he no longer requires, he shall not destroy the drug or cause it to be destroyed but shall dispose of it to a constable, or to a person who may lawfully supply that drug to him.

(5) Nothing in paragraph (1) or (3) shall apply to any person who is required to keep records only by virtue of Regulation 22(2) or (3) or 24(3).

(6) Nothing in paragraph (1) or (3) shall apply to the destruction of a drug which has been supplied to a practitioner or pharmacist for that purpose in pursuance of Regulation 6(2) or (3).

Revocations

1.5.27 **27.**—(1) The Regulations specified in Schedule 7 are hereby revoked.

(2) Notwithstanding paragraph (1), any register, record, book, prescription or other document required to be preserved under Regulation 22 or 23 of the Misuse of Drugs Regulations 1973 (S.I. 1973 No. 797) shall be preserved for the same period of time as if these Regulations had not been made.

(3) In the case of a prescription issued before the coming into operation of these Regulations, Regulation 16(1) shall have effect as if—

(a) in the case of a prescription containing a controlled drug other than a drug to which the provisions of Regulation 15 of the said Regulations of 1973 applied at the time the prescription was issued, sub-paragraphs (a) and (b) of that paragraph were omitted; and

(b) in any other case, for the said sub-paragraphs (a) and (b) there were substituted the words "unless the prescription complies with the provisions of the Misuse of Drugs Regulations 1973 relating to prescriptions".

1.5.28 SCHEDULE 1 **Regulation 3**

CONTROLLED DRUGS SUBJECT TO THE REQUIREMENTS OF REGULATIONS 14, 15, 16, 18, 19, 20, 23, 25 AND 26

1. The following substances and products, namely:—
(a) Bufotenine
Cannabinol
Cannabinol derivatives [not being dronabinol or its stereoisomers][1]
[2]Cathinone
Coca leaf
Concentrate of poppy-straw
Eticyclidine
Lysergamide
Lysergide and other N-alkyl derivatives of lysergamide
Mescaline
Psilocin
Raw opium
Rolicyclidine
Tenocyclidine

4-Bromo-2, 5-dimethoxy-*a*-methylphenethylamine
N,N-Diethyltryptamine
N,N-Dimethyltryptamine
2,5-Dimethoxy-*a*, 4-dimethylphenethylamine

NOTES
¹S.I. 1996 No. 2048.
²S.I. 1986 No. 233.

(*b*) any compound (not being a compound for the time being specified in sub-paragraph (*a*) above) structurally derived from tryptamine or from a ringhydroxy tryptamine by substitution at the nitrogen atom of the sidechain with one or more alkyl substituents but no other substituent;

(*c*) any compound (not being methoxyphenamine or a compound for the time being specified in sub-paragraph (*a*) above) structurally derived from phenethylamine, an N-alkylphenethylamine, *a*-methylphenethylamine, an N-alkyl-*a*-methylphenethylamine, *a*-ethylphenethylamine, or an N-alkyl-*a*-ethylphenethylamine by substitution in the ring to any extent with alkyl, alkoxy, alkylenedioxy or halide substituents, whether or not further substituted in the ring by one or more other univalent substituents;

(*d*) any compound (not being a compound for the time being specified in Schedule 2) structurally derived from fentanyl by modification in any of the following way, that is to say,

(i) by replacement of the phenyl portion of the phenethyl group by any heteromonocycle whether or not further substituted in the heterocycle;
(ii) by substitution in the phenethyl group with alkyl, alkenyl, alkoxy, hydroxy, halogeno, haloalkyl, amino or nitro groups;
(iii) by substitution in the piperidine ring with alkyl or alkenyl groups;
(iv) by substitution in the aniline ring with alkyl, alkoxy, alkylenedioxy, halogeno or haloalkyl groups;
(v) by substitution at the 4-position of the piperidine ring with any alkoxycarbonyl or alkoxyalkyl or acyloxy group;
(vi) by replacement of the N-propinoyl group by another acyl group;

(*e*) any compound (not being a compound for the time being specified in Schedule 2) structurally derived from pethidine by modification in any of the following ways, that is to say,

(i) by replacement of the 1-methyl group by an acyl, alkyl whether or not unsaturated, benzyl or phenethyl group, whether or not further substituted;
(ii) by substitution in the piperidine ring with alkyl or alkenyl groups or with a propano bridge, whether or not further substituted;
(iii) by substitution in the 4-phenyl ring with alkyl, alkoxy, aryloxy, halogeno or haloalkyl groups;
(iv) by replacement of the 4-ethoxycarbonyl by any other alkoxycarbonyl or any alkoxyalkyl or acyloxy group;
(v) by formation of an N-oxide or of a quaternary base.

2. Any stereoisomeric form of a substance specified in paragraph 1.
3. Any ester or ether of a substance specified in paragraph 1 or 2.
4. Any salt of a substance specified in any of paragraphs 1 to 3.
5. Any preparation or other product containing a substance or product specified in any of paragraphs 1 to 4, not being a preparation specified in Schedule 5.

1.5.29   SCHEDULE 2   **Regulation 3**

CONTROLLED DRUGS SUBJECT TO THE REQUIREMENTS OF REGULATIONS 14, 15, 16, 18, 19, 20, 21, 23, 25 AND 26

1. The following substances and products, namely:—

Acetorphine
Alfentanil
Allylprodine
Alphacetylmethadol
Alphameprodine
Alphamethadol
Alphaprodine
Anileridine
Benzethidine
Benzylmorphine (3-benzylmorphine)
Betacetylmethadol
Betameprodine
Betamethadol
Betaprodine
Bezitramide
[1][Carfentanil]
Clonitazene
Cocaine
Desomorphine
Dextromoramide
Diamorphine
Diampromide
Diethylthiambutene
Difenoxin
Dihydrocodeinone
    O-carboxymethyloxime
Dihydromorphine
Dimenoxadole
Dimepheptanol
Dimethylthiambutene
Dioxaphetyl butyrate
Diphenoxylate
Dipipanone
[3][Dronabinol]
Drotebanol
Ecgonine, and any derivative of
    ecgonine which is convertible to
    ecgonine or to cocaine
Ethylmethylthiambutene
Etonitazene
Etorphine
Etoxeridine
Fentanyl
Furethidine
[2][Glutethimide]
Hydrocodone
Hydromorphinol

Hydromorphone
Hydroxypethidine
Isomethadone
Ketobemidone
[2][Lefatamine]
Levomethorphan
Levomoramide
Levophenacylmorphan
Levorphanol
[1][Lofentanil]
Medicinal opium
Metazocine
Methadone
Methadyl acetate
Methyldesorphine
Methyldihydromorphine
    6-methyldihydromorphine)
Metopon
Morpheridine
Morphine
Morphine methobromide, morphine
    N-oxide and other pentavalent
    nitrogen morphine derivatives
Myrophine
Nicomorphine
Noracymethadol
Norlevorphanol
Normorphine
Norpipanone
Oxycodone
Oxymorphone
Pethidine
Phenadoxone
Phenampromide
Phenazocine
Phencyclidine
Phenomorphan
Phenoperidine
Piminodine
Pinitramide
Proheptazine
Properidine
Racemethorphan
Racemoramide
Racemorphan
Sufentanil
Thebacon

Thebaine
Tilidate
Trimeperidine
4-Cyano-2-dimethylamino-4,
    4-diphenylbutane
4-Cyano-1-methyl-4-phenylpiperidine

1-Methyl-4-phenylpiperidine-
    4-carboxylic acid
2-Methyl-3-morpholino-1,
    1-diphenylpropanecarboxylic
    acid
4-Phenylpiperidine-4-carboxylic acid
    ethyl ester

2. Any stereoisomeric form of a substance specified in paragraph 1 not being dextromethorphan or dextrophan.

NOTES
    [1]Inserted by S.I. 1986 No. 2330.
    [2]Omitted by S.I. 1986 No. 2330.
    [3]Inserted by S.I. 1995 No. 2048.

3. Any ester or ether of a substance specified in paragraph 1 or 2, not being a substance specified in paragraph 6.

4. Any salt of a substance specified in any of paragraphs 1 to 3.

5. Any preparation or other product containing a substance or product specified in any of paragraphs 1 to 4, not being a preparation specified in Schedule 5.

6. The following substances and products, namely:—

Acetyldihydrocodeine
Amphetamine
Codeine
Dextropropoxyphene
Dihydrocodeine

Ethylmorphine (3-ethylmorphine)
[1][Fenethylline]

[1][Glutethimide]
[1][Lefetamine]
Mecloqualone

Methaqualone
Methylamphetamine
Methylphenidate
Nicocodine
Nicodicodine (6-nicotinoyldihydro-
    codeine)
Norcodeine

Phenmertrazine
Pholcodine
Propiram
[2][Quinalbarbitone]

NOTES
    [1]Inserted by S.I. 1986 No. 2330.
    [2]Inserted by S.I. 1988 No. 916.

7. Any stereoisomeric form of a substance specified in paragraph 6.

8. Any salt of a substance specified in paragraph 6 or 7.

9. Any preparation or other product containing a substance or product specified in any of paragraphs 6 to 8, not being a preparation specified in Schedule 5.

SCHEDULE 3   **Regulation 3 1.5.30**

CONTROLLED DRUGS SUBJECT TO THE REQUIREMENTS OF REGULATIONS 14, 15 [EXCEPT TEMAZEPAM][1] 16, 18, 22, 23, 24, 25 AND 26

1. The following substances, namely:—

86 *Controlled Drugs*

(*a*) Benzphetamine
4[Buprenorphine]
1[Cathine]
Chlorphentermine
Diethylpropion
Ethchlorvynol
Ethinamate
Mazindol

Mephentermine
Meprobamate
Methylphenobarbitone
Methyprylone
Pentazocine
Phendimetrazine
Phentermine
Pipradrol
1[Temazepam]

(*b*) any 5,5 disubstituted barbituric acid 2[not being quinalbarbitone]

2. Any stereoisomeric form of a substance specified in paragraph 1³ [not being phenylpropanolamine].
3. Any salt of a substance specified in paragraph 1 or 2.
4. Any preparation or other product containing a substance specified in any of paragraphs 1 to 3, not being a preparation specified in Schedule 5.

NOTES
1Inserted by S.I. 1995 No. 3244.
2Inserted by S.I. 1986 No. 916.
3Inserted by S.I. 1986 No. 2330.
4Inserted by S.I. 1989 No. 1460.

1.5.31 SCHEDULE 4 **Regulation 3**

PART I

CONTROLLED DRUGS EXCEPTED FROM THE PROHIBITION ON POSSESSION WHEN IN THE FORM OF A MEDICINAL PRODUCT; EXCLUDED FROM THE APPLICATION OF OFFENCES ARISING FROM THE PROHIBITION ON IMPORTATION AND EXPORTATION WHEN IMPORTED OR EXPORTED IN THE FORM OF A MEDICINAL PRODUCT BY ANY PERSON FOR ADMINISTRATION TO HIMSELF; AND SUBJECT TO THE REQUIREMENTS OF REGULATIONS 22, 23, 25 AND 26

1. The following substances, namely—

Atamestane
Bolandiol
Bolasterone
Bolazine
Boldenone
Bolenol
Bolmantalate
Calusterone
4-Chloromethandienone
Clostebol
Drostanolone
Enestebol
Epitiostanol
Ethyloestrenol
Fluoxymesterone
Formebolone

Methenolone
Methyltestosterone
Metribolone
Mibolerone
Nandrolone
Norboletone
Norclostebol
Norethandrolone
Ovandrotone
Oxabolone
Oxandrolone
Oxymesterone
Oxymetholone
Prasterone
Propetandrol
Quinbolone

Furazabol
Mebolazine
Mepitiostane
Mesabolone
Mestanolone
Mesterolone
Methandienone
Methandriol

Roxibolone
Silandrone
Stanolone
Stanozolol
Stenbolone
Testosterone
Thiomesterone
Trenbolone

2. Any compound (not being Trilostane or a compound for the time being specified in paragraph 1 of this Part of this Schedule) structurally derived from 17-hydroxyandrostan-3-one or from 17-hydroxyestran-3-one by modification in any of the following ways, that is to say,

(a)   by further substitution at position 17 by a methyl or ethyl group;

(b)   by substitution to any extent at one or more of positions 1, 2, 4, 6, 7, 9, 11 or 16, but at no other position;

(c)   by unsaturation in the carbocyclic ring system to any extent, provided that there are no more than two ethylenic bonds in any one carbocyclic ring;

(d)   by fusion of ring A with a heterocyclic system.

3. Any substance which is an ester or ether (or, where more than one hydroxyl function is available, both an ester and an ether) of a substance specified in paragraph 1 or described in paragraph 2 of this Part of this Schedule.

4. The following substances, namely—
    Chorionic Gonadotrophin (HCG)
    Clenbuterol
    Non-human chorionic gonadotrophin
    Somatotropin
    Somatrem
    Somatropin

5. Any stereoisomeric form of a substance specified or described in any of paragraphs 1 to 4 of this Part of this Schedule.

6. Any salt of a substance specified or described in any of paragraphs 1 to 5 of this Part of this Schedule.

7. Any preparation of other product containing a substance or product specified or described in any of paragraphs 1 to 6 of this Part of this Schedule, not being a preparation specified in Schedule 5.[1]

NOTE
[1]Inserted by S.I. 1996 No. 1597.

PART II   **Regulation 3**   **1.5.32**

CONTROLLED DRUGS EXCEPTED FROM THE PROHIBITION ON IMPORTATION, EXPORTATION AND, WHEN IN THE FORM OF A MEDICAL PRODUCT, POSSESSION AND SUBJECT TO THE REQUIREMENTS OF REGULATIONS 22, 23, 25 AND 26

1. The following substances and products, namely:—

Alprazolam
Bromazepam
Camazepam

Ketazolam
Loprazolam
Lorazepam

Chlordiazepoxide
Clobazam
Clonazepam
Clorazepic acid
Clotiazepam
Cloxazolam
Delorazepam
Diazepam
Estazolam
Ethyl loflazepate
[1][Fencamfamin]
[1][Fenproporex]
Fludiazepam
Flunitrazepam
Flurazepam
Halazepam
Haloxazolam

Lormetazepam
Medazepam
[1][Mefenorex]
Nimetazepam
Nordazepam
Oxazepam
Oxazolam
[2][Pemoline]
Pinazepam
Prazepam
[1][Propylhexedrine]
[1][Pyrovalerone]
Temazepam
Tetrazepam
Triazolam
[1]N-Ethylamphetamine

2. Any stereoisomeric form of a substance specified in paragraph 1.

3. Any salt of a substance specified in paragraph 1 or 2.

4. Any preparation or other product containing a substance or product specified in any of paragraphs 1 to 3, not being a preparation specified in Schedule 5.

NOTES

[1]Inserted by S.I. 1986 No. 2330 and deleted by S.I. 1996 No. 2048.
[2]Inserted by S.I. 1989 No. 1460.

1.5.33   SCHEDULE 5   **Regulation 3**

CONTROLLED DRUGS EXCEPTED FROM THE PROHIBITION ON IMPORTATION, EXPORTATION AND POSSESSION AND SUBJECT TO THE REQUIREMENTS OF REGULATIONS 24 AND 25

1.—(1) Any preparation of one or more of the substances to which this paragraph applies, not being a preparation designed for administration by injection, when compounded with one or more other active or inert ingredients and containing a total of not more than 100 milligrammes of the substance or substances (calculated as base) per dosage unit or with a total concentration of not more than 2.5 per cent. (calculated as base) in undivided preparations.

(2) The substances to which this paragraph applies are acetyldihydrocodeine, codeine, dihydrocodeine, ethylmorphine, nicocodine, nicodicodine (6-nico-tinoyldihydrocodeine), norcodeine, pholcodine and their respective salts.

2. Any preparation of cocaine containing not more than 0.1 per cent. of cocaine calculated as cocaine base, being a preparation compounded with one or more other active or inert ingredients in such a way that the cocaine cannot be recovered by readily applicable means or in a yield which would constitute a risk to health.

3. Any preparation of medicinal opium or of morphine containing (in either case) not more than 0.2 per cent. of morphine calculated as anhydrous morphine base, being a preparation compounded with one or more other active or inert ingredients in such a way that the opium or, as the case may be, the morphine, cannot be recovered by readily applicable means or in a yield which would constitute a risk to health.

4. Any preparation of dextropropoxyphene, being a preparation designed for oral administration, containing not more than 135 milligrammes of dextropropoxyphene (calculated as base) per dosage unit or with a total concentration of not more than 2.5 per cent. (calculated as base) in undivided preparations.

5. Any preparation of difenoxin containing, per dosage unit, not more than 0.5

milligrammes of difenoxin and a quantity of atropine sulphate equivalent to at least 5 per cent. of the dose of difenoxin.

6. Any preparation of diphenoxylate containing, per dosage unit, not more than 2.5 milligrammes of diphenoxylate calculated as base, and a quantity of atropine sulphate equivalent to at least 1 per cent. of the dose of diphenoxylate.

7. Any preparation of propiram containing, per dosage unit, not more than 100 milligrammes of propiram calculated as base and compounded with at least the same amount (by weight) of methylcellulose.

8. Any powder of ipecacuanha and opium comprising—
  10 per cent. opium, in powder,
  10 per cent. ipecacuanha root, in powder, well mixed with
  80 per cent. of any other powdered ingredient containing no controlled drug.

9. Any mixture containing one or more of the preparations specified in paragraphs 1 to 8, being a mixture of which none of the other ingredients is a controlled drug.

SCHEDULE 6   **Regulation 3 1.5.34**

FORM OF REGISTER

PART 1

Entries to be made in case of obtaining

Date of which supply received	NAME	ADDRESS	Amount obtained	Form in which obtained
	Of person of firm from whom obtained			

PART II

Entries to be made in case of supply

Date on which the transaction was effected	NAME	ADDRESS	Particulars as to licence or authority of person or firm supplied to be in possession	Amount supplied	Form in which supplied
	Of person or firm supplied				

SCHEDULE   **Regulation 27**

<small>REGULATIONS REVOKED</small>

Column 1 Regulations Revoked	Column 2 References
S.I. 1973 No. 797	
The Misuse of Drugs (Amendment) Regulations 1974	S.I. 1974 No. 402
The Misuse of Drugs (Amendment) Regulations 1975	S.I. 1975 No. 499
The Misuse of Drugs (Amendment) Regulations 1977	S.I. 1977 No. 1380
The Misuse of Drugs (Amendment) Regulations 1979	S.I. 1979 No. 326
The Misuse of Drugs (Amendment) Regulations 1983	S.I. 1983 No. 788
The Misuse of Drugs (Amendment) Regulations 1984	S.I. 1984 No. 143

1986 No. 2331

1.6   **DANGEROUS DRUGS**

The Misuse of Drugs (Designation) Order 1986

Made - - -	*22nd December* 1986
Laid before Parliament	*13th January* 1987
Coming into Operation	*1st April* 1987

In pursuance of section 7(4) and (5) of the Misuse of Drugs Act 1971 (c. 38), on the recommendation of the Advisory Council on the Misuse of Drugs, I hereby make the following Order:—

1.6.1   **1.** This Order may be cited as the Misuse of Drugs (Designation) Order 1986 and shall come into operation on April 1, 1987.

1.6.2   **2.**—(1) The controlled drugs specified in Part I of the Schedule hereto are hereby designated as drugs to which section 7(4) of the Misuse of Drugs Act 1971 applies.

(2) Part II of the Schedule hereto shall have effect for the purpose of specifying those controlled drugs which are excepted from Part I thereof.

1.6.3   **3.** The Misuse of Drugs (Designation) Order 1977 (S.I. 1977 No. 1379) and the Misuse of Drugs (Designation) (Variation) Order 1984 (S.I. 1984 No. 1144) are hereby revoked.

SCHEDULE   **Article 2**

1.6.4   PART I

<small>CONTROLLED DRUGS TO WHICH SECTION 7(4) OF THE MISUSE OF DRUGS ACT 1971 APPLIES</small>

1. The following substances and products, namely:—

(a) Bufotenine
     Cannabinol
     Cannabinol derivatives
     Cannabis
     Cannabis resin
     Cathinone
     Coca leaf
     Concentrate of poppy-straw
     Eticyclidine
     Lysergamide

     Lysergide and other N-alkyl derivatives
     of lysergamide
     Mescaline
     Psilocin
     Raw opium
     Rolicyclidine
     Tenocyclidine
     4-Bromo-2, 5-dimethoxy-*a*, 4-methyl-
     phenethylamine
     N, N-Diethyltryptamine
     N, N-Dimethyltryptamine
     2, 5-Dimethoxy-*a*, 4-methyl-
     phenethylamine
     N-Hydroxy-tenamphetamine
     4-Methyl-aminorex

(b) any compound (not being a compound for the time being specified in sub-paragraph (*a*) above) structurally derived from tryptamine or from a ringhydroxy tryptamine by substitution at the nitrogen atom of the sidechain with one or more alkyl substituents but no other substituent;

(c) any compound (not being methoxyphenamine or a compound for the time being specified in sub-paragraph (*a*) above) structurally derived from phenethylamine, an N-alkylphenethylamine, *a*-methylphenethylamine, an N-alkyl-*a*-methylphenethylamine, *a*-ethylphenethylamine, or an N-alkyl-*a*-ethylphenethylamine by substitution in the ring to any extent with alkyl, alkoxy, alkylenedioxy or halide substituents, whether or not further substituted in the ring by one or more other univalent substituents;

(d) any compound (not being a compound for the time being specified in Part II of this Schedule) structurally derived from fentanyl by modification in any of the following ways, that is to say,

   (i)   by replacement of the phenyl portion of the phenethly group by any heteromonocycle whether or not further substituted in the heterocycle;
   (ii)   by substitution in the phenethyl group with alkyl, alkenyl, alkoxy, hydroxy, halogeno, haloalkyl, amino or nitro groups;
   (iii) by substitution in the piperidine ring with alkyl or alkenyl groups;
   (iv)   by substitution in the aniline ring with alkyl, alkoxy, alkylenedioxy, halogeno or haloalkyl groups;
   (v)   by substitution at the 4-position of the piperidine ring with any alkoxycarbonyl or alkoxyalkyl or acyloxy group;
   (vi)   by replacement of the N-propionyl group by another acyl group;

(e) any compound (not being a compound for the time being specified in Part II of this Schedule) that is structurally derived from pethidine by modification in any of the following ways, that is to say,

   (i)   by replacement of the 1-methyl group by an acyl, alkyl whether or not unsaturated, benzyl or phenethyl group, whether or not further substituted;
   (ii)   by substitution in the piperidine ring with alkyl or alkenyl groups or with a propano bridge, whether or not further substituted;
   (iii) by substitution in the 4-phenyl ring with alkyl, alkoxy, aryloxy, halogeno or haloalkyl groups;
   (iv)   by replacement of the 4-ethoxycaronyl by any other alkoxycarbonyl or any alkoxyalkyl or acyloxy group;
   (v)   by formation of an N-oxide or of a quaternary base.

2. Any stereoisomeric form of a substance specified in paragraph 1 above.
3. Any ester or ether of a substance specified in paragraph 1 or 2 above.

4. Any salt of a substance specified in any of paragraphs 1 to 3 above.

5. Any preparation or other product containing a substance or product specified in any of paragraphs 1 to 4 above.

PART II

1.6.5   <center>CONTROLLED DRUGS EXCEPTED FROM PART I</center>

1. The compounds referred to in paragraph 1(*d*) of Part I of this Schedule are—

> Alfentanil
> Carfentanil
> Lofentanil
> Sufentanil.

2. The compounds referred to in paragraph 1(*e*) of Part I of this Schedule are—

> Allylprodine
> Alphamerprodine
> Alphaprodine
> Anileridine
> Betameprodine
> Betaprodine
> Hydroxypethidine
> Properidine
> Trimeperidine.

Customs and Excise Management Act 1979

1.7   <center>**CHAPTER 2**</center>

An Act to consolidate the enactments relating to the collection and management of the revenues of customs and excise and in some cases to other matters in relation to which the Commissioners of Customs and Excise for the time being perform functions, with amendments to give effect to recommendations of the Law Commission and the Scottish Law Commission.

[22nd February 1979]

PART I

PRELIMINARY

Interpretation

1.7.1   **1.**—(1) In this Act, unless the context otherwise requires—

> ...
>
> "container" includes any bundle or package and any box, cask or other receptacle whatsoever;

"the customs and excise Acts" means the Customs and Excise Acts 1979 and any other enactment for the time being in force relating to customs or excise;

"the Customs and Excise Acts 1979" means—

this Act,

the Customs and Excise Duties (General Reliefs) Act 1979,

the Alcoholic Liquor Duties Act 1979,

the Hydrocarbon Oil Duties Act 1979,

the Matches and Mechanical Lighters Duties Act 1979, and

the Tobacco Products Duty Act 1979;

...

"exporter", in relation to goods for exportation or for use as stores, includes the shipper of the goods and person performing in relation to an aircraft functions corresponding with those of a shipper;

...

"importer", in relation to any goods at any time between their importation and the time when they are delivered out of charge, includes any owner or other person for the time being possessed of or beneficially interested in the goods and, in relation to goods imported by means of a pipe-line, includes the owner of the pipe-line;

"justice" and "justice of the peace" in Scotland includes a sheriff and in Northern Ireland, in relation to any powers and duties which can under any enactment for the time being in force be exercised and performed only by a resident magistrate, means, a resident magistrate;

"land" and "landing", in relation to aircraft, include alighting on water;

...

"prohibited or restricted goods" means goods of a class or description of which the importation, exportation or carriage coastwise is for the time being prohibited or restricted under or by virtue of any enactment;

...

"ship" and "vessel" include any boat or other vessel whatsoever (and, to the extent provided in section 2 below, any hovercraft);

"shipment" includes loading into an aircraft, and "shipped" and cognate expression shall be construed accordingly;

...

Time of importation, exportation, etc.

5.—(1) The provisions of this section shall have effect for the purposes **1.7.2** of the customs and excise Acts.

(2) Subject to subsections (3) and (6) below, the time of importation of any goods shall be deemed to be—

    (*a*)   where the goods are brought by sea, the time when the ship carrying them comes within the limits of a port;

(*b*)   where the goods are brought by air, the time when the aircraft carrying them lands in the United Kingdom or the time when the goods are unloaded in the United Kingdom, whichever is the earlier;

(*c*)   where the goods are brought by land, the time when the goods are brought across the boundary into Northern Ireland.

(3) In the case of goods brought by sea of which entry is not required under section 37 below, the time of importation shall be deemed to be the time when the ship carrying them came within the limits of the port at which the goods are discharged.

(4) Subject to subsections (5) and (7) below, the time of exportation of any goods from the United Kingdom shall be deemed to be—

(*a*)   where the goods are exported by sea or air, the time when the goods are shipped for exportation;

(*b*)   where the goods are exported by land, the time when they are cleared by the proper officer at the last customs and excise station on their way to the boundary.

(5) In the case of goods of a class or description with respect to the exportation of which any prohibition or restriction is for the time being in force under or by virtue of any enactment which are exported by sea or air, the time of exportation shall be deemed to be the time when the exporting ship or aircraft departs from the last port or customs and excise airport at which it is cleared before departing for a destination outside the United Kingdom.

(6) Goods imported by means of a pipe-line shall be treated as imported at the time when they are brought within the limits of a port or brought across the boundary into Northern Ireland.

(7) Goods exported by means of a pipe-line shall be treated as exported at the time when they are charged into that pipe-line for exportation.

(8) A ship shall be deemed to have arrived at or departed from a port at any time when the ship comes within or, as the case may be, leaves the limits of that port.

. . .

Penalty for improper importation of goods

1.7.3   **50.**—(1) Subsection (2) below applies to goods of the following descriptions, that is to say—

(*a*)   goods chargeable with a duty which has not been paid; and

(*b*)   goods for importation, landing or unloading of which is for the time being prohibited or restricted by or under any enactment.

(2) if any person with intent to defraud Her Majesty of any such duty or to evade any such prohibition or restriction as is mentioned in subsection (1) above—

(a)   unships or lands in any port or unloads from any aircraft in the United Kingdom or from any vehicle in Northern Ireland any goods to which this subsection applies, or assists or is otherwise concerned in such unshipping, landing or unloading; or

(b)   removes from their place of importation or from any approved wharf, examination station, transit shed or customs and excise station any goods to which this subsection applies or assists or is otherwise concerned in such removal, he shall be guilty of an offence under this subsection and may be detained.

(3) If any person imports or is concerned in importing any goods contrary to any prohibition or restriction for the time being in force under or by virtue of any enactment with respect to those goods, whether or not the goods are unloaded, and does so with intent to evade the prohibition or restriction, he shall be guilty of an offence under this subjection and may be detained.

(4) Subject to subsection (5) or (5A) below, a person guilty of an offence under subsection (2) or (3) above shall be liable—

(a)   on summary conviction, to a penalty of the prescribed sum or of three times the value of the goods, whichever is the greater, or to imprisonment for a term not exceeding six months, or to both; or

¹(b)   on conviction on indictment, to a penalty of any amount or to imprisonment for a term not exceeding seven years; or to both.

(5) In the case of an offence under subsection (2) or (3) above in connection with a prohibition or restriction on importation having effect by virtue of section 3 of the Misuse of Drugs Act 1971, subsection (4) above shall have effect subject to the modifications specified in Schedule 1 to this Act.

²(5A) In the case of an offence under subsection (2) or (3) above in connection with the prohibition contained in section 20 of the Forgery and Counterfeiting Act 1981, subsection (4)(b) above shall have effect as if for the words "2 years" there were substituted the words "10 years".

(6) If any person—

(a)   imports or causes to be imported any goods concealed in a container holding goods of a different description; or

³(b)   directly or indirectly imports or causes to be imported or entered any goods found, whether before or after delivery, not to correspond with the entry made thereof, he shall be liable on summary conviction to a penalty of three times the value of goods or £400, whichever is the greater.

(7) In any case where a person would, apart from this subsection, be guilty of—

(*a*)   an offence under this section in connection with the importation of goods contrary to a prohibition or restriction; and

(*b*)   a corresponding offence under the enactment or other instrument imposing the prohibition or restriction, being an offence for which a fine or other penalty is expressly provided by that enactment or other instrument, he shall not be guilty of the offence mentioned in paragraph (*a*) of this subsection.

NOTES

[1]See s. 12(1)(*a*) of the Finance Act 1988.
[2]Inserted by s. 23(1) of the Forgery and Counterfeiting Act 1981.
[3]S.I. 1984 No. 447; S.I. 1984 No. 526.
…

Offences in relation to exportation of prohibited or restricted goods

1.7.4   **68**.—(1) If any goods are—

(*a*)   exported or shipped as stores; or

[1](*b*)   brought to any place in the United Kingdom for the purpose of being exported or shipped as stores, and the exportation or shipment is or would be contrary to any prohibition or restriction for the time being in force with respect to those goods under or by virtue of any enactment, the goods shall be liable to forfeiture and the exporter or intending exporter of the goods and any agent of his concerned in the exportation or shipment or intended exportation or shipment shall each be liable on summary conviction to a penalty of three times the value of the goods or £400, whichever is the greater.

(2) Any person knowingly concerned in the exportation or shipment as stores, or in the attempted exportation or shipment as stores, of any goods with intent to evade any such prohibition or restriction as is mentioned in subsection (1) above shall be guilty of an offence under this subsection and may be detained.

[2](3) Subject to subsection (4) or (4A) below, a person guilty of an offence under subsection (2) above shall be liable

(*a*)   on summary conviction, to a penalty of the prescribed sum or of three times the value of the goods, whichever is the greater, or to imprisonment for a term not exceeding six months, or to both; or

[3](*b*)   on conviction on indictment, to a penalty of any amount, or to imprisonment for a term not exceeding seven years, or to both.

(4) In the case of an offence under subsection (2) above in connection with a prohibition or restriction on exportation having effect by virtue of

section 3 of the Misuse of Drugs Act 1971, subsection (3) above shall have effect subject to the modifications specified in Schedule 1 to this Act.

[4](4A) In the case of an offence under subsection (2) above in connection with the prohibition contained in section 21 of the Forgery and Counterfeiting Act 1981, subsection (3)(*b*) above shall have effect as if for the words "2 years" there were substituted the words "10 years".

(5) If by virtue of any such restriction as is mentioned in subsection (1) above any goods may be exported only when consigned to a particular place or person and any goods so consigned are delivered to some other place or person, the ship, aircraft or vehicle in which they were exported shall be liable to forfeiture unless it is proved to the satisfaction of the Commissioners that both the owner of the ship, aircraft or vehicle and the master of the ship, commander of the aircraft or person in charge of the vehicle—

(*a*)   took all reasonable steps to secure that the goods were delivered to the particular place to which or person to whom they were consigned; and

(*b*)   did not connive at or, except under duress, consent to the delivery of the goods to that other place or person.

(6) In any case where a person would, apart from this subsection, be guilty of—

(*a*)   an offence under subsection (1) or (2) above; and

(*b*)   a corresponding offence under the enactment or instrument imposing the prohibition or restriction in question, being an offence for which a fine or other penalty is expressly provided by that enactment or other instrument, he shall not be guilty of the offence mentioned in paragraph (*a*) of this subsection.

NOTES
[1]S.I. 1984 No. 447; S.I. 1984 No. 526.
[2]Inserted by s. 23(2) of the Forgery and Counterfeiting Act 1981.
[3]See s. 12(1)(*a*) of the Finance Act 1988.
[4]Inserted by s. 23(2) of the Forgery and Counterfeiting Act 1981.
...

Penalty for fraudulent evasion of duty, etc.

170.—(1) Without prejudice to any other provision of the Customs and Excise Acts 1979, if any person—   **1.7.5**

(*a*)   knowingly acquires possession of any of the following goods, that is to say—
    (i)   goods which have been unlawfully removed from a warehouse or Queen's warehouse;
    (ii)   goods which are chargeable with a duty which has not been paid;

(iii) goods with respect to the importation or exportation of which any prohibition or restriction is for the time being in force under or by virtue of any enactment; or

(b) is in any way knowingly concerned in carrying, removing, depositing, harbouring, keeping or concealing or in any manner dealing with such goods, and does so with intent to defraud Her Majesty of any duty payable on the goods or to evade any such prohibition or restriction with respect to the goods he shall be guilty of an offence under this section and may be detained.

(2) Without prejudice to any other provision of the Customs and Excise Acts 1979, if any person is, in relation to any goods, in any way knowingly concerned in any fraudulent evasion or attempt at evasion—

(a) of any duty chargeable on the goods;

(b) of any prohibition or restriction for the time being in force with respect to the goods under or by virtue of any enactment; or

(c) of any provision of the Customs and Excise Acts 1979 applicable to the goods, he shall be guilty of an offence under this section and may be detained.

[1](3) Subject to subsection (4) or (4A) below, a person guilty of an offence under this section shall be liable—

(a) on summary conviction, to a penalty of the prescribed sum or of three times the value of the goods, whichever is the greater, or to imprisonment for a term not exceeding six months, or to both; or

[2](b) on conviction on indictment, to a penalty of any amount, or to imprisonment for a term not exceeding seven years or to both.

(4) In the case of an offence under this section in connection with a prohibition or restriction on importation or exportation having effect by virtue of section 3 of the Misuse of Drugs Act 1971, subsection (3) above shall have effect subject to the modifications specified in Schedule 1 to this Act.

[3](4A) In the case of an offence under this section in connection with the prohibitions contained in section 20 and 21 of the Forgery and Counterfeiting Act 1981, subsection (3)(b) above shall have effect as if for the words "2 years" there were substituted the words "10 years".

(5) In any case where a person would, apart from this subsection, be guilty of—

(a) an offence under this section in connection with a prohibition or restriction; and

(b) a corresponding offence under the enactment or other instrument imposing the prohibition or restriction, being an offence for which a fine or other penalty is expressly provided by that enactment or other instrument, he shall not be guilty of the offence mentioned in paragraph (*a*) of this subsection.

NOTES
[1]Inserted by s. 23(3) of the Forgery and Counterfeiting Act 1981.
[2]See s. 12(1)(*a*) of the Finance Act 1988.
[3]Inserted by s. 23(3) of the Forgery and Counterfeiting Act 1981.

SCHEDULE 1   **Sections 50(5), 88(4) and 170(4)**

CONTROLLED DRUGS: VARIATION OF PUNISHMENTS FOR CERTAIN OFFENCES UNDER THIS ACT   **1.7.6**

1. Sections 50(4), 68(3) and 170(3) of this Act shall have effect in a case where the goods in respect of which the offence referred to in that subsection was committed were a Class A drug or a Class B drug as if for the words from "shall be liable" onwards there were substituted the following words, that is to say—

"shall be liable–
(*a*) on summary conviction, to a penalty of the prescribed sum or of three times the value of the goods, whichever is the greater, or to imprisonment for a term not exceeding 6 months, or to both;
(*b*) on conviction on indictment, to a penalty of any amount, or to imprisonment for a term not exceeding 14 years, or to both.".

2. Sections 50(4), 68(3) and 170(3) of this Act shall have effect in a case where the goods in respect of which the offence referred to in that subsection was committed were a Class C drug as if for the words from "shall be liable" onwards there were substituted the following words, that is to say—

"shall be liable—
(*a*) on summary conviction in Great Britain, to a penalty of three times the value of the goods or £500, whichever is the greater, or to imprisonment for a term not exceeding 3 months, or to both;
(*b*) on summary conviction in Northern Ireland, to a penalty of three times the value of the goods or £100, whichever is the greater, or to imprisonment for a term not exceeding 6 months, or to both;
(*c*) on conviction on indictment, to a penalty of any amount, or to imprisonment for a term not exceeding 5 years, or to both.".

3. In this Schedule "Class A drug", "Class B drug" and "Class C drug" have the same meanings as in the Misuse of Drugs Act 1971.

Criminal Justice (International Co-operation) Act 1990

1.8　　　　　　　　　　**CHAPTER 5**

Offences at sea

Offences on British ships

1.8.1　　**18.** Anything which would constitute a drug trafficking offence if done on land in any part of the United Kingdom shall constitute that offence if done on a British ship.

Ships used for illicit traffic

1.8.2　　**19.**—(1) This section applies to a British ship, a ship registered in a state other than the United Kingdom which is a party to the Vienna Convention (a "Convention state") and a ship not registered in any country or territory.

(2) A person is guilty of an offence if on a ship to which this section applies, wherever it may be, he—

(*a*)　has a controlled drug in his possession; or
(*b*)　is in any way knowingly concerned in the carrying or concealing of a controlled drug on the ship,

knowing or having reasonable grounds to suspect that the drug is intended to be imported or has been exported contrary to section 3(1) of the Misuse of Drugs Act 1971 or the law of any state other than the United Kingdom.

(3) A certificate purporting to be issued by or on behalf of the government of any state to the effect that the importation or export of a controlled drug is prohibited by the law of that state shall be evidence, and in Scotland sufficient evidence, of the matters stated.

(4) A person guilty of an offence under this section is liable—

(*a*)　in a case where the controlled drug is a Class A drug—
　　(i)　on summary conviction, to imprisonment for a term not exceeding six months or a fine not exceeding the statutory maximum or both;
　　(ii)　on conviction on indictment, to imprisonment for life or a fine or both;
(*b*)　in a case where the controlled drug is a Class B drug—
　　(i)　on summary conviction, to imprisonment for a term not exceeding six months or a fine not exceeding the statutory maximum or both;
　　(ii)　on conviction on indictment, to imprisonment for a term not exceeding fourteen years or a fine or both;

(c) in a case where the controlled drug is a Class C drug—
  (i) on summary conviction, to imprisonment for a term not exceeding three months or a fine not exceeding the statutory maximum or both;
  (ii) on conviction on indictment, to imprisonment for a term not exceeding five years or a fine or both.

(5) In this section "a controlled drug" and the references to controlled drugs of a specified Class have the same meaning as in the said Act of 1971; and an offence under this section shall be included in the offences to which section 28 of that Act (defences) applies.

Enforcement powers

20.—(1) The powers conferred on an enforcement officer by **1.8.3** Schedule 3 to this Act shall be exercisable in relation to any ship to which section 18 or 19 above applies for the purpose of detecting and the taking of appropriate action in respect of the offences mentioned in those sections.

(2) Those powers shall not be exercised outside the landward limits of the territorial sea of the United Kingdom in relation to a ship registered in a Convention state except with the authority of the Secretary of State; and he shall not give his authority unless that state has in relation to that ship—

(a) requested the assistance of the United Kingdom for the purpose mentioned in subsection (1) above; or
(b) authorised the United Kingdom to act for that purpose.

(3) In giving his authority pursuant to a request or authorisation from a Convention state the Secretary of State shall impose such conditions or limitations on the exercise of the powers as may be necessary to give effect to any conditions or limitations imposed by that state.

(4) The Secretary of State may, either of his own motion or in response to a request from a Convention state, authorise a Convention state to exercise, in relation to a British ship, powers corresponding to those conferred on enforcement officers by Schedule 3 to this Act but subject to such conditions or limitations, if any, as he may impose.

(5) Subsection (4) above is without prejudice to any agreement made, or which may be made, on behalf of the United Kingdom whereby the United Kingdom undertakes not to object to the exercise by any other state in relation to a British ship of powers corresponding to those conferred by that Schedule.

(6) The powers conferred by that Schedule shall not be exercised in the territorial sea of any state other than the United Kingdom without the authority of the Secretary of State and he shall not give his authority unless that state has consented to the exercise of those powers.

Jurisdiction and prosecutions

1.8.4   **21.**—(1) Proceedings under this Part of this Act or Schedule 3 in respect of an offence on a ship may be taken, and the offence may for all incidental purposes be treated as having been committed, in any place in the United Kingdom.

(2) No such proceedings shall be instituted—

(*a*)   in England or Wales except by or with the consent of the Director of Public Prosecutions or the Commissioners of Customs and Excise;

(*b*)   in Northern Ireland except by or with the consent of the Director of Public Prosecutions for Northern Ireland or those Commissioners.

(3) Without prejudice to subsection (2) above no proceedings for an offence under section 19 above alleged to have been committed outside the landward limits of the territorial sea of the United Kingdom on a ship registered in a Convention state shall be instituted except in pursuance of the exercise with the authority of the Secretary of State of the powers conferred by Schedule 3 to this Act; and section 3 of the Territorial Waters Jurisdiction Act 1878 (consent of Secretary of State for certain prosecutions) shall not apply to those proceedings.

Criminal Procedure (Scotland) Act 1995

1.9   **CHAPTER 46**

Sufficient evidence

Evidence as to controlled drugs and medicinal products

1.9.1   **282.**—(1) For the purposes of any criminal proceedings, evidence given by an authorised forensic scientist, either orally or in a report purporting to be signed by him, that a substance which satisfies either of the conditions specified in subsection (2) below is—

(*a*)   a particular controlled drug or medicinal product; or

(*b*)   a particular product which is listed in the British Pharmacopoeia as containing a particular controlled drug or medicinal product.

shall, subject to subsection (3) below, be sufficient evidence of that fact notwithstanding that no analysis of the substance has been carried out.

(2) Those conditions are—

(*a*)   that the substance is in a sealed container bearing a label identifying the contents of the container; or (*b*)   that the substance has a characteristic appearance having regard to its size, shape, colour and manufacturer's mark.

(3) A party proposing to rely on subsection (1) above ("the first party") shall, not less than 14 days before the trial diet, serve on the other party ("the second party")—

(*a*)   a notice to that effect; and
(*b*)   where the evidence is contained in a report, a copy of the report,

and if the second party serves on the first party, not more than seven days after the date of service of the notice on him, a notice that he does not accept the evidence as to the identity of the substance, subsection (1) above shall not apply in relation to that evidence.

(4) A notice or copy report served in accordance with subsection (3) above shall be served in such manner as may be prescribed by Act of Adjournal; and a written execution purporting to be signed by the person who served the notice or copy together with, where appropriate, the relevant post office receipt shall be sufficient evidence of such service.

(5) In this section—

"controlled drug" has the same meaning as in the Misuse of Drugs Act 1971; and
"medicinal product" has the same meaning as in the Medicines Act 1968.

NOTE
    The notice to be served in terms of s. 282(3) should follow the style referred to in the Act of Adjournal (Criminal Procedure Rules) 1996 at r. 27.3 and set out in Form 27.3.

PART B

CASES

CHAPTER TWO

Importation and Exportation   2.1

Introduction   2.2

The Misuse of Drugs Act 1971 provides by section 3 for the prohibition on the importation and exportation of controlled drugs. The offences — of which there are several — are to be found in the Customs and Excise Management Act 1979 and in particular sections 50, 68 and 170.

A. LAW: IMPORTATION   2.3

1. R. v. Hussain   2.3.1
(1969) 53 Cr.App.R. 448

A customs officer boarded a ship at Liverpool and found about 20 lbs. of cannabis resin concealed in a bulkhead panel in a cabin occupied by H. and two other crew members. At that stage H. said that the concealment had nothing to do with him, but that he would take the blame. The court later placed little importance on this admission because of language difficulties which existed at the time of discovery.

The ship went on to London and there H. was questioned more comprehensively. He said that while the ship was *en route* from Las Palmas to Liverpool the engineer and the carpenter came into the cabin with the cannabis resin. They concealed the cannabis resin in the bulkhead and told H. that he would have his throat cut if he said anything about it. He was promised a reward if he kept silent.

H. was charged with being knowingly concerned in the fraudulent evasion of the prohibition on the importation of cannabis resin contrary to section 304(*b*) of the 1952 Act and also the unlawful possession of controlled drugs contrary to section 13 of the 1965 Act. His defence amounted to a denial that the drugs were his and that he was a passive spectator. H. was convicted and sentenced to 18 months' imprisonment concurrent on each charge. He appealed against conviction.

WIDGERY, L.J. (at p. 451): "It seems perfectly clear that the word 'knowingly' in the section in question is concerned with knowing that a fraudulent evasion of a prohibition in respect of goods is taking place. If, therefore, the accused knows that what is on foot is the evasion of a prohibition against importation and he knowingly takes part in that operation, it is sufficient to justify his conviction, even if he does not know precisely what kind of goods are being imported. It is, of course, essential that he should know that the goods which are being imported are goods subject to a prohibition. It is essential he should know that the operation with which he is concerning himself is an operation designed to evade that prohibition and evade it fraudulently. But it is not necessary he should know the precise category of the goods the importation of which has been prohibited."

And later (at p. 452)

"This Court takes the view that there is no reason to suppose that the jury would associate the word 'smugglers' solely with those who seek to evade Customs duty. We think that in the ordinary use of language today the verb 'to smuggle' is used equally to apply to the importation of goods which are prohibited in import and, indeed, one sees the word used quite often in regard to illegal immigrants brought in secretly by night in small boats. We do not think the jury would have been in any way put off in their approach to this problem by reference [in the trial judge's charge to the jury] to 'smugglers' and 'smuggling'."

> Appeal *quoad* charge one dismissed and *quoad* charge two allowed for other reasons.

NOTE

This case is considered again in a number of later cases. The dicta relate to section 304 of the 1952 Act but the relevant phrase "being knowingly concerned in the fraudulent evasion of the prohibition" is repeated in section 170 of the 1979 Act.

2.3.2
2. R. v. Ardalan
[1972] 2 All E.R. 258

A. and four others became involved in a complicated set of arrangements which led to them being charged with conspiring together to acquire possession of a quantity of cannabis the importation of which was prohibited by the 1965 Act, knowingly and with intent to evade the prohibition contrary to section 304 of the 1952 Act. On conviction they appealed.

ROSKILL, L.J. (at p. 260): "Two things should be noted about this section. First, in the forefront of para (*a*) are the words 'knowingly and with intent to evade any prohibition or restriction for the time being in force.' There can be no doubt that those words set out the requisite state of mind to be possessed by the person charged before he can be convicted of an offence against the section. Secondly, the person charged must be shown to have acquired possession of the goods with the intent of which I have spoken, being goods with respect to the importation or exportation of which any prohibition or restriction is for the time being in force."

And later (at p. 261)

"If once ... there can be an offence committed at some point of time and at some place after importation (for example, acquisition at or near the airport), it is difficult to see why there should be any limit to that point of time or place provided always, of course, that the goods the subject-matter of the charge are goods which are the subject of a prohibition or restriction on importation and the acquisition is done knowingly and with intent to evade that prohibition or restriction. But subject to those two matters, this court sees no reason to think that on the true construction of section 304 any distinction can be drawn between the case of uncustomed goods on the one hand and goods the importation of which is prohibited or restricted on the other."

Appeals refused.

3. Byrne v. Low   2.3.3
[1972] 3 All E.R. 526

B. was convicted before justices of fraudulently evading the prohibition on importation of prohibited goods, *i.e.* indecent articles consisting of 1,000 magazines and 650 cine films, contrary to section 304 of the 1952 Act. The invoice price of the articles in question, expressed in Danish kroner, was equivalent to £2335. The accused was sentenced to a fine of £3000 or 12 months' imprisonment in default. He appealed to quarter sessions who varied the sentence by imposing a sentence of imprisonment, suspended, and substituting a penalty of £100 for the penalty of £3,000 imposed by the justices. Quarter sessions reduced the amount of the fine on the ground that, since the importation of the articles was prohibited, there would be no 'open market' for them, within the meaning of section 305(2) of the 1952 Act, by which to fix the value of the goods and so the maximum penalty which the court could impose under section 304 was one of £100.

On appeal, the Queen's Bench Division held that the appeal would be allowed and the case sent back for the fine to be re-assessed. For the purposes of section 305(2) any distinction between the so-called black and white markets was irrelevant; all that was necessary was to ascertain what was the price which would be paid by a willing buyer to a willing seller at the port of landing. An invoice from the overseas seller to the intended recipient would be a good, and sometimes the only and conclusive, guide to the open market value of the goods in question.

LORD WIDGERY, C.J. (at p. 529): "It is contended before us today, and I think clearly the contention is correct, that in deciding what is the open market value of goods of this kind, one is not restricted by the distinction between the so-called black market and white market. What is being sought is the price which a willing seller would accept from a willing buyer for these goods as landed at the port or airport at which they were originally landed. If we can ascertain what is the price which would be paid by a willing buyer to a willing seller at the port of landing, then that is the open market value of the goods for present purposes."

Appeal allowed.

NOTE

It is virtually inconceivable that those smuggling controlled drugs into the United Kingdom will produce an invoice showing the purchase price. However, this authority gives some guidance to the assessment of value, a matter of some importance given the prevalence of values put on controlled drugs by customs officers and the police. For further discussion on the topic see Kay "Aramah and the Street Value of Drugs" [1987] Crim.L.R. 814.

2.3.4   **4. R. v. Green**
                              [1976] Crim.L.R. 47

G. completed customs forms on August 6, to obtain clearance of a crate on a ship at Southampton. On August 20, customs officers opened the crate and found that it contained cannabis which was then replaced with peat. Thereafter G. rented a garage and in September the crate was delivered to it by a haulage contractor. G. supplied the contractor's name and address to others involved and G. was said to have admitted assisting to unload the crate at the garage. The trial judge held the offence to be a continuing one. G. was convicted of being knowingly concerned in the fraudulent evasion of the prohibition on the importation of cannabis, contrary to section 304(*b*) of the 1952 Act and conspiring to evade the prohibition on the importation of a controlled drug.

Held, the *actus reus* of the offence under section 304(*b*) was being concerned in the evasion or attempted evasion of the prohibition, not the successful evasion. Evasion was a continuing offence and did not cease when the goods were seized. Once imported the evasion continued until the goods ceased to be prohibited or, possibly, were re-exported. The renting of the garage to store the drug completed the offence. There was ample authority that the *actus reus* of conspiracy was the agreement to effect an unlawful purpose. It must follow that the fact that, unknown to the conspirators, the unlawful purpose could not be achieved was no defence.

Appeal dismissed.

2.3.5   **5. R. v. Hennessey**
                            (1978) 68 Cr.App.R. 419

H. drove a car to the continent and he returned the following day by way of Dover. There customs officers searched his car and found 28.14 kilogrammes of cannabis resin in the hiding places made by another accused. When the packets of cannabis resin were found H. said: "I don't know anything about them." About a month later he made a written statement in which he said that he thought he was bringing back "blue" films to England and the context in which he said it showed that he knew that what he claimed to be bringing back was a prohibited import. H. was convicted of being knowingly concerned in the fraudulent evasion of the prohibition of the importation of controlled drugs contrary to section 304(*b*) of the 1952 Act and he was sentenced to two years' imprisonment.

LAWTON, L.J. (at p. 423): "On his own story Hennessey did know that he was concerned in the fraudulent evasion of a prohibition in relation to goods. In plain English he was smuggling goods. It matters not for the purpose of conviction what the goods were as long as he knew that he was bringing into the United Kingdom goods which he should not have been bringing in."

Appeal dismissed.

6. Attorney-General's Reference (No. 1 of 1981)   2.3.6
[1982] 2 All E.R. 417

In a trial the prosecution showed that certain individuals had bought goods on shore and then made off with them seeking to evade capture. At the end of the prosecution case the judge held that in order for the word "fraudulent" to be satisfied, the prosecution had to prove that the individuals had done something which amounted to acting or telling lies to, or deceiving or attempting to deceive customs officers. As the evidence did not seem to him to amount to deceit in the traditional sense or to come within the definition of "fraudulent", the individuals were acquitted.

The Attorney-General referred for the court's opinion the question "Whether the presence of the word 'fraudulent' in section 170(2) of the Customs and Excise Management Act 1979 has the effect, that in prosecutions under that provision for fraudulent evasion or attempted evasion of a prohibition or restriction with respect to goods or of duty chargeable thereon, the prosecution must prove fraudulent conduct in the sense of (1) acts of deceit practised on a customs officer in his presence or merely (2) conduct deliberately intended to evade the prohibition or restriction with respect to, or the duty chargeable on, goods as the case may be."

Held, that in the court's opinion, what had to be "fraudulent" was not behaviour towards a customs officer but the evasion or attempt at evasion of the prohibition. Consequently, it was inappropriate to import narrow definitions of "fraudulent" from branches of the law dealing with fraud practised on other persons.

"Fraudulent" in section 170(2) had the effect that in prosecution under the subsection for fraudulent evasion or attempted evasion of a prohibition or restriction with respect to goods or duty chargeable thereon, the prosecution had to prove fraudulent conduct in the sense of dishonest conduct deliberately intended to evade the prohibition or restriction with respect to, or the duty chargeable on, goods as the case might be. There was no necessity for the prosecution to prove acts of deceit practised on a customs officer in his presence.

Opinion stated.

2.3.7   **7. R. v. Jakeman**
                        (1983) 76 Cr.App.R. 223

J. booked two suitcases containing cannabis onto a flight from Ghana to Italy and thereafter to England. The flight was diverted to France but J. did not collect the suitcases in Paris nor in London after they had been sent on. She was later arrested by customs officials. She told them that she had collected her suitcases on arrival at London, in the usual way. After further questioning and on being shown the unclaimed suitcases, she admitted they were hers and that she knew that they contained cannabis. J.'s version of events included an assertion that, in essence, she had decided not to go through with the venture and had torn up the baggage tickets and not collected her suitcases.

At the close of the defence case the judge, when asked, indicated his view that J.'s alleged intention to abandon her part in the importation before that importation took place provided no defence. J. changed her plea to guilty. She sought leave to appeal on the ground *inter alia* that the judge's ruling was wrong. It was submitted on her behalf that for an offence under section 170(2) to be made out the participation of an individual and the *mens rea* must continue throughout the offence, that is, until the aircraft touches down at London Airport.

Wood, J. (at p. 227): "For guilt to be established the importation must, of course, result as a consequence, if only in part, of the activity of the accused.

Although the importation takes place at one precise moment — when the aircraft lands — a person who is concerned in the importation may play his part before or after that moment. Commonly, the person responsible for despatching the prohibited drugs to England acts fraudulently and so does the person who removes them from the airport at which they have arrived. Each is guilty. *Wall* (1974) 59 Cr.App.R. 58 is an example of the former and *Green* (1975) 62 Cr.App.R. 74 of the latter.

What is suggested is that she should not be convicted unless her guilty state of mind subsisted at the time of importation. We see no reason to construe the Act in this way. If a guilty mind at the time of importation is an essential, the man recruited to collect the package which has already arrived and which he knows contains prohibited drugs commits no offence. What matters is the state of mind at the time the relevant acts are done *i.e.* at the time the defendant is concerned in bringing about the importation."

Application refused.

8. R. v. Neal   **2.3.8**
[1984] 3 All E.R. 156

N. and others were convicted of being knowingly concerned in the fraudulent evasion of the prohibition on the importation of a controlled drug; namely cannabis resin, contrary to section 170(2) of the 1979 Act and were sentenced to various terms of imprisonment.

Six hundredweight of cannabis resin was discovered at a farmhouse in Wales that belonged to one of the accused who later admitted that he knew that the substance had been imported. There was no evidence to link any one of the accused with the actual importation itself.

Each appealed on a point of law, namely that in the absence of such evidence of a link the convictions were wrong in law. Crown Counsel submitted at appeal that on its true construction section 170(2) is a sweeping up or catch-all provision intended to make it an offence for anyone, irrespective of whether or not he was a member of or associated with the original smuggling team, to deal with goods which he knows have been imported in breach of the law with the intent of fraudulently evading the long arm of the customs and excise.

GRIFFITHS, L.J. (at p. 60): "[Section 170(1)] clearly includes those who are not a part of the original smuggling team. For example, it includes anyone who acquires possession of goods unlawfully removed from a warehouse, or anyone who hides goods on which duty has not been paid, or anyone who carries goods the importation of which is forbidden; and there can be no warrant for reading into the language of the subsection the qualification 'provided they are part of the original team.'

The subsection is aimed at making it an offence for anyone in any circumstances to be a party to defrauding the Crown of duty or evading any prohibition or restriction on imports. The language of the subsection is so embracing and casts the net so wide that one is left to wonder what purpose is served by sub-s. (2), for it is difficult to think of any behaviour aimed at defrauding the customs and excise that would not be caught by sub-s. (1). However, sub-s. (2) has consistently appeared in similar form in a succession of Customs and Excise Acts as the final and sweeping up provision: see the Customs Consolidation Act 1853, s. 232, the Customs Consolidation Act 1876, s. 186 and the Customs and Excise Act 1952, s. 304(*b*).

We are satisfied that it was inserted by the draftsman with the intention of casting his net as widely as words enabled him (note his language), 'in any person' and 'in any way'. This was the view of Lord Salmon expressed in *DPP* v. *Doot* [1973] 1 All E.R. 940 at 954, [1973] A.C. 807 at 830–831. Lord Salmon was discussing the construction of the Customs and Excise Act 1952, but for all material purposes that is re-enacted in similar language in the present Act. He said: 'Section 304 [and I interpolate to say that this is the equivalent of the 1979 Act] is obviously a long stop for ss. 45 and 56 to catch anyone against whom actual importing, exporting or being concerned in actual importing or exporting cannot be proved although no doubt it is wide enough to cover importing and exporting also'."

Appeals dismissed.

NOTE

In *R. v. Watts and Stack* (1979) 70 Cr.App.R. 187 the prosecution had contended that there was an evasion of the prohibition on the importation of any goods, whenever goods of that description were dealt with in this country. The trial judge had accepted that for example the growing of cannabis plants in a back garden in this country would be an evasion of the prohibition on the importation of cannabis. W. and S. had been convicted and appealed on the basis that the trial judge had erred in leaving the case in the terms stated to the jury, there being no evidence of importation, nor any evidence.

At the Court of appeal Crown Counsel abandoned the line taken earlier and recognised that in order that there should be an evasion of a prohibition, it must be shown that the prohibited acts have been committed, and that "there can be no evasion of a prohibition on importation, unless a prohibited importation has taken place."

The court proceeded, following on that concession, to hold that on a true construction of the relevant section, in order to establish that any particular dealing with goods was done with intent to evade the relevant prohibition on importation, the onus was on the Crown to prove that intent must involve establishing a link or *nexus* between the *actus reus* of the offence and some prohibited importation.

At the hearing of the appeal in *Neal*, counsel for Neal and certain of the other appellants, relied on *R. v. Watts and Stack* for the proposition that the offence could only be committed by a person "involved in the initial smuggling operation". The court in *R. v. Neal* thought (at p. 163) that the language might just be susceptible of this construction but it was not read as such in its context. The court did not believe that the language was intended to do more than stress the importance of the prosecution leading evidence to establish the necessary intention to evade the prohibition and that it is not sufficient to rely solely on any statutory presumptions and a mere act of dealing.

"An act of dealing in a drug may or may not reveal an intention to evade the prohibition according to the circumstances in which it takes place. If no more can be proved than that a piece of cannabis changed hands in Piccadilly Circus, no doubt it would be foolish of the prosecution to proceed under this section of the 1979 Act, for it would be far-fetched to suggest that the real intent of such a transaction is to evade the prohibition on the import of cannabis ... there are ample powers available to prosecuting authorities under the drugs legislation to deal with such a situation by charging those involved either with possession of cannabis or the more serious offence of possession with intent to supply."

9. R. v. Taaffe   2.3.9
[1984] 1 All E.R. 747

T. smuggled a controlled drug into the United Kingdom intending fraudulently to evade a prohibition on importation but he believed mistakenly that the goods were currency and not controlled drugs. He also believed mistakenly that the importation of currency was prohibited. He was charged under section 170(2) of the 1979 Act with being knowingly concerned in the fraudulent evasion of the prohibition on the importation of a controlled drug contrary to section 3(1) of the 1971 Act.

At T.'s trial the judge ruled that even on T.'s version of events he was obliged to direct the jury to convict T. because T. believed that he was importing goods even though he did not know the precise nature of the goods involved. T. pleaded guilty.

Thereafter T. appealed against his conviction to the Court of Appeal where his appeal was allowed and his conviction quashed on the ground that the requisite *mens rea* for an offence under section 170(2) was actual knowledge and as T. believed that the substance he was importing was currency, the importation of which was not a criminal offence, his mistake of law did not convert the importation into a criminal offence.

The Crown then appealed to the House of Lords.

LORD SCARMAN (at p. 749): "Lord Lane, C.J. [in the hearing of T.'s case before the Court of Appeal] construed the subsection under which the respondent [T.] was charged as creating an offence not of absolute liability but as one of which an essential ingredient is a guilty mind. To be 'knowingly concerned' meant, in his judgment, knowledge not only of the existence of a smuggling operation but also that the substance being smuggled into the country was one the importation of which was prohibited by statute. The respondent [T.] thought he was concerned in a smuggling operation but believed that the substance was currency. The importation of currency is not subject to any prohibition. Lord Lane C.J. concluded … 'He [T.] … is to be judged against the facts that he believed them to be. Had this indeed been currency and not cannabis, no offence would have been committed.'

Lord Lane, C.J. went on to ask this question: 'Does it make any difference that [T.] … thought wrongly that by clandestinely importing currency he was committing an offence?'

The Crown submitted that it did. The court rejected the submission: [T.'s] … mistake of law could not convert the importation of currency into a criminal offence; and importing currency is what it had to be assumed that [T.] … believed he was doing.

My Lords, I find the reasoning of Lord Lane C.J. compelling. I agree with his construction of section 170(2) of the 1979 Act; and the principle that a man must be judged on the facts as he believes them to be is an accepted principle of the criminal law when the state of a man's mind and his knowledge are ingredients of the offence with which he is charged."

Appeal dismissed.

NOTE

In what circumstances can a man mistake controlled drugs for money?

Lord Scarman asserted that the principle that a man must be judged on the facts as he believes them to be is an accepted principle of the criminal law when the state of a man's mind and his knowledge are ingredients of the offence. Professor J. C. Smith, Q.C. has stressed that the principle is inconsistent with the view that "only reasonable mistakes will excuse": [1984] Crim.L.R. 356.

The accused pleaded guilty after a ruling by the trial judge that *the agreed facts* did not afford a defence to the charge. Precisely what was agreed between counsel is not stated in the report referred to above.

An indication of the agreed facts is given in an earlier report: *The Times*, April 16, 1983. Taaffe drove a car into the green lane of the ferry terminal at Sheerness and told the customs officer on duty that he had nothing to declare. The car was searched and it was noticed that the spare tyre was deflated.

In the tyre were found five packages containing cannabis resin. Then Taaffe was searched and taped to his back under his clothes were a further three packages of cannabis resin. When asked whether he knew what substance was in the packages, he said, "I am waiting to find out, because, if it is drugs ..." and that was the end of that answer. When asked what he did think was in them, Taaffe replied, "Money."

Taaffe does not appear to have given evidence.

The statute involved in the charge is common to England and Scotland and the *ratio* of *R. v. Taaffe* is thus highly persuasive in Scotland, but one cannot be sure that it will be followed here.

<table>
<tr><td>2.3.10</td><td align="center">**10. R. v. Shivpuri**
[1986] 2 W.L.R. 988</td></tr>
</table>

S. was found in London carrying a package containing a powdered substance and more such substance was found at his flat. The prosecution case was that at several police interviews S. admitted having drugs and under caution he typed his own confession statement and stated that he very deeply suspected that the substance was heroin. Analysis proved it to be merely vegetable material akin to snuff.

In evidence on his own behalf S. denied making any admissions about drugs and denied that the type of statement amounted to a confession because from testing the substance he knew that it was not drugs.

He was convicted on charges of attempting to be knowingly concerned in dealing with and harbouring a controlled drug namely diamorphine, the importation of which was prohibited contrary to section 1(1) of the 1981 Act and section 170(1)(*b*) of the 1979 Act.

S. appealed against conviction on the ground that, because the substances found in his possession were not drugs, he could not be guilty of attempting to be concerned in either dealing with or harbouring a controlled drug as charged. The Court of Appeal dismissed the appeal and the matter of conviction was taken to the House of Lords.

LORD BRIDGE (at p. 996): "The only *mens rea* required for the offence of possessing a drug in any specified class is knowledge that it was a controlled drug ... Irrespective of the different penalties attached to offences in connection with the importation of different categories of prohibited goods, *Reg. v. Hussain* [*supra*] established that the only *mens rea* necessary for proof of any such offence was knowledge that the goods were subject to a prohibition on importation ... the decision in *Reg. v. Hussain* has effectively been adopted and endorsed by the legislature and thus remains good law."

Appeal dismissed.

NOTE
For Scots lawyers there are two distinct difficulties in dealing with the decision in *Shivpuri's* case. First, the speeches in the House of Lords are concerned to a large extent with trying to find a true construction of section 1 of the 1981 Act, which does not apply in Scotland, and that in the context of section 170 of the 1979 Act. The point was accentuated by *Anderton v. Ryan* [1985] 2 W.L.R. 968, a difficult case involving the beliefs of an accused on a material aspect, which was required to be overruled in *Shivpuri's* case.

Secondly, the House of Lords had to consider *R. v. Courtie* [1984] 2 W.L.R. 330, an earlier decision of its own, where it had been held that the Sexual Offences Act 1967 created several different offences and, given that each needed proof of different factual ingredients, resulted in different penalties. The last named Act also did not apply to Scotland.

11. R. v. Ellis   2.3.11
(1987) 84 Cr.App.R. 235

Ellis and Street, together, and Smith, alone, appeared before different judges and admitted that they participated in importing large quantities of cannabis into England, concealed in secret compartments of motor cars. On being charged with contravening section 170(2) of the 1979 Act, the accused asked the judge for a ruling as to whether they had a defence in law if the facts were that they were aware that they were participating in the importation of prohibited goods but believed that such goods were pornographic goods which they believed to be subject to prohibition and which were in fact subject to prohibition.

In both cases the trial judges, holding that they were bound by *R. v. Hennessey* (1978) 68 Cr.App.R. 419, decided that they had no defence on those assured facts. The accused then changed their pleas to guilty and were sentenced. On appeal the cases conjoined for the same point of law arose in each.

In the Court of Appeal it was *held* that it was not necessary for the appellants to know the precise nature of the goods imported when charged with contravening section 170(2) of the 1979 Act, so long as they knew that there was a prohibition against their importation.

Appeals dismissed

2.3.12   **12. R. v. Caippara**
(1988) 87 Cr.App.R. 316

Customs officers intercepted two packets containing cocaine which had arrived in England by post from Bolivia. They were addressed to C., one to his home and the other to his place of business. In each packet, baking powder was substituted for cocaine by the officers. Each packet consisted of a note from C.'s sister asking for money, wrapped round a postcard which formed a container for the drug. The packets were re-assembled and delivered by a customs officer posing as a postman, the one to C.'s home where his wife received it in his absence, the other to his business, where C. accepted it.

Some hours after C. was questioned at his business address by customs officers and he told the officers that the packet was unsolicited. C. said that he had thrown away the envelope and postcard and kept the powder which he had folded into a fresh piece of paper inside a notebook. C. said that he assumed the powder was cocaine but he did not know what to do with it.

C. was charged *inter alia* with two charges of being knowingly concerned in the fraudulent evasion on the importation of a controlled drug contrary to section 170 of the 1979 Act. He was acquitted on the charge that related to the packet that was delivered to his home. A submission of no case to answer on the charge that related to the packet which was delivered to his business address was rejected and he was later convicted.

C. appealed on the ground that there was no evidence to show that he was knowingly concerned in any evasion on the prohibition on the importation of cocaine when the two envelopes arrived in England, and no offence had been committed as the cocaine had been replaced by the baking powder before he received it.

MAY, L.J. (at p. 319): "Even if the two envelopes did arrive wholly unsolicited, that which the appellant did at least with the contents of the envelope addressed to his workplace, and the envelope and the message within itself, in our view constituted quite sufficient material to enable the learned recorder properly to decide that there was a case fit to go to the jury."

And later (at p. 320)

"In many cases the authorities intercept contraband on its arrival in this country, substitute harmless material for the illegally imported goods and allow the container, suitcase or vehicle, whatever it may be, to go on its way so that they may discover to whom it is delivered thereafter and who handles or deals with it. By so acting, the authorities hope that they will be led either to the person for whom the contraband, such drugs, was ultimately intended and perhaps to the person who was responsible for arranging the unlawful importation in the first place. If such a substitution meant in law that any subsequent recipient of what he thought to be contraband could for this very reason be guilty of no offence, the consequences for the proper enforcement of the relevant provisions, for instance, the prohibition of controlled drugs, might be serious indeed. Fortunately, however, we do not think that the argument is in any way soundly based.

The statutory provision in the 1979 Act is drawn extremely widely [and his Lordship then cited Griffith L.J. in *Neal, supra*, paragraph 2.3.8]. It is important to note that there is nothing in section 170(2) of the 1979 Act which required the allegedly criminal activities of the person 'knowingly concerned' to be undertaken before the evasion or attempt at evasion of the prohibiter on the importation in order for an offence to be committed ... In the instant case the importation of the cocaine in the particular envelope can be said to have been complete when it arrived in this country from Bolivia ... Clearly, the appellant's sister's attempt to get the cocaine in the envelope to him undetected by the ordinary delivery of the airmail to him was fraudulent evasion of the prohibition on importation. The question for the jury was whether at any time before or after the arrival of the envelope in this country the appellant could properly be said to have been 'knowingly concerned' in that fraudulent evasion by his sister. We do not attempt any definition of the word 'concerned'. It is an ordinary English word with well-known and unspecialised meaning."

Appeal dismissed.

NOTE

This decision was the subject of a brief but trenchant commentary by Professor J. C. Smith, Q.C.: [1988] Crim.L.R. 173. The professor doubts the correctness of a conviction solely on the basis of the acts which the accused did after receiving the envelope and contents. Thus, he was convicted of being knowingly concerned in the fraudulent evasion of the prohibition on the importation of cocaine although, in fact, the only substance that he dealt with was baking powder.

The professor concedes that the court may have some force in its suggestion that the law would otherwise be unenforceable. But neither the court nor the professor consider the propriety of the customs and excise officers sending the drugs on in accordance with plan, when the controlled drugs might become lost to sight.

The professor also asks how a person properly can be said to be concerned in the fraudulent evasion of a prohibition on importation when the importation is complete before he ever knows anything about it? This may be contrasted with Caippara's case where the court stated explicitly that the statutory provision is drawn extremely widely: in law, the importation was complete when Caippara received the envelope and retained the controlled drugs.

2.3.13   **13. R. v. Panayi and Karte (No. 2)**
                              [1989] 1 W.L.R. 187

Customs officers boarded a yacht then within the territorial waters of the United Kingdom. On board were two men, P. and K., and 690 kilogrammes of cannabis resin. P. and K. said that the drugs had been loaded in Spain and were to be delivered to Holland. Their presence within United Kingdom waters was not deliberate but the result of navigational error and contrary winds and tides.

At their trial on a charge of being knowingly concerned in the fraudulent evasion of the prohibition on the importation of a Class B controlled drug, the trial judge directed the jury that the prosecution must prove no more than that P. and K. (1) knew that they were carrying controlled drugs; (2) knew that the importation of controlled drugs was contrary to British law; (3) entered territorial waters; and (4) knew that they were running the risk, in the circumstances then prevailing, of coming into a territorial waters and nonetheless went on to take that risk. On conviction P. and K. appealed on a point of law.

BUSH, J. (at p. 192): "We take the view that the Act of 1979 is clear in its terms, and that what the prosecution have to prove is that these accused were knowingly concerned in any fraudulent evasion or attempted fraudulent evasion. In simple terms they cannot be knowingly concerned in the fraudulent evasion unless they intend dishonestly to evade the restriction. They cannot knowingly be involved in the evasion of one of the essential ingredients, namely, the fact that they are within territorial waters, is unknown to them; provided of course that they never had any intention of entering the United Kingdom territorial waters. If they had the intention to evade the prohibition, the mere fact that they were further on in their journey than they anticipated would not assist them.

Though it is possible in some cases to equate recklessness with knowledge or general intent, this cannot be done in this kind of case where the specific intent is required of being knowingly concerned in any fraudulent evasion."

                                                        Appeals allowed.

NOTE
    This case had a peculiar history the precise details of which are set out in the judgment (at pp. 190–1). The net effect of the procedural changes was that at trial the prosecution was "labouring under an unnecessary hardship" and that the jury

were not asked to decide what was the real intended destination of these goods but asked to decide whether the entry into the United Kingdom territorial waters was deliberate or accidental or in effect recklessness. As Bush, J. observed "It is not for the court, even if pressed by the defence, to direct the prosecution how it should present its case."

It must be said that the decision in regard to "specific intent" is to be seen in terms of the English distinction between specific and basic intent. It may be that the Scottish courts would hold the same law on the point to be the same as in England but simply not refer to the intent being specific.

The court also indicated (at p. 194) that had the indictment contained as an alternative a charge of contravening section 5(2) of the 1971 Act then the accused would have had no defence. The court rather pointedly underlined that on indictment such a charge of simple possession carried a maximum of five years' imprisonment.

14. Montes v. H.M. Advocate   2.3.14
1990 S.C.C.R. 645

The appellants were charged with being knowingly concerned in the fraudulent evasion of a prohibition on the importation of cocaine by importing cocaine at Greenock, contrary to section 170(2)(b) of the 1979 Act. The Crown relied for proof of importation on evidence that cocaine was found in a ship which had, according to its master's declaration, sailed to Greenock from Georgetown, Guyana, that cocaine of the same type was found in the possession of the appellant J. in Glasgow, at a time when he was accompanied by the appellant V., and that J. was a former member of the ship's crew, and also on evidence from a police officer that cocaine came from South America.

Proof that the appellants, and particularly M. and L., were involved in the importation depended on evidence of various comings and goings by the appellants, of meetings and contacts among themselves and with members of the ship's crew, and of visits by them to the ship at Greenock. There was no evidence of surveillance of the ship before it reached Greenock.

The Crown also led evidence of a statement by J., made outwith the presence of the others, in which he admitted that the cocaine in his possession had been put on the ship in Colombia.

In his charge to the jury, the trial judge directed them that statements made by one accused incriminating other accused were not evidence against them unless they were present when they were made. But when he came to discuss the evidence which the jury could take into account in determining whether importation had been proved, he told them that they could have regard to J.'s statement. The appellants were convicted and appealed to the High Court on the ground of insufficiency of evidence and, so far as the appellants other than J. were concerned, on the ground that the judge had misdirected the jury in relation to the use that could be made of J.'s statement. In his report, the judge expressed the view that a statement by one accused outwith the presence of another was inadmissible against the latter only where it incriminated him, and that J.'s statement had not incriminated anyone but that it was relevant to the question of importation, mere importation not being a crime.

Held (1) that importation was a fact which required to be proved by the Crown and the trial judge had misdirected the jury by misdirecting them that what J. said was evidence on which they could rely in the case of the other appellants; but (2) that there was sufficient evidence for conviction without reference to J.'s statement, and accordingly there had been no miscarriage of justice; and appeals on this ground refused.

THE LORD JUSTICE-CLERK (ROSS) (at p. 666): "The advocate-depute submitted that the trial judge had correctly directed the jury that they had to consider whether the Crown had proved beyond reasonable doubt that the cocaine had been imported into the Port of Strathclyde between the dates specified. Moreover there was no dispute that 'imported' meant brought in from abroad, that is from outside the United Kingdom."

(At p. 667)

"[I]mportation was a fact which required to be proved by the Crown if guilt ... was to be established. What the Customs and Excise officers testified that the appellant [J.] had said to them was hearsay evidence, and so was not admissible against the co-accused as evidence of the facts alleged in the statement. In directing the jury that the evidence of the appellant [J.'s] answers was evidence upon which the jury could rely in the case of the other appellants, the trial judge, in my opinion, misdirected the jury.

Since there was a misdirection on the part of the presiding judge, the next question which arises is whether this led to any miscarriage of justice. Where there had been misdirection, it depends upon the circumstances whether it led to a miscarriage of justice, and where there is ample evidence to justify a conviction without relying on the evidence complained of, the proper conclusion is that no miscarriage of justice has occurred. In the present case, although the trial judge did misdirect the jury on this particular matter, I am of opinion that there was no miscarriage of justice because, without the evidence relating to the answers given by the appellant [J.] to the officers of Customs and Excise, there was quite sufficient evidence to justify the conviction of the other appellants. As I have already observed, the Crown case depended upon circumstantial evidence ... Even without the evidence relating to what the appellant [J.] said to the officers of Customs and Excise, I am of opinion that there was a strong circumstantial case against the other appellants, and that there was ample evidence to justify their conviction. That being so, I am satisfied that the misdirection to which I have referred did not lead to a miscarriage of justice."

Appeals refused.

15. R. v. Suurmeijer 2.3.15
[1991] Crim.L.R. 773

S. appealed against his conviction for being knowingly concerned in the importation of cannabis. He was the passenger in a car which was stopped by customs officers as it passed through the "Nothing to declare" channel at Sheerness Ferry Terminal. The driver, H., said he had hired the car and intended spending a few days in London. Both he and the appellant had single tickets. As the car was searched, H. was said to have begun to perspire and told the officers that he had lent the car to a friend for a few days before leaving Holland. The petrol tank was found to have been adapted and concealed 30.5 kg of cannabis. In interview, the appellant said that H. had proposed a trip to London for a couple of days and had paid for the tickets. S. had not seen the car until the day before departure. He denied knowing anything of the drugs.

Held, there was insufficient evidence upon which the jury could be sure that the appellant knew about the drugs in the petrol tank. If the prosecution relies upon the veracity and competence of witnesses whom both the judge and the jury have seen and had an opportunity to assess, the Court is generally very slow to interfere when the judge takes the view that the case should go to the jury. Here there was no question of assessing the reliability of witnesses. There was no dispute about the facts. The only question was whether by reason of his presence in company with H. in the car the jury could safely conclude that if H. knew about the drugs then the appellant must know about them also.

Appeal allowed.

16. Howarth v. H.M. Advocate 2.3.16
1992 S.C.C.R. 364

The accused were charged with being knowingly concerned in the fraudulent evasion of the prohibition on the importation of cocaine. There was evidence to suggest that they believed the drugs to be cannabis resin.

Direction that the Crown required to prove (1) that the drugs were cocaine, (2) that there had been dishonest conduct by the accused deliberately directed to evading or defeating the effect of the prohibition against the importation of controlled drugs, and (3) that the accused knew the goods were controlled drugs, but that the jury need not be concerned whether they knew the drug was cocaine as distinct from cannabis.

At the trial of the appellant Howarth and others, the trial judge in his charge to the jury gave them directions.

LORD PENROSE (at p. 366): "Now, ladies and gentlemen, to bring home guilt of that offence, the Crown must prove that an accused person was in some way knowingly concerned in the fraudulent evasion of the prohibition and I must tell you what that involves or what it requires.

Well, ladies and gentlemen, in the first place and this actually applies to all three charges, it must be proved as a matter of fact that the goods in question were the controlled drug cocaine, so that is the first fact of importance. In the second place, it must be proved that there was a fraudulent evasion of the prohibition. Now, what does that mean? Well, that means dishonest conduct deliberately directed to evading or defeating the effect of the prohibition against the importation of controlled drugs.

Now, can I give you that again because that's quite difficult. The fraudulent evasion of the prohibition means dishonest conduct deliberately directed to evading or defeating the effect of the prohibition against the importation of controlled drugs. Ladies and gentlemen, importation in this context is really quite a simple idea. It means bringing goods into the United Kingdom from a foreign country so there's not too much difficulty in that, so that, ladies and gentlemen, the crux of it is perhaps that if you are satisfied as a matter of fact that what was involved in this case was the controlled drug, cocaine, you would then have to be satisfied that what was on foot was a course of dishonest conduct to evade or get round the prohibition against that act, which is set out in the statute referred to, and the third factor which may or may not become the most difficult for you is that before a person can be convicted of this charge, it must be . established, proved, that the person was knowingly concerned in that operation of evasion. Now, ladies and gentlemen, 'concerned' in this context is a word of very wide meaning. It is intended to cover all of those who have played a part in the prohibited activity, whether or not they actually handled the drug, so it would involve those who plan and direct operations, those who finance operations, the people on the fringes as it were, just as much as it would affect those who arrange or engage in the transport of the goods or the loading and unloading of a cargo or whatever, so, ladies and gentlemen, 'concerned' is a word used by Parliament to ensure that this charge is comprehensive in its scope and catches all those who are involved in a practical way with the prohibited activity.

Well, ladies and gentlemen, it is not just concerned but it is knowingly concerned, and it must be demonstrated that the person who is shown to have been involved in or to have taken some part in the operation in some way was so involved knowingly. Now, ladies and gentlemen, what must he know? Well, it must be proved that the particular accused person knew that the goods being imported were prohibited goods, in this case controlled drugs. It is essential that it be proved that he knew that what he was doing was taking part in an operation designed to get round the prohibition and that it was in knowledge of that fact that he involved himself in it, but it is not necessary, ladies and gentlemen, for the Crown to establish that an accused person knew the precise character of the drugs. Now, take this case. There's not much point in taking examples away from it. You have heard evidence that might be held by you to indicate that people thought that cannabis was involved, whereas now the charges relate to cocaine. Ladies and gentlemen, you need not be concerned whether any person knew that the drug was cocaine as distinct from cannabis. What you must consider is whether it has been proved that people knew that they were dealing with controlled drugs and I hope that this is clear enough as a proposition in itself.

Now, ladies and gentlemen, another way of putting that is that the person who is involved need not know the precise character or capacity or type of drugs so long as he knew that he was dealing with the prohibited goods: controlled drugs.

Well now, ladies and gentlemen, can I try to summarise that so far? You have to consider whether it was proved or has been proved in fact that there was an importation within the scope of the provision, that is, an importation of controlled drugs. You must consider and before you can convict must be satisfied that it was fraudulent in the sense I have mentioned, that is, dishonest. You have to consider in the case of each accused person whether that accused person knowingly involved himself in or allowed himself to become involved in that enterprise in some capacity or other. The capacity need not involve actual handling of the goods at all or actual handling at the point of importation.

Now, ladies and gentlemen, I have already referred to the fact that in the first charge all three accused are charged together and as acting along with other persons. Now, the others are not named ... See whether it has been proved to your satisfaction that the drugs were imported in December and, if so, at what stage.

Well, ladies and gentlemen, the next issue, if you have come so far — and this of course is a whole series of 'ifs' as you will appreciate — if you have decided that it wasn't cocaine and decided that it wasn't imported you really don't have to consider anything else, the issue is at an end before you get to the point to which I'm now going to turn.

Has it been proved by the Crown that there was any fraudulent evasion of the prohibition on importation. It's a terrifying expression, ladies and gentlemen, but remember that fraudulent evasion simply means dishonest conduct deliberately intended to defeat the effect of the prohibition. Intention itself is seldom capable of direct proof. It's a matter of inference in the ordinary case from facts and circumstances. In this case, if you do conclude that there was an importation of cocaine using clandestine methods in a remote area of the country, using the cover of darkness for the handling of the goods and methods of secrecy described by [the witness] Forrest and cloak-and-dagger methods, then ladies and gentlemen, that would be the sort of material that you would consider in arriving at a conclusion whether it had been proved that there had been a fraudulent evasion.

Now, ladies and gentlemen, it would be after that you would come to what may be the most difficult issue in the case: has the Crown proved against the accused individually that he was knowingly concerned in that fraudulent evasion? Now, ladies and gentlemen, remember the direction that 'concerned in' has its ordinary meaning of being involved in the activity in some positive way. Knowledge would not suffice without active involvement, active involvement without proof of knowledge would not suffice for conviction ...

If ... you come to the view that one or more of [the accused] were involved in a common plan, then, in accordance with the directions on concert I gave you, that person may be responsible for the acts of others but, in the first instance and most importantly, you must consider what has been proved against each individually, including the question whether it has been proved that that person was involved in a common plan."

No ground of appeal attacked these directions.

Appeals refused.

NOTE

The point about the belief as to the actual substance being imported was commented upon at the hearing of the appeal against sentence: *Howarth v. H.M. Advocate*, 1992 S.C.C.R. 525, *infra* at paragraph **2.5.15**.

2.3.17   **17. R. v. Lucien**
[1995] Crim.L.R. 807

L. was intercepted at Gatwick Airport by a customs officer, having arrived on an incoming flight. Purporting to act under section 164 of the Customs and Excise Management Act 1979, the officer requested L. to hand over his shoes for examination, which he did. They were found to conceal a quantity of cocaine.

During a *voir dire*, the customs officer conceded that he had no reasonable grounds for suspecting that L. was carrying prohibited articles. Such grounds were required by section 164(1). The defence made a submission that the evidence that cocaine was found in shoes alleged to have been worn by L. should be excluded.

The judge ruled against the submission, relying (in view of the officer's concession) on section 78(2) rather than section 164 of the 1979 Act. Section 78(2) imposes a requirement on any person leaving or entering the United Kingdom to answer such questions put to him with respect to his baggage and anything contained therein or carried with him.

L. appealed against conviction on the ground that the judge had ruled incorrectly in that the customs officer was not entitled to rely on section 78(2) because L.'s shoes were neither part of his baggage nor "carried with him".

Held, by analogy with the case of *Brokelmann v. Barr* [1971] 3 W.L.R. 108 and section 6(1) of the Finance Act 1968, once it was understood that the carriage referred to in the 1979 Act — a statute in *par materia* with the Finance Act — was carriage by sea, air or (now) train and not by the individual, so the airline company which carried L. to the United Kingdom carried not only L. but, with him, his clothing as well as his baggage. The Court emphasised that section 78 of the 1979 Act did not provide an alternative basis for permitting customs officers to conduct rub-down, strip or intimate searches. That power existed only by virtue of section 164 of the Act.

Appeal dismissed.

NOTE
Section 6(1) of the Finance Act 1968 imposes a statutory declaration of "any thing contained in his baggage or carried with him" which has been obtained outside the United Kingdom or has been obtained without payment of duty or tax and for which there is no entitlement to exemption. *Brokermann v. Barr* concerned a car and it was held that the car was "carried with" the defendant since the carriage envisaged by section 6(1) of the 1968 Act was carriage by sea or air and things might be carried with a person in a ship or aircraft.

18. R. v. Latif and Shahzad   2.3.18
(1995) 1 Cr.App.R. 270

H. was an informant employed by the United States Drugs Enforcement Agency. He was introduced to the appellant S. who suggested an export of drugs into the United Kingdom. H. pretended that he knew an airline pilot who could be used as a courier. H. said that he would himself receive the drugs in London. Either S. or someone on his behalf would then collect the drugs from him. Twenty kilogrammes of heroin were delivered to H. and later carried to the United Kingdom by a British officer of Customs and Excise. H. came to England and eventually persuaded S. to join him to receive the heroin. A customs officer had procured a visa for S. through the British High Commission. S. and the appellant L. came to H.'s hotel where they were both arrested. S. and L. were convicted of being knowingly concerned in the fraudulent evasion of the prohibition on importation of a controlled drug, heroin, contrary to section 170(2)(b) of the 1979 Act. They appealed on the ground, *inter alia*, that neither of them was, on the prosecution evidence, guilty of the offence charged, and the judge should have accepted the submission that there was no case to answer.

Held, that the words "fraudulent evasion" extend to any conduct which is directed and intended to lead to the importation of goods covertly in breach of a prohibition on import.

SAUGHTON, L.J. (at p. 273): "Section 170(2) of the Customs and Excise Management Act 1979 provides: 'if any person is, in relation to any goods, in any way knowingly concerned in any fraudulent evasion or attempt at evasion … (b) of any prohibition or restriction for the time being in force with respect to the goods under or by virtue of any enactment … he shall be guilty of an offence under this section and may be arrested.'

The wording can be traced back at least to the Customs Consolidation Act 1853, *Attorney-General's Reference (No. 1 of 1981)* (1982) 75 Cr.App.R. 45, 48, [1982] Q.B. 848, 853.

Section 3 of the Misuse of Drugs Act 1971 provides that, with certain exceptions, the importation of a controlled drug is prohibited. But the section by itself creates no offence and imposes no sanction (*Whitehead and Nicholl* (1982) 75 Cr.App.R. 389). Mr Bolton, the customs officer who brought the heroin into the United Kingdom, committed a prohibited act. None of the exceptions extended to him. [Crown counsel] concedes as much. But that was not by itself a criminal offence. Mr Bolton's conduct would not have been prohibited if he had had a licence from the Secretary of State to import heroin, but he had none. [Counsel for the appellants] suggests that there would have been no fraudulent evasion by anybody if Mr Bolton had been the holder of a licence.

That leads to a fundamental question as to what section 170(2) means. At first sight we might have thought that there had to be some fraudulent person bringing the goods into this country and deceiving the Customs and Excise in the process. If that be right there was no completed offence in this case, for even without a licence Mr Bolton was not fraudulent and did not deceive anybody. His superiors knew what he was doing. Mr Shahzad and Mr Latif would not be guilty of the complete offence, but it is arguable they would be guilty of an attempt.

Such a construction of section 170(2) is not, in our judgment, correct. It would not catch the man who organises an importation by an innocent courier. There would be no fraudulent evasion by anybody in such a case, and the organiser could not therefore be knowingly concerned in the fraudulent evasion. [Counsel for the appellants] submitted that the organiser would be liable as the principal of the courier who acted as his agent. We do not find that suggestion of vicarious liability plausible.

In our judgment the words 'fraudulent evasion' include a good deal more than merely entering the United Kingdom with goods concealed and no intention of declaring them. They extend to any conduct which is directed and intended to lead to the importation of goods covertly in breach of a prohibition on import. We find support for that in the case of *Jakeman* (1983) 76 Cr.App.R. 223.

… There was a case for [the appellants] to answer and on the prosecution evidence they were guilty of the offence with which they were charged. We need not consider the argument for an alternative verdict of guilty of an attempt.

We would mention that [Crown counsel] was prepared to accept that at least an importation must occur if the full offence is to be committed.

That did him no harm as an importation did occur in the present case. It is generally wise to concede that which one does not need to defend. A similar concession was made and approved by this Court in *Watts and Stack* (1980) 70 Cr.App.R. 187. On the other hand, successful deceit of a customs officer is certainly not an essential element of the offence. Sometimes the customs officer knows in advance that a passenger is smuggling. Sometimes it is at once apparent to him. In any event, importation takes place before that stage."

Appeals dismissed.

B. LAW: EXPORTATION **2.4**

1. Garrett v. Arthur Churchill (Glass) Ltd **2.4.1**
[1969] 2 All E.R. 1141

C. bought an antique goblet on behalf of an American. The export of such a goblet was at the relevant time prohibited without a permit: section 56(2) of the 1952 Act. C. was instructed by the American to hand over the goblet to a third party in the knowledge that the third party would take it to America without the appropriate licence. C. handed it over and then lost all control of it.

C. was prosecuted for being knowingly concerned in the exportation of a good with intent to evade a restriction placed on such goods. At trial the magistrates held that the loss of control meant that C. was not concerned in the exportation of the goblet which took place thereafter. C. was acquitted. The Customs and Excise Commissioners appealed.

LORD PARKER, C.J. (at p. 1145): "A man can be concerned with the exportation of goods by doing things in advance of the time when the aircraft leaves, and certainly handing over goods for export the night before the aircraft leaves seems to me quite clearly to amount to being 'concerned in the exportation ... of ... goods'.

I do not think the justices asked themselves the correct question, because under section 56(2) the question is whether the respondent ... [C.], was knowingly concerned in the exportation of this goblet with intent to evade the prohibition. I agree with counsel for the respondents' submission that that is to be treated as all one phrase and that one has to ask oneself that question. The justices, as it seems to me, have divided up the phrase and considered whether he was knowingly concerned with the exportation and, having come to the conclusion that he was not, have found it unnecessary to consider whether if he were it was with intent to evade. As I have said, the matter must be looked on as one phrase and one question has to be answered."

Appeal allowed and case remitted to the
magistrates' court.

NOTE
Although not a drugs case this decision is likely to be of relevance.

2.5 C. SENTENCING: IMPORTATION

2.5.1 Class A: (i) Cocaine

2.5.2   **1. R. v. Ribas**
                    (1976) 63 Cr.App.R. 147

R. pleaded guilty to the fraudulent evasion of the prohibition on the importation of cocaine. R. was a Brazilian who was stopped when entering England. He was found to have 161 grammes of cocaine. It was of a very high degree of concentration; much of it was almost 100 per cent pure. It was said to have a wholesale value then of £3,000 and a retail value of £8,000. His explanation was that he was passing through London in the course of a business trip and that he intended using that quantity of cocaine over the few months that the trip would take. He was sentenced to eight years' imprisonment and he appealed against sentence. On appeal, counsel for R. submitted that smuggling was analogous to possession *simpliciter*.

BRIDGE, L.J. (at p. 150): "The view which this Court takes is that Parliament has provided for the smuggling of prohibited drugs to be treated as a category of offence on its own which is separate and distinct from the categories of possessing a drug once it has got into this country, which may either be simple possession or possession with intent. Up to the maximum penalty of 14 years' imprisonment, it seems to us the gravity of the smuggling offence depends primarily on the quantity smuggled and secondarily on all the other relevant circumstances. But if a large quantity, and a quantity certainly capable of providing a substantial commercial supply is brought into this country in contravention of the statutory prohibition on the importation then, irrespective of any specific intent to put that quantity into circulation, Parliament had provided for it to be treated as a grave offence. Importation, whatever the specific intent of the importer, as was pointed out by Lord Justice Shaw, in the course of the argument, involves at the very least the risk that the quantity imported will find its way on to the home market and the object of prohibition on the importation is to protect the home market, and to serve that supplies of these virulent drugs will not be made available here."

Appeal allowed and eight years' imprisonment
varied to five years' imprisonment.

NOTE
The court considered that the original term was not called for and varied the sentence accordingly.

In *R. v. Keane, The Times*, April 15, 1978, an Australian passing through London was found to have 194 grammes of cocaine. His appeal against three years' imprisonment was refused on the basis that the sentence was "moderate".

2. R. v. Rospigliosi   **2.5.3**
[1980] Crim.L.R. 664

R. pleaded guilty to harbouring cocaine with intent to evade the prohibition on importation and also to importing a separate quantity of cocaine. R. had kept at his flat, on behalf of a friend, about half a kilogramme of cocaine. The friend had brought that quantity into the country with a view to sale. R. also had about one gramme of cocaine which he had had sent to him for his own personal use. He was sentenced to eight years' imprisonment for harbouring and two years' imprisonment for importation, concurrent. He appeared against sentence.

Held, the sentence of two years for importation of a small quantity of cocaine for personal consumption was not open to criticism. The appellant was an intelligent young man who knew perfectly well that it was wrong to import such a drug into the country. The sentence of eight years was "a bit too much", accepting that the appellant's part had been limited to harbouring the drug, although a stern and severe sentence must be imposed to deter others from taking any part in harbouring or otherwise facilitating the distribution of dangerous drugs.

Appeal allowed and eight years' imprisonment
varied to six years' imprisonment.

3. R. v. Ford   **2.5.4**
(1981) 3 Cr.App.R. (S.) 70

F. and others were convicted or pleaded guilty to a variety of charges relating *inter alia* to importing cocaine. They were sentenced to terms of imprisonment ranging from 10 years' imprisonment to five years, according to the parts played by the individuals. All appealed against sentence.

LORD LANE, C.J. (at p. 73): "It scarcely needs emphasis that the smuggling of cocaine on this scale (the market value of this consignment was put at more than £200,000) must be sharply discouraged. At the moment cocaine is not in widespread use illegally in this country; but we are told that there has been something of a cocaine explosion in the United States; and, unhappily, what happens on that side of the Atlantic tends to travel across to England almost inevitably. It must be made absolutely plain that, whether cocaine is as dangerous as heroin or LSD, it is a class A drug, and that those who provide or try to provide distributors with that sort of drug will find themselves in prison for a very long time."

> Appeals for principal participants refused but appeals allowed and sentences varied for certain minor participants, partly in view of personal circumstances.

2.5.5   **4. R. v. Suermondt**
                        (1982) 4 Cr.App.R. (S.) 5

S. pleaded guilty to conspiring to import four kilogrammes of cocaine in two separate consignments, and being concerned in the importation of a further consignment of 5.9 kilogrammes of cocaine. He had been concerned in the purchase of cocaine in Peru, and its importation with a view to sale in the United Kingdom. The total estimated street value of the three consignments was said then to be about £1,400,000. He was sentenced to 10 years' imprisonment and appealed.

SKINNER, J. (at p. 7): "It is clear, as a result of the inquiries that have been made and a further report which has been put before this Court today, that on any showing cocaine is both addictive and dangerous and is a socially harmful drug. It may well be that it is less dangerous and less socially harmful than heroin but it seems to this Court that there is little profit in comparing its importation with the importation of heroin because if the appellant had been caught importing heroin on the scale of this importation of cocaine the sentence would have been very much higher and in the region of 14 to 15 years.

It may well be that because of the high price of cocaine its socially harmful effects are less obvious than the socially harmful effects of other drugs, but [counsel for the appellant] eventually submitted to us that cocaine should be considered on a par with amphetamines in its dangerous qualities and we are content to deal with the matter on that basis ... In the judgment of this Court this is a case where the overwhelming consideration to be borne in mind by the sentencer is one of deterrence. Here the appellant admitted taking three substantial consignments of a dangerous and addictive drug and, to use a cliché, took part in a game in which he was playing for high stakes, high profits on the one hand, if he avoided detection, a heavy sentence on the other if he got caught. In those circumstances, any personal consideration of the appellant must be outweighed by the deterrent considerations."

> Appeal dismissed.

NOTE

In *R. v. Taan* (1982) 4 Cr.App.R. (S.) 17, C.A. a deterrent sentence of 12 years was upheld on appeal. The quantity of drugs was worth a much larger sum and the court took the view that the appellant was not an underling in the sophisticated smuggling operation. *R. v. Parada* [1984] Crim. L.R. 631 is an example of "underlings" being sentenced. The appellants were described as "poor women from Bolivia who did not speak English." Appeals against sentence of six years' imprisonment were dismissed.

5. R. v. Martinez   **2.5.6**
(1984) 6 Cr.App.R. (S.) 364

M. was a citizen of Colombia who had lived in the United Kingdom since 1974. He was convicted of importing 23.7 grammes of cocaine with a street value of about £3,000 by receiving a letter addressed to him and containing the drug. He was sentenced to five years' imprisonment and appealed. It was said on his behalf by counsel that the sentence was excessive for a man of good character, and that the case was not covered by the reference in *R. v. Aramah* (1982) 4 Cr.App.R. (S.) 407 to importers of Class A controlled drugs in appreciable quantity, for whom a sentence of not less than four years is suggested.

LORD LANE, C.J. (at p. 365): "First of all it should be made clear that there is no distinction to be drawn between the various types of Class A drug. The fact that in the decision to which I have referred, namely *Aramah*, particular mention was made of heroin was because at that time, in terms of availability, heroin presented the greatest threat to the community. The same considerations as applied to heroin apply equally to other Class A drugs. Any idea that those who import or deal in cocaine or LSD, as it is known, should be treated more leniently is wrong.

This case concerns, as already indicated, the importation of cocaine hydrochloride. The illicit importation and abuse of this drug is on the increase. It is time to draw attention to the increasing abuse of cocaine and the dangers of its abuse and to dispel the myth which seems to obtain in some quarters that cocaine is merely some sort of social aid and is not addictive.

Cocaine is a powerful stimulant contained in the leaf of the coca plant which grows in abundance chiefly in the Andean regions of South America where climatic conditions are favourable to it.

Cocaine has apparently, over the years, retained an appeal to the wealthy, the influential and the intellectual. It is that type of user who has been responsible for perpetuating the false elitism which accompanies its use. Unhappily the abuse of cocaine has not been confined to that particular section of society. With the increased availability of the drug, all sections of the community now have access to it and are in danger of being tainted by its compelling addictive qualities.

International organisations have estimated the productive capacity of the Andean growing areas as in the region of 150,000 metric tonnes. About

15 per cent. of that total quantity is consumed by the natives of that part of the world themselves, who chew the leaves, 5 per cent. is used for pharamaceutical purposes and the balance of 80 per cent. of the total production is left to find its way to the illicit markets of the world. Up to date the United States of America has been the main market for the drug. We are told, and there is no reason to disbelieve it, that of the four to five million Americans who it is said regularly now use cocaine, no less than 200,000 are profoundly dependent on the drug.

It is possible, and it can only be a possibility, that due to the saturation of America by the drug, the traffickers are now looking to expand to other markets and it is accepted that Canada and Europe are likely to be the target for this activity.

Unhappily this prediction has already started to be justified. These are the figures: in 1972, 23 kilogrammes of cocaine were seized in Europe. By 1983 the figure was no less than 952 kilogrammes. The present surplus of the coca leaf in South America and the huge profits which traffickers can make between the purchase price in the Andes and the selling price in European countries will inevitably encourage further trafficking into Europe which will doubtless stimulate interest and demand by additional experimenters and users. With these profits to be made, further professional criminal involvement in the trade is inevitable with all that means.

The number of seizures of cocaine in the United Kingdom rose from 400 in 1982 to 700 in 1983. The actual amounts seized were 100 kilogrammes which is no less than five times the amount seized in 1982 and more than twice the previous peak of 40 kilogrammes in 1980. The United Kingdom is still very much in its infancy so far as cocaine abuse is concerned. However the increased quantities seized tend to suggest that an upward spiral has begun. Anything which these courts can do to prevent that spiralling will be done.

There are a number of different ways of taking cocaine. Some are more dangerous than others. These can result in an enormous craving for the drug and the addict tends to become compulsive and less able to control the amounts of the drug he uses. In addition to the psychological dependency resulting from the drug, there is no doubt that cocaine abuse results in a very serious physical addiction. Withdrawal symptoms are commonplace. It can also cause psychosis in the shape of a feeling of persecution which may have extremely dangerous consequences. It would be doing no one a service to describe in detail the various methods which users of this drug employ. Suffice to say that one expert has stated this: 'The bad or dangerous effects make cocaine potentially the most lethal drug of the 1980s.' It is just as well that those matters should be widely known.

So far as the present case is concerned, [counsel for the appellant] in a brief, but succinct and accurate submission suggested that this sentence was too long for this amount, namely £3,000 worth of cocaine hydrochloride, imposed on what he describes as a family man of good character, and correctly so described. Unhappily the good character of the importer, or the person dealing with importation is seldom of any weight when it comes to sentence. People who are employed to import are usually, for obvious reasons, selected largely because of their good character. The second submission which [counsel for the appellant] makes is a suggestion that the passage which I have read from the decision in *Aramah* does not cover the present situation, the words being 'It will seldom be that an importer of any appreciable amount of the drug will deserve less than four years.' But this was an appreciable amount of the drug. It was something more than a trivial amount. The learned judge in the circumstances was absolutely correct when imposing the sentence that he did."

Appeal dismissed.

6. R. v. Keach and Steele   2.5.7
[1985] Crim.L.R. 329

K. pleaded guilty to being concerned in the importation of 36.7 grammes of cocaine hydrochloride said to be worth £4,500. The drug was in cellophane packets hidden inside a can of shaving foam. S. (K.'s personal secretary) was found to be in possession of 0.4 grammes of the same substance and she admitted that she knew K. had possession of the large quantity. Sentenced to nine months' and three months' imprisonment respectively.

Held, importation of cocaine is prohibited irrespective of the intention of the importer with regard to the disposal of the drug. K. was clearly aware of the risks that he ran. An immediate custodial sentence was necessary for importation of such a large quantity of cocaine and the sentence could not be faulted as being too long. S.'s involvement in the offence was minimal, and due to her association with K. her sentence was varied to two months, suspended for two years.

Appeals dismissed and varied respectively.

NOTE
Keach is a well-known American actor and his trial was heavily covered by newspapers. Not least of the interesting facts arising from the case is the time that passed between date of conviction and date of hearing the appeal against sentence; 10 days.

7. R. v. Longley-Knight   2.5.8
(1988) 10 Cr.App.R. (S.) 147

L-K., a girl aged 16, pleaded guilty to being concerned in the importation of 197.42 grammes of cocaine, worth about £30,000. She had gone to

Holland with an older girl, the latter actually carrying the drug at the time they were stopped. L-K. was sentenced to 28 months' detention, the time having been reduced to allow for time spent in custody. The older girl was sentenced to 30 months' youth custody. L-K. appealed on the ground that as she had played a lesser part she should have received a lesser sentence.

Held, although the precise role played by the appellant was not clear, the court would assume that she had played a lesser role, and impose a shorter sentence on that ground. Teenagers who are tempted to be involved in the importation of drugs, particularly hard drugs, should be aware that the sentences which the courts would impose would be severe. An adult committing a similar offence would expect a sentence of seven years' or more imprisonment. The court thought that the just sentence for the appellant would have been 24 months: allowing a revision of two months in respect of the time spent in custody pending sentence, the proper sentence would be a term of 22 months' detention.

Appeal allowed and sentence varied.

2.5.9   **8. R. v. Dolgin**
(1988) 10 Cr.App.R. (S.) 447

D. pleaded guilty to being concerned in the importation of cocaine. A postal packet containing 124 grammes of cocaine was intercepted by the Customs and Excise and later delivered to D. who signed for it. His flat was searched immediately and customs officers found £3,750 in notes, a set of scales, a fold of paper containing traces of cocaine hydrochloride and cutting blades with similar traces.

D. admitted that he was a cocaine user, and had arranged for the substance to be sent to him from the United States. He claimed to have paid $4,000 for the cocaine and that it was entirely for his own consumption, to last him for the remaining few months of his stay in England.

In sentencing D. the judge at first instance determined that he had not benefited from drug trafficking, but rejected his assertion that the importation was solely for his own personal use. The basis for the latter was that the 124 grammes was estimated to have a street value of more than £21,000, and also the finding of scales with traces of cocaine.

D. received five years' imprisonment and appealed, arguing that it was a material fact that the importation was for personal use only, as opposed to sale, and that the assertion of personal use had been rejected without adequate evidence.

SIMON BROWN, J. (at p. 449): "[T]his Court does not accept that it is of any real materiality to an offence of this nature whether the importation is intended for onward supply or for personal use. Of course if it is a relatively small amount, obviously for personal use, that is of great relevance, but its relevance lies in its limited quantity. The vice in the offence consists in the very fact of importation, of increasing the stock of the prohibited drug within our shores. There is always the risk that the drug once here may be stolen, and there is the possibility, particularly if it is a large quantity, that even if the importer had not initially been intent on supply, as time passes he may become tempted for whatever reason to make supplies of it."

Later (at p. 50)

"We are not moved by his plea for mercy. In our judgment serious importations of this sort of a Class A drug necessarily involve severe sentences of this character."

Appeal dismissed.

NOTE

The importance of Dolgin's case is that it restates as a general principle that in sentencing importers of controlled drugs the critical factor affecting the severity of the sentence will be the quantity imported, rather than the purpose of the importation.

9. R. v. Roberts   2.5.10
(1989) 11 Cr.App.R. (S.) 575

R. was convicted of being concerned in the importation of cocaine: she pleaded guilty to conspiring to import cannabis. The appellant's luggage was searched at Gatwick Airport and found to contain cocaine worth £194,000 sewn into garments. She was sentenced to 11 years' imprisonment.

Held, the sentencer had decided, on ample evidence, that the appellant was more than a casual carrier but a member of an established team; the Court could not take account of personal circumstances, including the facts that the appellant had two children and a third had been born to her in prison. The sentence could not be altered.

Appeal dismissed.

10. R. v. Radjabi-Tari   2.5.11
(1990) 12 Cr.App.R. (S.) 375

The appellant pleaded guilty to evading the prohibition on the importation of cocaine. He had caused a parcel containing 989 grammes of cocaine, of 85 per cent purity, to be sent to him by post from abroad. He was sentenced to nine years' imprisonment.

Held, (considering *Aramah, infra*, and *Bilinski, infra*) the sentence was not so severe as to justify the Court in interfering.

Appeal dismissed.

2.5.12   **11. R. v. Garcia**
                         (1992) 13 Cr.App.R. (S.) 583

G. pleaded guilty to importing a Class A drug and possessing a Class A drug. The appellant approached a man and asked him to act as a courier in the importation of cocaine from South America. The man agreed to do so, but reported the matter to the Customs and Excise. The appellant arranged for the man to fly to South America and collect 5.33 kilogrammes of cocaine of between 50 per cent and 60 per cent purity. The appellant met the man on his return to England. A further quantity of cocaine was found in the appellant's flat. He was sentenced to 14 years' imprisonment.

Held, (considering *Bilinski, infra*) the principal feature that influenced the Court was the status of the appellant within a large and sophisticated organisation. The appellant was not a fringe operator; he was the kind of man who was seldom caught. Even giving due credit for the appellant's plea, the sentence was wholly appropriate for a major operator carrying major authority.

                                            Appeal dismissed.

2.5.13   **12. R. v. Valencia-Cardenas**
                         (1992) 13 Cr.App.R. (S.) 678

The appellant pleaded guilty to unlawfully importing cocaine. He was stopped by customs officers after arriving at Heathrow Airport and found to be carrying 70 pockets in his stomach. The packets contained 694 grammes of powder containing 85 per cent cocaine hydrochloride with an estimated street value of £130,000. He was sentenced to 10 years' imprisonment.

Held (considering *Aramah, infra, Ezeoke and others* (1988) 10 Cr.App.R. (S.) 440 and *Kouadio* (February 5, 1991), the appellant was a married man of previous good character who had agreed to commit the offence because of financial problems. In the light of the cases considered, the sentence should be reduced to eight years' imprisonment.

                                            Appeal allowed.

2.5.14   **13. R. v. Scamaronie and Pacheco-Nunez**
                         (1992) 13 Cr.App.R. (S.) 702

The first appellant pleaded guilty to being concerned in the importation of a Class A drug and the second appellant was convicted of the same offence. They were concerned in importing 20 kilogrammes of cocaine of 95 per cent purity in packages concealed in a diplomatic pouch. They were arrested in a hotel in London in possession of the cocaine. They were sentenced to 20 years' imprisonment in each case.

Held, the judge, having heard submissions, concluded that the first appellant was one of the prime movers in the conspiracy, and that he was more deeply involved than the second appellant. The first appellant had received an adequate discount for his plea of guilty; without the plea the appropriate sentence would have been in the region of 25 years.

Appeals dismissed

NOTE
The Court of Appeal was unimpressed by the appellants' misuse of the diplomatic bag, and to that extent there was a breach of trust.

14. Howarth v. H.M. Advocate   2.5.15
1992 S.C.C.R. 525

The appellants were convicted of being concerned in the importation of half a metric ton of cocaine, value at £100m. The first appellant was sentenced to 25 years' imprisonment and the second and third appellants to 15 years' imprisonment each. They appealed to the High Court against sentence.

Held, that those who engage in importing Class A drugs must expect severe sentences which must to some extent reflect the amount and value of the drugs involved, and that the sentences were not excessive; and appeals refused.

Observed, that if the first appellant had tendered an acceptable plea of guilty and there had been evidence that he genuinely believed he was involved with cannabis and not cocaine, a less severe sentence could have been pronounced.

NOTE
The High Court of Justiciary have accepted the point in *R. v. Bilinski* (1987) 86 Cr.App.R. 146.

15. R. v. De Arango and Loaiza   2.5.16
(1993) 96 Cr.App.R. 339

D. and L. (and others) were passengers flying from Bogota to Geneva via Heathrow. They were arrested by customs officers at Heathrow and their suitcases were searched. D. and L. were each found to have some four kilogrammes of cocaine, concealed in books, binders and records. The prosecution case was that D. and L. were couriers and after trial they were convicted of being knowingly concerned in the fraudulent evasion of the prohibition on the importation of a Class A controlled drug. D. and L. appealed against conviction on a point of law but that was dismissed. The court also considered appeals against sentence.

MᴄCᴏᴡᴀɴ, L.J. (at p. 405): "[Counsel for the appellants] points out, and we accept, that there is no reason to think that any of the four women was an organiser. They were couriers. He uses the colourful but accurate expression that they were 'expendable cannon fodder'. He draws attention quite properly to the devastating effect on them of the sentences, not merely the length of them, but the long years of separation from their children who cannot afford to visit them. These are all human matters which one readily accepts.

As the judge pointed out, as cannon fodder, they are sent out by evil men to do their dirty work for them. Anyone who, whether for money or for any other reason whatsoever, joins in the international trade in cocaine is literally trafficking in the misery and degradation and sometimes even the death of people who become hooked on it. As he pointed out, anyone who is caught doing that must expect a severe sentence.

Each of these four women was carrying about four kilos of cocaine. The jury was told that they could either convict them on the basis that they were part of a team and knew it, or that each was only guilty in respect of the amount that she carried in her suitcase. The jury found the former. They found, in other words, that each was contributing to the importation of 16 kilos of cocaine.

In those circumstances, in our judgment, they did fall to be dealt with in respect of the importation of 16 kilos of cocaine, a Class A drug, worth about £2.6 million. They did not plead guilty and therefore there is little or no mitigation. We are unable to say that these sentences were out of line with the *Aramah* [*infra*] guidelines. Consequently, we must dismiss their appeals.'

Appeals dismissed.

2.5.17   **16. R. v. Ashley**
                          (1993) 14 Cr.App.R. (S.) 581

A. pleaded guilty to importing cocaine. She had been stopped at an airport and found to have three packages strapped to her body with adhesive tape. The packages contained 926 grammes of cocaine, estimated to be worth £186,000. The appellant claimed that she had been recruited to import the drugs by a man, and was under the impression that the packages contained cannabis. She was to be paid £5,000 for acting as a courier. She was sentenced to 10 years' detention in a young offenders institution.

Held, it had been recognised in *Bilinski, infra* that a belief that the drugs imported were cannabis as opposed to Class A drugs could be a mitigating factor, but the sentencer was entitled to disbelieve the appellant's claim without hearing evidence on the ground that it was manifestly false. The sentence of 10 years made inadequate allowance for the mitigating factors — the appellant's plea of guilty and her youth. These factors would require some discount from the sentence which would otherwise have been justified; a sentence of seven years' detention in a young offenders institution would be substituted.

Appeal allowed.

17. R. v. McLean   2.5.18
(1994) 15 Cr.App.R. (S.) 706

McL. pleaded guilty to being knowingly concerned in the fraudulent evasion of the prohibition on the importation of a controlled drug, cocaine. The appellant was intercepted at Gatwick Airport, and found to have 171 packages containing cocaine in his possession, 143 of which he had swallowed. The cocaine weighed 288 grammes at 85 per cent purity. It was accepted that the importation was solely for the appellant's personal use. He was sentenced to six years' imprisonment.

Held (considering *Dolgin* (1988) 10 Cr.App.R. (S.) 447 and *Meah and Marlow* (1990) 12 Cr.App.R. (S.) 461), the fact that the drugs were for the appellant's personal consumption offered some mitigation. The sentence would be reduced to five years.

HARRISON, J. (at p. 708): "In our view, the fact that these drugs that were being imported were for the appellant's personal consumption, and that he fell to be sentenced on that basis, should afford some mitigation on his behalf. At the same time, we have to take into account that the mere fact that that amount of drugs was imported into this country does mean that there is a risk that as time passes they may find their way into other hands."

Appeal allowed.

18. R. v. Richardson   2.5.19
(1994) 15 Cr.App.R. (S.) 876

The first appellant was convicted of two counts of conspiracy to be knowingly concerned in the fraudulent evasion of the prohibition on the importation of the controlled drug, cocaine, one count of conspiracy to import cannabis, and assisting others to benefit from drug trafficking. This appellant was concerned in a conspiracy to import 44 kilogrammes of cocaine, a second conspiracy to import 144 kilogrammes of cocaine, and a third to import two tonness of cannabis. He was also concerned in remitting the proceeds of the sale of the first consignment to other conspirators abroad. He was sentenced to 25 years' imprisonment on each count relating to cocaine, with concurrent sentences for the other offences.

Held (considering *Aramah, infra, Bilinski, infra, Turner* (1975) 61 Cr.App.R. (S.) 67, *Garner* (unreported, March 1, 1991), *Scamaronie and Pacheco-Nunez, infra*), where a court had to deal with massive drug importations involving street values into millions of pounds, those involved in the higher echelons must expect in a contested case to receive sentences of the order indicated in *Scamaronie*. A plea of guilty should result in a substantial discount, as would assistance to the authorities; assistance offered after sentence would not usually attract a discount. The sentence of 25 years on the first appellant, who had pleaded not guilty and who had played a significant part in the conspiracies, could not be faulted. The sentence of 20 years on a second appellant did not make sufficient allowance for his plea; a sentence of 18 years would be substituted. The sentences on the other appellants were appropriate.

Appeal by R. dismissed.

2.5.20   **19. R. v. Bell**
                          (1995) 16 Cr.App.R. (S.) 93

B. was convicted of being knowingly concerned in the fraudulent evasion of the prohibition on the importation of a Class A controlled drug, cocaine. The appellant was stopped on his arrival at Gatwick Airport and found to have 387 grammes of cocaine concealed in bars of soap in his luggage. He was sentenced to eight years' imprisonment and ordered to pay £700 prosecution costs.

Held (considering *Van Hubbard* (1986) 8 Cr.App.R. (S.) 228), the sentencer was entitled to draw the inference that the appellant was more than a mere courier, and the sentence was not excessive.

MANCE, J. (at p. 94): "The judge expressly directed his mind to the case of *Van Hubbard* which we have looked at. He took into account what was said in the pre-sentence report and what counsel had said.

Before us it is submitted that the sentence was excessive. The pre-sentence report made no other recommendation but that a substantial custodial sentence was inevitable, and that has been accepted before us, but it is said that it was too long. In particular, it is said there was no basis for the judge's inference that the appellant was any more than a courier, and that the importation was not particularly large-scale.

We have heard those submissions. We have considered the case of *Van Hubbard*. This is a case where, in our view, the judge was entitled to draw the inference in the absence of any explanation, that the appellant was not merely a courier, but his role was nearer the source of supply. He did draw that inference after the trial, and we see nothing wrong with the sentencing exercise which he undertook.

Following a conviction, the appellant does not have the benefit of any mitigation which would, without doubt, have existed had he pleaded guilty, and in the circumstances we see no relevant distinction between this case and *Van Hubbard* and we consider that the sentence was correct."

Appeal dismissed.

20. R. v. Nwoko and Olokunle   2.5.21
(1995) 16 Cr.App.R. (S.) 612

N. pleaded guilty to two counts of being knowingly concerned in the fraudulent evasion of the prohibition on the importation of a controlled drug, cocaine. O. was convicted of one such count. The applicants were concerned in importing a quantity of cocaine by post. They were sentenced to five years' imprisonment and 10 years' imprisonment respectively, and recommended for deportation. The first applicant was a Nigerian citizen and if she returned to Nigeria would be liable under Nigerian law to be sentenced to a term of imprisonment for committing an offence in a foreign country involving narcotic drugs.

Held, the existence of the Nigerian law was an irrelevant factor for the purposes of sentencing. The sentences were perfectly proper.

SERVICE, L.J. (at p. 613): "On behalf of the applicant Nwoko [counsel] suggests that in the circumstances of this case a sentence of five years was excessive and should have been a sentence of a year less, namely a period of four years.

In the course of his submissions he drew our attention to a Nigerian decree, which provides, among other things, that: 'Any Nigerian citizen found guilty in any foreign country of an offence involving narcotic drugs who thereby brings Nigeria into disrepute shall be guilty of an offence under this subsection ... and liable to imprisonment for a term of five years without an option of a fine ...'

It is suggested by [counsel] that this factor was something which should have been taken into account by the sentencing judge because it put his client in, or at risk of double jeopardy.

With great respect to [counsel], we think this is an impossible proposition. Quite apart from the fact that it seems to us that a decree of the nature we have described is a matter which would concern the Home Office on questions of deportation and the like, the idea that the sentencing judge could or should, or indeed would be able to, do an exercise to try to discover whether or not the Nigerian authorities would apply the decree in the case of the applicant, would give an impossible task to any sentencing court. It seems to us that in an importation case of this kind the judge is fully entitled to ignore that factor, and indeed the factor is an irrelevant factor for the purposes of the sentencing exercise."

Appeal dismissed.

21. R. v. Aranguren   2.5.22
(1994) 99 Cr.App.R. 347

The Court laid down revised sentencing guidelines for offences involving Class A prohibited drugs. Instead of using the factor of monetary value of such hard drugs, as heretofore, the new yardstick for measuring the relative significance of any seizure of Class A drugs was by weight rather than street value. Thus, for the guidelines laid down in *Bilinski, infra*, the following should be substituted: where the weight of the drugs at 100 per cent purity was of the order of 500 grammes or more, sentences of 10 years' imprisonment and upwards were appropriate. Where the weight at 100 per cent purity was of the order of five kilogrammes or more, sentences of 14 years' imprisonment or more were appropriate.

Applying those new guidelines, the Court dismissed the appeals of Aranguren against eight years' imprisonment (621.3 grammes of differing purities equivalent to 521.515 grammes at 100 per cent purity), Aroyewumi and Bioshogun each against 10 years' imprisonment (1.19 kilogrammes of 85 per cent purity, equivalent to 1.01 kilogrammes at 100 per cent purity), Littlefield against 15 years' imprisonment (12.78 kilogrammes at 95 per cent purity equivalent to 12.14 kilogrammes at 100 per cent purity) and Gould against seven years' in respect of one Class A offence and three Class B offences — eight and a half years including other offences (1.18 kilogrammes of 92 per cent pure cocaine, equivalent to 1.08 kilogrammes at 100 per cent).

LORD TAYLOR, D.J. (at p. 349): "These are five appeals against sentences of imprisonment for offences of being knowingly concerned in the importation of cocaine or in one instance for possessing cocaine with intent to supply it. In each, the basis upon which the quantity of drugs seized was assessed at the trial has been challenged. Money values were put upon each seizure by Customs and Excise, purporting to be the amount realisable from the ultimate consumers. Although this approach of assessing the 'street value' has been adopted for some years, it is argued that figures used in the five cases under appeal were unrepresentative and unfair. More fundamentally, it is submitted that a more satisfactory basis for assessing the importance of a consignment of cocaine is by weight rather than by street value.

[The Court then considered *Aramah, supra, Martinez, supra*, and *Bilinski, infra*]

At the heart of these appeals is the method which has been used to assess street value and its application in these cases. We admitted expert advice on this topic on behalf both of the appellants and of the Customs and Excise.

Mr Aitken, called for the appellants, has worked in the field of drug abuse for 20 years and has been an independent consultant since 1975. Mrs Conners [formerly Miss Kwik] is a research analyst with long experience of prohibited drugs and is presently a research analyst with Customs and Excise based at the National Co-ordination Unit. They were the principal witnesses on each side but we also heard from two statisticians, Dr Balding for the appellants and Dr Bassett for Customs.

Also called, were Dr King, Director of the Forensic Science Laboratory at Aldermaston, two police officers experienced in drugs squads and, on behalf of the appellant Gould, Mr Poulter, a director of the National Drugs Advice Agency.

The practice has been to use four factors to determine street value. Two of these, the weight of the consignment and its purity at the time of seizure can be accurately measured. The other two factors, average purity at street level and average price at street level, have to be based on data obtained from a range of sources. Those averages have, the Customs maintain, to be taken into account because imports of a high purity are usually adulterated or 'cut' before they reach the consumer and because prices vary with the amount sold, with the locality and with current availability, amongst other factors. It was conceded, on behalf of the Customs Authorities, that the average deduced could only be a notional guide.

Average purity is assessed by assimilating the actual purity figures of seizures, region by region. Those figures are rounded down to the nearest 5 per cent (which favours defendants). They are analysed by the drugs intelligence laboratory and a national average is determined. Because the figures vary from time to time, they are revised quarterly.

Mr Aitken said that to bring average purity into account was unfair because although he agreed it was more likely than not that the drug would be 'cut', this was not necessarily so and in an individual case it might be unfair to build in that factor. We are satisfied on the evidence that 'cutting' occurs in a preponderance of cases, that for the purposes of a notional figure to be considered only as a guide and as one factor in the sentencing exercise, the Customs approach has been a proper one.

Average street price is again assessed by collating data from police investigations country-wide and producing therefrom a notional national average.

In recent times, the methods used have been refined in two respects. The figures obtained both as to street purity and street price from the 11 regional areas are weighted to take account of differing levels of availability and drug use and of population in different regions. Secondly, the quarterly reviews are brought promptly to the attention of officers valuing drugs for prosecution.

Despite best endeavours, however, Mrs Conners agreed that there are inherent difficulties about valuing drugs. First, as drugs are an illegal commodity, prices are not overtly established and anecdotal evidence obtained from witnesses by the police may not be frank. Indeed, dealers may claim to sell drugs at very low prices to reduce the court's assessment of 'benefit' liable to confiscation.

Secondly, price ranges vary from place to place, from time to time and are dependant upon purity. As already mentioned, although adulteration is very likely to take place, when dealing with a seizure at a port it cannot be proved conclusively that adulteration would have taken place. Prices may vary with quantities and since the drugs are addictive, users may be willing to pay large sums particularly if the drug is in short supply at any particular time or place. Finally a port seizure may leave the authorities in doubt as to whether the drug is for domestic consumption or for onward transmission to another country.

Notwithstanding these problems, we believe that the provision to the courts of street value estimates, for use only as a rough guide, has been a reasonable and fair approach. In *Patel* (1987) 9 Cr.App.R.(S.) 319, Watkins L.J. at p. 321, after listing some of the difficulties mentioned above, said: 'These are factors which obviously tend to cause the use of the street value of heroin as a yardstick to translate quantities of the drug into financial terms as an aid to sentencing to be regarded with caution. So long as it is relied upon as a rough yardstick, we see no reason why judges should not measure the length of sentence to some degree by it.'

Nevertheless, we are satisfied that the better way to measure the relative significance of any seizure of Class A drugs is by weight rather than by street value. All the parties before us and their expert witnesses were of that opinion. We have already summarised the reasons why street value is difficult to assess with any precision in a given case, even though the quarterly average figures afford a reasonable rough guide. The effect of this imprecision is that prosecution figures for average purity or average price may be challenged and where this occurs, the judicial response may vary. Some judges may follow the prosecution figure, some may take a mean figure between those of the prosecution and defence experts and some may assume, in the defendant's favour, that his expert is right.

However, there is another and very important reason for considering weight rather than street value. If cocaine or heroin is readily available, the price to the consumer drops. So the more imports the drugs profiteers can achieve, the lower the street value per gramme. By taking street values as the criteria rather than weight, the sentencing level for like quantities of the drug becomes lower as supplies become more plentiful. Although making large profits from importing prohibited drugs is morally reprehensible, the main mischief to which the prohibitions are directed by Parliament is the widespread pushing of addictive drugs harmful to the community. It cannot serve Parliament's purpose if the more drugs imported and therefore the lower the street price, the lower the level of sentencing.

We therefore propose to revise the sentencing yardsticks by expressing them in terms of weight rather than street value of the drugs. Clearly, it would not be fair to take the actual weight of the consignment regardless of its purity. To achieve an accurate and fair standard applicable to all cases, we agree with the experts that it is necessary to calculate what weight of the drug at 100 per cent purity is contained in each seizure. We are told and accept that no importation is in fact at 100 per cent strength since it is not prepared under laboratory conditions, though strengths of percentages in the 80s and 90s are achieved. However, by calculating in each case the weight at 100 per cent strength, a consistent approach can be made to the significance of each consignment. What then should the guidelines be? On behalf of the Customs and Excise, it has been submitted that a sentence of the order of 10 years would be appropriate for an importation of 500 grammes of heroin or cocaine at 100 per cent purity and sentences of 14 years and upwards for five kilogrammes or more at 100 per cent purity. These figures are put forward as being roughly in line with the general level of sentencing established under the system operating hitherto. It is argued for the appellants that the figures of half a kilogramme and five kilogrammes are too low in seeking to find the weight equivalent of £100,000 and £1 million respectively. They submit that too high an estimate of street value and too firm an assumption of 'cutting' have been made.

To check the suggested figures, we have compared the sentences they would support with the sentences actually passed in reported cases where the weight and purity of the drug is quoted. We are satisfied that the figures suggested would support sentences in line with those reported. To take, for example, the guideline case of *Bilinski*, the seizure was 3.306 kilogrammes of heroin, 90 per cent pure. Its street value was said to be £600,000. The equivalent weight of 100 per cent pure heroin would have been 2.73 kilogrammes, £100,000 worth of 100 per cent pure drug would therefore have been 2.73/6 kilogrammes = 455 grammes, approaching half a kilogramme. It was said in *Bilinski* (at p. 149) that 'a term of 12 years or thereabouts would have been appropriate ... in the absence of any mitigating factors.' £1 million worth would be 2.73/6 x 10 kilogrammes = 4.55 kilogrammes or approaching five kilogrammes.

Furthermore, we are of opinion that the figures suggested by the Crown are entirely appropriate to the gravity of importing Class A drugs in the light of the maximum sentences recently increased by Parliament. Accordingly, in our judgment, for the guidelines laid down in *Bilinski* in respect of Class A drug importations, there should be substituted the following. Where the weight of the drugs at 100 per cent purity is of the order of 500 grammes or more, sentences of 10 years and upwards are appropriate. And where the weight of 100 per cent purity is of the order of five kilogrammes or more, sentences of 14 years and upwards are appropriate.

We have been invited to broaden this judgment to include new guidelines covering the importation of such Class A drugs as LSD and Ecstasy (MDA), and the Class B drug amphetamine sulphate, but we do not think it is appropriate to do so. It has been emphasised by this Court many times that there is no basis for regarding any particular drugs as less harmful than other drugs within the same class. In relation to MDA, we are not aware of any case in this Court involving large scale importation and it would be wrong to speculate about the evidence that might be adduced in such a case, but there are numerous very recent reported decisions about the smaller scale supply of MDA. On the other hand, LSD appears often to be imported and supplied in the form of squares or measured in the equivalent of 'doses' so that the weight of a seizure is not usually given. We did not think it necessary, therefore, to add to the guidance recently given in *Attorney-General's References* (Nos. 3, 4 and 5 of 1992) (1993) 14 Cr.App.R.(S.) 191. Finally, there are now numerous reported decisions of this Court in which the production, importation and supply of amphetamine sulphate has been dealt with on broadly similar lines to cannabis offences, within the *Aramah* guidelines. The percentage purity of the substances involved in these cases at street level is usually low (normally in the range of 5 per cent to 10 per cent) but it may well be significantly higher in bulk supply. We emphasise the importance of taking into account the purity level as well as the weight or quantity in amphetamine sulphate cases but, subject to that, no further guidance is presently necessary.

[Counsel] argued that even if we substituted new guidelines, they should apply only in the future. If we found that the appellants or any of them were sentenced on the basis of a flawed assessment of street value under the *Bilinski* guidelines, fairness requires that the error should result in a reduction of sentence. We cannot agree. Having decided what is the proper basis upon which the magnitude of the drug seizures should be measured, our duty is to see whether by those criteria the sentences passed were either wrong in principle or manifestly excessive. Having stated the principles, we now apply them to the individual appellants."

[The Court then considered and dismissed the individual appeals.]

Appeals dismissed.

NOTE

The importance to the English courts of the decision in *R. v. Aranguren* cannot be overstated. The developments that led up to the change of general policy are set out in Henderson, "Sentencing Problems in Class A Drugs Cases" (1995) 6 K.C.L.J. 89.

2.5.23 Class A: (ii) Diamorphine

2.5.24   **1. R. v. Jusoh**
                          [1979] Crim.L.R. 191

J. was convicted of being concerned in the fraudulent importation of heroin. He was a member of the crew of a ship which arrived in Cardiff from Bangkok and in which customs officers found 27 pounds of heroin, said then to have an estimated street value in excess of £1 million. J. was alleged to have helped the primary conspirators hide the heroin aboard the ship in return for a quantity of cannabis. He was sentenced to 12 years' imprisonment.

Held, heroin was a pernicious drug whose effects were destructive to human life, and severe sentences were to be expected. However, it was not correct to impose an extremely long sentence on a minor participant in a conspiracy to import, in order to indicate what the major participants might expect if brought to justice. Without minimising the gravity of the offence, the court would reduce the sentence to eight years' imprisonment as he was not one of the "big fish."

Appeal allowed and sentence varied.

NOTE
   Shorter sentences were upheld in *R. v. Li* [1973] Crim. L.R. 454 and *R. v. Po* (1974) Halsbury's *Abridgements* 745, but the quantity in these cases was smaller.

2. R. v. Poh and To   2.5.25
(1981) 3 Cr.App.R. (S.) 304

P. and T. who came from Malaysia, were convicted of being concerned in the fraudulent evasion of the prohibition on the importation of heroin. They had been involved in an attempt to import two cars in which a total of 32 kilogrammes was concealed. The street value was said to have been £5 million. It was said that the heroin was destined not for this country but for France. Each was sentenced to (the then maximum of) 14 years' imprisonment and each appealed.

LORD ROSKILL (at p. 305): "The only question is whether the maximum sentences which the learned judge … thought it necessary to pass, are in any way excessive. It has been most eloquently urged upon us by [counsel for the appellants], who has said everything that could possibly be said for these two undeserving criminals, that the 14 year sentences, being the maximum, should have been reserved for the man who is said to have been behind the scene, whose name was apparently mentioned, but who has not been caught, that these two men were not the principals but were merely engaged in what was apparently called the 'Singapore' or 'Penang run.' This Court is quite unable to accept that submission. These men allowed themselves to be involved in the running of hard drugs on the most enormous scale.

   It has been said that one of them is now 64 and the other is 58, and it was suggested, both at trial and in this Court, that on humanitarian grounds these 14 year sentences were too long. In the view of this Court these men have forfeited all rights to have any humanitarian consideration to be taken into account at this stage. They were prepared to hazard the lives of literally hundreds, if not thousands, of people of all ages up and down the Continent of Europe. Why we in this Court are now being asked to extend mercy to them merely because of their age is something which this Court finds difficult to understand, however eloquently the plea may be put forward. It cannot be too clearly realised that if persons engage in this type of trade the penalties must be as heavy as the law allows them to be ... those sentences were not one day too long."

Appeals dismissed.

NOTE
This is an example of what in other circumstances the Court of Appeal in England has described as "premier league crime which merited premier league punishment": *R. v. Sutcliffe* (1995) 16 Cr.App.R. (S.) 69.

2.5.26   **3. R. v. Inglesias**
The Times, November 15, 1982

I. and others were convicted of being knowingly concerned in the fraudulent evasion of the prohibition on the importation of heroin. Sentences ranging from seven years to 12 years were passed and consequently applications were made for leave to appeal.

SIMON BROWN, J.: "The court had to say that the smuggling of heroin into this country from Pakistan was a matter of the gravest nature.

It dealt with death, for it only took a very few doses of heroin to give rise to addiction which could not be resisted — a physical addiction which involved a craving for more. In that condition those who suffered were vulnerable to the pressures of the unscrupulous operators who required assistance in the further dissemination of the drug.

The fact was that this country had been the centre for distribution of heroin from countries in the East, now from Pakistan.

The court had to make it clear that those who engaged in assisting the importation of heroin into this country would receive severe sentences."

Applications refused.

2.5.27   **4. R. v. Bilinski**
(1988) 9 Cr.App.R. (S.) 360

B. pleaded guilty to importing 3.036 kilogrammes of heroin with 90 per cent purity and a street value of about £600,000. He was a member of the crew of a Polish ship in which customs officers found three packets of heroin concealed behind a wiring duct. His fingerprints were found on the packets.

B. initially denied any knowledge of the packets but later admitted that he had agreed to bring the packages on board the ship for a payment of £3,500. He claimed to believe that the packages contained cannabis.

The packages were given to B. by the customs officers and they were malleable and wrapped in transparent plastic through which a white powder could be seen. A book apparently about cannabis was found in his cabin.

On sentencing B. to 12 years' imprisonment, the trial judge said that he considered B.'s alleged belief that the drug was cannabis was irrelevant and consequently declined to hear evidence about it. B. appealed against sentence.

LORD LANE, C.J. (at p. 362): "It is of course no answer to the charge of importing a Class A drug that the importer thought it was a Class B drug. The plea of guilty does not therefore indicate the nature of the appellant's belief. If his belief is irrelevant to sentence, the judge need not concern himself with what the belief might have been. If, however, belief is relevant and is in dispute, what should the judge do to ascertain the truth?

Is it relevant? On the one hand is the argument that anyone who chooses to engage in smuggling prohibited drugs must accept the risk that the drug is of a kind different from that which he believes or has been told it is. In addition there is the 'floodgates' argument expressed by [the trial judge to the effect that if he took such a belief into account then every courier or dealer would make a similar claim in relation to Class A drugs]. On the other hand, submits [counsel for the appellant], if a defendant genuinely has been misled as to the type of drug then in the light of the fact that the maximum sentence for importing heroin is imprisonment for life as against the 14 years' maximum for importation of cannabis, it would be unjust not to allow some mitigation at least of the punishment. The latter view is certainly that which has been taken by this Court in earlier decisions, of which *Ghandi* (1986) 8 Cr.App.R. (S.) 391 is one. In that case the primary question before the courts was whether the judge, having heard evidence from the defendant as to his belief that the heroin which he had imported was cannabis, was wrong in rejecting that evidence. Neither counsel nor the Court suggested that the defendant's belief was irrelevant.

We are of the view that the defendant's belief in these circumstances is relevant to punishment and that the man who believes he is importing cannabis is indeed less culpable than he who knows it to be heroin ... To what extend the punishment should be mitigated by this factor will obviously depend upon all the circumstances, amongst them being the degree of care exercised by the defendant ...

The next question is what the proper sentence should be for the carrier/importer of this quantity of 90 per cent. pure heroin. The guidelines in *Aramah* (1982) 4 Cr.App.R. (S.) 407, as was pointed out in *Gilmore, The Times,* May 21, 1986, must be updated to take account of the fact that the maximum sentence for the importation of Class A drugs has now been increased by the Controlled Drugs (Penalties) Act 1985, from 14 years to life imprisonment. It was suggested in *Aramah* that where the street value of the consignment is in the order of £100,000 or more, sentences of seven years and upwards are appropriate, and that 12 to 14 years' imprisonment is appropriate where the value of drugs involved is £1 million or more. The former figure should now be increased to 10 years and upwards and the latter to 14 years and upwards."

> Appeal allowed and 12 years' imprisonment
> varied to eight years' imprisonment.

NOTE

Bilinski's sentence was reduced on the basis of his guilty plea, the assistance that he gave the authorities and the possibility (in the absence of a finding to the contrary by the judge) that he might have believed the drugs to be cannabis.

In the judgment the court asked how the issue of mistaken belief as to the nature of the drugs should be determined. The answer provided was a hearing as provided for in *Newton* (1982) 4 Cr.App.R. (S.) 388: that procedure in Scotland is essentially a proof in mitigation.

R. v. Ocheja (1988) 10 Cr.App.R. (S.) 277 is a good example of the guidelines in *Bilinski* being applied. O. was found in possession of just over one kilogramme of heroin which she had imported from Nigeria. The street value was said to be worth £80,000. The trial judge sentenced O. to 12 years' imprisonment but on appeal that was reduced to nine years. Slightly lower sentences were passed for importing a slightly lower quantity of heroin in *R. v. Ezeoke* (1988) 10 Cr.App.R. (S.) 440.

2.5.28   **5. R. v. Faluade**
                           (1989) 11 Cr.App.R. (S.) 156

F. pleaded guilty to being concerned in the importation of heroin. She had been found at Gatwick Airport with 95 packages concealed on her body, which contained 210 grammes of 35 per cent heroin worth about £22,000. F. gave evidence that she did not know that the packages contained hard drugs but she was not believed by the trial judge. She was sentenced to four and a half years' imprisonment and appealed.

WALKER, L.J. (at p. 157): "This appellant was well aware that she was engaging herself in the very dangerous business of carrying hard drugs into this country. The amount was quite significant. It was, measured against amounts carried into this country in other cases, comparatively on the low side. But nevertheless it would have fed the appetite for drugs of a very large number of people had it been distributed and clearly a sizeable profit would have been made out of that as a result of retail sales.

Carriers are, it is true, sentenced upon a somewhat lower scale than those who are at the heart of the trade in drugs, but couriers who are fully aware of what it is they are doing, must expect when they carry hard drugs into this country to be punished severely ...

Bringing heroin into this country on such a scale is a matter which is viewed with the utmost seriousness and the public expect judges to punish severely those who lend their hands to it ...

Once a person knowingly acts as a courier bringing heroin into this country there is seldom, if ever, room for mercy. We see no room for it here."

Appeal dismissed.

6. R. v. Nweke   2.5.29
(1989) 11 Cr.App.R. (S.) 500

N. pleaded guilty to being concerned in fraudulently evading the prohibition on the importation of heroin. The appellant was detained at Heathrow Airport, where he was found to have 37 packages concealed in his body, which contained 172 grammes of powder containing about 25 per cent diamorphine. The value was estimated to be £15,480. The appellant had two previous convictions for importing cannabis. He was sentenced to six years' imprisonment.

Held (considering *R. v. Bilinski, supra* and *R. v. Olumide* (1988) 9 Cr.App.R. (S.) 364), the sentence was neither wrong in principle nor excessive.

Appeal dismissed.

NOTE
Although counsel for the appellants in *R. v. Olumide* (1988) 9 Cr.App.R. (S.) 364 and the above appeal stressed that their clients had pleaded guilty, the Court of Appeal was somewhat unimpressed with that because the appellants were what are known as "mules" or "body packets", having concealed the controlled drugs in their bodies.

In *R. v. Kouadio, The Times*, February 21, 1991 it was held that it was necessarily appropriate to assess the seriousness of the offence by reference solely to the quantity of controlled drugs involved. Some regard should be given to the method of importation, the degree of organisation and planning, and the difficulty of detection. Wright J. observed that a sentence had to be imposed where drugs were concealed in the courier's body which would deter others from engaging in such activities.

7. R. v. Hussain and Quddus   2.5.30
The Times, June 27, 1990

H. and Q. were convicted of the unlawful importation of diamorphine and were sentenced to 13 years' and 11 years' imprisonment respectively. Each appealed against sentence.

Held, the most important consideration in applying sentencing guidelines in cases of unlawful drug importation was the accused's position in the drug-smuggling operation.

H. was clearly very high up in the drug operation but there was no evidence of Q.'s involvement prior to the incidents which led to his arrest.

> Appeal by H. dismissed and by Q. allowed to the extent that 11 years' imprisonment varied to nine years.

2.5.31

8. R. v. Meah and Marlow
(1991) 92 Cr.App.R. 254

The appellants both pleaded guilty to importing substantial quantities of diamorphine, a prohibited Class A drug, on the basis that they intended to use the drugs for their own consumption. The trial judge was suspicious that he had not been told the truth about the destination of the drugs, but he did not hold a *Newton* (1983) 77 Cr.App.R. 13) inquiry (so that the circumstances of the offences could be investigated) and sentenced them: Meah to six years' imprisonment and Marlow to four years' imprisonment. On appeal against sentence, it was contended that they both came more within the possession category rather than the courier category.

Held, allowing the appeals, that in the circumstances a *Newton* inquiry should have been held; failing to do so the judge should have sentenced the appellants on the basis that their story was true; but not on the same basis as for mere possession of the drugs. The sentences would be varied, Meah to three years' imprisonment and Marlow to two years' imprisonment.

Per curiam if a judge thinks it right to sentence on the basis that drugs have been brought in for a defendant's personal consumption, it will still be a serious offence and, if the quantity is substantial, the result may well be imprisonment for a substantial period.

JUPP, J. (at p. 256): "When he passed sentences of six and four years respectively we think that the learned judge made a proper distinction between the two appellants, but we are told that certainly in the case of Meah, and it may also be so in the case of Marlow, counsel for Meah had come to the court prepared to face a *Newton* trial (see 1983) 77 Cr.App.R. 13). When one looks at the whole of the facts, the Court does not find it surprising that the judge declared himself suspicious that he was not being told the truth about the destination of the drugs. This Court would have been equally suspicious or more of a defendant saying through counsel that an importation of drugs in amounts like this concealed in this way at considerable risk to health was for his own consumption.

When a suggestion of this sort is made, the judge should hold? a *Newton* inquiry unless the suggestion is so absurd that it can be rejected out of hand. Having declined to hold a *Newton* trial, the learned judge in our view had to sentence on the basis that he had accepted that these large amounts of the drugs were in fact required and intended for use by the two appellants for their own consumption. That must make a considerable difference to the kind of sentence that he had to pass. The guideline in *R. v. Aramah* (1983) 76 Cr.App.R. 190 he kept to, but they were guidelines given when the Court was troubled about the importing by the gangs which have become such a pest now over quite some number of years. The learned judge in our view simply had to take into account, if he felt he had to accept it and if he did not accept it entirely he had to give the two appellants the benefit of the doubt, that the offence was bred out of their drug addiction and was merely a means of feeding it direct with the drugs they imported.

It has been argued before us that this ought to be treated in exactly the same way as a mere possession of drugs. We cannot accept that proposition. The importation was a fraudulent evasion of customs regulations and enactments. In this particular case both appellants went to enormous lengths to hide the drugs, taking considerable risks to health in doing so. In bringing drugs valued at £17,000 in one case and £6,806 in the other they were each of them increasing the stock of these dangerous drugs available in this country. Importing is a distinct offence from possessing. The penalties are different and in our view it is not right to say that this must be treated simply as a case of possession.

Nevertheless there must be a considerable reduction in sentence to reflect the fact that the drugs were for the appellants' own consumption. Accordingly, we must allow both of these appeals and substitute for the sentences passed by the learned judge a sentence of three years in the case of Meah and a sentence of two years in the case of Marlow. We should add this. We would be surprised if judges accepted this kind of a defence on its face value where drugs of this quantity are involved, without holding a *Newton* inquiry. If a judge does think it right to sentence on the basis that drugs have been brought in for a man's personal consumption, it will still be a serious offence and, if the quantity is substantial, the result may well be immediate imprisonment for a substantial period."

Appeals allowed and sentences varied.

NOTE
There are circumstances when a judge is entitled to treat the claims of an accused as manifestly false or wholly implausible: see, *e.g. R. v. Broderick* [1994] Crim.L.R. 139.

9. R. v. Afzal and Arshad   2.5.32
(1992) 13 Cr.App.R. (S.) 145

The appellants pleaded guilty to two offences of being concerned in evading the prohibition on the importation of heroin, and possession with intent to supply. The appellants were found in possession of three tins containing a total of 1,236 grammes of brown powder consisting of one per cent diamorphine. They were sentenced on the assumption that they were in possession of 1,236 grammes of heroin, which when "cut" about four times would have a street value of half a million pounds, to terms of twelve years' and eight years' imprisonment respectively. Subsequently, evidence was produced to show that the powder they had was so dilute that it would be unsaleable, or if sold would expose them to retaliation by dissatisfied customers. The case was referred to the Court by the Secretary of State under the Criminal Appeal Act 1968, s. 17(1)(a).

Held, the Court had stated in *R. v. French* (February 1, 1990) that the fact that a quantity of material containing heroin was below the average dilution was not a ground for reducing the sentence below the level indicated by the authorities in *R. v. Aramah, infra*, but a sentence below the normal bracket could be justified where the strength of the diamorphine was so low that the material was hardly recognisable as containing diamorphine in normal doses. It had been established in *R. v. Bilinski, supra*, that an offender's belief that he was importing cannabis, when in fact it was heroin, could be taken into account when imposing sentence: did the principle work the other way round? The Court could not accept the proposition that the appellants should be sentenced on the basis that the heroin was virtually valueless: a man who believed he was importing heroin of average strength was clearly more culpable than one who believed he was importing heroin which was unsaleable. It was clear that the appellants thought they were importing heroin of average saleable purity: it seemed that they had been deceived by their suppliers. Some reduction in the sentences was called for: sentences of eight years and five years would be substituted. Prosecution counsel should take care to ensure that the correct figures relating to street value were placed before the court.

Lloyd, J. (at p. 149): "It seems to us that we should approach the problem by looking at two factors, both at what the appellants have in fact done and also at what they thought they were doing. In other words, we must take account of the *actus reus*, and its consequences, as well as their *mens rea*. On that view some reduction from the 12 years and eight years passed by the learned judge is required because the *actus reus* here, though amply sufficient to support the conviction, would not have had such devastating consequences, as would have been the case if the same quantity of heroin had been of average strength."

Appeals allowed and sentences varied.

NOTE
The difficulties of relying on "street values" as a guide to sentencing in controlled drugs cases were discussed in *R. v. Patel* (1987) 9 Cr.App.R. (S.) 319.

In a commentary to *R. v. Afzal and Arshad* it was suggested that it would be better to rely on the quantity of pure drug involved rather than the variable concept of "street value" which (as was pointed out in *R. v. Patel*) varies both with time and place, and cannot be easily proved: [1991] Crim.L.R. 722.

10. R. v. Latif and Shahzad   2.5.33
(1994) 15 Cr.App.R. (S.) 864

L. and S. were convicted of being knowingly concerned in the fraudulent evasion of the prohibition on the importation of a controlled drug, diamorphine. S. formed an agreement in Pakistan to arrange for 20 kilogrammes of heroin to be imported into the United Kingdom. The heroin was supplied to a man who was an informer, and brought into the United Kingdom by a customs officer. S. was then persuaded to come to the United Kingdom to receive the heroin, and L. came with him. They were sentenced to 20 years' imprisonment (L.) and 16 years' imprisonment (S.).

Held (considering *R. v. Aramah, infra, R. v. Bilinski, infra* and *R. v. Scamaronie and Pacheco-Nunez, supra*), that the sentencer was entitled to treat the second appellant as a professional international trafficker and as the principal organiser of the importation. As there was no question of either appellant being led to do something that he would not otherwise have done, it was doubtful whether it was appropriate to consider entrapment as a mitigating factor. Neither sentence was too long.

Appeals dismissed.

NOTE
This case raised a point of law on appeal: see *supra* at paragraph **2.3.18**.

11. R. v. Patel and Varshney   2.5.34
(1995) 16 Cr.App.R. (S.) 267

P. was convicted in 1989 on two counts, and V. on one count, of being knowingly concerned in the fraudulent evasion of the prohibition on the importation of a controlled drug, heroin. The first count related to the importation of 823 grammes of powder, thought to be of 30 per cent purity, with a value of £66,463. The second offence, in which both appellants were concerned, involved 12.5 kilogrammes of powder concealed in carpets. The powder would have been worth £1,127,000 if of normal purity. P. was sentenced to 15 years' imprisonment and V. to nine years' imprisonment. The case was referred to the Court of Appeal by the Home Secretary on the ground that the powder involved in the second importation had been found to be of very low purity, between 2 per cent and 4 per cent, and contained between 310 and 316 grammes of pure heroin. The remainder of the powder was either phenobarbitone or an inert material.

The value of the heroin would have been about £104,000 and the phenobarbitone would have been worth £34,000. The percentage of heroin was so low that the appellants would have had difficulty in selling it at all. It was not commercially practicable to extract the heroin from the mixture.

Held, the question was what would have been the proper sentence on the appellants in the light of the evidence now available, and in the light of *R. v. Aroyemi* (1994) 16 Cr.App.R. (S.), in which the Court of Appeal had held that sentencing levels should be related to the weight of the pure drug involved in the consignment. The Court was entitled to draw the inference that the appellants thought that they were importing heroin of normal strength, and that they were importing 12.5 kilogrammes of saleable heroin. The position had been addressed in *R. v. Osei* (1988) 10 Cr.App.R. (S.) 289, where it was held that the fact that the purity of the consignment of heroin imported by a courier was only 1 per cent, and the weight of the heroin involved was 0.67 grammes, was not a major factor, and in *R. v. Afzal and Arshad* (1992) 13 Cr.App.R. (S.) 145, where the appellants were concerned with 1.236 kilogrammes of powder of 1 per cent purity. The Court of Appeal in that case did not accept the argument that a man's belief as to what he had done should not be taken into account in considering the gravity of the offence and what should be his sentence. The Court, in the light of that guidance, had concluded that the relevant factors were the quantity of drugs actually involved in the importation, the role of the individual defendant, and the element of *mens rea* on the part of the defendant. The appellants here thought that they were importing 12.5 kilogrammes of commercial grade heroin, probably of about 30 per cent purity; they thought they were engaged in a major importation of a large quantity of commercially saleable heroin. An analogy could be drawn with cases of attempt, where the actual substantive offence is never committed, but there was nevertheless an important element of criminality. Applying these considerations, the sentence of 15 years imposed on P. would be reduced to 12 years, concurrent with the nine years for the other importation; the sentence on V. would be reduced to eight years. The Court considered it appropriate to make such a reduction in sentence, in the light of the new evidence available to the Court and the fact that the matter had been referred by the Home Secretary.

Sentences varied.

2.5.35   **12. R. v. Daniel**
(1995) 16 Cr.App.R. (S.) 892

D. pleaded guilty to being knowingly concerned in the fraudulent evasion of the prohibition on the importation of a controlled drug. The appellant was stopped at Gatwick Airport and found to be in possession of 1.43 kilogrammes of heroin at 45 per cent purity, equivalent to 643.5 grammes of pure heroin, concealed in a briefcase. He was sentenced to nine years' imprisonment.

Held, accepting the appellant was a courier and was in desperate financial straits as a result of the illness of two of his children, the sentence reflected the plea of guilty and was not manifestly excessive.

Appeal refused.

Class A: (iii) Lysergamide **2.5.36**

1. R. v. Kemp **2.5.37**
(1979) 69 Cr.App.R. 330

K. and 14 others had produced chemically, lysergamide from a base material, ergotamine tartrate, on an enormous scale and it was made into tablets and distributed in this country and abroad, as far away as Australia.

Five indictments involving the 15 related to a conspiracy to manufacture, produce or supply the drug and covered a period of seven years between 1970 and 1977. Bearing in mind that the maximum sentence for an offence against section 4 of the 1971 Act was 14 years, the Court of Appeal upheld sentences of 13 years' imprisonment on K. and another as manufacturers, and sentences ranging from three to 11 years on the distributors.

ROSKIN, L.J. (at p. 346): "What we have said so far has concerned the ringleaders in this plot ... [they] were concerned quite deliberately, knowing full well what they were doing, in the manufacture and production of this vast quantity of LSD. But they of course needed channels of distribution for it was not much use having this vast quantity unless channels of distribution existed through which ... it could be moved around in this country, and out into Europe and indeed even to Australia, so that all the consequences of the evil in which these people were engaging might reach the far corners of the earth."

Further (at p. 347)

"We preface what we say with this general observation. We have often said in this Court that this Court will not, where a trial judge over a long period of time and talking all the care that Park J. took, allocates degrees of responsibility as he sees it, whether after trial or pleas of guilty, interfere with the trial judge's assessment, unless he can clearly be shown either to have overlooked some fundamental fact or in some respect to have gone wrong in principle. A trial judge hearing the evidence, seeing the accused, hearing the mitigation of counsel, watching the course of the trial, is in an infinitely better position than this Court, with all its experience, can possibly be in dealing with such a matter."

And later (at p. 348)

"In a very able argument partly founded on the evidence of Dr Mitcheson, a doctor from University College Hospital, [counsel for one appellant] asked us to say that the courts in dealing with sentences in Class A drug cases should, as it were, grade categories of Class A drugs. Because, as he claimed, what he called a tariff of sentences has been evolved to some extent in cannabis and also to some extent in heroin cases, and because Dr Mitcheson claimed that LSD was a less damaging drug than heroin, we should say that in this case the scale of sentences should be less than the scale evolved in heroin cases ...

What happened is this. The learned judge in January had passed a group of sentences on those who appeared before him on the early indictments. What he then said made it absolutely plain that he had, as other judges have — it is all part of general judicial reading knowledge — read widely into the literature relating to LSD. There are few judges either at first instance or in this Court who have not engaged in similar reading. He made it very plain that he was taking the view that LSD was a destructive and damaging drug.

Anticipating that the same view might be taken by the judge when he came to deal with those who were perhaps even more serious offenders, the defence perfectly naturally, sought to arm themselves with contrary medical evidence and to that end Dr Mitcheson was called.

There is no doubt, on his evidence, that certain attributes of LSD, if he is right, are less devastating than certain attributes of heroin. For example, it is said by him (and let it be assumed he is right — we express no view at all) that LSD is not an addictive drug. He also claimed, and other counsel relied upon this evidence, that LSD is not a drug which leads to violence ... Basing himself on certain research and a statistical sample which was referred to in his evidence, he expressed the view that, if the decision rested with him, LSD ought not to be a Category A drug.

Basing himself on that evidence [counsel] urged us to say that LSD cases in general, and these cases in particular, should be treated less seriously than heroin cases ... The learned judge also had the benefit of this argument.

There is a fundamental failing in this argument with all respect to counsel who urged it on us ... Parliament has decreed those drugs which are Category A, those drugs which are Category B and those drugs which are Category C ... No doubt a lawyer looking at that list sees several unfamiliar names. It is urged upon us that in a case where a trial judge was concerned with a drug with an unfamiliar name, he might require evidence to assist him as to the propensities of that particular drug. Therefore the learned judge in this case, so the argument went, ought to have given weight to Dr Mitcheson's evidence and graded LSD cases such as the present below the heroin cases in gravity.

As I have already said, there is a fallacy in that argument. It is no part of the duty of a trial judge nor of this Court to grade Category A drugs into classes ... The duty of the courts in Category A cases, whatever the drug involved, is to look at the evidence and assess the proper sentence to be imposed in the light of all the information made available. In the case of many drugs a trial judge can be assumed — cannabis is an obvious example — to have certain knowledge. In the case of heroin he may be assumed to have certain knowledge. In the case of LSD there is no reason to think why he should not be assumed to have certain knowledge. It is a matter for the judge what information, what assistance, what evidence he requires to help him in a particular case. No doubt the prosecution and the defence, in appropriate cases, will be ready to assist him with that information, assistance and if necessary evidence ..."

Finally (at p. 350)

"If crimes of drug abuse with LSD or heroin cannot be stopped by sentences such as the learned judge found necessary to impose in these cases, then something else has got to be done to stop it, and the only remaining weapon in the hands of the courts, reluctant as any court is to pass very long sentences, will be consecutive sentences."

Application for leave to appeal against sentence
refused.

2. Attorney-General's Refs. Nos. 3, 4 and 5 of 1992   2.5.38
(1993) 14 Cr.App.R. (S.) 191

The offenders pleaded guilty to conspiring to evade the prohibition on the importation of a Class A controlled drug (LSD). Two of the offenders pleaded guilty to offences on other indictments, involving supplying Ecstasy and amphetamine respectively. Two of the offenders flew to Amsterdam and bought a large quantity of LSD tablets, these were concealed inside greetings cards which were sent to various addresses in the United Kingdom by post. Eleven cards containing a total of over 19,000 squares were intercepted. The street value of the LSD was estimated at between £60,000 and £100,000; the Court proceeded on the basis of the lower figure. Sentences of two-and-a-half years' imprisonment were given for the conspiracy, with six months' imprisonment consecutive for the other offences in the case of two offenders. The Attorney-General asked the Court to review the sentences on the ground that they were unduly lenient.

Held, the Attorney-General submitted that two of the offenders were principal organisers, and that the conspiracy involved a major importation. The guidelines in *R. v. Aramah* (1982) 4 Cr.App.R. (S.) 407, as revised in *R. v. Bilinski* (1987) 9 Cr.App.R. (S.) 360, indicated a sentence of between seven and 10 years for offences involving Class A drugs worth up to £100,000, on a plea of not guilty. The sentences passed on the offenders were not only outside the guidelines in a way which a sentencer, taking into account individual circumstances, might properly deviate from the guidelines; they were very much below the guideline level. Applying the criteria laid down in *Attorney-General's Reference No. 4 of 1989*, (1989) 11 Cr.App.R. (S.) 517, and *Attorney-General's Reference No. 5 of 1989* (1989) 11 Cr.App.R. (S.) 489, the Court had no doubt that the sentences were unduly lenient. The Court had power to review only the sentences for conspiracy; the other offences, charged in different indictments, were triable either way and thus outside the scope of the Criminal Justice Act 1988, s. 35. The other indictments were relevant in the judgment of the Court because the two offenders concerned had committed the offence of conspiracy while on bail in respect of those offences, and in the judgment of the Court that did amount to an aggravating factor of the conspiracy so as to be relevant to the appropriate sentence. The Court bore in mind in one case the youth and good character of the offender, the fact that the offenders would shortly have been eligible for parole under the original sentences, and the element of double jeopardy, but had no doubt that the sentences were unduly lenient and should be increased. The sentences on two of the offenders for the conspiracy would be increased from two and a half years to five, and on the third offender, allowing for mitigating factors peculiar to him, to four years.

Sentences varied.

2.5.39 Class A: (iv) Ecstasy (MDMA, etc.)

2.5.40   **1. R. v. Bayley**
(1995) 16 Cr.App.R. (S.) 605

Two appellants were convicted of importing 58 kilogrammes of Ecstasy, 490 kilogrammes of cannabis and 980 grammes of cocaine; the third pleaded guilty to similar offences. B., the first appellant, obtained a refrigerated trailer which was taken to the Continent and loaded with drugs in concealed compartments. He was sentenced to 15 years' imprisonment for importing Ecstasy and nine years for importing cannabis and cocaine, all concurrent. The other appellants received sentences of 12 years.

Held, the sentence of 15 years for importing a large quantity of Ecstasy was perfectly proper. The total sentence on one of the other appellants, who had played a lesser role, and pleaded guilty, would be reduced from 12 to nine years.

2.5.41   **2. R. v. Blackburn**
(1995) 16 Cr.App.R. (S.) 902

B. pleaded guilty to being knowingly concerned in the fraudulent evasion of the prohibition on the importation of controlled drugs of Class A and Class B. The appellant was concerned in importing 15,500 tablets of Ecstasy and 22.5 kilogrammes of cannabis, concealed in hollow parts of a vehicle. He was sentenced to eight years' imprisonment for importing the Class A drug, and six years concurrent for importing cannabis.

Held, the sentencer was right to take a sentence of 12 years as the starting point for the importation of Ecstasy in the absence of a guilty plea. The discount of four years was generous in the circumstances and the sentence imposed in relation to the Class A drug was not excessive. The sentence for importing cannabis would be reduced to four years.

AULD, L.J. (at p. 904): "[Counsel], who appears on behalf of the appellant today, acknowledges that there is no significant distinction between the importation of Ecstasy tablets and other forms of Class A drugs. That is a sensible concession. Ecstasy tablets have a potentially lethal effect, as other cases before this Court have demonstrated, and one that may occur quite quickly.

[Counsel's] best point, as he put it, that this is a young man who was corrupted and used by his father, a convicted drugs smuggler himself, and that he acted out of loyalty to his father. He also pointed out that this was a single offence and that this was a young man of previous good character.

We take the view that the starting point which the judge took in this case, some 12 years had the matter been contested, and without the benefit of the particular matters of mitigation to which he referred, was about right. We consider also in the circumstances that the discount of four years that he gave from that period in respect of the more serious of the two offences was a generous discount. The case was overwhelming against the appellant.

The only point is whether a greater deduction from the sentence should have been made because of the family involvement and the corruption of this young man by his father.

The fact is that the appellant must have gone into this matter with his eyes open. He knew his father's record. He had not made just one or two visits to the Continent, he had made a number. He was clearly involved, as the judge said in sentencing him, more than as a mere courier. He took an important and clearly responsible part in the organisation of the transportation of the whole consignment. We take the view that the sentence imposed by the judge in respect of the count concerning the Ecstasy drugs was not excessive and was within the range of sentences for such an offence with the sort of mitigation that the appellant offered here.

It may be academic, but we should deal with the appeal against sentence in relation to the offence concerning the cannabis resin, the Class B drug. For that offence, as we have mentioned, the judge imposed a concurrent sentence of six years' imprisonment. We take the view that that was out of range for that class of offence and that an appropriate sentence would have been one of four years' imprisonment. To that extent and that extent only, we allow the appeal so as to substitute that lower sentence on that offence. It will be served concurrently, as before."

Appeal refused.

2.5.42   **3. R. v. Warren and Beeley**
                         [1996] 1 Cr.App.R. 130

The court laid down sentencing guidelines for offences involving the importation of the Class A prohibited drug Ecstasy, the common name for MDA (methylenedioxyamphetamine), MDMA (methylenedioxy-methylamphetamine) and MDEA (methylenedioxytyethylamphetamine). Regard should be had to the weight of the drug rather than to its street value. The tariff for involving Ecstasy would be maintained at substantially the same level as for other Class A drugs. It followed that for 5,000 tablets or more of Ecstasy the appropriate sentence would be in the order of 10 years' imprisonment or upwards, for 50,000 tablets or more, 14 years or more. That was on the basis that the tablets contained the average or near average amount of active ingredient. If analysis revealed a substantially different content in an individual case, the weight of the constituent would be the determinative factor.

Applying these guidelines, the court allowed the appeal of Warren (who pleaded guilty to importing 1,011 Ecstasy tablets) to the extent of reducing his sentence from six to five years' imprisonment. Beeley (who pleaded guilty to importing 1,585 tablets of Ecstasy) had his sentence reduced from seven to six years' imprisonment.

LORD TAYLOR, C.J. (at p. 121): "These two appeals have been listed together since they both concern the proper approach to sentencing for offences involving a prohibited Class A drug known as MDA or Ecstasy. In *R. v Aranguren and others [supra]*, this court gave guidance as to the sentencing approach and criteria for offences involving heroin and cocaine, but in the absence of sufficient evidence declined to do so in relation to Ecstasy. In the instant case we have had the advantage of receiving evidence from Mrs Gillian Connors, a Senior Officer with Her Majesty's Customs and Excise with extensive experience in the drugs field and presently a research analyst with the National Co-ordination Unit. We have also had oral evidence from Dr King, the Head of the Drugs Intelligence Laboratory at Aldermaston. From that evidence it emerges that Ecstasy is the collective and simple name given to three different drugs, each being a complex including amphetamine: MDA, MDMA and MDEA. All three are Class A controlled drugs. They broadly have similar effects. They are hallucinogenic stimulants and there is evidence that they can, in some situations, cause fatality.

There was evidence which was recited in *R.* v *Slater and Scott* (unreported, February 2, 1995, C.A.) showing that the drugs are capable of causing convulsions, collapse, hyperpyrexia, intravascular coagulation and acute renal failure. Those physical effects on the consumer may not be the only adverse effect of the drugs, which may very well affect the behaviour of the consumer in relation to others.

Ecstasy drugs have no clinical value and therefore all manufacture of them must be illicit and must be designed to produce drugs which offend against the legislation. The Ecstasy drugs seized in the United Kingdom come frequently from the Netherlands or Belgium, as well as other places, but there are illicit laboratories producing these substances in the United Kingdom. The drug usually comes in the form of a well-made tablet. There are capsules, but those are less common. Sometimes, though rarely, the drug comes in the form of loose powder. Dosage units vary between a content of 75 milligrams or 125 milligrams of the active constituent, but most tablets, we are informed, contain amounts close to the average of 100 milligrams. Accordingly, 5,000 tablets would be expected to contain a total of 500 grammes of the active constituent. From the manufacturer's point of view, the achievement of 100 milligrams or thereabouts is desirable: if less than that were included the tablet would be less marketable, and if more than that were included, then it would be more than is necessary or appropriate for an individual dose and the manufacturers would be unlikely to wish to exceed what was necessary for that purpose.

In the case of the powders the number of equivalent tablets can be calculated from the knowledge of the purity of the powder and the assumption that tablets will contain 100 milligrams or thereabouts of pure substance. The remainder of the tablet, apart from the active constituent, is made up of an inert binder, often a substance called lactose. Although not routinely carried out, there are no technical difficulties in the quantitative determination of the drugs content of either tablets or powders, whether by analysis of each individual tablet or the whole content of the powder or by sample.

There was also evidence before us that seizures of Ecstasy by Customs and by the police since 1989 have greatly increased. In 1993 there were over 2,000 seizures made by the Customs authorities and the police, the effect of which added up to a total of over two-and-a-half million doses. The seizures which were made are accepted to be only a fraction of the total amount available in the United Kingdom. The growth in the number and quantity of the seizures since 1989 points to an increase in the organisation and scale of operations in regard to that drug. Although over half of all the Ecstasy seizures was in the London area, there have been significant seizures elsewhere. The drug is readily available in all the major cities in the United Kingdom. That indicates that its importation and distribution are well organised. Individual seizures have been made of as large a quantity as 252 kilogrammes — almost one million doses.

The range of Ecstasy prices at street level is variable. The price varies considerably depending upon a number of factors such as the number of doses being purchased, the relationship between the buyer and the seller and the place of purchase. Because Ecstasy has become so widely available during the past few years the price has dropped considerably. In 1990 the national average price per tablet was £21. That dropped to £16.50 in February 1994 and has since further dropped to £13. Thus, if street value were to be a major criterion in determining the level of sentencing, the more Ecstasy imported, the lower would be its value and the lower would be the level of sentencing. This would clearly be contrary to public policy. It was this factor which prompted the court to alter the criteria in its guidance as to offences involving heroin and cocaine in *Aranguren* [(1994) 99 Cr.App.R. 347]. Since that case, regard should be had to the weight of the drug, rather than to its street value.

We consider the same applies to Ecstasy. The evidence, as we have said, is that most tablets contain amounts of the active constituent close to the average of 100 milligrammes and, accordingly, 5,000 tablets would contain 500 grammes. In *Aranguren*, the court held that importation of heroin or cocaine of 500 grammes or more at 100 per cent purity should merit sentences of 10 years and upwards; importations of 5 kilogrammes or more, 14 years and upwards. We consider that similar criteria should, by way of guidance, be applicable to importations of Ecstasy. In applying the criteria in that way we consider that the tariff in regard to offences concerning Ecstasy will be maintained substantially at the same levels as in relation to the other Class A drugs. It is to be assumed, since Parliament has so classified the drugs, that drugs within one class are to be regarded similarly.

It follows from what we have said that in general, for 5,000 tablets or more of Ecstasy, the appropriate sentence would be of the order of 10 years and upwards; for 50,000 tablets or more, 14 years and upwards. That is on the basis that the tablets are of the average (or near average) content mentioned above. If analysis shows a substantially different content in an individual case then the weight of the constituent will be the determinative factor so far as this particular criterion is concerned.

However, we wish to stress two matters: first, these criteria are by way of guidance only; and secondly, that the quantity of tablets or the weight of the constituent is only one factor to be considered in deciding the appropriate sentence. The role of the offender, his plea, any assistance he may have given to the authorities are some, but not all, of the other considerations which the court will have to weigh."

[The Court then considered and allowed the individual appeals.]

Appeals allowed and sentences varied.

4. R. v. Van Tattenhove and Doubtfire   **2.5.43**
[1996] 1 Cr.App.R. 408

This appeal arose out of convictions for importing substantial quantities of two controlled drugs, amphetamine sulphate and Ecstasy tablets. The issue at appeal related to the prosecution duty of disclosure and the procedure to be followed in regard to *ex parte* applications under English law. There were also appeals against sentence.

LORD TAYLOR, C.J. (at p. 411): "In cross-examination on behalf of Doubtfire it was suggested to Mr Welsh, the customs officer who took charge of the case, that Doubtfire might have been a 'cut-out', a person put in place by someone in charge of an illegal drug-running operation in order to insulate himself from detection and arrest."

And later (at p. 416)

"We turn to the question of sentence, which has been the subject of addresses by both counsel, and as to which the single judge gave leave in both cases. It is submitted that the sentence of 25 years' imprisonment was manifestly excessive. The importation was of an enormous amount of the two drugs [*i.e.* 493,620 tablets of Ecstasy said to have a street value of £10 million, and 146.55 kilogrammes of amphetamine sulphate, said to be worth over £23 million.]. This court has indicated in previous cases that where massive quantities of drugs are imported, then those who are in the higher echelons of the team involved must expect very long sentences of the order of 25 years' imprisonment or more. The argument in the present case is that the appellants were not in that league. It is submitted that they were at the bottom of the scale; that Van Tattenhove was merely a courier, and that Doubtfire was merely a casual unloader. They were both 'foot soldiers', rather than occupying any higher position.

The trial judge had an excellent opportunity of judging the roles of those involved because the case was tried over a period of four weeks. Moreover, both of the appellants gave evidence and were cross-examined. Therefore the judge had the opportunity not only of getting the flavour of the case as a whole, but of sizing up the calibre and capabilities of the two defendants before him.

[The Court then considered the facts and the comments of the trial judge.]

However, we have to look at the level of sentence. It is argued before us that, in the usual event of someone being caught who is the prime organiser and beneficiary of a huge importation of this kind, there clearly has to be a very long sentence. Sentences passed on persons lower than that in the hierarchy must leave room for the highest sentences to be imposed upon those at the top of the scale. The submission is that in passing sentences of 25 years' imprisonment the trial judge was leaving no room at the top for any 'Mr Big' who might have been higher up the hierarchy than either of the two appellants, should he be caught and brought to book. We think there is force in that submission. We bear in mind that someone who is at the top might expect, with an importation of this calibre, a sentence of somewhere between 25 and 30 years' imprisonment. Bearing that in mind, we consider that 25 years was too long for either of the appellants. We believe that the judge led more emphasis on the quantity of drugs than on the role of the offenders before him. That being so, we think that it is right that we should reduce these sentences. But we repeat: anybody who gets involved in any way with any importation of this kind, particularly if they are higher up than being mere foot soldiers, must expect long sentences. Accordingly, doing the best we can, we do not think that we should reduce these sentences by more than five years in each case. We therefore substitute sentences of 20 years' imprisonment for the sentences of 25 years imposed by the trial judge. To that extent only these appeals are allowed."

Applications for leave to appeal against
conviction refused. Sentences varied.

2.5.44 Class A: (v) Opium

2.5.45   **1. R. v. Gerami and Haranaki**
                              (1980) 2 Cr.App.R. (S.) 291

G. and H. were convicted of being concerned in fraudulently evading the prohibition on the importation of opium and related offences. They had arranged for 8.37 kilogrammes of prepared opium to be imported in the form of cigarettes, concealed in a tin ostensibly containing sweets. G. was found to have £5,000 on him when he was arrested. There was evidence that it was unlikely that the opium would be converted. Each was sentenced to eight years' imprisonment and appealed.

Held, the length of the prison term for G. was fully justified having regard to the quantity of opium, and evidence that the demand for opium in England outstripped supply and although it used not to be a locally abused drug, it was becoming one. In the case of H. he had not been the instigator of the offence, the sentence would be varied to six years. Both men were to be deported.

Appeals dismissed and varied respectively.

2.5.46 Class A: (vi) Morphine

2.5.47   **1. R. v. Ahmed**
                              (1980) 2 Cr.App.R. (S.) 19

A., an employee of an airline, pleaded guilty to being knowingly concerned in the fraudulent importation of morphine. He was a man of good character who had acted as a courier. He was caught attempting to carry 991 grammes of morphine through customs in a bag with a false bottom. Sentenced to seven years' imprisonment and appealed.

LORD LANE, C.J. (at p. 20): "991 grammes of powdered morphine which had a value on the street, we are told, of £250,000 ... He has a wife and three children who will suffer severely if the prison sentence is to be served.

Of course, one feels for the wife and children in this case, as one feels for the millions of people whose lives are made miserable by the trafficking in these drugs. It is very important that those who only act as couriers should be dealt with seriously when they are caught because if the couriers can be discouraged the trade will suffer a grave below."

Appeal dismissed.

Class B: (i) Amphetamine   **2.5.48**

1. R. v. Fitzgerald   **2.5.49**
(1994) 15 Cr.App.R. (S.) 236

F. and others were convicted of being concerned in the importation of amphetamines, or of conspiring to do so. They were concerned in arranging the importation by sea of 33.1 kilogrammes of amphetamine sulphate with a street value of between £800,000 and £2,900,000. The scheme was disclosed to the Customs and Excise by a man who was invited to take part and the participants were arrested as the amphetamine was being brought ashore. The principals were sentenced to 11 years' imprisonment each; those who had played lesser roles to seven years.

Held, the sentencer was entitled to infer that the principal actors were not new to drug smuggling and that the activities of the informer had not contributed significantly to their decision to commit the offence. The sentences of 11 years imposed on the principals were not excessive; the sentences of seven years on the two who had played lesser roles were excessive, having regard to the parts they had actually played, and would be reduced to five years and four years respectively.

Appeals variously refused and allowed.

2. R. v. Coughlan   **2.5.50**
(1995) 16 Cr.App.R. (S.) 519

C. was convicted of conspiring to import a controlled drug, amphetamine. The appellant was seen in a car from which a box containing

12 kilogrammes of amphetamine of 29 per cent purity was thrown. This box had been imported on a lorry, concealed in a load of bacon. The sentencer formed the view that the appellant was at the centre of the conspiracy. He was sentenced to 12 years' imprisonment, with a confiscation order in the amount of £100 under the Drug Trafficking Offences Act 1986.

Appeal allowed.

2.5.51 Class B: (ii) Cannabis

2.5.52
1. R. v. Hussain
[1962] Crim.L.R. 712

H. arrived at London Airport from Karachi in possession of three tins containing Indian hemp (cannabis) which he tried to take through customs without a licence. He pleaded guilty and he appealed against sentence.

Held, as both offences (unloading prohibited goods from an aircraft and possessing a dangerous drug without a licence) arose from the same transaction generally, the appropriate way was to make whatever sentences were given concurrent.

H. had committed a serious offence and to deter others, sentences of two and three years' imprisonment consecutive were varied to two and five years' concurrent.

Sentences varied.

2.5.53
2. D.P.P. v. Doot
(1972) 57 Cr.App.R. 600

D. and four other American citizens pleaded guilty to importing cannabis resin by concealing it in three separate vans which were then shipped to England. The street value of the total quantity was then said to be £90,000. In due course the case came before the House of Lords where the matter of sentence was also considered and observations made in speeches.

LORD SALMON (at p. 625): "It is surely no mitigation that the defendants intended to commit further crimes by exporting the prohibited drugs from this country. There is unfortunately a ready market in this country for these dangerous drugs. I do not doubt that if the respondents had received an acceptable offer for them here, it would have been accepted. However, this may be, it hardly seems in accordance with the rules of international comity that courts should treat the respondents with special leniency because their crimes were more likely to ruin young lives in the United States of America than in this country."

Later (at p. 628)

"Today, crime is an international problem — perhaps not least, crimes connected with the illicit drug traffic — and there is a great deal of co-operation between the nations to bring criminals to justice. Great care is also taken by most countries to do nothing which might help their own nationals to commit what would be crimes in other countries."

Convictions and sentences restored.

3. R. v. Klug   2.5.54
The Times, November 23, 1977

K. had been found to be in possession of cannabis oil in London when in the course of a journey from India to Germany. He appealed against a sentence of three years' imprisonment for illegal importation.

JOPP, J.: "The English courts could not merely say that as long as the importer of drugs went away there was no need to punish him. The country had to punish him for the importation of dangerous drugs even though they were intended for another country. Unless all the countries concerned co-operated, the movement of drugs from the Far East to Europe would never cease."

Appeal dismissed.

4. R. v. Williams   2.5.55
(1979) 1 Cr.App.R. (S.) 5

W., a Jamaican of good character, arrived at London Airport carrying suitcases containing 5.15 kilogrammes of cannabis said to be worth £5,000 in this country. He pleaded guilty and was sentenced to three years' imprisonment. He appealed.

CANTLEY, J. (at p. 6): "[T]his would on the face of it be a very serious case of an offence against the law forbidding the importation of this dangerous drug.

There are however some special circumstances relating to the appellant. He belongs to a sect in Jamaica called Rastafarians. There are persons in this country who profess whatever beliefs Rastafarians have. The Court was informed, and accepted, that Rastafarians make an extensive, and indeed spectacular use of cannabis. The Court was informed by counsel that this appellant would probably consume a pound or two of cannabis a week, smoking some of it and using the rest of it in some concoction in tea, and this was not only a pleasure, but a form of religious rite. The Court was also informed, and accepted, that the intention of the appellant to sell the cannabis, or some of it, was confined to selling it to Rastafarians in this country …

The Court is prepared to accept that this is not the ordinary case of commercial importation of cannabis, and that the appellant, having a settled and good job in his own country, was not a professional smuggler of drugs."

Appeal allowed and three years' imprisonment
varied to two years.

NOTE

The *ratio decidenti* given at the head of the report cited refers to the court making a distinction between professional smugglers and those who import for personal use and distribution "within a limited social group." That is rather to move from the particular to the general and perhaps, with respect, unjustifiably. It is submitted that the court restricted the concessionary approach to Rastafarians who use cannabis as part of their religious rites.

In *R. v. Forsythe* (1980) 2 Cr.App.R. (S.) 15 a sentence of 10 years' imprisonment on a Jamaican was reduced to five years, but only because it was excessive standing the general approach. That was referred to in *R. v. Bibi* (1980) 2 Cr.App.R. (S.) 177 where the Court of Appeal (Criminal Division) referred to the dangerous overcrowding of prisons and asserted that if imprisonment was necessary then it should be as short as possible, consistent with the protection of the public and the punishment and deterrence of offenders: *per* Lord Lane, C.J. (at p. 179), "What the court can and should do is to ask itself whether there is any compelling reason why a short sentence should not be passed. We are not aiming at uniformity of sentence; that would be impossible. We are aiming at uniformity of approach."

2.5.56   **5. R. v. Chisti**
(1981) 3 Cr.App.R. (S.) 99

C. pleaded guilty to being concerned in the fraudulent importation of cannabis. He had been concerned in an attempt to smuggle one-third of a ton of the substance in a wooden crate. He was sentenced to nine years' imprisonment and recommended for deportation. He appealed.

Held, anyone involved in such activity must expect a substantial sentence of immediate imprisonment, but the appellant was not the principal in the transaction for whom a sentence of nine years would have been appropriate. Appeal *quoad* imprisonment allowed but recommendation for deportation upheld.

Sentence varied to six years' imprisonment.

NOTE

In *R. v. Abdul* (1981) 3 Cr.App.R. (S.) 160, five years' imprisonment was reduced on appeal to three years where the cannabis smuggled amounted to 43.65 kilogrammes.

In *R. v. Nesbitt* (1981) 3 Cr.App.R. (S.) 221 the quantity of cannabis was 17 kilogrammes. On appeal against sentence, counsel referred to the brackets (the minimum and maximum) for smuggling controlled drugs in Class B: Lord Dunn, L.J. held (at p. 223) that "the limits of the brackets [in *Aramah*] are not sacrosanct, and the circumstances of particular cases may be such that the judge is justified in imposing a sentence which is larger than the normal limits accepted as being appropriate for the offence."

6. R. v. Aramah   2.5.57
(1982) 4 Cr.App.R. (S.) 407

A. was found sitting in the driver's seat of a vehicle parked at the West African Terminal of Tilbury Docks. Four other men standing at the vehicle ran away. The police searched the vehicle and found four plastic bags each containing a number of packages of herbal cannabis, weighing just over 59 kilogrammes. The street level value of that herbal cannabis was between £100,000 and £130,000. A. was found to have wire cutters in his pocket. A. held two previous convictions; one in 1968 for simple possession of cannabis and amphetamines for which he was fined a modest sum and one in 1972 for importing 88 kilogrammes of cannabis and possession of 14.2 kilogrammes for which he received three years' imprisonment. On being convicted for being concerned in the importation of the 59 kilogrammes he was sentenced to six years' imprisonment. He appealed against sentence only.

LORD LANE, C.J. (at p. 408): "[I]t may be of assistance if we make some general observations about the level of sentences for drug offences, since our list, as will have been observed, is entirely composed of such crimes.

Class 'A' drugs and particularly heroin and morphine

It is common knowledge that these are the most dangerous of all the addictive drugs for a number of reasons: first of all, they are easy to handle. Small parcels can be made up into huge numbers of doses. Secondly, the profits are so enormous that they attract the worst type of criminal. Many of such criminals may think, and indeed do think, that it is less dangerous and more profitable to traffic in heroin or morphine than it is to rob a bank. It does not require much imagination to realise the consequential evils of corruption and bribery which the huge profits are likely to produce. [Thirdly, this] factor is also important when considering the advisability of granting bail. Sums which to the ordinary person, and indeed the ordinary defendant, might seem enormous are often trivial for the trafficker in drugs.

The two main sources of supply are South-east Asia and South-west Asia. These two sources are in competition, one with the other, and with the stakes so high, this may be a fruitful source of violence and internecine strife. Fourthly, the heroin taker, once addicted (and it takes very little experimentation with the drug to produce addiction), has to obtain supplies of the drug to satisfy the terrible craving. It may take anything up to hundreds of pounds a week to buy enough heroin to satisfy the craving, depending upon the degree of addiction of the person involved. The only way, it is obvious, in which sums of this order can be obtained is by resorting to crime. This in its turn may be trafficking in the drug itself and disseminating accordingly its use still further.

Fifthly, and lastly, and we have purposely left it for the last, because it is the most horrifying aspect, comes the degradation and suffering and not infrequently the death which the drug brings to the addict. It is not difficult to understand why in some parts of the world traffickers in heroin in any substantial quantity are sentenced to death and executed.

Consequently anything which the courts of this country can do by way of deterrent sentences on those found guilty of crimes involving these Class 'A' drugs should be done.

Then I turn to the importation of heroin, morphine and so on: large scale importation, that is where the street value of the consignment is in the order of £100,000 or more, sentences of seven years and upwards are appropriate. There will be cases where the values are of the order of £1 million or more, in which case the offence should be visited by sentences of 12 to 14 years. It will seldom be that an importer of any appreciable amount of the drug will serve less than four years.

This, however, is one area in which it is particularly important that offenders should be encouraged to give information to the police, and a confession of guilt, coupled with considerable assistance to the police, can properly be marked by a substantial reduction in what would otherwise be the proper sentence.

Next, supplying heroin, morphine, etc. it goes without saying that the sentence will largely depend on the degree of involvement, the amount of trafficking and the value of the drug being handled. It is seldom that a sentence of less than three years will be justified and the nearer the source of supply the defendant is shown to be, the heavier will be the sentence. There may well be cases where sentences similar to those appropriate to large scale importers may be necessary. It is, however, unhappily all too seldom that those big fish amongst the suppliers get caught.

Possession of heroin, morphine etc. (simple possession): it is at this level that the circumstances of the individual offender become of much greater importance. Indeed the possible variety of considerations is so wide, including often those of a medical nature, that we feel it impossible to lay down any practical guidelines. On the other hand the maximum penalty for simple possession of Class 'A' drugs is seven years' imprisonment and/or a fine, and there will be very many cases where deprivation of liberty is both proper and expedient.

Class 'B' drugs, particularly cannabis

We select this from amongst the Class 'B' drugs as being the most likely to be exercising the minds of the courts.

Importation of cannabis: importation of very small amounts for personal use can be dealt with as if it were simple possession, with which we will deal later. Otherwise importation of amounts up to about 20 kilogrammes of herbal cannabis, or the equivalent in cannabis resin or cannabis oil, will, save in the most exceptional cases, attract sentences of between 18 months and three years, with the lowest ranges reserved for pleas of guilty in cases where there has been small profit to the offender. The good character of the courier (as he usually is) is of less importance than the good character of the defendant in other cases. The reason for this is, it is well known that the large scale operator looks for couriers of good character and for people of a sort which is likely to exercise the sympathy of the court if they are detected and arrested. Consequently one will frequently find students and sick and elderly people are used as couriers for two reasons: first of all they are vulnerable to suggestion and vulnerable to the offer of quick profit, and secondly, it is felt that the courts may be moved to misplaced sympathy in their case. There are few, if any, occasions when anything other than an immediate custodial sentence is proper in this type of importation.

Medium quantities over 20 kilogrammes will attract sentences of three to six years' imprisonment, depending on the amount involved, and all the other circumstances of the case.

Large scale or wholesale importation of massive quantities will justify sentences in the region of 10 years' imprisonment for those playing other than a subordinate role.

Supply of cannabis: here again the supply of massive quantities will justify sentences in the region of 10 years for those playing anything more than a subordinate role. Otherwise the bracket should be between one to four years' imprisonment, depending upon the scale of the operation. Supplying a number of small sellers — wholesaling if you like — comes at the top of the bracket. At the lower end will be the retailer of a small amount to a consumer. Where there is no commercial motive (for example, where cannabis is supplied at a party), the offence may well be serious enough to justify a custodial sentence.

Possession of cannabis: when only small amounts are involved being for personal use, the offence can often be met by a fine. If the history shows, however, a persistent flouting of the law, imprisonment may become necessary.

We turn now to apply those principles in so far as relevant to the present case. This was importation of a very large quantity of cannabis, 59 kilogrammes, the value of which, as I have already stated, was between £100,000 and £130,000. It seems to us that this was the very top of the range. There is no feature of the case which we can discover as a mitigating factor. The case was contested. Consequently, unlike the cases where there has been a plea of guilty, no discount can on this account be given to him. The fact that this man had been warned in the past, when he was convicted in 1972 of a very similar offence and then sent to prison for three years, shows that he is flouting the law. In those circumstances it seems to us that the sentence of six years was entirely appropriate."

Appeal dismissed.

NOTE

One commentator noted that the guidelines in *Aramah's* case "constitute a restatement of existing sentencing policy, and a convenient source of reference rather than a change of direction." [1983] Crim.L.R. 273. In Scotland the decision must be regarded, at the very least, as influential.

2.5.58   **7. R. v. Price**
                          (1985) 7 Cr.App.R. (S.) 190

P. pleaded guilty to being concerned in the importation of cannabis. The appellant, together with a number of others, went to Morocco in a yacht and bought a quantity of cannabis, which was then brought back to England. The prosecution estimated the total mount of cannabis to be between 60 and 80 kilogrammes and the defence did not object to this figure at the Crown Court, but on appeal it was claimed that the amount was nearer 40 kilogrammes. He was sentenced to a total of seven years' imprisonment, and ordered to forfeit a car and an amount of money found in his possession.

Held, in *R. v. Aramah, supra*, the Lord Chief Justice had indicated that medium quantities of over 20 kilogrammes would attract sentences of three to six years' imprisonment, and that large scale or wholesale importation of massive quantities would justify sentences in the region of 10 years for those playing other than a subordinate role. The Court had been referred to *R. v. Forsythe, supra*, and *R. v. Chisti, supra*, where the amounts involved were larger than in the present case, and the Court had reduced the sentence to five years and six years respectively. It was unnecessary to draw precisely the line between medium quantities and those which could justifiably be called large scale. Having regard to the appellant's previous convictions for drug offences, a sentence of seven years was appropriate within the *Aramah* scale, and would have been appropriate if the appellant had been convicted after a trial. The sentencer had not given sufficient discount for the appellant's plea of guilty; in the light of the appellant's guilty plea the sentence would be reduced to five and a half years.

                          Appeal allowed and sentence reduced.

NOTE

For similar cases see *R. v. Mitchell, infra*, and *R. v. Dundas* (1988) 9 Cr.App.R. (S.) 473.

2.5.59   **8. MacNeil v. H.M. Advocate**
      .   1986 S.C.C.R. 288

MacN. and five others were charged variously with (1) importing cannabis, or alternatively being concerned in importing cannabis and (2) possession with intent to supply. N., one of the five others, was convicted of charge (1) in the alternative (being concerned). He was sentenced to 10 years' imprisonment.

He appealed against sentence and on his behalf counsel submitted that N. had been convicted "only" of charge (1) in the alternative and that the trial judge did not make adequate distinctions between those convicted of that version of the charge and those convicted of the charge in the first alternative.

Held, that there is no room for the view that the offence libelled in the second alternative version of the charge is any less serious than the offence in the first alternative.

Appeal refused.

9. R. v. Mitchell   2.5.60
(1986) 8 Cr.App.R. (S.) 472

M. pleaded guilty to two charges of being knowingly concerned in the fraudulent evasion of the prohibition on the importation of cannabis. The first charge related to the importation of 191.5 kilogrammes of cannabis worth over a quarter of a million pounds, between March and June 1984. The other charge related to the importation between September and October 1985 of 645.7 kilogrammes of cannabis worth nearly a million pounds. He was sentenced to six years' imprisonment on charge one and 10 years' imprisonment on the other charge, both sentences concurrent. He appealed against sentence.

TUCKER, J. (at p. 473): "We have borne in mind the guidelines as to sentencing in this class of case laid down by the Lord Chief Justice in the well known case of *R. v. Aramah* (1982) 4 Cr.App.R. (S.) 407 where he said, 'Large scale or wholesale importation of massive quantities will justify sentences in the region of 10 years' imprisonment for those playing other than a subordinate role.' It was not suggested that 10 years was necessarily the highest sentence which would be appropriate.

In this case there was a massive importation. It followed an earlier importation which could certainly be described as substantial, if not also massive. The appellant could not complaint if consecutive sentences had been imposed. According to the judge, the appellant was not the mastermind, or at any rate the judge was not satisfied that he was the mastermind, but he was playing more than a subordinate role."

Appeal dismissed.

10. R. v. Daly and Whyte   2.5.61
(1987) 9 Cr.App.R. (S.) 519

The Court of Appeal (Criminal Division) considered two separate cases which had been conjoined for appeal purposes.

Daly was stopped at Heathrow on the way back from Spain. In his suitcase were found several plastic-wrapped slabs of cannabis resin; some of them inside socks. The total weight was 15 kilogrammes with an estimated street value of £37,500. He pleaded guilty to being knowingly concerned in the fraudulent evasion of a prohibition on the importation of a controlled drug. He was sentenced to five years' imprisonment and appealed against sentence.

Whyte was stopped at Heathrow on the way from Ghana to Germany. His suitcase was found to have a false top and bottom and smelled of glue. In the false bottom customs officers found hidden an amount just in excess of 12 kilogrammes of cannabis resin. He pleaded guilty to being knowingly concerned in the fraudulent evasion of the prohibition on the importation of a controlled drug. He was sentenced to four years' imprisonment and recommended for deportation. He appealed against sentence.

WATKINS, L.J. (at p. 520): "The leading guideline case for drug cases is the well known *Aramah* (1982) 4 Cr.App.R. (S.) 407. In respect of the importation of Class A drugs, the guidelines given by the court in *Aramah* have been updated (see *Bilinski* (1988) 9 Cr.App.R. (S.) 360, a case involving heroin). Nothing to that effect was said in *Bilinski* with regard to the importation of Class B drugs like cannabis. It was incumbent therefore, in our view, on the learned judge who passed sentence in this case to follow the guidelines in *Aramah*, the observations made in *Gilmore* (*The Times Law Reports*, May 21, 1986) notwithstanding.

In *Aramah* it was observed that medium quantities of over 20 kilogrammes of cannabis should attract sentences of three to six years' imprisonment, depending on the amount involved and all the other circumstances of the case. The amount here is, as we have said, below 20 kilogrammes. It follows therefore that, there being no serious accompanying circumstances to bear in mind, as the judge himself observed, the sentence appropriate to this offence would be something less than three years' imprisonment. It was not the most sophisticated offence. It was a crude attempt to bring cannabis into this country. A relatively small amount was involved. The proper sentence, in our judgment, is two years' imprisonment."

And later quoad Whyte J. (at p. 521)

"Here again we have to look at *Aramah* and apply the guidelines given there ... This was a more sophisticated attempt to bring in cannabis than that committed by Daly. Accordingly, he has to receive, in our judgment, a somewhat more severe punishment. The appropriate sentence in his case we think is two-and-a-half years' imprisonment."

Appeals allowed and sentences varied
respectively.

11. R. v. Adewoye
(1988) 10 Cr.App.R. (S.) 226

2.5.62

A. was stopped at Heathrow on his way into this country from Nigeria. His luggage was searched and it was found to contain 3.37 kilogrammes of herbal cannabis wrapped in packages concealed by his clothing. It was said that the value of that cannabis at street level was about £6,000. He pleaded guilty to being knowingly concerned in the fraudulent evasion of a prohibition on the importation of a controlled drug. He was sentenced to two years' imprisonment.

At the hearing of the appeal counsel for the appellant submitted that as the same court had held two years to be an appropriate sentence for the importation of 15 kilogrammes of a value of £37,500, as in *R. v. Daly, supra,* then two years would appear to be excessive in a case such as the present where the importation was very much less, only 3.37 kilogrammes to a value of £6,000.

STOCKER, L.J. (at p. 228): "This Court accepts that in this case it does seem that as the importation was substantially less in quantity than in the case of *Daly* and the value of the drug substantially less, it may well have been that the Court of Appeal in *Daly* would have reduced the sentence below the point of two years, but within the *Aramah* guidelines, had those amounts been comparable to the present one ...

We will allow the appeal. We consider that the appropriate sentence would be one of 18 months rather than the two years imposed by the learned judge.

Having said that, we wish to make it clear that judges cannot be expected to make minute comparisons of the precise amounts and values of the cannabis which may be imported in any given case before that judge. The amount involved here was within the general *Aramah* guidelines. We are reducing it only because of the factors that we have indicated. We are not intending to say in any way that a judge sentencing a person for importing cannabis must necessarily make a minute comparison of the precise amounts and values of the cannabis imported with sentences imposed in other cases."

Appeal allowed.

NOTE

R. v. Aramah (1982) 4 Cr.App.R. (S.) 407 and *R. v. Daly and Whyte Watson* (1988) 10 Cr.App.R. (S.) 256: W. and another woman travelled together and between them they were found to be in possession of a total of 12 kilogrammes of cannabis, concealed in packages of fish in their suitcases. W.'s suitcase contained 7.4 kilogrammes with a street value of just over £11,000. W. was sentenced to four years' imprisonment which on appeal was held not to be in line with the *Aramah* principles and it was reduced to two years. Roch, J. observed (at p. 257): "We remind ourselves that what was said in *Aramah* was said for the guidance of sentencing courts and was not intended to be construed and applied as if it were a section of an Act of Parliament." *R. v Harris* (1989) 11 Cr.App.R. (S.) 169 is a further example of importation of a "modest quantity" of a Class B drug (6.02 kilogrammes of herbal cannabis valued at about £4,000).

2.5.63

12. R. v. Sturt
(1993) 14 Cr.App.R. (S.) 440

S. was convicted of attempting to evade the restriction on the importation of cannabis. The appellant, through a company, rented a warehouse in Spain in which 217 kilogrammes of cannabis were found concealed in a load of ceramic tiles. The tiles were imported into England, after the cannabis had been removed. He was sentenced to nine years' imprisonment.

Held, the sentencer was justified in concluding that the appellant had played a major role in the enterprise and the sentence was appropriate.

Appeal dismissed.

2.5.64

13. R. v. Elder and Pyle
(1994) 15 Cr.App.R. (S.) 514

The appellants pleaded guilty to two counts of being knowingly concerned in the fraudulent evasion of the prohibition on the importation of a controlled drug; one count related to herbal cannabis and the other to cannabis resin. The appellants arrived in Dover and were found to be in possession of 200 grammes of cannabis resin and 700 grammes of herbal cannabis. They admitted buying the cannabis in Amsterdam for about £1,800, and bringing it back for their own consumption. It was accepted that they did not intend to supply others. They were sentenced to nine months' imprisonment, suspended, in each case.

Held, if the offences did not cross the threshold beyond which only a custodial sentence could be justified, there was no possible basis on which the sentence could be suspended; the sentencer did not identify any circumstances which made the case exceptional. The question was whether the offences were so serious that only a custodial sentence could be justified. In *Aramah, supra*, the Court had said that importation of small quantities of cannabis for personal use could be dealt with as though they were cases of simple possession. In the absence of any previous conviction for drugs offences on the part of either appellant, the Court had come to the conclusion that the offences did not cross the custody threshold and could properly be dealt with by a community sentence. The Court would substitute a community service order for 180 hours in each case.

Appeals allowed.

14. R. v. Klitkze   **2.5.65**
(1995) 16 Cr.App.R. (S.) 445

K. pleaded guilty to being knowingly concerned in the fraudulent evasion of the prohibition on the importation of a controlled drug. He was concerned in importing 15.28 kilogrammes of hemp cannabis concealed in a crate containing compressors. He was sentenced to five years' imprisonment.

Held, that this was a case of the importation of a not insubstantial quantity of cannabis in a sophisticated manner for personal gain. The starting point was somewhere in the region of four years, that could be reduced to reflect the appellant's personal background, plea of guilty and co-operation with the authorities to three years.

EBSWORTH, J. (at p. 46): "[T]his was a relatively sophisticated offence; it was an organised enterprise, and this appellant's role was not that of a mere courier being used by others for their part for a lump sum payment but it was a matter which was organised for his own commercial purposes. That, quite clearly, since there was going to be a distribution in this country, takes it outside the ordinary run of courier cases."

Appeal allowed and sentence varied.

D. SENTENCING: EXPORTATION   **2.6**

Class B: Cannabis   **2.6.1**

1. R. v. Otjen   **2.6.2**
(1981) 3 Cr.App.R. (S.) 186

O. was on a plane on a journey from Nigeria to Amsterdam. The flight was expected to land at Heathrow, and it did. Passengers completing the whole journey, of whom O. was one, were not expected to leave the plane. By chance the passengers were required to leave one plane that was being taken out of service and to board another.

A security check of hand luggage revealed two packages in O.'s possession. The packages contained in total 3.84 kilogrammes of herbal cannabis said to have a street value of £6,000 or so.

Later O. pleaded guilty to being knowingly concerned in the fraudulent evasion of the prohibition on the importation of controlled drugs. He admitted a number of previous convictions including smuggling cannabis. He was sentenced to two and a half years' imprisonment and recommended for deportation. He appealed against sentence.

On appeal counsel submitted that, firstly, it was a technical importation. It was an importation, because goods are imported into this country the moment the aircraft lands. Secondly, it was never intended that these drugs should be distributed in this country; they were always destined for Amsterdam. This appellant never anticipated that he would leave the aircraft or take any active steps to deceive the British authorities as to the presence of the drug.

GRIFFITHS, L.J. (at p. 188): "This is a case which has to be viewed against the undoubted fact that the drug trade is an international business carried on to the detriment of citizens in all civilised countries, and this country owes a duty to other civilised countries to do all in its power to deter this trade, whether or not the drugs are intended for consumption in this country or some other country. It would be quite wrong for this country to say, having apprehended a courier carrying a very large quantity of drugs: 'Well, we will have nothing to do with it, because the drugs were destined for another country.' If we were to take that attitude, it would be inviting all the couriers to use our airports for the purpose of distributing illegal drugs."

Appeal dismissed.

CHAPTER THREE

Conspiracy 3.1

Introduction 3.2

In Scotland conspiracy is a crime at common law. In England and Wales conspiracy is an offence created by section 1(1) of the Criminal Law Act 1977 and amended by section 5 of the Criminal Attempts Act 1981.

A. LAW 3.3

1. R. v. Ardalan 3.3.1
[1972] 2 All E.R. 258

For the facts of this case see *supra*, at paragraph **2.3.2**

ROSKILL, L.J. (at p. 261): "[Counsel for the appellant] criticised the learned judge by reference to the fact that at two places in the summing-up he is said not to have drawn the jury's attention sufficiently clearly to what it was of which they had to be sure before they could convict any of the appellants of conspiracy. He made particular complaint that the judge talked about 'the cartwheel type of conspiracy'; that he talked about 'sub-conspiracies' and that later on he talked about 'the chain type of conspiracy'. It is said that the learned judge never made plain to the jury to what it was they had to direct their attention.

It is right to say that these epithets, or labels, such as 'cartwheels' and 'chains' have a certain respectable ancestry and have been used in a number of conspiracy cases that from time to time have come before the courts. Metaphors are invaluable for the purpose of illustrating a particular point or a particular concept to a jury, but there is a limit to the utility of a metaphor and there is sometimes a danger, if metaphors are used excessively, that a point of time arises at which the metaphor tends to obscure rather than to clarify."

And later (at p. 262)

"Care must be taken that the use of words or phrases such as 'wheels', 'cartwheels', 'chains', 'sub-conspiracies' and so on are used only to illustrate and to clarify the principle and for no other purpose."

Appeals dismissed.

3.3.2   **2. D.P.P. v. Doot**
                           [1973] 1 All E.R. 940

D. and four other American citizens agreed in either Belgium or Morocco that they would import unlawfully cannabis resin into England with the object of re-exporting it to the United States. The controlled drug was concealed in three vehicles which were shipped to England. The vehicles, the controlled drug and the conspirators were all found at various times and places in England. They were charged on an indictment which libelled a locus of "in Hampshire and elsewhere" and they were convicted of conspiracy to import the controlled drug.

On appeal, the Court of Appeal quashed the conviction holding that the English courts did not have jurisdiction to try the offence charged since the essence of the offence was the agreement amongst them to do the unlawful act, the offence was complete when the agreement had been made and the agreement had been made abroad. The Crown appealed to the House of Lords.

LORD WILBERFORCE (at p. 943): "the truth is that, in the normal case of a conspiracy carried out, or partly carried out, in this country, the location of the formation of the agreement is irrelevant; the attack on the laws of this country is identical wherever the conspirators happened to meet; the 'conspiracy' is a complex, formed indeed, but not severally completed, at the first meeting of the plotters.

A legal principle which would enable concerting law breakers to escape a conspiracy charge by crossing the Channel before making their agreement or to bring forward arguments, which we know can be subtle enough, as to the location of agreements or, conversely, which would encourage the prosecution into allegation or fiction of a renewed agreement in this country, all this with compensating merit, is not one which I could endorse."

VISCOUNT DILHORNE (at p. 949): "Though the offence of conspiracy is complete when the agreement to do the unlawful act is made and it is not necessary for the prosecution to do more than prove the making of such an agreement, a conspiracy does not end with the making of the agreement. It continues so long as the parties to the agreement intend to carry it out. It may be joined by others, some may leave it. Proof of acts done by the accused in this country may suffice to prove there was at the time of those acts a conspiracy in existence in this country to which they were parties and if that is proved, then the charge of conspiracy is within the jurisdiction of the English courts, even though the initial agreement was made outside the jurisdiction."

LORD PEARSON (at p. 951): "A conspiracy involves an agreement express or implied. A conspiratorial agreement is not a contract, not legally binding, because it is unlawful. But as an agreement it has its three stages, namely (1) making or formation (2) performance or implementation (3) discharge or termination. When the conspirational agreement has been made, the offence of conspiracy is complete, it has been committed, and the conspirators can be prosecuted even though no performance has taken place [*R.* v. *Aspinall* (1876) 2 Q.B.D. 48, at pp. 58, 59], *per* Brett, J.A. But the fact that the offence of conspiracy is complete at that stage does not mean that the conspiratorial agreement is finished with. It is not dead. If it is being performed, it is very much alive. So long as the performance continues, it is operating, it is being carried out by the conspirators, and it is governing or at any rate influencing their conduct. The conspiratorial agreement continues in operation and therefore in existence until it is discharged (terminated) by completion of its performance or by abandonment or frustration or however it may be.

On principle, apart from authority, I think ... a conspiracy to commit in England an offence against English law ought to be triable in England if it has been wholly or partly performed in England. In such a case the conspiracy has been carried on in England with the consent and authority of all the conspirators. It is not necessary that they should all be present in England. One of them, acting on his own behalf and as agent for the others, has been performing their agreement, with their consent and authority, in England. In such a case the conspiracy has been committed by all of them in England. Be it granted that 'All crime is local' and 'The jurisdiction over the crime belongs to the country where the crime is committed' (*per* Lord Halsbury, L.C. in *Macleod* v. *Attorney-General for New South Wales* [[1891] A.C. 455, at p. 458]). The crime of conspiracy in the present case was committed in England, personally or through an agent or agents, by all the conspirators."

LORD SALMON (at p. 956): "It is obvious that a conspiracy to carry out a bank robbery is equally a threat to the Queen's peace whether it is hatched, say, in Birmingham or in Brussels. Accordingly, having regard to the special nature of the offence a conspiracy to commit a crime in England is, in my opinion, an offence against the common law even when entered into abroad, certainly if acts in furtherance of the conspiracy are done in this country. There can in such circumstances be no doubt that the conspiracy is in fact as well as in theory a real threat to the Queens' peace ...

If a conspiracy is entered into abroad to commit a crime in England, exactly the same public mischief is produced by it as if it had been entered into here."

Appeal allowed. Convictions restored.

NOTE

The speeches in the House of Lords in Doot's case were made on March 21, 1973. Since that date the law of England regarding conspiracy has been much changed with the introduction of the statutory offence: section (1) of the Criminal Law Act 1977, as amended by section 5 of the Criminal Attempt Act 1981. But Doot's case is still binding in England and Wales and is highly persuasive in Scotland, partly because the law relating to conspiracy in the latter is still in a relatively early state of development, comparatively.

In *R. v. Borro v. Abdullah* [1973] Crim.L.R. 513, counsel sought to distinguish the circumstances there from Doot's case: it was said, for example, that in an agreement to import cannabis resin into the United Kingdom there was no evidence that the Queen's peace was likely to be breached. The court held, in answer to that point, that it was not correct to say that the agreement did not threaten the Queen's peace. It involved the illegal possession of the drug within the jurisdiction, where it could possibly be dealt with other than by export.

3.3.3   **3. R. v. El-Ghazal**
                         [1986] Crim.L.R. 52

G. was asked by T. to arrange a meeting between T. and C. so that T. and C. could "make a deal about cocaine". The three met and T. and C. agreed that C. would purchase cocaine for T. It was also agreed that T. and C. should cheat the seller of his money. G. went with T. and C. to the meeting with the seller but G. left soon after as he said he knew the others were about to do "something funny" regarding payment. Later G. and T. visited C.'s flat but C. had already been arrested in possession of controlled drugs. There was no evidence that G. would have received any of the cocaine or made a profit out of the transaction.

On conviction G. appealed and it was *held* that the trial judge had left the matter to the jury correctly, namely that if they were sure that T. was asking to be introduced to C. so that one of them could obtain cocaine and G. knew that to be the purpose of the introduction then he was entering into an agreement to procure cocaine for one of them. There had been no suggestion that G. had pulled out at any stage.

Appeal dismissed.

3.3.4   **4. R. v. McGowan**
                         [1990] Crim.L.R. 399

M. was a qualified chemist who assisted another to produce holograms using amphetamine sulphate. Policemen found chemicals and notes both belonging to M. and both necessary to make amphetamine sulphate. He told the policemen that he would have made amphetamine sulphate and then sold it. At his trial on a charge of conspiracy to produce a controlled drug he denied these admissions to the police and offered an innocent explanation of his actions.

Counsel on both sides said in their speeches to the jury that the burden of proof rested on the Crown throughout. But the trial judge directed the jury that although the preliminary burden of proof was on the Crown, the burden of proving lack of knowledge or suspicion that the substance was a controlled drug was on M., on the authority of section 28(2) of the 1971 Act.

On conviction M. appealed and it was *held* that there had been a misdirection. In *R. v. Cuthbertson* [1981] A.C. 470, Lord Diplock had decided (at p. 481) that conspiracies were not "offences under the [1971] Act" for the purpose of seeking forfeiture of relevant articles by section 27 of that Act.

Section 28, relating to the burden of proof, should be construed similarly. Section 28(1) listed the offences to which that section applied and conspiracy was not one of them. The burden of proof remained throughout on the Crown where conspiracy was charged.

Appeal allowed and conviction quashed.

NOTE
The difficulty in McGowan's case arose out of the English practice of charging a conspiracy to contravene an Act of Parliament: a similar practice arose in *R. v. Siracusa* [1989] Crim.L.R. 712, where the charge was one of conspiring to be knowingly concerned in the fraudulent evasion of the prohibition on the importation of controlled drugs. It was held that the *mens rea* sufficient to support the commission of a substantive offence will not necessarily be sufficient to support a charge of conspiracy to commit that offence. That was certainly so in McGowan's case where different burdens applied in the conspiracy charge from those that would have been applied in a charge of producing a controlled drug.

5. R. v. Sansom   **3.3.5**
(1991) 92 Cr.App.R. 115

Four appellants, including S., were charged with conspiracy to evade the prohibition on the importation of controlled drugs. It was admitted that an agreement had been entered into to import cannabis resin from Morocco to a European country. It was the prosecution case that the intention was to import the drugs into England, whereas the defence maintained that the drugs were destined for Belgium. An English-owned vessel sailing from Morocco with the drugs met a British-registered fishing boat in the English Channel. The drugs were transferred to the fishing boat. The vessel sailed into Plymouth harbour where she was stopped. Those on board were arrested. The fishing boat sailed back up the Channel before being stopped the following day, in water claimed by the prosecution to be British territorial waters, and by the defence to be international waters. A large quantity of cannabis having been found on the boat, those on board were arrested. The common defence was that the object of the enterprise was to take the cannabis to Belgium, not to England. Various documents, not disclosed to the defence, were put to two of the appellants in cross-examination. A submission that the court had no jurisdiction to try the count of conspiracy, on the ground that the agreement was alleged to have been made abroad, and since the fishing boat was arrested outside territorial waters, no unlawful act in England in pursuance of the conspiracy had been established, was rejected. All four appellants were convicted.

On appeal it was contended, *inter alia*, that the court had no jurisdiction.

Held, that since there was clear evidence of an unlawful act in that one of the appellants had acted in England in pursuance of the alleged conspiracy which was still subsisting by commissioning the fishing vessel and sailing her to collect the cannabis, and sufficient evidence from which the jury could infer an intention to import the cannabis to England, the Court had jurisdiction to hear the charge of conspiracy.

Appeal allowed on another ground.

3.4 B. SENTENCING

3.4.1   **1. R. v. Kemp**
                                        (1979) 69 Cr.App.R. 330

K. and another had been sentenced to 13 years' imprisonment after being convicted of conspiring to manufacture, produce and distribute lysergide. Various distributors received sentences ranging from three to 11 years' imprisonment. All applied for leave to appeal against sentence.

ROSKILL, L.J. (at p. 352): "[T]he learned judge dealt with those who manufactured and produced at the top of the scale. He then graded those who were responsible for distribution towards the bottom.

The gravamen of the submissions ... has been that the learned judge got the apportionment of blame wrong, because one can perhaps be shown to have had fewer tablets in his possession than another or one can be shown to have made a lesser profit than another out of this distribution. So far as it is possible to gauge the truth in relation to quantities, either of cash or tablets, the point has a modicum of substance. But the sentences in these cases do not have to be assessed on a percentage basis by reference to who had what, who distributed what, who gained what. Some no doubt gained more than others.

What the learned judge had to do was apportion the blame, the degree of responsibility, as he saw it, and we see nothing wrong whatever with the sentences which he passed."

Application refused.

2. R. v. Carrington   3.4.2
Court of Appeal (Criminal Division) May 15, 1981

C. was convicted of conspiring to contravene the provisions of the 1971 Act. At the material times he was a detective sergeant in the Drugs Squad of the Metropolitan Police. That squad had seized 11 $\frac{1}{2}$ cwts. of cannabis which later should have been destroyed. Some of it was removed before destruction.

Thereafter C. supplied a man with about 950 lbs. of this cannabis. That man received something like £63,000 for his efforts in selling some of it. When C.'s house was searched £6,000 was recovered, "and admittedly represented", the proceeds of C.'s activities.

C. was sentenced to seven years' imprisonment and he appealed against sentence.

LORD LANE, C.J.: "[One] is bound to observe, if it needs observation, that this type of offence committed by this type of man, a sergeant in the Drug Squad at the Metropolitan Police, strikes at the very foundation of justice and that may be a cliché, but it is a necessary cliché in these circumstances. These types of offences undermine the whole administration of the criminal law. One does not have to attend very many trials in this part of the country to realise what the effect of this sort of behaviour by [a] police officer means so far as the administration of justice is concerned, what it means so far as deliberations of juries are concerned. It cannot be too strongly emphasised that these offences are as grave as any can be so far as justice is concerned and in those circumstances, though it grieves us in many ways to have to do it, we are bound to say that there is nothing wrong in the length of this sentence."

Appeal dismissed.

2. R. v. Shaw   3.4.3
(1986) 8 Cr.App.R. (S.) 16

S. used false names saying that he represented a real company and, later, that he was in business for himself. By this means he was able to purchase 112 $\frac{1}{2}$ litres of benzyl methyl ketone (BMK), an essential ingredient in the manufacture of amphetamine sulphate. The total cost of the BMK was about £7,700 which was paid in cash. Premises used by S. were searched and other chemicals were found, chemicals also necessary to manufacture amphetamine sulphate.

S. declined initially to assist the police but later offered information about others involved in the plan, and locations of a factory and so on if the prosecution was dropped. This was refused. At the subsequent trial S. explained that he thought the BMK was to be used in the manufacture of synthetic perfume. He was convicted of conspiracy to produce a controlled drug.

S. was sentenced to 10 years' imprisonment and he applied for leave to appeal against sentence. That was refused by a single judge and he renewed his application.

LEGGAT, J. (at p. 18): "The approach which this Court adopts, and has urged upon lower courts in sentencing in respect of drugs offences, was set out in the judgment of the Court delivered by my Lord, the Lord Chief Justice, in *Aramah* (1983) 76 Cr.App.R. 190. At page 193 the Court said this: 'Large scale or wholesale importation of massive quantities [of Class B Drugs] will justify sentences in the region of 10 years' imprisonment for those playing other than a subordinate role. Supply of cannabis: here again the supply of massive quantities will justify sentences in the region of 10 years for those playing anything other than a subordinate role.'

Manufacture is analogous with importation. This conspiracy to produce amphetamine unlawfully on a massive scale can only have been for illicit supply... .

As to the reference to vast profits, according to the estimate of the applicant's counsel, the value of the drugs which might, and one must assume would, have been manufactured was between £2 million and £7 million."

And later (at p. 19)

"[T]he inference might well be drawn, as the learned judge drew it, that the applicant was one of the ringleaders. On any view, he was not acting in any subordinate role. The larger the amount in which a man is shown to have been dealing, the nearer to the top of an organisation is he likely to be."

Application refused.

NOTE

In *R. v. Rubenstein and Grandison* (1982) 4 Cr.App.R. (S.) 202 (at p. 204) Lord Lane C.J. held that "the offence of producing a drug is closely analogous to the offence of smuggling drugs. Just as the gravity of smuggling depends primarily upon the quantity, so the gravity of producing depends primarily upon the quantity."

That point has been restated, it is submitted, in another form in *R. v. Shaw* when manufacture was said to be analogous to importation.

3.4.4 **4. R. v. Patel**
(1987) 9 Cr.App.R. (S.) 319

P. was convicted of conspiring to supply diamorphine and sentenced to 12 years' imprisonment, on the basis that the "street value" of the diamorphine (1.99 kilogrammes and 55 per cent purity) was about £750,000, and that was the sentencing range indicated for such an amount in *R. v. Aramah*. On appeal evidence was called by the appellant and the prosecution to establish the true street value of the drug.

WATKINS, L.J. (at p. 320): "In sentencing, His Honour Judge Rubin, with the case of *Aramah* in mind, said: 'When one is dealing with quantities in the region of one million pounds or upwards, the right sentence is one of 12 to 14 years ... it seems to me that you were the consignee ... of heroin worth ... something like three quarters of a million pounds on the market' and on that basis he passed a 12 year sentence. That estimate had been given at the trial and apparently had not been challenged. However, [counsel for the appellant] did challenge it before the Court who granted leave, stating, 'there should be available for the full court evidence to support the valuation contended for'.

Accordingly, the case was listed before this Court when the appellant called a witness from the agency Release, namely, its Assistant Director, Mrs Perry, who gave seemingly authoritative evidence that the value of the drug involved was £160,000 approximately or only just over a fifth of the amount that the learned judge had based his sentence on. Notice of the outline of this evidence had been with the prosecution in the form of an affidavit from the director of Release for approximately a month before the hearing. However, the prosecution had not served any counter notice of evidence on the appellant, but at the hearing called Detective Sergeant Naylor, the officer in the case, who gave evidence in support of his original valuation. Faced with those totally divergent figures, each coming from a reputable source, the Court adjourned the matter so that authoritative figures could be obtained from the Drug Squad and other official sources, observing that 'it is not right that this Court should proceed under any kind of misapprehension'.

When the case was relisted, the prosecution called Mr Galpin from the National Drugs Intelligence Unit, who are the national clearing house for all drug information. On hearing his evidence the earlier conflict of evidence was considerably easier to understand and there was a large measure of common ground between him and Mrs Perry.

The Court was here dealing with 1.99 kilogrammes of heroin at 55 per cent. purity and Mrs Perry was assuming that it would be sold on the street as good quality at between 40 and 55 per cent. purity. Dealing with London street value, he and Mrs Perry were agreed that the present price for a gramme of heroin of good quality was £80. This would be sold in 'wraps' for approximately $1/8$ of a gramme for £10 the wrap. Even medical heroin is not more than 90 per cent. pure. Smuggled heroin is never that pure and the heroin content diminishes as it is traded from hand to hand and 'cut' or adulterated with other substances to increase the bulk of the powder. The amount to which it has been cut will not be readily apparent to the purchaser at the point of purchase. As a rough guide, the lighter and less bitter the drug is, the more adulterated and weaker it is. But until he uses the drug he will have no accurate idea of the strength of it and could well buy poor quality for the price of good. The result of this is that on the street the same basic quantity of heroin could make double the amount of wraps if it is sold at 20 per cent. purity as if it is sold at 40 per cent. purity, and yet the wraps could be sold to even a moderately discerning purchaser for the same price per wrap.

The difference in this case arose from the fact that Mrs Perry was assuming a purity of upwards of 40 per cent. and Sergeant Naylor a purity of between seven and nine per cent. Her evidence was that with the regrettable increase of heroin on the market in recent years so users have become more discerning and have turned in increasing numbers from injecting to smoking, and diluted doses at seven to 15 per cent. purity would not be acceptable to smokers. Sergeant Naylor, on the other hand, said that in his experience the degree of purity varied from between 75 per cent. and 0.4 of one per cent. (clearly a 'rip-off' consignment) and that it was not unreasonable to work on the figures that he had taken. Mr Galpin assisted with some statistical information: of 85 quantities of drug seized in the first quarter of 1985, the mean purity was 40 per cent. But, as one would expect, as the drug became more cut in passing from hand to hand, the smaller the quantities, the less the purity. So of the 21 samples that were less than a gramme (*i.e.* more representative of what would be likely to change hands on the street) the mean purity was 30 per cent., though he suggested that this figure should be regarded as too high, because a gramme was too high a ceiling for a sample designed to reflect street trade. He clearly had in mind a figure between 15 per cent. and 20 per cent. At 10 per cent., he conceded that the user would regard it as 'bad gear' and would not patronise that supplier again for choice, but would still regard heroin that impure as a saleable commodity, *i.e.* as being above the 'rip-off' level.

It would be apparent from that evidence that:
(1) The so called street value of heroin depends very much on the assumption as to purity made in the calculations. Different assumptions can give very different results.
(2) The street value of this drug varies considerably from city to city — in some cases by nearly two to one; and
(3) An all too ready availability of the drug can result in a fairly substantial drop in the market price.

These are factors which obviously tend to cause the use of the street value of heroin as a yardstick to translate quantities of the drug into financial terms as an aid to sentencing to be regarded with caution. So long as it is relied upon as a rough yardstick we see no reason why judges should not measure the length of sentence to some degree by it.

With those words of warning in mind, we examine the yardstick used by the judge in this case. It seems to us, had he the benefit of the evidence which we have heard, he would have estimated a street value for the heroin he was concerned with at a figure of a little in excess of £300,000. With that assistance he may well have concluded that a sentence of 10 years' imprisonment would have been appropriate. That is our conclusion.

Accordingly, we quash the sentence of 12 years' imprisonment and substitute for it one of 10 years' imprisonment. To that extent this appeal is allowed."

Appeal allowed and sentence varied accordingly.

5. R. v. Hutton and Aslam   3.4.5
(1988) 9 Cr.App.R. (S.) 484

The appellants pleaded guilty to conspiring to supply heroin. A. admitted supplying H. with heroin on two occasions: the amount was between three and four grammes with a value of something over £300. H. admitted receiving heroin from A. but his admission was not limited to two occasions. They were sentenced to four years' imprisonment (H.) and six years' imprisonment (A.).

Held (considering *Bilinski, supra*), earlier decisions had now to be considered in the light of what was said in *Bilinski* and the fact that Class A drugs were now treated more seriously as a result of Controlled Drugs (Penalties) Act 1985, which increased the maximum term for importing a Class A controlled drug from 14 years to life. However, it was important to bear in mind what was decided in *Bilinski*, which involved a very substantial importation of heroin, worth about £600,000. The sentence was reduced on account of the appellant's plea and the assistance he had given to the authorities by naming his suppliers. The sentence which would have been considered appropriate on the facts of *Bilinski* if the case had been contested, 12 years, was reduced on account of these factors to eight years. *Bilinski* was a valuable authority, demonstrating the increased gravity with which cases of importing or supplying heroin are treated, and also showing the importance which is attached by the Court to any assistance which is given to the authorities by persons who plead guilty which will help to clear up other trafficking in heroin. The Court would look at the sentences on the appellants in the present case, treating them on the same basis except for one mitigating feature. In the case of A., having regard to the quantity and his plea of guilty, the appropriate sentence would be four years' imprisonment. In the case of H., there was the added feature of the assistance he gave to the authorities, for which he should receive some discount additional to that received for the plea. His sentence would be reduced to three years' imprisonment.

Appeal allowed and sentences varied.

6. R. v. Hopes   3.4.6
(1989) 11 Cr.App.R. (S.) 38

H. pleaded guilty to conspiring to supply a controlled drug, being concerned in the importation of a controlled drug and being in possession of a controlled drug. He was "at the heart of the conspiracy."

H. recruited others and provided the money. The conspiracy materialised in the importation of two and a half kilogrammes of heroin of 90 per cent purity, which arrived in the United Kingdom in March 1986. He was himself the carrier and he had discussions with another about future deliveries. The street value of the quantity actually brought in was said to be £2 million.

H. was sentenced to 16 years' imprisonment concurrent on each of the first two charges with no separate penalty on the third. He appealed against sentence.

STAUGHTON, L.J. (at p. 41): "These drugs cases pose a difficult problem for the sentencer because one has no sympathy whatever for the defendant, and therefore the danger is that one may allow one's disgust at the offence and its consequence to override all other considerations. However, not so long ago Parliament increased the maximum sentence for this type of offence to life imprisonment. In *Bilinski* (1987) Cr.App.R. (S.) 360, this Court said that for a major importation of a Class A drug on this scale one should look at a sentence of 14 years and upwards.

We are not here dealing simply with the importation of two and a half kilogrammes of heroin, whether the street value is £2 million or less. We are dealing with a conspiracy to import on a large scale for a continuing period of time. People were engaged, arrangements were made, and had it not been detected it would have caused further importations on a very large scale.

In those circumstances, despite the plea of guilty and the appellant's help to the police, we do not feel able to say that the sentence of 16 years' imprisonment was wrong."

Appeal dismissed.

3.4.7   **7. R. v. Taylor**
                    (1991) 12 Cr.App.R. (S.) 665

The appellants pleaded guilty to conspiring to produce amphetamine sulphate. Two of the appellants were employed in a chemical company as laboratory assistants; they attempted to produce amphetamine sulphate over a period of about a year, without success: they did attempt to sell a diluted and adulterated version of a substance which they had purchased through their employers. They were sentenced to two years' imprisonment or detention in a young offenders institution.

Held, sentences of 12 months' imprisonment or detention in a young offenders institution would be sufficient.

8. Attorney-General's Reference No. 16 of 1991   **3.4.8**
(1992) 13 Cr.App.R. (S.) 653

The offender, William Clark, was convicted of conspiring to supply a Class A drug (heroin), possessing heroin with intent to supply, possession of a firearm with intent to commit an indictable offence, false imprisonment and unlawful possession of ammunition. It was shown that for a period of about six months before his arrest the offender was a dealer of heroin in a substantial way, acting as a wholesaler supplying to others who were dealing in heroin at street level. It was alleged that the offender bought two ounces of heroin each day for about £1,000 per ounce and sold it again for £3,200. The offender's profits from drug trafficking were assessed at £200,000 for the purposes of the Drug Trafficking Offences Act 1986. The offences of false imprisonment and possession of a firearm and ammunition related to an incident in the course of which the offender threatened a former girlfriend with a gun, which was fired out of a window; the incident ended in a siege by armed police. Sentenced to seven years' imprisonment for the conspiracy to supply heroin, with 12 months' consecutive for the false imprisonment and firearm offences. The Attorney-General asked the Court to review the sentence on the ground that it was unduly lenient.

Held, the sentence for the heroin offence was well below what might have been expected for supplying heroin in this quantity and for this amount of profit. The sentence was unduly lenient, and fell outside the proper bounds of the sentence which a judge could legitimately impose. The sentence for conspiring to supply heroin would be increased to 10 years, with five years' concurrent for possession with intent to supply; the sentences for the firearm offences would be increased to three years, consecutive to the 10 years, making a total of 13 years.

LORD LANE, C.J. (at p. 655): "We have been helpfully referred to a number of authorities on the question of the proper length of sentence so far as supplying of heroin is concerned. There is perhaps no need for us to refer in any detail to the well known case of *Aramah*, [*supra*], or the equally well known case of *Bilinski*, [*supra*]. It is plain on the basis of those two cases and upon other cases which have been cited to us, namely the cases of *Ashraf*, [*infra*] and *Patel*, [*supra*], that this sentence in respect of the heroin is well below what one would have expected to be imposed for supplying heroin in this quantity and at this sort of profit.

We have been asked in a concise address by [counsel for the offender] to treat this as a case which might just pass as being within the proper limits of a judge's discretion, particularly a judge as experienced as this one undoubtedly was.

Unhappily we do not feel able to agree with that submission. It seems to us that this sentence was unduly lenient, in that it fell outside the proper bounds of a sentence which a judge in these circumstances could legitimately impose. Our view is that on count 1, the conspiracy to supply a Class A controlled drug, the sentence should be one of ten years' imprisonment; on count 2, the possession with intent to supply 49.16 grammes of heroin should have been one of five years' imprisonment to run concurrently with the 10. So far as the rest of the counts are concerned, the possession of the firearm and the possession of the ammunition should each be visited by a term of three years' imprisonment. The false imprisonment which was part of the same story should be met by a term of one year's imprisonment, all those three sentences to run concurrently with each other, but consecutively to the 10 years on the first two counts. The total sentence therefore will be one of 13 years' imprisonment, as opposed to the eight years imposed by the learned judge. To that extent this reference succeeds."

Sentences varied.

NOTE

The circumstances of an appeal against sentence resulting in an increased sentence can vary between Scotland, on the one hand, and England and Wales, on the other: compare section 118(4)(b) of the Criminal Procedure (Scotland) Act 1995 with section 36 of the Criminal Justice Act 1988; the latter power can be used only where the offence concerned is triable only on indictment and conspiracy is always triable only on indictment, even though the intended offence is an either way offence.

3.4.9   **9. R. v. Couzens and Frankel**
(1993) 14 Cr.App.R. (S.) 33

The appellants were convicted of conspiring to produce a Class A drug (MDMA). The appellants were alleged to have produced the drug experimentally on a small scale within the United Kingdom, with a view to producing it on a large scale in Yugoslavia, where it was not prohibited. They were sentenced to nine years' imprisonment (Frankel) and six years' imprisonment (Couzens).

Held, the sentencing judge was entitled to take into account the appellant's intention to produce the drug abroad on a large scale. The sentences were appropriate.

Appeals dismissed.

3.4.10   **10. R. v. King**
(1993) 14 Cr.App.R. (S.) 252

The first appellant pleaded guilty to conspiring to produce a controlled drug, amphetamine sulphate. The first appellant purchased a rabbit farm and arranged its conversion to a sophisticated factory for the production of amphetamine. When the premises were raided by police, equipment and chemicals capable of producing amphetamine with a potential street value of between £5 million and £10 million. He was sentenced to 10 years' imprisonment.

Held, the sentencer had taken 12 years as the upper limit from which to compute the various sentences on the different defendants. He had allowed the first appellant a discount of two years for his plea, which was entered only after his co-defendant had given evidence against him. There were no grounds for criticising the sentence.

Appeal dismissed.

11. R. v. Rescorl   **3.4.11**
(1993) 14 Cr.App.R. (S.) 522

The appellants (with one exception) pleaded guilty to conspiracy to import cannabis, and all pleaded guilty to conspiracy to supply cannabis. They were concerned in an attempt to import 320 kilogrammes of cannabis by sea. The appellant Rescorl, who was considered to be a prime mover, was sentenced to nine years' imprisonment with a confiscation order in the amount of £21,000.

Held, this was a major operation involving cannabis worth over £1 million. The sentence of nine years, allowing for the appellant's plea, was perfectly proper in principle. The confiscation order would be reduced to £10,000.

MACPHERSON, J. (at p. 524): "This Court is wholly satisfied that this was a major conspiracy involving a large weight of drugs, probably 800 pounds with a street value of over £1 million, so we are told. It may be that there are other cases where more is brought in, but this was a major importation and we are not persuaded that a starting point of nine years was wrong or can be criticised. It could mean that after a contest the sentence would have been 11 or 12 years, but in the judgment of this Court, in respect of Miss Rescorl nine years was a perfectly proper sentence in principle."

Appeal dismissed.

12. R. v. Murphy   **3.4.12**
(1994) 15 Cr.App.R. (S.) 329

The appellants were convicted of conspiring to produce amphetamine. They were concerned with others in ordering various chemicals required to produce amphetamine and metylamphetamine. They were sentenced to five years' imprisonment in each case.

Held, the sentences were not excessive.

BLOFELD, J. (at p. 330): "This case was before a very experienced judge who has close knowledge of the drug scene in Liverpool — unhappily a city which is plagued with drug problems. In due course, he came to sentence all three men. He took the view that Barrett, having pleaded guilty, although he was by far the most important of these three men he had to sentence, should be sentenced to five years' imprisonment. Counsel for the appellants both submit that the sentences passed on their clients were too long in comparison. They say that the part they each played, in respect of Murphy and Kenny, indicated that they were effectively minnows. This Court does not agree. They both played an important role, even though they were subsidiary, in a very serious conspiracy. If successful, it might have caused untold havoc to many innocent lives."

Appeal refused.

CHAPTER FOUR

Production and Supply **4.1**

Introduction **4.2**

The Misuse of Drugs Act 1971 provides by section 4 for offences relating to the production of a controlled drug and to the supply of a controlled drug to another.

A. LAW: PRODUCTION **4.3**

(i) Production **4.3.1**

1. R. v. Farr **4.3.2**
[1982] Crim.L.R. 745

F. admitted to the police that on one occasion two people arrived at his house and asked to use his kitchen. He agreed even though he knew that these two people produced "pink heroin". F. was charged with an offence under section 4(2) and he was convicted. He had not been charged with an offence of allowing his premises to be used for the production of a drug under section 8 of the 1971 Act.

Held, on appeal that F.'s conviction would be quashed. There must be established some identifiable participation in the process of producing a controlled drug before a person could be convicted under section 4. There would have been no answer to a charge of contravening section 8 of the 1971 Act but F. was not charged with that. Sections 4 and 8 are not mutually exclusive.

Appeal allowed.

NOTE
Appended to the above report is a commentary concerning a "speculative interpretation" to the effect that section 4(2) excludes the ordinary (English) law of aiding and abetting. Being "concerned in" is said to cover much that would amount to aiding and abetting under the general law and might, it is said, be held to be intended to take the place of the general law: [1982] Crim.L.R. 745–6.

It is also worth recalling that section 37(1) of the 1971 Act provides that "produce", where the reference to producing a controlled drug, means producing it by manufacture, cultivation or any other method, and "production" has a corresponding meaning.

4.3.3   **2. R. v. Russell**
                                (1992) 94 Cr.App.R. 351

Russell was charged, *inter alia*, with being in unlawful possession of a controlled drug (count 2) and supplying the same (count 2A). He had converted cocaine hydrochloride (a Class A prohibited drug) into free base cocaine by mixing the former with bicarbonate of soda and heating it. The result was a series of marble-like chips, free base cocaine, which was chemically different from cocaine hydrochloride. At his trial, after legal argument, the judge ruled that producing free base cocaine, or "crack", by the method described above, amounted to "production" of a controlled drug, for the purposes of section 4(2) of the 1971 Act. The appellant was thereupon re-arraigned and pleaded guilty to counts 1 and 5.

On appeal against the judge's ruling, *held*, that the conversion of one form of a Class A prohibited drug (cocaine hydrochloride) described in paragraph 4 of Sechedule 2 to the Misuse of Drugs Act 1971 into a substance described in paragraph 5 of that Schedule but not in paragraph 4, amounted to a "production" of the drug for the purposes of section 4(2) of the 1971 Act. It was the production of a substance, not by manufacture or cultivation but by other means, as defined by section 37(1) of the 1971 Act with physical and chemical features different from the cocaine hydrochloride from which it had sprung, even though it shared the same generic term — cocaine. Accordingly, the judge's ruling was correct and the appeal would be dismissed.

LORD LANE, C.J. (at p. 353): "The first and principal ground of appeal is that the learned judge was wrong to rule as he did that the conversion of cocaine hydrochloride into free base cocaine amounted in law to the production of a controlled drug. It was after that ruling that the appellant changed his plea to one of guilty on counts 2 and 2A.

The appellant in counts 2 and 2A was charged under sections 4(2)(b) and 4(2)(a) respectively of the Misuse of Drugs Act 1971, which provide that it is an offence for a person to produce or to be concerned in the production of a controlled drug. The particulars under these two counts stated that the controlled drug was of Class A, namely free base cocaine. The appellant's contention, put shortly, is that the converting of cocaine hydrochloride into free base cocaine does not amount to producing a Class A drug, because all that is being done is to change one form of cocaine (*i.e.* a salt of cocaine) into another form, namely free base cocaine.

The method of conversion is this. Cocaine hydrochloride, which is in a salt or powder form, is mixed with bicarbonate of soda and water and then heated. The result is a series of marble-like chips. That is the free base cocaine. The two forms were conceded to be chemically different and to have different physical properties. That is to say, cocaine hydrochloride is soluble in water, free base cocaine is not. Cocaine hydrochloride has a high melting point at 195 degrees centigrade and is not therefore suitable for smoking. Free base cocaine has a comparatively low melting point at about 90 degrees centigrade, vaporises easily and is therefore easy to smoke or inhale. Indeed that is the purpose of making it.

The following definitions are provided by the Act: By section 37, 'Produce', where the reference is to producing a controlled drug, means producing it by manufacture, cultivation, or any other method, and 'production' has a corresponding meaning. 'Controlled drug' has the meaning assigned by section 2 of the Act. Section 2 provides 'that the expression means any substance or product for the time being specified in Parts I, II, or III, of Schedule 2 of the Act.' Part I of Schedule 2 (Class A drugs), paragraph 1, lists, *inter alia*, the following substances and products: Coca leaf, cocaine. Paragraphs 2 and 3 are not material for the present purposes. Under paragraph 4 there is included, 'Any salt of a substance for the time being specified in any of paragraphs 1 to 3.' This would therefore include cocaine hydrochloride but not free base cocaine. Under paragraph 5 is included 'Any preparation or other product containing a substance or product for the time being specified in any of paragraphs 1 to 4.' This would include free base cocaine.

It is self-evident that the conversion of the coca leaf, by natural or chemical means, into cocaine hydrochloride would amount to production of cocaine hydrochloride — a salt of cocaine — although the generic drug, *i.e.* cocaine, remains the same. Thus, conversion of one form of Class A drug into another form of the same genus may be production. In our judgment, the conversion of the salt (described in paragraph 4 of Schedule 2) into a substance described in paragraph 5 but not in paragraph 4 amounts to a production. It is the production of a substance (not by manufacture or cultivation but by 'other means') with physical and chemical features different from the cocaine hydrochloride from which it springs, albeit sharing the same generic term, cocaine. In our judgment the ruling of Judge Morgan Hughes was correct and this ground of appeal fails."

Appeals dismissed.

The Court certified, under section 33(2) of the Criminal Appeal Act 1968 that the following point of law of general public importance was involved in its decision *viz.*: "Whether the conversion of one substance which is a controlled drug into a chemically and physically different substance which is also a controlled drug can constitute 'production' of a controlled drug within the meaning of the Misuse of Drugs Act 1971?" Leave to appeal to the House of Lords was refused.

4.3.4 *(ii) Conspiracy to produce*

4.3.5   **1. R. v. Nock**
                              [1978] Crim. L.R. 483

N. and A. were tried on indictment charging them with conspiracy to contravene section 4 of the 1971 Act. In evidence it was established that they agreed together to obtain cocaine by separating it from other substances contained in a powder. They had obtained the powder believing that it was a mixture of cocaine and lignocaine and that they could produce cocaine from it. In fact the powder was lignocaine hydrochloride, which contained no cocaine, so that it was impossible to produce cocaine from it. Convictions were upheld in the Court of Appeal and the matter went to the House of Lords.

Held, that it was decided (in English law) in *Houghton* v. *Smith* [1975] A.C. 476 that steps on the way to the doing of something which was thereafter done (or would have been done if not interrupted by some supervening event) and which was not a crime, could not be regarded as attempts to commit a crime.

In the instant case the question arose whether when two or more persons agreed on a course of conduct with the object of committing a criminal offence but, unknown to them, it was not possible to achieve their object by the course of conduct agreed on, they committed the crime of conspiracy.

N. and A. had agreed to pursue a course which could never in fact have produced cocaine. They submitted that there was no agreement in general terms to produce cocaine if and when they found a suitable material. The limited agreement they made could not in any circumstances have involved the commission of an offence created by the 1971 Act.

                                                         Appeals allowed.

4.3.6   **2. R. v. Harris**
                              (1979) 69 Cr.App.R. 122

H. and four others attempted to make amphetamine. They had the correct chemical formula, but when they mixed the chemicals concerned in a pan on a stove, they failed to produce amphetamine. This was not only because one ingredient was wrong but also because they lacked knowledge of the proper process.

H. was convicted of conspiracy with others to do an unlawful act, that is conspiracy to produce a controlled drug contrary to section 4(1) of the 1971 Act. H. appealed against conviction on the ground that the alleged conspiracy was one which, in relation to himself and the others concerned, was impossible to fulfil and thus he could not come within the offence charged.

Held, on appeal, that H. and the others had acquainted themselves with the proper process to produce amphetamines and thus had entered into an agreement to do an unlawful act which was inherently possible of consummation and, accordingly, the conviction was correct.

Appeal dismissed.

NOTE
The distinction between these two cases is that the agreement in *R. v. Nock* was to do something that was in fact scientifically impossible whereas in *R. v. Harris* the agreement was to do something that was in fact scientifically possible but had not been achieved on the occasion that formed the basis of the charge.

B. LAW: SUPPLY   **4.4**

(i) Supply   **4.4.1**

1. R. v. Holmes   **4.4.2**
[1976] Crim.L.R. 125

Counsel for H. submitted at trial, in answer to a charge of supplying controlled drugs, that where a person held drugs on behalf of himself and others then the whole group were in joint possession of the drugs. It followed, it was said, that a division of the drugs within the group could not be a supply within the meaning of the relevant section of the 1971 Act. The trial judge rejected the submission, the defence did not call evidence and H. was convicted and appealed against conviction.

Held, that the court must give the word "supply", which by section 37(1) of the 1971 Act includes distribution, its ordinary everyday meaning, so that a person who purchased drugs for himself and others could "supply" the drugs to others. As the defence had not led evidence because of the trial judge's ruling, the matter was sent back for a rehearing before a different judge.

Appeal allowed.

NOTE
Section 37(3) of the 1971 Act provides that for the purposes of that Act "the thing which a person has in his possession shall be taken to include anything subject to his control which is in the custody of another." The effect of the decision in *Holmes'* case is that A. may be convicted of supplying B. with a controlled drug even though the controlled drugs belonged to B.
In *R. v. Buckley* [1979] Crim.L.R. 664, following *Holmes*, the scenario of A. and B. described above arose and it was held that given section 37(1) whatever A. was doing he was certainly "distributing" the controlled drugs to B. and an appeal against conviction in these circumstances was dismissed.

4.4.3   **2. R. v. Dempsey**
                                    (1986) 82 Cr.App.R. 291

Michael Dempsey was in lawful possession of physeptone, a heroin substitute. Before going to a toilet to inject himself Michael gave some of the physeptone, itself a controlled drug, to Marueen Dempsey, a woman with whom he lived. Michael was arrested after having injected himself and Maureen was arrested as she walked away from the toilet. She told the police that she was taking care of the physeptone as there was a danger that Michael might inject himself with too much of the drug if he had immediate access to it all.

Michael was charged with supplying a controlled drug to Maureen contrary to section 4(3)(*a*) of the 1971 Act, and Maureen was charged with contravening section 5(2) of the same Act. At the end of the prosecution case the judge was asked to rule whether Michael and Maureen had a defence on the facts. The judge ruled that neither had a defence, whereupon both changed their pleas to guilty.

Michael appealed against conviction and the question to determine was whether by handing ampoules of the drug to Maureen to hold for him temporarily, he could be said to have supplied the drug to her.

LORD LANE, C.J. (at p. 293): "The word 'supply' is defined in the Shorter Oxford Dictionary as follows '... To fulfil, satisfy (a need or want) by furnishing what is wanted. To furnish, provide, afford (something needed, desired or used) ...' Those are the two definitions which seemed to be relevant to the particular circumstances. It is an act, so it seems, which is designed to benefit the recipient.

It does not seem to us that it is apt to describe the deposit of an article with another person for safe-keeping, as was the case here. The argument was canvassed in argument of a person who hands his coat to a cloakroom attendant for safekeeping during the show in a theatre or cinema. It could scarcely be said that the person handing the coat supplies it to the cloakroom attendant. Nor do we think it makes any difference that the cloakroom attendant wishes in one sense to get the coat, thinking that he may get a tip at the end of the evening. That is not the sort of wish or need which is envisaged by the definition of the offence. That sort of transfer is a transfer for the benefit of the transferer rather than the transferee."

                          Appeal *quoad* Michael Dempsey allowed.

NOTE

Maureen's appeal is considered, *infra* at paragraph **5.4.96** in relation to the statutory defence in section 5(4).

3. R. v. Taylor
[1986] Crim.L.R. 680

4.4.4

T. was a registered medical practitioner. He was charged with supplying a controlled drug by issuing National Health Service prescriptions on some 800 occasions to 70 people for various quantities of methadone, and all this within a six-month period. At trial it was submitted that even assuming that a registered medical practitioner acted unlawfully and in bad faith in prescribing a controlled drug, the mere issuing of a prescription authorising a pharmacist to dispense such a drug did not amount to supplying within the meaning of the 1971 Act.

Held, by the trial judge, acceding to defence counsel's submission that supplying within the meaning of the 1971 Act involves the physical passage of the substance involved from the supplier to the supplied. To hold otherwise, it was said, would be to equate issuing a prescription with handing over the substance involved and would do violence to the ordinary meaning of the word "supply." The 1971 Act is a criminal statute and ought to be construed strictly.

NOTE

As this case was decided by a court of first instance in England the decision is neither binding nor persuasive in Scotland. There must be some doubt as to whether this decision would be followed in Scotland. The pharmacist hands over the controlled drug to the recipient but the pharmacist is clearly acting in good faith on the authority of the prescription and is thus an innocent agent. However, the pharmacist acts as he does having received a prescription so that the prescription may be seen as assistance in the supplying of the controlled drugs with prior consent.

In Scotland it could be argued that the doctor was art and part guilty of the offence. He could also be charged with aiding and abetting the commission of the offence.

On the matter of a registered medical practitioner acting unlawfully and in bad faith in prescribing a controlled drug (to himself) see *R. v. Dunbar* [1982] 2 All E.R. 188 and brief commentary at (1982) 74 SCOLAG 169.

4. R. v. Lubren and Adepoju
[1988] Crim.L.R. 378

4.4.5

The two appellants were seen by police officers emerging from a flat belonging to Miss C. where officers found heroin. The two appellants, and Miss C., were charged with unlawfully supplying a Class A drug "to another." The prosecution case was that the appellants had gone to the flat to supply the drug to Miss C., but in her absence had left it with someone else, F. (The prosecution did not allege supply to F.) At the close of the prosecution case a successful submission of no case to answer was made on behalf of Miss C. on the basis that she could not be concerned in supplying the drug to herself. As regards the appellants, however, the trial judge permitted an amendment to the indictment deleting Miss C.'s name as a defendant and inserting it as the "another" to whom supply was made. The appellants were convicted and appealed.

Held, the word "another" on an indictment means someone not named on the indictment: *R. v. Brian Smith* (unreported, February 14, 1983) and *R. v. Ferrara* (unreported, July 17, 1984) followed. There was no evidence of supply by the appellants to a person not originally named on the indictment and the judge accordingly ought to have acceded to their submissions of no case to answer. By allowing a late amendment the judge deprived the appellants of the chance of an acquittal on the indictment as it stood, even though the appellants had not been prejudiced in their defence.

Appeal allowed and conviction quashed.

4.4.6

5. R. v. Connelly
[1992] Crim.L.R. 296

C. was convicted of supplying a controlled drug, amphetamine (Count 8). She had three co-accused. R. pleaded guilty to possession of a Class B drug (Count 2) and possession with intent to supply (Count 9). L., R.'s boyfriend, pleaded guilty to possession of a Class A drug and F. pleaded guilty to two counts of supplying a Class B drug.

The Crown's case was that R. was the organiser of a drug run. The appellant flew to Amsterdam and smuggled the amphetamine back inside a body belt. R. and L. met at a flat in Brighton where co-accused F. lived with his girlfriend, G. R. collected the drugs from the appellant and supplied some of them to F. She then left with the rest of the drugs and was arrested with £8,000 worth of amphetamines in her possession.

As originally indicted, all four co-accused were charged in Count 1 with being concerned in supplying the amphetamine to another. Before the prosecution case was opened the point was taken that the other person was intended on the prosecution case to be one of the four co-accused named in that count in the indictment and that this must fail following the Court of Appeal's decision in *Lubren and Adepoju* [1988] Crim.L.R. 378. As a result, Count 8 was added to the indictment charging the appellant alone with supplying the amphetamine to R.

It was argued before the Court of Appeal that, *inter alia*: (i) it was an abuse of the process of the court for the prosecution to have been allowed to drop Count 1, on which the appellant would have been entitled to have been acquitted had the matter gone to the close of the prosecution case, and to substitute Count 8; and (ii) that following *Lubren and Adepoju* the person to whom the supply was alleged to have been made could not be one of those named in the same indictment, so that Count 8 itself was bad.

Held (i) the trial judge had been right to allow the amendment to the indictment; it was a purely technical point which was remedied by the prosecution at the stage before the case was opened to the jury and it was impossible to say that any injustice had resulted; (ii) the Court had, throughout its judgment in *Lubren and Adepoju* used the word "indictment" as opposed to "count." However, the reasoning behind that decision and the previous decisions of *Smith* (unreported, February 14, 1983) and *Ferrara* (unreported, July 17, 1984) was that as a matter of plain English, where A., B. and C. were charged with supplying a drug to another, that other could not be A., B. or C.. The cases did not hold that the other person could not be somebody who was a defendant on the same indictment; each count was in law a separate indictment. There was therefore no substance in the submission that Count 8 was bad in law.

Appeal dismissed.

NOTE
This decision is perhaps of more importance to English lawyers for the procedural points.

6. R. v. X.   **4.4.7**
[1994] Crim.L.R. 827

X. was convicted of possessing with intent to supply 1,211 tablets of amphetamine sulphate. He was a registered police informer and had in the past given the police information on a suspected drug dealer, R. His defence was that he had the drugs in pursuit of an arrangement with police officers to pass them to R. who would then sell some to an undercover officer. In his summing-up the judge directed the jury that if they believed X.'s account, they must decide if that constituted supply (having given them guidance on the meaning of the word derived from *Maginnis* [1987] 1 A.C. 303). If it did not, they would acquit. If it did, he asked them to add to a rider to their guilty verdict indicating that they believed that he intended the drugs to eventually get into police hands, and it was this course that the jury followed.

On appeal it was argued that the intention to pass the drugs to R. did not fall into the meaning of supply given by Lord Keith in *Maginnis* at page 309. It was not in X.'s mind to supply the drugs to R. because they were not to be given to R. to fulfill his wants or requirements.

Held, that the submission confused motive with intention. If what is contemplated or intended is supply (in the *Maginnis* sense), the supplier's motive is not relevant. The Court derived some assistance from *Finch* (unreported, July 20, 1992), in which the trial judge's statement that if a person acquires drugs with a view to supplying them to another and then informs on that other then he is guilty of the offence, was said, albeit *obiter*, to be correct by Lloyd L.J..

Appeal dismissed.

NOTE

The commentary by Sir John Smith to the above report is of interest for he noted that "it seems that whether there is a 'supply' of drugs depends on the intention of the alleged supplier when he delivers possession to another. If A. delivers drugs to B., intending B. to be a mere custodian who will return the drugs on demand and not use them for any purpose of his own, there is no 'supply.' If B. returns the drugs to A. intending that A. will use them by consumption or by sale to another or otherwise, there is a supply by B. to A.. If, therefore, in the present case X. delivered the drugs with the intention that R. should sell them to another, he intended to supply the drugs to R.. The judge's direction to the jury that they should acquit if they did not think that this amounted to a 'supply' in the ordinary meaning of the word, was too favourable. Even if X.'s sole motive for so doing was to entrap R., he was still guilty of the offence: *Yip Chiu-Cheung* [1994] Crim.L.R. 824.

So far as conviction was concerned, it was immaterial whether X. was acting for the purposes of law enforcement or not. As regards sentence, it was a most material consideration. Questions of fact relating only to sentence are decided by the judge, not the jury. The rider to the verdict was presumably a matter which the judge could take into account but the decision was his: *Warner v. Metropolitan Police Commissioner* [1969] 2 A.C. 256, where the judge having (rightly, as the law then was) directed the jury that it was immaterial whether the defendant knew the thing in his possession was a controlled drug, asked them, after a verdict of guilty whether he did know?"

4.4.8 *(ii) Offer to supply*

4.4.9   **1. Haggard v. Mason**
                                  [1976] 1 All E.R. 337

H. purchased 1,000 tabs of what was believed was lysergide (LSD) which he intended to resell. H. was introduced to a third party to whom he offered to supply a quantity of lysergide, an offer that was accepted. It transpired that the substance was not a controlled drug. On being convicted of offering to supply a controlled drug to another, H. appealed.

LAWSON, J. (at p. 340): "It matters not in relation to the offence of offering to supply that what is in fact supplied pursuant to that offer, the offer having been accepted, is not in fact a controlled drug. Of course if the charge had been supplying a controlled drug, it is clear that the fact that a controlled drug was not in fact supplied would mean that that offence could not have been established."

Appeal refused.

2. R. v. Gill
(1992) 97 Cr.App.R. 215

4.4.10 G. was arrested after being observed taking money for a bag containing pills. The bag was found to contain vitamin pills. The appellant claimed that his intention was to cheat his customers by offering to supply Ecstasy but actually supplying vitamin C tablets. Appealing against his conviction for conspiracy to supply a controlled drug, contrary to section 4(1)(b) of the 1971 Act, he contended that a pretence to offer to supply a controlled drug did not constitute an offence; that the Crown must prove, in the absence of evidence that the drugs were prohibited drugs, that at the very least the appellant believed that they were prohibited drugs.

Held, that on a true construction of section 4(1)(b) of the 1971 Act, the offence was complete when the offer was made regardless of whether the offerer intended to carry the offer into effect by actually supplying that drug. The fact that what was charged was a conspiracy rather than the substantive offence could not make any difference.

Appeal dismissed.

3. R. v. Goodard   4.4.11
[1992] Crim.L.R. 588

G. appealed against conviction of offering to supply a controlled drug to another. He had changed his plea after a ruling by the trial judge. The appellant had been arrested by officers investigating an allegation of robbery. In interview he admitted that he had obtained money from a man by offering to get him cannabis. At the conclusion of the prosecution it was submitted that there was no case to answer, that the appellant had not intended to supply the cannabis but had obtained the money by deception. The assistant recorder rejected the submission.

Held, there is nothing in section 4(1)(b) of the 1971 Act which provides that the person who makes the offer must intend to supply the controlled drug. The offence is complete when the offer to supply a controlled drug is made, quite regardless of whether the offerer intends to carry the offer into effect by actually supplying the drug. The construction contended for by the applicant would make it almost impossible for the Crown to meet a defence that the defendant did not intend to carry out the offer. That could not have been the intention of Parliament and it was contrary to the plain meaning of the words. If a defendant having been convicted of this offence persuaded a judge that it was not his intention to carry the deal into effect, that may be a matter of mitigation but it could not be a defence.

Appeal dismissed.

NOTE
    The learned commentator said, in regard to this case, that the *actus reus* of the offence is the making of the offer and the appellant intended to make the offer, even if he did not intend to carry it out. An intention to cause the *actus*

reus of an offence is generally a sufficient *mens rea* in the absence of any specific requirement of an ulterior intent. An argument to the contrary in this case might be that the mischief at which the Act is aimed is obviously the misuse of drugs and no misuse of drugs was intended or foreseen by the appellant. But this hardly seems sufficient to require the inference of a requirement of an ulterior intent.

4.4.12   **4. R. v. Mitchell**
                                      [1992] Crim.L.R. 723

It was alleged that M. approached an off-duty police officer and offered to sell him some "nice hash." The officer declined, went away and returned with another plainclothes officer. M. said to him, "you've changed your mind. £20 for the hash." He was arrested and searched. On him was found a grassy substance which was not a drug. He was charged with offering to supply a controlled drug, namely cannabis. At his trial he denied making any offer. The count was amended by leave of the judge to an offer to supply "cannabis ... *or cannabis resin*" because prosecution evidence has confirmed that "hash" meant cannabis resin as opposed to herbal cannabis. The judge directed the jury that it did not matter whether M. had any controlled drug in his possession or whether he intended to supply a controlled drug or something bogus, so long as he made an offer. M. was convicted and appealed, submitting that the judge misdirected the jury.

Held, that it had been decided in *Haggard v. Mason* [1976] 1 All E.R. 337 that an offence of offering to supply a controlled drug (as opposed to an offence of supplying a drug) could be established without it being proved that the substance was a controlled drug. M.'s counsel had sought to distinguish the present case from *Haggard v. Mason* because in that case, unlike the present one, the defendant believed that the substance on offer was a controlled drug. However, the relevant part of section 4(3)(a) was the offer, which could be by words or conduct. The offer in words in this case completed the offence and the nature of the substance was irrelevant: if the offer had been by conduct, it might have been relevant whether the substance was a controlled drug. It had also been submitted that the defence in section 28 of the 1971 Act (lack of knowledge or belief in facts alleged) could avail M., but section 28 did not apply to an offer to supply by words.

Appeal dismissed.

NOTE

Consistently with the present decision, *R. v. Goodard*, *supra*, established that it is not necessary to prove that a person charged with offering to supply a controlled drug intended to put the offer into effect.

4. R. v. Showers   4.4.13
[1995] Crim.L.R. 400

S. was charged with offering to supply cocaine. An undercover police officer approached S. who asked him what he wanted. The officer replied that he wanted "a stone" (meaning crack cocaine). After some haggling and argument the officer paid S. £25 for a cream coloured substance which turned out to be a peanut wrapped in cellophane. S. was convicted and appealed, submitting that he should not have been convicted of the offence because to his knowledge the substance was not a drug.

Held, it was clear that it was not necessary to prove an intent to supply a drug in order to establish the offence of offering to supply it: *Gill, supra, Goodard, supra*. The conversation between S. and the officer showed that an offer had been made by S.

Appeal refused.

(iii) Concerned in the supplying   4.4.14

1. R. v. Hughes   4.4.15
(1985) 81 Cr.App.R. 334

H. and T. arranged to meet D. and C. Later the police saw H., D., and C. each give something to T. Immediately thereafter T. went into a chemist shop and thereafter obtained controlled drugs on the authority of a medical prescription. T. left the chemist shop and handed something to D. and C. and, a short time later, to H. It was then that D. and C. left together. There was a shout of "police" and a chase took place and H. ran away. The police caught H. but a search revealed nothing criminative on his person.

After trial H. was acquitted by a jury of unlawful possession of the controlled drugs concerned but he was convicted of being concerned in the unlawful supply of a controlled drug to another contrary to section 4(3)(*b*) of the 1971 Act. The Crown case against H. was that he was concerned in the unlawful supply of the controlled drug to D.

H. appealed on the basis that the trial judge failed to direct the jury properly, or indeed at all, on the meaning of the expression "concerned in" in the relevant subsection of the 1971 Act.

Goff, L.J. (at p. 347): "After stating the terms of section 4 of the 1971 Act, his Lordship referred to *R. v. Blake and O'Connor* (1978) 68 Cr.App.R. 1.

That was a case relating to an offence under section 4(3)(*c*) of the Act, under which, as we have seen, it is an offence to be concerned in the making to another, in contravention of the subsection, of an offer to supply a controlled drug.

So the difference between [s. 4(3)](*b*) and [s. 4(3)](*c*) is that in (*b*) there has to be an actual supply in which the accused was concerned whereas under (*c*) it is enough that there was an offer to supply in which the accused was concerned. The case of *Blake* was concerned with (*c*)."

After the facts in *Blake* were outlined his Lordship held that: … "It appears to us that, for an offence to be shown to have been committed by a defendant contrary to subsection (*b*) or subsection (*c*), as the case may be, the prosecution has to prove (1) the supply of a drug to another, or as the case may be, the making of an offer to supply a drug to another, in contravention to section 4(1) of the Act; (2) participation by the defendant in an enterprise involving such supply or, as the case may be, such offer to supply; and (3) knowledge by the defendant of the nature of the enterprise, *i.e.* that it involved supply of a drug or, as the case may be, offering to supply a drug."

Appeal allowed and conviction quashed.

4.4.16   **2. McCadden v. H.M. Advocate**
1986 S.C.C.R. 16

McCadden was charged that while acting along with others he was concerned in the supplying of diamorphine to other persons, including a man called Cunningham who was charged on the same indictment with possession of diamorphine. The evidence was that Cunningham acted as a courier and that McCadden drove him to a cafe outside which there was a man called McQuade.

McCadden pointed out McQuade to Cunningham, who left the car and joined McQuade. Then McQuade came over to the car and spoke to McCadden who drove off leaving Cunningham and McQuade together. Thereafter Cunningham and McQuade met a man called Paterson who gave Cunningham a bag.

The bag contained 490.8 grammes of heroin with a purity of 45 per cent. According to the evidence of experienced drugs squad officers, the street value of such a quantity of heroin could vary between £225,000 and £596,000.

There was also evidence of visits by Paterson and McCadden to McQuade's house, of a visit made by McCadden to London, and of an attempt by McCadden to avoid arrest.

On conviction McCadden was sentenced to 10 years' imprisonment and he appealed against conviction.

THE LORD JUSTICE-CLERK (ROSS) (at p. 18): "[Counsel for the appellant] before us has attacked the sufficiency of the evidence of knowledge and he has pointed out that there was no direct evidence that he had been found in possession of any of the paraphernalia of a drug dealer or a drug user. No doubt that is so, but of course evidence of that kind is not essential to establish knowledge upon his part. Knowledge is something which required in this case to be inferred from the circumstantial evidence."

Appeal refused.

3. Kerr v. H.M. Advocate   4.4.17
1986 S.C.C.R. 81

K.'s flat was searched by the police. They discovered scales and weights designed for weighing in grammes which had been hidden behind an ordinary set of kitchen scales in a corner of the kitchen. Minute particles of light brown powder amounting to about one milligramme were present on both scale-pans of the scales designed for weighing in grammes and the powder was found to contain diamorphine. Beside these scales and weights were found a mirror and a box of glucose, the functions of which, as part of a diamorphine dealer's paraphernalia, were explained in evidence to the jury. There were also found in a drawer in the kitchen, beside some scarves and other articles, a number of plastic bags and pieces of polythene.

Moreover, next door to K.'s flat, was another flat then empty and under renovation. A scarf was pinned to the side of the letter-box inside this empty flat. This scarf was retrieved by the police through the letter-box, without the door of the empty flat having to be opened. It had apparently been pinned there so that it could be recovered without opening the door of the empty flat. In the scarf were three plastic bags containing substantial or dealer quantities of diamorphine.

There was evidence that there were similarities in the plastic found in K.'s house and in the scarf. There was evidence that a part of a bag found in K.'s flat could, because of its shape and because of painting on it, have been part of the same bag.

A woman living with K. was never at any time said by anyone to be involved but she identified to the police the scarf referred to as belonging to her, although she denied that at trial. K. admitted knowledge of the paraphernalia in his flat. When he was cautioned and charged, K. replied "You didn't find any smack in my house."

K. was convicted of an offence under section 4(3)(*b*) of the 1971 Act and he appealed.

LORD HUNTER (at p. 87): "Subsection 3(*b*) of section 4, which is the relevant provision, makes it an offence for a person to be concerned in the supplying of a controlled drug to another in contravention of subsection (1) of section 4. The said subsection (1), read short, provides, *inter alia*, that it shall not be lawful for a person to supply a controlled drug to another. I am not sure that it assists in the interpretation of the words 'to be concerned in', where they are used in this and other statutes, by seeking for analogues, although no doubt analogues such as 'involved' or 'implicated' could be discovered. I prefer, for myself, to apply the statutory language as it stands, since it conveys a clear meaning. Nor, in my opinion, is it helpful in a particular case to attempt to delimit forms of participation in the supplying of controlled drugs which may result in a conviction under section 4(3)(*b*). I doubt also whether it is altogether helpful to treat such a provision in a United Kingdom statute merely as it were a form of statutory concert. Under section 46 of the Criminal Procedure (Scotland) Act 1975 the charge 'guilty, actor or art and part' is implied in all Scottish indictments. Judging from its terms and the context in which it occurs, I consider that section 4(3)(*b*) was purposely enacted in the widest terms and was intended to cover a great variety of activities both at the centre and also on the fringes of dealing in controlled drugs. It would, for example, in appropriate circumstances include the activities of financiers, couriers and other go-betweens, lookouts, advertisers, agents and many links in the chain of distribution. It would certainly, in my opinion, include the activities of persons who take part in the breaking up of bulk, the adulteration and reduction of purity, the separation and division into deals and the weighing and packaging of deals."

THE LORD JUSTICE-CLERK (ROSS) (at p. 89): "I agree that a jury should have no difficulty in understanding what is meant by 'to be concerned in the supplying of' a controlled drug to another. I find myself in complete agreement with the interpretation of this statutory provision as expounded by Lord Hunter. In particular, I agree that a contravention of section 4(3)(*b*) may be established even though there has been no actual supply of the controlled drug to another person; the offence which the statute creates is being concerned in the supplying of a controlled drug to another, not being concerned in the supply of a controlled drug to another. To give an example, if a man were to assist a drug user by introducing him to a supplier of controlled drugs, that could involve the former being concerned in the supplying of a controlled drug to another even though no actual supply took place on the occasion in question."

Lord Brand agreed with the opinion of Lord Hunter.

Appeal refused.

4.4.18   **4. Kyle v. H.M. Advocate**
                                      1988 S.L.T. 601

K. and another were convicted on an indictment containing charges of contravening sections 4(3)(*b*), 4(3)(*a*) and 5(3), all of the 1971 Act. The evidence justifying conviction on each of these charges was the same. In charging the jury the trial judge had said that if the jury found the accused guilty of the charges of contravening section 4(3)(*a*) and section 5(3) then the charge of contravening section 4(3)(*b*) would become academic. Both accused were convicted of the charges of contravening sections 4(3)(*b*), 4(3)(*a*) and 5(3), all of the 1971 Act, and appealed.

THE LORD JUSTICE-CLERK (ROSS) (at pp. 603–4): "So far as the indictment is concerned, it was, of course, competent to libel cumulatively the alleged contravention of sections 4(3)(*b*), section 4(3)(*a*) and section 5(3) which were the subjects of charges 1, 2 and 3. For a person to be found guilty of being concerned in the supply of a controlled drug (s. 4(3)(*b*)), it is not necessary for any supply to have actually taken place. As Lord Hunter pointed out in *Kerr*, s. 4(3)(*b*) was enacted in the widest terms and was intended to cover a great variety of activities both at the centre and also on the fringes of dealing in controlled drugs. Even if an accused has been found guilty of supplying a controlled drug in terms of s. 4(3)(*a*), and of possession of a controlled drug with intent to supply it to another in terms of s. 5(3), it does not follow that he cannot also be convicted of being concerned in the supplying of a controlled drug to other persons in terms of s. 4(3)(*b*) provided that the evidence relied on in relation to the charge under s. 4(3)(*b*) is supplementary to that relied on for the charges under s.4(3)(*a*) and s. 5(3). Thus, for example, there might be evidence of actings of the accused which related to a period either before or after the time when he supplied the controlled drug (s. 4(3)(*a*) or when he had possession of the controlled drug with intent to supply (s. 5(3)). In the present case, however, the trial judge informed the jury that the evidence relied on for charges 2 and 3 constituted the entire evidence in relation to charge 1. In that situation, for the jury to convict the appellants of charge 1 as well as charges 2 and 3 was to convict them twice in respect of the same set of facts, and that was something which the jury were not entitled to do.

The trial judge sought to deal with the matter by imposing concurrent sentences on the first three charges, but, in my opinion, he ought to have made it clear to the jury that in the circumstances of this case it was not open to them to convict the appellants of charge 1 if they were finding them guilty of charges 2 and 3."

Lord Robertson agreed with the Lord Justice-Clerk.

LORD DUNPARK (at p. 604): "For the reasons given by your Lordship in the chair I agree that both these appeals should be refused except for the appeals against conviction on charge 1, which should be sustained and that conviction quashed …

As these three offences are separate and distinct statutory offences, it is not necessary for the Crown to libel them as alternative offences. Evidence which is insufficient to prove actual supply or possession with intent to supply may nevertheless establish that an accused person was concerned in some way in the supplying to others. Moreover, there may be evidence which entitles a jury to convict on all three of these offences."

> Appeal allowed and conviction on charge 1
> quashed.

4.4.19   **5. Tudhope v. McKee**
                                    1987 S.C.C.R. 663

For the facts of this case see *infra*, paragraph. **10.3.5.**

NOTE

Reconciling the Scottish decision with the English one is very difficult. In *Hughes, supra,* Goff, L.J. held specifically that in the offence of being concerned in the unlawful supply of a controlled drug contrary to section 4(3)(*b*) there must be a *de facto* supply. In comparing the offence of being concerned in the supplying of such a drug to another — section 4(3)(*b*) — there must be an actual supply whereas in the offence of being concerned in the making to another of an offer to supply such a drug — section 4(3)(*c*) — there need not be an actual supply. Secondly, it was held that the prosecution in relation to section 4(3)(*b*) must prove (i) the supply of a drug to another; (ii) participation by the accused in an enterprise involving such a supply; and (iii) knowledge by the accused of the nature of the enterprise, *i.e.* that it involved supplying a controlled drug.

Any commentary on *Hughes* may proceed along two lines. First, the facts as narrated in the report (p. 346) do not show that Hughes himself was actually concerned in the supply of anything. At most the evidence shows that he was merely present when some sort of deal was concluded. There is no evidence that he was involved in such supply as actually occurred nor is there evidence as to why he met the others or what was in fact handed over to him. There was in short little justification for his conviction.

A second line is that raised by Fortson (at p. 131) who suggests somewhat tentatively that the report of *Hughes* does not reveal whether the offence in section 4(3)(*b*) was considered in the context of the statutory defence in section 28 of the 1971 Act. It is submitted that that observation is too circumspect an observation: rather there is no suggestion in the headnote or the rubric that the statutory defence was considered and nor does the court mention the matter in the judgment, which it surely would have done had it been raised by counsel. Accordingly, *Hughes* may be considered to have been decided on the basis that the elements of the offence that the prosecution have to prove were not established in that case.

What does the prosecution have to prove in this regard? The four Scottish decisions taken together provide a comprehensive answer: *McKee* asserts that the accused has to prove that he probably did not know, for example, that controlled drugs were being supplied; *McCadden* asserts that knowledge may be inferred from the circumstances and that the accused need not be the one actually to supply the drugs; *Kerr* is authority for the wide spectrum of transactions and activities that may be drawn into the offence, and *Kyle* is authority for the proposition that the offence in terms of section 4(3)(*b*) is wholly different from others in sections 4 and 5 and is therefore not necessarily an alternative. For an example of a failure to direct a jury in accordance with *Kyle* see *Martin v. H.M. Advocate,* 1989 S.C.C.R. 546.

4.4.20   **6. Higgins v. H.M. Advocate**
                                    1989 G.W.D. 5–198

H. was convicted of a number of charges of contravening the 1971 Act. He appealed those convictions and appeared on his own behalf at the

appeal. The main point put forward by H. was that he had been convicted
of two charges arising out of the same *species facti.*

THE LORD JUSTICE-GENERAL (EMSLIE): "The appellant was indicted for trial
... upon a number of charges. The result of the trial was that the appellant
was found guilty of charge (2), charge (4) and charge (5) on the indictment.
Charge (2) is a charge that in the period 24th March 1986 to 4th May 1986
he was concerned in the supply of cannabis resin at Patio Cottage of which
he was the tenant. That was libelled as a contravention of section 4(3)(b) of
the Misuse of Drugs Act 1971. Charge (4) is a charge relating to 4th May
1986 and that was a charge of possession of cannabis resin, on that day at
Patio Cottage. Charge (5) is a charge of possession of cannabis resin at that
cottage on that day, with intent to supply it to another, contrary to section
5(3) of the statute. Mr Higgins, on his own behalf, has attacked his conviction
on charges (4) and (5) upon a single ground and that was that there was
insufficient evidence to permit the jury to draw the inference that he had
practical control and was in a position to exercise practical control over a
substantial block of cannabis which figured in the evidence ...

In these circumstances, accordingly, the appeal fails on the first ground
which of course means that we have to pass to the second submission
based on the second note of appeal. In this submission we are concerned
with conviction on charges (2) and (5) which we have already described.
The submission of Mr Higgins shortly stated is that according to our law
no person can be found guilty of more than one offence arising out
of the same species facti. Against the background of that proposition in
law the appellant's submission was that in relation to both charges (2)
and (5) the sheriff rehearsed to the jury precisely the same evidence,
including evidence about the possession of the large sum of money. His
submission accordingly was that the jury were invited to convict him of
both charges arising out of precisely the same evidence, including evidence
about the possession of the large sum of money. His submission
accordingly was that the jury were invited to convict him of both charges
arising out of precisely the same species facti. There was a certain initial
attraction in that submission, but we have come to be of the opinion that
it is unsound for one reason and one reason only. The jury had to decide
so far as charge (5) was concerned whether the block of cannabis was
held with an intent to supply it to others. It was accordingly legitimate for
the jury to look at the sum of money as a factor and perhaps a minor
factor, in throwing light upon the character of the possession, but when
they came to charge (2), which was concerned with a tract of time in the
past, although the sum of money was the same, the significance of the
evidence of the finding of the money bore a different aspect. The sheer
size of the sum of money and the way in which it was constituted was apt
to throw a significant light on the past, although on the face of it the same
pieces of evidence did not all have the same part to play in relation to

each of the charges. In the circumstances of this case, we are satisfied that the submission made under the second note of appeal fails because of the difference which we have detected, in relation to the money, in the species facti, which supported the conviction on each of the charges. In all the circumstances accordingly the appeal will be refused on both propositions which were advanced in support of the note of appeal."

Appeal refused.

NOTE
The Opinion of the Court is to be found at 1990 S.C.C.R. 268.

4.4.21   **7. Youngson v. H.M. Advocate**
                          1989 G.W.D. 29–1309

Y. appealed against his conviction *inter alia* of a contravention of section 4(3)(b) of the 1971 Act and his ground of appeal was a misdirection by the trial judge.

Held, the judge had accurately commented that there was no evidence that Y. wanted drugs for his own use and therefore it could be said that he was concerned in supplying them to another.

Appeal refused.

4.4.22   **8. McDowall v. H.M. Advocate**
                          1991 S.C.C.R. 197

M. was charged with possessing cannabis resin with intent on February 23, 1989, contrary to section 5(3) of the 1971 Act and with being concerned in the supply of cannabis resin between January 1, 1989 and February 23, 1989, contrary to section 4(3)(b) of the same Act. The evidence against him arose out of a search of his house (the locus in both charges) during which quantities of cannabis resin were found along with tick lists relating to prior transactions. The sheriff in his charge to the jury referred to evidence "common" to both charges, and did not direct the jury, in accordance with *Kyle v. H.M. Advocate*, 1988 S.L.T. 601, that they could not convict on two charges arising out of the same *species facti*. The appellant was convicted on both charges and appealed to the High Court.

Held, that the jury were entitled to treat the tick lists as relevant to both charges, so that the description of the evidence as common was not misleading, and that although it would have been better if a direction had been given in accordance with *Kyle*, there was no material risk in this case of the appellant being convicted twice on the same *species facti*, and accordingly there had been no miscarriage of justice; and appeal refused.

THE LORD JUSTICE GENERAL (HOPE) (at p. 199): "The appellant is William Hugh McDowall who was charged on indictment in the sheriff court at

Ayr with three offences under the Misuse of Drugs Act 1971. The first charge was one of possession of a controlled drug, namely cannabis resin, with intent to supply it to another, contrary to section 5(3) of the Act. The second was a charge of simple possession, contrary to section 5(2). The third was one of being concerned in the supplying of cannabis resin in contravention of section 4(1), contrary to section 4(3)(b). It is a feature of the way in which the indictment was framed that charges (1) and (2) related to the same date and the same place. The date libelled was 23rd February 1989 and the place was a house in Girvan where the appellant resided at that time. So far as charge (3) is concerned, that charge related to a period between 1st January 1989 and 23rd February 1989, but the place libelled was the same. The appellant pled not guilty, but in the event he was found guilty on all of these charges and he was sentenced to three years' imprisonment on charges (1) and (3) and to one year's imprisonment in respect of charge (2), these sentences to run concurrently. An appeal has been presented against both conviction and sentence and [counsel] appeared today to argue the various grounds of appeal.

We shall deal at this stage with the first ground which has argued against conviction. This states that: 'The presiding sheriff failed to charge the jury in accordance with the law as laid down in *Kyle* v. *H.M. Advocate* ... as a consequence of which the jury convicted the appellant of contraventions of both sections 5(3) and 4(3)(b) of the Misuse of Drugs Act 1971 upon the same body of evidence.'

It can be seen from the way in which this ground of appeal has been framed that it contains two essential propositions. The first is that it was necessary for the sheriff to give a direction in accordance with what was said in *Kyle*, and secondly that in this case the convictions on these two charges did in fact proceed upon the same body of evidence.

In presenting this argument [counsel] referred us to various passages in the sheriff's charge. The background to these passages is that a number of things were found in the house when the police conducted their search. Things found in a box on a table, in a coat and also in a tobacco tin in the living-room, when examined, proved to be cannabis resin of various quantities. In various drawers in the kitchen of the house the police also found a card and an envelope with lists of names and sums of money and notebooks with names and sums of money with various calculations and figures. The police regarded these various documents as tick lists, that is to say as lists of supplies of drugs to persons on credit who are expected to pay for them at a later date. Having reminded the jury of what was found in the house the sheriff said: 'The point of the Crown's argument is that, while one or two of these might be explained as simple possession, the more you have and the different sizes and varieties you have point towards intention to supply, and they say, relying on common evidence, "Being concerned in the supplying."'

Referring to the tick lists, he said: '[I]f you put the interpretation upon it or even upon part of it, which the police have suggested, then it is easier to see how there is an intention to supply and being concerned in the supply to others.'

As [counsel] pointed out, this was a reference to the first and third charges on the indictment, and he criticised the use of the phrase 'common evidence.' He also submitted that the sheriff should then have directed the jury that they could not rely on the same evidence in respect of more than one charge. No such direction was given, but the issue in the present case is whether the evidence relating to these two charges could really be said to have been the same evidence or, as it may more accurately be put for the purposes of this case, evidence of the same species facti.

In *Kyle* the various charges, including the equivalents of charges (1) and (3) on the indictment in this case, related to the same date, and the evidence was confined to activities in the lounge bar of a public house on that date. Here the dates libelled in the two charges are not the same, since charge (3) relates to a period between 1st January and 23rd February 1989. Charge (1) relates only to the date when the search was carried out. And the evidence consisted not only of evidence about the quantity of the cannabis resin found in the various containers in the living-room, all of which was relevant to the charge of possession on that date with intent to supply, but also of the results of the search in the kitchen which produced the tick lists and various other documents in the drawers which clearly related to transactions in the past. In our opinion the jury were entitled to regard the tick lists as material which could be used for two purposes and not only one. These lists were relevant to the intention with which the drugs were being possessed on the date of the search, and they were also relevant to the appellant's activities in the past.

We were referred to the learned advocate-depute to *Higgins v. H.M. Advocate* [1989 G.W.D. 5–198] where a similar question arose as to whether the jury had been invited to convict the appellant on two charges arising out of the same species facti. The Lord Justice-General referred to the evidence as being 'apt to throw a significant light on the past, and although on the face of it the same pieces of evidence had parts to play in both charges, the same pieces of evidence did not all have the same part to play in relation to each of the charges.'

As he put it, the finding of money which was the critical fact in that case bore a different aspect as regards the past from what it did about the future. Looking at the matter in this way we consider that for the sheriff to describe the evidence on which the Crown relied as common evidence was not so misleading as to give rise in itself to a misdirection. As for the question whether it was essential for the sheriff to give a direction in terms mentioned by the Lord Justice-Clerk in *Kyle* at p. 129, that is to say that the jury could not also find the appellant guilty of charge (3) in this case if they were minded to find him guilty on charge (1) on the basis of the same evidence, we answer it in the negative. It would have been better if such a direction had been given, but in the circumstances of this case the important evidence relating to the tick lists was clearly relevant to both charges. It was relevant to the past course of conduct which was the subject of charge (3) and to the nature of the possession which was the subject of charge (1). There was no material risk in this case therefore of the appellant being convicted twice on the same species facti. So we do not consider that the absence of such a direction in the present case could be said to amount to a miscarriage of justice. For these reasons we are not persuaded that there is substance in this first ground of appeal."

Appeal refused.

NOTE
This and other cases are discussed by Bovey in "Duplication in Charges" (1995) 41 J.L.S. 306.

9. Clements v. H.M. Advocate   4.4.23
1991 S.L.T. 388

Two accused persons were charged, along with four other men on an indictment, with, *inter alia*, a contravention of section 4(3)(b) of the 1971 Act, in respect that on June 26 and 27, 1988 at various addresses in England, on a train travelling between London and Edinburgh and at various addresses in Edinburgh they were concerned in the supplying of cannabis resin to other persons. No evidence was led at the trial to show that the two accused travelled to Scotland on either of the two days or that they had ever been to Scotland prior to their arrest. The evidence led by the Crown was solely to the effect that both accused had been involved in collecting seven kilogrammes of cannabis resin in London and in giving it to a co-accused who had travelled from Scotland, and who thereafter returned to Scotland by train. Both accused were convicted and appealed on the ground that the Scottish courts did not have jurisdiction to try the accused because the only evidence against them was their actings in London and there was nothing in the 1971 Act which overcame the presumption that a criminal statute was not intended to have extra-territorial effect.

Held, (1) that the problem in this case was one as to territorial limitation as between different jurisdictions within the United Kingdom which depended on constitutional practice and not international comity, and (2) that the determinative factor so far as jurisdiction over the accused was concerned was the place where the drugs were to be supplied, the accused's knowledge or ignorance of that place being immaterial, and there was nothing in precedent, comity or good sense to inhibit the Scottish courts from treating as justiciable here acts in contravention of section 4(3)(b) of the 1971 Act committed in another part of the United Kingdom which formed part of the chain in the supplying of controlled drugs to persons present in Scotland.

Observed, per the Lord Justice-General (Hope) that the interests of justice were best served by trying all those who participated in the chain together in the same courts.

THE LORD JUSTICE GENERAL (HOPE) (at p. 394): "There is nothing in precedent, comity or good sense to inhibit the Scottish court from treating as justiciable here acts in contravention of s. 4(3)(b) of the 1971 Act committed in another part of the United Kingdom which formed part in the chain of the supplying of controlled drugs to persons present in Scotland. The only argument to the contrary was that submitted by senior counsel which, as I have said, has no relevance to the present case since we are not concerned with the extra-territorial effect of the 1971 Act. No other authorities were cited to us to the effect that what I consider to be in accordance with common sense and the interests of justice could not be done in this case.

For these reasons, I am of the opinion that the determinative factor, so far as jurisdictions over the appellants in this case is concerned, is the place where the drugs were to be supplied. This is consistent with the structure of s. 4, because the purpose of subs. (3)(b) is to strike at all those whose activities may assist in the contravention of s. 4(1)(b). The underlying mischief at which these provisions are directed is the supply or offer to supply of a controlled drug to another, and to look to the place of the mischief as the place where jurisdiction can be established against all those involved would be consistent with the idea that the courts of the place where the harmful acts occur may exercise jurisdiction over those whose acts elsewhere have consequences: see Lord Diplock's discussion of this point in *R. v. Treacy* [[1971] A.C. 537] at p. 562. This is not to say that the courts of other parts in the United Kingdom might not also have jurisdiction in an appropriate case. But, as Lord Diplock pointed out, the risk of double jeopardy is avoided by the common law doctrines in bar of trial, in England, of autrefois convict and, in Scotland, that the accused has tholed his assize.

That is sufficient for the disposal of these appeals. I should add that, had it been necessary to do so, I would have held that, there being sufficient evidence to infer that Clements knew that the drugs were to be taken to Scotland, he was undoubtedly subject to the jurisdiction of the Scottish courts in this matter. This is because in his case there was evidence of an intention that his actings should have harmful effects here. But, since I consider that proof of knowledge or intention as to the destination of the drugs is not necessary to establish jurisdiction in the case of this offence, I am of opinion that no relevant difference exists between the position of the two appellants."

Appeals refused.

NOTE

It is of interest that in *McMorrow v. H.M. Advocate*, 1987 G.W.D. 39–1416 it was observed in the High Court of Justiciary that if the appellant was a courier then he was concerned in the supply of drugs.

10. Rodden v. H.M. Advocate   **4.4.24**
1994 S.C.C.R. 841

R. was charged along with another man, B. with being concerned in the supply of a controlled drug, contrary to the 1971 Act, s. 4(3)(b). The two accused were in a car driven by the appellant which was stopped by the police. Both men left the car and were searched, with negative results. After the accused had driven off, the police discovered some substances which they rightly suspected were drugs and which they believed had been dropped by the accused. They kept a watch on the locus and after about 20 minutes the two accused returned and began an agitated search of the locus. The police then found some of the suspected drugs in B.'s possession.

At the trial, B.'s position was that he had been looking for a key. The sheriff directed the jury that if B. was concerned in the supply of a controlled drug, by inference the appellant must also have been so concerned, because he was helping B. to look for the drug. Both accused were convicted and the appellant appealed to the High Court on the ground, *inter alia*, that the sheriff had failed to direct the jury that the Crown must prove that the appellant knew that B. was looking for a drug.

Held, that where two people are charged art and part in a contravention of section 4(3)(b), it must be proved that there was knowledge on the part of each accused that drugs were involved in the transaction in question, that the real question in this case was whether there was sufficient evidence to entitle the jury to draw the inference that the appellant knew that drugs were involved, and that there was sufficient evidence to justify the jury in drawing that inference, and that, although the sheriff's charge left something to be desired, the jury must have appreciated that what they were being asked to determine was whether the appellant and B. were acting together when they were seen searching for what turned out to be a controlled drug, and that accordingly there had been no miscarriage of justice; and appeal on this ground refused.

THE LORD JUSTICE-CLERK (ROSS) (at p. 844): "We are bound to say that the sheriff's directions regarding the case against the appellant are not entirely satisfactory and indeed are somewhat confusing. On one view the sheriff appears to be telling the jury that they were entitled to find the appellant guilty if they were also finding the co-accused guilty.

However that may be, we are satisfied that in the present case there was no miscarriage of justice. The Crown case against both the appellant and his co-accused clearly was that they were acting together in concert. Where two or more accused are charged with acting art and part in the contravention of section 4(3)(b) of the Act of 1971, it must be established by sufficient evidence that there was knowledge on the part of each accused that drugs were involved in the transaction in question

(*McCadden* v. *H.M. Advocate* [1986 S.C.C.R. 16]; *Tudhope* v. *McKee* [1988 S.L.T. 153]).

Accordingly the real question in the present case must be whether there was sufficient evidence to entitle the jury to draw the inference that the appellant knew that drugs were involved in the transaction in question. We are satisfied that there was sufficient evidence to justify the jury in drawing that inference. The appellant and his co-accused were both searched when they were stopped at the locus initially. The appellant was still with his co-accused when they returned to the locus and they were both seen looking around in an agitated and anxious way and on their hands and knees. There was thus ample evidence that the two of them were engaged together in the exercise of looking for some object on the ground. The matter does not end there because since two pieces of cannabis resin were subsequently found in the possession of Mr Black and were identified as two of the pieces which the police had seen earlier, it follows that the appellant must have been present when his co-accused discovered and took possession of and retained those two pieces of cannabis resin. He must have known perfectly well what they were looking for and that his co-accused found what they were looking for. On the basis of that evidence we are satisfied that the jury were entitled to conclude that when they were seen at the locus on their hands and knees looking for something, the appellant and his co-accused were engaged together in a common criminal purpose, namely that they were concerned in the supplying of a controlled drug. Section 4(3)(b) is enacted in very wide terms and covers a great variety of activities in relation to dealing in controlled drugs (*Kerr* v. *H.M. Advocate* [1986 J.C. 41]). The present case appears to us to be a clear case of two people being found guilty art and part of contravening the provisions of section 4(3)(b) of the Act of 1971. Although the sheriff's charge leaves something to be desired, we are satisfied that the jury must have appreciated that the case before them was based on concert and that what they were being asked to determine was whether the appellant and his co-accused were acting together when they were seen in an agitated and anxious way to be searching at the locus for something which turned out to be a controlled drug. For the foregoing reasons we are satisfied that the directions which the sheriff gave did not produce any miscarriage of justice."

Appeal refused.

4.4.25   **11. Dickson v. H.M. Advocate**
                              1995 S.L.T. 703

D. was tried on indictment with *inter alia* being concerned in the supply of the drug MDA, commonly referred to as Ecstasy, between February 1, 1993 and May 6, 1993, and possessing MDA with intent to supply it to others on May 6, 1993, contrary to sections 4(3)(b) and 5(3) respectively of the 1971 Act. The evidence against the accused consisted of the recovery of a quantity of MDA on May 6, 1993. The trial judge directed the jury that if they decided that the accused was buying in bulk and separating the drug into smaller deals with a view to selling the deals for profit the proper verdict would be guilty of both charges because that would indicate that the accused was more actively involved in the general chain of distribution than mere possession with intent to supply to other persons. The accused was convicted and appealed on the ground of misdirection.

Held, (1) that there was a misdirection since the passage complained of was an invitation to the jury to convict on both charges on the same set of facts: the possession of drugs which had been bought in bulk with a view to sale for profit was a typical case under section 5(3) and it was involvement in other transactions, usually over a period of time before or after the date when the accused was found in possession of the drugs, which allowed also a conviction under section 4(3)(b); (2) that the directions were accordingly confusing and gave rise to the risk of a miscarriage of justice; and appeal allowed and conviction under section 4(3)(b) quashed.

THE LORD JUSTICE GENERAL (HOPE) (at p. 705): "The appellant is Kevin Robert Kent Dickson who was found guilty in the High Court at Forfar of various charges under the Misuse of Drugs Act 1971. Among these were three charges which related to the Class A controlled drug known as methylenedioxyamphetamine, or MDA for short, commonly referred to as 'Ecstasy'. Charge 1 was one of being concerned in the supplying of this controlled drug between 1 February 1993 and 6 May 1993, contrary to s. 4(3)(b) of the Act. Charge 4 was one of having this controlled drug in his possession in a house in Dundee on 6 May 1993, with intent to supply to another or others, contrary to s. 5(3). Charge 5 was one of having the controlled drug in his possession on that date and in the same house at Dundee, contrary to s. 5(2) of the 1971 Act. The appellant has appealed against his conviction on charge 1 only, on the ground that there was a miscarriage of justice due to misdirections by the trial judge. He does not challenge his conviction on charges 4 and 5, for which he received substantial periods of imprisonment.

The point which the trial judge was dealing with in the passages to which our attention has been drawn in this case is the familiar one which arises where charges are brought under more than one provision of the Misuse of Drugs Act 1971 in the light of the same facts and circumstances. It is well established that an accused cannot be found guilty of more than one offence on the same set of facts. Authority for that is to be found in *Kyle* v. *H.M. Advocate*, 1988 S.L.T. 601. But there is no rule of law which prevents an accused from being convicted on more than one charge in regard to his possession of controlled drugs, so long as the evidence relied on in respect of each charge is not the same evidence. If there is additional evidence to support a conviction on other charges as well as the one to which a jury directs its first attention, then it will be open to the jury to convict on those other charges also having regard to that additional evidence.

In the present case, the grounds of appeal do not suggest that there was a lack of evidence to support the conviction on these three charges. The complaint is that the directions which the jury were given were confusing and that the trial judge, although making the general point which we have just mentioned correctly, resorted to examples the effect of which was to lead to a miscarriage of justice.

The trial judge began his discussion of this matter in his charge where he told the jury that they had to consider whether each charge was, or was not, established against the accused independently. He stressed that the jury could not convict of more than one charge on precisely the same set of facts or inferences and he then went on to give further directions to explain how that direction operated in the present case. He took as his starting point charge 5, which was the charge of simple possession, and in a passage which has not been criticised to any extent he explained to the jury what the difference was between that charge and charge 4, which was the charge of possession with intent to supply to others. He made it clear that, if the jury were minded to find the accused guilty of both these charges, they would require to conclude on the evidence that he was in possession of some of the Ecstasy which was found in his possession for his own use and some of it with intent to supply it to others. That part of his directions was, we think, entirely in accordance with sound principle, and it was not said to have given rise to any difficulty.

The passage which has been challenged is that where he came to deal with charge 1. In this passage he gave directions to the jury as to how they could find the appellant guilty of this charge as well as charges 4 and 5. He began by giving them the familiar direction about the meaning of the phrase 'concerned in the supplying to others of controlled drugs', in s. 4(3)(b) of the 1971 Act. This direction was taken from a passage in Lord Hunter's opinion in *Kerr v. H.M. Advocate*, 1986 J.C. 41. He ended this passage by stressing that, unless the jury were satisfied that there were circumstances which took the case beyond either simple possession or possession with intent to supply to others, it would not be open to them to convict on this charge. Those parts of this passage are not criticised either in this appeal.

The point which has given rise to the appeal emerges where the trial judge sought to give examples of how the jury might be able to distinguish between the facts appropriate for a conviction on charge 1 as compared with those appropriate for a conviction on charges 4 and 5. The first example which he gave was if the jury decided that the accused was buying in bulk and separating the drug MDA into smaller deals with a view to selling them for a profit. Taking that set of facts as his example, he then said that the proper verdict would be to find the appellant guilty of charge 1 as well as charge 4, because it would be obvious from those facts that he was intending to pass the drugs on to other people. He added that it would be possible for the jury on these facts to convict the appellant on charge 5 also if they thought that some of the drug was to be held back for the appellant's own use.

In our opinion that passage, without further explanation, amounted to a misdirection, because it was an invitation to the jury to convict the appellant on both charge 1 and charge 4 on the same set of facts. The trial judge told the jury that they could, and should, convict him of charge 1 as well as charge 4 if they thought that the appellant was buying in bulk and separating the drugs which were in his possession into smaller deals with a view to selling them for a profit. But the question whether or not the drugs were bought in bulk or were to be sold for profit was not to the point, as there was nothing here to distinguish between the facts appropriate to a conviction on charge 4 and the additional facts on which a conviction on charge 1 would also be appropriate. The possession of a quantity of controlled drugs which have been bought in bulk with a view to their sale for profit is a typical case for a conviction under s. 5(3). It is the involvement in other transactions, usually over a period of time before or after the date when the accused was found to be in possession of them, which enables him to be convicted also of an offence under s. 4(3)(b) of the Act. The trial judge then went on to give a further example of the distinction between a person who is actively involved in the general chain of distribution as compared to somebody who is merely the passive recipient of drugs from others. But here again it appears to us that he failed to distinguish clearly enough between the facts appropriate to a conviction on charge 1 as compared with those appropriate to a conviction on charge 4. The use of the word 'passive' was misleading, as it suggested that the actions of purchase from others and of separating into deals were sufficient in themselves to enable the distinction to be drawn. These actions, typically, are those which will show that a person who is in possession of controlled drugs is in possession of them with intent to supply them to another or others. Something more, by way of involvement in other transactions, is needed if the accused is to be convicted also of being concerned in the supplying of controlled drugs.

In his reply to counsel's submissions, which we have in effect summarised in what we have said so far, the advocate depute submitted that the directions which the trial judge gave in this passage were in accordance with the evidence which the jury had heard and that they could be properly understood against that background. He gave us a brief account of his understanding of what the evidence was in this case. On this point however we are in some difficulty because the trial judge in his brief report has not told us what the evidence was, although he says that the example of the additional *species facti* which he gave to the jury was in accordance with the evidence. Although the advocate depute did give us, as we say, a brief summary of what the evidence was, this was disputed by counsel as not being in accordance with his recollection. In these circumstances we do not feel able to draw any conclusions on this point. All we can say is that, if the directions which the trial judge gave were in accordance with the evidence, they failed to make it clear to the jury where the additional evidence was which would have justified a verdict of guilty on charge 1 as well as charge 4.

It is important in cases of this kind, where juries are being told that they cannot convict on more than one charge on the same set of facts, for directions which are intended to give examples of this to be related to the evidence which has been led in the case. Furthermore, it is important that the jury should be properly guided as to the distinction between s. 5(3) charge and a s. 4(3)(b) charge, and as to how that distinction can be made in the light of the evidence. As we have said, typically a s. 4(3)(b) charge will involve some activities extending over a period of time. The wording of charge 1 suggests that that was indeed what the Crown was seeking to prove in this case. By way of contrast a s. 5(3) will normally be related to the finding of particular drugs in the accused's possession on one particular occasion, which indeed was what was alleged on charge 4. It is unfortunate that in the passages to which our attention has been drawn the trial judge did not mention the time element, or mention other facts and circumstances which might have indicated that the appellant's activities extended beyond his possession of drugs on 6 May 1993 into a more extended activity involving other transactions as well as that which resulted in his possession of those drugs on that date.

We have reached the conclusion that the jury's verdict on this charge must be set aside. In our opinion the passage of the charge was confusing and it gave rise to the risk of a miscarriage of justice. We are not satisfied that it would be right for us in all the circumstances of this case to attempt to analyse the evidence with the assistance of a further report from the trial judge, in order to see whether this misdirection nevertheless did not give rise to a miscarriage of justice. This is because we cannot know what the jury made of that evidence, in view of the way in which they were told they could find the appellant guilty of charge 1 as well as charge 4. For these reasons we have decided that the course which we must take in this case is to allow the appeal and quash the conviction on charge 1."

Appeal allowed.

4.4.26

12. Douglas v. Boyd
1996 S.C.C.R. 44

B. and her father were charged with a contravention of section 4(3)(b) of the 1971 Act. The evidence led by the Crown was that B.'s father sold the drugs involved on an occasion on which B. was not present. A fortnight later B. requested payment on behalf of her father from the person who had bought the drugs. The sheriff upheld a submission of no case to answer and acquitted B. The procurator fiscal appealed to the High Court by stated case.

Held, that the sheriff had not attached proper significance to the fact that what was in issue was "being concerned in the supplying" of a controlled drug and that, in any event, so far as supply in this case was concerned, the process of supply could not be said to have been at an end at the stage when B. went to the person who had been supplied and demanded payment for the drug on behalf of the supplier, and the sheriff was wrong to hold that there was insufficient evidence to convict the respondent; and appeal allowed, and case remitted to the sheriff to proceed as accords.

Appeal allowed.

(iv) Concerned in the making of an offer to supply   4.4.27

1. R. v. Blake and O'Connor   4.4.28
(1978) 68 Cr.App.R. 1

Policemen saw O. approach a group of people in central London and they heard him ask if they liked cannabis. When they asked where they could get some of the drug, O. replied that he had a friend who lived in a flat nearby who could "fix them." When they arrived at B.'s flat, B. said to O. "Is it [the cannabis] they want?" Then B. appeared to realise that some of the people present were policemen and he left pretending not to know O.

Both B. and O. were charged with contravening section 4(3)(c) of the 1971 Act. Neither B. nor O. gave evidence at their trial, and the jury were directed that before B. could be guilty there would have to be some previous arrangement between him and O. Both B. and O. were convicted.

On appeal it was argued for B. that as B. did not know of the offer made outwith his flat, he could not be guilty of the offence charged.

EVELEIGH, L.J. (at p. 2): "The Court has been invited to say that the offence of being concerned in the making to another of an offer requires a specific and close involvement in the particular offer that was made in Piccadily on that day, and, if we understand counsel's argument properly, he is saying that Blake, not knowing that that particular offer was made, could not be guilty of that offence. This Court rejects that submission. It is clear that section 4(3)(c) has been particularly widely drawn to involve people who may be at some distance from the actual making of the offer. It is not necessary, on the facts of this case, to go more closely into the precise meaning of that section."

Appeal dismissed.

NOTE

This case is also reported at [1979] Crim.L.R. 464. That report does not include reference to the question asked by B. of O. and neither report gives any indication of whether there was an answer to that question and, if so, what O. said. That question, it is submitted, reveals the existence of some knowledge common to B. and O.

The appeal court regarded it as enough that B. had arranged with O. that O. should make offers to supply the drug to someone. When O. made such an offer to an individual then B. was "concerned in" the making of that offer. At appeal Eveleigh, L.J. pointed out that O. might not have been convicted if the jury had concluded that O. was merely giving the interested parties information as to where they could get the cannabis.

The last point was explained by one of the counsel involved in the case who added that it was not entirely a matter of semantics to say there is a difference between making an offer to supply drugs and informing a person of a drug supplier who might be in a position to supply a drug: [1979] Crim.L.R. 684.

That distinction may in certain circumstances be a correct one to make but the Appeal Court held the jury to be perfectly justified in coming to the verdict they did, particularly as no other explanation was given for the conduct of B. and O. at the relevant time.

4.5   C. SENTENCING: PRODUCTION

4.5.1   **1. R. v. Shaw**
                      (1988) 10 Cr.App.R. (S.) 93

S. pleaded guilty to possessing a controlled drug with intent to supply, and producing a controlled drug. Policemen had searched his house and found 66 cannabis plants and equipment for cultivating them and converting the leaves: a further 44 plants were found growing in the cellar. It was claimed that S.'s methods were such that he was unlikely to succeed in producing a commercially marketable quantity of cannabis. He was sentenced to five years' imprisonment and appealed.

IAN KENNEDY, J. (at p. 94): "The case therefore remains on the basis, that it is asserted upon the appellant's behalf that it is unlikely that his production would ever have been a commercial success. That clearly is an important matter in the context of a case such as this."

(At p. 95)

"Of [the viability of the venture] the learned [trial] judge said this: 'To say that you intended only to see what you could produce, that you thought the product you were going to produce was of such an inferior quality nobody would buy it, is again absolute rubbish.' We would not ourselves disagree with that proposition. Perhaps it was inferior, I do not know. I am not interested. The fact is it was controlled; these blocks contained controlled drugs. Of course you intended to sell them and if during the course of selling them the buyers felt that they had been swindled or were deceived, then no doubt you would have said 'That is too bad.' Again, we would not dissent from the learned judge's comments. But the facts remain that the question that had to be evaluated for the purpose of sentence was not simply the fact that this man had produced a controlled drug, but also concerned the degree of danger that his operation presented to the public in general. It might be that, if the purchasers complained, he would say that it was 'too bad.' But then they would not come back for more, and particularly in an area such as the Isle of Wight, the prospect of this becoming a substantial business would be remote."

Appeal allowed and sentence of two years' imprisonment imposed.

NOTE

The decision of the appeal court contains (*ibid*. at p. 94) a description of how, as a result of a misunderstanding between individuals, the plants were not examined scientifically for the THC (tetrahydrocannibinol) content to be measured. Thus the issue of the weakness or the strength of cannabis, having been raised by the defence, could not be proved by them or refuted by the prosecution.

2. R. v. Richard   **4.5.2**
(1994) 15 Cr.App.R. (S.) 249

Two appellants pleaded guilty to attempting to produce a controlled drug, amphetamine, and a third to permitting premises to be used for the purpose. Police officers searching the premises of he third appellant found equipment and material suitable for the production of amphetamine sulphate. After hearing evidence the sentencer found that the appellants intended to produce about one kilogramme of amphetamine sulphate for commercial gain. The first appellant was sentenced to three years' imprisonment and the others to 30 months' imprisonment.

Held, it was possible that the amount of amphetamine which would have been produced was less than the sentencer had found it to be; the sentence on the first appellant would be reduced to two years and on the other appellants to 18 months' and 12 months' imprisonment respectively.

Appeals allowed.

3. R. v. Marsland   **4.5.3**
(1994) 15 Cr.App.R. (S.) 665

M. pleaded guilty to producing a Class B drug, cannabis. Police officers searching the appellant's premises were shown a room in which 22 mature cannabis plants were growing: the room had been adapted for the purpose. A further 55 cannabis plants in various stages of growth were found in other parts of the house. The appellant claimed that he was producing cannabis solely for his own use, and he was sentenced, to 18 months' imprisonment, on that basis.

Held, (considering *Proud* (1987) 9 Cr.App.R. (S.) 119) the sentence of 18 months was too long; an appropriate sentence would be nine months.

Appeal allowed.

4.5.4   **4. Henderson v. H.M. Advocate**
1996 S.C.C.R. 71

H., a first offender, pleaded guilty in the High Court to a charge of producing cannabis, contrary to section 4(2)(a) of the 1971 Act. She was sentenced to 18 months' imprisonment and appealed to the High Court where it was submitted on her behalf that as the cannabis was grown for her own use the offence should be treated in the same way as simple possession of cannabis.

Held, (1) that it was a misconception to treat a contravention of section 4(2)(a) as equivalent to an offence of simple possession which was usually transient and in small quantities, while in the case of production the activity involved a degree of planning with a conceived beginning and end in view, and that the maximum sentences provided for each of these offences showed that it was the intention of Parliament that the production and cultivation of cannabis should be seen as offences of an entirely different character from simple possession and (2) that the court's duty was to apply the law in accordance with policy disclosed by the sentences provided for by Parliament, and that looking at the matter in that light the sentence was not excessive; and appeal refused.

Observed, that it would have been a misdirection if the trial judge had sentenced the appellant on the basis that her activity was carried out with the intention of supplying cannabis to others or dealing in the cannabis, the appellant not having been charged with these offences.

Appeal refused.

4.6 D. SENTENCING: SUPPLY

4.6.1 (1) Class A: *(i) Diamorphine*

4.6.2   **1. R. v. Macauley**
(1968) 52 Cr.App.R. 230

M. had been convicted of supplying six diamorphine tablets to a boy, who was 15 years' old, apparently for onward transmission. M. was sentenced to the then statutory maximum of 10 years' imprisonment.

EDMUND DAVIES, L.J. (at p. 232): "Ten years was the maximum sentence, and the fact of itself causes the Court to pause and ask itself anxiously whether that was the right sentence to impose. Holy Writ has in dread terms declared what is the fitting fate of those who place a stumbling block in the path of the young. And Parliament has rightly had regard to the growing menace of drug addiction. Anyone supplying a mere child, a boy of 15, with a hard drug is doing a most terrible deed which calls for grave punishment."

Appeal dismissed.

2. R. v. Ogunmokum   4.6.3
Court of Appeal (Criminal Division) January 16, 1975

O. and others were convicted of a large number of offences relating to the possession and supply of diamorphine in London. O. was sentenced to imprisonment and appealed.

BROWNE, L.J. (p. 2): "People who were buying for their own use were dealt with in the Magistrates' Courts. The next level were what are called 'runners' — the link between the buyers and pushers. Many of the 'runners' were addicts themselves, selling heroin in order to raise the money to supply their own requirements. Most of those concerned in the first trial were 'runners.' In the arguments in the other case this morning the phrase 'addict-pushers' was used to describe some, at any rate, of these people."

Appeals dismissed.

3. R. v. Chatwood   4.6.4
[1980] 1 All E.R. 467

C. had pleaded guilty to possessing diamorphine and to supplying the same drug. He was sentenced to three years' imprisonment on the supply charge and six months concurrent on each of the possession charges. That, it was said on appeal, was excessive.

FORBES, J. (at p. 472): "A sentence of three years for supplying heroin cannot, in the view of this court, be regarded as excessive or wrong in principle."

Appeal dismissed.

4. R. v. Ashraf and Huq   4.6.5
(1981) 3 Cr.App.R. (S.) 287

This case is considered *infra* at paragraph **5.4.39**

4.6.6
5. R. v. Gee
(1984) 6 Cr.App.R. (S.) 86

G. was convicted of supplying controlled drugs by selling diamorphine and methadone in order to obtain money to purchase diamorphine for himself. He pleaded guilty to a number of offences, some of which were committed while on bail for others. He was sentenced to six years' imprisonment and appealed.

MUSTHILL, J. (at p. 90): "[It is] essential to realise that there are gradations in the gravity of offences of this type, and it is essential in each case for the Court to do its best to place the particular offences at the correct part of the scale of seriousness.

Where do the present offences lie on the scale? At the bottom of the scale is the small social supplier, the man who does supply drugs, but only within the limited circle of friends and not for gain. Markedly higher up the scale, though substantially below the top of it, is the small professional middleman who supplies drugs in order to make a profit. It seems to us that this appellant lies between the two points on the scale which we have identified."

Appeal allowed and four years' imprisonment
substituted.

NOTE
Further along the scale from *R. v. Gee* is the case of *R. v. Doyle* (1988) 10 Cr.App.R. (S.) 5. There D. was found in possession of a bag containing 3.39 grammes of powder of which 25 per cent was diamorphine, estimated to be worth £179. D. admitted using heroin himself, and that he had been selling heroin in small packets for a few weeks. Appeal against seven years' imprisonment dismissed.

4.6.7
6. R. v. Guiney
[1985] Crim. L.R. 751

G. pleaded guilty to two charges of supplying diamorphine and possessing 534 milligrammes of diamorphine with intent to supply. He had been arrested in possession of the quantity of diamorphine stated which was in 20 paper wraps, and £375 in cash. He admitted that he had bought the drugs the previous day and had sold some to customers. He claimed that he sold only to friends and existing addicts. He was sentenced to six years' imprisonment. On appeal counsel for G. submitted that the sentence was excessive in the light of *R. v. Gee, supra.*

Held, that the appellant in *R. v. Gee* had come somewhere between the small-scale social supplier supplying friends without profit, and the small-scale professional middleman supplying drugs for profit. The same description would fit the appellant in this case. As one of the more important functions of the Appeal Court is to achieve consistency the same result would follow.

> Appeal allowed and four years' imprisonment substituted.

7. R. v. Ansari   4.6.8
[1986] Crim.L.R. 128

A. was stopped while driving his car, and found to be in possession of 35 grammes of diamorphine. His house was searched and a total of four ounces of diamorphine was found buried in the garden. A. admitted that he had bought the controlled drugs in London and that he had supplied small quantities to three other people, including his wife. It was accepted that he had not been concerned in any importation of diamorphine from abroad. A. pleaded guilty to a number of drugs-related charges, including supplying charges, and he was sentenced to a total of seven years' imprisonment.

On appeal, it was accepted that the amount of diamorphine involved did not place it at the higher end of the scale. The age and good character of A. were not significant, as some persons were sought out by organisers of the trade to form the chain of distribution. The court accepted that A. was not a professional dealer as there was no evidence of dealing outside a small circle of friends, who were probably all addicts.

The court was of the view that the range of sentences for dealing in hard drugs should be reconsidered, having regard to the deadly nature of dealing in these drugs, but the court was not at this juncture concerned with that. The court could not criticise the trial judge but on a comparative basis the sentence was somewhat severe.

> Appeal allowed and seven years' imprisonment varied to five years.

8. R. v. Kelly   4.6.9
(1988) 9 Cr.App.R. (S.) 385

K. pleaded guilty to possessing diamorphine and to supplying it. He was found in possession of a very small quantity of it and a friend who was with him was found in possession of about one twentyfourth part of a gramme. K. had given that quantity to his friend. Sentenced to 12 years' imprisonment for supplying diamorphine and 12 months concurrent for possession, K. appealed.

STOCKER, L.J. (at p. 387): "One must emphasise that we are here dealing with heroin, a drug very prevalent and potentially lethal when used. The courts have, over and over again, pointed out the gravity of offences relating to heroin".

And later (at p. 388)

"This was a case of social supply of one small fold of heroin amounting to about [one twentyfourth part of a gramme], a very tiny amount. There was no question of sale or purchase entered into. We form the view that that was just about the smallest amount which could be concerned in the offence of supplying and must put the case absolutely at the bottom end of the sentencing range, though there is no doubt at all a substantial prison sentence, even for so modest a supply ... was appropriate."

Appeal allowed and sentence varied to two years' imprisonment.

4.6.10   **9. R. v. Green**
(1992) 13 Cr.App.R. (S.) 613

G. pleaded guilty to supplying heroin. The appellant was recorded on video supplying heroin in a street. He admitted making between £140 and £175 per day in this way. He was sentenced to 18 months' imprisonment on each count concurrent. The appellant had been diagnosed as suffering from sickle cell anaemia at the age of 16 months, and suffered form the disease in a very severe form. The appellant had suffered from anaemia and jaundice, and had required blood transfusions on many occasions. Management of his illness was severely impaired by his imprisonment, and there was a risk of serious deterioration leading to sudden death if specialist facilities were not available.

Held, the sentencer indicated that a sentence of five years would have been appropriate, but reduced it to 18 months because of the appellant's condition. While it was vitally necessary that those who peddle drugs should be dealt with severely, the special circumstances of the case persuaded the Court to suspend 14 months of the sentence, so that the appellant would be released immediately.

Appeal allowed.

4.6.11   **10. R. v. O'Brien**
(1994) 15 Cr.App.R. (S.) 556

O'B. pleaded guilty to four counts of supplying a Class A drug, heroin. The appellant shared a vial of heroin, which he had bought for £30, with a group of young people; the heroin was of dangerously high purity. All of those who took the heroin became ill, and one died. It was accepted that the appellant had not supplied the heroin with a commercial motive. He was sentenced to five years' imprisonment.

Held, the Court took into account the fact that the supply was not on a commercial scale, that the appellant was not aware of the purity of the heroin and the personal mitigation. The sentence of five years was excessive; a sentence of three years would be substituted.

Appeal allowed and sentence varied.

NOTE
The Court in *R. v. O'Brien* was influenced by decisions not before the trial judge. Those cases involved the supply of a controlled drug in similar circumstances and not for a commercial motive and, separately, manslaughter: *R. v. Cato* (1976) 62 Cr.App.R. 41; *R. v. Dalby* (1982) 74 Cr.App.R. 348 and *R. v. Clarke and Purvis* (1992) 13 Cr.App.R. (S.) 552.

Class A: *(ii) Lysergamide* **4.6.12**

1. R. v. Vickery **4.6.13**
[1976] Crim.L.R. 143

V. pleaded guilty to supplying LSD. He had bought a car from another person for 200 LSD tablets, a fur coat and £25. He then assisted the other person to find buyers for the tablets. V. was sentenced to three years' imprisonment. He had three previous convictions relating to drugs. He appealed against sentence.

Held, that LSD tablets were a very dangerous form of drugs and three years' imprisonment could be regarded as the minimum sentence for supplying them, in the absence of extenuating circumstances. In the present case there was an element of aggravation because V. had helped the other man to sell the tablets.

Those who supplied drugs should be treated much more severely than those who possessed them, as had been recognised by Parliament. The sooner it was appreciated that those who supplied drugs would get severe sentences the better it would be.

Appeal dismissed.

NOTE
This approach was followed later in *R. v. Musgrove* (1982) 142 J.P. 406 where a student bought LSD and sold it to his friends at cost price. No profit was made in these transactions, and the appellate court was clearly sympathetic to the character of the appellant, but nevertheless dismissed an appeal against a sentence of three years' imprisonment.

2. R. v. Virgin **4.6.14**
(1983) 5 Cr.App.R. (S.) 148

V. pleaded guilty *inter alia* to supplying LSD after selling five tablets of the substance to a young man for £10. V. was also found to be in possession of enough LSD to provide about 48 doses. He was sentenced to three and a half years' imprisonment concurrent on the two charges relating to the supply of LSD with concurrent sentences for the other offences. He appealed against sentence and it was then submitted that he only supplied drugs in a small way to enable him to buy others for his own consumption. In short V. contended that he was the last link in the chain of supply.

SHELDON, J. (at p. 150): "The extreme dangers of LSD are, or should be, common knowledge and need no emphasis. They are such that, bearing in mind the relative ease with which the drug can be distributed by any who might wish to do so, those who are convicted of supplying it must anticipate a substantial prison sentence ... In a recent social inquiry report ... the reporting officer said that the appellant was 'shocked by the length of prison sentence he received' and that it was to be anticipated that it would have a salutory effect on any future involvement by him with drugs. So it is to be hoped — such indeed is one purpose of a sentence such as this."

Appeal dismissed.

4.6.15 Class B: *(i) Cannabis*

4.6.16   **1. R. v. McAuley**
(1979) 1 Cr.App.R. (S.) 71

M. pleaded guilty to a number of charges concerning cannabis, especially to supplying it. He had been frank with the police when arrested and he admitted supplying cannabis but he said, and it was accepted by the Crown, that only a circle of his friends had been supplied. On being sentenced to 18 months' imprisonment he appealed.

SWANWICK, J. (at p. 72): "The danger is that such circles are apt to widen as the news gets round and as more people become addicted or take up the habit, learning no doubt from one another."

Appeal dismissed.

4.6.17   **2. R. v. Platt**
(1980) 2 Cr.App.R. (S.) 307

P. pleaded guilty to several charges of supplying cannabis. He was sentenced to 15 months' imprisonment concurrently for each charge. He had bought eight ounces of cannabis in Reading and he resold it in parcels of one or one half ounce in Cornwall. The purchase price was £180 and the resale price about £256, making a profit of £76. Sentence was appealed.

BOREHAM, J. (at p. 309): "This was a substantial amount of cannabis. The profit, though not vast, was by no means negligible. He was deliberately distributing amongst a substantial number of people, and in these circumstances, he had no ground for complaining about the result."

Appeal dismissed.

NOTE
In *McNab v. H.M. Advocate*, 1986 S.C.C.R. 230 the appellant pleaded guilty to offering to supply cannabis resin, in three pieces said to have a street-value of £40, to two policemen in a public house. The sheriff took the view that the appellant had acted in the knowledge of the attitude of the courts to such offences, and imposed a sentence of nine months' imprisonment, which was appealed. On appeal it was held that the sheriff was entitled to take the view he did, and that the sentence could not possibly be regarded as excessive and appeal refused.

3. R. v. Hill   4.6.18
(1988) 10 Cr.App.R. (S.) 150

H. pleaded guilty to four offences relating to the possession or supply of cannabis. Police officers observed abnormal numbers of persons visiting his house for short periods: several were stopped and found to be in possession of small quantities of cannabis. When policemen entered the house, H. attempted to swallow a bag containing 55 grammes of cannabis in the form of 32 individually wrapped pieces. It was accepted that H. had been dealing in cannabis from his house on a regular basis and over a period of time, although the precise period was disputed. H. appealed against a sentence of 30 months' imprisonment.

AULD, J. (at p. 152): "It is true that the appellant was not a large-scale drug-dealer making large profits. He was a retail distributor supplying small quantities from his home. Nevertheless he appears to have established a regular clientele and to have been operating on a well-organised and commercial basis. As I have said, on the information before the learned judge, he was making a profit of at least £100 a week out of this regular dealing. As the learned judge in his sentencing remarks described it, this was 'a supply on a very considerable scale to quite a large number of people.' Without such distribution outlets at the end of the drug distribution network, wholesale drug dealers and importers on a large scale could not flourish. Nevertheless, in our view, the sentence here was near the top end of the bracket for offences of this sort. The court was concerned with cannabis resin. Although the supply was on a regular basis to a large number of people the amounts involved were comparatively small. We think that perhaps greater recognition should have been given to the appellant's plea of guilty in the matter. In all the circumstances the view of the court is that a total sentence of 21 months' would have been more appropriate."

NOTE
	The scenario presented by the facts in this case is familiar to that encountered frequently by those in practice so that the case is a useful guide to sentencing levels. One difference for Scots lawyers is the discount on a guilty plea: such an inducement is frequently referred to in English decisions but is not part of Scottish practice *c.f. Strawhorn v. McLeod*, 1987 S.C.C.R. 413.

4.6.19					**4. Miller v. H.M. Advocate**
					1995 S.C.C.R. 314

M., aged 33, was the mother of four children of whom three, including a ten-month-old baby, were her personal responsibility. She was a good mother. She was convicted of supplying a small amount of cannabis and of possessing cannabis to a value of between £360 and £600 with intent to supply it to another. She was sentenced to four years' imprisonment on each charge, concurrently, and appealed to the High Court against sentence.
	Held, that in view of the effect of imprisonment on her children, and particularly the baby, there was room for a degree of leniency which ought to have been available in other similar cases; and sentences reduced to three years' imprisonment on each charge.

NOTE
	The High Court of Justiciary asserted firmly that it would continue, so long as it had the power to do so, to assert the right of judges to exercise leniency wherever that is appropriate: *H.M. Advocate v. McKay*, 1996 S.C.C.R. 410. In that case the respondent was a reformed addict who was then assisting others who had allegedly suffered similarly.

4.6.20					**5. Gibson v. H.M. Advocate**
					1992 S.C.C.R. 855

G. pleaded guilty to supplying cannabis resin, contrary to section 4(3)(a) of the 1971 Act. She was found in possession of about £35 worth of cannabis resin and also pleaded guilty to a charge of unlawful possession of cannabis resin, contrary to section 5(2) of the 1971 Act. She was sentenced to nine months' imprisonment on the supply charge and appealed to the High Court against the sentence as excessive, she being a first offender and the supply being to friends only.
	Held, that it was undoubtedly the position that offences such as supplying controlled drugs should attract severe sentences, but that the court must always have regard to the circumstances of any particular case and in the present case the sheriff had not attached sufficient weight to the fact that the appellant was a first offender, that the quantity involved

was very small, and that any supply took place among friends; and appeal allowed and sentence of imprisonment quashed and order for 180 hours' community service substituted.

Appeal allowed.

NOTE
The supply of controlled drugs can produce judicial rhetoric, *e.g.* in *MacBeth v. H.M. Advocate*, 1987 G.W.D. 34–1224 there was reference to the appellant having a "corrupting influence in a rural community" and the degree of his material contribution.

However, the unlawful nature of controlled drugs and their supply (taken with economies of scale) mean that an individual is frequently deputed to obtain controlled drugs for others.

The High Court of Justiciary has been told on very many occasions that the accused or appellant has been supplying controlled drugs merely "socially" or to like-minded "friends."

Such an explanation need not always be accepted unquestioningly but it is heard too often to be invariably wrong and the appellate judges seem prepared to have regard to the restricted nature of the ultimate market.

For examples of social supply see: *Donaldson v. H.M. Advocate*, 1987 G.W.D. 4–117; *Lyall v. H.M. Advocate*, 1987 G.W.D. 10–327; *Andrew v. H.M. Advocate*, 1987 G.W.D. 11–366; *Laurie v. H.M. Advocate*, 1988 G.W.D. 25–1069; *Cunningham v. H.M. Advocate*, 1988 G.W.D. 37–1522 (where there is a reference to the distinction between "commercial" and "technical" supply); *McCabe v. H.M. Advocate*, 1988 G.W.D. 8–317; *Wade v. H.M. Advocate*, 1989 G.W.D. 5–205; *Galt v. McGlennan*, 1990 G.W.D. 23–1277; *Ferguson v. H.M. Advocate*, 1991 G.W.D. 34–2067; *Linden v. Heywood*, 1992 G.W.D. 6–289; *Whitelaw v. H.M. Advocate*, 1992 G.W.D. 4–184; *Martin v. H.M. Advocate*, 1992 G.W.D. 9–481; *Laing v. Hillary*, 1992 G.W.D. 14–802; *Brown v. H.M. Advocate*, 1992 G.W.D. 15–872; *Wilson v. H.M. Advocate*, 1993 G.W.D. 40–2411; *Cadis v. H.M. Advocate*, 1993 G.W.D. 11–744; *Shaw v. H.M. Advocate*, 1993 G.W.D. 29–2577; *Nelson v. Russell*, 1994 G.W.D. 14–883; *Guy v. H.M. Advocate*, G.W.D. 15–943; *McNeill v. H.M. Advocate*, 1994 G.W.D. 28–1692; *Carlin v. H.M. Advocate*, *infra*; *Grieve v. H.M. Advocate*, 1994 G.W.D. 35–2069; *Hurles v. Hamilton*, 1995 G.W.D. 2–62; *Burns v. H.M. Advocate*, 1995 G.W.D. 3–133; *Shand v. Donnelly*, 1995 G.W.D. 29–1527; *Hendry v. H.M. Advocate*, 1996 G.W.D. 4–202; *McIntyre v. Hamilton*, 1996 G.W.D. 11–635; *Russell v. H.M. Advocate*, 1996 G.W.D. 22–1266; *Campbell v. Lees*, 1996 G.W.D. 25–1431; *Cunningham v. Lees*, 1996 G.W.D. 28–1674; and *Geddes v. Ruxton*, 1996 G.W.D. 29–1746.

6. R. v. Steventon   4.6.21
(1992) 13 Cr.App.R. (S.) 127

S. pleaded guilty to supplying cannabis, possessing cannabis with intent to supply, and possessing cannabis. Police officers searching the appellant's house found about 730 grammes of cannabis resin in two places. A man in whose company the appellant was arrested admitted buying cannabis from the appellant. S. admitted that he had been dealing in cannabis over a period of about three months. Financial investigations for the purposes of the Drug Trafficking Offences Act 1986 showed unexplained financial transactions over a period of two and a half years. He was sentenced to a total of three years' imprisonment, with a confiscation order in the amount of £1260.

Held, treating the appellant as a medium level retailer, the sentence was too long: a sentence of two years would be substituted.

Simon Brown, J. (at p. 129): "When one turns to the well-recognised guideline decisions upon this area of sentencing, one finds that the bracket for the supply of other than huge quantities of cannabis is specified, if that be the correct term, as between one and four years' imprisonment 'depending upon the scale of the operation. Supplying a number of small sellers, wholeselling if you like comes at the top of the bracket. At the lower end will be the retailer of a small amount to a consumer.'

That passage from the well known decision in *Aramah* (1982) 4 Cr.App.R. (S.) 407 founds [counsel's] helpful and cogent submission before this Court. Accordingly, accepting that this appellant is properly to be regarded as essentially a medium level retailer, clearly not a wholesaler, but equally clearly not a small time low-grade supplier, one's starting point is midway within the bracket of one to four years to which we have referred. That would place the starting point at something of the order of two and a half years. That tariff, of course, is appropriate to contested cases. Here there was a plea of guilty which must in the ordinary way attract a discount.

In the result the Court is disposed to accept the essential thrust of counsel's argument upon this appeal that the three-year sentence passed here is too long and at odds with the guidelines that so closely govern sentencing in this particular area of offending. In our judgment it is appropriate, having regard to the plea, to reduce the sentence here from three years' imprisonment to one of two years' imprisonment. This may best be achieved simply by reducing the sentence to two years on count 1, the other sentences running in any event concurrently. The consequence is that the total sentence produced is one of two years' imprisonment. To that extent this appeal succeeds."

Appeal allowed.

4.6.22　　　　　　　　　　**7. R. v. Nolan**
　　　　　　　　　　(1992) 13 Cr.App.R. (S.) 144

N. pleaded guilty to supplying cannabis. He arranged for a group of schoolboys to buy half an ounce of cannabis from a friend for £50. He was sentenced to four years' imprisonment.

Held, although the amount of cannabis involved would not normally justify a sentence as long as four years, there was the element of corruption of the boys which had led to three of them being expelled from school. In spite of the seriousness of the offence the sentence was too high and a sentence of two and a half years would be substituted.

Appeal allowed.

8. R. v. Weeks 4.6.23
(1993) 14 Cr.App.R. (S.) 94

W. was convicted of supplying a controlled drug, cannabis. The appellant was observed to supply another man with three grammes of cannabis for £10. He was sentenced to 12 months' imprisonment.

Held, (considering *Finkhouse, supra)* the sentence of 12 months was excessive; a sentence of six months was appropriate.

TURNER, J. (at p. 95): "Reference was made to a case in this Court of *Pinkhouse* [*supra*], which was an example of an offence of supplying cannabis on a small scale. But we venture to think that the only assistance that that case has been to us was the passage in the judgment of Leggatt J. at page 19, where he said: 'But in the judgment of this court it is unhelpful in a case such as this to refer to other cases the sentences in which were dependent on their own peculiar facts and did not in any sense constitute guideline cases.' We agree with those observations.

We have each separately given careful consideration to the level of sentence in this case and have come to the conclusion that 12 months was indeed excessive. We have come to the conclusion that the appropriate sentence would have been, on these special facts peculiar to this case, one of six months' imprisonment. The sentence therefore of 12 months' imprisonment is quashed and six months substituted for it."

Appeal allowed.

9. R. v. Vickers 4.6.24
(1993) 14 Cr.App.R. (S.) 317

V. pleaded guilty to supplying cannabis and to possessing cannabis. The appellant, a man aged 49, was approached by three boys, aged between 12 and 15, who asked him for cannabis. The appellant took the boys to his parents' house and gave one of them a small amount of cannabis in the form of a cigarette, which the youngest boy attempted to smoke. The appellant then showed the boys some pornographic material. He was sentenced to 30 months' imprisonment.

Held, there were many different degrees of supplying, from sharing a small amount with a friend to dealing on a commercial scale. The present case was near the bottom of the scale, but not at the bottom of it, because the appellant took the initiative in inviting the boys to his room and because they were relatively young. The appropriate sentence would be nine months' imprisonment.

SEDLEY, J. (at p. 318): "It is unlikely that any of the three boys was materially corrupted by the episode. The drug in question was not Class A, and the judge was wrong to treat the distinction between Class A and Class B drugs as one without a material difference. Parliament itself has made the distinction and the courts can take note of the fact that different classes of prohibited drugs may differ in the harm they are likely to do.

There are also many different degrees of supplying. They travel from sharing a small amount with a friend to dealing on a commercial scale. The present case was at the lower end of this scale, but not at the bottom of it, because the appellant took at least part of the initiative in inviting the boys to his room to smoke cannabis, and because they were relatively young.

The error in the judge's approach requires this Court to look again at the sentences he passed on the appellant, but it does not follow that they will necessarily be wrong. However, so far as the offence of supplying is concerned, the guidance given by this Court in *Aramah* [*supra*] is that, whereas commercial supplying ought ordinarily to attract a sentence of between one and four years, non-commercial supplying (*e.g.* at a party) 'may well be serious enough to justify a custodial sentence.' The implication of this formulation is that there will be cases of supplying in which a custodial sentence can be avoided. This case may be on the margins. But it is less grave than the least serious forms of commercial supplying.

We consider in the circumstances that the appropriate sentence, and the one we propose to substitute, is nine months on the first count.

On the second count there was no indication that this was anything but the possession of a small amount of cannabis by a man otherwise of good character. In the circumstances we propose to impose a sentence of one month concurrent with the first mentioned sentence on this count."

Appeal allowed.

4.6.25 *(ii) Concerned in Supply: General Considerations*

4.6.26   **1. Beattie v. H.M. Advocate**
                              1986 S.C.C.R. 605

B. was charged that he was concerned with the supply of controlled drugs (the "main charge") "in respect that" and there then followed 30 "sub-charges" of contraventions of various sections of the 1971 Act including section 4(3)(*b*); the charge concluded "all of which is contrary to the Misuse of Drugs Act 1971, section 4(3)(*b*)." The maximum sentence available for a contravention of section 4(3)(*b*) was 14 years' imprisonment and a fine, and none of the contraventions referred to in the charges carried a higher penalty. After the jury had been empanelled, the appellant pleaded guilty to the main charge, and also to some of the sub-charges in whole or in part. The trial judge treated this as a plea to a number of separate charges and imposed separate sentences on each of the sub-charges, some of which were consecutive to others, so that the total sentence was one of 16 years' imprisonment. He also imposed fines on some of the sub-charges, the fines to be recoverable by civil diligence.

The appellant appealed on the ground that a sentence of imprisonment in excess of 14 years was incompetent, and also on the ground that it was incompetent to impose a fine in addition to the maximum sentence of imprisonment, because the imposition in default of payment would then be incompetent. He also appealed against the sentences as excessive.

Held (1) that the maximum sentence available did not depend on the form of the plea tendered, but depended on the nature of the charge which was one of contravening section 4(3)(*b*) in a number of specified respects, that the trial judge had erred in treating each sub-charge as a separate charge, and that maximum period of imprisonment available was 14 years; and sentence of imprisonment quashed, and substituted by a sentence of 14 years' imprisonment on the main charges, and separate but concurrent sentences of imprisonment on each sub-charge; and

(2) that imprisonment in default of payment of the fines, if that ever arose, would be imprisonment for failure to pay them and not for a contravention of section 4(3)(*b*); and that the fines were therefore competent.

NOTE
This case is perhaps of more interest for the drafting of indictments (see Sheriff Gordon's comments *ibid.* at p. 613). However it is an indication — and a warning — that the maximum sentence is used.

For further discussion about the appellant's sentence see *Beattie, Petitioner*, 1992 S.C.C.R. 812 which is probably of more interest in relation to the competency of petitions to the nobile officium.

Further examples of sentences for being concerned in the supply of controlled drugs are *McIntosh v. H.M. Advocate*, 1986 S.C.C.R. 496 and *Dowell v. H.M. Advocate*, 1986 G.W.D. 5–96. Imprisonment and fines were imposed and upheld on appeal in *R. v. Fox* [1986] Crim.L.R. 518.

2. R. v. Spinks   4.6.27
[1987] Crim.L.R. 786

S. and a friend had agreed to purchase a small quantity of diamorphine for immediate consumption. S. purchased £10 worth of diamorphine which was consumed by them. S. pleaded guilty on the basis that his involvement with his friend amounted to a supply of his friend. S. was sentenced to 12 months' imprisonment and he appealed.

The appeal court did not accept the submission that the sentence should have been on the same level as for simple possession as this was an act of supply, albeit on a very limited scale, and the sentence should have been slightly more than would have been appropriate for simple possession.

Twelve months was held to be too severe and the sentence was varied to allow the appellant's immediate release. The appellant had apparently been in custody for just over two months and that was equivalent then to a sentence of about three months' imprisonment.

Appeal allowed.

NOTE

This case may usefully be contrasted with *McWilliams v. H.M. Advocate*, 1985 S.C.C.R. 419. That, strictly speaking, involved the supply of diamorphine, but the facts were similar: McW.'s friend was suffering so severely from withdrawal symptoms resulting from drug use, that McW. thought that he had to help and he did so by sharing his own quantity of diamorphine with the friend. McW. was unrepresented and he submitted to the court that "three years for sharing his own fix with a friend must be an excessive sentence." The High Court of Justiciary disagreed and refused the appeal.

4.6.28

3. R. v. Falshaw
(1993) 14 Cr.App.R. (S.) 749

F. pleaded guilty to being concerned in supplying amphetamine sulphate. The appellant admitted being involved in the supply of two kilogrammes of amphetamine sulphate which were found in the possession of a co-defendant. The appellant was treated as the organiser of the enterprise. He was sentenced to seven years' imprisonment.

Held, it was impossible to apply precisely the guidelines given in *Aramah*, *supra*, in respect of cannabis to amphetamines; although both were Class B drugs, amphetamine was of considerable greater value when measured by weight. The Court would treat the case as in the same category as one involving cannabis of medium quantity, which would indicate a sentence within the bracket of one to four years, or three to six years. In *R. v. Morgan* (1985) 7 Cr.App.R. (S.) 443, a case of conspiracy to manufacture amphetamine on a large scale, sentences of six to eight years were upheld on appellants, two of whom had been convicted following a contested trial. The present offence was not so serious as that in *Morgan*. The Court had concluded that after a guilty plea the sentence of seven years was substantially in excess of the proper bracket for this sort of offence, and a sentence of four years would be substituted.

Appeal allowed.

4.6.29

4. Carlin v. H.M. Advocate
1994 S.C.C.R. 763

C. pleaded guilty to possessing amphetamine with intent to supply it to others and to being concerned in its supply to others. It was agreed that the appellant and four of his friends had combined to buy the amphetamine for their own use and that there was no intention to sell it. The sheriff imposed a sentence of one year's imprisonment and the appellant appealed to the High Court.

Held, that this is an explanation which is being put forward increasingly frequently in cases of this kind and it must be emphasised that whether drugs are bought upon that basis or are bought with the intention of selling them, the court takes a serious view of anyone who has possession of controlled drugs with the intention of supplying them to others or who is concerned in the supplying of drugs to others, whether those others are friends and associates or whether they are strangers, and that the sentence was not excessive.

THE LORD JUSTICE-CLERK (ROSS) (at p. 765): "[Counsel for the appellant] has emphasised that the appellant pled guilty upon a basis which had been agreed between the Crown and the defence, that basis being that the appellant and four of his friends had combined their financial resources to enable them to buy amphetamine for their own use in a larger quantity than they would normally have done individually, on the basis that the price of the drug was considerably cheaper when bought in quantity. It was therefore contended that this was not a proper commercial transaction with drugs and there was no question of these drugs being sold for profit. This is an explanation which is being put forward increasingly frequently in cases of this kind and it must be emphasised that, whether drugs are bought upon that basis or are bought with the intention of selling them, the court takes a serious view of anyone who has possession of controlled drugs with the intention of supplying them to others and likewise the court takes a serious view of anyone who is concerned in the supplying of drugs to others, whether those others are friends and associates or whether they are strangers.

[Counsel] submitted that the sheriff had not attached sufficient weight to the basis upon which the plea of guilty had been made but we do not feel that that criticism is justified, having regard to what the sheriff says in his report. In his report the sheriff says: 'I therefore proceeded on the basis that even if the appellant did not have the drugs with the intention of selling them for profit, the quantity was such that a custodial sentence and not community service was necessary.'

[Counsel] also maintained that the sheriff had not attached sufficient weight to the personal circumstances of the appellant. The sheriff tells us that he considered the reports and that he heard what was said on the appellant's behalf. We accept that the social enquiry report is in favourable terms and it to the appellant's credit that he comes from a stable background, that he has a good work record and that he appears now to have given up drugs. We were provided with references and also a statement to the effect that since being released on interim liberation the appellant has obtained employment. The appellant has a number of previous convictions but we readily accept what [counsel] says to the effect that they are minor, that none were on indictment and he has not suffered a custodial sentence before.

The question for us must be whether the sentence imposed by the sheriff can, in all the circumstances, be regarded as excessive. It appears to us that the sheriff did have regard to the explanation put forward to the effect that the drugs were not to be sold for profit. The sheriff was entitled to have regard to the quantity of drugs involved and, in our judgment, he was also fully justified in taking the view that even if the appellant had obtained these drugs with the intention of sharing them with his friends, the offence was still a serious one which merited a custodial sentence. It has been repeatedly said in these courts that those who choose to traffic in drugs will be dealt with and that applies not only to those who sell drugs commercially, but also those who supply them on any other basis, because by acting in that way they would enable drugs to pass from the suppliers to the ultimate consumers.

Nothing which has been said today would persuade us that the sentence could be regarded in this case as excessive and accordingly the appeal against sentence must be refused."

Appeal refused.

NOTE
Interestingly, in *Pope v. H.M. Advocate*, 1995 G.W.D. 16–894 the judge was entitled (said the appeal court) to refuse to accept claims by the co-accused that the controlled drugs found were to supply to each other only, where they had declined an opportunity to give evidence.

4.6.30　　　　　　　　　　**5. R. v. Edwards**
(1992) 13 Cr.App.R. (S.) 356

E. pleaded guilty to two counts of being concerned in the supply of a Class A controlled drug. The appellant on two occasions was concerned with others in selling small quantities of "crack" cocaine. He was sentenced to four years' imprisonment.

Held, the sentence was not manifestly excessive.

AULD, J. (at p. 357): "In sentencing him the judge said that he took into account his plea of guilty, his good character and the other matters advanced by counsel in mitigation. He went on to observe that it was clear from the evidence that the appellant was a small time dealer in crack, which he, the judge, regarded as possibly the most dangerous and addictive form of cocaine. He said that he was thus concerned in spreading the degradation, despair and suffering which that drug inflicted on those who used it, his only reason for doing so being financial greed.

By way of appeal from that sentence of four years' imprisonment, [counsel] attractively and incisively urged four matters in mitigation which he maintained should have brought the sentence below the level of four years' imprisonment imposed by the judge. They were these: that the appellant was drawn into the drug trafficking which was already prevalent in the area where he lived and which gave rise to the police undercover operation; that he derived little profit from the transactions; that he was not a prime mover in the group who were selling crack cocaine in that area, and that he had pleaded guilty and was a man of good character.

Those who deal in cocaine crack, even at the lower end of the scale and who come to it for the first time, deal in rapid addiction and degradation, as the judge in his sentencing remarks observed. Without such dealers the lethal traffic in this dangerous drug would not exist. This Court has made plain in the guideline case of *Aramah* [*supra*] and the subsequent case of *Satvir Singh* (1988) 10 Cr.App.R. (S.) 402, that for the supply of such a drug it is seldom that a sentence of less than five years will be justified. [Counsel] in his able submission acknowledged that guideline and the fact that the sentence here fell within that general framework.

Here the appellant was actively, and authoritatively, engaged in touting cocaine in an area where such traffic appears to have been rife. All the signs were, certainly on the second occasion, that he was doing a brisk business. He was entitled to some credit for his pleas of guilty and for his previous good character and, to the extent urged by [counsel], for the other matters mentioned in his address today. In our view, the sentence of four years' imprisonment, a year less than the normal minimum indicated by this Court for this class of offence, adequately reflected those mitigating factors. The sentence was not manifestly excessive. Accordingly this appeal is dismissed."

Appeal dismissed.

6. H.M. Advocate v. McPhee   4.6.31
1994 S.C.C.R. 830

McP., who was aged 19, pleaded guilty to offences of supplying, being concerned in the supply of, and unlawfully possessing LSD, a Class A drug, contrary to sections 4(3)(a) and 5(2) respectively of the 1971 Act. The section 4(3)(a) charge related to the supply of a single tab of LSD to two girls, aged 13 and 14. The other charges arose out of admissions by the respondent. The sheriff sentenced him to one year's probation with the special conditions that he perform 200 hours of unpaid work and attend a drugs rehabilitation project. The Lord Advocate appealed to the High Court against the sentence as unduly lenient.

Held, that the sheriff had not attached sufficient weight to the ages of the persons concerned or to the repeated warnings given by the High Court to the effect that persons dealing in controlled drugs, and particularly Class A drugs, will be severely dealt with, and that, where a 19-year-old has supplied such drugs to 13- and 14-year-olds, however small the amount, a custodial sentence would be almost inevitable unless there were strong mitigating circumstances; and appeal allowed and sentence quashed and sentenced totalling three years' detention substituted.

THE LORD JUSTICE-CLERK (ROSS) (at p. 836): '[W]here a nineteen-year-old has supplied a Class A drug to thirteen- or fourteen-year-old children, however small the amount, we would have thought that a custodial sentence would be almost inevitable unless there were strong mitigating circumstances.

We have considered this case very carefully and we have reached the clear conclusion that the disposal adopted by the sheriff, namely probation, was unduly lenient. That being so, it is necessary for this court to consider what the appropriate disposal is. In doing so this court must of course take into account the provisions of section 207(2) and (3) of the Criminal Procedure (Scotland) Act 1975. Thus this court would not be entitled to impose detention upon the respondent unless it was satisfied that no other method of dealing with him was appropriate. When we have regard to all the circumstances of this case and in particular the fact that this nineteen-year-old respondent supplied the drug, which was a Class A drug, to these two young girls, we are satisfied that the only appropriate disposal is a custodial sentence. It is then necessary for this court to consider what the appropriate periods of detention would be in respect of these charges. In selecting these sentences, we have borne in mind, as [counsel for the respondent] invited us to do, that the respondent was originally sentenced on 5 May 1994 and that he has had this matter hanging over his head since, but we are quite clear that, for an offence of this kind, custodial sentences must be imposed which will reflect the gravity of the offences and make it clear to the respondent and to others that conduct of this kind will not be tolerated. We accordingly quash the probation order made by the sheriff and in substitution for that, in respect of charge (1), we sentence the respondent to detention in a young offenders institution for a period of three years, and in respect of charge (3) we sentence him to detention for a period of twelve months. These sentences will run concurrently."

Appeal allowed.

4.6.32   **7. H.M. Advocate v. Lee**
                         1996 S.C.C.R. 205

The respondent, who was aged 18 at the time of the offence, was put on deferred sentence for two years on a charge of being concerned in the supply of Ecstasy, contrary to section 4(3)(b) of the 1971 Act. The Lord

Advocate appealed to the High Court against the sentence as unduly lenient.

Held, inter alia, that to hold that the disposal in this case was appropriate would plainly contradict what was said in *H.M. Advocate v. McPhee,* 1994 S.L.T. 1292 and would be contrary to the sentencing policy the court has felt obliged to follow in the public interest in order to do what it can to deter and punish those who engage in the supply to others of Class A drugs; and appeal allowed and respondent sentenced to four years' detention.

THE LORD JUSTICE-GENERAL (HOPE) (at p. 212): "In our opinion the observation by the Lord Justice-Clerk in *H.M. Advocate v McPhee* [1994 S.L.T. 1292] to which we were referred by the advocate-depute provided clear guidance as to what was appropriate in this case. He issued a plain warning to the public, and guidance to sentencers generally, about the way in which offences of the kind which the respondent committed in this case would require to be dealt with by the court. The requirement is for an immediate and substantial custodial sentence, to punish the defender, to deter others and to protect the public. It is only if there are strong mitigating circumstances that any other disposal will be appropriate.

If we were to hold that the disposal which was decided on by the trial judge in this case was appropriate, as we were invited to do by [counsel for the appellant] that plainly would contradict what was said in *McPhee*. It has not been suggested in this case that there were any circumstances which could be described as strong mitigating circumstances. It would also be contrary to the sentencing policy which this court has felt obliged to follow in the public interest in order to do what it can to deter and to punish those who engage in the supply to others of Class A drugs. This is the only way in which the court can fulfil its responsibility to the public in these cases. It must be brought home to those who engage in this activity for their own gain, or who may be tempted to do so, that the offence of trafficking in Class A drugs is a very serious one. The supply of these drugs, especially to young people frequenting a disco, is an evil practice, in view of the risks which are faced by those who take these dangerous drugs in such circumstances. The court must deal severely with these cases and normally a substantial custodial sentence will be inevitable.

The trial judge has cast doubt in his report of the deterrent effect of custodial sentences. He has suggested that it must be for the Lord Advocate to demonstrate that they are an effective deterrent if he is to succeed in demonstrating that an order deferring sentence was inappropriate. This, however, is not a matter which can be determined by the court, one way or the other, by evidence. The effectiveness of a deterrent sentence is not an issue which is, in that sense, justicable. Moreover, the aim of deterring others from engaging in similar criminal activity is well established as a proper objective in the mind of the sentencer. The assumption is that they are deterred, not just by the fear of being detected, but by what is likely to happen to them if, on being detected, they are convicted of the offence. And the declared aim of deterring others from committing similar crimes has an important function in reassuring the public that the gravity of these offences is appreciated by the court. Furthermore, any deterrent effect which a publicly pronounced sentence may have in reducing the incidence of crime is most likely to be felt in cases where the criminal activity involves planning or premeditation, as in the case of drug trafficking. So those who are tempted to engage in the supply of controlled drugs by dealing with them in the street must be made aware of the fact that they are likely to face long custodial sentences if they are detected. The risk of such a sentence is a factor which they must take into account. Therein lies its value as a deterrent, whereas the risk of detection might be thought to be worth taking if offences of this kind could be expected to be dealt with leniently.

So far as the circumstances of this case are concerned we have not found anything which would justify a non-custodial disposal. We have taken account of all that has been said about the respondent's personal circumstances, including the absence of previous convictions and the effect of a custodial sentence on his employment. But in view of the gravity of the offence we consider that the only appropriate way of dealing with this case is by means of a custodial sentence to date from today's date. The sentence of this court is that the respondent be detained in a young offenders institution for a period of four years."

Appeal allowed.

4.6.33 *(iii) Concerned in Making an Offer to Supply*

4.6.34 **1. R. v. Ng and Dhali**
[1978] Crim.L.R. 176

N. was met by a third party who wanted to buy diamorphine and N. arranged for the sale of the diamorphine from D. to the third party. N. pleaded guilty at the outset and he was sentenced to five years' imprisonment. D. was sentenced to eight years' imprisonment.

On appeal N.'s sentence was reduced to four years' imprisonment as he had pleaded when he did and he had given evidence against D. and others involved in the deal. It was impossible to say that D.'s sentence was wrong.

Appeal by N. allowed in part. Appeal by D.
dismissed.

CHAPTER FIVE

Possession and possession with intent to supply   **5.1**

Introduction   **5.2**

The Misuse of Drugs Act 1971 provides by section 5 for restriction of possession of controlled drugs. In particular, section 5(2) makes it an offence for a person to have a controlled drug in his or her possession. Section 5(3) makes it an offence for a person to have a controlled drug in his or her possession, whether lawfully or not, with intent to supply it to another. Section 5(4) provides for certain related statutory defences. The concept of possession is central to the legal problems arising from controlled drugs and regard must be had to earlier case law.

A: LAW   **5.3**

(i) Cases prior to the 1971 Act   **5.3.1**

1. R. v. Irala-Prevost   **5.3.2**
[1965] Crim.L.R. 606

I-P. was a passenger in a car on a journey from North Africa to England. A large quantity of drugs was concealed in the car. He was charged *inter alia* with possession of the drugs. His defence was that he was unaware of the presence of these drugs.

On conviction an appeal was taken on the matter of the judge's charge to the jury. It was held that it was incumbent on the judge to say something to the jury to make them realise that some degree of control must be established, but that had not been done.

Appeal allowed

2. Warner v. Metropolitan Police Commissioner   **5.3.3**
[1969] 2 A.C. 256

W. was charged with having dangerous drugs in his possession without authority. The police had seen W. driving a van. A search of the van revealed three cases in the back, one of which contained scent bottles. Another case contained 20,000 amphetamine sulphate tablets.

W. had been to a cafe where he ordinarily collected scent from a man. The cafe proprietor told W. that a parcel from that man was under the counter. W. had found two parcels there, one containing scent and the other containing the drugs. W. said to the police that he assumed that both contained scent.

At his trial the jury were directed in regard to possession that if W. had control of the box which turned out to be full of amphetamine sulphate tablets then the offence was committed. It was only relevant mitigation that W. did not know the contents.

On appeal the House of Lords held that where drugs were contained in a parcel the prosecution had to prove not only that the accused possessed the parcel but also that he possessed its contents, for a person did not (within the meaning of the Act) possess things of whose existence he was unaware. A mistake as to the quality of the contents, however, did not negate possession.

Lord Reid (at p. 279): "The object of this legislation is to penalise possession of certain drugs. So if *mens rea* has not been excluded what would be required would be the knowledge of the accused that he had prohibited drugs in his possession: it would be no defence, though it would be mitigation, that he did not intend that they should be used improperly. And it is a commonplace that if the accused had a suspicion but deliberately shut his eyes, the court or jury is well entitled to hold him guilty. Further it would be pedantic to hold that it must be shown that the accused knew precisely which drug he had in his possession. Ignorance of the law is no defence and in fact virtually everyone knows that there are prohibited drugs. So it would be quite sufficient to prove facts from which it could properly be inferred that the accused knew that he had a prohibited drug in his possession. That would not lead to an unreasonable result."

(At p. 280)

"The problem here is whether the possessor of a house or box or package is necessarily in possession of everything found in it, or, if not, what mental element is necessary before he can be held to be in possession of the contents."

(At p. 281)

"In considering what is the proper construction of a provision in any Act of Parliament which is ambiguous one ought to reject that construction which leads to an unreasonable result. As a legal term 'possession' is ambiguous at least to this extent: there is no clear rule as to the nature of the mental element required. All are agreed that there must be some mental element in possession but there is no agreement as to what precisely it must be."

Lord Morris of Borth-Y-Gest (at p. 286): "The word 'possession' is much to be found in the vocabulary of the law and it cannot always be given the same meaning in all its diverse contexts. But the notion of being in possession of drugs is not one which as a rule should present difficulty in comprehending. A useful start in considering an Act of Parliament is to take the plain literal and grammatical meaning of the words used ... I think that the notion of having something in one's possession involves a mental element. It involves in the first place that you know that you have something in your possession. It does not however involve that you know precisely what it is that you have got."

(At p. 288)

"The problem presented in this case is, in my view, purely one of construction and interpretation. The intention of Parliament is to be ascertained. Parliament used words to express its intention. The words that are employed must be considered in their context and in the setting of the purpose which Parliament has proclaimed. What, then, does 'possession' mean? Does 'possession' involve that someone must knowingly have control over something? Does 'possession' further involve that there must be knowledge, either in general or with precision, as to what the thing is?'

(At p. 289)

"The question resolves itself into one as to the nature and extent of the mental element which is involved in 'possession' as the word is used in the section now being considered. In my view, in order to establish possession the prosecution must prove that an accused was knowingly in control of something in circumstances which showed that he was assenting to being in control of it: they need not prove that in fact he had actual knowledge of the nature of that which he had.... .

A jury must not convict unless they are satisfied that possession in an accused has been proved. There can be no rigid formula to be used in directing a jury. Varying sets of facts and circumstances will call for guidance on particular matters. The conception to be explained, however, will be that of being knowingly in control of a thing in circumstances which have involved an opportunity (whether availed or not) to learn or to discover, at least in a general way, what the thing is. The same result might follow if it was a matter of indifference whether there was such opportunity or not. If there is assent to the control of the thing, either after having the means of knowledge of what the thing contains or being unmindful whether there are means of knowledge or not, then ordinarily there will be possession. If there is some momentary custody of a thing without any knowledge or means of knowledge of what the thing is or contains — then, ordinarily, I would suppose that there would not be possession. If, however, someone deliberately assumes control of some package or container, then I would think that he is in possession of it. If he deliberately so assumes control knowing that it has contents he would also be in possession of the contents. I cannot think that it would be rational to hold that someone who is in possession of a box which he knows to have things in it is in possession of the box, but not in possession of the things in it. If he had been misinformed or misled as to the nature of the contents or if he had made a wrong surmise as to them it seems to me that he would nevertheless be in possession of them. Similarly, if he wrongly surmised that a box was empty which in fact had things in it, possession of the box (if established in the way which I have outlined) would involve possession of the contents."

LORD GUEST (at p. 299): "[T]here must, in relation to possession, be some conscious mental element present.

In the end of all, however, the meaning of 'possession' will depend upon the context."

LORD PEARCE (at p. 305): "I think that the term 'possession' is satisfied by a knowledge only of the existence of the thing itself and not its qualities, and that ignorance or mistake as to its qualities is not an excuse. This would comply with the general understanding of the word 'possess.' Though I reasonably believe the tablets which I possess to be aspirin, yet if they turn out to be heroin I am in possession of heroin tablets. This would be so I think even if I believed them to be sweets. It would be otherwise if I believe them to be something of a wholly different nature. At this point a question of degree arises as to when a difference in qualities amounts to a difference in kind. That is a matter for a jury who would probably decide it sensibly in favour of the genuinely innocent but against the guilty."

LORD WILBERFORCE (at p. 310): "What is prohibited is possession — a term which is inconclusive as to the final shades of mental intention needed, leaving these to be fixed in relation to the legal context in which the term is used."

Appeal dismissed.

NOTE

Warner's case was concerned with section 1(1) of the 1964 Act. The two questions that arose on appeal were, first, whether the offence of unlawful possession created by section 1 was one of absolute liability and, secondly, what was meant by the phrase "have in his possession"? The two questions were not easily separated and the whole matter was analysed by many lawyers, most notably by Goodhart, "Possession of Drugs and Absolute Liability" [1968] 84 L.Q.R. 382.

The terms of section 5 of the 1971 Act differ from the earlier statutes and that Act contains, as a result of *Warner's* case, the statutory defence in section 28. The case continues as an authority on the concept of possession, even though much of the recent analysis of the speeches is critical; Bovey at p. 40, *et seq.* But what precisely is *Warner* an authority for? In *R. v. McNamara* (1988) 152 J.P. 390 at p. 394 Lord Lane, C.J. observed that: "Unhappily it is not altogether easy to extract from the speeches of their Lordships the *ratio decidendi.*" However, it would seem to be the position now that the prosecution must prove that the accused had custody or control of the container and that he knew that he had that custody or control. Further, it must be shown that the accused knew that the container over which he had custody and control contained something. For the prosecution to prove these matters is to prove a prima facie case to answer. How an accused meets the case depends on the facts and circumstances of the whole affair forming the basis of the charge. An accused person now has the advantages of the defences in section 28 of the 1971 Act which did not exist at the time of the decision in *Warner's* case. To that extent large parts of their Lordships' speeches are otiose." This case was discussed but not applied in *R. v. Waller* [1991] Crim. L.R. 381.

3. R. v. Fernandez   5.3.4
[1970] Crim.L.R. 277

F. was a merchant seaman. He was to be paid to take a package with him to England. He was told that the package contained sticks for smoking and he had an idea that this referred to marijuana cigarettes. The package broke open while he had it and he saw the content. He was aware that if the customs authorities found the package he would be in trouble. He said that he did not know that the package contained drugs and there was nothing that aroused his suspicions. On conviction he appealed.

Held, that in "package" cases prima facie the prosecution satisfy the onus on them by proving that the accused was in physical control of articles which were dangerous drugs. But if the suggestion is made that he was mistaken as to the nature of the goods then it may be necessary to consider what his mental state was. Further, if the accused took the package into his possession in a situation in which he should certainly have been put on inquiry as to the nature of what he was carrying, and yet he deliberately failed to pursue an inquiry and accepted the goods in circumstances which must have pointed the finger of suspicion at their nature and the propriety of his carrying them, then it was a proper inference that he accepted whatever they were, and it was not open to him to say that he was not in possession of the goods because he did not know what they were.

Appeal dismissed.

4. Lustman v. Stewart   5.3.5
1971 S.L.T. (Notes) 58

L. and others were attempting to set up in a country area of Scotland a self-sufficient community and were at the relevant time living communally. Acting on information the police obtained a search warrant for the premises. In a room there were several ashtrays with ends of hand-rolled cigarettes. When L. was cautioned and charged he replied "There are things which happen here which I can't control."

Following conviction L. appealed on the ground that there was no finding-in-fact that the drug was actually in the custody of any individual, nor were there facts and circumstances to entitle the sheriff to come to the conclusion that it was in their custody. The High Court of Justiciary held that the findings-in-fact fell just short of what was sufficient for conviction and, without issuing opinions, the conviction was quashed.

Appeal allowed.

5.3.6   **5. R. v. Searle**
[1971] Crim.L.R. 592

S. and others used a vehicle for a touring holiday. Drugs were found in that vehicle and S. and the others were charged with possession of them. The prosecution case was put on the basis of joint possession. None of the accused gave evidence but all were convicted and appealed.

Held, that the charge to the jury in effect equated knowledge with possession. However, mere knowledge of the presence of a forbidden article in the hands of a confederate was not enough: joint possession had to be established. The sort of direction which ought to have been given was to ask the jury to consider whether the drugs formed a common pool from which all had the right to draw at will, and whether there was a joint enterprise to consume drugs together because then the possession of drugs by one of them in pursuance of that common intention might well be possession on the part of all of them.

Although there was ample evidence to justify a conviction it was impossible to say with certainty that all of the accused were guilty.

Appeal allowed.

5.3.7   **6. R. v. Buswell**
[1972] 1 W.L.R. 64

B. was prescribed amphetamine tablets as treatment for drug addiction. He thought that these particular drugs had been destroyed accidentally. He obtained a similar prescription to replace those thought to have been destroyed.

Later he discovered the first drugs prescribed still to be in existence and he consumed some. The police found the remainder and he was charged with unlawful possession and after trial he was convicted. He appealed.

PHILLIMORE, L.J. (at p. 66): "I suppose there are very few households in this country which do not contain a few little bottles with some drugs, possibly specified in the schedule, which have not been consumed in the course of treatment and which have been kept at the back of the medicine cupboard and forgotten. To suggest that a member of the household who received them under a perfectly proper lawful prescription is in unlawful possession once the treatment is concluded seems to this court to be an extraordinary proposition."

Appeal allowed.

7. MacKay v. Hogg
(1973) S.C.C.R. Supp. 41

5.3.8

M. was asleep naked on a couch in the house of another and his clothes were on a chair beside him. The police arrived and his clothes and the chair were searched and no drugs were found. Some little time later, 16 tablets containing the drug lysergide were discovered on the seat cover of the chair. No one had had anything to do with the chair, except M. between the two police searches. The learned sheriff inferred that on the evidence only M. could have placed the tablets where they were found and held a charge of unlawful possession proved. M. appealed.

Held, that all that could be reasonably inferred from the findings-in-fact was that M. must have moved the tablets by hand from some unknown part of the householder's living-room to the seat cover of the chair. This "fleeting contact" between M. and the tablets was not, in the context of the other findings in this case, enough to justify a finding that he had them in his possession within the meaning of the subsection. Conviction quashed "in these quite unusual and exceptional circumstances."

Appeal allowed.

(ii) Possession of Minute Quantities of Controlled Drugs   5.3.9

1. Hambleton v. Callinan
[1968] 2 All E.R. 943

5.3.10

C. and another were arrested by the police on suspicion of being in unlawful possession of drugs. They were asked for and gave to the police samples of urine. On analysis the samples were found to contain amphetamine powder and barbiturate. The justices found that with regard to the charge relating to unlawful possession of the amphetamine powder in the urine samples, the powder was not in their possession in the terms of section 1(1) of the 1964 Act. The prosecution appealed the acquittal.

LORD PARKER, C.J. (at p. 945): "When, as here, something is literally consumed and changed in character, it seems to me impossible to say that a man is in possession of it within the meaning of this Act, and accordingly I would dismiss this appeal.

But before leaving the matter, I confess that I myself can see no reason why in another case the time when the possession is said to have taken place should not be a time prior to the consumption, because as it seems to me the traces of, in this case, amphetamine powder in the urine is at any rate *prima facie* evidence — which is all that the prosecution need — that the man concerned must have had it in his possession, if only in his hand prior to raising his hand to his mouth and consuming it."

Appeal dismissed.

5.3.11   **2. R. v. Marriott**
                                [1971] All E.R. 595

M. was found to be in possession of a knife and on forensic analysis the blade had a minute quantity of cannabis resin attached to the tip of the blade. He was charged with being in possession of a quantity of cannabis.

On appeal against conviction on the ground that the trial judge had misdirected the jury, *held* that the prosecution had to prove not only that the accused had unauthorised possession of cannabis resin but also that he had reason to know at least that there was some foreign substance on the blade of the penknife.

Appeal allowed.

NOTE
   It would seem that the surrounding circumstances had suggested that the knife had been used previously to cut up cannabis resin but as that had not been charged these matters were irrelevant.

5.3.12   **3. Keane v. Gallacher**
                                1980 S.L.T. 144

G. was charged with possession of cannabis resin. Two minute quantities of that substance had been found in a tin and a plastic bag respectively which were recovered in his room. The former weighed 10 milligrammes and the latter weighed less than one milligramme. At his trial it was argued *inter alia* that there was an onus on the Crown to prove that the quantity of cannabis resin found in his possession was "usable" and that this the Crown failed to do. This was upheld and G. was acquitted. The Crown appealed.

THE LORD JUSTICE-CLERK (WHEATLEY) (at p. 148): "[I]n this context it is inappropriate to rely on the ordinary maxim of *de minimis*, and that if the quantity of the drug found is so minute that in the light of commonsense it amounts to nothing, it should be treated as such. That latter point in our view is associated with the requirement that the controlled drug must be capable of proper identification as such before a conviction can be recorded. In all the other English cases the decisions were based on these two foregoing considerations and not on the 'usable' test. With respect, we cannot agree that the 'usable' test as distinct from the 'identifiable' test can be legitimately read into the requirement of section 5(1). It was first introduced by a side-wind in *R. v. Worsell* [[1969] 2 All E.R. 1183] and adopted for the first time as a ground of decision in *R. v. Carver* [[1978] Q.B. 472]. On our reading and interpretation of section 5(1) this innovation is not justified."

(At p. 149)

"Where identification of the matter found as being a controlled drug is satisfactorily established then on our view of the law this point [*de minimis*] does not arise, since at the point of time of the discovery of the material the person was in possession of a controlled drug."

Appeal allowed.

4. R. v. Boyesen   5.3.13
[1982] 2 W.L.R. 882

B. was charged with unlawful possession of five milligrammes of cannabis resin. He had been found by a policeman to be carrying a small metal tin in which was a polythene bag containing traces of a brown substance. Evidence was given for the prosecution that the brown substance was cannabis resin, that it was visible to the eye and a reasonable quantity and that it was tangible and manipulable.

At trial the defence submitted that the prosecution had to prove possession of a quantity of the drug sufficient to be usable in a way that the Act was intended to prohibit. That submission was overruled by the judge. On conviction the matter was taken to the Court of Appeal which allowed the appeal. The Crown appealed to the House of Lords.

LORD SCARMAN (at p. 886): "Possession is a deceptively simple concept. It denotes a physical control or custody of a thing plus knowledge that you have it in your custody or control. You may possess a thing without knowing or comprehending its nature: but you do not possess it unless you know you have it."

(At p. 888)

"If it be said that an 'identification' test is itself not expressly stated in the subsection, I would reply that it is implicit. Unless the thing possessed is shown by evidence to be a controlled drug, there is no offence.

If I were disposed, which I am not, to add to the subsection by judicial interpretation words which are not there, I would not accept the words suggested, *i.e.* capable of being used in a manner prohibited by the Act. The uncertainty and imprecision of such a criterion of criminal responsibility would in themselves be mischievous. But, further, the view that possession is only serious enough, as a matter of legal policy, to rank as an offence if the quantity possessed is itself capable of being misused is a highly dubious one. Small quantities can be accumulated. It is a perfectly sensible view that the possession of any quantity, which is visible, tangible, measurable, and 'capable of manipulation' … is a serious matter to be prohibited if the law is to be effective against trafficking in dangerous drugs and their misuse."

(At p. 889)

"The question is not usability but possession. Quantity is, however, of importance in two respects when one has to determine whether or not an accused person has a controlled drug in his possession. First, is the quantity sufficient to enable a court to find as a matter of fact that it amounts to something. If it is visible, tangible and measurable, it is certainly something. The question is one of fact for the commonsense of that tribunal …

Secondly, quantity may be relevant to the issue of knowledge … If the quantity in custody or control is minute, the question arises — was it so minute that it cannot be proved that the accused knew he had it? If knowledge cannot be proved, possession would not be established."

Appeal allowed.

NOTE

Boyesen ended some degree of uncertainty in English law and reconciled apparently conflicting decisions of the Scots and English courts on a common statute. The uncertainty arose from the various tests established by the English courts: in *R. v. Worsell* [1969] 2 All E.R. 1183 the test seemed to be sufficient quantity for use but in *R. v. Graham* [1969] 2 All E.R. 1181 the test seemed to be whether the quantity was weighable and measurable. In *Bocking v. Roberts* [1974] Q.B. 307 it was asserted by a majority of the judges that the test was whether the quantity was measurable. The last test was doubted in *R. v. Colyer* [1974] Crim.L.R. 243 and *R. v. Hieorowski* [1978] Crim.L.R. 563 but applied in *R. v. Carver* [1978] Q.B. 472. These matters were discussed and analysed at length in a variety of articles noted in Part C of this work.

The apparently conflicting decisions of the Scots and English courts on a common statute were the subject of a Parliamentary question on January 11, 1980. The Solicitor-General for Scotland was asked if he was satisfied that these judgments were compatible with the uniform application of the 1971 Act. The reply was that a different test was now being applied in each jurisdiction and that in his view the Scots test was the correct one but that there was no anomaly in the law only in the application of it as it then was.

5.3.14 *(iii) Cases under the 1971 Act: Possession*

5.3.15

1. Allan v. Milne
1974 S.L.T. (Notes) 76

A. and three others shared a flat and paid into a fund which was used to settle the rent. The police searched the flat but found nothing incriminating.

They returned to the flat a fortnight later and found a quantity of cannabis, a chillum pipe and a set of scales for measuring small weights. No incriminating replies were made to caution and charge and no explanation was offered.

The sheriff found that the four were well aware that the cannabis and the pipe were concealed beneath the sink. Any of the four had access to the cannabis and pipe and could control the use to which they were put. The cannabis and pipe were held to be in the joint custody and possession of all four.

These findings-in-fact were justified on the reasoning that three of the students had lived in the flat for over a year and the fourth had been there for at least a period of weeks. There was nothing to suggest that anyone else had placed the drugs in the flat. The first search negated the defence of ignorance. They appeared to be on close terms.

The quantity of cannabis found was such that it was likely to be more than enough for one person's use. The kitchen and the living-room appeared to be used communally. The scales were found openly on the kitchen table and were not of the sort in ordinary kitchen use. In the absence of evidence to the contrary the only reasonable inference from these circumstances was that all the students had knowledge of the presence of the cannabis in the flat, and of its whereabouts. Any occupant had access to the cannabis and could use it as he or she chose.

All four occupants were convicted of possession and appealed to the High Court of Justiciary which, without issuing opinions, held that the findings-in-fact were sufficient for conviction.

Appeal refused.

2. Calder v. Milne   5.3.16
High Court of Justiciary, unreported, February 18, 1975

C. shared a flat with three others and although C. had exclusive use of a room as a bedroom, other occupants were permitted to use the room as a sitting-room if they wished. Occasionally C.'s girlfriend shared his room although she was not present on the relevant date nor the previous night. Policemen obtained a warrant and searched C.'s room in his absence and there found two cigarette-ends in a waste paper basket which also contained waste paper. Cannabis was found in those cigarettes. C. in evidence conceded that he had smoked cannabis on an earlier occasion and he had flushed the reefer ends away. He claimed that the cigarette ends found by the police were not his. The sheriff disbelieved the last point and held the charge proved.

On appeal the Crown observed in their opinion that there was no finding-in-fact as to when C. was last in his bedroom before the search and there was nothing to show when he last slept in the room or in the house. In all those circumstances, it is quite impossible to hold that the possession of the cannabis in question had been brought home to C.

Appeal allowed.

5.3.17
3. R. v. Wright
[1976] Crim.L.R. 248

W. was in a car with others including B. A police car was following and W. was seen to throw something from the car. This turned out to be a small tin containing cannabis. He was charged with unlawful possession of the cannabis.

W. said in evidence that he did not have any cannabis and that he was not aware that others in the car had any. He did not know that the car behind was a police car. B. had given him the tin. W. did not know what the tin contained but he threw it out of the window when told to do so by B. He knew that B. used cannabis and on being told to throw the tin away it occurred to W. that it might contain drugs.

W. was convicted and appealed on the ground that the judge had not given the jury proper directions as to the mental element of possession. It was held that it was clear from *R. v. Warner* (1968) 52 Cr.App.R. 373 that for the purposes of the 1964 Act, a distinction was to be made between mere physical control and possession, which connoted a mental element. If a person was handed a container and at the moment he received it did not know or suspect, and had no reason to suspect, that it contained drugs and if, before he had time to examine the contents, he was told to throw it away and immediately did so he could not be said to be in possession of the drugs so as to be guilty of an offence against section 5 of the 1971 Act. As such a direction had not been given the conviction was quashed.

Appeal allowed.

5.3.18
4. Coffey v. Douglas
High Court of Justiciary, unreported, May 26, 1976

C. was in a house when the police arrived and knocked at the door. He looked out of the window, saw the policeman, closed the window and between half a minute and two minutes later opened the door. In that interval before the policemen were admitted, they heard a scuffling noise and the sound of the lavatory being flushed. Once in the house the policeman found floating in the lavatory pan three cigarette ends, later shown to contain cannabis resin.

On conviction of unlawful possession an appeal was taken to the High Court of Justiciary. No formal opinion was delivered but in disposing of the appeal their Lordships were satisfied that the sheriff ought not on the evidence to have drawn the inference that C. had deposited the cigarette ends at the relevant time. The lavatory was no doubt flushed but there was no evidence whatever that the cigarette ends had been exposed recently to water: for all the court knew, the cigarette ends might have been there before the lavatory was flushed at the time the police arrived.

Appeal allowed.

5. McKenzie v. Skeen   5.3.19
1983 S.L.T. 121

Policemen searched a flat and found a suitcase which M. said belonged to her. In that suitcase was found a small glass jar with a lid which was in position. The jar contained a quantity of seeds and 10 milligrammes of cannabis in the form of small flakes. This cannabis was amongst the seeds and might not be seen through the brown-coloured glass of the jar. The seeds were clearly visible. On conviction an appeal was taken on the basis that there was insufficient evidence to establish knowledge on M.'s part.

THE LORD JUSTICE GENERAL (EMSLIE) (at p. 121): "[F]or the purposes of [s. 1 of the 1964 Act] a person cannot be said to be in possession of an article which he does not realise was there at all. What was required, therefore, was proof that the alleged possessor was aware of the existence of the thing which he is said to have possessed and since the section did not demand proof of knowledge of the quality of the thing possessed, if that thing turned out to be a controlled drug proof of the offence was complete. Has the Misuse of Drugs Act 1971 made the fundamental change for which in this case the Crown contends? [The Crown had argued that the onus was on the accused to prove that she did not know that she had any particular article found under her control.] In my opinion the answer is emphatically in the negative."

LORD CAMERON (at p. 122): "The Act of 1971 does not define what is meant by 'possession' except that by section 37(3) it is provided: 'For the purposes of this Act the things which a person has in his possession shall be taken to include any thing subject to his control which is in the custody of another.' This would in my opinion warrant the inference that the concept of possession is in respect of an article subject to the control of the possessor and the concept of control would imply knowledge that the article in question was subject to her control. Control is not a function of the unconscious.

The word 'possession' is the critical word in [s. 1 of the 1964 Act and s. 5 of the 1971 Act] and 'possession' of the drug is of the essence of the offence created. There is nothing in the Act of 1971 which in any way points to a different interpretation being given to the same word appearing in the same context in both statutes. If Parliament had wished to intend that the word should bear a different meaning it would have been easy by specific definition to do so. This has not been done and therefore I am of opinion that proof of knowledge of possession of the article itself though not of its nature or quality is essential proof of the offence created by section 5(2) of the Act of 1971."

Appeal allowed.

5.3.20   **6. R. v. Peaston**
(1979) 69 Cr.App.R. 203

P. occupied a bedsitting-room in a house of such accommodation. He received through the post in an envelope a film capsule containing 7.7 grammes of amphetamine. This envelope had been pushed through the letter-box by the postman with other letters, and someone had placed these letters on the hallway table. P. was unaware of the envelope's arrival.

A policeman arrived with a search warrant, took the envelope to P.'s room and gave it to him. He opened it and handed the contents to the policeman. He was charged and in due course convicted of unlawful possession of the drug. He appealed on the ground that on the admitted facts he could not be said to be in "possession."

Held, that since P. had ordered the supplier to send the drug through the post to his address, he was properly to be regarded as in possession of the envelope containing it when it arrived through the letter-box of the house in which he as living.

Appeal dismissed.

5.3.21   **7. Mingay v. Mackinnon**
1980 J.C. 33

M. lived in a communal flat in which he had a bedroom where he alone slept. The living-room was in common use. There were no locks on the doors in the flat. A considerable quantity of cannabis and paraphernalia connected with its consumption were found in the living-room. On the facts stated, it was found that there was a clear inference that M. was aware of the presence of cannabis and its consumption in the flat. In his bedroom a cigarette-end containing cannabis was found in an ash-tray. On conviction, M. appealed.

LORD CAMERON (at p. 35): "It was, however, not enough for the prosecutor to demonstrate, if a conviction was to be secured, that the appellant had knowledge of the articles and drugs in the flat and that smoking of cannabis resin was taking place there on a very large scale. It was in addition essential for the prosecution to establish that in addition to knowing about the drugs and the articles, and the smoking of cannabis resin in the flat, cannabis resin, or some of it, was in the possession and control of the appellant."

Appeal allowed.

NOTE
Mingay was distinguished in *Crowe v. MacPhail*, 1986 S.C.C.R. 549. In the latter the appellant was convicted of possessing a small quantity of cannabis resin. It had been found in the ash-tray adjacent to the bed occupied by him in a prison cell. That cell was shared by another prisoner, and its door was open for a considerable part of the day. On being cautioned and charged C. made a reply which was construed as an admission *viz.*, "It wasn't exactly in my possession, it was under my ashtray. There is a difference." Appeal against conviction was refused. For an example of a case where there was held on appeal to have been insufficient evidence for conviction see *Young v. H.M. Advocate*, 1986 S.C.C.R. 583. Another prison case is *Feeney v. Jessop*, 1991 S.L.T. 409.

8. Cheshire Chief Constable v. Hunt   5.3.22
(1983) 147 J.P. 567

H. and others had on their own admission smoked cannabis which belonged to another person who admitted ownership of it. They were found guilty of possession of cannabis for the purposes of section 5(2) of the 1971 Act. That was so notwithstanding that the charge alleged possession of an unspecified amount.

Appeal refused.

9. R. v. Martindale   5.3.23
[1986] 1 W.L.R. 1042

M. had in his pocket a leather wallet containing a very small amount of cannabis resin. He claimed that the controlled drug had been his but that it had been in the wallet upwards of two years and he had forgotten about it. He sought a ruling from the trial judge as to whether on these facts he had a defence. The judge ruled that the assumed facts did not constitute a defence. Thereafter M. pleaded guilty and applied for leave to appeal.

LORD LANE, C.J. (at p. 1044): "Possession does not depend upon the alleged possessor's powers of memory. Nor does possession come and go as memory revives or fails. If it were to do so, a man with a poor memory would be acquitted, he with a good memory would be convicted."

Application refused.

NOTE
Martindale was followed in *Gill v. Lockhart*, 1988 S.L.T. 189. Similar circumstances are narrated in *Williamson v. H.M. Advocate*, 1988 G.W.D. 24–1013.

5.3.24
10. R. v. Hunt
[1986] 3 W.L.R. 1115

A paper fold containing a white powder was found at H.'s house. The analyst's report showed that the powder contained "morphine mixed with caffeine and atrophine." At trial the defence submitted that there was no case to answer. The argument was that there had been no evidence of the proportion of morphine or to the effect that the powder was not compounded as specified in paragraph 3 of the Schedule 1 to the Misuse of Drugs Regulations 1973 which set out exceptions.

The trial judge decided against that submission and H. changed his plea to guilty. He appealed against conviction and the Court of Appeal (Criminal Division) held that the burden of proving that the preparation of morphine fell within the relevant exception lay upon H. The conviction was upheld. H. appealed to the House of Lords.

LORD GRIFFITHS (at p. 1127): "[I]f the linguistic construction of the statute did not clearly indicate upon whom the burden should lie the court should look to other considerations to determine the intention of Parliament such as the mischief at which the Act was aimed and practical considerations affecting the burden of proof and, in particular, the ease or difficulty that the respective parties would encounter in discharging the burden. I regard this last consideration as one of great importance for surely Parliament can never lightly be taken to have intended to impose an onerous duty on a defendant to prove his innocence in a criminal case, and a court should be very slow to draw any such inference from the language of a statute."

(At p. 1130)

"[I]f the burden of proof is placed upon the defendant he may be faced with very real practical difficulties in discharging it. The suspected substance is usually seized by the police for the purposes of analysis and there is no statutory provision entitling the defendant to a proportion of it. Often there is very little of the substance and if it has already been analysed by the prosecution it may have been destroyed in the process."

(At p. 1131)

"[A]s this question of construction is obviously one of real difficulty I have regard to the fact that offences involving the misuse of hard drugs are among the most serious in the criminal calendar and, subject to certain special defences the burden whereof is specifically placed upon the defendant, they are absolute. In these circumstances, it seems to me right to resolve any ambiguity in favour of the defendant and to place the burden of proving the nature of the substance involved in so serious an offence upon the prosecution."

LORD MACKAY OF CLASHFERN (at p. 1131): "I consider that this case emphasised the need for absolute clarity in the terms of the analysts' certificate founded on by the prosecution in cases of this sort and, in my opinion, it would be wise where there is any possibility of one of the descriptions in the relevant Schedule applying to the substance which is the subject of the certificate that the analyst should state expressly whether or not the substance falls within that description as well as stating whether or not it is a controlled drug within the meaning of the Act of 1971."

Appeal allowed.

NOTE

This is another example of a case concerning controlled drugs raising profound issues in criminal law. The decision in *Hunt's* case has been widely considered: most notably, and critically, Professor Glanville Williams analysed the speeches in the context of the general principles involved in "The Logic of Exceptions" [1988] C.L.J. 261. For other discussion see Healy [1987] Crim.L.R. 355; Mirfield [1988] Crim.L.R. 19 and 213; J. C. Smith (1987) 38 N.I.L.Q. 223; Peiris (1987) 7 L.S. 279; Zuckerman (1987) 103 L.Q.R. 170 and Birch [1988] Crim.L.R. 221.

11. R. v. Lewis   5.3.25
[1988] Crim.L.R. 517

L. was the sole tenant of a house in Wales in which amphetamine and cannabis were found. He had not been present during the search but he had seen the warrant which the police had left behind. He explained that the tenancy was a device which he used to obtain state benefits to which he was not entitled. L. had never intended to live in the house and he visited there only occasionally. Others went to the house. L.'s wife and the landlord corroborated the infrequent visits. L. said further that he never looked in the cupboards and took little notice of what was on the premises; he never suspected the presence of drugs.

On conviction L. appealed on the ground that the judge, relying on *Warner, supra*, had misdirected the jury on the meaning of possession. It was held that it was not necessary to direct the jury that they had to be satisfied that L. had actual knowledge that the articles were under his control before they could convict. The speeches in *Warner* seemed to reflect a number of different shades of meaning and approaches to the meaning of "possession." It was not easy to distil a majority conclusion.

The Court of Appeal followed the approach of Lord Scarman in *R. v. Boyesen, supra*, who adopted and applied Lord Wilberforce's description of "possession" in *Warner*. The effect of that was whether, on the facts, the defendant had been proved to have, or ought to have imputed to him, either the intention or knowledge that what he possessed was in fact a prohibited substance.

Appeal dismissed.

NOTE

Professor J. C. Smith, Q.C., provided the analysis of *Lewis* for the commentary to the above report and commences with the observation that "Once again the courts are in difficulties in trying to extract a sensible and workable proposition from *Warner*." The difficulty, he advises, arises because possession has become the criterion of guilty although it is a neutral concept, not involving blame or fault.

5.3.26   **12. Wood v. Allan**
                                     1988 S.L.T. 341

W. was charged with unlawful possession of a controlled drug and the matter proceeded to trial. The evidence revealed that the police were in W.'s house when he produced a medicine bottle. W. opened the bottle but it was taken from him by a policeman before W. could do anything further.

The bottle was found to contain between 12 and 15 tablets. All the tablets, except two, appeared to the policeman to accord with a label attached to the bottle which bore to show the tablets had been prescribed through regular medical and pharmaceutical channels.

The two tablets referred to were of a different colour to the bulk, and on analysis the two tablets were found to be Tuinal tablets containing disubstituted barbituric acids, a Class B controlled drug. At the close of the Crown case it was submitted that there was no case to answer on the ground that neither the unlawfulness of the possession of the drugs had been established nor that the drugs were not prescribed for medicinal purposes as provided for by subordinate legislation. W. was convicted and appealed on the ground of insufficiency of evidence.

THE LORD JUSTICE GENERAL (EMSLIE) (at p. 343): "[W]e are quite satisfied that it was sufficient for the Crown to establish what they did establish, namely that the appellant had in his possession on the date libelled, a Class B drug, a controlled drug. Having established that, the Crown was entitled to say that the court should convict the appellant unless the appellant had brought himself within the exception described in reg. 10(2).

It is important to notice just what the regulation requires an appellant to establish. It is not enough to establish the appellant's (or the accused's) presence within an excepted class under reg. 10(2) to show that he had in his possession a bottle of pills with a chemist's label on the outside. It is essential, if an accused is to bring himself within the exception, that he should prove possession of the drug, which would otherwise be possessed unlawfully, for administration for medical purposes in accordance with the directions of the practitioner. A number of considerations would be important — the date on which the bottle of pills or tablets was supplied; the directions on the label governing the administration of the contents; and it would be essential for the accused, in a case such as this, to show that his possession of the drugs at the relevant time was for administration at the relevant time for medical purposes in accordance with current directions of a practitioner issued to him."

Appeal refused.

NOTE

The High Court of Justiciary in the foregoing case approved of the dictum of Melford-Stevenson, J. in *R. v. Ewens* [1967] 1 Q.B. 322 at p. 330: that was to the effect that an accused person knows "perfectly well" whether he falls within an exception and has or should have readily available to him the means by which he could establish whether or not he is within the excepted class. However, in *Wood's* case the Court held that the exception in the subordinate legislation was covered by section 312(*v*) of the Criminal Procedure (Scotland) Act 1975. That provides in Scots law that proof in relation to exceptions, provisos, excuses or qualifications is not required of the prosecution.

13. R. v. Strong; R. v. Berry   5.3.27
The Times, January 26, 1989

B. was driving a car which was followed and stopped by the police. S. was sitting on the rear seat beside a child's seat. A third man was sitting in the front passenger seat. The car was searched and controlled drugs were found; (i) 54.3 grammes of herbal cannabis was found in a plastic bag wrapped in a jumper which was under the child's seat in the rear; (ii) 830 milligrammes of cannabis resin was found under a mat by the driver's seat; and (iii) 260 milligrammes of cannabis resin was found between the backrest and seat in the rear.

In addition to the drugs in the car, some digital kitchen scales with a plastic tray were found under the front passenger's seat. When questioned all three men denied any knowledge of the presence of drugs in the car. B. said the scales had come from his home which he shared with the third man. After trial all three men were convicted but only S. and B. appealed. The ground was that the trial judge had been wrong to reject submissions regarding the sufficiency of evidence.

LORD LANE, C.J.: "[T]he case against the two appellants differed markedly.

The prosecution put the case on the basis of joint possession. That is to say the prosecution set out to prove that each of the three defendants jointly had control of one or more of the three packages of cannabis.

Realistically speaking, if joint possession of one package was proved, it followed that the prosecution would succeed on all three.

What then did joint possession in these circumstances entail? It had to entail that, although no one of them had the packages or any of them on his person or in his pockets, yet each had the right to say what should be done with the cannabis — a right shared with his colleagues.

As Lord Widgery, giving the judgment of the Court of Appeal said in *R. v. Searle* (unreported, July 5, 1971): 'The sort of direction to which the deputy recorder should have opened the jury's mind was to ask them to consider whether these drugs formed a kind of common pool from which all had a right to draw.'

If Strong might not have known about the presence of the cannabis in the car — in other words, unless he was proved to have known about the cannabis — he could not be in joint control of it. It stood to reason that knowledge in such circumstances was a *sine qua non* of possession."

However, even if he did not know about its presence, that was not enough. The mere fact that someone, for instance, had told him that there was cannabis in the car would not be enough to saddle him with possession.

In short, mere presence in the same vehicle as the drug and in particular where there was no evidence of knowledge could not amount in the circumstances of the present case to evidence from which the jury could properly infer possession, whether individual or joint.

There was no evidence which could properly be said to call for an explanation from Strong ...

So far as Berry was concerned, the position was different. He was, with [the third man], the joint owner of the car. They were both entitled to drive it and in it were the three packages, all concealed more or less.

On its own these facts read against the background of possession and driving of the car would be a sufficient basis for the jury to infer control, in the absence of any credible explanation from him.

What must have put the matter beyond doubt was the presence of the scales under the front seat. The only explanation given at that stage was that they had been lent to a friend to weigh some wool. They had been fetched back from her but, surprisingly, had not found their way back to the kitchen in the [shared house]."

Appeal by S. allowed and conviction quashed.
Appeal by B. dismissed.

NOTE

In a similar type of case the High Court of Justiciary held in regard to section 23(2)(a) of the 1971 Act that "in the absence of any obvious innocent reason for C.'s presence in the suspected car the police were entitled to conclude reasonably that he was in possession of drugs": *Campbell v. H.M. Advocate, infra*, at paragraph **5.3.32**.

5.3.28

14. Hughes v. Guild
1990 S.C.C.R. 257

H. and B. lived together, apparently as man and wife. They shared a flat, of which they were the sole occupants. Police officers saw H. and B. enter their own flat. The officers went in with H. and B. and showed them a search warrant. Thereafter a quantity of cannabis resin was found on the mantelpiece in the living room. There were two small pieces, each wrapped in separate pieces of a carrier bag. Also found in the living room was a knife lying in front of the fireplace, a piece of carrier bag in the fireplace, and two packets of torn cigarette papers. The blade of the knife was found on examination to have trace amounts of cannabis resin adhering to its cutting edge.

H. and B. were charged with unlawful possession of a controlled drug. At trial after the Crown evidence had been led a submission of no case to answer was rejected. H. did not give evidence. B. gave evidence but both were convicted and thereafter appealed against conviction.

THE LORD JUSTICE GENERAL (HOPE) (at p. 531): "As in all cases of this type, the matter is one of fact and circumstance. One must resort to inferences, because the pieces of the controlled drug were not found in the hands or in the pockets of the appellants. Each fact must be seen in the context of all the facts as a whole if its true significance is to be assessed ... the key to the matter is whether the inference of knowledge can be drawn ... once knowledge is established in such case, it is a relatively short step to say that there was control also. Section 37(3) of the [1971] Act tells us that the things which a person has in this possession shall be taken to include anything subject to his control which is in the custody of another. That extends the meaning of possession, but it also shows that control is necessary for there to be possession and that the power to dispose of the article is the essence of control. Mere knowledge of the presence of the article is not enough, because the person must be in a position to exercise practical control over it in some way ... when knowledge is established, in a situation where the persons charged are the only occupiers and the packages containing controlled drugs are open to view in their own dwelling-house, it seems almost inevitable that they are the persons who have control over them in a practical sense. This is because, for all practicable purposes, they can do what they want with them, dispose of them or use them to retain them and place them wherever they choose."

And later (at p. 532)

"I prefer to approach each case on its own against the general background of what is necessary in principle to establish possession."

Appeals dismissed.

NOTE

The Court held knowledge and control proved on the facts of this case. That reasonable decision was subjected to criticism; see Ferguson, "Joint Possession of Controlled Drugs" 1990 S.L.T. 233.

The requirement of knowledge and control for possession is asserted in *Murray v. MacPhail*, 1991 S.C.C.R. 245.

For similar cases see *Lynch v. H.M. Advocate*, 1991 G.W.D. 24–1364; *Milligan v. Friel*, 1992 G.W.D. 31–1803; *McGill v. MacDougall*, 1993 G.W.D. 38–2456 and *Douglas v. Normand*, 1994 G.W.D. 18–1108. For a discussion of these cases, see Bovey, "Possession: The Retreat From Control" (1994) 41 J.L.S. 58.

See also *McTurk v. H.M. Advocate*, 1997 S.C.C.R. 1 at pp. 4 and 5.

5.3.29   **15. Davidson v. H.M. Advocate**
                              1990 S.C.C.R. 699

D. was charged with possession, and possession with intent to supply, of cannabis resin. The cannabis was found under his co-accused's bed beside a set of electric scales he had bought for her three days before. The appellant did not live with the co-accused, but he was in the bedroom when the police raided her house and later told them that he had gone there to get cannabis. When the police came into the room, he climbed out the window. At his trial, a submission was made of no case to answer on the ground that there was no evidence that he had control of the cannabis. The trial judge repelled the submission and the appellant was convicted. He appealed to the High Court.

Held, that the jury were entitled to have regard to the appellant's flight from the police and to the presence of the scales beside the cannabis, and that there was just sufficient evidence to go to the jury.

THE LORD JUSTICE-CLERK (ROSS) (at p. 701): "In the ground of appeal which has been lodged, it is said that the Crown failed to establish possession. It was accepted that there was ample evidence of the appellant's knowledge of the presence of cannabis resin in the house referred to in these charges, but it is said that there was insufficient evidence to entitle the jury to hold that he had control of the drug. It is of course well recognised that for possession these two elements must be present, both knowledge and control. Knowledge, as we say, is conceded and the issue was whether there was sufficient evidence to permit the jury to conclude that the appellant had control over the cannabis resin. A submission of no case to answer was made in relation to these charges and the trial judge rejected the submission and the defence proceeded to lead evidence. The issue which is raised by the ground of appeal is whether the trial judge was well founded in rejecting the submission.

In his report the trial judge tells us that he was persuaded by the advocate-depute that there was sufficient evidence on the basis, first, that the appellant had admitted that he had supplied electric scales to his co-accused which were found beside the cannabis resin under her bed and, secondly, that his precipitous escape through her window on the arrival of the police and his subsequent concoction of a false alibi were so eloquent of guilt as to amount to an adminicle of evidence which the jury were entitled to take into account. There is no doubt that the evidence relied on for proof of control was very slender but we have come to the conclusion that it was just sufficient and that the trial judge was correct in rejecting the submission and allowing the matter to go before the jury. There was, as the trial judge tells us, evidence that the cannabis resin was found under the bed of the appellant's co-accused [...]. She was the tenant of the house in question and the appellant lived elsewhere. But in addition to the cannabis resin there was also found under the bed a set of electric scales and a cutting board used for cutting cannabis resin. There was evidence of a statement made by the appellant to two police officers to the effect that he had, at the request of his co-accused, supplied her with electric scales and had delivered them to her house some three nights before 7th June. Furthermore, there was evidence that on 7th June the appellant was in [the co-accused's] bedroom when the police raided her house. He apparently told the police at a later stage that he had gone to her house to get cannabis. So the situation was that when police arrived, the appellant was not only aware that there was cannabis resin in the house but he was in the room where the cannabis resin was and beside the cannabis resin there were electric scales which he admitted having supplied to his co-accused. In addition to that, as we say, when the police arrived he made off through the window of the bedroom, and we are satisfied that that was in the circumstances here something to which the jury were entitled to have regard. As the trial judge says, no doubt there are a number of possible explanations for the appellant's flight from the house but we are satisfied that the jury were entitled to rely on that evidence and the evidence regarding the scales, which, as we say, were found beside the cannabis in the room where the appellant was before he began his flight. In these circumstances we have come to the conclusion that there was just sufficient evidence to go to the jury and that accordingly there was no miscarriage of justice in the trial judge's allowing the case to go to the jury because there was sufficient evidence both of knowledge and control."

Appeal refused.

16. Croal v. H.M. Advocate   5.3.30
1991 G.W.D. 40–2445

On appeal against conviction, *held* that where 340 squares impregnated with lysergide placed in a cigarette packet hidden in a cupboard in a common stair had been replaced by the police with a similar dummy packet, and after the police had kept watch and seen C. enter the stair, C. had been found in the cupboard with the packet lying among rubbish on the floor, and where he could not substantiate his excuse for being in the cupboard, there was sufficient evidence of possession, albeit fleeting, of the packet and its contents. (C. did not dispute that it was possible to infer from such possession, possession of the drugs which had been found there a few days before.) The trial judge had sufficiently directed the jury that the essential elements of possession were control and knowledge and that if they accepted the evidence of the police they were entitled to infer that the packet had been in C.'s possession. The jury had been addressed by counsel on the circumstances. There was no difference in principle between contact which was prolonged and that which was fleeting.

Appeal refused.

NOTE
    This decision seems to be inconsistent with *MacKay v. Hogg, supra*, at paragraph **5.3.8**.

5.3.31   **17. Morrison's Application**
                                       [1991] N.I. 70

A bottle containing a liquid suspected of being alcohol was found in A.'s shared cell. The governor found them both guilty under rule 31(7) of the Prison Rules (Northern Ireland) 1982 of possessing an unauthorised article. They applied for judicial review.

Held, (1) the concept of possession was not excluded from "has in his cell" in rule 31(7); (2) the governor had to be satisfied that the person charged was in possession of the article; (3) the finding of an article in a two-man cell was not sufficient proof that both were in possession of it; and (4) in the absence of evidence pointing to one of the prisoners or to them both, it was not possible to say which of them was guilty.

CARSWELL, J.: "The governor was on more uncertain ground, however, when he dealt with the evidence against each applicant of his possession of the bottle. Each raised the possibility that some other person could have put the bottle in the cell when its occupants were elsewhere. The governor plainly was unimpressed by such a suggestion, and did not believe the applicants when they told him that they had never seen the bottle and knew nothing of it. I consider that he was entitled so to conclude and to reject the defence that the bottle could have been the property of some other person and that it had nothing to do with either of the applicants.

    Each applicant was charged with having the unauthorised article in his cell. I consider that although Rule 31(7) contains the phrase 'has in his cell, room or possession', this does not mean that the concept of possession is not involved in the earlier words of the rule 'has in his cell'. On the contrary, I am of the view that, just as in *R. v. Murphy, Lillis and Burns* (1971) N.I. 193 having a firearm with one was held to involve possession plus a more personal element, so here it is necessary for the governor to be satisfied that the person charged with having an unauthorised article in his cell was in possession of that article. The governor quite clearly recognised this, as appears from his reference in various places in the transcript to the need to prove possession.

    What he does not appear to have understood with the requisite clarity was the difficulty of establishing possession when the only evidence is that the object was in a place or room occupied by two or more persons, and the evidence does not point to a connection with one rather than the other or others or to a joint possession. This was the difficulty which faced the Crown in *R. v. Whelan* [1972] N.I. 153, where a firearm was found in a bedroom occupied by three brothers, the only adult males in the house. The Court of Criminal Appeal held that there was insufficient evidence that any of the three was in possession of the gun, although it was virtually certain that one at least of them must have been, nor was there evidence on which they could properly be held to have been in possession. Lowry L.C.J. said at pages 156–7: 'Every argument of logic and commonsense would indicate that there was a very strong case that at least one of these men was in possession of this gun, and it is quite clear that none of them had a licence or permit to have the gun and no explanation is forthcoming as to what the gun was doing in this house. It appears to the court, however, that this is a case which could well be approached on the basis that guilt existed in the alternative, that is to say, that one, or possibly two, of these men might have been guilty while the remaining two or one, as the case may be, were or was innocent of the offences which have been included in the indictment and that the difficulty, in fact the impossibility, of laying the blame conclusively at the door of one accused is not a warrant for permitting or inviting a finding of guilty against each of them.'

This situation is mirrored in the present case. The bottle was found in the cell, which was occupied by the two applicants. Both denied any knowledge of it. The governor was, as I have held, entitled to reject their defence that an outside person placed it there and to conclude that it must have been one or both of the applicants. That is nevertheless insufficient proof that it can be laid to the door of either. The governor clearly was of the view that to find an article in a two-man cell is sufficient proof that both were in possession of it. I cannot accept that as correct. It was quite possible that either was in sole possession of the bottle, and that the other was not involved. In the absence of evidence pointing to one of them or to a joint possession one cannot say which was guilty and cannot convict either of possession. Cases may occur in which such evidence may be forthcoming, and where a governor may properly conclude after hearing it that A. had the article whereas B. was not in possession, in which event he should find the case proved against A. and dismiss the charge against B. In others there may be sufficient evidence that both were in joint possession, in which event both may be correctly convicted. An analogous case may be found in my decision in *In re Moen's Application* (1990, unreported), where I held that the background of the case was such that the governor was entitled to hold that the two occupants of a cell acted in concert to carry out a forbidden act which could not be proved to have been done physically by either.

One can readily sympathise with governors holding adjudications in which difficult legal concepts such as possession have to be dealt with.

They may not have the benefit of legal training, and have to exercise fairness and common sense in their disposition of the cases. Fortunately, in the large majority of cases these qualities will stand them in very good stead. When one comes to a case which depends on a correct appreciation of the elements which must be proved to establish possession, however, their decisions cannot stand unless they are in accordance with the law. I am compelled to conclude that the governor did not appreciate the law correctly in these cases and so misdirected himself in what had had to be proved against the applicants. On the evidence which appears from the transcripts I do not consider that there ever was a prima facie case against either applicant of possession of the bottle, nor was it furnished by their own evidence given at the adjudication.

I shall therefore make an order of certiorari quashing the adjudication against each applicant."

Application granted.

5.3.32

18. Campbell v. H.M. Advocate
1992 S.C.C.R. 35

C. and two co-accused were charged with possession of cannabis resin with intent to supply it to another. The police had received information that the two co-accused had hired a car and had reason to believe that the car was to be used to take drugs from Glasgow to Oban. They accordingly set up a roadblock and stopped the car. The two co-accused were in the front of the car and the appellant in the back. There was a slab of cannabis resin under a front seat at the appellant's feet and a holdall on the seat beside him. The holdall belonged to the appellant. The police detained and searched all three accused. A knife with traces of cannabis was found in the appellant's holdall. The appellant was convicted and appealed to the High Court on the ground that the police were not entitled to detain and search him.

Held, (1) that the police, given the information that they had received, were entitled to conclude reasonably that the appellant was in possession of drugs, and they had therefore authority to detain and search him; and (2) that there would have been sufficient evidence to convict the appellant without his admission of ownership of the holdall, since he was found in the car with the slab of cannabis at his feet and the holdall at his side.

The Lord Justice-Clerk (Ross) (at p. 37): "The appellant is Duncan McNeil Campbell who was found guilty at the sheriff court at Oban of charge (1) on an indictment which was a charge of contravening section 5(3) of the Misuse of Drugs Act 1971. That was a charge that along with two co-accused in a motor vehicle he unlawfully had in his possession a controlled drug, namely cannabis resin, with intent to supply it to another. He has appealed against conviction and the note of appeal contains three grounds of appeal. Today on his behalf [counsel] has intimated that he is no longer insisting on grounds two and three and he has concentrated upon ground one. Ground one is to the effect that it is alleged that the search of the appellant by the police was illegal and that his detention was illegal. The sheriff in his report describes the circumstances which gave rise to this prosecution. It appears that on Friday evening, 12th January, police officers at Oban received a telephone call giving them reliable information that the appellant's two co-accused had hired a motor vehicle, registered number [...], for the purpose of making a return journey to Glasgow that night. The police officers had reasonable grounds to suspect that the purpose of the journey was to obtain controlled drugs in the Glasgow area and bring them to Oban. The sheriff further informs us that acting on this information the police set up a roadblock on the outskirts of Oban and that at about 2 a.m. on Saturday, 13th January the car was stopped at the roadblock and was found to contain three persons. These three persons were the appellant and his two co-accused. The two co-accused were apparently in the front driving and passenger seats and the appellant was in the rear seat behind the front passenger seat. The sheriff tells us that lying on the floor under the front passenger seat was a plastic binbag containing a slab of a substance about 4" x 3" x 1" which was subsequently identified as cannabis resin. On the rear seat next to the appellant was a holdall bag containing personal clothing and a knife which was found to have minute particles adhering to its blade which [were] subsequently identified as cannabis resin. The appellant admitted ownership of the bag and the personal clothing but denied any knowledge of the knife.

In presenting the appeal [counsel] has maintained that when the two co-accused and the appellant were detained the police had not yet searched the car and were not aware of the presence of the slab or the holdall bag. He informed us that the history of the matter was that the three individuals were detained and removed to the police station in a police vehicle and that their vehicle, that is the vehicle in which they had been found, was then driven to the police station where it was searched and these items were discovered. [Counsel's] submission was that so far as the appellant was concerned the police had not been entitled to detain him in terms of section 23(2)(a) of the Misuse of Drugs Act 1971. Under reference to the case of *Wither* v. *Reid* [1979 S.L.T. 192] [counsel] stressed that the section in question had been referred to in that case to the effect that the statute was a penal statute which had to be construed strictly. He recognised that having regard to what the sheriff says in his report the police no doubt had reasonable grounds to suspect that the two co-accused were in possession of a controlled drug and thus to search them and detain them for the purpose of a search but he maintained that in the circumstances that right did not extend to the appellant who was merely found to be a third individual in the car when it was stopped. [Counsel] founded on the case of *Lucas* v. *Lockhart* [(1980) S.C.C.R. Supp. 256]. That was a case where the police had stopped a car in order to enquire about the ownership of the car and having done so recognised the driver as being a person with whom they had had dealings previously in connection with drug offences. They then proceeded to search the driver and also two passengers, one of whom was the appellant in that case, who was found to have in his possession a quantity of cannabis. It was conceded upon appeal in that case that in the circumstances the police were not entitled to exercise their power of search under section 23(2) to search the appellant in that case. It must be recognised, however, that that case differs materially from the present case on its facts because the vehicle in the case of *Lucas* had not been stopped because there was any suspicion that drugs were being conveyed in the vehicle but it had been stopped for an entirely different purpose, namely to enquire about the ownership of the vehicle. Moreover in the case of *Lucas* the sole suspicion which the police entertained when they stopped the vehicle was in connection with the driver of that vehicle and its ownership. There was no question in the case of *Lucas* of the police ever having had suspicion that the vehicle was in some way involved in drug dealing. None the less, [counsel] maintained that in the circumstances of this case the mere fact that the appellant was present in the car in the company of two other men who were suspected of being involved with drugs was no justification for detaining and searching him under the powers contained in section 23(2).

The advocate-depute, on the other hand, maintained that in the circumstances the police were entitled to detain and search all the individuals whom they found in the car. They had received information not merely that the two co-accused were likely to be involved in obtaining controlled drugs, but information that this particular car had been hired for the purpose of conveying these two men to and from Glasgow in order to obtain controlled drugs in the Glasgow area and bring them to Oban. When they accordingly set up a roadblock and stopped the car the situation was not merely that the co-accused were suspected of being involved but this particular car was suspected of being used for the conveying of drugs. In these circumstances the advocate-depute maintained that when the police discovered not two men but three men in the car they had reasonable grounds to suspect that all the individuals in the car were in possession of controlled drugs and accordingly to search and detain all three. In this connection the advocate-depute founded on the case of *Guthrie v. Hamilton* [1988 S.L.T. 823]. That case was of course different on its facts but in our opinion the principle which was approved of in that case is also applicable in the circumstances of the present case. In that case the police had obtained a warrant under section 23(3) in respect of premises and they were engaged in searching the premises when the appellant called at the house. He was detained on the doorstep and found to be in possession of drugs. At his trial it was suggested that the evidence of the drugs found in his possession had been illegally obtained but it was held that the search of him had been properly carried out under section 23(2). In the course of the opinion delivered in that case it was pointed out that the real question was whether the facts and circumstances gave the police reasonable grounds to entertain the particular suspicion and the following was stated in the opinion (at p. 826): 'In the present case the situation was that because the police had reasonable grounds to suspect that controlled drugs were in the possession of a person in the premises […], they applied for and obtained a search warrant. When a caller came to the door during the search, and that caller had no obvious innocent reason for being there, we are of the opinion that the police officers were justified in suspecting that the caller was a person in possession of controlled drugs. We agree that the situation might well have been different if there had been some obvious innocent explanation for the caller's presence.'

In the present case when the vehicle was stopped by the police with the prior knowledge which they had and the vehicle was found to contain not merely the two men whose names the police officers already had but a third party, namely the appellant, we are satisfied that in the circumstances the police officers were entitled to conclude reasonably that that person, namely the third party, was in possession of drugs and that therefore they had authority to search him and to detain him for the purpose of searching him. Accordingly we are satisfied that the detention and search of the appellant were in the circumstances legal.

In the course of presenting his submissions [counsel] stressed that the appellant had been detained before the articles were found in his car and before he admitted ownership of the holdall bag and the personal clothing in it and denied knowledge of the knife. The advocate-depute, however, pointed out that there would have been sufficient evidence to warrant conviction of the appellant even without the admission because the fact of the matter was that he was found in the car with the slab of cannabis under the front seat behind which he was sitting, that is at his feet, and with his holdall at his side. We agree with the advocate-depute that that is indeed the situation and for all these reasons we are satisfied that there was no miscarriage of justice in this case and the appeal against conviction must accordingly be refused."

Appeal refused.

19. Bain v. H.M. Advocate
1992 S.L.T. 935

5.3.33

An accused person was charged, along with his girlfriend, with possessing amphetamine sulphate with intent to supply to another. The drugs were found in open view in a room in the girlfriend's house, of which she was the tenant. The accused normally lived at a different address but occasionally stayed at his girlfriend's house. He had attended the house at least once a week and had taken charge of arrangements which were being made for a new kitchen or an improvement of the kitchen in that house. The sheriff charged the jury that in these circumstances the accused was in a position the equivalent of an occupier and, accordingly, could have the requisite knowledge and control of the drug. The accused was convicted and appealed, contending that there had been no evidence to show that he had any such knowledge or control.

Held, that it was always a question of facts and circumstances in each case whether the inference could be drawn that an individual who was the occupier of premises had the necessary knowledge and control for possession, but that the evidence in this case was not sufficient to enable the inference to be drawn.

Appeal allowed.

5.3.34

20. R. v. Conway and Burkes
[1994] Crim.L.R. 826

C. was convicted of possessing cannabis. She was acquitted of possession with intent to supply. Her cohabitee, B., was convicted of conspiracy to import drugs, assisting a drugs trafficker and possession of drugs with intent to supply. Three quantities of drugs were found at C.'s house — 226 grammes hidden in a cavity behind the bathroom door; 5.3 grammes in a tobacco tin on the bedside table and 3.5 grammes hidden in a man's shoe on top of the wardrobe. Substantial amounts of cash were also found. The appellant initially said the money had belonged to her late husband but subsequently admitted that it belonged to B.

Counsel submitted, *inter alia*, that the judge had erred in directing the jury on the offence of simple possession that permitting the drug to remain rather than getting rid of it was sufficient.

Held, something more than knowledge must be proved. If the word "permission" is used to describe the second ingredient, it must be stressed that mere acquiescence is not enough. There must be something more, something positive which may be express or implied but which emphasises that there must be evidence of encouragement at least, or something similar. The judge had made no reference to control of the premises. He should have given some indication of how the test, whether by reference to permission or any other particular phraseology, should have been applied in the circumstances of the case.

Appeal allowed.

NOTE

In *R. v. Lewis, supra*, it was held that where controlled drugs were found in a house of which the accused was the sole tenant it was not necessary for the jury to be directed that they had to be satisfied that he had actual knowledge that he had the controlled drugs under his control. It was enough that he had the opportunity to find out that they were there. It has been submitted that that principle was wrong: [1988] Crim.L.R. 517.

That criticism has been reasserted: the decision in *R. v. Conway and Burkes* was correct in requiring knowledge of the presence of the controlled drugs as the first essential and that it is not enough where the controlled drugs may be under the exclusive control of another person in the house. The learned commentator added that where they are or may be under the exclusive control of another, the accused's liability, if any, will be that of a secondary party; [1994] Crim.L.R. 827.

It is submitted that both *R. v. Lewis* and *R. v. Conway and Burkes* ought to be examined very closely before reliance is placed upon them in support of any proposition because in neither report is there any reference to the extent of knowledge that requires to be proved given the strict nature of liability and the statutory defence available to the accused in terms of section 28 of the 1971 Act: see *Tudhope v. McKee*, 1987 S.C.C.R. 663.

21. Bath v. H.M. Advocate   5.3.35
1995 S.C.C.R. 323

B. was charged with contraventions of section 5(2) and (3) of the 1971 Act in connection with drugs which were found concealed under the windscreen-motor cover in the engine compartment of a car which had no bonnet. The car, on which the appellant was due to start work, was in a lock-up garage which was rented by the appellant and his father. The trial sheriff repelled a submission of no case to answer and the appellant was convicted. He appealed to the High Court.

Held, that the case was similar to other cases where drugs are found concealed in a drawer or a cupboard in premises to which the accused and at least one other person have access, in which case there requires to be some other evidence that the accused was aware of the presence of the drugs, that in the present case the appellant's father also had access to the garage and there was no evidence that the car had yet been worked on, so that it would not have been possible for the jury to say which of the two men put the drugs under the cover and knew that they were there, and that the sheriff should have upheld the appellant's submission of no case to answer.

Appeal allowed and convictions quashed.

NOTE
In *McAllen v. H.M. Advocate*, 1996 G.W.D. 37–2137 the controlled drugs were not concealed and hence the case distinguished from *Bath v. H.M. Advocate*.

22. Sim v. H.M. Advocate   5.3.36
1996 S.C.C.R. 77

S. was tried on a charge of possessing a controlled drug with intent to supply it to others, contrary to section 5(3) of the 1971 Act. The police had searched the appellant's house and had found an opaque unsealed plastic grocery bag, inside which were 16 transparent self-sealing plastic bags each containing about 100 capsules of Temazepam.

The judge directed the jury that the Crown required to prove that the appellant knew that the bag and its contents were in his physical control and that he knew the general character of the contents of the bag, but did not need to prove that he knew they were particular drugs. The appellant was convicted and appealed on the ground that the judge should have directed the jury that the Crown required to prove that he was aware that he was in possession of the contents of the bag.

Held, the judge's directions were correct.

THE LORD JUSTICE GENERAL (HOPE) (at p. 78): "The appellant is Frances David Sim, who was found guilty in the High Court at Glasgow of having in his possession the controlled drug Temazepam with intent to supply it to another or others; contrary to section 5(3) of the Misuse of Drugs Act 1971. He was sentenced to four years' imprisonment. There is no appeal against sentence, but the appellant has appealed against his conviction on the ground that there was a misdirection by the trial judge on the elements required for proof of the case against him on this charge.

It is said in the ground of the appeal that in his charge the trial judge stated that there were three essential elements to the charge as to each of which the jury would be required to be satisfied beyond reasonable doubt before they could return a verdict of guilty. It is then said that in setting out the elements the trial judge failed to inform the jury that there must be evidence from which it could be inferred that the appellant knew he was in possession of an illegal drug. As the trial judge has pointed out in his helpful report, a direction in the terms suggested by this ground of appeal would have been a misdirection of law, as it would be contrary to what was said in *McKenzie* v *Skeen* [1983 S.L.T. 121].

In support of that ground of appeal, however, [the solicitor advocate] directed his challenge to what the trial judge said in his charge ... when he was dealing with the possession of controlled drugs. The trial judge made it clear ... that it was not sufficient in law for someone merely to have physical control of a handbag or other bag. He said that that person must also know that he had had that physical control. He then went on to say this. 'To put me in possession I would require to know the existence of the package in my bag. I would not require to know the precise character of the bag or its contents, namely that they were particular drugs, but I would need to know that the packet and its contents were in my bag.'

Thereafter, in explaining how those principles could be applied to the evidence in the case, which resulted from the finding of a white plastic bag in the bedroom wardrobe of the appellant's bedroom, the trial judge said this ... 'The Crown must, however, prove that he knew that the bag, with contents, was in his physical control, and that he knew the general character of the contents of that bag.'

[The solicitor advocate] submitted that the direction ... which contained the statement that to put the accused in possession he would require to know the existence of the package in his bag, was a misdirection. He said that it implied that it would be sufficient for possession that the person was aware that he had the packet only, whereas what was required was awareness of the existence of the thing which turned out to be controlled drugs. It was not enough that he was aware simply that he was in possession of the container or the wrapping. He had to be aware that he was in possession of the contents. He accepted, however, that the trial judge had given a direction which was sound in law and consistent with the opinions in *McKenzie* v *Skeen*, where he said that what the Crown required to prove was that the accused knew that the bag with contents was in his physical control and that he knew the general character of its contents. In the end his submission came to be that there was a confusion between these two statements which would be likely to have misled the jury and accordingly there was a miscarriage of justice.

In our opinion, reading these passages together and in their whole context, there was no such confusion. We considered that it was quite clear what the trial judge was saying in this part of the charge. He was basing his direction correctly upon the opinions in *McKenzie* v *Skeen*. What he was doing was to develop the matter, first by reference to an illustration and then by applying that illustration to the evidence which was before the jury in this case. He was making it clear how the principles in *McKenzie* v *Skeen* fell to be applied to that evidence. The matter was summed up by him perfectly properly, as a proper development of the previous passages, in the passage to which [the appellant's solicitor advocate] quite rightly took no objection. In our opinion, therefore, this appeal is entirely without substance. There was no misdirection in this case and no miscarriage of justice."

Appeal refused.

23. Docherty v. Brown   5.3.37
1996 S.C.C.R. 136

D. was charged with a contravention of sections 5(3) and 19 of the 1971 Act in that he took possession of a number of tablets which he believed to contain, but which did not in fact contain, a controlled drug with intent to supply the drug to others, and "did thus attempt to have said controlled drug in your possession with intent to supply it to another." He took a plea to the relevancy of the charge on the ground that since the tablets did not contain a controlled drug, no offence against the statute could have occurred, and accordingly no relevant charge of attempt could be brought. The sheriff repelled the plea and the appellant appealed to the High Court.

Held (by a Bench of five judges), (1) that the fact that it is impossible to commit the complete crime does not preclude the Crown from charging the accused with an attempt; (2) that, when considering whether a relevant charge of attempted crime has been laid, it is not necessary to consider whether or not it was impossible for the completed crime to be committed, and that all that the court requires to do is to consider whether the accused had the necessary *mens rea* and had taken matters further by doing some positive act towards execution of his purpose; and (3) that where the accused knows of the impossibility of what he is attempting to do, there can be no attempt, and that a charge such as the present would be irrelevant unless it were libelled that the accused believed that the tablets of which he had taken possession contained controlled drugs.

Appeal refused.

5.3.38 *(iv) Cases under the 1971 Act: Possession with intent to supply*

5.3.39

1. R. v. King
[1978] Crim.L.R. 228

M. gave evidence at his trial that he would on occasions make a reefer cigarette, smoke it in part and pass it to others who would do likewise and return it to him. This process would be repeated. Counsel for K. was invited to address the court as to whether the passing round of a reefer cigarette could be supply within the meaning of section 5(3) of the 1971 Act. During the course of the argument the question arose as to whether an intent to supply was a real or constructive intent.

Held (a) that section 5(3) of the 1971 Act requires a real intent to supply, a willingness to do what is referred to, and that there must be a real likelihood that this will be done.

(b) That section 5(3) must be given its ordinary everyday meaning following *Holmes v. Chief Constable of Merseyside Police* [1976] Crim.L.R. 125, and that it appears to mean the passing of possession from one person to another, following the dicta of Lord Parker C.J. in *Mills* [1968] 1 Q.B. 522. Where, as here, a person passes round a cigarette among several people in circumstances where some or all of them contemplate only taking a puff and passing it on, that does not constitute supplying the material in the cigarette as it exists. It is only a supply if at the beginning the defendant has the material in his possession and at the end it has come into the possession of another in the sense that the other can do with it as he wishes. The control over a cigarette exercised by an individual within a circle of smokers is not such a degree of control as to make it a "supply" by the defendants within the meaning of section 5(3).

2. R. v. Moore
[1979] Crim.L.R. 789

5.3.40

M. had persuaded two girls who had never smoked cannabis before to leave a public house with him to "go for a smoke." M. was arrested outside the public house as he was rolling a reefer. He admitted an intention to share the reefer with the two girls. It was submitted at his trial that following *R. v. King, supra*, on M.'s stated intention there was not sufficient to make it a "supply" within the meaning of the Act.

Held that "supply" should not be given so narrow a definition. In this case there was an offer of consumption and therefore an offer to supply. The trial judge declined to follow *R. v. King*.

NOTE

The decisions in the cases of *King* and *Moore* are inconsistent with each other and the matter requires resolution by the Court of Appeal, especially since both the cases are decisions of the Crown Court. The commentary on *R. v. Moore, supra*, at p. 790 states that "If there is a supply in a case like the present it must consist in the transfer of control of the reefer. As the defendant would have put it into the hands of the girls with the intention that they should use the drug, it seems that the better view is that there is a supply. If the girl were to smoke the whole reefer, it would seem clearly right to regard her as having been supplied. The fact that the cigarette was to be shared and held by each for only a short time would seem to amount to a difference in degree rather than in principle."

3. R. v. Greenfield
[1983] Crim.L.R. 397

5.3.41

The police found G. in his car with a plastic bag containing some cannabis. He denied that it was his and said that it belonged to an unnamed person who had left it in the car after having been given a lift. The cannabis was to be handed back by G. on demand and this man intended to supply it to others. On conviction of possession with intent to supply, G. appealed on the ground of misdirection by the trial judge.

Held, that the question was whether the intention undoubtedly held by G. that the drug should be supplied by the unknown man to a third person was sufficient for an offence by the 1971 Act. The words "with intent to supply" predicated an intent on the part of the person who possessed to supply, not an intent that someone other that the person in possession should supply.

Appeal allowed.

NOTE

Accompanying the above reports is a commentary by Professor J. C. Smith, Q.C., *ibid.* at p. 398, and there it is questioned why the appellant's intention to deliver the cannabis on demand to the unknown man was not sufficient intention to supply, relying on *R. v. Mills*. He makes the additional point that the "supply" may be no more than a passing of possession and the fact that the unknown man is not a "consumer" but rather a middleman is irrelevant in law. The appellant's counsel wrote to the Editor of the Criminal Law Review on the point: [1983] Crim. L.R. 575. The professor's point had been considered in the Court of Appeal. Counsel seemed to be of the view that it does not follow that the appellant could be said to be supplying the cannabis to the unknown man when he was merely returning physical custody of it to that unknown man and it had never ceased to be under that unknown man's control. It was a question of ordinary English usage and the Court of Appeal had decided the case on the basis that the appellant did not have an intent to supply the cannabis to the unknown man.

5.3.42　　　　　　　　　**4. Morrison v. Smith**
　　　　　　　　　　　　　　　1983 S.C.C.R. 171

M. admitted the unlawful possession of methadone. At the same time in her house there were found other drugs to a value of several hundred pounds in all. She denied any knowledge of these drugs. A charge of possession of these drugs with intent to supply was held proved and she appealed. The sheriff had based his finding of an intent to supply on the value, quantity and diversity of the drugs concerned. The drugs were lerorphanol, morphine, methylphenidate and ethylmorphine hydrochloride.

THE LORD JUSTICE GENERAL (EMSLIE) (at p. 174): "In this case the starting point was the finding of the appellant in possession of a substantial quantity of assorted drugs — four different drugs of substantial value. The appellant offered no explanation for her possession, negativing the idea that it was possession with intent. Her evidence was that she knew nothing about them and that evidence the sheriff rejected."

　　　　　　　　　　　　　　　　　　　　　　　　　Appeal allowed.

NOTE

　　Morrison's case was considered in Shiels, "Possession of Controlled Drugs with Intent to Supply" (1984) 89 SCOLAG 23. There it was argued that in Scotland there appeared to be an evidential burden on an accused to, at the least, place doubts on the prosecution's contention that there was an intention to supply. Moreover it was argued that in the Scots courts the intention to supply can be inferred objectively from the circumstances in which possession is discovered, at least in the absence of an explanation to the contrary from the accused. In England the test is subjective on the authority of *King's* case and the intention must be a "real" intent and not a constructive one and there must be a willingness to do this and a "real" likelihood that this will be done. That article met with a swift rejoinder: Bovey, "Possession of Controlled Drugs With Intent to Supply (*A Second View*)" (1984) 91 SCOLAG 48. The contrary view there was that there was no difference between Scots and English law on the relevant point.

5. R. v. Delgado   5.3.43
[1984] 1 All E.R. 449

D. told the court at his trial that two friends had stolen a bag containing a substantial quantity of cannabis. They had had nowhere to keep it and he had been asked to keep the bag for a couple of hours and later to deliver the bag to them at a certain time and place. He was arrested by the police on his way to deliver the bag to his friends. He was convicted of possession with intent to supply and he appealed against that conviction on the basis that the trial judge had erred in law.

SKINNER J. (at p. 452): "[W]e are driven back to considering the word 'supply' in its context. The judge himself ruled on the dictionary definition which is a fairly wide one. This court has been referred to the *Shorter Oxford English Dictionary* which gives a large number of definitions of the word 'supply', but they have a common feature *viz.* that in the word 'supply' is inherent the furnishing or providing of something which is wanted.

In the judgment of this court, the word 'supply' in section 5(3) of the 1971 Act covers a similarly wide range of transactions. A feature common to all of those transactions is a transfer of physical control of a drug from one person to another. In our judgment questions of transfer of ownership or legal possession of those drugs are irrelevant to the issue whether or not there was intent to supply."

Appeal dismissed.

NOTE
   A commentator on this case was of the view that: "The very wide meaning given to 'supply' extends the offence far beyond the mischief at which it is aimed. If A. is in possession of a controlled drug, class C, and he gives it to B. to look after until he asks for it back, A. is liable to a maximum of five years for supplying the drug but B. is now liable to 14 years for being in possession with intent to supply. This may be an unavoidable consequence of giving 'supply' its natural meaning: but it may be that a charge, simply of possession contrary to section 5(2) would more accurately reflect the gravamen of the defendant's conduct." [1984] Crim.L.R. at p. 170. The commentator's approach is open to challenge if it is accepted that for the mischief which the legislation strikes at is the circulation of drugs. It follows that any act that promotes the circulation of controlled drugs is a wrongful one.

6. R. v. Downes   5.3.44
[1984] Crim.L.R. 552

D. was convicted of possession of cannabis resin with intent to supply. She admitted that a box and some cash belonged to her but she denied that documents, drugs, notebooks or scales belonged to her. She denied possessing the cannabis resin with intent to supply. The prosecution case was that D. and another were in joint possession of the drugs with intent to supply.

D. appealed on the ground of misdirection by the trial judge. *Held*, that unless two persons in joint possession of a controlled drug were engaged in a joint venture to supply the drugs to others, the mere fact that one knew of the other's intention to supply them, but had no intention to supply them himself, did not constitute the necessary intent for the purpose of an offence under section 5(3) of the 1971 Act.

Appeal allowed.

5.3.45   **7. Donnelly v. H.M. Advocate**
1984 S.C.C.R. 419

D. was charged with possession of heroin with intent to supply. The Crown case depended on the total quantity of drugs in D.'s possession and on their having been made up into saleable quantities. Her defence was that the drugs belonged to another person called Colin Stewart. On conviction she appealed.

Lord Dunpark (at p. 421): "[I]f the appellant intended to part with all or some of the drugs in her possession to Colin Stewart, even for his own use, she intended to supply Colin Stewart and it matters not whether his intention was to use them himself or to supply others."
(At p. 422)
"[W]here a large quantity of controlled drugs, separately packaged in quantities normally sold in the streets, are found in the possession of a person, it is open to a jury to infer that that person intended to supply them to another. If the appellant in this case did no more than allow Colin Stewart to uplift drugs in her physical possession, she was thereby supplying them to another, namely Colin Stewart."

Appeal refused.

NOTE
The High Court of Justiciary in the Opinion approved of *R. v. Delgado, supra*, and distinguished Donnelly's case from *R. v. Downes, supra* on the facts.

5.3.46   **8. Morgan v. H.M. Advocate**
1985 S.C.C.R. 245

M. was charged with possession of controlled drugs, namely diamorphine and methadone, with intent to supply the same to another or alternatively with unlawful possession of controlled drugs namely diamorphine and methadone, both contrary to the relevant sections of the 1971 Act. She was convicted of the first alternative in respect of the diamorphine and the second alternative in respect of the methadone. She appealed on the ground that the verdict was incompetent.

Held, that there was no inconsistency in the verdict which was competent.

Appeal dismissed.

9. R. v. Maginnis
[1987] 2 W.L.R. 765

5.3.47

M. was charged with possession of cannabis resin with intent to supply it to another. His evidence was that the package, which had been found under the driver's seat of his car, had been left there the previous evening by a friend. He declined to name that friend but said, "I expected him to come round and pick it up." On conviction M. appealed and that appeal was allowed by the Court of Appeal. The Crown then appealed to the House of Lords.

LORD KEITH OF KINKEL (at p. 767): "[T]he issue in the appeal is concerned with the meaning properly to be ascertained in the usual way by reference to the ordinary natural meaning of the word together with any assistance which may be afforded by the context.

The word 'supply' in its ordinary natural meaning, conveys the idea of furnishing or providing to another something which is wanted or required in order to meet the wants or requirements of that other. It connotes more than the mere transfer of physical control of some chattel or object from one person to another. No one would ordinarily say that to hand over something to a mere custodier was to supply him with it. The additional concept is that of enabling the recipient to apply the thing handed over to purposes for which he desires or has a duty to apply it. In my opinion it is not a necessary element in the conception of supply that the provision should be made out of the personal resources of the person who does the supplying. Thus if an employee draws from his employer's store materials or equipment which he requires for purposes of his work, it involves no straining of language to say that the storekeeper supplies him with those materials or that equipment, notwithstanding that they do not form part of the storekeeper's own resources and that he is merely the custodier of them. I think the same is true if it is the owner of the business who is drawing from his own storekeeper tools or materials which form part of his own resources. The storekeeper can be said to be supplying him with what he needs. If a trafficker in controlled drugs sets up a store of these in the custody of a friend whom he thinks unlikely to attract the suspicions of the police, and later draws on the store for the purposes of his trade, or for his own use, the custodier is in my opinion rightly to be regarded as supplying him with drugs. On the assumed facts of the present case ...

the defendant had been made custodier of the drugs by his unnamed friend, who, having regard to the quantity of the drugs, may legitimately be inferred to have been a trader. If on a later occasion the defendant had handed the drugs back to his friend, he would have done so in order to enable the friend to apply the drugs for the friend's own purposes. He would accordingly, in my opinion, have supplied the drugs to his friend in contravention of section 4(1). It follows that in so far as he was in possession of the drugs with the intention of handing them back to the friend when asked for by the latter, he was in possession with intent to supply the drugs to another in contravention of section 4(1) and was thus guilty under section 5(3)."

Appeal allowed. Conviction restored.

NOTE

Lord Keith (at p. 771) drew a distinction between *R. v. Delgado, supra*, and *R. v. Dempsey, supra*. In essence the distinction was that in the former the drugs would ultimately be put back into circulation, whereas in the latter the custodier had no intention of using the drugs for her own use. In short the transfer must be for the purposes of the transferee. The decision in *Donnelly v. H.M. Advocate*, *supra*, accorded with that view and it was approved: Lord Keith added that the "desirability of these statutory provisions, applicable as they are both in England and in Scotland, being interpreted alike in both jurisdictions needs no emphasis." Of the judges, three agreed with Lord Keith in supporting the Crown appeal. A dissenting speech was made by Lord Goff of Chieveley (at p. 772) and his Lordship's view of the word "supply" as used in relation to goods, connotes the idea of making goods available to another from resources other than those of the recipient." The present case concerned "a deposit of goods" and section 5(3) "creates an offence which is evidently directed at those who are 'pushing' controlled drugs. But a person with whom controlled drugs are deposited is not, in my opinion, necessarily involved in 'pushing' them." (at p. 774).

In *R. v. Kearley* [1991] Crim.L.R. 284 it was held that evidence from policemen of there being telephone and personal callers to a house was admissible to prove the commercial supply of controlled drugs.

5.3.48   **10. McDowall v. H.M. Advocate**
                              1991 S.C.C.R. 197

McD. was charged with possessing cannabis resin with intent to supply on February 23, 1989, contrary to section 5(3) of the 1971 Act, and with being concerned in the supply of cannabis resin between January 1, 1989 and February 23, 1989, contrary to section 4(3)(b) of the same Act. The evidence against him arose out of a search of his house during which quantities of cannabis resin were found along with tick lists relating to prior transactions.

The sheriff in his charge to the jury referred to evidence "common" to both charges, and did not direct the jury, in accordance with *Kyle v. H.M. Advocate*, 1988 S.L.T. 601, that they could not convict on two charges arising out of the same *species facti.* The appellant was convicted on both charges and appealed to the High Court.

Held, that the jury were entitled to treat tick lists as relevant to both charges, so that the description of the evidence as common was not misleading, and that although it would have been better if a direction had been given in accordance with *Kyle v. H.M. Advocate,* there was no material risk in this case of the appellant being convicted twice on the same species facti, and accordingly there had been no miscarriage of justice.

THE LORD JUSTICE GENERAL (HOPE) (at p. 200): "[A] number of things were found in the house when the police conducted their search. Things found in a box on a table, in a coat and also in a tobacco tin in the living-room, when examined, proved to be cannabis resin of various quantities. In various drawers in the kitchen of the house the police also found a card and an envelope with lists of names and sums of money and notebooks with names and sums of money with various calculations and figures. The police regarded these various documents as tick lists, that is to say as lists of supplies of drugs to persons on credit who are expected to pay for them at a later date."

(At p. 201)

"We were referred by the learned advocate-depute to *Higgins v H.M. Advocate* [1989 G.W.D. 5–198] where a similar question arose as to whether the jury had been invited to convict the appellant on two charges arising out of the same species facti. The Lord Justice-General referred to the evidence as being 'apt to throw a significant light on the past, and although on the face of it the same pieces of evidence had parts to play in both charges, the same pieces of evidence did not all have the same part to play in relation to each of the charges.' As he put it, the finding of money which was the critical fact in that case bore a different aspect as regards the past from what it did about the future. Looking at the matter in this way we consider that for the sheriff to describe the evidence on which the Crown relied as common evidence was not so misleading as to give rise in itself to a misdirection. As for the question whether it was essential for the sheriff to give a direction in terms mentioned by the Lord Justice-Clerk in *Kyle* at p. 603, that is to say that the jury could not also find the appellant guilty of charge (3) in this case if they were minded to find him guilty on charge (1) on the basis of the same evidence, we answer it in the negative. It would have been better if such a direction had been given, but in the circumstances of this case the important evidence relating to the tick lists was clearly relevant to both charges. It was relevant to the past course of conduct which was the subject of charge (3) and to the nature of the possession which was the subject of charge (1). There was no material risk in this case therefore of the appellant being convicted twice on the same species facti. So we do not consider that the absence of such a direction in the present case could be said to amount to a miscarriage of justice."

Appeal refused.

NOTE
    The brief report of *Higgins v. H.M. Advocate* cited above does not contain the Lord Justice General's Opinion but the relevant part is set out in 1991 S.C.C.R. 201.

5.3.49   **11. Mattison v. H.M. Advocate**
1991 S.C.C.R. 211

M. was charged on indictment with (i) possessing cannabis resin with intent to supply it to another, contrary to section 5(3) of the 1971 Act, and (ii) possession of cannabis resin, contrary to section 5(2) of the same Act. He had been found in possession of a number of small pieces of cannabis which were in his jacket, and also of a much larger piece in his rucksack, but the charges did not specify in any way what cannabis resin it was to which they referred. The Crown accepted a plea of guilty to the section 5(2) charge and went to trial on the section 5(3) charge. The accused gave evidence that all the cannabis resin in his possession was for his own use, and his solicitor told the jury that he had already pleaded to possession of all the cannabis resin he had. In his charge to the jury the sheriff told them to disregard that plea, and said, "Suffice it to say that the accused accepts that he was in possession of the cannabis resin but that fact must not sway you one way or the other." The appellant was convicted and appealed to the High Court on the grounds (1) that it was not open to the Crown to obtain a conviction on the section 5(3) charge after accepting a plea of guilty to the section 5(2) one; (2) that the sheriff had failed to direct the jury that they could not convict of more than one offence on the same *species facti*; and (3) that in the passage in his charge referred to he had excluded the defence from their consideration.

    Held, (1) that the Crown could not competently maintain that this was not a case of simple possession after accepting a plea of guilty to that effect without amending the charges so as to indicate to which cannabis each related, and that by accepting a plea to the section 5(2) charge in the terms in which it was libelled, they had deprived the jury of an opportunity of examining the evidence in order to decide upon what facts verdicts of guilty on the two charges might be returned, and that there had accordingly been a miscarriage of justice; (2) that a direction in the terms sought would have been meaningless, since there was only one charge before the jury; and (3) that the sheriff had not directed the jury to disregard the defence of simple possession.

THE LORD JUSTICE GENERAL (HOPE) (at p. 213): "Three arguments were presented in support of the appeal against the appellant's conviction on charge (2). The first was that it was not open to the Crown to obtain a conviction on that charge because the Crown had already accepted the appellant's plea of guilty to a charge of a simple possession. These, it was said, were two offences arising out of the same species facti. The second was that the sheriff misdirected the jury by failing to direct — and no such direction was given by him — that they could not convict the appellant of more than one contravention of the Misuse of Drugs Act 1971 arising out of the same species facti. The third was that, by making the comment which we have just quoted, the sheriff wrongly excluded from the consideration of the jury the appellant's defence that he had contravened section 5(2) of the Act and that his plea of guilty had been accepted by the Crown.

Of these points by far the most important is the first, and in our opinion it is decisive of this appeal. There is no doubt that it was open to the Crown to charge the appellant cumulatively with all three offences under the Misuse of Drugs Act 1971 which were libelled in this indictment. It is in accordance with normal practice for a person who is found to be in possession of such a large quantity of drugs as the appellant had with him in this case to be charged at the same time with simple possession and with possession with intent to supply. It is not unusual for a charge of being concerned in the supplying of the controlled drug to be included as well as when, as in this case, there is evidence from which inferences to that effect can be drawn. Of course, as was recognised in *Kyle* v *H.M. Advocate* [1988 S.L.T. 601] an accused cannot be found guilty of more than one offence arising out of the same species facti. Where there is such a risk that that may occur the trial judge must make it clear to the jury that they cannot find the accused guilty of more than one charge on the same evidence. Provided such a direction is given there will be no miscarriage of justice if the jury find the accused guilty of more than one charge, provided there was sufficient evidence for guilt upon each of them to be established."

Appeal allowed.

12. Martin v. H.M. Advocate   5.3.50
1992 S.C.C.R. 356

M. was charged on indictment with possession of cannabis resin, contrary to section 5(2) of the 1971 Act (charge (5)), and with possession of cannabis resin with intent to supply it to another, contrary to section 5(3) of the same act (charge (3)). He was also charged along with another person with obstructing the police in the exercise of their powers of search under the 1971 Act. When cautioned and charged with charge (5) the appellant had replied, "It was just for personal use". His possession of cannabis resin was not in dispute at the trial, the question being whether he had it with intent to supply.

In his charge to the jury the sheriff left it open to the jury to convict on both charges (3) and (5) and the appellant was convicted of both. He appealed that conviction.

Held, that as the prosecutor had not irrevocably and finally committed himself to the position that charges (3) and (5) were to be treated as alternatives, the sheriff was correct in leaving the matter to the jury.

THE LORD JUSTICE GENERAL (HOPE) (at p. 362): "We are left with a final point of criticism which relates to the issue of whether the jury were entitled to proceed to convict the appellant on both charges (3) and (5). The submission by [counsel for the appellant] was that, while it was open to the Crown to charge the appellant cumulatively with these charges and while on a proper reading of the indictment the charges were brought cumulatively against him, the prosecutor had elected to ask the jury to convict on only one or other of the two charges and had in effect reduced the charges to the position where they were being left to be considered only in the alternative. No criticism was made of the sheriff's directions ... to the effect that there was sufficient evidence to justify a conviction on both charges. But in the light of what the procurator fiscal was said to have decided to do when addressing the jury it was submitted that a conviction on both charges was not open, and the sheriff was wrong to leave it to the jury to decide for themselves whether to convict on both. The learned advocate-depute, however, asked us to look more closely at what it is said both in the charge to the jury and in the sheriff's report as to what exactly took place when the procurator fiscal addressed the jury. It appears that the procurator fiscal depute did not commit himself irrevocably and finally to the position that these charges were to be treated only as alternatives. The sheriff says in his report that the fiscal's position was that these charges ought properly to be treated as alternatives but he left the matter open. The sheriff for his part decided that, unless he could say that the evidence made it impossible for the jury to convict on both, he ought to leave the indictment as it stood and leave it to the jury to decide whether they should convict on both. In our opinion that decision was the correct one in the circumstances as they have been described to us in the sheriff's report and as we find it in what the sheriff says in his charge. Accordingly we reject the argument that this case ought to have been dealt with on the basis of alternatives only, and in our opinion there was no miscarriage of justice in the fact that the jury were left to decide whether the appellant was guilty on both charges.

It was submitted that there were various other defects of a relatively minor character, in the charge, both in terminology and content. We have considered these in the light of the evidence which is summarised in the sheriff's report and in the charge pointing to the guilt of the appellant on charge (3). We should say that so far as charge (5) is concerned, in view of the terms of the appellant's admission to the police and what was in issue at the trial, we are quite satisfied that there was no miscarriage of justice in regard to his conviction on that charge. So far as charge (3) is concerned, there was evidence that three pieces of cannabis resin were found in the dwellinghouse. There was also evidence that scales and a tin in which some cannabis resin was found were in the house when the police were called, and as to the finding of money and the behaviour of the appellant when the police arrived, all of which was available to entitle the jury to draw the inference that he was in possession of cannabis resin with intent to supply to others. For that reason, in regard to the minor criticisms that were made, we are not persuaded that the jury were likely to have been misled given the nature of the evidence."

Appeal refused *quoad* charges (3) and (5).

13. Lockhart v. Hardie   5.3.51
1994 S.C.C.R. 722

H. was charged with being in possession of cannabis resin with intent to supply it to others, contrary to section 5(3) of the 1971 Act, and with possession of cannabis resin, contrary to section 5(2) of the same Act. In both cases the locus was said to be at a hotel and in a police office. The respondent had been arrested at the hotel in connection with an alleged assault and taken to the police station where he was placed in a cell and searched and was found to be in possession of a quantity of cannabis resin. The sheriff accepted that the respondent was in possession of a dealer's stock of the drug but acquitted him of the section 5(3) charge on the ground that there was no evidence suggestive of possession at the hotel and that no sane person could have an intent to supply when he was locked up in a police cell. The respondent was convicted of the section 5(2) charge. The procurator fiscal appealed to the High Court by stated case against the acquittal on the section 5(3) charge.

Held, that intent to supply denotes supply taking place in the future and there is no need for the Crown to prove that at the particular time when an accused is found in possession he has some intent to make an immediate supply to some other person; and appeal allowed and conviction on the section 5(2) charge quashed and case remitted to the sheriff to convict of the section 5(3) charge as libelled, there being no ground in the evidence for deleting the reference to the hotel.

THE LORD JUSTICE-CLERK (ROSS) (at p. 723): "This is a Crown appeal at the instance of the Procurator Fiscal, Aberdeen. The respondent is Ewen Scott Hardie. The respondent appeared in Aberdeen Sheriff Court in answer to a complaint containing five charges. The sheriff explains in this case that what has given rise to the present stated case relates to two charges on the complaint. These were charges (3) and (4), charge (3) being a charge of contravening section 5(3) of the Misuse of Drugs Act

1971 and charge (4) a charge of contravening the provisions of section 5(2) of the same Act. In both charges the locus was described as Marriott Hotel, Riverview Drive, Dyce, and Grampian Police Sub-Divisional Office, Bucksburn, Aberdeen. The sheriff convicted the respondent of charge (4), but acquitted him of charge (3). It is against that decision of the sheriff that the Crown have appealed.

The sheriff has set out the findings in the case quite clearly. Having done so, he explains that when he convicted the appellant of charge (4), he did so under deletion of the reference to the Marriott Hotel. We are not satisfied that that was the proper course for the sheriff to have taken. Having regard to the terms of the findings in fact in the case, we are satisfied that there was no ground for his deleting the reference to the Marriott Hotel. The appellant was detained there and conveyed from there in a police car to the police station, where a subsequent search revealed the controlled drugs. The reasonable response must be that the appellant had possession of the controlled drugs from the time he was detained. However, the issue before us is the sheriff's decision to acquit the respondent of the more serious charge, that of contravening section 5(3). The sheriff in his note explains that what concerned him in the case was whether he was entitled to find the respondent guilty, on the facts stated, of possession with intent to supply, which the Crown was inviting him to do. He was satisfied that the appellant had possession at least at the police station, although, having regard to the findings, we are satisfied that he ought to have held that there was possession also at the earlier stage in the Marriott Hotel. The sheriff was satisfied that the quantity, the wrapping of the drugs into recognisable deals and their value pointed to supply rather than personal use and indeed finding in fact 23 is in the following terms 'That the quantity of drugs found, the wrapping of the drugs into recognisable deals and the value suggested a dealer's stock rather than a user's supply.'

That being so, it is surprising to find that the sheriff acquitted the respondent of that charge. He states his reason for doing so as follows. 'My difficulty, and the reason I found as I did and acquitted the respondent, was that I could not sensibly deduce that any sane person could have had intent to supply anyone when he was locked up in a police cell.'

The advocate-depute submitted that the sheriff, in making that statement, was taking too restricted a view of what is required for a conviction under section 5(3) of the Act of 1971. Section 5(3) provides as follows. 'Subject to section 28 of this Act, it is an offence for a person to have a controlled drug in his possession, whether lawfully or not, with intent to supply it to another in contravention of section 4(1) of this Act.'

The sheriff appears to have thought that, before there could be a conviction, there would require to be some present or immediate intent to supply someone else. We are not satisfied that that is so. The advocate-depute pointed out that there is no need for the sheriff to be satisfied as to the identity of any other person to whom supply is intended nor is it necessary for the sheriff to be satisfied as to the precise point of time at which any future supply is intended nor where it is intended to make that supply. Intent to supply denotes supply taking place sometime in the future and we are certainly satisfied that there is no necessity for the Crown to prove that at the particular time when an accused is found to be in possession, he has some intent to make an immediate supply to some other person. Accordingly we are satisfied that the sheriff adopted too restrictive an approach to section 5(3) and, on the basis of the findings in fact which the sheriff made, we are satisfied that he ought to have convicted the appellant of charge (3).

The advocate-depute accepted that if there was to be a conviction under charge (3), the sheriff was not entitled also to convict of charge (4), as that would involve convicting the respondent twice on the same species facti, [counsel] who appeared for the respondent, did not seek to oppose this appeal and accordingly we shall answer the one question in the case in the affirmative. We shall then quash the conviction of the respondent on charge (4) and we shall remit the case to the sheriff with a direction that he should convict the respondent of charge (3) as libelled."

Appeal allowed.

B. SENTENCING: POSSESSION	**5.4.1**
General Principles	**5.4.2**
1. R. v. McCay [1975] N.I. 5	**5.4.3**

M. and seven others were convicted of offences relating to the possession of, supply of and incitement to use certain drugs. One case was an appeal against sentence with the leave of a single judge, while the seven others were applications for leave to appeal. The appeals were heard in the Court of Criminal Appeal in Northern Ireland.

LORD LOWRY, C.J. (at p. 5): "We observe first that the learned county court judge made the correct general approach by condemning the practice of taking drugs otherwise than on doctor's orders. This practice is a crime. The fact that the offender is usually the main sufferer distinguishes it from most other crimes, but cannot obscure the social evil which results. One may feel sympathy with the plight of an addict while maintaining a necessarily severe attitude in the interests of those who may be tempted to do likewise and indeed in the interests of the accused. The present cases do not exemplify physical or psychological addiction, but this fact removes one circumstance which is likely to promote a lenient approach.

There are, as in almost every criminal field, cases amongst drug takers and even suppliers — though they are both exceptional — in which great leniency may be justified, and a judge with the duty of sentencing will be vigilant, in the interests of the community as well as the accused, to recognise them.

The learned judge properly condemned even more the heinous practice of supplying drugs or providing a setting conducive to their uses, practices which are more sordid and worthy of punishment where the offender profits financially. He enumerated three principles:

1. Possession of a drug is less serious than supplying it to another;
2. Introducing drugs to someone with no previous experience is more serious than supplying drugs to someone who is already using them;
3. Possession or supplying LSD or heroin is worse than possessing or supplying cannabis.

As to the third point there is, no doubt, a further distinction to be made between heroin and LSD, but the latter is said to be so unpredictable as to constitute a grave danger to its users. We agree with the learned judge that it would be wrong to encourage the impression that so-called 'soft' drugs are not dangerous and destructive. Point is added to the learned judge's remarks by the emergence of liquid cannabis in concentrated form.

It may be helpful if we try to frame certain further principles:

4. In connection with offences of supplying and permitting premises to be used, a previous conviction for a similar offence should weigh heavily against the accused;
5. A previous clear record in connection with drug offences is relevant but is not in itself a clear indication against a custodial sentence;
6. In possession cases, and to a lesser extent in cases of supply and permitting premises to be used, a previous criminal record unconnected with drugs is of minor importance;
7. Severe sentences, including custodial sentences of any kind, are of assistance in signifying the community's rejection of drug-taking and its hostility to traffickers in drugs and even to those who supply them free of charge;
8. The importance of drugs, especially when done for gain, ought to be very severely punished;
9. One who runs an establishment or organises parties or groups to encourage drug-taking should normally receive a heavy prison sentence;
10. The same principle applies strongly to those who in relation to drugs corrupt young people in this fashion or otherwise;
11. The fact that the offences involve a group or 'cell' of people may constitute a circumstance calling for heavier punishment than would be appropriate in purely individual cases."

Appeals dismissed.

Class A: (i) Cocaine **5.4.4**

1. R. v. Layton **5.4.5**
(1988) 10 Cr.App.R. (S.) 109

L. was sentenced to 30 months' imprisonment for possessing 5.6 grammes of cocaine, and to various other terms for a variety of other offences. L. appealed only in relation to the sentence for unlawful possession of a controlled drug.

Held, that the sentence of 30 months was wholly out of accord with proper sentencing principles and much too long. A just and proper sentence for a first offence of possessing cocaine would be three months' imprisonment and the sentence would be reduced accordingly.

Appeal allowed and sentence varied.

NOTE
The Court considered *R. v. Omashebi* (1981) 3 Cr.App.R. (S.) 271 which was in point; see also *McCreadie v. Walkingshaw*, 1991 S.C.C.R. 761.

2. Campbell v. H.M. Advocate **5.4.6**
1986 S.C.C.R. 403

C. pleaded guilty to possession of 790 milligrammes of cocaine and to possession of cannabis. He was sentenced to three years' imprisonment on the first charge and to six months' imprisonment on the second. He appealed against the three year sentence as excessive.

Held, as the substance was a Class A controlled drug and the appellant had previous convictions for contraventions of the 1971 Act, the sentence was not excessive.

Appeal refused on that ground.

NOTE
The High Court of Justiciary agreed to backdate the sentence in view of the appellant's willingness to plead guilty at an earlier date.

3. R. v. Beveridge **5.4.7**
(1993) 14 Cr.App.R. (S.) 211

B. was stopped by police officers while in his car and found to be in possession of a paper wrap containing 173 milligrammes of cocaine and a flick-knife with a six inch blade. He was sentenced to six months' imprisonment for possessing cocaine and six months consecutive for having an offensive weapon.

Held, (considering *Layton* (1988) 10 Cr.App.R. (S.) 109 and *Lutzo* (1989) 11 Cr.App.R. (S.) 495), the sentence of six months for possessing cocaine was fully justified, as was the consecutive sentence for having an offensive weapon.

Appeal dismissed.

5.4.8   **4. R. v. Scarlett**
                              (1995) 16 Cr.App.R. (S.) 745

S. was convicted of possessing a small quantity of cocaine and pleaded guilty to possessing cannabis resin. The appellant was stopped by police officers who found seven small pieces of crack cocaine, amounting to 1.69 grammes, in an umbrella he was carrying. He also admitted possession of 0.96 grammes of herbal cannabis and 0.89 grammes of cannabis resin. He was sentenced to six months' imprisonment for possessing cocaine, and one month concurrent for possessing cannabis.

Held, (considering *Layton* (1988) 10 Cr.App.R. (S.) 109 and *Lutzo* (1989) 11 Cr.App.R. (S.) 495), the authorities to which the Court had been referred confirmed that the sentence passed was within the bracket for offences of possession of Class A drugs. A longer sentence might have been justified.

Appeal dismissed.

5.4.9   Class A: (ii) Diamorphine

5.4.10   **1. R. v. Fraser**
                              [1967] 3 All E.R. 544

F. pleaded guilty to unlawful possession of 24 heroin tablets and he was sentenced to six months' imprisonment. Leave to appeal against sentence was sought.

LORD PARKER, C.J. (at p. 545): "As a general matter, this court would like to emphasise that they are dealing solely with heroin, and where heroin is concerned, this court is satisfied that in the ordinary way, if there are no special circumstances, the public interest demands that some form of detention should be imposed. Heroin is, as has been termed in argument, a killer, and it must be remembered that anybody who takes heroin puts himself body and soul into the supplier or the supply. Such persons have no moral resistance to any pressure that may be brought to bear on them. Accordingly, as I have said, this court is clearly of opinion that a sentence of detention, in the absence of special circumstances, is the proper sentence."

Application refused.

2. R. v. Long
(1984) 6 Cr.App.R. (S.) 115

5.4.11

L. and another, both addicts, pleaded guilty to possessing diamorphine (heroin). It was accepted that the drug was solely for their own personal use. Each was sentenced to nine months' imprisonment, with six months' suspended. Each appellant had a previous conviction for possessing cannabis.

MICHAEL DAVIS, J. (at p. 116): "We take the view that the correct sentences in this case should be immediate custodial sentences. We think three months, which was the unsuspended part of the sentence, was correct."

Appeal refused.

3. Hoy v. McLeod
1983 S.C.C.R. 149

5.4.12

H., a heroin addict, pleaded guilty to possessing heroin and cannabis. At the time of the offence he was on probation for possessing controlled drugs. The sheriff imposed a sentence of 12 months' imprisonment on the heroin charge and of three months' imprisonment concurrently on the cannabis charge. H. appealed against the sentence on the heroin charge.

THE LORD JUSTICE GENERAL (EMSLIE) (at p. 151): "There can be no quarrel with his [the sheriff's] decision that a sentence of imprisonment was necessary. The only question is whether by imposing the maximum sentence of imprisonment permitted by law, the sheriff has gone too far, too fast, and has selected a sentence which can be seen to be excessive in all the circumstances. From the report it looks as if the sheriff had regard to what he called the interests of society in a long sentence of imprisonment for the appellant. We find it difficult to know precisely what the sheriff had in mind but one thing he ought not to have in mind was the suggestion that the appellant was in any way involved in the supply of drugs and, indeed, his history brought out in the schedule of previous convictions, demonstrates that although he has been convicted of contraventions of the Misuse of Drugs Act before they have all been contraventions by way of possession. We are satisfied ... that there was no justification for imposing the maximum sentence in this case and that the whole objectives which the sheriff had in mind could be achieved by a shorter sentence than that. For these reasons we shall quash the sentence of 12 months' imprisonment upon the ground that we are satisfied that it is excessive, and we shall substitute for that sentence a sentence of six months' imprisonment."

Appeal allowed in part.

5.4.13   **4. Ramsay v. H.M. Advocate**
                                    1984 S.C.C.R. 409

R. pleaded guilty to possession of 1.56 grammes of diamorphine on two occasions. The trial judge observed that he treated the case as a serious case of drug addiction and he imposed a sentence of four years. Appeal was taken against sentence on the grounds that it was harsh and oppressive.

THE LORD JUSTICE GENERAL (EMSLIE) (at p. 410): "Drug addiction is not a crime and it looks as if the learned judge in proceeding to sentence has exceeded the bound of what would be an appropriate sentence for possession and possession alone. From the information we have, this registered drug addict was consuming about one gram of heroin a day... What he was found to possess was little more than a day's supply of the drug which he appeared to need to feed his addiction. In addition to taking drugs, of course, we have heard that he consumed about two bottles of vodka a day. The daily cost must have been immense and it is not perfectly clear where the money came from. Leaving that on one side, the question is, what is an appropriate sentence to impose upon a drug addict possessing the quantities of heroin with which this case is concerned? In our judgment it was not four years' imprisonment, in spite of the record which contained two previous convictions for possession of drugs, but one of two years' imprisonment."

                                                    Appeal allowed in part.

NOTE
    This case was followed closely by *R. v. Bassett* (1985) 7 Cr.App.R. (S.) 75 where it was held that curing an offender of drug addiction was an improper reason for passing a long sentence of imprisonment. The most recent case is *R. v. Lawrence* (1988) 10 Cr.App.R. (S.) 463.

5.4.14   **5. Money v. H.M. Advocate**
                                    1988 S.C.C.R. 127

M. was convicted on indictment of possessing 580 milligrammes of diamorphine. He was sentenced to 24 months' imprisonment. He appealed against the sentence on the ground that it was excessive.

THE LORD JUSTICE GENERAL (EMSLIE) (at p. 128): "The appeal is presented upon the basis that the appellant had four packets of heroin in his possession for his own use. The total quantity amounted to 580 milligrams. The value of the drugs in his possession was not high and the sentence, because of that circumstance and various personal circumstances, could be seen to be excessive. Although the appellant has a very bad record he has no convictions under the Misuse of Drugs Act. He is married with a daughter aged three and a half. It is said that he had been abusing drugs for about 18 months but has now broken contact with drugs and, if released, has employment promised to him.

While we are satisfied that the sentence could be regarded as a severe one for possession of heroin, the question is not severity but whether the sentence ought to be treated by us as an excessive one. We observe that the trial judge says that the sentence may have been rather higher than would normally be imposed. We are not inclined to agree with that submission. As far as we can see, the sentence, though a severe one, cannot be described as an excessive one in all the circumstances."

Appeal refused.

6. Meighan v. Jessop   5.4.15
1989 S.C.C.R. 208

M. pleaded guilty to unlawful possession of heroin and disubstituted barbituric acid. Traces of these drugs were found in a substance on a spoon and on a piece of paper in M.'s possession. He was placed on deferred sentence to be of good behaviour for a year. By the time of the deferred diet he had obtained employment as a drugs counsellor. The sheriff imposed fines of £150 and £50 respectively and M. appealed against these as excessive.

THE LORD JUSTICE CLERK (ROSS) (at p. 209): "It is the fact that the quantities of drugs found were small, described as traces, we think, in the sheriff's report, but be that as it may, it is evident to us that if the appellant had not behaved himself and improved himself during the period of deferment he could well have expected a custodial sentence. The sheriff, it seems to us again, has reflected the appellant's contribution to his own future welfare by not sending him to prison and by selecting fines which, having regard to his means [a salary of £10,000 per annum] can only be described as relatively small."

Appeal refused.

7. R. v. Lutzo   5.4.16
(1989) 11 Cr.App.R. (S.) 495

L. pleaded guilty to possessing a Class A controlled drug, heroin. The appellant was arrested, and admitted that two wraps of paper containing 283 milligrammes of 44 per cent heroin found near where he was arrested belonged to him. The appellant had seven previous convictions, mostly for offences related to the possession and supply of drugs. He was sentenced to 12 months' imprisonment.

Held, (considering *R. v. Aramah* (1982) 4 Cr.App.R. (S.) 407 and *R. v. Long* (1984) 6 Cr.App.R. (S.) 115) the sentencer was wrong to say that

12 months was the minimum proper sentence. An immediate custodial sentence was not wrong in principal, but 12 months was too long: a sentence of six months would be substituted.

Appeal allowed and sentence varied.

5.4.17

8. R. v. Gallagher
(1990) 12 Cr.App.R. (S.) 224

G. pleaded guilty to possessing heroin. He was found with 3.3. grammes of 33 per cent heroin in his possession. The appellant pleaded guilty on the basis that the heroin was for his own consumption. He was sentenced to 12 months' imprisonment.

Held, although the appellant was in possession of the heroin for his own consumption and was an addict, it was necessary to mark the disapproval of society for an offence of this type by a prison sentence. In view of the amount and the appellant's personal circumstances, the sentence would be reduced from 12 months to six.

Appeal allowed and sentence varied.

5.4.18

9. Munro v. H.M. Advocate
1994 S.C.C.R. 220

M. pleaded guilty to being in possession of 36 deals of heroin, valued at £720, on the basis that she was unaware of the presence of the heroin until shortly before she was stopped by the police. She believed that the heroin had been put into her jacket pocket by her boyfriend and it was her intention to return the heroin to him. She was sentenced to two years' imprisonment and appealed to the High Court.

Held, that it could not be said that, with a drug of this nature which the appellant intended to hand to another, the appellant was not properly dealt with by the sentence imposed.

LORD ALLANBRIDGE (at p. 222): '[T]he appellant was intending, having discovered this substantial quantity of heroin which is a dangerous Class A drug, not to hand it to the police but to apparently give it to another, namely her boyfriend, whose property she thought it was. It is quite clear that the judge took into account the mitigating features to which we have already referred and made due allowance for them. We have done the same and we are not satisfied that in a case of this nature, where the sentence would have been higher due to the nature of the drug and the quantity and value of the drug had there not been mitigating features, the mitigation taken into account by the temporary judge was sufficient."

Appeal refused.

Class A: (iii) Ecstasy (MDMA, etc.)   **5.4.19**

1. Ravenall v. Annan   **5.4.20**
1992 S.C.C.R. 658

R., a 35-year-old first offender, was convicted on summary complaint of being in possession of £20 worth of Ecstasy. The sheriff took the view that the practice of the High Court required him to impose a custodial sentence and sentenced the appellant to six months' imprisonment. The appellant appealed to the High Court on the ground that the sentence was excessive.

Held, that the sheriff had a mistaken impression of the policy of the High Court, that each case must be treated on its merits and that in this case a custodial sentence was inappropriate; and appeal allowed and sentence of imprisonment quashed and a fine of £250 substituted.

Appeal allowed.

2. R. v. Cox   **5.4.21**
(1994) 15 Cr.App.R. (S.) 216

C. pleaded guilty to possessing 16 Ecstasy tablets and was convicted of possessing 1.5 grammes of crack cocaine. He was sentenced to 12 months' and 18 months' detention respectively in a young offenders institution concurrent.

Held, (considering *R. v. Layton* (1988) 10 Cr.App.R. (S.) 109) it was open to the sentencer to say that the two offences taken together were so serious that only a custodial sentence could be justified, but sentences of 12 months and 18 months were outside the proper range; sentences of three months' detention in a young offenders institution on each count concurrent would be substituted.

Appeal allowed.

Class A: (iv) Amphetamine   **5.4.22**

1. R. v. Campbell   **5.4.23**
(1992) 13 Cr.App.R. (S.) 630

C. was convicted of possessing a Class A drug and acquitted of possessing a Class A drug with intent to supply. The appellant was found in possession of 106 capsules each containing amphetamine sulphate and a strip of card impregnated with LSD. The sentencer made comments which appeared to imply that he was sentencing the appellant as a dealer.

Held, the appellant fell to be sentenced for simple possession; the correct sentence was 12 months' imprisonment.

Appeal allowed.

5.4.24
2. McMillan v. H.M. Advocate
1992 S.C.C.R. 900

McM. was convicted of possessing seven packets of amphetamine, with a street value of between £70 and £105, with intent to supply them to others, contrary to section 5(3) of the 1971 Act. She had been charged on indictment with a number of drugs offences along with her cohabitee, who was a dealer in drugs. She was sentenced to six months' imprisonment and appealed to the High Court.

Held, that it could be said that the appellant's position was one of a woman living with a man dealing in drugs who unfortunately succumbed to the temptation of dealing to a very limited extent herself, that these circumstances were exceptional, and that, in view of the good background report and her good record, the sentence was excessive; and appeal allowed and sentence quashed and order for 200 hours' community service substituted.

Appeal allowed.

5.4.25 Class B: (i) Cannabis

5.4.26
1. R. v. Jones
(1981) 3 Cr.App.R. (S.) 51

J. was convicted of possessing 3.2 grammes of cannabis resin. He had an earlier conviction of cultivating and possessing cannabis and had been fined. He was sentenced to three weeks' imprisonment which was suspended, and fined £50. He appealed against the suspended sentence.

GLIDEWELL, J. (at p. 52): "The main point which he makes in his note of appeal is that a sentence of imprisonment of any sort, suspended or not, for an offence of possessing a small quantity of cannabis, when there is, as in this case, no suggestion that he was supplying or doing anything of that sort, because the possession was purely for his own use, is wrong, even though he has a previous conviction. In respect of that he points out that something like five years had elapsed between his earlier conviction and the offence which led to this conviction. The Court is disposed to agree with the point he makes."

Appeal allowed.

NOTE

In *R. v. Minott* (1979) 143 J.P. 392 the Court of Appeal upheld a sentence of three months' imprisonment for the possession of 2.32 grammes of cannabis. Thereafter in *R. v. Leaman* (1979) 1 Cr.App.R. (S.) 256 the same court varied a sentence of four months' imprisonment for the possession of 2.1 grammes of cannabis to a fine of £10. But in *R. v. Osborne* (1982) 4 Cr.App.R. (S.) 262 it was held that *Jones, supra,* was not to be taken as a blanket decision that no cases of possession ever qualify for a custodial sentence.

2. R. v. Hall
(1981) 3 Cr.App.R. (S.) 228

5.4.27

H. pleaded guilty to simple possession of 83.3 grammes of cannabis and he was sentenced to six months' imprisonment. He had three previous convictions for possession of cannabis. On appeal the sentence was varied to one of three months' imprisonment.

THOMPSON, J. (at p. 229): "He had three previous convictions for having cannabis for his own use. He does not seem to learn and therefore he does not excite a great deal of sympathy. But we take the view that, in spite of his record, he, a 29-year-old man who came from Jamaica in 1967, can have his sentence reduced to some extent."

Sentence varied.

NOTE
    In *R. v. McLaren* (1979) 1 Cr.App.R. (S.) 285 the appellant had six previous convictions over a 20 year period and he admitted to being a confirmed smoker of cannabis and had been all of his life. A sentence of two years' imprisonment was varied to nine months.

3. R. v. Robertson-Coupar
(1982) 4 Cr.App.R. (S.) 150

5.4.28

R-C. was convicted of possession of cannabis. She had one similar conviction for possession of a small quantity, *viz.* one-eighth of an ounce of cannabis. She was sentenced to one month's imprisonment which was suspended. On appeal this was varied to a fine of £50.

GRIFFITHS, L.J. (at p. 151): "The appellants were not legally represented. They presented their own defence ... they presented a defence on the grounds of conscience.
    Whatever the merits or demerits of the arguments about cannabis, the fact remains that for the moment it is a criminal offence to smoke it. It cannot be smoked in this country with impunity. Those who do choose to smoke it and cultivate it must expect to receive punishment for it. There is a bigger stake here than the merits or not of cannabis and that is the fact that if you choose to live in our society you must obey the laws for the time being in force. If you want to go and smoke cannabis, it would appear from the material placed before us that there may be other places where you can go and live and do so.

But in a series of decisions of this court it has been said that where the offence is one of possession of cannabis in very small quantities for one's own consumption, as a general rule it is not appropriate to impose a sentence of imprisonment. The proper penalty in the ordinary course of events is a financial one. But I would say this, that even for the possession of cannabis, if there is continuous and persistent defiance of the law there may come a time when the courts will have no alternative but to impose a custodial sentence. The law cannot countenance a continual flouting of the statute."

Sentence varied.

NOTE
It is interesting that sentencing policy in England has changed in so short a period for in *R. v. Mollins* [1973] Crim.L.R. 62 it had been held that possession of cannabis ought to attract a period of imprisonment, albeit suspended. A short sentence of immediate imprisonment for simple possession was upheld in *R. v. Minott* [1979] Crim.L.R. 673. In any event in *R. v. Robertson-Coupar* and *Jones* (1981) 3 Cr.App.R. (S.) 51 it appeared to be the policy that a sentence of imprisonment, immediate or suspended, would not normally be appropriate on a second conviction for possession; the point, according to Dr D. A. Thomas, at which the continuous flouting of the statute leaves the court with the obligation to consider a custodial sentence seems to be about the fourth or fifth conviction: [1982] Crim.L.R. 536.

In *McCarrol v. H.M. Advocate*, 1987 G.W.D. 10–328 one of the grounds of appeal was that the judge had attributed to the appellant the view that cannabis resin was harmless and could be dealt with by the appellant with impunity and that this had influenced the sentence. On appeal, it was accepted that the appellant did not hold such views. On the other hand, the appellant did seem to hold these views in *Coyle v. Wilson*, 1990 G.W.D. 14–750.

5.4.29   **4. R. v. Osborne**
                       (1982) 4 Cr.App.R. (S.) 262

O. was convicted of possessing 3.83 grammes of cannabis. He had six previous convictions for offences involving cannabis over a period of 15 years, and had previously been sentenced to imprisonment for possessing a large quantity of cannabis in 1968 and for supplying drugs in 1972.

On appeal against a sentence of three months' imprisonment it was *held* that in ordinary circumstances, possession of a very small quantity of cannabis for one's own use would not result in a custodial sentence, but the case of *Jones*, *supra*, was not to be taken as a blanket decision that no cases of possession ever qualify for a custodial sentence. The sentence was varied to allow the immediate release of O. after three weeks' imprisonment.

Appeal allowed in part.

NOTE

In *R. v. Aldred* (1983) 5 Cr.App.R. (S.) 393, 28 days' immediate imprisonment for possessing just less than one milligramme of cannabis was varied to a fine of £75. He had no previous convictions for drugs offences although he had some for other matters. He had never been subject to an immediate sentence of imprisonment before. See also *R. v. Francis* [1989] Crim.L.R. 158.

5. Grundison v. Brown   5.4.30
1987 S.C.C.R. 186

G., a first offender, pleaded guilty to possessing 226 milligrammes of cannabis resin, with a value of about 50 pence. The sheriff fined him £100 and he appealed to the High Court of Justiciary on the ground that this was excessive.

THE LORD JUSTICE GENERAL (EMSLIE) (at p. 187): "In all the circumstances we are inclined to think that the sentence was excessive and that for this first offence of its kind the appropriate penalty would have been an admonition. We shall quash the fine and admonish Mr Grundison, but in saying that we want to make it quite clear that if Mr Grundison is convicted again of possession of cannabis resin or anything else, the conviction will stand in his record and he cannot expect to be treated in the same way again."

Appeal allowed.

NOTE

The policy of the High Court of Justiciary was reaffirmed in *Simpson v. Hamilton*, 1988 S.C.C.R. 163. However, in *Cleland v. McLeod*, 1988 S.C.C.R. 509 a fine of £125 on a first offender was upheld on appeal.

6. R. v. Rigby   5.4.31
(1992) 13 Cr.App.R. (S.) 111

R. pleaded guilty to possessing amphetamine and cannabis resin, and to handling and attempting to use a stolen prescription form. The appellant was found in possession of 77 grams of powder containing between 2.5 and 9 per cent amphetamine, and 21.9 grams of cannabis resin. He received a stolen prescription form and used it to attempt to obtain 23 Temazepam tablets from a pharmacist. He was sentenced to 200 hours' community service.

Held, there was no error in the total sentence imposed.

Appeal dismissed.

NOTE

If nothing else this authority serves to indicate how difficult it can be to categorise cases.

5.4.32
7. R. v. Cocks
(1992) 13 Cr.App.R. (S.) 166

C. pleaded guilty to possessing cannabis. He had been found in possession of 2.82 grammes of herbal cannabis and a total of 7.10 grammes of amphetamine sulphate. The appellant had served two previous sentences of imprisonment for possessing controlled drugs with intent to supply. He was sentenced to 12 months' imprisonment.

Held, (considering *R. v. Aramah* (1982) 4 Cr.App.R. (S.) 407) in the ordinary way, a sentence of imprisonment would not be passed for possession of small amounts of Class B drugs for personal consumption, but the appellant had committed similar offences on three previous occasions, and his record could be taken into account in considering whether a sentence of immediate imprisonment was justified. However, the sentence was much too long; a sentence of three months' imprisonment would be substituted.

Appeal allowed.

5.4.33
8. O'Neill v. H.M. Advocate
1994 S.C.C.R. 223

O'N. was convicted of simple possession of 2.699 grammes of cannabis resin, valued at between £8 and £13.50. He had one similar previous conviction. He was sentenced to six months' imprisonment and appealed to the High Court against the sentence.

Held, that either a fine with no time to pay or 30 days' imprisonment would have been appropriate; and appeal allowed and sentence quashed and sentence of 30 days' imprisonment substituted.

Appeal allowed.

5.4.34
9. McCleary v. Walkingshaw
Calderwood v. Walkingshaw
1996 S.C.C.R. 13

McC. and C. were each convicted of possessing small quantities of cannabis. The sheriff fined them £250 and £300 respectively, having adopted a policy of imposing deterrent sentences to try to prevent his districts being infected by drug abuse. The appellants appealed to the High Court against the sentences.

Held, that the sheriff was perfectly entitled to take the policy decision he did, it being well recognised that particular problems in particular areas of the country may require deterrent sentences for local reasons and that it had not been demonstrated that the sheriff failed to have regard to the circumstances of each offender and offence.

LORD SUTHERLAND (at p. 14): "The appeals really arise because of what the sheriff tells us about a policy decision which has been taken by him. He tells us that in the particular area of his sheriff court, that is the area around Kirkcudbright, there has up until now been a shortage of problems relating to drug offences. There appears, however, to be an increase in these offences becoming apparent. He says that he has made it clear in the past that he wishes to impose deterrent sentences to try to prevent this corner of the country being infected by drug abuse. He tells us that when such offences as the present ones have been dealt with by way of fines, fines in the region of £150 to £200 have been imposed and, as this does not appear to have proved to be effective, he has concluded that penalties for drug-related offences must be increased until they can be seen to be having a deterrent effect. He appreciates that the level of fine imposed may well be higher than fines imposed in other sheriff courts for similar offences but he says that it is necessary to respond to public and police concern regarding this problem in his area.

In both appeals counsel argued that the sheriff had misdirected himself on the matter of policy. [Counsel] on behalf of McCleary argued that each case had to be dealt with on its own merits. The sheriff has talked about a general sentencing policy of the court and this is something which would relate to all offences, whereas deterrent sentences are matters which should only relate to the individual circumstances of a particular offence or particular offender. [Counsel for Calderwood] said that the policy imposed by the sheriff here appears to be blanket and uniform and the sheriff has not indicated any concern with the circumstances either of the offender or, more importantly, the circumstances of the offence. She referred to the case of *Sopwith* v *Cruickshank* [1959 S.L.T. (Notes) 50], where a sheriff in Ayr had in a considerable number of cases arising out of road traffic matters, albeit all different matters, disqualified on a blanket basis for a period of 12 months and it was held that such an approach was entirely improper.

As far as the present sheriff's policy decision is concerned, in our view he was perfectly entitled to take the policy decision which he did. It is well recognised that particular problems in particular areas of the country may require deterrent sentences to be imposed for particular local reasons and the sheriff has explained to us, in the present case, what his reasons were for deciding that deterrent sentences were necessary in cases of this kind. In our view that was a view which he was fully entitled to take. Of course, it follows that even though he has decided to impose fairly severe penalties for deterrent reasons in cases of this type, he must still have regard in each individual case to the circumstances of the particular offence and the circumstances of the particular offender. It was argued that in these two cases he has failed to do that because he has set out virtually nothing in his report about either the circumstances of the offence or the circumstances of the offender. In our view it is fairly clear that the sheriff has accepted in both cases that the amounts of cannabis involved were of a minimal nature and of course the quantity involved was referable to personal use only. It is also clear that he has recognised that neither offender was in a position to pay a large fine for financial reasons.

We are not satisfied that it has been demonstrated that the sheriff has failed to have proper regard to the circumstances of each offender or to the circumstances of each offence. Undoubtedly, the levels of fine which he has imposed in these two cases are substantially higher than fines which might be found from other sheriff court areas for offences of simple possession of a very small quantity of cannabis. However, as we have indicated, the sheriff is entitled to take the view that a deterrent policy is necessary and, provided that he has proper regard to the circumstances of the offender and the offence, his approach cannot be challenged. As we have said, we do not consider that he has failed to take these matters properly into account in these cases and accordingly both appeals must be refused."

Appeals refused.

NOTE

The High Court of Justiciary has on other occasions deferred to the sheriff's local knowledge, *e.g. Hamilton v. Stewart*, 1989 G.W.D. 10–431; *Hughes v. Webster*, 1989 G.W.D. 29–1327; *McLean v. Walkingshaw*, 1992 G.W.D. 3–127; *Boyle v. Normand*, 1992 G.W.D. 14–803; *Cardno v. H.M. Advocate*, 1992 G.W.D. 23–1314; *Weir v. MacDougall*, 1992 G.W.D. 39–2307; *Russell v. Henderson*, 1996 G.W.D. 9–494; and *Rowlands v. Hingston*, 1997 G.W.D. 14–611.

5.4.35 *(ii) Possession with intent to supply*

5.4.36 Class A: (i) Cocaine

5.4.37 **1. R. v. Atkins**
(1981) 3 Cr.App.R. (S.) 257

A. was found in a street to be in possession of 17.9 grammes of cocaine hydrochloride said to be valued at £1,000 or thereabout. He was sentenced to three years' imprisonment for possession of it with intent to supply. He was unemployed and there were no relevant convictions. The appeal against sentence was on the ground that it was excessive for a man of good character.

PHILLIPS, J. (at p. 257): "The fact remains that, taking the least serious view of the matter established by the evidence, he was shown to have been part of a chain of distributors, of some sort or another, of the supply of hard drugs for illicit purposes, and therefore would be playing an active part in the chain. Anything beyond that would be speculation."

Appeal refused.

NOTE
   This case was reported also at [1982] Crim.L.R. 128 and the commentary there describes the sentence as being relevant to the "smaller scale retail dealer." Similarly in *R. v. Davies* [1983] Crim.L.R. 46, D. pleaded guilty to possessing 6.5 grammes of cocaine with intent to supply with a street value of £500. Appeal against a sentence of 15 months' imprisonment was refused. The court observed that it "was inevitable people supplying hard drugs would be sent to prison and as a general rule the sentence of imprisonment would be measured in terms of years rather than months."

Class A: (ii) Diamorphine   5.4.38

1. R. v. Ashraf and Huq   5.4.39
(1981) 3 Cr.App.R. (S.) 287

A. pleaded guilty to possessing 45 grammes of heroin and to supplying it on one occasion. A. was arrested after H. had provided information about him. H. had given the information when he himself was arrested for possession of an offensive weapon and found to have two packs of 52 grammes of heroin. The street value of the latter quantity was said to be £5,200. Sentences of seven years' imprisonment for A. and 10 years' imprisonment for H. were appealed.

MAY, J. (at p. 288): "Beginners or not, anyone who trades in dangerous drugs, particularly heroin, must expect, when caught very severe sentences. Those who deal are caught perhaps more frequently than those who supply to them, and it may be that if those who deal and those who are minded to deal realise the courts will pass severe sentences, they will be less inclined to indulge in their dangerous and miserable trade."

Appeal refused.

2. R. v. Hyam   5.4.40
(1983) 5 Cr.App.R. (S.) 312

H. pleaded guilty to a number of offences concerning controlled drugs. He had agreed to supply two plain-clothes police officers with four ounces of heroin at a price of £4,000. The drug was found in his possession on arrest. A total of £2,250 in cash was later found in bundles at his home. He was sentenced to six years' imprisonment for possessing heroin with intent to supply it to another, with concurrent and lesser sentences on the other charges. He appealed against the sentence of six years' imprisonment.

PETER PAIN, J. (at pp. 314–15): "The view which this Court takes is that there are the gravest reasons for suspecting that the appellant was a supplier on a much larger scale than [another man involved in the case] but when one looks at the way the matter was gone into, there really was not enough solid evidence to show that that was the case. After all, to have money in bundles of £100 may be highly suspicious, but it is not an uncommon way of bundling money, and to rely on the word of [the other man involved in the case] is not a very sound basis. On the other hand, it was quite apparent from the nature of the whole transaction that the appellant was nearer the source of the supply.

Having regard to the guidance given in *Aramah*, we take the view that the sentence of six years was rather too much in the circumstances. While the appellant is more to blame than [the other man involved in the case] in the matter, nonetheless there was a disparity. We therefore quash the sentence on count 3 of six years' imprisonment for possessing heroin with intent to supply and we substitute a sentence of four years' imprisonment."

Appeal allowed in part.

NOTE

In the period after Hyam was convicted and before his appeal was held, the Court of Appeal (Criminal Division) issued the judgment in *Aramah* (1983) 76 Cr.App.R. 190.

5.4.41   **3. R. v. Mansoor**
(1983) 5 Cr.App.R. (S.) 404

M. agreed to supply a detective with heroin and made arrangements to meet him. At the agreed time and place M. and others appeared and in due course M. was arrested holding a bag. That bag was found to contain 321 grammes of heroin. M. was convicted of conspiracy to contravene the Misuse of Drugs Act 1971 and possession of heroin with intent to supply another. He was sentenced to nine years' imprisonment and he appealed against that sentence.

SKINNER, J. (at pp. 404–7): "The value of [321 grammes of heroin] has been a matter for some discussion, if not dispute, on this appeal. During the trial there was evidence from a police officer, which at that stage was unchallenged, that the street value of the heroin to its eventual users would be £192,700. It was on that basis that the learned judge passed his sentence.

The price being demanded [by the appellant] in the car was only £8,400. [Counsel for the Crown], who has assisted us on this question of value, says that at that stage in the chain of transactions leading to the ultimate user his evidence would be that they would expect the price to be somewhere between £15,000 and £16,000. [Counsel for the appellant] ... says on the other hand that at that stage the value would not be as high as that. On his evidence, having been adulterated a number of times by intermediate handlers of the goods, the ultimate value was between £19,000 and £22,000. The Crown accept that the price at the time of arrest was somewhere between £60 and £70 per gramme, the difference between the ultimate valuations being accounted for by the amount of adulteration which might or might not take place in the meantime.

We have taken into account the doubts we have expressed about the evidence that the learned Recorder received about the value, and, on the other hand, the very substantial quantity involved with the promise of more being available. A heavy sentence here was certainly not wrong in principle. However having regard to the facts which were not before the learned Recorder, we think the sentence was excessive in length. There were no mitigating features here; there was no plea of guilty, no admission of guilt; but looking at the facts as they appear to this Court, it seems to us that the proper sentence would be seven years' imprisonment rather than nine."

Appeal allowed in part.

NOTE
    In the period after Mansoor was convicted and before his appeal, the Court of Appeal (Criminal Division) issued the judgment in *Aramah* (1983) 76 Cr.App.R. 190.

4. R. v. Juhasz   5.4.42
(1986) 8 Cr.App.R. (S.) 408

J. was the occupier of a flat. Two people were seen going there for a few minutes on the same day. When these two were stopped they were found to be in possession of heroin. J. was stopped later the same day and found to be in possession of two packets of heroin. In J.'s flat was found a quantity of plastic bags, a set of scales and squares of paper. J. admitted selling heroin to those who had left his flat, and that he had bought a fresh supply for resale; he claimed to have about 10 to a dozen customers. He was sentenced to 18 months' imprisonment on each of the counts for supplying heroin and three years on the count for possession with intent to supply, all consecutive. The sentences were appealed on the basis that they should not have been consecutive, and that the total was too long.

DRAKE, J. (at p. 410): "One [of the points made in support of appeal against sentence] is that in all the circumstances, the sentences passed on this appellant should not have been consecutive since all of the transactions related to the same afternoon and were, in effect, part of the same occasion of police observation. With that submission, this Court agrees. The sentences, in the view of this Court, clearly should not have been consecutive; whatever sentences were passed, they should have been made concurrent ...

Then we have to come to the problem of whether or not the total sentence of imprisonment was too long. Our attention was drawn to two authorities, namely *Gee* (1984) 6 Cr.App.R. (S.) 86 and *France* (1984) 6 Cr.App.R. (S.) 283. The court also drew the attention of the appellant's counsel to a more recent authority, that of *Guiney* (1985) 7 Cr.App.R. (S.) 200, in which the Lord Chief Justice gave the argument. In the case of *Guiney*, a sentence of seven years' imprisonment for a small supplier, supplying only to his friends, was reduced to four years' imprisonment. However, it is to be observed that in that case the appellant pleaded guilty, and the Lord Chief Justice, having reduced the sentence, also said that if such trafficking went on, the time would come when the courts might have to pass sentences for small-scale trafficking in heroin well in excess of the four years suggested as the proper term in *Gee* and other cases ...

We have come to the conclusion that the proper sentence in this case, and in the circumstances of this particular appellant, for these offences, is one of five years' imprisonment. Accordingly, we propose to quash the sentences of 18 months, 18 months and three years on counts 1, 2 and 3 which were consecutive sentences, and substitute instead sentences totalling five years in all ... Therefore, we substitute five years concurrent on counts 1, 2 and 3, we leave the three years concurrent for possession with intent to supply on count 3."

Appeal allowed in part.

5.4.43   **5. R. v. Carter**
(1986) 8 Cr.App.R. (S.) 410

C.'s flat was searched and the police found a total of 5.6 grammes of heroin, of which C. claimed that 2.6 grammes was for his use and that of his girlfriend. He admitted selling heroin in small quantities to a few people to make sufficient profit to enable him to buy heroin for personal use. He was sentenced to six years' imprisonment concurrent on each count of supplying heroin and four years concurrent for possessing heroin with intent to supply. On appeal against sentence it was argued that C. had supplied only to a small and regular number of persons, there was no question of selling to inexperienced people, and that the sentence was at variance with the guidelines in *Aramah* (1982) 4 Cr.App.R. (S.) 407.

TAYLOR, J. (at p. 412): "The mitigation put forward on behalf of the appellant was repeated by [counsel] on his behalf today. It was this, that he dealt only to fund his own habit and not for excessive profit, there was a small and regular number of customers, there was no question of going out on a random basis selling to inexperienced people and thereby corrupting them into the use of drugs. Reliance was placed upon the appellant's previous good character, and of course on his plea of guilty. He had at one stage undergone treatment to rid himself of the addiction but that had failed. ...

The next point taken was that the sentence was at variance with the standards laid down in guidelines in the well-known case of *Aramah* (1982) 4 Cr.App.R. (S.) 407. It was suggested that the proper sentence in relation to an offence of this kind on the *Aramah* guidelines would be of the order of three years' imprisonment with a plea of guilty.

However [counsel for the appellant] cited three authorities: *Gee* (1984) 6 Cr.App.R. (S.) 86; *Guiney* (1985) 7 Cr.App.R. (S.) 200; and *Hyam* (1983) 5 Cr.App.R. (S.) 312. In all of those cases he suggested, and correctly in the judgment of this Court, that the level of dealing was much the same as in the present case. In each of those cases the sentence originally imposed was six years' imprisonment, and it was reduced in each case to four years. Accordingly the contention of three years could be sustained as [counsel for the appellant] conceded during the course of argument.

But whilst it is true that a strict application of the *Aramah* guidelines might well show that this sentence of six years' imprisonment was excessive, there are three points to be made. The first is, that they are only guidelines and they are not to be applied rigidly. Secondly, it is important to use the specific words which my Lord, the Lord Chief Justice, used in *Aramah* in relation to this type of case in order to arrive at what would be the appropriate sentence by the guidelines. What the learned Lord Chief Justice said was simply this: 'It is seldom that a sentence of less than three years will be justified and the nearer the source of supply ... the heavier will be the sentence.' It is not possible to argue from that that a sentence of three years is appropriate and that no higher sentence could be justified in that class of case.

But the third point is perhaps the most important, since time has moved on. It is best expressed in the last paragraph of the judgment of the learned Lord Chief Justice in the case of *Guiney* which was cited to us, where he said this 'before leaving the case, we feel it important to make this observation. It might very well be that in future if the menace of heroin continued to increase in the way that it has, and if particularly Parliament sees fit to raise the maximum sentence for this type of offence, the scale of penalties which are reflected in the cases of *Gee* and *Hyams* and other similar cases dealing with heroin will have to be raised, and in future it may very well be that a person in the position of this appellant may have to be sentenced to terms of imprisonment well in excess of the four years suggested as a proper term in *Gee* and other cases and now of course followed by this Court in the present case.'

Observations about the possible need to raise the level of sentencing were also made in the case of *Gilmore* (unreported — May 20, 1986). In the course of giving the judgment of the Court, Mr. Justice Drake said this: 'The experience of all the members of this court is that the number of serious drug offences is on the increase, and has been on the increase since the time when *Aramah* was before the court in 1982. We think that without violating the guidelines the time has clearly come when it is necessary to move up the level of sentencing for serious drug offences.'

It is right to observe that since these two cases were decided the scourge of drug abuse, and in particular of heroin, has certainly not abated, it has increased. Furthermore, Parliament has raised the level of sentencing with effect from September 17, 1985. The offences in this case were committed in December 1985. Accordingly, the guidelines which were appropriate before September 1985 are now no longer directly in point.

For those reasons this Court takes the view that the sentence of six years' imprisonment which was imposed upon this appellant would have been an appropriate sentence, but for one factor to which I must now refer. That factor was the plea of guilty. It is important in this class of case, as has been emphasised on many occasions, that however serious the offending, proper discount should be given for a plea of guilty. The extent of the discount must vary of course, depending upon the circumstances. In the present case it may well be said that the appellant had very little option but to plead guilty. He was in the flat when the police arrived. He had thrown the heroin in the flat when it was searched. He therefore cannot claim to have as large a discount in terms of sentence as might be appropriate in another case.

That said, this Court takes the view that some discount should be made. Looking at the sentence of six years and all the circumstances of this case, it does not appear that an appropriate allowance was made. For those reasons the Court is prepared to reduce the sentence from six years' imprisonment to five years' imprisonment. That will be concurrently on each of the two counts 2 and 3 of the indictment. Overall therefore the sentence will be reduced from six years to five years. To that extent and to that extent only this appeal is allowed."

Appeal allowed in part.

NOTE
See also *R. v. Eliot* [1989] Crim.L.R. 306 for a similar result.

5.4.44   **6. Cunningham v. H.M. Advocate**
                                  1988 S.C.C.R. 514

C. pleaded guilty on indictment to possessing heroin and other drugs with intent to supply them to another. The drugs in question constituted one deal, the weight of which was not given in the law report. It was said to be worth £25. The drugs were originally obtained by C.'s brother-in-law, who was an addict, and it was C.'s intention to pass the drugs on to a third party on behalf of the brother-in-law, the intended transaction being non-commercial. C. had a number of fairly minor previous convictions. He had served only one previous custodial sentence, in 1972. He had no previous convictions for drug offences. The sheriff imposed a sentence of six months' imprisonment and C. appealed against sentence.

THE LORD JUSTICE-CLERK (ROSS) (at p. 516): "The sheriff in his report has explained why he imposed the sentence which he did. He explains that in the Kilmarnock area the supply and use of drugs is prevalent; he tells us to that repeated warnings have been given to the effect that cases under section 5(3) will be treated seriously by the courts and he expresses the view that a prison sentence is to be expected for such an offence whether the supply has been commercial or what might be described as technical. He concludes that there was nothing in the present case to take it out of the ordinary. He goes on to explain that he felt he could impose a lighter sentence than normal because of the mitigating factors put before him, and that is his explanation for selecting the sentence of six months. In our opinion, nothing which had been said today would suggest that the approach by the sheriff was in any way flawed. The sheriff had regard to all relevant matters. He was clearly entitled to take the view that any offence of this kind, whether supply was on a commercial basis or not, was a serious matter and one which contributes to the use of drugs by others."

Appeal refused.

7. R. v. Satvir Singh   5.4.45
(1988) 10 Cr.App.R. (S.) 402

S. was convicted of a variety of drugs offences but principally of possession of about 80 grammes of heroin with intent to supply it to others. He was sentenced to a total of eight years' imprisonment made up of one sentence of eight years on the principal charge of possession with intent to supply and other concurrent sentences. The sentence was appealed.

Held, that in *R. v. Aramah* it was said that it would be seldom that a sentence of less than three years would be appropriate for possession with intent to supply. That level of sentence would increase as the gap narrowed between the supplier and the main source of supply.

However since the decision in *Aramah's* case the Controlled Drugs (Penalties) Act 1985 increased the maximum to life imprisonment. That meant that the starting point for this type of offence should in general now be five years at least, both for supplying and possession with intent to supply.

The assistance which the court could derive from the amount of drug actually found in the possession of the offender was limited, it was the scale and nature of the dealing that was important. S. was shown to be a regular dealer in heroin, who used sophisticated means of concealment and had large sums of cash to hand. There were no mitigating features, and S. as a medical practitioner should have known the addictive effect of heroin and the results of addictions.

The court held the correct sentence to be one of seven years' imprisonment, but a second matter occurring while S. was on remand was ordered to run consecutively. As that sentence was 12 months, the net effect was one of no change.

Appeal allowed in part.

5.4.46   **8. Walker v. H.M. Advocate**
                           1987 S.C.C.R. 379

W. was convicted of possessing heroin, and of possessing Class B drugs with intent to supply, contrary to sections 5(2) and 5(3) respectively of the 1971 Act. She had two previous convictions in 1977 for possessing drugs. She was sentenced to one year's imprisonment on each charge, the sentences to be consecutive. She appealed against the sentences as excessive, and argued *inter alia* that she had given the drugs to a friend so that the friend might give some back to her, thus rationing her use of drugs, and that the offence of possession with intent to supply was therefore merely technical.

Held, that whether the supply was technical or commercial, a sentence of one year's imprisonment for a contravention of section 5(3) was inadequate in the case of a person with two previous convictions for unlawful possession of drugs, and the same was true of a contravention of section 5(2); and sentences increased to two years' imprisonment on each charge, to run concurrently.

THE LORD JUSTICE-CLERK (ROSS) (at p. 383): "Charge (10) was a charge of possession of Class B drugs with intent to supply them to another. In the grounds of appeal reference is made to the defence case that her intention was to supply her co-accused only, who in turn would resupply her, thus rationing her with drugs. The trial judge says that he has no recollection of counsel for the appellant suggesting to the jury in his speech that the appellant intended to supply her co-accused. [Counsel for the appellant], on the other hand, maintains that he does recollect making such a suggestion, and he submitted that if the jury accepted that suggestion any supply would be technical and not commercial.

In our opinion, whether or not the supply is regarded as commercial or technical, the sentence imposed of one year's imprisonment in respect of charge (10), far from being excessive, was inadequate. In his report to us the trial judge says that he considers that it would be easier to criticise his sentences as too light rather than excessive, and with that statement we find ourselves in agreement. A sentence of one year's imprisonment for a contravention of section 5(3) of the Act of 1971 in respect of an individual who had previous convictions for the unlawful possession of drugs, is in our opinion inadequate."

                                        Appeal refused and sentences increased.

NOTE
It is likely that the appellant was unimpressed by the result of her appeal. However, the real interest lies in the purported distinction between technical or commercial supply. The 1971 Act makes no such distinction but it is clear that in mitigation many accused and appellants seek to explain their actions with explanations that distance them from supply for profit.

It is recognised that some supply is merely that of the routine task: in *Robinson v. H.M. Advocate*, 1987 G.W.D. 27–1044 the appellant was recognised by the trial judge to be "a messenger boy". See also *Robertson v. H.M. Advocate*, 1993 G.W.D. 25–1554. In *Hepburn v. H.M. Advocate*, 1987 G.W.D. 31–1426 the appellant was "an unpaid courier." In *Burnett v. H.M. Advocate*, 1991 G.W.D. 37–2246 the appellant was "a courier", and thus, presumably, paid for his efforts: see also *Beham v. H.M. Advocate*, 1993 G.W.D. 6–410. However, in *McGregor v. H.M. Advocate*, 1992 G.W.D. 20–1169 the appellant was "a link in the chain of supply rather than a dealer himself", although the appellate judges there thought the distinction to be of little significance. Merely to say that the supply would follow from holding drugs for another has not impressed the appellate judges: *Foote v. H.M. Advocate*, 1995 G.W.D. 21–1179. The reason for such judicial scepticism is illustrated in *McDougall v. H.M. Advocate*, 1996 G.W.D. 20–1161 where it was noted that "the use of persons without convictions as custodians of drugs was becoming more prevalent." In short, assertions of comparatively innocent activities will be examined: in *Wright v. H.M. Advocate*, 1991 G.W.D. 11–656 the appellants were said to be "just street-runners" but it was clear that they showed considerable knowledge and initiative and were "properly described as part of a skillful and professional gang."

However, the economies of scale make the purchase of bulk sensible and the illegal nature of controlled drugs tends to result in a limited knowledge of suppliers and their whereabouts. Those caught up in supply charges may justifiably and honestly place themselves in the category of non-profitable or technical supply. There are many cases of that nature, especially with the "social supply to friends": see, *supra*, at paragraph **4.6.20**.

9. R. v. Stark   5.4.47
(1992) 13 Cr.App.R. (S.) 549

S. pleaded guilty to possessing heroin with intent to supply. He was found in possession of 1.03 grammes of heroin. Two further quantities of heroin were found at his home, amounting to 26 grammes. The street value was estimated at £25,000. He was sentenced to four years' imprisonment.

Held, the appellant had been diagnosed some time previously as HIV positive and more recently AIDS had developed. His life expectancy was now very limited, it was estimated at between 12 months and two years.

The appellant's condition made life in prison particularly hard. The Court was asked to reduce what was otherwise a perfectly appropriate sentence to allow the offender to be released and to die with dignity. The Court had every sympathy with that desire, but it was not the province of the Court to manipulate a sentence in this way. The appellant had appeared before the Crown Court and the indictment was allowed to lie on the file because of his condition; shortly afterwards he was arrested again in possession of heroin and the prosecution obtained leave to proceed on the indictment. This showed that there was a grave risk that the appellant would continue to traffic in drugs as long as he was able to do so. It was not for the Court to manipulate the sentence; this was a matter for the exercise of the Royal Prerogative of mercy.

Appeal dismissed.

5.4.48
10. R. v. Arif
(1994) 15 Cr.App.R. (S.) 895

A. pleaded guilty to possessing a Class A drug with intent to supply. Police officers searching his flat found two parcels, one containing 494 grammes of powder containing 20 per cent heroin, the other containing 492 grammes of powder containing 13 per cent heroin. A further series of bags contained a total of 298 grammes of powder containing 17 per cent heroin. The appellant claimed that he was in possession of the heroin on behalf of another person, and the trial judge, after hearing evidence, found that the appellant had taken possession of the heroin, knowing that it was heroin, but intending to retain the drug only until he was required to hand it over. He was sentenced to six years' imprisonment.

Held, the criminality of one who provided safe haven for drugs was less than that of a courier, and it was unfair to the appellant to equate his activities with those of a courier. The sentence would be reduced to four and a half years.

Appeal allowed and sentence varied.

5.4.49 Class A: (iii) Lysergimide

5.4.50
1. R. v. Bennett
(1981) 3 Cr.App.R. (S.) 68

B. was convicted of possessing 25 LSD tablets with intent to supply them to others. He had purchased the tablets for £1.50 each. He was sentenced to three years' imprisonment on that charge and he received concurrent sentences on other less serious charges. It was accepted that he had supplied LSD only among his friends. He appealed against sentence.

Jupp, J. (at p. 70): "The learned judge said that the possession of drugs with a view to supplying them to others, whether they be friends or not, has to be taken seriously. He added that he did not think the appellant was a very efficient or important drug dealer, but that in the interests of the public, possession with intent to supply and offences involving supplying had to be treated seriously. In the judge's words: 'No-one knows, once someone starts taking drugs, where it is going to end.' In our view the learned judge was quite right to take that view of this offence, albeit that the supply was only, as far as the evidence goes, to friends.

In our view, however, sentences for this type of offence must be severe because, as the learned judge said, no-one knows where it will end when someone first starts taking drugs. Anybody who supplies in order to facilitate the taking of drugs is guilty of a very serious offence."

Appeal dismissed.

2. R. v. Bowman-Powell   5.4.51
(1985) 7 Cr.App.R. (S.) 85

B-P. pleaded guilty to possessing "92 doses" of LSD with intent to supply. He admitted that he intended to sell about half of these doses to a regular set of friends and customers. He had previous convictions for drug offences. He appealed against a sentence of four years' imprisonment.

Lawton, L.J. (at p. 87): "A great deal has happened in the last few years with regard to drug cases. Their supply is becoming more and more common and the public are becoming more and more concerned about it. The time has come when it must be made clear to those who supply drugs, particularly those who supply Class A drugs like LSD, that they can expect to lose their liberty for a long time. We can see nothing wrong with this sentence of four years' imprisonment."

Appeal dismissed.

NOTE
The court distinguished between *R. v. Bowman-Powell* and *R. v. Virgin* (1983) 5 Cr.App.R. (S.) 148 on the basis that the former had previous convictions involving controlled drugs which the latter did not.

3. Mullady v. H.M. Advocate   5.4.52
1988 S.C.C.R. 113

M., who had a number of previous convictions on summary complaints for dishonesty, but no previous convictions for drug offences, was convicted of possessing a quantity of lysergide, a Class A drug, valued at about £100, with intent to supply it to others, and with offering to supply lysergide to a named person. He was sentenced to four years' detention on each offence, the sentences to be concurrent, and appealed to the High Court against the sentences as excessive.

Held, that a sentence of four years is the minimum sentence which is appropriate for trafficking in such drugs.

LORD BRAND (at p. 114): "In our opinion no ground has been urged upon us which would justify us in interfering with the sentences imposed, which were four years concurrent on each charge. As has been said repeatedly in this court, contraventions of the Misuse of Drugs Act and in particular trafficking in Class A drugs must be regarded as very, very serious offences which the court will do its upmost to suppress. A sentence of four years' imprisonment is the minimum sentence which is appropriate for trafficking in these drugs."

Appeal refused.

5.4.53   **4. R. v. Andrews**
                         (1992) 13 Cr.App.R. (S.) 504

A. pleaded guilty to possession of a Class A drug with intent to supply and to possession of cannabis. He was found in possession of two pieces of card impregnated with 20 doses of LSD and one and a half grammes of cannabis. The appellant admitted that he had bought the LSD for £80 and that it was his practice to sell it to his friends without making any profit. He admitted that he had supplied two or three friends with two or three doses. He was sentenced to 18 months' detention in a young offenders institution with a confiscation order of £144.

Held, (considering *Kelly* (1987) 9 Cr.App.R. (S.) 181) the Court had said in *Kelly* that a sentence of two years was the bottom of the sentencing range for supplying Class A drugs in small quantities on a social basis. The considerations applied in *Kelly* applied to this case; the gravity of an offence of dealing in LSD must be properly marked. It would not be right to reduce the sentence.

Appeal dismissed.

5.4.54 Class A: (iv) Ecstasy (MDMA, etc.)

5.4.55   **1. R. v. Broom**
                         (1993) 14 Cr.App.R. (S.) 677

B. pleaded guilty to possessing a Class A drug, Ecstasy, with intent to supply, and possessing a Class B drug, amphetamine. The appellant was found by police in possession of a bag containing 190 tablets of Ecstasy and 47.8 grammes of 9 per cent amphetamine powder. He admitted that he intended to sell the drugs and expected to make a profit of about £1,000. He was sentenced to three years' imprisonment.

Held, the appellant was dealing in drugs for profit: the sentence was at the top end of the scale for this offence, but was not wrong in principle or manifestly excessive.

OTTON, J. (at p. 678): "The appellant himself was not an addict. Very often we hear in this Court that a person who has become addicted to a Class A drug such as heroin can only feed their unfortunate addiction by dealing in drugs in order to finance their own purchases to satisfy their addiction. This is not such a case. He enjoys the late night dancing and drug scene and in order to be able to afford that, when he is unemployed, he quite ruthlessly deals in drugs selling them in the market and using the profit to satisfy his predilection for the drug scene.

In those circumstances this Court, as did the court below, must take a serious view of the case. It is true that the value of the drugs, £4,500 was not as high as is often seen in this Court. This was trade in Ecstasy at its most pernicious and a severe sentence was called for. We acknowledge that the sentence is at the top end of the scale for this type of offence. It is quite another thing to say that the sentence was either wrong in principle or manifestly excessive. We are not satisfied that either of those situations has arisen. We see nothing wrong with this sentence and we are not disposed to interfere with it."

Appeal dismissed.

2. R. v. Veeraswamy   5.4.56
(1993) 14 Cr.App.R. (S.) 680

V. was convicted of two counts of possessing a Class A drug with intent to supply and one of having counterfeit currency notes. Police officers found about 50 Ecstasy tablets and some counterfeit currency notes at her home. She was sentenced to five years' imprisonment for possessing controlled drugs, and six months concurrent for having counterfeit currency.

Held, it was conceded that the sentence could not be faulted in principle, but the appellant was a married woman with four children whose husband was serving a prison sentence. It had been held in *R. v. Parkinson* (unreported, November 4, 1976) that a court might mitigate a sentence to avoid exceptional hardship. As the quantity of drugs which had been found in the appellant's possession put her in the lower end of the scale for this type of offence, the Court would extend mercy to the appellant and substitute a sentence of three years' imprisonment.

Appeal allowed.

3. R. v. Allery   5.4.57
(1993) 14 Cr.App.R. (S.) 699

A. was convicted of possessing a Class A drug with intent to supply. The appellant was stopped by police officers at a motorway service area, and seen to throw away a bag containing 19 tablets of Ecstasy. Further tablets were found at his home. He was sentenced to five years' imprisonment.

Held, Parliament had determined that Ecstasy would be a Class A drug and it was for the Court to determine the relative dangers of various classes of drugs. The sentence was not excessive.

Application refused.

5.4.58   **4. R. v. Bryant**
                    (1993) 14 Cr.App.R. (S.) 707

B. pleaded guilty to possession of a Class A drug, Ecstasy, with intent to supply. He was found in possession of Ecstasy tablets, and admitted intending to sell them at a night club. He admitted selling cannabis, Ecstasy and other drugs on a number of previous occasions. He was sentenced to a total of four years' imprisonment.

Held, the sentence would be reduced to three years' imprisonment.

Appeal allowed.

5.4.59   **5. R. v. Burton**
                    (1993) 14 Cr.App.R. (S.) 716

B. pleaded guilty to possessing Ecstasy tablets with intent to supply, possessing amphetamine sulphate with intent to supply, possessing cannabis resin, possessing a firearm without a certificate and possessing ammunition without a certificate. Police officers searching the appellant's premises found 1,470 Ecstasy tablets, a quantity of amphetamine sulphate, 300 grammes of cannabis, a revolver and ammunition, and other items related to the sale of drugs. The estimated street value of the Ecstasy tablets was between £22,000 and £28,000. He was sentenced to six years' imprisonment for possessing Ecstasy tablets, concurrent terms for possessing amphetamine sulphate and cannabis, and 18 months consecutive for the firearm offences (a total of seven and a half years).

Held, Ecstasy was a Class A drug because it had dangerous side effects and could cause death. If the sentence of six years had stood alone, it would not have been excessive. It was within the ordinary guidelines, and there was no reason to distinguish between different categories of Class A drugs. However, this was the first custodial sentence imposed on a man of 25, and the sentencer had not paid sufficient regard to the principle of totality. The sentence of six years would be reduced to five, leaving a total of six years and six months' imprisonment.

BELDAM, L.J. (at p. 718): "We therefore turn our attention to the sentence of six years for possessing with intent to supply the drug Ecstasy. The reason why this drug is classed as a Class A drug is quite plainly because of the dangerous side effects which it has been shown to have on occasions, capable of causing, for example, liver damage and even death. We consider that the sentence of six years' imprisonment on that count, had it stood alone, was not excessive. It is accepted by counsel that it was within the ordinary guidelines laid down in the cases, and we see no reason, and indeed the courts have often said that there is no reason, to distinguish between categories of drugs classified in Class A because of their dangerous nature."

Appeal allowed.

6. R. v. Kempley   5.4.60
The Times, April 15, 1994

K. appealed against a sentence of five years' imprisonment after having been convicted of possessing Ecstasy with intent to supply.

Held, there had to be a deterrent element in any sentence imposed on someone found in possession of Ecstasy with intent to supply.

RUSSELL, L.J.: "One only had to read the newspapers to learn that frequently Ecstasy was administered in discos and the like to young girls who perhaps had taken alcohol.

That had the most horrifying consequences, as anyone concerned with drug addiction must realise. The court took the view that there had to be a deterrent element in the sentence imposed on anyone found in possession of Ecstasy with the intention that it should be used by others.

The sentence imposed was not wrong in principle and, although heavy for a first offender, was not too long."

Appeal dismissed.

NOTE
It may also be seen to be a deterrent to be fined and imprisoned and it is competent to impose both: *Scott v. H.M. Advocate*, 1988 G.W.D. 24–1021.

7. R. v. Jones   5.4.61
(1994) 15 Cr.App.R. (S.) 856

J. was convicted of possessing a Class A drug with intent to supply. He was found outside premises where a "rave" was about to take place, in possession of 27 $^3/_4$ tablets of Ecstasy. He was sentenced to four years' imprisonment.

Held, Parliament had deliberately and advisedly classified Ecstasy as a Class A drug: a sentence of two years would have been justified in the circumstances.

WRIGHT, J. (at p. 857): "The facts are very simple. At about 5.00 a.m. on Sunday, August 2 — which, we understand, possibly surprisingly, is about the time of day at which the activities in such premises begin — the appellant was found to be sitting in a motor vehicle just outside the entrance of one of the largest 'house' or 'techno' garages in South London — 'rave' premises known as the 'Ministry of Sound.' He had in his possession 27 $^3/_4$ tablets of Ecstasy. It was apparent, as the jury found, that he was intending to sell them to the customers of these premises who were, at that time, beginning to arrive in large numbers.

The street value of the drugs was somewhere between £325 and £425. The cannabis drugs, which formed the subject of the other minor charges were 14 grams of herbal cannabis and six grams of cannabis resin.

The learned judge in passing sentence took into account, and expressly said that he did take into account the Practice Statement of October 1, 1992. He also stressed that the dangers of Class A drugs such as this kind needed no further emphasis.

This appellant is somewhat older than those who are often to be found in dealing in drugs of this kind. He is 31. His counsel, to whom we are indebted for a concise and persuasive argument, effectively has abandoned, we think rightly, the grounds of appeal that were originally laid before the court. He has concentrated upon this appellant's personal circumstances. He points out, as is plain from the papers, that this man has a very limited previous record of criminality. This is, indeed, his first custodial sentence of any significance and he has only one previous conviction involving the use of illegal drugs. That was as long ago as 1983. He has, in fact, been out of trouble since 1988.

Since he left school at the age of 16 he has had virtually a continuous career in employment in the building industry, improving his position steadily as time went on and earning a comfortable living. That, we are told, came to an end through no fault of his own some short time before this offence was committed, when he lost his job — a fate that has overcome many people in the building industry in recent years.

In the circumstances, we are told, and we are prepared to accept that under the pressure of lack of money and general financial difficulties, he has become addicted, if he had not been before, to drugs such as 'E', got into bad company, and as a result found himself in a position where he committed the offence for which the jury convicted.

There can be no doubt, however, that he was intending to supply this particular Class A drug. The evidence upon which the jury convicted him was overwhelming.

In the well known case of *R.* v. *Aramah* (1982) 4 Cr.App.R. (S.) 407 this Court established that a bracket of one to four years for small scale dealing in cannabis was appropriate. But the subsequent case of *R.* v. *Bilinski* (1987) 9 Cr.App.R. (S.) 360 also made it clear that when one is dealing with Class A drugs the offence of supply, or possession with intent to supply, will seldom justify a sentence of less than five years' imprisonment.

It may well be that synthetics such as MDMA [Ecstasy] do not have the evil effects that heroin or LSD may have, but they are still Class A drugs and Parliament has advisedly and deliberately classed them in the same group as heroin, cocaine and other hard drugs of that variety.

The wave of these drugs, that is now said to be inundating such places of entertainment as discos and nightclubs, is something that gives rise to grave anxiety.

This Court had to consider the problem of MDMA in the case of *R. v. Allery*, [*supra*]. When Beldam L.J. gave the judgment of the Court he [equated Ecstasy with heroin and cocaine]. This appellant, therefore, has been convicted of possession with intent to supply a drug which is regarded by the courts as being on a par with heroin and cocaine.

In such circumstances, following, as we do, the case of *Bilinski*, a sentence of five years' imprisonment would have been eminently justified in circumstances such as these. The appellant was treated entirely reasonably by the learned judge. It might even be said that a sentence of four years was lenient. In the circumstances, this appeal must be dismissed."

Appeal dismissed.

8. R. v. McLaughlin   5.4.62
(1995) 16 Cr.App.R. (S.) 357

McL. pleaded guilty to possessing a Class A drug with intent to supply. He was a passenger in a car which was stopped by police officers. He was searched and found to be in possession of 1,000 Ecstasy tablets. He claimed to be acting as a courier for others. He was sentenced to five years' imprisonment.

Held, this was a serious offence and those who played minor roles in the distribution of drugs must expect severe sentences. On the basis that the offence was an isolated incident, the sentence was excessive: a sentence of four years' imprisonment would be substituted.

GAGE, J. (at p. 358): "In mitigation, it was said that this was a one-off occasion, when he was acting as a courier for a person he would not name.

The appellant is a self-employed contract cleaner. He had one finding of guilt and six previous convictions, mostly for road traffic offences. In 1982 he was convicted of an offence of robbery and sentenced to three years' imprisonment. There was a pre-sentence report before the court which set out his home circumstances and his employment history.

Before this Court counsel takes three points. First, it is submitted that the basis of the sentence was not the basis of the plea. It is said that the appellant was acting as a courier, doing it for a friend, and that this was a one-off occasion when he had a mistaken belief as to the nature of the drugs. It is submitted that the sentence did not reflect this comparatively minor role. However, it is to be noted, as we have indicated, that when asked the name of his friend, he refused to give it. It is also submitted that the sentence did not reflect his plea of guilty, and that it was manifestly excessive when viewed against his own home circumstances. It is submitted that the consequences for him of the sentence were disastrous. His fiancée had left him, his business had collapsed and his house had been sold.

The Court regards this offence as a serious one. Even those who play minor roles in the distribution of drugs must expect substantial sentences. However, in our view, on the basis of the appellant's plea, the judge put him a little too high up the scale in the distribution of the drugs. On the basis that it was a one-off incident, we think there is force in the submission that the sentence was excessive. Accordingly, we propose to quash the sentence of five years' imprisonment and to substitute therefor a sentence of four years' imprisonment. For these reasons and to that extent the appeal is allowed."

Appeal allowed.

5.4.63   **9. R. v. Kingham**
(1995) 16 Cr.App.R. (S.) 399

K. pleaded guilty to two counts of possessing a Class A drug with intent to supply. He was found in possession of a total of 199 Ecstasy tablets and 79 tablets of LSD. The appellant claimed to have obtained the drugs for use at a party and that he did not expect to make any profit from the transaction. He was sentenced to four years' imprisonment with a confiscation order for £341.

Held, the sentence could be reduced to three years' imprisonment.

LONGMORE, J. (at p. 400): "The prosecution in their opening before the judge did not specifically allege that the appellant had made any profit. However, the judge said in passing sentence that he had the greatest doubts about this being a non-profit making exercise and that the quantity and street value of the drugs warranted a substantial period of imprisonment. He took into account that the appellant had no previous convictions for this sort of offence, that the offences were immediately admitted and that he had pleaded guilty.

[Counsel] now, on his behalf, says in the first place that it should be treated as a non-profit making exercise, and secondly, he points to authority in the form of *R. v. Broom* and *R. v. Bryant* (1993) 14 Cr.App.R. (S.) 677 and 707 respectively. In those cases tablets of a similar quantity and a not dissimilar value were found on the respective defendants and sentences of three years were imposed, it being acknowledged that three years was somewhat towards the top of the scale.

We have taken into account those arguments. We think it right that here there was at least no aggravation of the offence by reason of any substantial profit being made and we think that in the circumstances it is right to reduce the four year sentence. In our view the appropriate sentence is three years."

Appeal allowed.

10. R. v. Asquith   5.4.64
(1995) 16 Cr.App.R. (S.) 453

A. pleaded guilty to possessing a Class A controlled drug with intent to supply. He was found in a car park in possession of 48 tablets of Ecstasy. He claimed that he had them in order to take them into a club, and retain them until the owner of the tablets sold them; A. would then be given five tablets as reward for his assistance. He was sentenced to three years' detention in a young offenders institution.

Held, decisions of the Court in cases involving Ecstasy indicated that Ecstasy was a drug in the same category as heroin and cocaine and that the normal starting point for possession of such a drug with intent to supply was five years.

HOLLAND, J. (at p. 454): "The appellant was stopped in a car park outside a Doncaster leisure club. Upon searching him, 48 tablets containing Ecstasy were found in a bag in his sock. It was accepted that they had been given to him by a man called Thompson. It was further accepted that Thompson was a drug dealer and that the object of giving these drugs to this appellant was to ensure that they could be taken into the leisure club by somebody who was not subject to suspicion. Once this appellant had taken the drugs into the leisure club, he was then to hold them until such time as Thompson made sales. As and when Thompson sold one or more drugs, this young appellant would then dispense them from the store that he held.

The recompense that would be due to this appellant for this service was a free sample for his own use. It seems that he anticipated receiving some five tablets of Ecstasy, which are said to have had a value of £15 each. Thus it was that the total recompense anticipated had a value of some £75.

To those facts various other matters serve to be added for the purposes of sentencing. First, this young man had no previous like convictions. Secondly, it was accepted that he had no financial gain in contemplation, only the free sample already referred to in this judgment. Thirdly, he had the advantage of a supportive pre-sentence report, which unrealistically recommended probation.

When sentencing the learned recorder took further into account his plea of guilty, but felt that the involvement of this young man with a Class A drug in the fashion described meant that a substantial custodial sentence was inevitable, hence the three years.

In considering this appeal, this Court is acutely conscious that one pernicious recurring feature of the world of drug dealing is the cynical use of comparative innocents to undertake the fetching, the carrying and the storing. That use serves, if successful, to divert attention away from the dealers at the centre of the dealing. There is, secondly, the feature that if caught it is hoped the courts will be sympathetic to such comparative innocents.

In this regard this Court is only too familiar with the pathetic couriers, exploited persons of hitherto good character emanating from West Africa or the West Indies, each bringing very substantial quantities of drugs into this country.

It is again becoming familiar to this Court that young men like this appellant, who are on the periphery of drug dealing, come into the court because they have contributed vital but menial assistance for modest reward, typically free drugs.

With respect to all these persons, this Court is profoundly reluctant to give credence to any belief that relative innocents can play a role in drug dealing with impunity. All who enter into drug dealing, in any capacity, must, as the learned recorder pointed out, expect a custodial sentence, and a substantial one at that. That much has been realistically conceded by [counsel] in his helpful submission to this Court.

What he submits, though, is this. The length of the sentence was manifestly too long, and, in essence, he has pressed for a reduction of sentence to two years.

In presenting that argument he has properly taken advantage of a point raised for the consideration of this Court by the single judge. The single judge referred to the case of *R.* v. *Broom* (1993) 14 Cr.App.R. (S.) 677 [*supra* at paragraph **5.4.55**].

[Counsel] admits that here his client can be distinguished from that appellant. His client was involved with a very much lesser quantity of this drug. Further, his client had a lesser role in the matter, in that, as appears from the facts, his client was not the principal dealer but merely, as it were, a temporary employee of such. Thus it is, [counsel] submits, that if three years represents the top of the bracket for this class of offence, then it would be appropriate to accede to his submission that the length of the sentence was manifestly excessive and that a more appropriate sentence should be a lesser one, say, two years.

This Court has given anxious consideration to that argument, well advanced as it has been. But this Court has already reminded itself of the other decisions that are reported dealing with this matter of possession of Ecstasy with intent to supply. Those decisions make the following apparent. First, they underline the fact that we are dealing with a Class A drug, that is a drug in the same category, as, for example, heroin and cocaine. The second feature arising from a perusal of these other decisions is that the starting point for the consideration of a court when having to sentence a person involved in possession with intent to supply is, in truth, five years. It is from that particular level that the court may, if the facts allow, discount to a lower level; typically discounting if, as here, there has been a plea of guilty.

But what further and very clearly emerges from the decisions ... is that three years with all respect to the division of this Court in *Broom* so far from being at the top end of the scale, is essentially right at the centre of it. Indeed, as [counsel] had to concede, there is only one decision that is reported in which this Court upheld a sentence of less than three years, and that was in the wholly exceptional circumstances that arose in the case of *Catterall* (1993) 14 Cr.App.R. (S.) 724, in which a sentence of three years was set aside and a sentence of two years was substituted.

This Court, therefore, in considering [counsel's] submission, has had to do so in the light of these other decisions and in the light of the bracket as clearly established by those decisions.

What this Court has to say is this. In sentencing this appeal to three years the learned recorder was, in truth, sentencing precisely as it might be discerned to be appropriate from those decisions. Plainly, if he looked at them and asked himself, 'Is this such a case that I can make so substantial a distinction from what is the norm as to pass a lesser than a three year sentence, as was done in *Catterall*?', then he was bound to say to himself that there was nothing particularly significant about the facts of this case which would lead to that departure from what otherwise would be the normal sentence. Indeed, as was pointed out to [counsel] in the course of argument, whereas it is true that this appellant had a role, as it were, as an 'employee', nonetheless there were aggravating circumstances. What he was being employed to do was to introduce the drugs into a leisure club, so that there they would be distributed. A leisure club is just the type of place for introduction to these drugs.

It is in those circumstances that, notwithstanding the way in which the matter was presented to this Court, we find ourselves quite unable to say that the length of the sentence was manifestly excessive. In truth, this Court takes the view that it was precisely the right length of sentence for this type of offence. In those circumstances this appeal fails."

Appeal refused.

11. R. v. Spalding
(1995) 16 Cr.App.R. (S.) 803

5.4.65

S. pleaded guilty to possessing a Class A drug with intent to supply. He was found in possession of 54 tablets of Ecstasy. He pleaded guilty on the basis that he was looking after the tablets for a friend who was a dealer, and intended to return them to him. He was sentenced to 30 months' imprisonment.

Held, the evil of holding drugs for a dealer was that it protected the dealer from detection; anyone holding drugs, for whatever motive, must expect a sentence of imprisonment. The Court had accepted in *R. v. Arif*, *supra*, that a minder should normally not be dealt with as severely as a courier. The sentence would be reduced to 18 months.

Appeal allowed.

5.4.66   **12. R. v. Slater and Scott**
                         (1995) 16 Cr.App.R. (S.) 870

The first appellant was convicted and the second appellant pleaded guilty to possessing a Class A drug with intent to supply. Police officers searching Scott's flat found Ecstasy tablets worth £1 million and other items, and £55,000 in cash. The prosecution alleged that the flat was being used as an Ecstasy factory. The first appellant was sentenced to 13 years' imprisonment and the second appellant to 12 years' imprisonment.

Held, the sentencer was justified on the evidence in inferring that the premises were to be used for the production of drugs. The sentence of 13 years after a trial on the appellant was entirely in accord with recognised sentencing precedent. The sentencer, however, had not allowed the second appellant sufficient credit for his plea of guilty; his sentence would be reduced to 10 years.

OGNALL, J. (at p. 871): "The facts giving rise to this matter may be shortly summarised. Slater had a council flat [...] to which it seems Scott had free access. Police were keeping observations on this flat and saw Scott enter the premises. They followed and arrested him. He was searched. The police found 501 Ecstasy tablets in a bag, a smaller bag with fewer tablets of the same kind and £200 in cash. A search of the premises disclosed something over £1 million worth of Ecstasy tablets, something of the order of 137,000 capsules containing, in this context, an innocuous substance; a cutting agent; 15 kilogrammes of Mannitol; and something over £55,000 in cash.

In those circumstances and having regard to those substances, the Crown alleged at the trial that the flat was being used as an Ecstasy warehouse and factory. It was submitted to the jury, and indeed to the learned sentencing judge, that the Mannitol and the Ecstasy were to be mixed to manufacture tablets going under the nickname in drug circles of 'Dennis the Menace' with a total retail value in excess of £2.5 million.

It was contended, nonetheless, on behalf of the two men before the court that there was no actual evidence to support the contention that any technical manufacturing process designed to mix the substances had actually taken place. It was further submitted in both their cases after the conviction of Slater that the two men were not, as is sometimes described, 'drug barons' in their own right, but were part of an organisation within which, it had to be acknowledged, they should be put quite high up on the scale of responsibility and culpability.

In dealing with this matter the learned sentencing judge was at pains to elicit from the Crown any assistance they could give as to the respective degrees of culpability of these two men. In that regard [counsel], appearing for the Crown to assist the learned judge, as he has assisted us today, said this: 'As far as their relative positions as between themselves, there is nothing I can say which would distinguish the one from the other, and so their position in the organisation, clearly, is a joint one. That is the way the prosecution put it.' That then was the factual basis upon which one of these men pleaded guilty and the other was convicted by the jury.

Of their antecedent circumstances it is sufficient to say of the applicant Slater that he is now 54 years of age and of previous good character. There was a pre-sentence report about him which, understandably and realistically, having drawn attention to his history, made no recommendation other than to recognise an inevitable and substantial custodial sentence. The appellant Scott at 32 unfortunately has a number of convictions going back to 1981. But once again, no doubt because in the context of this case his record paled into virtual insignificance, the learned sentencing judge did not take those past convictions into account when passing sentence. Once again in his case the pre-sentence report outlined his earlier history, suggesting that upon his (the appellant's) account to the author of the report, he was acting as a caretaker for others in this very serious enterprise, and in the event offered no alternative proposal other than to recognise a substantial sentence of immediate custody. So much for the circumstances of these two men.

On behalf of the appellant Scott, [counsel] takes a number of points. First, he submits, as was submitted to the learned judge, that this man and his father ought not to be sentenced as drugs barons — as the persons in overall charge of the enterprise and destined to make the major slice of profit from it. Accordingly, he submits that the learned judge, who took 13 years for the applicant Slater as a starting point after a trial, started too high. Secondly, he reminds us that the judge was told, and accepted, that there was nothing to distinguish between these two men in respect of their relative culpability and criminality. Thirdly, he submits that in those circumstances a sentence only one year less than that passed on the father after the father's trial did not give adequate discount properly to reflect the plea of guilty. [Counsel] contends that even accepting that Scott's plea was relatively late in the day and even acknowledging that he was caught virtually red handed, nonetheless in passing a sentence with a discount of only one year — a discount which [counsel] graphically describes as only a sliver less than Slater's sentence — the learned judge did not pay proper or sufficient need to recognised sentencing principles so far as discount for pleas of guilty are concerned.

On behalf of Slater, [counsel] makes the following submissions. First, she reminds us of his erstwhile good character, which he had borne into the middle years of his life. She too submits that it was wrong of the learned judge to start with a sentence as high as 13 years. This man, she submits, was (a) not a drug baron; and (b) she invites this Court to conclude that, notwithstanding the nature and amount of materials found within the premises, it would be wrong to conclude that they reflected the threshold of actual production of this pernicious Class A drug. Those who are essentially [counsel's] submissions in support of his renewed application for leave to appeal against the sentence.

We deal with the renewed application first. It is to be observed that good character in the context of offences of this gravity is, as the Court has observed on numerous occasions, of relative unimportance. Secondly, we are each quite satisfied that there was indeed material before the sentencing judge from which he could properly infer that the materials found upon the police raid represented all necessary steps to mark the inception of the production of the drug as the Crown contended; in other words, if it was not actually a drugs factory it was very close indeed to the conversion of those premises into a factory for production of those goods. It is to be noted what the learned judge said in passing sentence in this case, and I quote from page 1 of the transcript: 'I begin with the fact that Ecstasy is a Class A drug. In a case in the Court of Appeal in 1993 called *Allery* the Court described it as a "synthetic amphetamine derivative". The judgment of the Court said that they had material which indicated that it was capable of causing convulsions, collapse, hyperpyrexia, discriminated intravascular coagulation and other very unpleasant consequences and was also capable of causing acute renal failure, and that, of course, acute renal failure, frequently, if not, invariably, leads to death. They commented that Parliament had been well advised to include this as a dangerous drug in the Class A. Even without that material it is plain from its mere characterisation of Class A that it is to be seen in the same category as, for instance, heroin and cocaine.'

With those observations each member of this Court entirely agrees. The production or the immediate precedent steps to production of a drug of this kind in huge quantities constitutes a very grave crime indeed.

We have considered in those circumstances whether it can properly be said, as [counsel] contends, that a sentence, albeit a very long one, of 13 years' imprisonment after a trial is outside the brackets laid down by these courts for offences of that gravity. We have taken into account, of course, the circumstances of this applicant as placed before us by his counsel. But at the end of the day we are in no way persuaded that a sentence, albeit a long one, was in any way excessive, still less manifestly so. A sentence of 13 years' imprisonment for this offence after a trial was entirely in accord with recognised sentencing precedent. For those reasons this renewed application must be refused.

I turn now to the appellant Scott. It seems to us in his case there is a deal of substance in the submissions made by [counsel] on his behalf. Given that 13 years, as we conclude, was the appropriate sentence for Slater, it seems to us that the learned judge did not give sufficient cognisance to the fact that his son had pleaded guilty to circumstances where the Court could not distinguish the degree of his involvement and criminality from that of Slater. We think that, paying due regard to the principle of discount here, the learned judge ought to have passed a sentence upon Scott, in the light of his plea of guilty, of 10 years' imprisonment. Accordingly, and for those reasons, in the case of Scott the sentence of 12 years' imprisonment is quashed and in place thereof there is a sentence of 10 years' imprisonment. To that extent only in his case the appeal against sentence is allowed.'

Application refused. Appeal allowed.

Class B: (i) Amphetamine   **5.4.67**

1. R. v. Davies   **5.4.68**
(1978) 142 J.P. 388

Police searched D.'s house and found two grammes of amphetamine divided into 11 packets. D. and her husband lived on social security and for some time had used the money to buy amphetamine for resale at a profit. She was sentenced to nine months' imprisonment and appealed. On appeal the court said the trial judge had to decide between the public interest, calling for punishment, and D.'s deteriorating personal circumstances. The decision that it was a case in which it was important to emphasise that those who possessed drugs with intent to supply should receive an immediate custodial sentence was one with which there was nothing to entitle the court to interfere.

Appeal dismissed.

2. R. v. Hole   **5.4.69**
(1991) 12 Cr.App.R. (S.) 766

H. pleaded guilty to possessing amphetamine sulphate with intent to supply. She was arrested at a railway station in possession of six ounces of amphetamine sulphate worth about £2,000. She was sentenced on the basis that she had just started to deal in drugs. She was sentenced to six months' imprisonment.

Held, taking into account that the appellant was a young woman with two young children and no significant previous convictions, the sentence was neither excessive nor wrong in principle.

Appeal dismissed.

5.4.70 **3. R. v. Morley**
(1994) 15 Cr.App.R. (S.) 86

M. pleaded guilty to possession of a Class B drug with intent to supply. The appellant was seen by police officers carrying a bag which was found to contain nearly 10 kilogrammes of amphetamine of one per cent purity with an estimated street value of between £143,000 and £191,000. It was accepted that the appellant was acting as a courier. He was sentenced to four years' imprisonment.

Held, it was recognised that the value per pound of amphetamine was much higher than that of cannabis. Given the appellant's subordinate role and the absence of any previous conviction for a drug related offence, the sentence would be reduced to three years.

Appeal allowed.

5.4.71 **4. R. v. Lyth**
(1995) 16 Cr.App.R. (S.) 68

L. pleaded guilty to possessing a Class B drug, amphetamine sulphate, with intent to supply. The plea was accepted on the basis that the appellant was in possession of the drug, worth about £7,500, on behalf of a supplier and would give the drug back to the supplier. He was sentenced to four years' imprisonment.

Held, the sentence was high, on the basis of which the plea was accepted. A sentence of two years' imprisonment would be substituted.

Appeal allowed.

5.4.72 Class B: (ii) Cannabis and cannabis resin

5.4.73 **1. R. v. Harnden**
(1978) 66 Cr.App.R. 281

H. pleaded guilty to possessing three-quarters of a pound of cannabis resin with intent to supply. The value was said to be in the order of £360. H. was sentenced to three years' imprisonment and he appealed against that sentence.

LORD WIDGERY, C.J. (at p. 282): "It is very important to point out that this young man had a set of scales, because in this particular trade possession of a set of scales is so often the badge of a supplier."

Appeal allowed.

NOTE
   The appeal was allowed and a sentence of Borstal training was substituted. This case, however, is of more interest, it is submitted, for the Lord Chief Justice's observations on scales. A set of scales was an important evidential point in *Davidson v. H.M. Advocate*, 1990 S.C.C.R. 699; see also *Hepplewhite v. Russell*, 1997 G.W.D. 15–648.

2. R. v. Smith   5.4.74
(1980) 144 J.P. 207

S. pleaded guilty to two counts of possessing cannabis resin with intent to supply. In one count the quantity was 540 grammes and in the other 420 grammes. The drug had admittedly been purchased for resale to half a dozen friends and the gain to S. was to be a supply of the drug for himself without cost. S. was sentenced to 12 months' imprisonment. On appeal it was submitted that the sentence would have a disastrous effect on his new career and that he would benefit from, and respond to, a community service order. The court said that this was the kind of case in which S. must have appreciated that he was liable to be imprisoned if he was detected. On appeal it was said that all the mitigating circumstance were urged on the trial judge and the sentence he passed was not a heavy one.

Appeal refused.

3. R. v. Lawless   5.4.75
(1981) 3 Cr.App.R. (S.) 241

L. pleaded guilty to a count of possessing 906 grammes of cannabis resin with intent to supply it to others. He claimed that he had bought that quantity for £1,600 with a view to keeping some for himself and supplying two friends "throughout the winter." He was sentenced to two years' imprisonment and he appealed.

CANTLEY, J. (at pp. 241–2): "As there was evidence, which was not challenged at the hearing, that this quantity of cannabis could make up to 8,000 cigarettes, it appeared to the trial judge that this involved a very heavy consumption by the five or six friends. He therefore very naturally viewed this explanation with considerable suspicion. However, apart from certain suspicious circumstances, there was nothing before the court to challenge successfully (and the prosecution did not seek to contradict) his account that he was buying this cannabis not to peddle it as a dealer, but as a member and agent of what one might term a social syndicate of cannabis smokers. Of course when such a syndicate is found and the member who obtains its supplies is caught, there must be punishment. A sentence of imprisonment is certainly appropriate.

However, the appellant is a man with a previously good record and this is not an ordinary case of possessing with intent to supply, in the sense that this cannot safely be treated as a case of possessing with intent to trade commercially in cannabis."

The court therefore varied the two years' imprisonment to nine months' imprisonment and as the appellant had been in custody of that period his immediate release was ordered.

Appeal allowed.

5.4.76   **4. R. v. Shead**
                    (1982) 4 Cr.App.R. (S.) 217

S. was convicted of possessing 21 grammes of cannabis resin with intent to supply it. The controlled drug had an estimated street value of £500. He was sentenced to 18 months' imprisonment. On appeal against sentence it was held that as the appellant was a dealer in Class B drugs, albeit in a relatively small way, that must attract a prison sentence of some substance; however, having regard to his good character and the relatively minor scale on which he was dealing a sentence of 12 months' would be more appropriate.

Appeal allowed in part.

5.4.77   **5. R. v. Daudi**
                    (1982) 4 Cr.App.R. (S.) 306

J.D. and H.C.D. pleaded guilty to possessing cannabis which cost £600 with intent to supply. It was accepted that they had purchased the cannabis on behalf of fellow members of the Rastafarian sect, and that they had no commercial motive in obtaining the controlled drug. They appealed against sentences of three months' detention and six months' imprisonment respectively.

GRIFFITHS, L.J. (at p. 307): "The fact remains that these two men, whatever their motives, quite deliberately committed an offence which is regarded as very serious and sentences of six months' imprisonment and three months' detention respectively for supplying a very large quantity of herbal cannabis cannot possibly be considered as wrong in principle or excessive. It is not possible for this Court to apply the law other than evenhandedly. It would be a denial of justice to say that 'because you are a Rastafarian you are entitled to be treated entirely differently from other members of the community if you choose to break the law relating to the supply and distribution of cannabis.' Therefore this Court has come to the conclusion that, despite everything that has been said on behalf of these men by [counsel], there are no grounds upon which it would be right, or indeed fair to the community as a whole, to discriminate in their favour. Sadly, they must pay the price of consciously and knowingly breaking the law. They have received what can be regarded as sentences right at the lower end of the bracket for the offences which they committed."

Appeals dismissed.

NOTE

Rastafarians are members of a Jamaican cult which regards Ras Tafari (the former emperor of Ethiopia, Haile Selassi) as God. Members of the sect are said to make extensive use of cannabis resin as part of the rituals of their religion.

A similar plea was submitted by counsel in *R. v. Dallaway* (1984) 148 J.P. 31. The court there, which included Lord Justice Griffiths, held that whatever the religious views of the appellant his activities were unlawful and a sentence of 12 months' imprisonment for possessing three and a half grammes of cannabis with intent to supply was upheld.

6. R. v. Macdonald   5.4.78
(1983) 5 Cr.App.R. (S.) 22

M. pleaded guilty to possessing about one kilogramme of cannabis with intent to supply. The controlled drug was in several pieces and a pair of scales was also found. The trial judge held M. to be "a supplier in general." On appeal against a sentence of 24 months' imprisonment, the sentence was varied to nine months' imprisonment.

PAIN, J. (at p. 24): "Having regard to the fact that the learned judge found that [M.] did not merely have a small amount of cannabis to supply to his friends, but he had a large amount for supply in general, we think that this is not a case that comes right at the bottom end of the scale. On the other hand, it is a case which was not very far up the scale. We would have thought that a sentence of 21 months' imprisonment would have been the sort of sentence that would have been consistent with the decision in *Aramah*. One also has to look at the fact that the trial judge allowed a reduction of six months for the misfortunes which [M.] had met with in life, and we feel that we too ought to allow for that. Instead of a sentence of 21 months, therefore, we think that it would be appropriate to impose a sentence of 15 months' imprisonment."

Appeal allowed in part.

NOTE

In *R. v. Sanderman* (1989) 11 Cr.App.R. (S.) 165 a sentence of two years' imprisonment was upheld for possessing cannabis with intent to supply but there the appellant had several previous convictions for offences related to drugs, including one for conspiracy to supply cannabis resin. For further examples of this approach by the court see *R. v. Hill* (1988) 10 Cr.App.R. (S.) 150 and *R. v. Daley* (1989) 11 Cr.App.R. (S.) 243. The guidelines in *R. v. Aramah* for sentencing for Class B controlled drugs were held to still apply by the decision in *R. v. Hedley* (1990) 90 Cr.App.R. (S.) 70.

5.4.79
7. R. v. Chatfield
(1984) 5 Cr.App.R. (S.) 289

C. and another were found in a car in Doncaster with about two kilogrammes of cannabis with an estimated street value of £5,000. They claimed that they had travelled up from Kent to Yorkshire and they were only couriers and were to receive about £2,000. Each pleaded guilty to possession with intent to supply and each was sentenced to 30 months' imprisonment. They appealed.

WATKINS, L.J. (at p. 290): "Some people in this country seem to regard the supplying of cannabis as an innocuous occupation. They are gravely mistaken in doing so. This Court cannot regard it so, because the public at large does not do so and neither does Parliament. The supply of such drug in any circumstances is a very serious matter. The taking of cannabis leads to the taking of other serious drugs such as heroin. Accordingly, as judges up and down the country who have to deal with offences of this kind are only too painfully aware, cannabis is on the lower level of progression towards taking and dealing in a very serious and damaging drug. Those who peddle cannabis, and help others to peddle it, must expect, when caught, to be severely dealt with."

Appeal dismissed.

5.4.80
8. Donnelly v. H.M. Advocate
1984 S.C.C.R. 93

D. was convicted of possessing "a large amount" of cannabis resin with intent to supply. As he had already spent 106 days in custody awaiting trial, the judge restricted the sentence to one of 18 months' imprisonment. The judge also noted that there was a considerable drug problem in Dundee and that the court must make examples of those convicted of "trafficking" in drugs with intent to supply. D. appealed against sentence.

THE LORD JUSTICE GENERAL (EMSLIE) (at pp. 94–5): "We are not persuaded that the sentence can be described as excessive. It has been pointed out in this court recently, and on several occasions, that those who traffic in drugs can only expect severe sentences at the hands of the court and in all the circumstances we are not persuaded that 18 months' was a sentence which has to be reduced because it is excessive ... It does not, nowadays, follow that those who possess drugs with intent, or those who supply them, can reasonably look forward to at least one trial in the summary court before appearing under solemn procedure."

Appeal dismissed

9. Varley v. H.M. Advocate   5.4.81
1985 S.C.C.R. 55

V. pleaded guilty to possessing 669 grammes of cannabis resin with intent to supply. That quantity of controlled drug had a street value of £2,500. The explanation put forward for V. was that he intended to supply only a limited circle of friends. He had two minor previous convictions, one for possessing, and one for cultivating, cannabis. He was sentenced to four years' imprisonment and he appealed.

THE LORD JUSTICE GENERAL (EMSLIE) (at p. 57): "It is very clear to us that the Lord Justice-Clerk proceeded to sentence accepting that even if the supply intended was for a limited circle of people, the quantity and other circumstances could not be ignored altogether ... It is well known that this court is determined to pass severe sentences for possession of drugs, Class A or Class B, with intent to supply others, and in examining this particular crime, we are quite unable to say that a four year sentence was an excessive one. It appears to us to have been restricted to four years by giving close attention to the good features in the appellant's history."

Appeal dismissed.

NOTE
  For a similar case see *Hudson v. H.M. Advocate*, 1990 S.C.C.R. 200.

10. Wright v. Houghton   5.4.82
1987 S.C.C.R. 674

W. was convicted on a summary complaint of possessing cannabis resin with intent to supply. He had about £75 worth of the controlled drug and also £360 of money. He was sentenced to 12 months' imprisonment. He had served previous prison sentences but he had no previous convictions for offences involving controlled drugs. He appealed against sentence.

THE LORD JUSTICE-CLERK (ROSS) (at p. 676): "In view of the circumstances, although the appellant had no previous convictions for this type of offence, we are satisfied that the sheriff was entitled to impose the maximum sentence of 12 months. It has been repeatedly said in these courts that a serious view will be taken of offences under section 5(3) of the Misuse of

Drugs Act 1971 and if, despite these warnings, persons like the accused commit these offences they must accept the consequences."

Appeal dismissed.

NOTE

Hemphill v. H.M. Advocate, 1989 S.C.C.R. 433 shows a similar reluctance by the High Court of Justiciary to interfere with the maximum sentence of three years' imprisonment given to a man appearing on indictment before a sheriff. That sentence was held not to be excessive for possessing 334 milligrammes of cannabis resin with intent to supply it to another.

5.4.83   **11. R. v. Finkhouse**
                       (1990) 12 Cr.App.R. (S.) 17

F. pleaded guilty to possessing a controlled drug with intent to supply, permitting premises to be used for the purpose of smoking cannabis and supplying a controlled drug. Police officers searching her home found 23 small portions of cannabis wrapped in clingfilm. It was accepted that the appellant had supplied a total of about five-eighths of an ounce of cannabis, over a period of three or four weeks. She was sentenced to two years' imprisonment.

Held, the sentence was longer than appropriate: a sentence of 15 months would be substituted, with nine to serve and the balance suspended.

LEGGATT, J. (at p. 19): "On her behalf [counsel] urges that she was a socially isolated woman who obtained the drug for use of herself and her friends. He underscores the fact to which I have already referred that the second and third counts in the indictment were formulated against her in consequence of her own admissions.

[Counsel] seeks to refer to two previous decisions of this Court: *Hill* (1988) 10 Cr.App.R. (S.) 150, in which for offences involving the provision of small quantities of cannabis to a considerable number of buyers a sentence of 21 months' imprisonment was imposed, and *McDonald* (1983) 5 Cr.App.R. (S.) 22, in which a significant quantity of cannabis was in the possession of the defendant for general supply for gain, and a sentence of 15 months' imprisonment was imposed. But in the judgment of this Court it is unhelpful in a case such as this to refer to other cases, the sentences in which were dependent upon their own peculiar facts, and which did not in any sense constitute guideline cases. Nor is it helpful, in the light of the mitigation such as is available to this appellant, to speak in terms of tariff sentences.

Those who regard the possession and use of cannabis as socially acceptable and morally unexceptional, no doubt make it more difficult for themselves to observe the law. But the possession of cannabis with intent to supply others and the supplying of others, as well as facilitating its use by making the offender's own premises available for that purpose, are criminal offences, of all of which, upon her own admission, this appellant was guilty.

Those are the matters that the Court must balance against the circumstances that the appellant was of previous good character, that she pleaded guilty, that she was no more than 22 years old at the time when the offences were committed, and was, in the light of the social enquiry report, somewhat immature. She made no profit by the offences and the quantity of cannabis involved was small, that is to say, she had evidently supplied a total of five-eighths of an ounce in five separate wrappings, and there remained in her possession 23 amounts of one-eighth of an ounce each. The total value of the cannabis concerned was probably no more than £300. Moreover she had been concerned with these matters for a period of no more than three or four weeks, concerned, that is, other than by way of use for her own purposes.

It was said in the court below that by reason of the seizure of £400 in cash by the police, a sum subsequently returned to her, she had been put in a position of difficulty, because it was in fact her grant money rather than the proceeds of the sale of cannabis.

The point finally made by [counsel] on the appellant's behalf is that the learned recorder seems to have been excessively influenced by the fact that those to whom the appellant had supplied the drug were themselves students, and as such were vulnerable, because the other side of the point is of course that the appellant was herself a student and in that sense herself vulnerable.

Taking all these matters into account and bearing in mind the need not only to punish this appellant but to deter others, the conclusion of this Court is that the sentence imposed by the learned judge was longer than appropriate. We accordingly quash the sentence of two years' imprisonment and substitute for it a sentence of 15 months' imprisonment. We further order that after the appellant has served nine months of the sentence, the remainder of it shall be held in suspense. To that extent this appeal is allowed."

Appeal allowed.

12. R. v. Sanck   5.4.84
(1990) 12 Cr.App. R. (S.) 155

S. pleaded guilty to possessing cannabis with intent to supply, and possessing cannabis. The appellant's room was searched and two pieces of cannabis were found, one of 0.8 gramme and one of 17 grammes. S. maintained that all the cannabis was for his own use. He was sentenced for possessing cannabis with intent to supply to a conditional discharge and a fine of £1,000 and for possession of cannabis to a fine of £200; ordered to pay £440 towards the cost of the prosecution with various orders for the forfeiture of drugs, money and related equipment.

Held, the appellant was entitled to succeed on the argument that it was wrong to impose a fine and a conditional discharge on the count for possession with intent to supply, in the light of *McClelland* (1951) 35 Cr.App.R. 22. The conditional discharge would be quashed. The Court did not accept that the amount of the fines was excessive. The charge of possession with intent was a serious matter which would normally attract a custodial sentence, and it had been shown that the fines were within the appellant's means.

Appeal allowed.

5.4.85   **13. R. v. Elder**
(1990) 12 Cr.App.R. (S.) 337

E. pleaded guilty to possessing cannabis with intent to supply, and possessing cannabis. He was found in possession of two quantities of cannabis, of which he admitted that 31 grammes were for sale. He was sentenced to two and a half years' imprisonment.

Held, if the appellant had pleaded not guilty, he might have expected to receive two years to two and a half years: as he had pleaded guilty the appropriate sentence was 21 months.

LLOYD, L.J. (at p. 338): "On September 22, 1989 at Lincoln railway station the police stopped the appellant on suspicion of possessing drugs. They asked him if he was in possession of a controlled substance. He replied: 'No.' Asked if he was sure, he then said: 'You'd better have this then,' and removed a small tin from the bib of his dungarees. This was found to contain a small quantity of cannabis resin, the subject of count 2. He was then arrested. After being cautioned he said: 'Yes, you'd also better have this', and produced from another pocket a single deal of cannabis resin wrapped in cling film (also covered by count 2) and a bag containing 22 wraps of cannabis resin, the subject of count 1. He also produced a pocket knife, the blade of which showed traces of cannabis resin. He admitted that he used the knife for cutting the deals.

In interview he admitted that the 22 deals were for sale at £5 each; the rest was for his own use. He said he had bought an ounce three days earlier for £110. The 22 wraps weighed 33 grammes, the rest weighed 4 $^1/_2$ grammes.

The appellant was born in November 1963, so he is now 26. He was unemployed at the time and living in a rented room. He has 10 previous court appearances, mainly for offences of dishonesty. Four have resulted in custodial disposals, including nine months' imprisonment for the supply, possession with intent and simple possession of amphetamine. We do not know the quantities.

There was no social enquiry report before the court. The prison report ordered on the direction of the single judge was satisfactory.

The judge in sentencing said that the appellant was quite plainly an important link in the chain of supply. He said that he had in mind a sentence of three years but in view of the plea of guilty he reduced it to two and a half years.

Counsel submits quite simply that three years for a small scale operation of this kind would have been too long on conviction. We agree with that submission. It was an exaggeration to describe this appellant as an important link in the chain of supply, except in the sense that every link is an important link. The appellant was operating at the very bottom end of the market. On a fight, having regard to his previous convictions, he might have expected to receive two to two and a half years: on a plea the appropriate sentence was no more than 21 months.

We therefore allow the appeal, quash the sentence of two and a half years and substitute a sentence of 21 months."

Appeal allowed.

14. R. v. Cook   **5.4.86**
(1990) 12 Cr.App.R. (S.) 374

C. pleaded guilty to possessing cannabis resin with intent to supply and possession of cannabis resin. His house was searched and a small piece of cannabis and £1,030 in cash was found. Later, his mother's house was searched and three blocks of cannabis resin amounting to 631 grammes was found. He was sentenced to three years' imprisonment with a confiscation order in the amount of £1,030.

Held, a sentence of two years would be adequate.

McCULLOUGH, J. (at p. 375): "On July 15, 1989 his house in Huddersfield was searched. A small amount of cannabis was found on the top of a curtain pelmet, and hidden between the jacket of the hot water tank and the tank itself was £1,030 in cash.

At interview that afternoon the appellant claimed that he had forgotten about the small piece of cannabis over the curtain and said that the £1,030 had been lent to him by his girlfriend for purposes of his business.

Later the same day his mother's house was searched. 630 grammes of cannabis resin in three separate blocks were found hidden upstairs, with a street value, we are told, of about £2,000.

He was re-interviewed and said that he was looking after this cannabis resin for someone else whom he was afraid to name. He had thought that it was worth only about £150. That, in view of his earlier conviction, is less than credible.

The issues of whose was the £1,030 and what it represented were decided by the judge after he had heard evidence; they were resolved against the appellant. Hence the confiscation order.

In submissions here [counsel] says simply that a three year sentence was too long for the major count. The appellant had pleaded guilty, as against which has to be set the fact that he had lied, and lied on oath, about how he came to have the money. In the absence of any evidence of the scale of his dealing he should not, it is said, have been put so near the top of the *Aramah* bracket of one to four years for suppliers of less than massive quantities. We think that there is substance in this submission.

[Counsel] drew attention to the case of *MacDonald* (1983) 5 Cr.App.R. (S.) 22, which concerned a man who had pleaded guilty to the possession of approximately one kilogramme of cannabis or cannabis resin with intent to supply it generally. His sentence was reduced to one of 15 months' imprisonment. A reading of the report shows that but for certain strong mitigating factors, personal to that particular man, the court would have thought that a sentence of 21 months, rather than 15 months, appropriate. We bear that in mind, but we also bear in mind the lack of frankness, going to the extent of lying on oath about the source of the money, and the fact that these offences followed less than six months after his conviction for simple possession in February 1989.

We are not persuaded that the sentence should come below two years, but we think that two years would have met the justice of the case. We propose to quash the sentence of three years' imprisonment and substitute a term of two years."

Appeal allowed.

NOTE

The gravamen of the offence is the intention to supply, so that the over-valuing of drugs is not fatal: *Hitchison v. H.M. Advocate*, 1991 G.W.D. 15–926.

5.4.87   **15. White v. H.M. Advocate**
1991 S.C.C.R. 555

W. was charged with possession of a substantial quantity of cannabis resin with intent to supply it to another, contrary to section 5(3) of the 1971 Act. The cannabis resin was found in a kitchen cupboard in her house in the course of a search by police officers. She was in the house at the time of the search and had stayed there the previous night, but evidence was led that she used the house only occasionally and that other persons, such as her brother, had access to it. When the police asked the appellant about the nature of the drugs which they had found, she replied, "I'm saying nothing about it."

W. was convicted and appealed to the High Court against conviction on the ground of insufficient evidence. The Crown conceded that unless the reply quoted could be construed as showing knowledge of the presence of drugs, there was insufficient evidence for conviction, but sought to argue that it could be so construed by reason of the words "about it."

Held, (1) that the reply could not be construed as indicating knowledge of the presence of the drugs; and (2) that there was insufficient evidence for conviction.

Appeal allowed and conviction quashed.

16. McQueen v. Hingston   **5.4.88**
1992 S.C.C.R. 92

McQ. pleaded guilty to possessing nine and a half grammes of cannabis resin, contrary to section 5(2) of the 1971 Act. He admitted a number of previous convictions, including contraventions of that Act in 1971, 1981 and 1988. He had five children, and was employed as a car salesman, earning between £300 and £600 a week. The sheriff sentenced him to sixty days' imprisonment and he appealed to the High Court.

Held, that in view of the appellant's circumstances and the fact that his last offence was three years earlier, the sentence was excessive.

LORD COWIE (at p. 94): "There is no doubt that this was a very serious offence, particularly since it was committed in a public place, but having regard to the personal circumstances of the appellant and the fact that his last offence was three years ago, we have decided that to impose a custodial sentence was excessive. What we shall do therefore is quash the period of sixty days' imprisonment and fine the appellant the sum of £1,500."

Appeal allowed.

NOTE
It has been said repeatedly that to have possession of controlled drugs with intent to supply is a very serious offence, *e.g. Bennett v. H.M. Advocate*, 1987 G.W.D. 24–811.

17. R. v. Black   **5.4.89**
(1992) 13 Cr.App.R. (S.) 262

B. was convicted of possession of cannabis with intent to supply. He was arrested following a disturbance and threw away a number of packages containing a total of 29.6 grammes of cannabis resin. He was found to be in possession of £165 in cash and a small amount of powder containing 12 per cent cocaine. He was sentenced to six months' detention in a young offenders institution.

Held, the sentencer was right to take the view that the offence was so serious that a non-custodial sentence for it could not be justified. The question was whether the period of detention adequately reflected the mitigating factors; the Court considered that the appropriate sentence would have been three months.

AULD, L.J. (at p. 263): "[Counsel], with great clarity, has made a number of submissions on the appellant's behalf. She points out, as was pointed out to the judge below, that there was no evidence that he had been a regular supplier of cannabis in the past, that the amount involved here was small, that he was of good character, living in a good home, that he was only young, 19 at the time, 20 now. [Counsel] urged upon us that, although such an offence might normally require a custodial sentence in the case of an adult offender, it did not have that 'extra serious quality' here (an expression which she derived from the decision of this Court in *R. v. Scott* (1990) 3 Cr.App.R. (S.) 23) to warrant a sentence of detention in a young offenders institution.

This young man was peddling cannabis. As [counsel] acknowledged in her helpful submissions to the Court, such an offence almost always demands a custodial sentence. In the guideline case of *R. v. Aramah* (1982) 4 Cr.App.R. (S.) 407, this Court indicated when dealing with adult offenders that for a person at the lower end of the supply chain, the retailer of a small amount to a customer, the usual minimum is one year's imprisonment. That is so even when the defendant is a first time offender. Custody is frequently the appropriate disposal, even when the supply is social and not of a commercial nature. It is plain that this young man, who had been unemployed for some time, was not short of money and was peddling cannabis, albeit on a small scale.

The judge was right to take the view that, if the appellant had been over 21, the nature and gravity of the offence was such that he would impose a sentence of imprisonment. In our view, he was also right to take the view that the offence here was so serious that a non-custodial sentence for it could not be justified and to order detention in a young offender institution.

The question is whether the period that he imposed adequately reflected the important mitigating factors that [counsel] urged upon the court so well. In our view, the appropriate sentence here would have been one of three months' detention in a young offender institution. We shall accordingly substitute that sentence for the one passed by the judge."

Appeal allowed.

5.4.90 **18. R. v. Friend**
(1993) 14 Cr.App.R. (S.) 77

F. pleaded guilty to possessing 58 grammes of cannabis resin with intent to supply. The cannabis was found concealed at his address, made up into small packets. About £2,000 in cash was found at the same time. The Court was invited to deal with the appellant as a small time dealer supplying people whom he knew. He was sentenced to 12 months' imprisonment.

Held, the sentence was not wrong in principle or manifestly excessive.

Appeal dismissed.

19. R. v. Fyffe   5.4.91
(1994) 15 Cr.App.R. (S.) 13

F. pleaded guilty to possessing a Class B controlled drug with intent to supply. He was stopped by police officers at a motorway service area and found to be in possession of 80 nine-ounce bars of cannabis resin. The appellant claimed that he had agreed to collect a package in Liverpool and deliver it in Perth; he did not realise until after he had received it that it contained drugs. He was sentenced to four years' imprisonment.

Held, it was accepted that the appellant was a courier. The sentence was outside the guidelines indicated in *R. v. Aramah, supra*, and would be reduced to two years' imprisonment.

Appeal allowed.

20. R. v. Lyall   5.4.92
(1995) 16 Cr.App.R. (S.) 600

L. pleaded guilty to producing cannabis and was convicted of possessing cannabis with intent to supply. The appellant took a tenancy of a house and created a sophisticated intensive cannabis growing unit, adapting a room so as to produce humidity and warmth. It was suggested that the system might have produced up to three kilogrammes of cannabis in a year. He was sentenced to three and a half years' imprisonment for producing cannabis and possessing cannabis with intent to supply, on each count concurrent, with six months consecutive for a bail offence.

Held, the previous cases involved production of cannabis on a much smaller scale, this was a carefully planned and professional operation, with the intent of growing cannabis for sale and profit. The sentence of three and a half years could not be characterised as manifestly excessive.

SERVICE, L.J. (at p. 601): "[Counsel] also drew our attention to two cases: that of *R. v. Snow* (1988) 10 Cr.App.R. (S.) 93 and *R. v. Stearn* (1982) 4 Cr.App.R. (S.) 195. In both of those cases the cultivation of cannabis had resulted in terms of two years' imprisonment. It was therefore suggested by [counsel] that the sentence of 42 months in respect of the production and possessing with intent were out of line with the cases in the books.

We do not accept that submission. An examination of *Snow* reveals, as indeed the learned recorder pointed out in the course of his sentencing remarks, that that was a case where there was a plea, and it was also a much less grand scale of production of cannabis than in the present case. Almost exactly the same remarks can be made in respect of the case of

Stearn, which was what one could describe as a home-grown production, not of the professional nature which appears to be this case.

As the recorder said, and as is abundantly clear, this present case is one of a carefully planned and professional operation, with the intention of growing and cultivating cannabis for sale for profits. It was in truth a cannabis factory. A great deal of skill and experience had been put into the venture, and as the recorder pointed out, he viewed, after trial, the appellant as being the instigator and responsible for involving the younger co-accused. There is also the fact that so far as the charge of possessing with intent is concerned, the appellant lacked the mitigating feature of a plea of guilty.

We have considered [counsel's] arguments carefully over the short adjournment, but we are unable ourselves to categorise the term of 42 months on the production and possessing with intent as being manifestly excessive. They were substantially greater than the class of *Snow* and *Stearn*, and when one adds the factors that were not present in those cases, namely the fact that there was a trial rather than a plea of guilty, plus the different league of sophistication in the production of this controlled drug, it seems to us that the sentence is not out of line with authority and cannot be validly criticised."

Appeal dismissed.

5.4.93   **21. Paterson v. McGlennan**
                              1995 S.C.C.R. 42

P., who was aged 17 at the time of the offences, pleaded guilty on August 31, 1994 to possessing cannabis with intent to supply it to another and with supplying it to another, the offences having been committed in April 1993. On September 20, 1994 he was sentenced to four months' detention on each charge, concurrently. He had been of good behaviour between April 1993 and September 1994 and was said to have turned over a new leaf. He appealed to the High Court against the sentences as excessive.

Held, that an offence of this nature would normally inevitably attract a custodial sentence, but the circumstances of the present case were somewhat exceptional in that there was an 18 months' delay between the commission of the offence and the sentence; and appeal allowed and sentence quashed, and order for 240 hours' community service substituted.

Appeal allowed.

NOTE
    In his report to the High Court of Justiciary the sheriff made it clear that he was influenced by *Stephen v. H.M. Advocate*, 1993 S.C.C.R. 660 where the Lord Justice General (Hope) again drew attention to the repeated statements from the appellate judges that those who traffic in controlled drugs, whether Class A or Class B, will be dealt with severely.

C. STATUTORY DEFENCE: SECTION 5(4)   **5.4.94**

1. Meider v. Rattee   **5.4.95**
[1980] C.L.Y. 530

E. was a registered drug addict and he had lawful possession of an ampoule of methadone. E. gave that quantity of drug to D. to look after. The aim of D.'s possession was to assist E. in reducing his intake of the drug. D. was found by the police to have possession of the drug some 48 hours after E. had given it to her.

D. was charged with unlawful possession of methadone and at her trial the defence was that she came within section 5(4)(*b*) as it was not "reasonably open to her" to deliver the ampoule to anyone other than E. She was convicted and appealed.

On appeal it was held that assuming (*dubutante*) that D.'s "purpose" within the subsection was to "deliver" it to E. rather than to keep it for him, it could not possibly be said that delivery to an authorised person was not reasonably open to D. during the 48 hours between a Friday and a Monday. The words "such a person" in the subsection meant delivery to any authorised person not E. only.

Appeal dismissed.

2. R. v. Dempsey   **5.4.96**
[1986] Crim. L.R. 171

Mr D. was a registered drug addict. He obtained lawfully 25 ampoules of physeptone. Mrs D. held some of the ampoules while her husband went into a public lavatory and injected himself with the remainder. The defence was that Mr D. had given the ampoules to Mrs D. for safe-keeping and to prevent him using too much of the drug. Both were convicted.

On appeal it was held *quoad* Mrs D. that her actings did not come within the terms of section 5(4)(*b*) of the 1971 Act. She took possession of the drug for the purpose of removing it from the custody of a person lawfully entitled to it; she did not take reasonable steps to deliver it into the custody of such a person as soon as possible after taking possession. Neither did she fall within regulation 6(*f*) or regulation 10(2) of the Misuse of Drugs Regulations 1973 which permit possession for administration of medical and other purposes or conveying the drug to a person authorised by the regulations to possess it.

Appeal dismissed.

NOTE
R. v. Dempsey is noted above at paragraph **4.4.3** in relation to "supply".

CHAPTER SIX

6.1 Cultivation of cannabis plant

6.2 *Introduction*

The Misuse of Drugs Act 1971 provides by section 6 that it is an offence to cultivate any plant of the *genus* cannabis.

6.3 A. LAW

6.3.1   **1. Tudhope v. Robertson**
                          1980 S.L.T. 60

Two accused persons were charged with cultivating plants of the *genus* cannabis. At their trial the Crown led evidence that the police observed the plants growing in pots at the window of the bedroom occupied by the accused. The police did not find any implements by which the plants could be tended when they searched the room, although some cannabis seeds were found in a paper bag. The sheriff acquitted both accused of the charge and the procurator fiscal appealed by stated case.

THE LORD JUSTICE GENERAL (EMSLIE) (at p. 63): "The sheriff was plainly wrong. He did as the Crown suggested take too narrow and restricted a view of the verb 'to cultivate', in the context in which it appears, in relation to plants in a pot. There was ample evidence to demonstrate sufficient cultivation to lead to conviction of the offence libelled. That evidence lay in the positioning of the plants to secure the light necessary to growth, the condition of the plants, the presence of the seeds, and the object which the respondents had in mind in having the plants in their house at all."

Appeal allowed.

NOTE
    The defence solicitor has referred at trial to the definition of "cultivate" in the *Shorter Oxford English Dictionary* (1973 ed.) *viz.*: "1. To bestow labour and attention upon; to till 2. To produce or raise by tillage." It defines "cultivation" in relation to plant as follows: "The improvement of a plant by labour and care." The sheriff had accepted this definition as conveying the essence of the meaning of the word.

2. Taylor v. Chief Constable of Kent   **6.3.2**
(1981) 72 Cr.App.R. 318

The defendant was the occupier of a house in which five cannabis plants were found in a bedroom which he did not occupy. He knew of the presence of those plants, which had been cultivated by another occupant of the house who had been convicted of that offence. T. was convicted before justices of being the occupier of premises where he permitted or suffered the production of a controlled drug contrary to section 8 of the 1971 Act. He appealed on the ground that he had committed no offence in that it was not proper to equate production of a drug with cultivation of a plant under the 1971 Act.

DONALDSON, L.C. (at p. 321): "[S]ection 8 makes it an offence to permit or suffer the producing of a controlled drug on the premises. 'Produce' is defined in section 37(1) as follows, 'where the reference is to producing a controlled drug, means producing it by manufacture, cultivation or any other method' one can substitute in section 8 for the word 'produce' the words 'produce by cultivation.' He was charged with knowingly permitting or suffering the production by cultivation of a controlled drug."

Appeal dismissed.

NOTE
Counsel for the defendant had said on appeal that it appeared that the production of a controlled drug in terms of section 4 of the 1971 Act was being equated with the cultivation of a plant by section 6 of the same Act. That, it was argued, could not be right as Parliament could not have intended to produce the same offence in almost consecutive sections. The Divisional Court observed that while that was a good argument in relation to an original Act of Parliament, it lost much of its force when applied as here to an amendment to an Act of Parliament. The amendment referred to was the expanded definition of "Cannabis" in section 37(1) of the 1971 Act as provided for by section 52 of the Criminal Law Act 1977.

3. R. v. Champ   **6.3.3**
(1981) 73 Cr.App.R. 367

The appellant was a herbalist who had a window box which contained a plant which turned out to be a cannabis plant. She was charged with cultivating a plant of the *genus* cannabis. Her defence at her trial was that she had as a herbalist acquired knowledge over the years of herbal remedies, that she thought the plant was hemp and had been told by an old gypsy that the plant cannabis was good for certain ailments. The trial judge ruled that it was not necessary for the prosecution to prove that the appellant knew that she was cultivating cannabis. The appellant was convicted and appealed on the ground that the judge's ruling was wrong in law.

LAWTON, L.J. (at p. 369): "Two considerations must be borne in mind: (1) what kind of offence is created by the section and (2) is it a defence, having regard to the wording of the section and of section 28, to which subsection (2) is subject, that the defendant did not know that she was cultivating a plant of the *genus* Cannabis? It is clear from the terms of subsection (1) that the plant Cannabis will not be cultivated unless the cultivation is allowed by regulation. It is also clear from the provisions of sections 1 to 5 of the Act that it is a regulatory Act. The object of Parliament clearly was to regulate the production, importation, export and use of drugs, which are controlled drugs. It follows, therefore, that the ordinary rule *viz.* that when an offence is created, unless there are indications to the contrary, *mens rea* is necessary and has to be proved by the prosecution, may not apply. But, even if there are indications that it is an absolute offence, courts must be very careful indeed before they decide that there is no need to prove *mens rea*. The court has to look at the context of the Act in which the penal provision comes.

It is to be noted that s. 6(2) starts by providing that the offence is subject to s. 28 of the Act. That section shows that Parliament intended that there should be certain defences to a charge of an offence which is regulatory. The heading of s. 28 is: 'Proof of lack of knowledge, etc., to be a defence in proceedings for certain offences.' Section 28(1) provides: 'This section applies to the offences under any of the following provisions of this Act, that is to say s. 4(2) and (3), s. 5(2) and (3), s. 6(2) and s. 9.

One of the objects of s. 28 is to provide a defence to charges under s. 6. Section 28(2) provides: 'Subject to subsection (3) below' — which is not relevant in this case — 'in any proceedings for an offence to which this section applies it shall be a defence for the accused to prove that he neither knew of nor suspected nor had reason to suspect the existence of some fact alleged by the prosecution which it is necessary for the prosecution to prove if he is to be convicted of the offence charged.

What facts did the prosecution have to prove? These were (1) that the appellant was cultivating something; (2) that she was cultivating a plant; and (3) that she was cultivating a plant of the genus Cannabis. The appellant sought to show that she did not know that she was cultivating a cannabis plant. Subsection (2) of section 28 makes it clear that she had to prove that defence. There was no burden on the prosecution to prove that she knew that she was cultivating a plant of the genus Cannabis. On the contrary, she had to prove that she did not know that she was doing so.

It follows, in our judgment, that on the clear terms of the statute the burden of proof was on her."

Appeal dismissed.

NOTE

This case is a clear authority placing the legal burden of proof as regards *mens rea* on the accused, and in accordance with normal principle the standard of proof will be proof on a balance of probabilities: *R. v. Carr-Briant* [1943] K.B. 607. The accused in this case had to prove that she did not know that she was cultivating a plant of the genus cannabis. The accused had not met the standard required of her, for, on her own admission, she thought she was growing hemp, a common name for cannabis *sativa*.

B. SENTENCING 6.4

1. R. v. Lansdowne 6.4.1
[1967] Crim.L.R. 716

L. pleaded guilty to possessing about 7,000 grammes of cannabis which he had grown for his own consumption. He was sentenced to 18 months' imprisonment and appealed.

Lord Parker, C.J.: "Growing cannabis for one's own use is a matter which will attract imprisonment."

Appeal allowed in part. Sentence varied to six
months' imprisonment.

NOTE
In contrast in *Grant v. Scott* (1991) G.W.D. 14–855 the High Court of Justiciary disapproved of a period of imprisonment and substituted community service.

2. R. v. Brown 6.4.2
[1973] Crim.L.R. 62

B. pleaded guilty to *inter alia* cultivating cannabis plants. He was found to be growing 119 plants in the back garden of his house. He said that they were grown for the use of himself and his co-defendant who lived with him. He was sentenced to 18 months' imprisonment and appealed.

Held, on the appeal that the court took the view that it would be right to approach the case as one of self-supply. Although growing cannabis for one's own use was not necessarily such a serious matter as supplying drugs to others, the court agreed with what was said in *R. v. Lansdowne*, *supra*, that those who did so were at risk of a prison sentence.

Appeal allowed in part. Sentence varied to six
months' imprisonment.

3. R. v. Anderson 6.4.3
[1977] Crim.L.R. 757

A. pleaded guilty to *inter alia* cultivating cannabis. Police found 53 fairly well-developed plants growing in A.'s house and 30 growing in the open.

Indoors they found a quantity of leaves being dried and several tins containing dried and crushed leaves. One eight-inch high plant would, according to the evidence, produce about one pound of marketable leaf. The quantity of dried and crushed leaf could be sold for £180 per pound. He was sentenced to 12 months' imprisonment and applied for leave to appeal.

Held, that the trial court had reached the conclusion that A.'s purpose in growing cannabis was to supply it to others as well as to himself. It was difficult to see how they could have come to any other sensible conclusion. It had been submitted that A. had not been charged with possession with intent to supply others. However, it was open to the court to consider his purpose in growing such a large quantity, to infer that it was for the purpose of supplying it to the public, and to take that into account in fixing the sentence.

Application refused.

6.4.4

4. R. v. Lawrence
[1981] Crim.L.R. 421

L. pleaded guilty *inter alia* to cultivating cannabis plants and not guilty to possessing a controlled drug with intent to supply. The last charge was ordered to lie on the file. A large number of cultivated cannabis plants were found growing in a wood and L. admitted that he had planted them and that he was looking after them. He claimed that all the cannabis was for his own use. He was sentenced to six months' imprisonment, suspended, for cultivation, with a fine of £200. On appeal against sentence the Court of Appeal (Criminal Division) had noted that the trial judge in passing sentence has observed that he could not get out of his mind the strong suspicion that L. was growing cannabis so that some of it might get into other people's hands. The appeal court had been led to the view, having regard to the trial judge's observations and the nature of the sentence, that the judge had not succeeded in banishing from his mind the allegation of possession with intent to supply, for which L. was not to be sentenced. The sentence of imprisonment, albeit suspended, was inappropriate, and the fine was excessive. The sentence of imprisonment was quashed and the fine reduced to £100.

Appeal allowed and fine imposed.

6.4.5

5. R. v. Stearn
(1982) 4 Cr.App.R. (S.) 195

S. pleaded guilty to producing a controlled drug, cannabis, possessing cannabis and supplying cannabis. A total of 44 cannabis plants had been found growing in his house, greenhouse and garden. S. admitted selling cannabis among his friends at about £20 per ounce; he had earned about £1,500 from his first season's crop. He was sentenced to a total of three and a half years' imprisonment. He appealed against sentence.

LORD LANE, C.J. (at p. 196): "We are told that he is having a tough physical time in open prison. That is a matter which we can only applaud ... It was perfectly plain that an immediate sentence of imprisonment was necessary. We find it quite impossible to say that there is any ground which would justify us releasing him at this stage. The displeasure of society at the distribution of this type of drug on this scale will not go unmarked." His Lordship then considered certain personal facts in mitigation and reduced the sentence to two years' imprisonment.

Appeal allowed in part.

NOTE

All of these cases may be considered together. It seems that from an early stage English judges have been prepared to infer self-supply or supply to others from the circumstances of each case. There is, however, no statutory authority for such a distinction for section 6 of the 1971 Act provides only for cultivation *simpliciter*. As a matter of substantive law, cultivation can be equated with production: *Taylor v. Chief Constable of Kent, supra*. In the earlier cases cultivation with intent to supply appeared to attract short terms of imprisonment. In *R. v. Stearn, supra*, where cultivating cannabis plants was charged as production, a more substantial term of imprisonment was passed. The whole matter might benefit from legislative revision.

6. R. v. Case   **6.4.6**
(1992) 13 Cr.App.R. (S.) 20

C. pleaded guilty to producing cannabis and to possessing cannabis resin. Police officers searching his house found three cannabis plants in pots, and a small quantity of cannabis mixed with tobacco. He was sentenced to three months' imprisonment, with a suspended sentence activated with the term reduced to six months, consecutively.

Held, considering *R. v. Robertson-Coupar and Baxendale* (1982) 4 Cr.App.R. (S.) 150, the law regarded the production of cannabis more severely than simple possession, the maximum penalty for production was 14 years, as opposed to five years for possession. The comments in *R. v. Robertson-Couper and Baxendale* were made with reference to possession rather than cultivation. The sentencer was correct to take a more serious view of production, and his approach to sentencing was entirely correct.

Appeal dismissed.

CHAPTER SEVEN

7.1 Occupiers of premises

7.2 *Introduction*

The Misuse of Drugs Act 1971 provides by section 8 that it is an offence for a person knowingly to permit or suffer certain activities to take place on premises. It is essential for such an offence that a person has a particular status, namely the occupier of premises or someone concerned in the management of them.

7.3 A. LAW

7.3.1 *(i) "Occupier"*

7.3.2   **1. R. v. Tao**
                                [1976] 3 All E.R. 65

Tao was an undergraduate at Cambridge and lived in a hostel owned by his college. A furnished room had been allocated to him at the hostel. He paid the college for the use of the room and lived there from the time that he first went to Cambridge. Police were called to the hostel because of a small fire in T.'s room but he was not present.

On entering the room the police smelled burning cannabis and found traces of cannabis resin in the room. T. was convicted of permitting the room to be used for the smoking of cannabis, contrary to section 8(*d*) of the 1971 Act. He appealed, arguing that, although he was in occupation of the room, he was not "the occupier" of the room within section 8.

ROSKILL, L.J. (at p. 67): "The real controversy in this court, and it was the real controversy on a submission before the judge, was whether or not the appellant was 'the occupier' of room 17. It was argued that he was not. At the outset of his argument counsel for the appellant was 'in occupation' of room 17, but he drew a distinction between being 'in occupation' and being 'the occupier'. At first sight, with all respect, that is a somewhat fine distinction. But it was said that the phrase 'the occupier' being undefined in the Act, one had to construe this Act as a penal statute, which it undoubtedly is, and should give a narrow meaning to the phrase 'the occupier'.

The fact that whereas in many Acts one finds the phrase 'the occupier' defined, there is no comparable definition in this Act, suggests to this court that it was the intention of Parliament, in framing section 8, to leave it to the tribunal of fact to determine whether, on the facts of each particular case, a given person was 'the occupier' of the premises in question.

One cannot consider the meaning of the phrase 'the occupier' without also considering the other half of this part of the section ...

One asks what is the mischief against which this section is aimed. If one asks that question, it seems to this court plain that the object is to punish those persons who are able to exclude from their premises potential offenders who wish to smoke cannabis in those premises but do not do so, by making such persons themselves guilty of an offence if they knowingly permit or suffer any of the forbidden activities, these persons being either 'the occupier' or 'concerned in the management' of those premises.

This suggests that Parliament was intending not that a legalistic meaning should be given to the phrase 'the occupier' but a commonsense interpretation, that is to say, 'the occupier' was to be regarded as someone who, on the facts of the particular case, could fairly be said to be 'in occupation' of the premises in question, so as to have the requisite degree of control over those premises to exclude them from those who might otherwise intend to carry on those forbidden activities I have already indicated. That is the way in which this court would approach the question of construction ...

It seems to us that the correct legal analysis of the appellant's right of occupation of that room was this: he had an exclusive contractual licence from the college to use that room ... It was, in our view, clearly a licence which gave him not merely a right to use but a sufficient exclusivity of possession, so that he can fairly be said to be 'the occupier' of that room for the purpose of section 8 ... It is in every case a question of fact and degree, whether someone can fairly be said to be 'the occupier' for the purpose of that section."

Appeal dismissed.

2. R. v. Campbell   7.3.3
[1986] Crim.L.R. 595

The Campbell brothers were charged with allowing premises to be used for smoking cannabis contrary to section 8 of the 1971 Act. At the trial counsel invited the judge to rule on a point of law arising from an agreed set of facts as to whether the brothers were "occupiers". One brother lived in a certain house with his mother. He held a party there with her permission but in her absence. The second brother attended the party although he lived elsewhere. The police raided the party. On being interviewed, the brothers agreed that cannabis had been smoked by guests at the party.

The brother who had held the party assumed responsibility for it. The second brother agreed that his mother had left both her sons in charge and that if someone ought to be charged with an offence then as between the mother and sons, the sons were responsible.

Held, that to be "the occupier", the person charged must be proved to have had, whether lawfully or otherwise, such an exclusive possession of the premises at the material time as to enable him to prevent the smoking of cannabis in them. Not every transient use of premises or physical ability to remove another from the premises would enable the court or jury to find the nature, extent and degree of possession sufficient for a finding that the person was the occupier of the premises. On the agreed facts the parents remained occupiers but had delegated to their sons their authority to licence the entry of guests during their absence overnight. In these circumstances the children did not become "occupiers" for the purpose of an offence under the Act.

NOTE

The meaning of the phrase "the occupier" in section 5 of the 1965 Act was considered in *R. v. Mogford* [1970] 1 W.L.R. 998. There, the accused were sisters then aged 20 and 15 and living with their parents at the parents' home. The parents went on holiday. The police went to the house and discovered cannabis being smoked there. The trial judge ruled on the question of whether the girls were the occupiers of the premises. Nield, J. held that for persons to be occupiers of premises within section 5 of the 1965 Act, they had to have legal possession of and control over the premises; and that on the facts, the girls as daughters of parents temporarily away on holiday, were not in legal possession of the premises and their control over the premises did not amount to the nature and measure of control envisaged by the Act. This case was considered, still in relation to section 5 of the 1965 Act, in *Christison v. Hogg*, 1974 S.L.T. (Notes) 33. There the appellant had been the occupier of a particular flat but it had been condemned as unfit for human habitation. Nevertheless, the appellant continued to live there as a squatter, that is to say, without legal right or title to do so. When the police discovered that the smoking of cannabis resin had taken place in the flat, the appellant claimed that he was not an occupier within the meaning of the Act. He was convicted and appealed. In upholding the conviction, the Lord Justice General (Emslie) held in the course of an opinion: "No violence is done to the wording of the section if the words 'the occupier' are construed as bearing their ordinary meaning and connotation. In our opinion, 'the occupier', within the meaning of the section, is a person who has possession of the premises in question in a substantial sense involving some degree of permanency and who, as matter of fact, exercises control of the premises and dictates their use. Every case will depend on its own facts. We see no reason to restrict the interpretation of the words 'the occupier' to describe one who has a legal right or title to inhabit the premises" (*ibid*. at p. 34). The High Court of Justiciary declined to accept the construction placed on the term "the occupier" by Nield J. in Mogford's case: the Scots judges looked at the mischief struck at by the section rather than being persuaded by the strict legal reasoning of the English judge. It is submitted that while the terms of section 8 of the 1971 Act are different from the earlier provisions, the mischief struck at by all sections remains the same.

3. Bamber v. MacKinnon
1996 S.L.T. 1180

M. was charged on a summary complaint with a contravention of the Fire Precautions Act 1971 in respect that, being the occupier of premises, he used them in such a manner that a fire certificate was required when no certificate was in force. The accused was the owner of a guest house and restaurant and held a restaurant licence for the premises. He was out of the country for two weeks on holiday at the time of the offence and had left two women in charge of the day to day running of the guest house. The sheriff, holding that the accused was in no position to exercise any form of control or supervision when on holiday and was therefore not the occupier of the guest house, acquitted the accused. The Crown appealed.

Held, that somebody who was away temporarily on holiday remained the "occupier" of the premises if he was in fact the owner/occupier before he left and had every intention of remaining as such when he returned.

Appeal allowed.

NOTE
In this case, *Christison v. Hogg*, *supra*, was applied.

4. R. v. Bradbury
[1996] Crim.L.R. 808

B. was convicted of allowing premises to be used for the supply of amphetamine and Ecstasy and of possessing those drugs. C., her boyfriend (the prosecution said), had been arrested for supplying drugs about five months before her arrest, and the prosecution case was that at least from then she was aware that he was suspected of supplying drugs. She was the tenant of a flat. Officers who had been observing the flat arrested C. outside the flat. He shouted "police, drugs squad, hide your drugs" outside the block of flats and at the communal door. After some delay, access was gained and B.'s flat was searched. The drugs were found in a number of places within the flat. Some were wrapped for retail sale. A cash-box containing £620 and a passport in C.'s name were also found. B. had left the flat shortly before the search was executed. She was arrested the next day. The police had not previously been aware of B., and although previous observations of the flat had been made, there had been nothing seen to lead the police to believe that drug-dealing had been going on from the flat. The defence case was that although C. had previously been her boyfriend, she had told him about two months before their arrest that the relationship was over. He found that difficult to accept. He lived more or less permanently at the flat, but she only spent the occasional night there. She had tried to get him to leave, but had not argued with him because he was prone to violence. She said that on the day of the search, she had not heard C. shout anything and was unaware of the presence of drugs in the flat. Defence counsel posed the question for the jury — if a tenant is visiting infrequently does she have control simply through knowledge? In his summing-up, the judge told the jury that the "short and simple" answer to that question was provided by B.'s answer in cross-examination that had she found any drugs in the flat, she would have telephoned the police. "That", said the judge, "is exercising control."

On appeal, it was argued that by such a direction the judge gave the impression that pure acquiescence would amount to control; and that the judge wrongly reminded the jury of the shouted warnings (which on the prosecution case explained B.'s hasty exit from the flat) without telling them that before they could rely on the warnings they must be satisfied that B. had heard them.

Held, (1) the jury should have been told that mere acquiescence was not enough. There had to be assistance or encouragement, as indicated by the court in *R. v. Conway and Burkes* [1994] Crim.L.R. 826 and *R. v. Bland* [1988] Crim.L.R. 41. The subject of control was extremely important in cases of this sort and the direction was a misdirection. (2) The court was satisfied that the words of C., which had been admitted before the jury (despite the strict position as to whether or not they were admissible, about which the Court declined to say anything) could only have any relevance if it were first established that B. had heard the words. To remind the jury of the evidence without directing them to that effect was a misdirection, and in view of the questions of control and knowledge being dealt with, it was a significant misdirection.

Appeal allowed.

7.3.6 *(ii) "Concerned in the management"*

7.3.7   **3. R. v. Josephs and Christie**
                         (1977) 65 Cr.App.R. 253

J. and C. ran a card school in the basement of a house owned but not occupied by the local council. They were in a sense squatters there without lawful authority as trespassers. The police raided the premises and there found packs of cannabis; many of the packs were in the possession of a man who had been with J. and C.

At trial it was argued that J. and C. could not be concerned with the management unless there was some sort of authority giving them a legal right. *De facto* management of a card school was insufficient. It was also said that it did not matter what the authority was, merely some sort of legal authority.

LORD WIDGERY, C.J. (at p. 254): "If in truth a man was exercising control over premises, running them or organising or managing them, the fact that he was not lawfully in possession of them was irrelevant."

Appeal dismissed.

NOTE
It would appear that the judgment of Lord Widgery, C.J. is derived from a consideration of the mischief being struck at by the section. A broader view of that mischief was taken by Lord Parker, C.J. in *Yeandel v. Fisher* [1965] 3 All E.R. 158 when he took note "of the fact that drugs are a great danger today, and legislation has been tightening up the control of drugs in all aspects." It was held in that case that the appellants had been rightly convicted of being concerned in the management of premises used for certain purposes connected with controlled drugs as section 9(1)(*b*) of the 1964 Act created an absolute offence.

(iii) "Knowingly permit" **7.3.8**

4. R. v. Thomas **7.3.9**
[1976] Crim.L.R. 517

T. was convicted of permitting cannabis to be smoked in premises occupied by him. He appealed on the ground that having regard to the word "knowingly" in the section the trial judge had summed up the matter incorrectly.

Held, the word "knowingly" added nothing to the offence created by section 5(*a*) of the Dangerous Drugs Act 1965. The word, according to the appeal judges, was probably added to make it plain that there must be either knowledge of the offending state of affairs or wilful blindness, and that reasonable grounds for suspicion was not enough. And perhaps also it was added to eliminate all risks of introducing that constructive knowledge, to be imputed from neglect to make such inquiries as a reasonable and prudent person would make, which generally speaking had no place in the criminal law.

NOTE
In *R. v. Ashdown* (1974) 59 Cr.App.R. 193 it was held, in relation to section 5 of the 1965 Act, that a co-tenant of premises who knowingly permits another co-tenant to smoke cannabis or cannabis resin on premises had committed an offence.

B. SENTENCING **7.4**

1. R. v. Hooper **7.4.1**
[1984] Crim.L.R. 637

The Court of Appeal (Criminal Division) has held that it was "absolutely right" to impose a custodial sentence on someone who allowed his

premises to be used for the smoking of cannabis, whether or not he was a
person of good character.

Appeal refused.

NOTE

Similarly, in *R. v. Pusser* (1983) 5 Cr.App.R. (S.) 225, six months' immediate
imprisonment upheld on the licensee of a public house for permitting the premises
to be used for the purpose of smoking cannabis. Tudor Evans, J. held, at p. 226,
that:

"The appellant was plainly warned by the police. The evidence was
overwhelming that he knew perfectly well what was taking place in the public
house and, so far as the evidence showed, at no time did he take the slightest step
to stop it, although he had been told by the police that the proper course was to get
in touch with them and seek their assistance. It may well be that by permitting
these activities to go on in the public house he was able to attract a large number
of people to use it and so make a larger profit. In our judgment, a sentence of
immediate imprisonment was fully merited, and we do not come to the conclusion
that the sentence passed was in any way excessive."

Many of the earlier reported cases concern the offences under the 1964 Act
and 1965 Act but the detail of the case is so sparse as to make these cases of
limited value: *cf. R. v. Blake* [1966] Crim.L.R. 232, *R. v. Omer* [1966] Crim.L.R.
457, *R. v. Andrew* [1967] Crim.L.R. 376 and others. However, it would appear
that the aggravating factors for sentencing purposes are inactivity in the face of
overt criminal actions and the suggestion of financial gain, or evidence of actual
gain, in some way connected to the offence.

7.4.2   **2. R. v. Gregory**
                          (1993) 14 Cr.App.R. (S.) 403

G. pleaded guilty to possessing a Class A drug with intent to supply,
possessing a Class A drug, possessing a Class B drug, and permitting
premises to be used for smoking opium. Police officers searching the
appellant's flat found 8.5 grammes of powder containing between 23 per
cent and 54 per cent heroin, tablets of methadone hydrochloride, and 13.84
grammes of cannabis resin. Three people who were present at the flat
when the police arrived admitted that they had gone there for the purpose
of using heroin. G. was sentenced to six months' imprisonment for
possessing heroin with intent to supply, three months for possessing a
Class A drug, three months for possessing a Class B drug, all concurrent,
and 15 months consecutive for allowing premises to be used for smoking
opium, with a suspended sentence activated consecutively.

Held, in relation to Class B drugs, it might be that it would be
appropriate to pass a non-custodial sentence in respect of an offence of
this kind, but any criminal conduct which facilitated the use of a Class A
drug must be regarded as serious, even without a commercial motive. It
was submitted that the appellant had not corrupted those who used his
flat, or profited from them; he had provided the venue in which they

could take Class A drugs in comparative safety. The sentence of 15 months was too long; a sentence of six months would be substituted, consecutive to the other sentences.

Appeal allowed and sentence varied.

3. R. v. McLellan
(1994) 15 Cr.App.R. (S.) 351

7.4.3

McL. pleaded guilty to permitting premises to be used for supplying cannabis, supplying cannabis, and supplying Ecstasy. She supplied cannabis from her home, in conjunction with her husband and her son; and she sold a single tablet of Ecstasy to a caller. She was sentenced to three years' imprisonment for supplying the Class A drug, with eight months and 12 months' imprisonment concurrent for the other offences.

Held, any sale of a Class A drug must attract a substantial sentence, but the sentence could be reduced from three years to two.

LORD TAYLOR, C.J. (at p. 353): "In passing sentence, the learned recorder bore in mind that the appellant's case before him was that she had simply handed over the packets to the man Bromley without thinking, that she had been foolish, and that she had not been involved personally on other occasions in actually supplying the drugs. He indicated that he dealt with the case on that basis and that a longer sentence would have been imposed had he not accepted the appellant's own account of the extent of her offending.

The submission which is made, and attractively made, by [counsel] on behalf of this appellant is that for a single tablet of a Class A drug (Ecstasy) valued only at £15, a sentence of three years was excessive. We have considerable sympathy with that submission. We have taken into account the cases of *R. v. Kelly* (1989) 9 Cr.App.R. (S.) 385, and *R. v. Spinks* (1987) 9 Cr.App.R. (S.) 297, which both concerned the supply of a very small amount of Class A drug where sentences less than that imposed upon this appellant were imposed. In the case of *Kelly*, two years; and in the case of *Spinks*, an even shorter sentence.

Standing back from this case and looking at it in the round, it is clear that drug dealing went on at this house, principally through the son, although with the collusion and non-interference of the parents. It may seem unfair that this appellant should have received so much longer a sentence, by reason of this one tablet to which she was party in the sale, than the father or the son. We consider that, nevertheless, any sale of a Class A drug must attract a substantial sentence. Balancing those factors, we think it proper to reduce the sentence in this case from three years; but we do not feel it right to reduce it to a sentence any less than two years. Accordingly, we substitute two years for the three years on count 5. The other sentences which were passed by the learned recorder remain, making two years' imprisonment in all.''

Appeal allowed.

NOTE

Permitting premises to be used for supplying controlled drugs is not to be equated with the actual supply of controlled drugs: see *Freeburn v. H.M. Advocate*, 1987 G.W.D. 23–845.

Chapter Eight

Offences under corresponding law   **8.1**

Introduction   **8.2**

The Misuse of Drugs Act provides by section 20 that the assisting in or inducing the commission outside the United Kingdom of offences punishable under a corresponding law is in itself an offence.

A. LAW   **8.3**

1. R. v. Vickers   8.3.1
[1975] 2 All E.R. 945

V. admitted that in 1973 he had agreed, in England and elsewhere, with another that V. would acquire a truck, would collect a number of speaker cabinets in London and transport them to Italy knowing that thereafter cannabis from a source unknown to V. would be fitted into the cabinets and shipped by other persons to the United States in contravention of federal legislation there. He pleaded guilty to conspiring to contravene section 20 but he appealed. This was done on the ground that the trial judge had erred, in the particular procedural circumstances of this case, in holding that the admitted facts amounted to a conspiracy to contravene section 20.

SCARMAN, L.J. (at p. 950): "It is a short point of construction of the Act. We say this not in any spirit of disrespect for the very careful and comprehensive argument of counsel for the appellant, but because, in our view, a concession, properly made by him at the outset of his submissions, is fatal to his case. The concession was that, as a matter of everyday speech, it could be said that what the appellant agreed to do was to assist in the commission of the offence under American law of illegally importing a prohibited drug into the United States of America. This submission, however, was that the words of the section must be narrowly construed as covering only acts directly concerned with the actual importation. In our view Parliament chose the plain English phrase 'assist in the commission of' so as to leave to the jury the opportunity of exercising a commonsense judgment on the facts of a particular case."

And later (at p. 951)

"[W]e find nothing in its provisions that compels us to construe the offence under section 20 of assisting as being one of strict liability. In ordinary English one who assists knows what he is doing and the purpose with which it is done."

Appeal against conviction dismissed.

8.3.2   **2. R. v. Evans**
(1976) 64 Cr.App.R. 237

E. left England and went to Brussels where he met a man. That man gave E. a suitcase containing cannabis and E. flew to Canada and gave the suitcase to another person. E. returned from Canada to Brussels and then to England.

The actings of E. amounted to an offence under Canadian law and he was convicted in England of contravening section 20 of the 1971 Act. The grounds of appeal included *inter alia* the question whether there had been any act done by E. in England which was capable of amounting to "assisting" in the commission of the offence charged.

Held, that there was sufficient evidence of "assistance" in that, having made his agreement, E. picked up the ticket provided for him and flew to Brussels knowing that the purpose of his journey was the transportation of cannabis from Brussels to Canada.

Appeal against conviction dismissed.

8.3.3   **3. R. v. Panayi and Karte**
[1987] Crim.L.R. 764

P. and K. had picked up a quantity of cannabis in Spain and were to take it to Holland. Their yacht was arrested off the Isle of Wight. It was proved that the law of the Netherlands prohibited the importation of cannabis.

The trial judge overruled a submission that there could be no conviction unless the substantive offence had been committed in Holland. Consequent on that ruling guilty pleas were made and appeals taken.

Held, that on a true construction of section 20 a person cannot be guilty of the offence of assisting the commission in a place outside the United Kingdom of an offence unless the offence outside the United Kingdom is committed. It was not committed in this case.

Appeals allowed.

NOTE
See also *R. v. Ahmed* [1990] Crim.L.R. 648.

B. SENTENCING   **8.4**

1. R. v. Faulkner and Thomas   **8.4.1**
[1977] Crim.L.R. 679

F. and T. had imported cannabis from Pakistan to Denmark. On the second such journey they passed through London and were stopped and found to have cannabis for their own use. That cannabis had been paid for from their earnings from the journey to Denmark.

On appeal against sentence, they argued that although the maximum sentence under section 20 of the 1971 Act was 14 years' imprisonment, the maximum sentence in Denmark for the same offence was six years and therefore a *pro rata* lower sentence ought to have been imposed.

Held, that the maximum sentence under the corresponding law of the country into which the drugs are imported was an irrelevant consideration. Where cases of planned international drug trafficking are brought before the sentencing court on the scale which existed here then there must be severe sentences for breaches of section 20 of the 1971 Act. The sentences of four years were therefore not excessive.

Appeals against sentence dismissed.

NOTE
In relation to being concerned in the international carrying of controlled drugs, the English courts do not accept that they should necessarily restrict their penalties to those likely to be imposed in the country of intended importation: see *R. v. Maguire* [1996] Crim.L.R. 838 and *R. v. Wagenaar and Pronk* [1996] Crim.L.R. 839.

2. R. v. Derrick   **8.4.2**
(1981) 145 J.P. 351

D. and others had been concerned in the importation of cannabis from North Africa to Spain. D. had bought a car in England and arranged for the petrol tank and boot to be altered for the purpose of concealing the drugs. He had also been involved in the purchase of airline tickets necessary for the venture. On conviction of contravening section 20 of the 1971 Act D. was sentenced to six years' imprisonment.

On appeal against sentence it was *held* that the evidence did not show that D. was the leader of the enterprise so as to justify a higher sentence and that it was difficult to determine the exact part played by him. Clearly he was an active and important participant in the offence. After anxious consideration the court concluded that the sentence was marginally higher than his established part merited. The sentence was reduced to five years' imprisonment.

Appeal against sentence allowed in part.

CHAPTER NINE

9.1 Powers to search and obtain evidence

9.2 *Introduction*

The Misuse of Drugs Act 1971 provides by section 23 for various powers to search and obtain evidence and by section 24 for a power of arrest.

9.3 *(i) Section 23(2) of the 1971 Act*

9.3.1   **1. Balloch v. Pagan**
High Court of Justiciary, unreported, November 25, 1975

In the course of a summary trial the procurator fiscal asked policemen who had searched a man whether they had reasonable grounds to suspect that the man was in possession of cannabis. The answer to that question was yes. When the policemen were asked to elaborate upon it, they begged leave not to do so as they felt their answers might be prejudicial to the interests of that man. There was no cross-examination of the general proposition that there were reasonable grounds to suspect possession.

The man appealed against his conviction of possession of the cannabis found during the search. The ground of appeal was that the evidence relating to the finding of the material found to be cannabis was improperly admitted in respect that it did not appear clearly, at least from the sheriff's findings, that the search was lawfully carried out.

The High Court upheld the conviction and was of the opinion that the sheriff was entitled to find in these circumstances that there had been reasonable grounds for suspicion.

Appeal dismissed.

9.3.2   **2. R. v. Littleford**
[1978] Crim.L.R. 48

A policeman gave evidence at a trial that at about 2 a.m. he saw a motor car parked in a public car park. He suspected that the car had been stolen and he requested information by radio from the police computer. He was informed that the car was suspected of being involved in drug trafficking. In the course of a search six grammes of cannabis resin were found in the back of the car.

After the objection was heard, the trial judge held that section 23 gives the police officers power to search a person or any vehicle when he has reasonable grounds to suspect that a person is in possession of a controlled drug. In this case it was the vehicle that was suspected, not the accused. The search was illegal but in all the circumstances the evidence of the search and of the result was admitted.

Evidence admitted.

NOTE
The trial judge reached his decision on a literal construction of the statute for section 23(2) refers to powers where "any person is in possession." As a matter of common sense, however, someone must possess the car and on the face of it that person may reasonably be suspected of possessing the contents.

3. Wither v. Reid   **9.3.3**
1979 S.L.T. 192

The police suspected that a woman was in possession of controlled drugs. She was told that she was being arrested and that she would be searched for controlled drugs. She was taken to a police station and a search was started. The woman resisted violently. In the event no such drugs were found but she was charged with police assault. At the trial on that charge the sheriff acquitted the woman on the view that the search was illegal, as it followed on an arrest which was itself illegal.

While section 24(1) of the 1971 Act permitted arrest without warrant, the conditions under which such an arrest might be made were not present in this case. Section 23(2)(*a*) permitted detention for the purpose of search, but in this case the police had arrested the accused, told her so and then purported to search her under section 23(2)(*a*). The Crown appealed by stated case.

The High Court held that the findings-in-fact clearly showed that the accused was arrested unlawfully. It was not an arrest under section 24 of the 1971 Act, but was a purported action under section 23(2)(*a*). The latter section did not give authority to arrest, only to detain for a limited purpose. There was a vital distinction between arrest and detention. If the police were proceeding under section 23(2)(*a*) they should have done so explicitly. The search was thus unlawful and the accused was entitled to use force to resist it.

THE LORD JUSTICE-CLERK (WHEATLEY) (DISSENTING) (at pp. 195, 196): "[I]t is easy to understand the respondent's annoyance, in the light of her personal knowledge that she was not in possession of any drugs, at being subjected to what she considered was humiliation and indignity, but if the police had reasonable grounds for suspecting that she was in possession of a controlled drug, then assuming that the police acted legally in taking her to the police station for the purpose of conducting a search, and it was explained to her that it was, it was her legal duty to submit to and not resist such a search even although she knew in her own mind that there was no justification of it ...

Later (at p. 196)

"[T]he whole procedure followed the pattern of section 23(2)(*a*) apart from the fact that Detective Sergeant Souden told the respondent that she was under arrest and not just being detained ... The issue may be put this way. Is the criterion what was said or what was done? ... As she could have been detained and taken to the police station for that purpose [of a search] ... I do not consider that the fact that Detective Sergeant Souden used the wrong word vitiates the procedure which was otherwise unimpeachable. I accept that a penal statute must be construed in favour of the subject when a doubt arises, but I do not consider this error in terminology should vitiate a conviction."

LORD KISSEN (at p. 196): "Whatever may have been in the mind of the detective sergeant, he did tell the respondent that she was under arrest. He purported to arrest her. I cannot see how the later explanation to the respondent, apparently based on section 23(2)(*a*), can alter what he specifically said he was doing. His apparent confusion about his powers cannot, in my opinion, mean that he was not putting her under 'arrest', as he himself clearly thought he was doing despite the explanation."

LORD ROBERTSON (at p. 197): "There is a vital distinction between 'arrest' and 'detention' ... [A] penal statute must be construed strictly. In my opinion, in deference to the rights of the citizen, it must be made perfectly clear to the person against whom action is being taken under section 23(2)(*a*) that that is what is being done and that he is not being arrested ... The police also should know the law and if they were proceeding under section 23 they should have done so explicitly."

Appeal dismissed.

NOTE

This decision is an example of the advice — "Whenever possible use the words of the Act." The Lord Justice-Clerk's dissenting view taken with the decision in *Balloch v. Pagan, supra*, would have given drugs officers extremely wide powers. The majority view of the Bench follows not only the strict letter of the state but emphasises, indeed exemplifies, the rule of construction that penal statutes must be interpreted where there is doubt in a way that preserves the liberty of the subject. As the Lord Justice General (Cooper) observed in *McGovern v. H.M. Advocate*, 1950 J.C. at p. 37, "unless the principles under which police investigations are carried out are adhered to with reasonable strictness, the anchor of the entire system for the protection of the public will very soon begin to drag." In *Gellatly v. Normand*, 1997 G.W.D. 12–499, it was held that the duty to give an explanation before a strip search was not absolute.

4. Lucas v. Lockhart   **9.3.4**

(1980) S.C.C.R. Supp. 256

A car was being driven by S. with two passengers in it, one of whom was Lucas. The police stopped the car to inquire about ownership, but recognised S. as being a person with whom they had had dealings a week before in connection with drug offences. They then proceeded to search S. and the other passenger, and when they found no drugs they decided to search Lucas, who was found to have in his possession two grammes of cannabis.

Lucas was found guilty after trial and he appealed to the High Court on the ground that the police officers did not have reasonable grounds for suspecting that he was in possession of a controlled drug, and had no right to search him under section 23(2) of the 1971 Act.

Held, (1) that in the circumstances the police were not entitled to exercise their power of search under section 23(2) to search the appellant; and (2) that as the appellant had not agreed to the search its irregularity should not be excused.

THE LORD JUSTICE GENERAL (EMSLIE) (at p. 258): "The sheriff convicted because after battle had been joined on the admissibility of the evidence requisite to any conviction the sheriff took the view that the evidence on which conviction depended had been lawfully obtained. The point arises in this way. Cannabis resin was found in the possession of the appellant when his person was searched in the circumstances described in the stated case. The search was carried out upon the purported faith of the statutory warrant granted to police officers by section 23(2) of the Act of 1971. The issue at the trial, and the only issue at the trial, was whether or not the police officers were entitled on the facts found and in the circumstances to exercise their power of search at all under that section. Having answered the burning question at the trial in a way adverse to the appellant it is not surprising that the first question in the case in these terms: 'In the circumstances found proved, did the police officers have reasonable grounds for suspecting that the appellant was in possession of a controlled drug, thus entitling them to search the appellant under section 23 of the Misuse of Drugs Act 1971?'

To that question there is only one answer, and it is given consent of the Crown. The answer is no. For the appellant, [counsel] then submitted that although in certain circumstances evidence illegally obtained may be admissible the necessary circumstances do not exist in this case. In reply the Crown sought to defend the conviction, notwithstanding the irregularity of the search, by pointing to an alleged agreement to be searched by the appellant ... We are entirely satisfied that these passages ought not to be read as indicating a voluntary submission to search on the part of the appellant. If the sheriff had thought that this man, the appellant, was a volunteer in the matter of search he would not have had to waste his time or ours upon a consideration of the statutory warrant under which the search purported to be carried out. We are therefore not prepared to read the passages as indicating any more than that the appellant, at a certain stage, ceased to resist the demands of the police officers that he come out and be searched. In these circumstances the learned advocate-depute has conceded that the conviction could not be justified in this case and he would not attempt to support it further".

Appeal allowed.

9.3.5   **5. R. v. Green**
[1982] Crim.L.R. 604

G. hailed a taxi and as he was about to enter it a woman of scruffy, unkempt appearance accosted him, saying that she was a policewoman and that she wished to question him about an incident which she had just witnessed. G. had been seen talking to a third party who was known to the police to be a drug addict and dealer. A struggle ensued and G. was charged with assault.

On conviction G. appealed *inter alia* on the ground that the policewoman's actions were unlawful in that although section 23(2)(*a*) entitled a police officer in certain circumstances to detain a person in order to search him, the section did not entitle the officer to detain that person in order to question him, which was the admitted reason for the appellant's detention.

It was *held*, that the submission relating to section 23(2)(*a*) was ill-founded. The right to detain in order to search must necessarily involve the right to detain and question and search. There was no obligation, because of the detention, to search.

Appeal allowed on other grounds.

NOTE

It would be an absurdity to expect police officers to carry out the whole of their powers in terms of section 23(2)(*a*) or 23(2)(*b*) in silence. Almost certainly there would be some conversation between the police officers and the detainee. But what sort of questioning does the English appeal court envisage here for the police officers in their jurisdiction? Is it only a narrow extent of questioning incidental to the search itself or does it go much further to include extensive questioning? Further, it is also the view of the learned commentator on this case in the *Criminal Law Review* that "stopping in order to find grounds for searching is surely not permissible."

9.3.6   **6. Johns v. Hamilton**
1988 S.C.C.R. 282

Policemen entered a private club after one constable had received information that someone in the premises had a "reefer" cigarette. They entered the club without permission or a warrant, although no one objected. J. was searched and found to have cannabis resin in his possession. At trial for unlawful possession of that controlled drug, objection was taken to evidence of the finding of the substance: the search was said to be unlawful. It was conceded by the Crown that there was no urgency involved but it was argued that the search was lawful under section 23(2). On conviction J. appealed.

Appeal allowed.

THE LORD JUSTICE-CLERK (ROSS) (at p. 285): "It thus appears plain that so far as section 23(2) is concerned, it is enabling the police to search and detain a person whom they come upon, whereas if there is any question of premises requiring to be searched steps require to be taken under section 23(3). The somewhat odd feature of the present case is this, that it was submitted on behalf of the appellant to the sheriff that there was no suggestion of any urgency which might have excused the failure of the officers to apply for a warrant under section 23(3), and the surprising feature is that the procurator fiscal accepted that there was no evidence of urgency in this case. No doubt this is because there had been evidence to that effect from the police. If there was no question of urgency in this case, then there was no reason why the officers should not have taken steps to obtain a warrant under section 23(3). In the circumstances we are satisfied that what the officers did was not and could not be justified in the circumstances by section 23(2)."

NOTE
    In the commentary on this case the case editor added that "different considerations apply where the police are already lawfully on the premises and then form a suspicion that someone else on the premises is in possession of a drug."

7. R. v. Longman   9.3.7
(1989) 88 Cr.App.R. 148

Police officers obtained a warrant to enter the appellant's premises to search for drugs pursuant to section 23 of the 1971 Act. In plain clothes they gained entry by a subterfuge, tricking the appellant into opening the door and forcing their way in stating they were police officers and had a warrant. The appellant reacted by shouting to a man in the house, whom one of the officers found in a room with drug paraphernalia about to administer cocaine to himself. The appellant lunged at one of the officers with a knife; but was disarmed before he inflicted any injury. He was convicted, *inter alia*, of attempted wounding with intent to resist lawful arrest and with obstructing a constable when exercising his powers under section 23 of the 1971 Act.

On appeal, *inter alia*, that the recorder had erred in ruling that for the entry and search of the appellant's premises and his subsequent detainer to be lawful it was not necessary for the requirements of section 16(5) of the Police and Criminal Evidence Act 1984 to be complied with before the police entered the premises in question; and, further, she had erred in her summing-up to the jury in defining the word "produce" in relation to the warrant in section 16(5)(b) as "available to be seen."

Held, that (1) under section 16 of the Police and Criminal Evidence Act 1984 and the code of practice made under that Act, entry to the premises may be effected in the circumstances such as the instant case before there is any requirement for a constable to identify himself to produce his warrant card or produce the search warrant as required by section 16(5). Further, it was recognised in the code, and also in section 23 of the Misuse of Drugs Act 1971, that the use of force, or its counterpart subterfuge in the instant case, was permissible to gain entry; if it were not so, then the whole object of the exercise would be frustrated. Thus, the recorder's ruling was correct and the police officers' entry into the premises was lawful.

(2) A warrant or warrant card was "produced" in compliance with section 16(5)(b) and (c) of the 1984 Act when the occupier of the premises was given an opportunity to inspect it. Thus, although it would have been better if the recorder had defined the word produced as made available to be inspected rather than made available to be seen; the jury could have been in no doubt that before the warrant and warrant card, the latter had obstructed the police in the exercise of their powers of search under section 23 of the 1971 Act by shouting to the man in the house, and the appellant had thereby deprived himself of the opportunity of inspecting the aforesaid documents before he was arrested.

Appeal dismissed.

9.3.8
8. Weir v. Jessop
1991 S.C.C.R. 242

W. was charged with possession of drugs, contrary to section 5(2) of the 1971 Act. The drugs had been found in his possession when he was searched by a constable who was acting on information that an unidentified person was involved with drugs on the fourth landing of a block of flats. When the police came to the locus W. was the only person there. He was asked if he was involved in using drugs and replied, "No", but added that he had been involved with drugs in the past. He was then searched. Objection was taken at W.'s trial to evidence of the search on the ground that the constable who searched him had no reasonable grounds to suspect that he was in possession of drugs. The objection was repelled and W. was convicted and appealed to the High Court.

Held, that in the whole circumstances the constable had reasonable grounds to suspect that the appellant was in possession of drugs.

THE LORD JUSTICE-CLERK (ROSS) (at p. 244): "[Counsel] also drew attention to *Lucas* v. *Lockhart* [(1980) S.C.C.R. Supp. 256] and she relied upon that case in support of a proposition that police officers were not entitled to exercise their powers of search under section 23(2) merely because they recognised a particular individual as someone who had some previous involvement with drugs. That was no doubt so in the case of *Lucas* v. *Lockhart* but the circumstances of the present case are different. In determining whether or not the constables had reasonable grounds to suspect that the appellant was in possession of drugs, we are of opinion that the whole circumstances must be looked at and that means the fact that they received a radio call asking them to investigate an anonymous report that an individual on the fourth landing of this block of flats was involved in the misuse of drugs. That is the first circumstance. The next circumstance is that the police proceeded to that very place, namely the fourth landing, and found only one person there, namely the appellant. The matter does not rest there because the conversation which we have referred to took place in the course of which the appellant, although denying that he was involved in using drugs, volunteered that he had been involved with drugs in the past. When all these circumstances together are taken into account, we are satisfied that the constable did have reasonable grounds for the suspicion and that accordingly he was entitled to carry out the search in question. that being so, the sole issue which was raised in this appeal must be determined in favour of the Crown."

Appeal refused.

9. Devlin v. Normand 9.3.9
1992 S.C.C.R. 875

D. was charged with being in possession of drugs in a prison with intent to supply them to a prisoner she was visiting. When she was in the visitors' room at the prison, D. was asked by a prison officer if she had anything in her mouth. She replied that she did not. The officer, who believed that she had something in her mouth, then asked D. to open her mouth and she did so. She was not cautioned nor told under what authority the request was being made. A package was then seen in her mouth, and the officer asked her to hand it to him, which she did. It contained controlled drugs. At D.'s trial the Crown relied on the package as evidence. D. objected to its admissibility on the ground that it had been obtained by an irregular search. The sheriff repelled the objection and convicted. D. appealed to the High Court.

Held, that what happened was analogous to the situation where an individual is asked to open a handbag or show what is in his pockets; that if such an individual declines to comply with the request and any force is used then one could say that a search had taken place, but if the individual voluntarily complies with the request, there is no question of any search having taken place.

Appeal refused.

9.3.10　　　　　　　　　　　**10. Simpson and McDermott v. Scott**

High Court of Justiciary, unreported, June 23, 1993

Police officers had reasonable grounds for suspecting that the appellants and a co-accused were in possession of a controlled drug in a caravanette. They followed the caravanette and stopped it. One of the police officers showed the warrant card to the occupants of the vehicle and shouted that they were plain clothes officers and intended to carry out a search for controlled drugs. All the doors of the caravanette were locked and the occupants did not unlock them. The police made no request to the occupants to open the doors and eventually had to break a window to gain access.

Held, that it must have been obvious to the occupants of the caravanette that the police wished to enter the vehicle in order to undertake a lawful search for controlled drugs and in these circumstances a request for them to open the doors would have been a mere formality. Since it was obvious that the police required access to the caravanette a formal request to that effect was not needed and the intention of the appellants to obstruct the police officers was therefore established.

THE LORD JUSTICE GENERAL (HOPE): "The issue in this case revolves around the absence of a request to open the doors of the vehicle before the police officer smashed the window with his baton to gain access to it. [Counsel], who appeared for both appellants, pointed out that intention was of the essence of the offence created by this subsection. He submitted that it was necessary in the circumstances of this case that there should have been a request by the police officers to open the van. This was because there had to be material before the sheriff to justify him in concluding that the appellants had formed the deliberate intention of obstructing the police officers in the exercise of their duty. He accepted that a failure to do something might constitute obstruction, but in this case that failure could only be held to amount to an intentional obstruction if it was preceded by a request. Time was also a material factor in this case. He accepted that, as is frequent in cases of this kind, time was of the essence. But he said that it did not follow from the fact that the police officers had to respond quickly to what was happening that there was a deliberate intention on the part of the appellants to obstruct them.

In regard to his proposition that intention was an essential element, [counsel] referred us to *Carmichael v. Brannan*, 1985 S.C.C.R. 234 at p. 240, where Lord Cameron said that the obstructing must be intentional in order that an offence be committed. But it was not disputed by the advocate-depute that, since the word 'intentionally' appears in the subsection, intention is a necessary element if there is to be a conviction of obstructing the police in terms of section 23(4)(a) of the 1971 Act. He submitted however that it was necessary to have regard to the whole circumstances. Where a request was made, that could be taken into account as part of the circumstances. But it was not an absolute requirement that a request should be made. He drew our attention to the background to the incident, which began with a pursuit by several police vehicles leading eventually to the van being brought to a halt. It was plain when the police officers emerged from their vehicles and especially when Constable Lowe showed his police warrant and shouted that they were police officers and intended to carry out a search for controlled drugs, what the purpose was for which the police had stopped the vehicle. Their attempts to gain access to it were followed by a further shout by Constable Lowe that they were police officers and that they intended to carry out a search for controlled drugs. He accepted that time was brief, but he submitted that there was no requirement in this case that there should be any formal request in view of the whole nature and circumstances of the event.

We consider that the question whether or not a request is required is a matter of circumstances. No hard and fast rule can be laid down about this as [counsel] very properly recognised in the course of his argument. Account therefore has to be taken in this case of the circumstances which led to the vehicle being stopped, of the nature of the vehicle to which the police wished to gain access and the various steps which were taken by the police prior to the smashing of the window with the baton. The evidence which emerged in the course of the Crown case was sufficient to entitle the sheriff to hold that it was obvious to the appellants that the police wished to enter the vehicle in order to undertake a lawful search for controlled drugs. One has to ask therefore in these circumstances what the purpose would have been of their making a request. What would it have added to the state of knowledge of the appellants and ... in these circumstances? It was said that a request was necessary in order to focus the issue more clearly, but it seems to us that, in the light of what had already happened in this case, that would have been no more than a formality. And if the request was purely a formality, given that the matter was already obvious to the occupants of the vehicle, it does not seem to us that this was an essential element in order to establish that the appellants had the necessary intention to obstruct the police officers.

Taking account of all these circumstances, we consider that the sheriff was entitled at the end of the Crown case to conclude that there was sufficient material available to him to hold that it was obvious what the police were wishing to do, and that since this was obvious, a formal request to the same effect was not needed in this case. When it came to the end of the case he was entitled to make the findings which he did in the light of the evidence."

Appeals refused.

NOTE

A brief report, *sub nom.*, *McDermott v. Scott* appears at 1993 G.W.D. 28–1747.

9.3.11   **11. Normand v. McCutcheon**
                              1993 S.C.C.R. 709

McC. and another were charged with contraventions of section 23(4)(a) of the 1971 Act. At their trial, two constables gave evidence that they had observed them engaging in what appeared to be drug dealing, had approached them, shown them their warrant cards and taken hold of them. Each respondent had thereafter put something in his or her mouth, made swallowing motions and refused to spit out when asked by the police to do so. Only one constable gave evidence that when the police approached the respondents, one of the officers told them that they were being detained under section 23. The sheriff held that in the absence of corroboration of that constable's evidence there was insufficient evidence that the respondents knew the reason for their detention and acquitted them. The prosecutor appealed to the High Court by stated case.

Held, that the evidence that the police had shown the respondents their warrant cards, the evidence of the actings of the respondents before the police approached them, and the evidence of their actings thereafter for which there was no other explanation than that they knew why they were being detained, provided sufficient corroboration of the evidence of the constable who said they were told they were being detained under section 23; and appeal allowed and case remitted to the sheriff with a direction to convict.

                                                            Appeal allowed.

9.3.12   **12. Stuart v. Crowe**
                                 1993 S.L.T. 438

During a search by the police of a house of a suspected drugs dealer under a warrant granted in terms of the 1971 Act, the accused arrived and was searched by the police but nothing of a drug related nature was found on his person. His car was then searched and a number of shirts were found but nothing of a drug related nature was found. The accused was detained under section 2 of the Criminal Justice (Scotland) Act 1980. The police thereafter applied for and were granted a warrant under section 23(2) of the 1971 Act to search the accused's house where certain documents of a potentially drug related nature were found. Thereafter, the police obtained another warrant under the 1971 Act to search the accused's garage premises where drug related material was found. The accused was subsequently indicted along with *inter alios* the person whose house had first been searched, on a charge under section 1 of the Trade Descriptions Act 1968 in relation to the shirts, and various contraventions of the 1971 Act. The accused before his trial sought suspension of the two warrants on the ground that the police had no reasonable grounds for applying for them under the 1971 Act.

Held, that if at the time when the accused arrived at the premises the police had reasonable grounds to entertain a suspicion that he was involved with drugs, which was the reason for the police's searching these premises, then that suspicion also gave the police reasonable grounds for taking the matter further and obtaining a warrant to search the accused's premises.

Bill refused.

13. McLeod v. Lowe   9.3.13
1993 S.L.T. 471

McL. was charged with *inter alia* obstructing police officers in the exercise of their powers under the 1971 Act by refusing to permit them to search him and struggling with them, contrary to section 23(4) of the 1971 Act. The evidence disclosed that a report was received by the police of an alleged contravention of the 1971 Act at an hotel. On arrival at the hotel the police were given certain information by the hotel staff and were taken to one of the bars where the officers' attention was directed to the accused. The police told the accused that he was being detained under the 1971 Act as they had information which led them to believe that he was in possession of a controlled substance. Outside the hotel, when the accused was told that he was to be searched, he became aggressive, abusive and unco-operative, he lashed out and broke free from the grasp of the police and ran away, but was eventually captured. A search did not reveal the possession of any controlled drug. In the course of the trial the defence had objected to the Crown's attempt to lead evidence from the police officers as to what was said to them by the hotel staff. The sheriff sustained the objection on the ground that only the hotel staff, who were not led in evidence, could testify as to whether they had pointed out the accused.

A submission of no case to answer was made on the ground that there was no evidence to show that the police had reasonable cause to suspect that the accused was in possession of drugs and accordingly the police had no right to detain him. The sheriff repelled the submission and convicted the accused, who appealed.

Held, (1) that the sheriff had erred in upholding the objection since what was at issue was the information on which the police acted and evidence as to that could competently have been given either by the hotel staff or by the police themselves; (2) (Lord Murray dissenting) that the evidence before the sheriff was insufficient to show that the police officers had reasonable grounds to suspect that the accused was in possession of drugs since it was impossible to determine whether the police officers had such reasonable grounds without knowing what it was the officers were told by the hotel staff; and (3) that having regard to how it came about that no evidence was led regarding what the police officers were told by the hotel staff, the appeal court ought to bear additional evidence upon this matter in terms of section 452(4)(b) of the 1975 Act and appeal continued and hearing of additional evidence ordered.

Per LORD MURRAY (DISSENTING) (at p. 475): "Whether or not there was a case to answer turned entirely on whether the findings were sufficient to justify the inference that the police had reasonable grounds to suspect that the accused was in possession of controlled drugs and not whether any suspicion was in fact justified, and accordingly the sheriff was entitled to repel the submission."

THE LORD JUSTICE-CLERK (ROSS) (at p. 475): "I agree with the advocate depute that the sheriff's decision in which he upheld the objection to this evidence was misconceived. What was at issue was the information upon which the police acted. Evidence about that could competently have been given by either the hotel staff or the police officers themselves. The evidence of the police officers to this effect would not have proved the truth of what they were told by the hotel staff but it could have proved that the statements were made. In other words what the Crown were endeavouring to lead from the police witnesses was primary hearsay which was admissible as direct evidence that the statement was made irrespective of its truth or falsehood (Walker and Walker, *Law of Evidence in Scotland*, p. 394). Subsequently at p. 396 it is observed that it is frequently necessary to prove that a statement has been made, and it is stated: 'The party leading the evidence does so merely to establish that the statement was made. He is probably not concerned with its truth, and indeed his case may be that it was untrue.' I accordingly agree with the advocate depute that the sheriff was wrong to have upheld the objection to the evidence which it was sought to take from the police officers as to what was said to them by members of the hotel staff.

In my opinion the evidence before the sheriff was not sufficient to show that the police officers had reasonable grounds to suspect that the appellant was in possession of drugs. It is not possible to determine whether the police officers had such reasonable grounds without knowing what it was that the police officers were told by members of the hotel staff. The sheriff did not have this information, and in the absence of that information he was not entitled to conclude that the police officers were acting within their powers in making a detention and search under s. 23(2) of the 1971 Act. On the other hand it is no fault of the respondent that the sheriff did not have this information. The sheriff would have had that information if he had repelled the objection to the evidence as he should have done. In these circumstances without knowing what the police officers were told by the hotel staff, it is impossible to determine whether the sheriff was entitled to make finding in fact 3. In terms of s. 452(4)(b) this court in hearing a stated case has power to hear any additional evidence relevant to any alleged miscarriage of justice. Having regard to how it came about that no evidence was led regarding what the police officers were told by the hotel staff, I am of opinion that the present case is one where the court ought to exercise this discretionary power and ought to hear additional evidence upon this matter. It is only when this court has been apprised of what the police officers were told by the hotel staff that this court will be able to determine whether there has been any miscarriage of justice as suggested by the appellant. I would accordingly move your Lordships to continue the appeal, and to order the hearing by this court of additional evidence as to what was said to the police officers by members of the hotel staff.''

LORD MURRAY (at p. 475): "I read the findings in this stated case to the effect that communication of suspicion that a drugs offence was being committed at a named hotel was made by telephone to the police. In consequence they attended at the hotel where they were received by hotel staff and taken to a particular bar where a particular person, the appellant, was pointed out to them. The appellant was then detained for search. Accordingly I am unable to agree with the expression of opinion by Your Lordship in the chair that the findings are insufficient to justify the inference which the sheriff drew that the police had reasonable grounds to suspect that the appellant was in possession of controlled drugs. The central issue in the appeal, whether or not there is a case to answer, turns entirely upon that point, not on whether any suspicion is in fact justified. However, in light of the sheriff's mistaken exclusion of material and relevant evidence through ill founded objection on the part of the appellant's agent, I entirely agree that it is appropriate in this case for the court to exercise its powers under s. 452(4)(b) of the 1975 Act to hear additional evidence upon the matter.''

LORD GRIEVE (at p. 476): "This case raises important issues. As was pointed out in *Dryburgh v. Galt*, 1981 S.L.T. at pp. 155–156, the legitimacy of police officers proceeding on information received depends on the source and content of that information. In my opinion it is not possible for a court to decide whether a police officer had reasonable grounds to suspect that a person was in possession of a controlled drug, until it knows on what information the police officer had proceeded. The facts will vary from case to case, but the kind of information on which a police officer can legitimately proceed to detain and search a suspect is to be found in the case of *Dryburgh* and *Weir v. Jessop*.

The course which your Lordship proposes we should take would enable the court to decide, bearing in mind the general considerations set out in *McNicol v. Peters*, whether or not the police officers in this case had reasonable grounds to suspect that the appellant was in possession of controlled drugs at the material time. In my opinion without the information which the additional evidence will provide it is not possible to answer any of the questions in the stated case. I agree that the case should be dealt with in the way in which your Lordship proposes, and for these reasons which your Lordship gives."

Appeal dismissed.

9.3.14   **14. R. v. Hughes**
[1994] 1 W.L.R. 876

A constable told the appellant, H., that he wished to search him. H. was seen to take something from a pocket and put his hand to his mouth. He refused to spit it out and began to chew. The constable held H.'s jaw with one hand and with the other hand held the outside of his nostrils, causing him to extrude a wrapper containing cannabis. H. pleaded not guilty to a charge of unlawful possession of a controlled drug. The judge rejected a submission that admission of the constable's evidence would be unfair, and H. was re-arraigned, pleaded guilty and was convicted. The judge granted a certificate on the question whether what the constable had done amounted to an "intimate search" within section 118(1) of the Police and Criminal Evidence Act 1984, whether the constable was in breach of the Police and Criminal Evidence Act 1984 Code of Practice regarding search and whether the evidence should have been excluded under section 78(1) of the 1984 Act. H. appealed against conviction.

Held, dismissing the appeal, that an "intimate search" as defined by section 118(1) of the Police and Criminal Evidence Act 1984 required some physical intrusion into a body orifice of a person by some physical examination, rather than a mere visual examination in order to cause the person to extrude what was contained in the body; that, although the constable's actions constituted a "search" for the purposes of the 1984 Act, merely causing the appellant to spit something out did not amount to an intimate search of a body orifice, and did not come within section 55(5); that, since the constable had a general duty to prevent the destruction of any evidence that might be material to possible proceedings, he had to act swiftly, and albeit there had been breach of the Code of Practice C in regard to search in general, it was not such that the evidence should have been excluded, under section 78 of the 1984 Act, as having an adverse effect on the fairness of the proceedings; and that, accordingly, the appeal was without merit.

Per curiam, it would be absurd if section 55 of the 1984 Act required a visual examination of an open mouth to be conducted by a registered nurse or medical practitioner because such an examination was an intimate body search.

15. Graham v. Orr   **9.3.15**
High Court of Justiciary, unreported, November 1, 1994

G. was arrested after failing a roadside breath test and was taken to a police station. He was released from arrest when the specimens of breath which he had given were found to contain a level of alcohol below the statutory limit. He was told that his car was to be kept in the police pound until he had provided a clear breath test. He became agitated on being given this information by a constable who then became suspicious because of G.'s behaviour. This was a vague suspicion which had not been brought to the point of suspecting G. of having committed any particular offence. The constable then went out to look at G.'s car. He opened the door and saw a plastic bag which contained cannabis resin stuffed into a parcel shelf in the area of the front passenger seat. At G.'s trial, objection was taken to the admissibility of the evidence of the finding of the bag and its contents but the sheriff admitted the evidence and convicted G.

Held, that the constable's actions amounted to a search of the appellant's car in order to see what was inside it; that the constable had no power at common law to search the vehicle and that in the circumstances the evidence of what was found inside the car was inadmissible.

THE LORD JUSTICE GENERAL (HOPE): "The appellant is Thomas James Graham who went to trial in the sheriff court at Inverness charged with the unlawful possession of cannabis resin, contrary to section 5(2) of the Misuse of Drugs Act 1971 and with the unlawful possession of cannabis resin with intent to supply it to another, contrary to section 5(3) of that Act. It was alleged that these offences were committed on 7 November 1992 at the Police Station in Aviemore.

The charges arose out of an incident when the appellant was arrested after failing a roadside breath test and taken to Aviemore Police Station. He was released from arrest when the specimens of breath which he had given for the purpose of testing on the Camic machine gave readings which were below the statutory minimum. But he was told that his car was to be kept in the police pound until he had provided a clear breath test. He became agitated on being given this information by Constable Scott, who then became suspicious because of the appellant's behaviour. The constable went out to look at the car, and it was as a result of what he found in it that the appellant and his co-accused, who was his companion in the car, were charged with the offences under the Misuse of Drugs Act of which they were later brought to trial and convicted.

Objections were taken in the course of the evidence of the Crown witnesses to evidence being led about what Constable Scott had seen in the motor car when it was parked in the police pound. There was also an objection to the detention of the appellant on the ground that the police officer had no reasonable grounds for suspecting him of being in possession of controlled drugs. Those two objections were related to the same point, as to whether the evidence of what Constable Scott saw in the car was inadmissible. The objections were repelled, and the motion of no case to answer which depended upon them was refused. The appellant gave evidence, but he was subsequently convicted and was sentenced to periods of imprisonment. An application has now been made for a stated case in order to challenge the conviction on the ground that the sheriff erred in repelling the submission that there was no case to answer.

It is clear that the whole matter depends upon a single point, which is whether the sheriff was in error in admitting the evidence about what Constable Scott found when he opened the door of the car and looked inside it. It was upon the basis of what he found having looked inside the car that everything else proceeded, including the further search of the car when the plastic bag was removed from it and the detention of the appellant. [Counsel for the appellant] submitted that what Constable Scott did was indeed to search the car. The basis for this was what the sheriff had narrated in finding 7, which states 'Constable Scott was suspicious about Graham's agitated behaviour when told that the car was going to be kept in the police pound. He went out to look at the car. On opening the door he saw a plastic bag stuffed crudely into a broken parcel shelf in the area of the front passenger seat.' Although at the outset of his argument [counsel] submitted that the car had been improperly appropriated by the police and ought not to have been detained in the police pound, we understood him to accept that ultimately the appellant did agree that the car could remain there until he provided a clear breath test, and he did not in the end seek to make anything of this point. The point which he did develop was related to the basis in law, if any, which the constable had for opening the door of the car. In the course of his evidence the constable said that he had become suspicious about something in view of the appellant's behaviour, but that he did not know quite what. It was on the basis of that vague suspicion, which had not been brought to the point of suspecting the appellant of having committed any offence, that the constable then did what he did. [Counsel] said that the constable was not entitled to search the car in these circumstances.

In his reply the advocate depute submitted that the police officer was entitled to check the car to see if it contained any object which might explain the suspicious behaviour of the appellant. He accepted that it was difficult in the circumstances to argue that the constable had a power to search the car at common law at that stage. He also accepted that until Constable Scott had found the plastic carrier bag inside the car he had no basis for conducting a search in terms of section 23(2) of the Misuse of Drugs Act 1971. The whole argument therefore upon which the Crown case rested was that this was not truly a search at all, but merely a check. The submission was that a search had not been commenced merely by the opening of the door of the car in these circumstances. The advocate depute referred to *Baxter v. Scott*, 1992 S.C.C.R. 342, but he accepted that the circumstances of that case were not directly analogous. The explanation for what was done there was not related to any suspicion on the part of the police officers that there was anything incriminating in the car. The reason given in that case was that it was police policy to search motor vehicles to see if there was anything dangerous or perishable in their custody. In the present case the explanation was a different one, and the advocate depute accepted that if there was an irregularity it could not be excused for the same reason as in that case.

In our opinion the constable had no power at common law to search the appellant's motor car. It is quite clear from the narrative of the constable's evidence that, while he was suspicious about something, his suspicion had not developed to the point of suspecting that the appellant had committed any offence. We can find nothing in the narrative of this evidence which would have justified a search under the common law power, and we consider that the advocate depute was right not to attempt to press that point. The question then is whether what the constable did amounted to a search. The narrative which we have been given is that he had previously locked the car retaining the keys. What he did was to go back to the car, unlock the door and open it. He then looked inside it and saw the plastic bag stuffed into the parcel shelf. It was not until he had opened the car door that he saw the bag. In our opinion his actions can only be explained as amounting to a search of the car in order to see what was inside it. No doubt it is a question of degree whether premises have been invaded to the extent necessary to amount to a search of them, but in the present case the search began as soon as Constable Scott opened the car door. It follows that, since on the facts of this case what Constable Scott was doing was to conduct a search of the car without having a power to do so, the evidence of what he found inside the car was inadmissible.

It has not been disputed that once that conclusion has been reached everything else that follows in this case is subject to the same objection, and that the sheriff had no basis upon which he could properly convict the appellant of the charges in this complaint."

Appeal allowed.

NOTE
This appeal was reported as Crown Office Circular No. A48/94.

16. Black v. D.P.P.   **9.3.16**
[1995] C.L.Y. 159

B. was detained on suspicion of possession of drugs. He was found in the house of a known drug dealer, his brother, and responded to his detention with aggressive behaviour. B. appealed against his conviction under section 23(4)(a) of the 1971 Act on the ground that the police did not have reasonable grounds in terms of section 23(2)(a) to suspect that he was in possession of a controlled drug.

Held, that (1) B. was visiting his brother and had a valid reason to be at the house. The fact that his brother was a known drug dealer could not give rise to reasonable grounds for suggesting that B. was in possession of drugs; (2) his aggressive behaviour after being detained could not retrospectively provide reasonable grounds.

Appeal allowed.

9.3.17   **17. Gavin v. Normand**
                             1995 S.L.T. 741

G. was tried on summary complaint with a contravention of section 1(1) of the Prevention of Crime Act 1953. G. called at a house which was being searched for controlled drugs by police officers under a warrant obtained in terms of section 23(3) of the 1971 Act. When asked why he was there, G. stated that he wanted to buy some cannabis resin. G. was then searched and a knife was found in his possession. Objection was taken to the admissibility of the evidence of the finding of the knife on the ground that the search was unlawful as the police officers had no reasonable grounds for suspecting that the accused was in possession of controlled drugs. The sheriff repelled the objection and convicted the accused who appealed, contending that his reply to the police indicated that he was not in possession of controlled drugs.

Held, (1) that the police were not bound to accept every word which the accused said and it was enough for them that the accused had admitted that he was in some way connected with dealing in drugs; (2) that the police were accordingly entitled to conclude that the accused might have some drugs in his possession and to search him.

THE LORD JUSTICE GENERAL (HOPE) (at p. 741): "The appellant is George Murdoch Gavin who went to trial at the sheriff court in Glasgow, charged with having with him without lawful authority or reasonable excuse in a public place an offensive weapon, namely a knife, contrary to s. 1(1) of the Prevention of Crime Act 1953. The public place referred to in the charge was the common close of a house [...] in Glasgow. In the course of the evidence which was being led on behalf of the Crown, an objection was taken by the appellant's solicitor to the admission of evidence about the finding of the knife in the appellant's possession when he was searched by police officers. That evidence was admitted subject to competency and relevancy. Later, when a motion of no case to answer was made, that motion was repelled. The appellant then gave evidence on his own behalf but he was found guilty of the charge. An application has now been made for a stated case, in which it is stated that the sheriff erred in law in repelling the appellant's objection that the search was unlawful in all the circumstances of the case, and in allowing the evidence obtained as a result of the search to be admitted into the proceedings.

It is clear from what the sheriff tells us that if the evidence relating to the search was inadmissible there would have been insufficient evidence for the conviction. The whole point therefore turns upon the circumstances of the search and whether that evidence was admissible. From the findings in fact it appears that on the date in question police officers were engaged in a search of the flat at [...], under the sanction of a search warrant which they had obtained in terms of the Misuse of Drugs Act 1971, s. 23. It must be assumed that the warrant had been granted under subsection (3) of that section which relates to the search of premises. At about 7 pm, while the search was still in progress, the appellant knocked at the door of the flat. A plain clothes police officer responded to the knock and invited the appellant to say why he was there. The appellant's reply was 'I'm here to buy some blaw.' The word which he used is a slang term for cannabis resin. He was then invited to enter the house, and he was then detained there for the purposes of a search in terms of s. 23 of the Act. In this instance, since this was a search being conducted of a person who had not been found in the house, it would appear that the search was under subs. (2) of the section. The finding is that the police officers involved had reasonable grounds to suspect that the appellant was in possession of a controlled drug. It was that last finding which counsel for the appellant challenged in the course of his submissions to us today.

As we understood his submissions, the argument was that the evidence did not justify the conclusion which is drawn in that finding. Counsel drew out attention to *Guthrie v. Hamilton*, 1988 S.L.T. 823, in which it was said that, as the caller at the premises had no obvious innocent explanation for being there, the police were entitled to suspect that he was in possession of controlled drugs. The submission was that that was not the correct approach, having regard to the terms of the statute. Counsel emphasised that what the statute required was reasonable grounds to suspect that the person was in possession of controlled drugs. He said that, in the light of the reply which the appellant had given in response to the question put to him by the police officer, it was clear that the reason why the appellant had come to the house was to obtain drugs. It could not be inferred from what he said that he was already in possession of them, and unless there was a reasonable ground for suspicion that he was already in possession of a controlled drug, there was no basis upon which the search could properly have been carried out.

In his reply the learned advocate depute submitted that it was open to the police to conclude that any person who called at the house was there for the purpose of dealing in drugs, and that this was reinforced when one examined what the appellant said in reply to the question put to him by the police officer. What the appellant had said was that he was there to buy drugs. But, far from absolving the appellant, this enhanced the suspicion that he was in some way connected with dealing in drugs, and that was enough to justify the suspicion which the police officers formed about him. He drew our attention to *Stuart v. Crowe*, 1993 S.L.T. [438] at p. 440F where the Lord Justice-Clerk said this: 'It appears to us to be a matter of common sense that if, as here, police officers are searching premises because they suspect that there are controlled drugs on these premises and someone arrives at the premises, the police are entitled to suspect that that person is also involved with controlled drugs and therefore to search his person.'

It was in reliance on that passage, and on the general submissions which he also made, that the learned advocate depute invited us to refuse this appeal.

The sheriff tells us in his note that the police officers said in their evidence that they had been informed that the flat was one where drugs were bought and sold. They anticipated that on occasion drugs would be delivered there, and they formed the view that any callers at the door should be considered suspect and should be searched. The police officers said that they were influenced in their decision to search the appellant by the comment which he made at the door, but that that was not the sole reason.

It is clear from that description of their evidence that the police officers, in conducting the search of these premises in the light of the information which they had been given, were entitled to be suspicious of any person who came to the door of those particular premises. We are not concerned therefore with the question as to whether the police are entitled to search any person who comes to any premises. This was a case where a search was already being conducted under warrant of premises which were thought to be associated with drug dealing. The significance of the remark made by the appellant in response to the question put to him by the police officer was that it confirmed that he was in some way associated with dealing in drugs. But the officers were not bound to accept every word that he said. It was enough for them that he had admitted that he was in some way connected with dealing in drugs. They were entitled to conclude that he might have some drugs in his possession as a result of this, and that was a sufficient basis for them to form the reasonable suspicion which would entitle them to search him.

For these reasons we are satisfied that the sheriff was right to repel the objection and to find that there was a sufficient basis in the evidence for a conviction. We shall answer the three questions in the case in the affirmative and refuse the appeal."

Appeal refused.

18. Ireland v. Russell   9.3.18
1995 S.L.T. 1348

An accused person was tried on summary complaint for a contravention of section 5(2) of the 1971 Act. At about 1 a.m. on the date of his arrest, two police officers, who approximately two months earlier had received information that the accused was involved in the possession and supply of controlled drugs, saw the accused in the street, for the first time since they had received that information, and detained him in order to search him. The accused was found to be in possession of a quantity of cannabis resin. Objection was taken to the search on the ground that the police had no reasonable grounds for suspecting that the accused had drugs because the officers' information was too old. The sheriff repelled the objection. The accused was convicted and appealed by stated case. The sheriff made no finding that the police had reasonable grounds for suspecting that the accused was in possession of controlled drugs or that the police believed that they had such grounds.

Held, that in the absence of evidence which could show a sound basis for the police having reasonable grounds for suspicion, they were not entitled to search the accused; and appeal allowed and conviction quashed.

Observed, that there was no question that if any specific period of time had elapsed, that disabled the police from acting upon information they received.

THE LORD JUSTICE-CLERK (ROSS) (at p. 1348): "This is the appeal of Mark Ireland. He went to trial at the sheriff court at Cupar on a complaint libelling a contravention of s. 5(2) of the Misuse of Drugs Act 1971. He was found guilty of the charge and against this conviction he has appealed by way of stated case. Today on his behalf counsel has explained that the sole issue raised in this case relates to whether or not the search which the police officers carried out of the appellant on 29 August 1994 was lawful. The sheriff in his findings explains that on 29 August 1994, around 1 am, in a street in Cupar, the appellant was approached by two police officers. They had received confidential information approximately two months earlier to the effect that the appellant was involved in the supply and possession of drugs. Apparently one of the officers had made some attempt to trace the appellant at his then given address on three or four occasions, but had been told that he was working away from Cupar. The officers' purpose in seeking to trace the appellant was to investigate this information which the police had received regarding his alleged involvement with drugs. The sheriff tells us that further inquiries had been made over the course of the time before 29 August, but these had all proved unsuccessful. The 29 August was the first occasion upon which the police officers had seen the appellant. Finding 6 is to the following effect: 'When he [PC Mithie] and Sergeant Prentice approached the appellant, PC Michie informed the appellant that he was detaining him for the purposes of a search under s. 23 of the Act and read from the aide memoire provided for the purpose in the following terms: 'I have reason to suspect that you are in possession of controlled drugs and would advise you that I am detaining you for the purpose of a search under the Misuse of Drugs Act 1971 and must caution you that you do not need to say anything but anything you do say will be noted and may be used in evidence.'

It was in these circumstances that the appellant was searched and a substance wrapped in clingfilm was found in the right pocket of his jeans. This proved to be cannabis resin. Counsel maintained that in the circumstances as described by the sheriff the police officers had not had reasonable grounds for suspecting that the appellant had drugs in his possession at the time and that accordingly, their search of him was not lawful. They had purported to search by virtue of the terms of s. 23(2) of the Misuse of Drugs Act 1971. Before the sheriff, objection had been taken to this evidence and the suggestion appears to have been that the information upon which the police proceeded was too elderly to justify a search under s. 23(2). The sheriff, in the note annexed to the case, points out that the police had searched him on the first opportunity they had, having attempted to trace him unsuccessfully before, and he attached significance to the fact that the information which the police had received some two months earlier related not only to the fact that the appellant may have been in possession of drugs, but that he may have been concerned in the supply of drugs, and in these circumstances the sheriff concluded that the police were entitled to search him on that basis on this occasion. Counsel, on the other hand, maintained that in the circumstances they were not so entitled.

The advocate depute maintained that the time lapse was a matter of facts and circumstances and that when regard was had to the whole circumstances the sheriff had been well founded in acting as he did. Where the police are proceeding upon information received, it is not possible to lay down any rule as to the period within which they must act upon that information by way of search, if a search is to be lawful. There is no question of saying that if any specific period of time has elapsed, that disables the police from acting upon the information. We say that because the question must be whether at the time when they stopped the appellant for the purpose of searching him they had a sound basis for concluding that they had reasonable grounds for suspecting that he had drugs in his possession at the time. It is of importance that the power which the police were purporting to exercise on this occasion relates to their powers of stopping and searching. Before they could be justified in invoking these powers they would require to satisfy the sheriff, if the matter was challenged, that at that time they had reasonable grounds to suspect that the appellant had drugs in his possession. Much might depend upon the place where the appellant was seen and the circumstances attending the police seeing the appellant and deciding to exercise the power which they had under s. 23. All that we are told in this case is that they encountered the appellant at 1 am in a street in Cupar. It is not suggested that he was acting in any way suspiciously, and no further specification is given of the place where he was. When the police did approach him, all that we are told in finding 6 is that there was read out to him a statement to the effect that they had reason to suspect that he was in possession of controlled drugs. But there is no finding to the effect that they had reasonable grounds for any such suspicion and there is nothing in either the findings or the note which the sheriff has written suggesting that there was evidence before the sheriff from the police officers to the effect that they believed that they had reasonable grounds for such a suspicion, and no evidence as to what the basis was for their believing that the appellant had drugs in his possession at that time. That being so, we have come to the conclusion that the sheriff was incorrect in allowing evidence of the search to be led. Having regard to the whole circumstances, and the absence of evidence from the police officers which could show a sound basis for their having reasonable grounds at the time to suspect that the appellant was in possession of drugs, we are not satisfied that they were entitled to carry out this search in terms of s. 23(2). It follows that the sheriff ought to have upheld the submission of no case to answer."

Appeal allowed

19. Cooper v. Buchanan   9.3.19
1996 S.C.C.R. 448

The police received information that a man B., who was travelling in a car with a companion, was in possession of controlled drugs. They stopped the car and found that B. was driving it and that C., the appellant, was a passenger. A constable told C. that she was being detained for the purpose of a search under section 23 of the 1971 Act and asked if she was in possession of a controlled drug. She then produced a quantity of cannabis resin. She was subsequently charged with a contravention of the 1971 Act and at her trial objection was taken to the evidence being led of the finding of the drug, on the ground that the police were not entitled to search her. The sheriff repelled the objection and convicted C., who appealed to the High Court.

Held, that the power to search the vehicle extended to things found in the vehicle and to persons travelling in it with the suspect at the time it was stopped, the crucial point being that it was information relating to the presence of B. travelling in a vehicle in possession of drugs which led the police to stop the vehicle in the first place.

THE LORD JUSTICE GENERAL (HOPE) (at p. 449): "The only issue which was raised at the trial related to the admissibility of evidence given by police officers of their search of the motor-car in which the appellant had been travelling as a passenger when it was stopped by them and in regard to the obtaining by them of evidence against the appellant in the course of the search. The sheriff held that the evidence relating to what occurred when the constable informed the appellant that they proposed to search her was admissible. It was to this single point that the application to challenge the conviction was directed, namely that the police officers who were conducting the search had no information which specifically related to the appellant when they stopped the car so their evidence of what happened when they said that they proposed to search her was inadmissible.

According to the findings which the sheriff has made, the police had received certain information to the effect that a person named Glen Banner was travelling north on the A9 in a motor-car and that he was believed to be in possession of controlled drugs. They were also made aware that there was a companion with him in the car. Acting on that information, which, it has to be stressed, related to the possession of controlled drugs by one of the occupants of the vehicle, the police officers stopped the car at Drumossie Brae. They found that its occupants were Glen Banner, who was driving the car, and the appellant, who was the front-seat passenger. The appellant was informed that she was to be detained for the purposes of a search in terms of the powers given to the police under section 23(2) of the Misuse of Drugs Act 1971 and she was then cautioned. She was then asked whether she was in possession of a controlled drug or drugs. Thereupon, without waiting to be searched, the appellant responded by producing from between her legs a piece of resinous substance which appeared to be adhering in some way to the front passenger seat and was not in fact on her person. She produced this substance to the police officer and said, 'That belongs to me.' She was taken to the police headquarters in Inverness and searched there, but nothing incriminating was found on her person. It was in the light of that evidence that the sheriff held that the appellant had in her possession cannabis resin at Drumossie Brae on the Perth to Inverness road, contrary to section 5(2) of the 1971 Act.

Section 23(2) of the 1971 Act provides that if a constable has reasonable grounds to suspect that any person is in possession of a controlled drug in contravention of the Act or of any regulations made thereunder, he may (a) search that person and detain him for the purpose of searching him and (b) search any vehicle or vessel in which the constable suspects that the drug may be found. [Counsel], who appeared for the appellant today, submitted that the sheriff had misdirected himself in finding that the police were entitled to search the appellant. That submission was made under reference to the finding to the effect that the information which they had received was that it was not the appellant who was in possession of the controlled drug but Glen Banner, who was the driver of the motor-car. [Counsel] pointed out that in the proposed adjustments for the appellant the sheriff had been asked to make a specific finding to this effect, namely that the police officers had no information causing them to suspect that Banner's companion was in possession of any controlled substance. The sheriff has not made any such finding, but he has noted in his comment on the adjustment that this was a correct statement which could already be deduced from other findings. We can therefore proceed upon the basis that the proposed adjustment correctly records the state of the police evidence.

In support of his submissions [counsel] referred to *Lucas* v *Lockhart* [(1980) S.C.C.R. Supp. 256] where a car which was being driven with a driver and two passengers in it was stopped by the police. In that case, however, the reasons why the police stopped the car was in order to make enquiries about the ownership of the vehicle. It was only when the vehicle had been stopped that they appreciated that the driver was a person with whom they had previously had dealings in connection with drug offences and they proceeded to search him. A search of one of the passengers in the car was held to be beyond their powers under section 23(2) in these circumstances. It was upon these grounds that that case was distinguished in *Campbell* v *H.M. Advocate* [1993 S.L.T. 245], which was a case where the police had received information that a car had been hired for the purpose of being used to take drugs from Glasgow to Oban. They set up a road block and stopped the car and carried out a search of all the people within the vehicle as well as of the vehicle itself. It was held that, in view of the information which they had received, the police were entitled to conclude that the appellant, who was one of the people in the vehicle, was in possession of drugs and they therefore had authority to detain and search him.

In the present case the sheriff took the view that the power to search the suspected person extended to the vehicle in which he was travelling in which the drug might be found. He said it was illogical, in exercise of that power, to include the vehicle but not any person within it, and it was on that view that he was of opinion that the inevitable inference from the statute was that the occupant or occupants of the vehicle might be searched as well as the vehicle. [Counsel] accepted that people who were found within a motor-car might be regarded as an integral part of the vehicle for this purpose, but he submitted that everything depended upon the nature of the suspicion which was entertained by the police at the outset. In this case the suspicion related to the individual and not to the vehicle, and therefore there was no basis upon which the police were entitled to search the appellant.

In our opinion, that is to take too narrow a view of the powers available to the police in the circumstances of this case. The information which the police had was that the person named Glen Banner was travelling in a motor-car in possession of the controlled drugs. They had reasonable grounds to suspect that he was in possession of controlled drugs in contravention of that Act. In terms of section 23(2) they were entitled to search him and the vehicle within which he was travelling, in order to discover whether he was carrying controlled drugs with him in the course of his journey. In our opinion, the power to search the vehicle extended to things found within the vehicle and to persons travelling in the same vehicle with the suspect at the time when it was stopped. The crucial point in this case, which distinguishes it from *Lucas* and makes it similar to *Campbell*, is that it was information relating to the presence of Banner within a vehicle in possession of drugs which led the police to stop the vehicle in the first place. It was this information which entitled the police to search both the vehicle in which he was suspected of travelling in possession of controlled drugs and the appellant, who was travelling as a passenger in that vehicle at the time when it was stopped by them."

Appeal refused.

9.3.20   **20. Wilson v. Brown**
                              1996 S.C.C.R. 470

W. was a patron at a rave, entry to which was controlled by stewards, who searched him for drugs with his consent and found nothing. The stewards later received information which led them to seek to search the appellant again. He refused to be searched and was put out of the premises. The stewards then saw him in an area known to be frequented by drug dealers. When they approached, W. threw several things to the ground which appeared to be drugs. The stewards then took W. back into the building in order to detain him pending the arrival of the police. The police came in about 20 minutes, but, before that, the stewards searched W. against his will and found drugs under his shirt. This search was carried out because it was management policy for searches to be carried out when stewards suspected that patrons might be carrying drugs.

W. was subsequently charged with possession with intent to supply of the drugs found by the stewards and at his trial objection was taken to the evidence of the search. The Crown conceded that the search was irregular, but sought to have the irregularity excused. The sheriff held that the search was justified because of the stewards' suspicions and because, in the interests of their safety, it was very prudent to search W. in case he was carrying weapons. The sheriff admitted the evidence and convicted W., who appealed to the High Court.

Held, that when regard was had to the fact that the stewards had no authority whatsoever to carry out any personal search of the appellant and bearing in mind that there was no question of urgency and that the search was carried out because they believed it was management policy to do so, the search could not properly be excused.

Observed, that if the stewards had suspected that the appellant was carrying weapons, the search might have been justified in the circumstances.

Appeal allowed and conviction quashed.

NOTE
This discussion is a matter of general application of rights and duties: for discussion, see Ferguson, "A Bouncer's Right To Search" (1996) 41 J.L.S. 227.

(ii) Section 23(3) of the 1971 Act **9.4**

1. H.M. Advocate v. Cumming **9.4.1**
1983 S.C.C.R. 15

After the panel was indicated on a charge of contravening the 1971 Act, a preliminary diet was held on joint motion of both parties. This was done to determine whether articles obtained during a search made under a warrant in terms of section 23(3) were admissible in evidence.

The warrant had been obtained after information was given on oath to a justice of the peace that there were reasonable grounds for suspecting that controlled drugs were "in the premises occupied by James Cumming, at [...]." The warrant was printed on a sheet of paper immediately below the deposition containing the information about the panel and it was undated. A date was appended to the signature of the justice of the peace. The warrant did not include the name of the authorised constable, and referred only to "the said premises at aforesaid."

Held, inter alia, that the failure to specify by name the constable authorised to enforce the warrant and the failure to specify the premises to be searched were both breaches of section 23(3). Further, these breaches were not irregularities which could be excused or condoned, but that they rendered the warrant incompetent, and that articles recovered under it would not be admissible in evidence.

Evidence inadmissible.

SHERIFF SCOTT ROBINSON (at p. 18): "Infringements of the formalities of the law in relation to matters such as search warrants and the method of their execution are not to be lightly condoned ...
And (at p. 19)
"Urgency may well excuse a search without any warrant in very special circumstances but once a warrant had been obtained I can see no reason why proper care should not have been taken to complete the warrant in proper form."

NOTE
The warrant referred to is reprinted in 1983 S.C.C.R. at p. 16. Even on the most liberal of approaches the Crown was bound to find itself in difficulty given the number of parts of the warrant left blank. For an example of the admissibility of evidence concerning controlled drugs discovered without a

warrant in circumstances of urgency, see *Walsh v. MacPhail*, 1978 S.L.T. (Notes) 29.

9.4.2   **2. Allan v. Tant**
                                      1986 S.C.C.R. 175

T. was charged with unlawful possession of opium in his house. At his summary trial evidence was led that police constables had visited his house. There a man was found smoking something that the police constable thought smelled like cannabis. One of the constables then gave sworn information to a justice of the peace that she had reasonable grounds to suspect that controlled drugs were in the possession of T. as the occupier of a locked room in his house. A search warrant was granted under section 23(3).

At the conclusion of the Crown case the sheriff sustained a submission of no case to answer and acquitted the accused. His reasoning was that the police constable who had given sworn evidence had no reasonable grounds for suspecting that controlled drugs were in the possession of any person within the locked room and outlined his reasons for so deciding. The Crown appealed to the High Court where the appeal was upheld and the case remitted to the sheriff to proceed.

THE LORD JUSTICE-CLERK (ROSS) (at p. 178): "It is thus clear that what the sheriff did was to go behind the warrant. In our opinion, this is something which he was not entitled to do. If a warrant is *ex facie* invalid, as where it contains the wrong name or address or where it is not signed, a sheriff will be justified in holding that the procedure followed thereon was unwarranted (*H.M. Advocate v. Bell* [1984 S.C.C.R. 430]). But a sheriff is not an appellate judge and he has no jurisdiction to review the granting of a warrant.

The High Court has power to suspend an illegal search warrant; *Bell v. Black and Morrison* [(1865) 5 Irv. 57] but a sheriff has no such power. Unless and until a warrant has been suspended or reduced or set aside, the warrant stands."

                                                          Appeal upheld.

9.4.3   **3. McCarron v. Allan**
                                      1988 S.C.C.R. 9

McC. was searched on the authority of a warrant in terms of section 23(3) of the 1971 Act. The warrant was for a named dwelling-house and "any persons found therein." While the police were searching that house, McC. came to the door holding a cigarette in his hand. A policeman answered the door and invited him in.

The cigarette was taken from McC. Later analysis showed the cigarette to contain cannabis resin and he was charged with unlawful possession of that controlled drug. At his trial there was an objection to the evidence of the cigarette on the basis that he had not been found in the named premises. The objection was repelled and the evidence having been allowed the charge was proven.

On appeal it was *held* that as McC. had accepted the invitation to enter the house, he was a person found therein and consequently the taking of the cigarette was authorised by the warrant and the appeal dismissed.

4. Bell v. H.M. Advocate   **9.4.4**
1988 S.C.C.R 292

B. and another were charged on indictment with contraventions of the 1971 Act. During the High Court trial the Crown sought to lead evidence obtained under search warrants bearing to be granted under section 23(3) of the 1971 Act.

The search warrant was a document consisting of a single sheet of paper. At the top of that sheet was set out the information on which was given on oath by a constable that there were grounds for suspecting the presence of drugs in specified premises. The rest of the document set out the warrant which authorised search of "the said premises".

Objection was taken to the Crown's attempt to lead the evidence referred to on the ground that the premises were not named in the warrants. The objection was repelled and convictions later followed. Appeal was taken against the trial judge's decision.

THE LORD JUSTICE GENERAL (EMSLIE) (at p. 294): "No statutory form of warrant is provided by the statute and various police authorities have devised for themselves a standard form of warrant in which there are blank spaces for the entry of various particulars."

And (at p. 295)

"[Counsel for the appellants] conceded that, if one looked at the form as a whole, there could not be the slightest doubt that the said premises in the warrant itself were the premises identified precisely in the information on oath which immediately precedes the warrant. It was accepted that, looking at the form as a whole, there was no lack of clarity as to the extent of the constable's authority under the warrant nor was there any lack of fair notice of the identity of the premises which the warrant authorised the constable to search. It could not be suggested that the appellant suffered any prejudice, but the technical argument was that section 23(3) had to be construed strictly and that what was essential to the validity of any warrant was that the premises should be 'named in the warrant.' It was not sufficient that they should be identified clearly by reference in the warrant. We were informed that objection to the validity of the Strathclyde Police warrants under section 23(3) has been taken in various courts, including the High Court, with different results. In some cases the objection had been sustained. In others the objection had been repelled ...

The test must be whether on examination of the warrant contained on the single sheet of paper the occupier of premises to whom it is shown will be able to satisfy himself that the constable has authority to search those premises. In other words, does the warrant clearly identify the premises which the constable has power to search? Section 23(3) speaks of 'the premises named in the warrant'. In our opinion it is quite unrealistic to read the warrant in this case by itself, shutting one's eyes to the information on oath which immediately precedes it on the single sheet. The warrant authorised search of 'the said premises'. The antecedent is clearly the premises at 29 Melville Street, identified in the information on oath, on the faith of which it was granted. Common sense requires us to say that in these circumstances the premises to be searched are sufficiently 'named in the warrant' within the meaning of section 23(3)."

Appeal refused.

NOTE

The warrant that formed the basis of the appeal is reprinted in the judgment with words, figures and dates in bold to indicate that they had been entered in manuscript: see *supra*, at pp. 294–5.

The point on appeal was a very narrow one but clearly required to be settled in view of the varying decisions in other cases. In particular, in *H.M. Advocate v. Scott*, unreported, High Court of Justiciary at Glasgow, March 7, 1988, Lord Clyde specifically decided the same point the other way and sustained an objection. His Lordship's reasoning is set out in an opinion which is reprinted *supra*, at pp. 296–7.

9.4.5   **5. Guthrie v. Hamilton**
                                    1988 S.C.C.R. 330

The police obtained a search warrant in terms of section 23(3) in respect of certain premises. While they were searching those premises G. called at the door. He was detained on the doorstep and was found to be in possession of cannabis. At trial for unlawful possession, objection was taken to evidence of that controlled drug as having been obtained illegally. The objection was repelled on the ground that the search was authorised by section 23(3). On conviction there was an appeal.

THE LORD JUSTICE-CLERK (ROSS) (at p. 332):"The sheriff in his note explains that he had considerable doubt as to whether the ambit of the search warrant was wide enough to authorise the police to search a person found on the doorstep of the house. [Counsel for the appellant] maintained that the sheriff was correct to have entertained these doubts. We do not agree. In our opinion the terms of the warrant were such that the police were entitled to search any person found in the premises. The premises which are referred to in the warrant are the premises at 45 Church Street, Inverkeithing. These premises must, in our opinion, include not merely the mid-terraced house itself but also the garden ground, the path leading to the front door and certainly the doorstep itself. The findings show that when police detained the appellant he was standing on the doorstep of the house. Accordingly, in our opinion, he clearly was a person who was found in the premises at that time. That being so, the police were fully justified in terms of the warrant in searching the appellant who was in the premises at the material time.

This is sufficient for the disposal of this appeal but argument was also presented to us to the effect that the police officers would not have been entitled to search and detain the appellant in terms of section 23(2) of the Act of 1971. Their right to search and detain him for the purpose of searching him under that subsection would depend upon whether they had reasonable grounds to suspect that he was in possession of a controlled drug at the time. [Counsel for the appellant] maintained that there were in the findings no objective factors supporting the proposition that they had reasonable grounds to suspect that he was in possession of drugs at the time. Under reference to *Dryburgh v. Galt* [1981 S.C.C.R. 26] and *McNicol v. Peters*, [1969 S.L.T. 261] [counsel for the appellant] addressed submissions to us on the question of whether the test was a subjective or an objective one. In our opinion, however, it is unnecessary to consider that aspect of the matter in this case. In a situation of this kind, as the Lord Justice-Clerk made plain in *McNicol v. Peters*, the real question is whether the facts and circumstances give the police reasonable grounds to entertain this particular suspicion.

In the present case the situation was that because the police had reasonable grounds to suspect that controlled drugs were in the possession of a person in the premises at 45 Church Street, they applied for and obtained a search warrant. When a caller came to the door during the search, and that caller had no obvious innocent reason for being there, we are of opinion that the police officers were justified in suspecting that the caller was a person in possession of controlled drugs. We agree that the situation might well have been different if there had been some obvious, innocent explanation for the caller's presence. If he had been a postman, or a milkman, or a visiting clergyman, then no doubt the police would not have been justified in entertaining that suspicion. But that was not the situation, and finding 10 makes it plain that each of the two constables suspected that the appellant had called at the house either to obtain or deliver drugs."

Appeal refused.

6. Baird v. H.M. Advocate   9.4.6
1989 S.C.C.R. 55

B. was charged on indictment with contraventions of the Misuse of Drugs Act 1971. Evidence had been obtained on the authority of a search warrant. That warrant was a production and it was listed on the indictment.

B. obtained a preliminary diet on the issue of whether this warrant was *ex facie* void for uncertainty as it bore to proceed on information that drugs "and/or" documents were suspected to be present.

The sheriff held that the warrant was not invalid, and B. appealed to the High Court of Justiciary.

THE LORD JUSTICE-CLERK (ROSS) (at p. 58): "The submission on the appellant's behalf was that the warrant in this case was invalid in respect that the necessary information on oath had refrained from electing between section 23(3)(*a*) and 23(3)(*b*) if the [1971] Act as being the grounds in respect of which he asserted that he had reasonable suspicion."

And later (at p. 59)

"The warrant in question contains a crave seeking a warrant and then contains the decision of the sheriff who records that he has examined the informant on oath and has considered the foregoing application and is satisfied that there is reasonable ground for suspicion. [Counsel for the appellant] maintained that there was ambiguity in the warrant but we do not agree that there is any ambiguity at all. It cannot be said that using the expression 'and/or' constitutes ambiguity. To the contrary, having read this warrant we are satisfied that the warrant is certain. As was made plain in the case of *Allan* v. *Tant* [1986 S.C.C.R. 175], it is not for the sheriff to go behind the warrant. That means that one looks at the warrant, and, looking at this warrant, we are satisfied that it is *ex facie* valid. We do not consider that the fact that the preamble contains the words 'and/or' in any way makes this warrant uncertain or *ex facie* invalid."

Appeal refused and decision of sheriff
affirmed.

9.4.7   **7. H.M. Advocate v. Strachan**
                                      1990 S.C.C.R. 341

S. was charged on indictment and at his trial in the sheriff court objection was taken to the leading of evidence obtained under a warrant on the ground that the warrant was invalid because of the absence of the designation of the sheriff concerned.

The procurator fiscal had presented a petition to the sheriff at Aberdeen craving him to take the oath of a named constable and to grant warrant to search named premises occupied by S., all in terms of section 23(3) of the 1971 Act.

The narrative of the oath and the warrant were typed and signed on the back of the petition. The narrative of the oath stated "Aberdeen, 2nd August 1989 in the presence of   compeared the said detective constable" etc. and was signed by the officer and the sheriff. It was followed by an interlocutor granting warrant as craved, and signed by the sheriff. The sheriff's signature was preceded in each case by the word "sheriff".

The sheriff at the trial repelled the objection and delivered an opinion holding that the omission of the sheriff's name and designation did not render the warrant invalid and the evidence was held to be admissible.

Objection repelled.

NOTE
It is a question of circumstances as to whether a defect can be excused: Sheriff C.N. Stoddart *Criminal Warrants* (1991) p. 109.

8. H.M. Advocate v. Rae 9.4.8
1992 S.C.C.R. 1

The accused were tried on indictment on, *inter alia*, charges under the 1971 Act in respect of which the Crown intended to lead evidence of articles found as the result of a search carried out under the authority of an *ex facie* valid warrant granted by a justice of the peace. The officer who had sworn the information on which the warrant was granted, and who had given evidence at an earlier abortive trial of the accused, was not available to give evidence. The justice who granted the warrant had indicated on precognition that she had no recollection of the warrant and that it was not her practice to seek information from a police officer who requested a warrant from her, and the Crown did not propose to call her as a witness. At the outset of the trial a motion was made by the accused for an adjournment to enable them to take a bill of suspension in the High Court with the purpose of challenging the warrant, any such challenge in the course of the trial being precluded by the decision in *Allan v. Tant*, 1986 J.C. 62.

Held (1) that the motion was competent; but (2) that it was not appropriate to grant it, because: (a) if a police officer says on oath before a justice of the peace that he has information that there is reasonable ground for suspecting the presence of drugs, the justice is entitled to grant a warrant without further enquiry and that, accordingly, it was extremely doubtful whether prima facie grounds existed for challenging the warrant; (b) it would be possible to challenge the warrant by bill or petition to the nobile officium after the trial in the event of the accused being convicted; and (c) to grant the motion would involve further delay in a trial in which the 110 days had already been extended; and motion refused.

Observed, that it might have been appropriate to obtain a preliminary diet in order to resolve what course required to be followed.

In the course of the trial, objection was taken to the leading of articles recovered under the warrant in the absence of evidence from the officer who had obtained it or the justice who had granted it.

Held, that such evidence was unnecessary, and that unless there was some reason on the face of the warrant to doubt that it had been regularly granted, it could be spoken to by any officer who had acted under its authority; and objection repelled.

LORD MCCLUSKEY (at p. 2): "Well, this is a motion made by counsel on behalf of the first accused, Gerald Rae, and concurred in by counsel acting on behalf of the second accused, Gillian McGurk or Rae, to adjourn the proceedings in the present case in order to allow a bill of suspension to be taken to a full quorum of the High Court, the purpose of that bill of suspension being to challenge the warrant which is Crown Production No. 7. That warrant, Crown Production No. 7, is conceded to be ex facie valid, but counsel seeks an opportunity by adjournment and bill of suspension to challenge the warrant on the grounds that it was not granted as required by the statute, namely the Misuse of Drugs Act 1971, section 23(3). Because the proceedings at this trial are fully recorded as required by section 274 of the Criminal Procedure (Scotland) Act 1975, I may not detail all the submissions that were made to me and I should confine myself therefore to giving my reasons for refusing this motion.

The background is that counsel informed me that this case was indicted for trial to commence on Monday, 10 June 1991 and before that date, namely on or about 6 or 7 June, the Crown had served a section 81 notice on the defence which disclosed that a witness, namely the justice of the peace who signed the warrant, Crown Production No. 7, was to be added to the list of witnesses on the indictment. It appeared that this was done because the witness George Soutar, to whom that warrant had been granted, had suffered an illness and was unable to give evidence. Following upon the service of that section 81 notice the justice of the peace whose name appeared on the notice was precognosced by agents acting for both accused persons and on the basis of the precognition it was suggested that a bill could be taken to indicate that the statutory requirements of section 23(3) had not been complied with. I should note, before I turn to the purely legal question that arises, that George Soutar, the person who applied for and received the warrant, Crown Production No. 7, apparently gave evidence as a Crown witness in earlier proceedings on the same indictment against the same accused in this court in March of 1991 and that was before he became ill of course. I was not informed that at that stage there was any challenge whatsoever to the warrant which he had obtained.

Two questions arise for me. The first is whether or not it is competent to grant a motion of the kind which is made and the second one is whether, if it be competent, I should grant it or not. I was referred to only two cases. One was *Allan* v *Tant*. That case illustrated that a trial judge cannot go behind a warrant which is ex facie valid. The reason given for that decision in the opinion of the court is to the effect that 'a sheriff is not an appellate judge and he has no jurisdiction to review the granting of a warrant. The High Court has power to suspend an illegal search warrant (*Bell* v *Black and Morrison* [(1865) 5 Irv. 57]), but a sheriff has no such power.'

In my reading of that case the reasoning would apply equally to a judge in the High Court, sitting in solemn proceedings. He is not an appellate judge when he sits in that capacity and no authority was quoted to me to show that he could suspend an illegal search warrant. In *Allan* v *Tant* [1986 J.C. 62] it was said that 'Unless and until a warrant has been suspended or reduced or set aside, the warrant stands.'

On this basis it appears that the only remedy for someone who seeks to reduce a warrant is to take proceedings before a quorum of the High Court sitting as an appellate court. No doubt that court would have power to remit to one of its number or to some other person to hear evidence if that was thought necessary, but the court itself would, in my opinion, have to decide the matter.

The other case to which I was referred was *Bell* v *Black and Morrison*. That is authority for the proposition that a warrant may be reduced after execution but it does not otherwise bear upon the problem before me. It appears to me clear that there must exist some procedure for challenging a warrant which is ex facie valid. If no procedure exists, then the person seeking to mount such a challenge would be able to use the jurisdiction of the High Court, the nobile officium jurisdiction of the High Court and that of course cannot be exercised by a single judge. I note that from a number of recent cases, and it will be sufficient to refer to one, the case of *Evans*, Petitioner [1991 S.C.C.R. 160] that if necessary, and indeed in the course of a High Court trial, the High Court of Justiciary can convene and determine an urgent matter raised by petition to the nobile officium. On the face of it, therefore, it does appear that — whether by a bill of suspension or by petition to the nobile officium asking the court to entertain a bill of suspension as a matter of extreme urgency — there must be some remedy which the person seeking to challenge the warrant could take. I am surprised that no such step has been taken since 10th or 12th June when it appears that a precognition of the justice of the peace was obtained.

I can conceive of circumstances in which the nature of the challenge was such that it would be desirable or perhaps even necessary in the interests of justice to resolve the question of the warrant by means of enquiring into the circumstances in which it came to be granted and I therefore do not rule out the possibility of granting such a motion. It appears to me it would be competent for me to grant the motion and I therefore turn now to consider whether or not I should.

I decided I should not grant it. In the first place, it appears to me to be extremely doubtful in prima facie grounds exist for challenging this warrant. In terms of the statute it is provided: 'If a justice of the peace ... is satisfied by information on oath that there is reasonable ground for suspecting' and then certain words follow, 'he may grant a warrant authorising any constable ... to enter ... the premises framed in the warrant.'

I have read the section short. It is in my opinion quite clear that the information itself which has to be placed before the justice of the peace is not necessarily information about the circumstances which had given rise to the reasonable grounds for suspecting the presence of drugs or documents envisaged by the section. If an officer of the police appears before a justice of the peace and, on oath, says that he has such information, then in my opinion the justice of the peace is entitled, without further enquiry, to grant the warrant. The court has plainly proceeded upon that view in a number of cases to which I was not referred and I should briefly mention two of them. In *Bell* v *H.M. Advocate* [1988 S.L.T. 820] the warrant which was before the court was in these terms, and I quote from p. 822:

'STRATHCLYDE POLICE

At **Glasgow** the **5th** day of **February** nineteen hundred and 87 years appears before me, one of Her Majesty's Justice of the Peace for the District of **Glasgow Brian Adams** a Constable of the Strathclyde Police, who affirms on oath that there are reasonable grounds for suspecting that controlled drugs specified in the schedule to the Misuse of Drugs Act 1971, and in contravention of said Act, and Regulations made thereunder are in the premises at **29 Melville St Glasgow** occupied by **Bell/Robertson.**'

It is plain in that case, where the validity of the warrant was upheld, [that] no more information was said to be laid before the justice of the peace than was said to be laid before the justice of the peace in the present case. A similar conclusion can be arrived at by studying the terms of the warrant contained in the case of *Baird* v *H.M. Advocate* [1989 S.C.C.R. 55]. The precognition which was read over to me, in part, or the slightly different precognition which was intimated to me by counsel for the second accused, is in terms which do not indicate that the warrant was granted by the justice of the peace without having a police constable state on oath before her that the police constable had reasonable grounds for suspicion. It appears to me therefore that the basis of the bill of suspension would be unsound and the bill would be likely to fail. Secondly, if it is competent to proceed by a bill of suspension, whether or not combined with the petition to the nobile officium, it appears to me that it would be possible to proceed by such a bill during or indeed after the trial itself and to combine such proceedings with a section 228 appeal arguing that there has been a miscarriage of justice in respect that the jury were allowed to hear evidence which should not have been admitted, it being admitted on the basis of warrant which was invalid. I also refer to the fact that, as I have indicated earlier, there has been some delay, and in the circumstances I do not consider it a justifiable delay, in proceeding to apply to the High Court by petition to the nobile officium.

The last consideration is that this is the second trial involving these charges and these accused persons. I was informed on Friday [14 June 1991] when this matter was first before me that the 110-day period had already been extended and indeed I had to extend it myself again on that occasion for seven days. Plainly, if I were to grant the present motion and allow a bill of suspension to begin its progress through the system, I would have to extend the 110-day period yet again. It appears to me to be contrary to the whole spirit of the legislation about delay in relation to trials. I should add also that the proper course in my view might have been — although in the absence of any fuller argument on it I don't want to express a final view on it — to apply to the court under section 76 of the 1975 Act and to obtain a preliminary diet in order to resolve what course required to be followed and this of course was not done. I should say, finally, I am disappointed that the arguments presented to me were so thin and showed little sign of the careful research to which the High Court is properly entitled. Of course, I sympathise with counsel who had been instructed late, but it has been the practice in my experience for counsel not to make that a reason for not doing full research and I am not satisfied that I had a full argument presented to me on all these matters. I shall refuse the motion."

Thereafter, in the course of the trial, objection was taken to evidence of articles recovered under the search warrant.

On June 17, 1991 Lord McCluskey delivered the following opinion.

LORD McCLUSKEY (at p. 5): "This is an objection taken to the line of evidence. There is no question unanswered at the present time. At present the police officer was asked, 'Did Detective Inspector Pollock produce a warrant?' and the answer to that question was, 'Yes, he did', and at that point objection was taken to the line of evidence. It was made clear that the objection is to be taken in relation to everything that followed upon the attempt by police officers to proceed on the authority of Crown Production No. 7, which bears to be a warrant to conduct certain searches at 43 Gartside Street, Glasgow, occupied by Rae.

The Crown have already made it plain that the court is not to hear the evidence either of the police officer named on that warrant and signing as 'informant' or of the justice of the peace who, on the face of the warrant, apparently granted it at Glasgow on 30 November 1990. The underlying question is therefore whether or not any such evidence is necessary. It is plain from the case of *Allan* v *Tant* that if no warrant is ex facie valid there can be no enquiry at the trial into the circumstances lying behind the granting of it. It is also plain from the case of *Bulloch* v *H.M. Advocate* [1980 S.L.T. (Notes) 5] that an ex facie defect in a warrant cannot be cured by leading evidence at the trial. Accordingly it is difficult to see what point there can be in presenting such evidence to the jury.

Against that background I consider the case of *Boyle* v *H.M. Advocate* [1990 S.C.C.R. 480], to which I have been referred. Although that was a case dealing with a warrant granted under the Taxes Management Act 1970, section 20, as amended, both the sheriff and the court made certain observations in relation to the procedure at common law or under the Misuse of Drugs Act, section 23(3), which is the statutory provision which governs the present case. Although these observations are obiter, at least in the sense that what was being decided in *Boyle* was the validity of a notice in writing issued under the provisions of the 1970 Act, none the less these observations are of high authority insofar as they deal with the position of ... common law warrants or warrants under section 20(3) of the Misuse of Drugs Act 1971.

The passage upon which both counsel have made submissions was that of the opinion of the court read by the Lord Justice-General on p. 489C, and I quote: 'Unless there be some reason on the face of the notices themselves to doubt that the procedure has been regularly carried through as required by the statute, it is sufficient that the notices themselves are produced and spoken to by the investigator to demonstrate that the appropriate procedure has been followed.'

In the context these observations are intended to apply to warrants granted at common law or under section 23(3) of the Misuse of Drugs Act 1971. It is plain that a warrant which authorises a search of this character can be granted by a sheriff on the petition or request of the procurator fiscal and neither of these officers would give evidence. It appears to me that by analogy and indeed by reference to the passage quoted from the opinion of the court, the same rule applies here. If the notices themselves appear, on their face, to the valid then they can be spoken to by any person authorised by the notice itself to use it, and in this case the warrant is to authorise either the informant, Constable Soutar, or any constable of Strathclyde Police to enter the premises and to search or carry out certain other activities there. It appears to me that any such constable acting within the terms of that warrant is properly in the role of 'investigator' within the meaning of the passage contained in the opinion of the court in *Boyle* and accordingly I repel the objection to the line of evidence and will do so formally when the court reconvenes tomorrow morning."

At the close of the Crown case all the charges against the second accused were withdrawn, and she was acquitted. At the conclusion of the trial on June 21, 1991 the first accused was acquitted of all the charges against him.

Accused acquitted.

9. Main v. Lockhart
1993 S.C.C.R. 347

M. was stopped by a police officer in the course of a routine check while he was driving his car. The officer received information that M. had previous convictions for drugs offences. The officer saw a carrier bag lying on the floor of the car. M. told him that it contained money but refused to allow him to search it. M. was allowed to drive off, but was stopped shortly afterwards by the same officer and two colleagues. A search was then made and the bag was found to contain over £16,000. M. was detained on suspicion of theft of the money.

Thereafter another constable obtained a warrant under section 23(3) of the 1971 Act to search M.'s house. M. was subsequently charged on summary complaint with possession of drugs, contrary to section 5(2) and (3) of the 1971 Act. Prior to his trial he brought a bill of suspension seeking to have the search warrant declared invalid on the ground that there was no reasonable ground to suspect the presence of drugs in his house.

Held, that the presence of the money in M.'s car and his previous convictions provided a reasonable basis for suspecting that the money was the result of activities in connection with the supply of drugs and that evidence relating to that activity might be present within his premises.

Bill refused.

10. McKelvie v. Macnaughton   9.4.10
High Court of Justiciary, unreported, July 4, 1995

McK., the complainer in this appeal, was charged with possession of controlled drugs. Prior to the trial a Bill of Suspension was taken to suspend *simpliciter* a warrant granted in terms of section 23(3) of the 1971 Act to search the complainer's house for controlled drugs. The Bill averred that no reasonable grounds existed at the time of the application for the grant of the warrant for suspecting that controlled drugs were in McK.'s possession at his house.

The circumstances were that on September 23, 1994 an unsealed envelope was posted through the letter box of a certain house in Peterhead. The occupants of the house opened the envelope and found that it contained £600 in £20 notes, together with a handwritten note stating that more money was to be delivered the following afternoon. The house was two doors away from a David Stephen's house and police officers had received information to the effect that he was concerned in the supply of controlled drugs and that he regularly travelled to the north of England to uplift drugs which he would then take to Peterhead to an unknown person who on receiving the drugs would distribute them.

The occupants of the house contacted the police and handed the money, envelope and handwritten note to them. They were asked to inform the police should anyone call to claim the money. The following day David Stephen called at the house and explained to the occupant that someone who was due him money had inadvertently put it through the wrong letter box and asked the occupant if he had knowledge of the money. The occupant said that he had received the money and had handed it over to the police. The same David Stephen and McK. attended at Peterhead Police Office and explained to police officers there how David Stephen had loaned McK. the money to buy a motor vehicle and that McK. had posted the money through the wrong letter box. The police officers did not believe this information and were of the opinion that the money was connected to a drugs deal.

Both McK. and David Stephen were detained in terms of section 2 of the Criminal Justice (Scotland) Act 1980 and the warrant to search McK.'s house was obtained from a justice of the peace. During the search of McK.'s house cannabis resin and cocaine were found.

Held, that there was reasonable grounds to suspect that controlled drugs were to be found at the complainer's house on the basis: (1) that the police had information that David Stephen was a drugs dealer; (2) that the envelope contained a large sum of money made up in £20 notes, which was a denomination commonly associated with drug dealers, and a note stating that more money was to be delivered the following day; (3) the complainer had associated himself with David Stephen in that the two of them together had presented themselves at the police station seeking the return of the money; and (4) they put forward an explanation which the police officers did not believe.

The justice of the peace was therefore entitled to grant the warrant and the court refused to pass the Bill.

Appeal refused.

NOTE
This case is reported as Crown Officer Circular No. A23/95.

9.4.11   **11. Hammond v. Howdle**
                                           1996 S.L.T. 1174

Two accused persons were charged on separate indictments libelling *inter alia* contraventions of section 5(2) of the 1971 Act. On the day before the alleged offences the police had applied to the sheriff for a search warrant on the basis that there were reasonable grounds for suspecting that controlled drugs were in the possession of a person or persons on the premises of a named public house. The sheriff granted the warrant. The accused in due course sought suspension of the warrant on the ground that as the police intended to search patrons of the public house, whoever they might be, they had no proper basis for seeking the warrant under section 23(3) of the 1971 Act.

Held, that the crucial point was the connection between controlled drugs and the premises and it was not necessary that a view should be formed as to precisely who was in possession of the drugs; and bill refused.

THE LORD JUSTICE GENERAL (HOPE): "No point has been taken in the argument today by counsel for the complainers about the manner of the execution of the warrant. His argument was directed only to the question whether it was granted in accordance with the power given by s. 23(3) of the Act. In terms of that subsection, if a justice of the peace, a magistrate or a sheriff is satisfied by information on oath that there is reasonable ground for suspecting that any controlled drugs are, in contravention of the Act or any regulations made thereunder, in the possession of a person on any premises, he may grant a warrant authorising any constable acting for the police area in which the premises are situated at any time or times within one month from the date of the warrant to enter, if need be by force, the premises named in the warrant and to search the premises and any person found therein. The basis upon which the warrant was granted in this case is challenged is that the requirements of the statute were not fulfilled, in respect that it was not known by the police who were to be in the premises so they were not in a position to say that they had reasonable grounds for suspecting that any particular person would be on these premises in the possession of controlled drugs in contravention of the statute.

The application which was made to the sheriff by the constable stated: 'It appears to the informant, from information received by him, that there are reasonable grounds for suspecting (a) that controlled drugs are specified in Sched 2 to the Misuse of Drugs Act 1971, as amended, are, in contravention of said Act or regulations made thereunder, in the possession of a person or persons on the premises at the Blue Bull hotel, including that part thereof known as the Kat House, High Street, Lockerbie, occupied by Alistair McLeod, and (b) that document as specified in s. 23(3)(b) of said Act are in the possession of a person or persons at said premises.'

Following upon that preamble the informant craved a warrant in the terms prescribed in subs. (3). On the face of this application it was framed entirely in accordance with the provisions of the subsection, and we have found nothing in its terms which would suggest that there was no proper basis upon which the sheriff could grant a warrant in the exercise of the power given to him by the statute.

As regards the argument that the police were not in possession of any information which would enable them to suspect that any particular person was in possession of controlled drugs on these premises, counsel drew our attention to ans. 4 in the answers for the respondent. In that answer it is admitted that the intention of the police was to search patrons of the public house for drugs. It is also admitted that the police were not in a position, at the date of the application for the warrant, to specify those persons they wished to search, nor were they in a position to charge any person. It is explained that they were not aware of individual persons who would attend said premises, but that they had reasonable grounds to suspect that controlled drugs would be in possession of persons on said premises. The argument was that in the light of that answer it was clear that the police had no proper basis for seeking a warrant in terms of para (a) of s. 23(3) of the Act.

In our opinion that argument is based upon a misunderstanding of the basis upon which a warrant may be sought under this paragraph. What is required is that there should be reasonable grounds for suspecting that 'a person' on the premises concerned is in possession of controlled drugs. It is not necessary that a view should be formed as to precisely who that person may be. The name of the person is not important, and indeed counsel did not suggest that it was. Nor is it important that in any other way the individual or individuals should be identified. The crucial point is the connection between controlled drugs and the premises, and the existence of a reasonable ground for suspecting that a person on the premises, whoever he or she may be, is in possession of the controlled drugs. It seems to us that the averments and admissions in ans. 4 in no way contradict the basis upon which this warrant was being sought under para (1) in terms of the information which was put before the sheriff. This was a warrant which was obtained in accordance with the statutory provisions, and we are not persuaded that there is any ground for holding that it was invalid. Accordingly we shall refuse to pass the bill in each case."

Appeal refused.

9.4.12   **12. Rollo v. H.M. Advocate**
                          1996 S.C.C.R. 874

The police, acting under a warrant, took possession of a Memomaster, which was described as an electronic notepad, access to the contents of which was controlled by a password. The Memomaster was an essential production in the trial of R. for contraventions of the 1971 Act. He was convicted and appealed to the High Court on the ground that the contents of the Memomaster were inadmissible in evidence because it was not a document in terms of section 23(3)(b).

Held, that the essence of a document is that it is something containing recorded information of some sort, and that it does not matter that the information requires to be processed in some way such as translation, decoding or electronic retrieval, or that it is protected in some way against unwanted access.

Observed, that section 23(3)(b) is limited to documents of the kind described in the subsection, and does not confer on the police power to remove other items such as coins or tombstones which fall within the meaning of "documents" but plainly are not related to or concerned with the transactions or dealings to which the subsection refers.

Appeal refused.

(iii) Section 23(4) of the 1971 Act **9.5**

1. Farrow v. Tunnicliffe **9.5.1**
[1976] Crim.L.R. 126

Police constables were not satisfied with a superficial search of F. and a girlfriend whom they suspected of supplying a controlled substance. F. and the girlfriend were detained and taken to a police station for a more thorough search. As a result of an incident on the way to the police station, F. was charged with intentionally obstructing a constable in the exercise of his powers under the 1971 Act.

At a summary trial it was argued that the power to detain did not include the power to take a person away to search him. This argument was rejected by the justice who convicted F. and he appealed.

Held, that section 23(2)(*a*) gave the police the right to search and detain a suspect for the purpose of searching him and this was intended to operate parallel to section 24 which gave the police the right of arrest on suspicion of certain offences. F.'s argument that the police constables ought to have arrested him before taking him away failed. Further, if a male constable wished a female subject to be searched it was obviously right that he could take the suspect to a police station to be searched by a female police constable.

Appeal dismissed.

2. R. v. Forde **9.5.2**
(1985) 81 Cr.App.R. 19

F. was seen to be in a group of four people in an area frequented by drug addicts and F. later conceded that he was a drug addict. The two police constables saw something being passed to F. who started to walk away. He was called upon to stop but he did not. When a policeman caught up with him, F. put something in his mouth and swallowed it. He was arrested and later said that it was a drug obtained on prescription. F. was charged with contravening section 23(4)(*a*) by intentionally obstructing a constable in the exercise of his powers under section 23. On being convicted, F. appealed on the ground that there were said to be defects in the summing-up.

LORD LANE, C.J. (at p. 22): "Putting the terms of section 23(4)(*a*) into perhaps more conventional language, X, the defendant commits an offence if he does any act which obstructs a constable who is lawfully detaining him or trying to detain him for the purpose of searching him for illicit drugs. Providing that — there are two provisos to be observed — X knows that the constable is detaining him or trying to detain him in order to search him for drugs; and, secondly, the obstruction is intentional, that is to say the act viewed objectively, through the eyes of a bystander, did obstruct the constable's detention or search, and viewed subjectively, that is to say through the eyes of the defendant himself, was intended to obstruct.

If the detainee was of course told in terms what the reasons were for his detention, then that puts the question of his knowledge beyond doubt. But there may be very many occasions, of which this is one, where the detaining act has to be done before the constable has an opportunity to explain what it is that he is doing and why he is doing it. But whatever the circumstances may be, if the jury are satisfied that the reasons are obvious, and must have been so to the detainee, the requirement in our judgment is satisfied."

Appeal dismissed.

9.5.3   **3. Carmichael v. Brannan**
                              1985 S.C.C.R. 234

Four men were charged with contravening section 23(4)(*a*). When the case was first called, a plea to the relevancy was taken. The charge on the complaint narrated that, having been informed of the existence of a lawful search warrant, various actions were done *viz.*, refusing to open a door, jumping from a verandah to the ground, jumping from one verandah to another for concealment, and swallowing certain items. The sheriff held that in view of the terms of section 23(1)(*a*) and the expression "intentionally obstruct", the charge was relevant if only in relation to the refusal to open the door to the policemen. The Crown appealed to the High Court against the decision that the remaining actions described were irrelevant. The High Court allowed the appeal and remitted the case to the sheriff to proceed as accords.

LORD CAMERON (at p. 239): "The word 'obstructs' [in relation to s. 23(4)(*a*)] stands by itself unconditioned in its association with other substantives, and relates to obstruction of a person in exercise of his powers under the Act. In order to ascertain what are the limits of the offence it is necessary to see what these powers are; these are powers exercisable under a warrant granted by a magistrate in virtue of section 23(3). Such a warrant empowers a search of premises and *any persons found therein* (emphasis added) [by his Lordship] ...

The word 'obstructs' stands by itself in the relevant section of the Act, unconditioned and uncontrolled by the presence of other verbs in the context of the subsection. The only limitation to be placed on the interpretation of 'obstructs' is that the obstructing must be intentional in order that an offence be committed. There is no basis, as was the case in [*Curlett* v. *McKechnie*, 1938 J.C. 176] ... for the construction to be limited by the application of the ejusdem generis rule. In these circumstances the word itself is capable of use to describe actual physical restraint or hindrance or can be used in a figurative sense, so that in my opinion anything done which is done with intention to hinder officers in the discharge of their duty under the warrant renders the doer obnoxious to the charge which is brought here against all the respondents. The offence is therefore not limited to personal and physical obstruction of officers in discharge of their duty. To place or to seek to place oneself in a position where a search of the person cannot be achieved is as much a breach of the section as physical resistance or opposition to a search of the person. The only limiting or controlling factor is, as I have said, that the obstruction be 'intentional', a word which does not require further exposition except perhaps to note that 'intentional' is the opposite of accidental ...

The action of [one of the respondents] ... in swallowing a substance for the time being at least, effectively withdrew that substance from examination and, if necessary, possession by the officers and, if that action were proved, would in my opinion be one of intentional obstruction of the officers in execution of their duty."

4. Butler v. Lowe   9.5.4
1990 G.W.D. 13–651

B. appealed against conviction under section 23(4)(a) of the 1971 Act.

Held, that the police had reasonable grounds for suspecting that B. might be in possession of a controlled drug, although none was subsequently found, where B. was in a group in a public house and one member was seen to light a cannabis cigarette.

Appeal refused.

NOTE
cf. Gauld v. Normand, 1996 G.W.D. 1–7 where there were five factors which taken together constituted reasonable grounds for suspecting possession of a controlled drug, *viz.* (i) a locus known for drug dealing; (ii) hesitation on seeing the police; (iii) placing something in the mouth on seeing the police; (iv) a stranger at the known locus; and (v) a swallowing of the items in the mouth.

5. Dunne v. Normand   9.5.5
1993 G.W.D. 3–155

D. had been observed by two police officers making what they suspected was a "reefer type cigarette" containing cannabis, and on being approached he had ripped it up and thrown it to the ground.

Held, there was sufficient evidence for conviction under section 23(4)(a) of the 1971 Act for obstructing the police in the exercise of their powers under section 23 of the Act. No evidence had been led that the part of the cigarette recovered had contained cannabis or another illicit substance, but since there was no other explanation for D.'s behaviour the sheriff had been entitled to conclude that he had known that the police were intending to act under the powers conferred by section 23 of the Act.

THE LORD JUSTICE-CLERK (ROSS): "This is an appeal by Martin Dunne. He is appealing by means of a stated case against his conviction on charge (2) on a complaint, that was a charge of contravening section 23(4)(a) of the Misuse of Drugs Act 1971. The charge libelled that he had intentionally obstructed two police officers in the exercise of their powers under section 23 of the Act of 1971 and attempted to destroy a reefer-type cigarette.

[Counsel] appeared for the appellant today and has put forward the appeal on his behalf. She drew attention to the terms of section 23 of the Misuse of Drugs Act 1971 …

Reference should also be made in this connection to section 23(2)(c) which empowers a constable to seize and detain, for the purpose of proceedings under the Act, anything found in the course of a search which appears to the constable to be evidence of an offence under the Act. For the sake of completeness we also refer to section 23(4) which makes it an offence if a person intentionally obstructs a person in the exercise of his powers under section 23.

The circumstances giving rise to this prosecution are clearly contained in finding 3 in the stated case. That finding is in the following terms. 'When seen by police constables, the appellant was in the process of making a long cigarette consisting of two lengths of normal cigarette paper filled with tobacco. The police officers were suspicious that the appellant was rolling a cigarette containing cannabis known as a "reefer-type cigarette". The police officers approached the appellant. They intended to detain the appellant under section 23 of the Misuse of Drugs Act 1971 in order to search the appellant and seize the reefer-type cigarette as a production. The appellant was not aware that the police officers were approaching him until the police officers were some two feet from him, when the appellant looked up. When he saw the police officers he stood up, ripped up the reefer-type cigarette and threw it on the ground. The appellant was only spoken to by police officers after this time.'

The subsequent findings reveal that the police officers recovered some of the reefer-type cigarette from the ground and there was no evidence that it had contained cannabis or any other illicit substance.

[Counsel] maintained that the appellant could not be convicted of the charge because there was no finding in fact that he had known what the police officers were intending when they approached him. It is true that there is no express finding to that effect but the matter is dealt with by the sheriff in his note and in the course of his note he expresses the view that there was ample evidence to show that the appellant knew that the police intended to act under the powers conferred upon them under section 23 of the Act of 1971 because, as soon as he saw them, he tore up the reefer-type cigarette which he was in the process of making. As the sheriff puts it, the tearing up was deliberate and not accidental.

It is plain from the terms of finding 3 that events all took place very quickly. The appellant was not apparently aware of the presence of the police officers, nor that they were approaching him, until they were only two feet away from him. It appears that as soon as he saw them he stood up and attempted to destroy the reefer-type cigarette which he was in the course of making. In these circumstances we are not surprised that the sheriff concluded that the only reasonable explanation for his behaviour was that he was obstructing the police officers. [Counsel] was unable to suggest any other explanation for the appellant's behaviour as soon as he saw the police officers.

The appellant himself gave evidence in this case and gave a different account of events. He maintained that he was smoking an ordinary cigarette and that when he had finished it, he stubbed it out on the ground. He denied rolling any cigarette and maintained that he had finished his cigarette as the police were coming towards him. That evidence was plainly not accepted by the sheriff, who says that he did not believe the appellant's evidence and considered he was lying. The result is that no other explanation was put forward by the appellant for the behaviour which the sheriff has described in finding 3.

In these circumstances, it appears to us that there was indeed sufficient evidence to justify the sheriff in drawing the inference that the appellant must have known that the police were intending to act under the powers conferred upon them by section 23 of the Act of 1971, since that is the only possible explanation for his behaving as he did."

Appeal refused.

NOTE
The Opinion of the court is reproduced at 1993 S.C.C.R. 713.

6. Annan v. McIntosh   **9.5.6**
1993 S.C.C.R. 938

McI. was charged on summary complaint with a contravention of section 23(4)(a) of the 1971 Act in that he obstructed two constables "who were then in the exercise of their powers" under the section "and did put an article into [his] mouth" and swallow it. He took a plea to the relevancy of the charge on the grounds that it did not specify that the constables had reason to suspect that the article in question was a controlled drug, or what powers they were exercising at the time. The sheriff upheld the plea and dismissed the charge. The prosecutor appealed to the High Court by bill of advocation.

Held, (1) (the respondent conceding the point) that it was not necessary to libel that the article was or was suspected to be a controlled drug; and

(2) that, although more specification would have been preferable, it was not necessary to make it clear whether the police were acting under section 23(2) or 23(3), there being no other relevant powers and no relevant difference when it came to the actions of the respondent between the two powers; and bill passed and case remitted to the sheriff to proceed as accords.

THE LORD JUSTICE GENERAL (HOPE) (at p. 940): "The principal issue which was raised in the debate, according to the report by the sheriff, was whether it was necessary for the charge to state that the article which the respondent put into his mouth, chewed and then swallowed was a controlled drug or, in any event, that the police officers had reasonable grounds for suspecting that that article was a controlled drug. The sheriff concluded that it was necessary for one or other of these matters to be specified in the charge in order to make it relevant. As he puts it in his appeal, there would not be a contravention of section 23 unless the officers were being obstructed or hindered in the execution of their duty, which was to seize controlled drugs. Accordingly, for the respondent to put something in his mouth and swallow it once the officers had commenced to exercise their powers was not in itself a breach of the section.

The Lord Advocate drew our attention to the discussion of this point in *Carmichael* v *Brannan* [1985 S.C.C.R. 234]. In that case the charge alleged that officers were in possession of a lawful search warrant and that one of the accused, named Stephen Francis Pollard, in knowledge that that was the case and that the officers had obtained entry in the exercise of the warrant for the purposes of a search, had placed an unknown substance into his mouth and swallowed it, contrary to section 23(4)(a) of the Act. At p. 240 Lord Cameron observed that the suggestion that the swallowing of an unknown substance could not be construed as seeking to hide evidence of a crime was fallacious. He went on to say this. 'The object was in the possession of Pollard and his person was liable to be searched, and it was clearly an object which could be comprised in the search and, if its character was or appeared to be of a criminal character, liable to be taken possession of and taken for examination.'

As the Lord Advocate put it under reference to that discussion, the circumstances under which the action was said to have been taken by the respondent indicated an intention to defeat the search which was being conducted. So the sheriff was not right in concluding that it was necessary for the libel to state in terms that the article was a controlled drug or was suspected to be such by the police officers.

We need not elaborate upon this point because [counsel] accepted, in the light of what was said in *Carmichael* v *Brannan*, that this part of the sheriff's reasoning was unsound. He went on, however, to draw attention to what he maintained was a lack of specification in the charge about the nature of the powers which the police officers were exercising at the time.

All that is stated in the charge is that the police officers were then in the exercise of their powers under section 23 of the Act. The sheriff has assumed, for the purposes of his report, that the power which was being exercised was that under section 23(3), that is to say, the power conferred on police officers when a warrant has been issued to them in terms of this subsection. We were informed by the Lord Advocate that that was the position in the present case and that this was the power which the police officers were seeking to exercise. Nevertheless, said [counsel], the charge ought to have stated that a warrant was in existence and that the respondent had been informed that that was the case in order to provide a relevant basis for a complaint under section 23(4)(a).

In our opinion it would have been preferable for more specification to have been given on this in the charge and we note that this was done in the charge to which the argument in *Carmichael* v *Brannan* was addressed. On the other hand, when one considers the structure of section 23, it is clear that the powers to which reference is made in subsection 4(a) must be powers under subsection (2) or under subsection (3). There are no other relevant powers so far as the present case is concerned and there is no relevant difference as far as we have been able to detect, when it comes to the actions of the respondent as libelled in this case between these two powers. In either case what the police officers were confronted with in the course of this search was a person who was swallowing an article, from which it could be inferred that it was his intention to defeat any search of his person which they might carry out. It does not therefore appear to us that there is any material point to be made as to which of the two powers specified in the subsection was being exercised in this case. It would, of course, be necessary as a matter of evidence to establish that the police officers were in the exercise of powers given to them by the section. But that is a separate matter and we consider that the charge itself was sufficiently relevant to enable evidence to that effect to be led."

Appeal allowed.

NOTE

Swallowing or attempting to swallow substances in order to keep them from the police is fairly common: see *Carmichael v. Smith*, 1990 G.W.D. 36–2054; *McGeachie v. H.M. Advocate*, 1994 G.W.D. 12–743; and *Malcolm v. Walkingshaw*, 1994 G.W.D. 17–1062. There are, however, other means of obstructing the police: in *Wilson v. H.M. Advocate*, 1987 G.W.D. 26–992 the appellant merely ran away when arrest was imminent, actions which were described by the court as being "at the bottom end of the scale." In *Hamilton v. H.M. Advocate*, 1991 G.W.D. 2–107 the substance of interest to the police was thrown on a fire, and in *Young v. H.M. Advocate*, 1991 G.W.D. 16–984 the item was thrown out of a window: see also *Gilmour v. H.M. Advocate*, 1992 G.W.D. 38–2247. In *Brown v. Russell*, 1995 G.W.D. 22–1215 the appellant ran upstairs, remained there for some time and then returned to the front door and attempted to prevent the police from entering the house. A different order of seriousness is *Marshall v. Normand*,

1996 G.W.D. 18–1054, where the appellant injected himself with a substance in a syringe on being confronted by police officers, and in doing so he caused blood to spray in the direction of the police officers, causing a potential health hazard. It would seem to be a reasonable inference from the brief dicta in these cases that the sentencing rule is that the less serious the obstruction the greater the likelihood that a sentence for obstructing is ordered to run concurrently with other related charges.

CHAPTER TEN

Statutory defences

10.1

Introduction

10.2

The Misuse of Drugs Act 1971 provides by section 28 for certain statutory defences related to knowledge. The aim of the section appears to be to limit criminal responsibility that would otherwise apply as a result of strict possession and the "container" case law. Section 28 provides for a general defence of lack of knowledge (such as ignorance or mistake of fact) in relation to certain offences.

CASES

10.3

1. McKenzie v. Skeen
1983 S.L.T. 121

10.3.1

THE LORD JUSTICE GENERAL (EMSLIE) (at p. 121): "It will be observed at once that this subsection [section 28(2)] is extraordinary in that it appears to restrict the prescribed defence to proof of ignorance 'of the existence of some fact ... which it is necessary for the prosecution to prove.' Why it was thought necessary so to provide is astonishing since no conviction could possibly be returned on the evidence as a whole unless the Crown proved all that required to be proved."

Appeal allowed.

NOTE
This case is discussed *supra* at paragraph **5.3.19** in relation to possession of controlled drugs.

2. R. v. Ashton-Rickhardt
[1978] 1 All E.R. 173

10.3.2

A.-R. was found asleep in his car late at night by the police. The police searched the car and found a reefer cigarette in the pocket of the driver's door. On analysis that cigarette was found to contain cannabis resin. A.-R. denied that the reefer was his but stated that no-one else had been in the car with him that night. He was charged with unlawful possession of a controlled drug contrary to section 5(2) of the 1971 Act.

The trial judge's charge to the jury omitted an assertion that the burden of proving knowledge by A.-R. of the presence in the car of the article containing the controlled drug rested on the Crown and directed that it was for A.-R. to disprove that he had knowledge that the article was in the car or that it contained a controlled drug. A.-R. was convicted and appealed.

ROSKILL, L.J. (at p. 178): "[I]t is sought to say that the effect of section 28(1) and (2) and perhaps (3) of the 1971 Act is to alter the meaning to be given to 'possession' so that the Crown no longer has to prove beyond reasonable doubt that the accused person knew that he had the 'thing', as it has been called, in his possession. Counsel for the Crown did not shrink from saying that section 28 removed from the shoulders of the Crown on to those of the accused the 'burden of disproof' of knowledge that he had the 'thing' in his possession …

The argument is that the effect of [section 28(2) and (3)] … is to put the whole burden of disproving knowledge on the accused. We think that argument is wrong as a matter of construction of the section … whatever the precise scope of the various subsections of section 28 may be, their manifest purpose is to afford a defence to an accused person where no defence had previously existed …

It would be very odd indeed if one effect of section 28, which we said a moment ago is plainly designed to afford a defence where no defence had previously existed, was at the same time to remove from the shoulders of the Crown the burden of proof of one of the essential elements of the offence as stated by the House of Lords in *Warner* v. *Metropolitan Police Comr.* [[1968] 2 All E.R. 356]. It seems to us plain that there is nothing in section 28 which in any way alters the burden which rests on the Crown so that when they seek to prove unlawful possession of a controlled drug, proof of possession involves proof of knowledge by the accused that he had control of the 'thing' in question, as the House of Lords decided in *Warner's* case."

(At p. 179)

"In our view, 'possession' in section 5(1) and (2) means the same as the House of Lords held it to mean in *Warner* v. *Metropolitan Police Comr.* and section 28 does not in any way affect that meaning."

Appeal allowed.

NOTE

R. v. Ashton-Rickhardt is discussed in detail in the article by Ribero and Perry "Possession and Section 28 of the Misuse of Drugs Act 1979" [1979] Crim.L.R. 90. There the writers argue that there can be discerned in the case law at least eight distinct "modes or situations" of possession. These are considered in regard to the operation of section 28. That article cannot be considered fully without reference to a reply: Mathias, "The Application of Section 28 of the Misuse of

Drugs Act 1971 to Possession" [1980] Crim.L.R. 689. Ribero and Perry conclude (at p. 107) that section 28(2) is incapable of application in respect of the possession of controlled drugs. That proposition is based on one of the principles from *R. v. Ashton-Rickhardt, supra,* at p. 178 that section 28 provides fresh defences which come into play upon the prosecution discharging their burden of proof in establishing a prima facie case of possession. Mathias (at p. 692) finds the phrase "it shall be a defence" in section 28(2) to be ambiguous in meaning either that provision is being made for a new defence or that an onus of proof is being placed on the accused. Mathias prefers the latter and submits (at p. 693) that in *R. v. Ashton-Rickhardt* the Court of Appeal wrongly rejected the submission that section 28(2) puts the burden of proving absence of knowledge upon the accused in order to rebut the prima facie case established by the prosecution on proof of custody of a controlled drug. The problem is essentially a matter of the construction of legislation.

3. R. v. Champ
(1981) 73 Cr.App.R. 367

10.3.3

LAWTON, L.J. (at p. 369): "[O]n the clear terms of the statute the burden of proof was on [the accused]".

NOTE
   This case is discussed at paragraph **6.3.3** in relation to section 6 of the 1971 Act.

4. R. v. Young
[1984] 2 All E.R. 164

10.3.4

Y., a soldier in Germany, had previously sold a man a small quantity of lysergide. A further meeting was arranged for the same purpose. As Y. and the men were negotiating a sale the police arrested Y. and as they approached Y. he swallowed what he had in his hand. He later vomited and the substance was recovered and analysed. Y. had been drinking although assessments varied as to the degree of intoxication. There was at the trial by court martial strong evidence from the defence that Y. was seriously affected by drink and was almost incapable.

   Y.'s condition was an important issue and his defence to a charge of possessing a controlled drug with intent to supply it rested on section 28(2) and (3) of the 1971 Act. The assistant Judge Advocate-General had directed the court that it was not a relevant consideration that Y. was, by reason of his intoxication, unable to hold a belief or register a suspicion that what he had in his possession was a controlled drug. The court was further directed that the test to be applied was that of the belief or suspicion of a reasonable sober man. On conviction the appeal focused principally on the direction referred to.

KILNER BROWN, J. (at p. 671): "For the appellant it is contended that 'had reason to suspect' [in section 28(3)(*b*)(i)] is not the same thing as 'reasonable grounds for belief.' Reliance is placed on the decision of the Divisional Court in *Jaggard* v. *Dickinson* [1980] 3 All E.R. 716, [1981] Q.B. 527. That is authority not binding on this court, but nevertheless persuasive for the proposition that, where there is an exculpatory statutory defence of honest belief, self-induced intoxication is a factor which must be considered in the context of a subjective consideration of the individual state of mind. The objective test of a reasonable sober man is irrelevant. Accepting and applying this decision as we do, it would lead to the conclusion that, in so far as the belief and suspicion are concerned, there would have been a misdirection in the instant case. But it leaves untouched the problem created by the introduction of the third limb, which is an integral part of the exculpatory defence. The remaining question is whether a reason is something entirely personal and individual, calling for an entirely subjective consideration, or involves the wider concept of an objective rationality. We are of the opinion that it is the latter. It follows therefore that, in our judgment, it was correct direction that the self-induced intoxication did not avail. Moreover, it was an unnecessary gloss to introduce the concept of the reasonable sober man. Nevertheless, this gloss did not vitiate the fundamental direction that the self-intoxication was no defence. The drunkenness relied on could not assist in considering whether or not the accused had no reason to suspect. The effect of this conclusion is that self-induced intoxication is not a relevant consideration in exercise of this statutory defence."

Appeal dismissed.

NOTE

When the burden of proof does shift to the accused under section 28, the standard of proof is on a balance of probabilities: *R. v. Carr-Briant* [1943] K.B. 607. Fortson, *The Law on the Misuse of Drugs* (1988), notes (at p. 159) that the accused is also required to meet a subjective and an objective test if his defence is under section 28(2) or 28(3)(*b*)(i). Thus he must prove: "(i) that he did not know the existence of the relevant fact (subjective); and "(ii) that he did not suspect the existence of the same (again subjective); and "(iii) that he had no reason to suspect the existence of that fact. The last requirement is objective." The objective nature of the last limb to section 28(3)(*b*)(i) means that there is a limit to the extent to which an accused can be judged on the facts as he believed them to be. It is at this point that a divergence of views has developed between writers.

Lord argues (at p. 88) that if an accused is in possession of a substance that he knows of as "blues" he may think that the term "blues" is common parlance for a substance that is not a controlled drug. In fact, Lord says, the term "blues" is common parlance for amphetamine. To borrow the terminology of a series of contract cases, the accused must be mistaken as to the identity of a substance and not merely its attribute (such as its name) in order to have a defence under section 28. Fortson argues (at p. 160) that a phrase popularly used to denote a controlled drug is likely to be sufficient reason to cause a person to suspect that the substance which he possesses, bearing that description, is in fact a controlled drug.

5. Tudhope v. McKee
1987 S.C.C.R. 663

10.3.5

McK. was sitting in a court when she passed a small package to her brother who was then a prisoner. He thereafter put the item into his mouth. After a struggle with a policeman and a court official the package was recovered. It was found to consist of a balloon containing several pieces of cannabis resin. The contents of the balloon could not be seen to be a controlled drug merely by looking at it for the contents were completely covered. At the trial the sheriff sustained a submission of no case to answer and acquitted McK. of a charge of being concerned in the supply of a controlled drug to another. The submission was to the effect that the Crown had failed to raise an inference of knowledge on her part as to the nature of the substance. The Crown appealed.

THE LORD JUSTICE-CLERK (ROSS) (at p. 666): "[I]t was not necessary in the present case for the Crown to establish that the respondent knew what was in the package. As is clear from *McKenzie* v. *Skeen* [1983 S.L.T. 121], the necessity for the Crown to establish knowledge on the part of the possessor that he had the article which turned out to be a drug arose from the construction placed upon the word 'possession.' Section 4(3)(*b*) is not concerned with possession. In my opinion the offence described in section 4(3)(*b*) is an offence of strict liability subject only to the defence afforded by section 28 of the Act. Thus, if the respondent can establish lack of knowledge on her part as to what was in the package, she may be able to establish a defence under section 28(3), but the onus will be upon her to establish such lack of knowledge."

LORD MCDONALD (at p. 666): "The sheriff held that the respondent had no case to answer because the Crown had not proved that she knew that the package which was undoubtedly in her possession and which she undoubtedly transferred to the prisoner McKee contained a controlled drug. In my opinion such knowledge may be proved by inference from proved facts and circumstances. I do not read the decision in *McKenzie* v. *Skeen* [1983 S.L.T. 121] as, in any sense, running counter to that proposition. The decision in *McCadden* v. *H.M. Advocate* [1986 S.C.C.R. 16], where knowledge was inferred on the part of an individual who took part in an elaborate plan involving the handing over of a bag containing heroin to a courier although he never had possession and was not directly a party to the transfer, is an example of knowledge being inferred from circumstantial evidence.

In the present case the sheriff recognised this but felt unable to draw the necessary inference. In my opinion, the facts and circumstances here were sufficient to raise an inference of knowledge on the part of the respondent such as to call for some explanation on her part. In other words, there was a case to answer.

The sheriff accepted that the package was transferred by the respondent to the prisoner in a furtive and clandestine manner but declined to draw an inference of knowledge from that fact because the transferee was a prisoner in custody. Notwithstanding this the respondent obviously knew she was handing over something illicit. The drug was rapped in a yellow balloon which in turn was wrapped in cling film. In these circumstances I would be prepared to infer that the package contained a controlled drug and that the respondent knew it. There was in short a case for her to answer."

LORD WYLIE (at p. 667): "It is well settled that, for the purposes of section 5(2) of the Act of 1971, proof of knowledge of possession of the article itself though not of its nature or quality is essential proof of the offence (*McKenzie* v. *Skeen*). The circumstances of the present case clearly satisfy that test, so far as any contravention of that section would have been concerned. The respondent had actual physical possession of the package. In any proceedings under that section it would of course have been open to the respondent to found on the provisions of section 28(3)(*b*)(i) ... Subject to that qualification the section imposes a strict liability ...

In the present case the starting-point is that the respondent was in possession of the package which she passed in the direction of [the co-accused] ... and in these circumstances it was not essential for the Crown to establish that she was aware of the nature of the contents. It would of course be open to her to establish, if she can, the defence for which statutory provision is made by section 28."

Appeal allowed.

NOTE

There have been two commentaries on this case: Sheriff Gordon at 1987 S.C.C.R. pp. 668–9 and Ferguson, "Knowledge of things?" at 1988 S.L.T. (News) 159. Sheriff Gordon identifies two problems in the case. The first is that the three judges differ in their reasons. Mr Ferguson is a little more blunt: 'It is impossible to hold that all three views can be correct." (at p. 160). The latter observation is all the more interesting on considering Mr Ferguson's own report on this case in the *Scots Law Times*: he is able in his report to distil a single *ratio* from these opinions 1988 S.L.T. 153 at p. 154. The second problem, identified by Sheriff Gordon is said by him to be "inherent in the existence of a specific offence of 'being concerned in' supplying drugs, since that phrase may also be thought to contain its own *mens rea*." The commentary continues that the "whole problem in the case would not have arisen if the Crown had charged the respondent with what they proposed to prove against her — the actual supply of drugs." It is difficult to understand the logic of this proposition for the Crown on the face of the summary complaint proposed to prove that the respondent was concerned in the supplying of controlled drugs. That charge was on the face of it a good one standing the evidence as summarised by the sheriff. The problem arises by way of the interpretation of a difficult Act, not from the actings of the Crown. Sheriff Gordon observes further that "being concerned in, sounds very much like being art and part in, and to say, as a general proposition, that the offence of being concerned in the supplying of drugs does not require *mens rea* has a slightly odd ring to it." The case of *Kerr (D.A.) v. H.M. Advocate*, 1986 S.C.C.R. 81 is considered in more detail above (at para. 4.4.17). For present purposes, reference need only be made to Lord Hunter's opinion (at p. 87) where he doubted "whether it is altogether helpful to treat such a provision [*i.e.*, section 4(3)(*b*)] in a United Kingdom statute merely as if it were a form of statutory concert. Under section 46 of the Criminal Procedure (Scotland) Act 1975 the charge 'guilty, actor or art and part' is implied in all Scottish indictments."

Lord Hunter continues: "Judging from its terms and the context in which it occurs, I consider that section 4(3)(*b*) was *purposely enacted in the widest terms* and was intended to cover a great variety of activities both *at the centre and also on the fringes* of dealing in controlled drugs. It would, for example, in appropriate circumstances include the activities of financiers, couriers and other go-betweens, lookouts, advertisers, agents and many links in the chain of distribution. It would certainly, in my opinion, include the activities of persons who take part in the breaking up of bulk, the adulteration and reduction of purity, the separation and division into deals and the weighing and packaging of deals." (emphasis added).

The importance of *Tudhope v. McKee*, it is submitted, lies in the reassertion of the importance of section 28 as a statutory defence. Thus, in the context of *McKee's* case, provided the Crown can link the accused generally to the supply of controlled drugs then the prima facie case has been made out. By section 28 it is for the accused to assert that he or she has probably made out a defence.

The person's "furtive and clandestine" activity in *Tudhope v. McKee* was matched by "furtive and nervous" behaviour in *McQuillan v. H.M. Advocate*, 1997 G.W.D. 17–763.

6. R. v. McNamara   **10.3.6**
(1988) 152 J.P. 390

The police were searching a house when McN. appeared outside on his motor cycle. On the back of the motor cycle the police found a box which contained cannabis. McN. was arrested and after caution he said that he was not the dealer but only the carrier. He admitted that it was cannabis and said that he had been told by someone, whom he refused to identify, to deliver it as instructed. In evidence McN. said he thought the material he was delivering was pornographic or pirated video films. On conviction McN. appealed on the grounds of misdirection.

LORD LANE, C.J. (at p. 393): "[Counsel for the appellant] submits that the prosecution must prove, as part of their duty, knowledge on the part of the defendant what the nature of the contents of the box were. He is forced to concede however that if his argument is correct, then the words of section 28(3) … are otiose. He is unable on his argument to provide those words with a sensible meaning.

The operation of section 28 of the Misuse of Drugs Act 1971, to say the least, is not free from difficulty … If one reads [section 28(2)] literally, they seem in effect to cast upon the defendant the burden of disproving all facts adduced by the prosecution in support of the charges. This, one imagines, cannot possibly have been the intention of the draftsman.

One therefore starts off with the proposition that the prosecution must prove basic possession. That sounds simple. It is not, because the basic concept of possession is itself an extremely difficult one to understand."

(At p. 394)

"Unhappily it is not altogether easy to extract from the speeches of their Lordships [in *R. v. Warner* [1968] 2 All E.R. 356] the *ratio decidendi*. But doing the best we can, and appreciating that we may not have done full justice to the speeches, the following propositions seem to us to emerge.

First of all a man does not have possession of something which has been put into his pocket or into his house without his knowledge; in other words something which is 'planted' on him, to use the current vulgarism. Secondly, a mere mistake as to the quality of a thing under the defendant's control is not enough to prevent him being in possession, for instance, if a man is in possession of heroin believing it to be cannabis or believing it perhaps to be aspirin.

Thirdly, if the defendant believes that the thing is of a wholly different nature from that which in fact it is, then the result, to use the words of Lord Pearce, would be otherwise. Fourthly, in the case of a container or a box, the defendant's possession of the box leads to the strong inference that he is in possession of the contents of whatsoever it is inside the box. But if the contents are quite different in kind from what he believed, he is not in possession of it."

(At p. 395)

"It seems to us, in order to make sense of the provisions of section 28, and also to make as clear as can be possible the decision in *Warner*, the draftsman of the Act intended that the prosecution should have the initial burden of proving that the defendant had, and knew that he had, in these circumstances the box in his control and also that the box contained something. That, in our judgment establishes the necessary possession. They must also of course prove that the box in fact contained the drug alleged, in this case cannabis resin ... Once the prosecution proved that the defendant had control of the box, knew that he had control and knew that the box contained something which was in fact the drug alleged, the burden, in our judgment, is cast upon him to bring himself within these provisions."

Appeal dismissed.

NOTE

For further discussion of this case in its context see Patient, "Possession, Warner and section 28", 1989 J.C.L. 105. For some further discussion of the general issues, see *R. v. Vann* [1996] Crim.L.R. 52 at p. 54.

7. Sinclair v. H.M. Advocate
1990 G.W.D. 1–13

10.3.7

S. appealed against conviction under section 5(3) of the 1971 Act.

Held, that directions that the effect of section 28 of the 1971 Act was that if one possessed a packet and did not know or look at what was inside, if one could satisfy the jury that one neither believed or suspected, nor had reason to suspect the presence of controlled drugs, one was entitled to be acquitted, were proper and adequate.

Appeal refused.

8. R. v. Rautamaki
[1993] Crim.L.R. 691

10.3.8

R. was convicted in an English court of possession with intent to supply. A carrier bag of Ecstasy tablets was found in an understairs cupboard. He said that a regular passenger of his mini-cab had asked him to look after the carrier bag, saying that it contained steroids, but he had told the investigating officers that he did not know who had left them. He admitted that this was a lie, explaining that he was in a state of shock at the time. Two of the grounds of appeal related to corroboration.

Held, the judge had correctly said that the case was not one in which the law required the Crown to corroborate its case that R. knew the tablets were Ecstasy. There was therefore no need for him to explain what was meant by corroboration given that corroboration in its strict sense applied only when there was a witness whose evidence stood in need of corroboration.

It was also contended that the judge should have told the jury that the lie could only provide evidence of guilty knowledge if R.'s consciousness of guilt was his only reason for telling it. Although a lie might be told for a single reason, a person who lied might have more than one reason operating on his mind leading him to lie. R. admitted he had lied, and gave shock as the reason. Some reasons for lying are inconsistent with guilt, for example, a lie told by an innocent man to make the truth of his innocence more plausible. Shock and guilt were not inconsistent reasons for the lie told by R.

It was important that the jury be told that the lie could only be indicative of guilt if it was told because R. was guilty and trying to conceal his guilt and not only because he was shocked. It was not considered that, following the summing-up, the jury could have been left with the impression that anything less than the consciousness of guilt would suffice to make the lie probative of guilt. In a case in which a defendant insisted to the end that he had not told a lie, or while admitting to a lie offered no explanation of it, a direction on the assessment of the significance of lies was likely to have to remind the jury that lies might be told for a variety of reasons consistent with innocence and perhaps offering examples. In this case, R.

admitted telling a lie and gave a reason for it. There were therefore only two explanations for the lie: shock or consciousness of guilt. It was not necessary for the judge to canvass the possibility of other explanations for the lie.

Having admitted possession of a Class A drug with the intention of supplying, by returning the tablets to the passenger, the onus of proving his innocence was on R. under section 28 of the 1971 Act. Section 28(3) provided that he was not to be acquitted by reason only of proving that he neither knew nor suspected, nor had reason to suspect, that the substance was the particular controlled drug alleged. He could only be acquitted if he proved on the balance of probabilities that he neither believed nor suspected, nor had reason to suspect, that the substance was a controlled drug. Whilst it seemed that section 28 was referred to in the course of the trial, the summing-up was based on the proposition that the onus of proving its case beyond a reasonable doubt rested upon the Crown. It was unfortunate that neither side had corrected the judge.

Appeal dismissed.

NOTE

In relation to the point concerning the burden of proof, it has been noted that it would seem to be beyond doubt that it was on the accused R.: [1993] Crim.L.R. 692. The prosecution is obliged to prove "basic possession": *R. v. McNamara, supra*, but this may amount to no more than proof that R. knew he had the carrier bag in his understairs cupboard and that he was aware that it had something in it. In fact, R. admitted that he knew the bag contained tablets, so the prosecution were able to prove more than the bare minimum requirement. Thereafter, provided of course that the prosecution could also show that the tablets were in fact Ecstasy, the onus was on R. to show, under section 28(3), that he neither knew, nor suspected, nor had reason to suspect that the tablets were a controlled drug of any kind. This would have been an uphill struggle for R., given the circumstances in which he claimed to have come into possession of the bag, and it is hardly surprising that a conviction was returned even though the jury were not directed that the onus of proof was on R.

CHAPTER ELEVEN

Forfeiture   **11.1**

Introduction   **11.2**

The Misuse of Drugs Act 1971 provides by section 27 for certain powers of forfeiture. These powers are open to the courts in addition to the powers of punishment contained in Schedule 4 of the 1971 Act.

The powers in section 27 provided to be too simplistic for the complex financial transactions surrounding the supply of controlled drugs and the wealth generated as a result of that supply.

Parliament has provided more detailed powers for England and Wales with the Drug Trafficking Offences Act 1986 (which does not much extend to Scotland) and for Scotland in the Proceeds of Crime (Scotland) Act 1995.

The 1986 Act has generated case law in England and Wales but that is not binding in Scotland nor is it persuasive given that the 1986 Act does not apply in the latter jurisdiction and that the terms of the 1986 Act and the 1995 Act are different.

CASES   **11.3**

1. R. v. Beard   **11.3.1**
[1974] 1 W.L.R. 1549

B. and others were convicted of being concerned in the illegal importation of controlled drugs. Money found in B.'s flat was part of the proceeds of sale of drugs. That money was ordered to be forfeited.

CAULFIELD, J. (at p. 1551): "I have no doubt that the word 'anything' which is a very general description of personal property, includes money...

My powers under section 27(1) are virtually unrestricted. I can order the destruction of the property, or I can order that it should be dealt with in such a manner as the court may order. Obviously, I must adopt a judicial not a whimsical approach as regards the words 'in such a manner as the court may order.'"

Forfeiture granted.

2. Haggard v. Mason   **11.3.2**
[1976] 1 All E.R. 337

H. was convicted of offering to supply a controlled drug to another contrary to section 4(3)(*a*) of the 1971 Act. The substance involved turned out in fact not to be a controlled drug. The justices also ordered the forfeiture of a sum of £146 which had been found in H.'s possession. On appeal it was *held, inter alia*, that the justices had no power under section 27 to order the forfeiture of the money found in H.'s possession and the forfeiture order was varied accordingly.

Order quashed.

NOTE

The judgment is exceedingly short on the point of forfeiture. No reason or explanation is given as to why there was no power. It seems a reasonable inference that there was no evidence to show that the money related to the offence.

11.3.3   **3. R. v. Morgan**
                            [1977] Crim.L.R. 488

M. pleaded guilty to possessing cocaine and cannabis resin with intent to supply it to another. He was found to have £393 in cash. On being sentenced the money was ordered to be forfeited under section 27. The appeal was principally against the terms of imprisonment imposed but the forfeiture order was also considered. It was *held* on appeal that the money was no doubt part of M.'s working capital for trade in drugs, but it did not appear to justify an order under section 27. The order was made without jurisdiction and was quashed.

Order quashed.

NOTE
This case was followed in *R. v. Llewellyn, infra* at paragraph **11.3.10**.

11.3.4   **4. R. v. Menocal**
                            [1979] 2 All E.R. 510

M. pleaded guilty to being knowingly concerned in the fraudulent evasion of the prohibition on the importation of cocaine. She was sentenced to a period of imprisonment and an order was made for the forfeiture of £4,371 found in M.'s handbag when she was arrested. Questions arose as to whether that order of forfeiture had been made properly, in the context of English criminal procedure. On appeal, *held* that the order had not been made timeously.

LORD SALMON (at p. 516): "All prison and other sentences against a convicted person, including money penalties and forfeitures of money in relation to an offence, have two purposes: (i) to punish the offender and (ii) to support the public good by discouraging the offender and other potential criminals from committing such an offence in the future."

Order quashed.

5. R. v. Cuthbertson   **11.3.5**
[1980] 2 All E.R. 401

C. and others produced and supplied a controlled drug on a large scale and consequently they made enormous profits. Two of those involved in the conspiracy transferred a substantial part of their share in the profits to bank accounts abroad. On conviction the trial judge ordered the forfeiture, under section 27 of the 1971 Act, of those assets which had been traced as representing the proceeds of their criminal enterprise. Appeal was taken against the nature and extent of the orders of forfeiture and the matter called ultimately in the House of Lords.

LORD DIPLOCK (at p. 403): "This is a pure question of construction of section 27 read in the context of the Act of which it forms a part. The question should not be approached with any preconception that Parliament must have intended the section to be used as a means of stripping professional drug traffickers, such as the appellants, of the whole of their illgotten gains, however laudable such a consummation might appear to be. Parliament's intention must be ascertained from the actual words which Parliament itself approved as expressing its intention when it passed the Act in the terms in which it reached the statute book ...

The words of the section, in my view, speak for themselves clearly, without resort to extraneous aids."

(At p. 404)

"The fact that the section is a penal provision is in itself a reason for hesitating before ascribing to phrases used in it a meaning broader than they would ordinarily bear."

(At p. 405)

"I would apply a purposive construction to the section considered as a whole. What does it set out to do? Its evident purpose is to enable things to be forfeited so that they may be destroyed or dealt with in some other manner as the court thinks fit. The words are apt and, as it seems to me, are only apt to deal with things that are tangible, things of which physical possession can be taken by a person authorised to do so by the court and which are capable of being physically destroyed by that person or disposed of by him in some other way. To ascribe to the section any more extended ambit would involve putting a strained construction on the actual language that is used, and, so far from there being any grounds for doing so, it seems to me that if it were attempted to extend the subject of orders of forfeiture to choses in action or other intangibles this would lead to difficulties and uncertainties in application which it can hardly be surprised that Parliament intended to create ...

So one limitation on the subject matter of an order for forfeiture is that it must be something tangible. There is also another: that what is forfeited must be shown 'to relate' to an offence under the Act *of which a person has been convicted by or before the court making the order.* For the purposes of section 27 one is therefore looking for an offence which is not only an offence under the Act but also an offence which in its legal nature is of a kind to which something tangible and thus susceptible to forfeiture can be said to 'relate'."

(At p. 406)

"Forfeiture is a penalty; justice requires that it should not be imposed by a court in the absence of a finding or an admission of guilt ...

No machinery whatever is provided by the section for effecting the assignment of choses in action or creating and realising the charges on real and personal property which 'following the assets' in this kind of way would entail. It is practical considerations of this kind which, in my view, lend weight to the conclusion based on the ordinary meaning of the actual language of the sections. They make it clear that, in the case of a sole offender, orders of forfeiture under section 27 can never have been intended by Parliament to serve as a means of stripping the drug traffickers of the total profits of their unlawful enterprises; and the difficulties of using the section for this purpose are but multiplied when the offences are joint: assets in such a case would have to be followed down multiple trails, whether or not the substantive offences were linked by a general conspiracy charge."

LORD SCARMAN (at p. 407): "[A]nything' in the context of section 27(1), is any tangible thing ... section 27 is concerned not with restitution, compensation or the redress of illegal enrichment but with forfeiture. Counsel for the appellants put it correctly, though strangely, when he suggested that forfeiture was limited to 'the accoutrements of crime', by which I took him to mean, in workaday English, the tools, instruments or other physical means used to commit the crime."

Appeals allowed.

NOTE

The decision of the House of Lords in *R. v. Cuthbertson*, that there had been no jurisdiction to order forfeiture of the appellants' assets under section 27 was widely commented on when it became known and, indeed, it was criticised in the House of Commons: H.C. Deb. Vol. 987 col. 1742 (July 3, 1980). One academic commentator was moved to say that the result was "extraordinary, not to say incredible" *cf.* [1980] Stat.L.R. 166 at p. 167 and see reply at [1981] Stat.L.R. 64.

The matter did not end with the appeals to the House of Lords for *The Times* (November 12, 1980) reported that the Inland Revenue had issued large claims for back-tax on what had hitherto been undisclosed income. The importance of this case lies in putting Parliament on notice as to what could be involved in a major case. The opinion of the House of Lords that the terms of section 27 of the 1971 Act did not permit the "following of assets' is clearly the starting point for the later legislation.

6. R. v. Ribeyre   11.3.6
[1982] Crim.L.R. 538

R. pleaded guilty to possessing cocaine with intent to supply it to others and to other offences involving cannabis. He was sentenced to two years' imprisonment and ordered to forfeit *inter alia* £700. R. had admitted that this sum was the proceeds of drug sales. That order was appealed.

Held, that there was power to order the forfeiture of the money under either section 27 of the 1971 Act or section 43 of the 1973 Act. The money had not been shown to be related to the offences of which the appellant was convicted, as was required by section 27, nor was it demonstrated that it was intended to be used in connection with future offences, as was required by section 43.

Appeal *quoad* money allowed.

7. R. v. Khan   11.3.7
[1982] 3 All E.R. 969

K. was convicted on one charge of possessing heroin with intent to supply it to another and he pleaded guilty to another. He was sentenced to 10 years' imprisonment, fined £10,000 and ordered to forfeit (i) a motor car under section 27 of the 1971 Act and (ii) a house at 4 Burnham Road, St Albans under section 43 of the 1973 Act. The sentence was appealed.

It was conceded by the Crown that section 43 of the 1973 Act did not apply to real property, but only to personal property. Further, standing Lord Diplock's dicta in *R. v. Cuthbertson*, above it was held that there was no jurisdiction for forfeiture.

Appeal *quoad* house allowed.

NOTE
   This case is irrelevant in Scotland as the Powers of Criminal Courts Act 1973 does not apply there. There is therefore no authority concerning the forfeiture of heritage in Scotland.
   The rule in *R. v. Khan* was applied in *R. v. Pearce* [1996] Crim.L.R. 442, but in the latter case it was observed that in cases where property was used for the purpose of cultivating cannabis, it might be appropriate for the court to deal with the matter by imposing a fine equal to or less than the value of the property concerned.

11.3.8   **8. Donnelly v. H.M. Advocate**
                                1984 S.C.C.R. 93

D. pleaded guilty to possessing 36 grammes of cannabis with intent to supply and he was sentenced to 18 months' imprisonment. £1,047 of money found in his house was ordered to be forfeited. He appealed *inter alia* on the ground that forfeiture was incompetent.

THE LORD JUSTICE GENERAL (EMSLIE) (at p. 95): "Upon the question of forfeiture, [counsel for the appellant] argued that the forfeiture of the money found was incompetent. It could not be justified, he argued under reference to a number of cases in England, under section 27(1) of the Misuse of Drugs Act 1971 and it could not be justified either under section 223(1) of the Criminal Procedure (Scotland) Act 1975. In reply the learned advocate-depute conceded that if the order depended upon the justification given by section 27(1) it could not be supported, and with that concession we entirely agree. Section 27(1) could not protect this order if that is all that we have to look at in determining the competency of the forfeiture. Coming, however, to section 223 of the Act of 1975, a different question arises, because we have to examine what was one to see whether it can be supported by the power given to the court in that section. Now the section says this:

'Where a person is convicted of an offence and the court which passes sentence is satisfied that any property which was in his possession or under his control at the time of his apprehension—

    (*a*) has been used for the purpose of committing, or facilitating the commission of, any offence; or

    (*b*) was intended by him to be used for that purpose, that property shall be liable to forfeiture.'

Now in this case the learned advocate-depute has argued that the order of forfeiture was competent under both head (*a*) and head (*b*) or either of them in section 223(1). In our opinion the order was competent, under section 223(1)(*b*). In the circumstances of this case the judge was entitled to be satisfied that the money found concealed in the flat in association with the paraphernalia of trafficking, and, indeed, the cannabis resin, was intended to be used by the appellant for the purpose of committing an offence and, for that matter, an offence under the Misuse of Drugs Act 1971. The intention was there to be seen and it arises as a reasonable inference from the material which was before the trial judge."

Appeal refused.

NOTE

    The point in *Donnelly v. H.M. Advocate* is that the court is saying that although the money is not related to the offence of which the appellant was convicted it might be related to a *future* offence, presumably to buy more controlled drugs.

For further discussion see "Forfeiture and Confiscation": Scottish Law Commission Discussion Paper No. 82 (June 1989) at para. 2.4 *et seq.*.

9. R. v. Chresaphi   **11.3.9**
Court of Appeal (Criminal Division) unreported, March 27, 1984

C. was convicted after trial of being concerned in the supply of heroin and he was sentenced to 21 months' imprisonment. The evidence showed that when the police searched D.'s bedroom they found £3,520 in bundles of £100. C.'s female cohabitee told the police that the money had been obtained by C. in the drug business. C. said on oath that the money was not from the drugs business but from his work and that it was being "kept out of the sight of the taxman." A forfeiture order was made by the trial judge and C. appealed against the making of that order.

CAUFIELD, J.: "The learned recorder went to a great deal of trouble to listen to arguments from the defence and the Crown before making a forfeiture order of £2,000 against the appellant: that is £2,000 of the £3,520 that had been found. He assuaged his conscience in this way, by saying that he thought that some of the money that had been found related to the offence. So he chose a figure, which cannot be measured with accuracy, of £2,000. One cannot say how much money was related to the offence, and while not asserting that the learned recorder was guessing — that may sound too vulgar — the learned recorder really was imagining what sum could be attributable to the offence.

The court has listened to the submissions which have been made by the appellant and by the respondent. The point is very simple. It is this: was there evidence before the learned recorder upon which he could be satisfied that the money found in the bedroom related to the offence? The simple answer to that question is that there was not any evidence upon which the learned recorder could decide that part of the money, namely £2,000, was related to the offence. Indeed, learned counsel for the Crown made that concession in the first few minutes of submission. The point is elementary, it is simple."

Appeal allowed.

NOTE
This case simply illustrated the error of speculating in such a matter.

10. R. v. Llewellyn   **11.3.10**
(1985) 7 Cr.App.R. (S.) 225

L. pleaded guilty to possessing cannabis with intent to supply and to two charges of possession of cannabis and amphetamines. Police searching L.'s house found these controlled drugs and also found separately £400 in cash which was in a polythene bag in L.'s wife's handbag. The trial judge having heard the evidence outlined, concluded that L. was dealing commercially and that the money was the proceeds of the sale of another quantity of cannabis on an earlier occasion. L. was sentenced to nine months' imprisonment and the £400 was ordered to be forfeited under section 27 of the 1971 Act. An appeal was taken up with respect to the forfeiture order only.

STUART-SMITH, J. (at p. 227): "It is important to notice that the offence charged in this indictment related to May 16, and the cannabis in the appellant's possession on that date. What is submitted on the appellant's behalf is that the £400 was in fact his working capital and could not relate to the cannabis in his possession on May 16.

In support of that submission counsel for the appellant relies on three authorities. The first is *Morgan*, which is more fully reported in Thomas's "Current Sentencing Practice" at p. 9086, decided on February 28, 1977. The judgment of the court was given by Lawton, L.J. After setting out the words of the section to which I have referred, in which he emphasised the words 'an offence' and also emphasised the words relating to 'the offence,' the Lord Justice said this: 'In our judgment, the words relate to the offence to which this appellant was convicted. He was convicted of having drugs in his possession with intent to supply. In other words he was going to sell them. He would not have required his working capital for that purpose. In our judgment therefore it follows that there was not sufficient evidence to justify the trial court in coming to the conclusion that it was satisfied that the possession of the £393 related to the offence of which he was convicted.'

That case was followed in *Ribeyre* (1982) 4 Cr.App.R. (S.) 165. We were also referred to the case of *Cuthbertson* [1980] 2 All E.R. 401 and the speech of Lord Diplock at page 405 to the same effect.

It seems to this court that these words apply to the facts of this case. It is impossible to see how the £400 related to the cannabis which he had in his possession with intent to supply. It may well have related to the cannabis which he had in his possession before May 16 and no doubt the learned judge's findings of fact on that issue were fully justified. That unfortunately does not mean that the court was able to make the forfeiture order. The words of the statute are clear and must be strictly interpreted."

Appeal allowed.

NOTE

The decision in *R. v. Llewellyn* was followed in *R. v. Cox* [1987] Crim.L.R. 141: there a forfeiture order for the forfeiture of £2,520 was quashed as there was no evidence that the money related to the offences charged to which the accused pleaded guilty. See also *R. v. Boothe* (1987) 9 Cr.App.R. (S.) 8; *R. v. Askew* [1987 Crim.L.R. 584; *R. v. Neville* [1987] Crim.L.R. 585; *R. v. Simms* [1988] Crim.L.R. 186; and *R. v. O'Farrell* [1988] Crim.L.R. 387.

In *R. v. Slater* [1986] 1 W.L.R. 1340 the Crown argued that forfeiture was competent as the money found had been used to commit or facilitate the commission of offences by persons other than the accused *viz.*, his customers. This attempt failed standing the terms of section 43 of the Powers of Criminal Courts Act 1973, but that section does not apply in Scotland.

These cases cited above have been overtaken by the Drug Trafficking Offences Act 1986 but "they will remain relevant to other cases where the offender has apparently profited without creating a loss which can be the subject of a compensation order." [1987] Crim.L.R. 586.

The English approach in *R. v. Llewellyn* may be contrasted with that of the Scottish courts in *Donnelly v. H.M. Advocate*, but the legislation in the two countries is different.

11. R. v. Churcher   **11.3.11**
(1986) 8 Cr.App.R. (S.) 94

C. pleaded guilty *inter alia* to charges of supplying controlled drugs and possession of controlled drugs with intent to supply. He was sentenced to imprisonment and a forfeiture order was made for two sums of money, £610 and £577, which were found in his possession at the time of his arrest.

C. claimed that one sum of money was a loan from his mother, and that the other had been withdrawn from a building society. Counsel for C. offered at trial to call evidence in support of these contentions but that was not accepted by the trial judge.

On appeal against the forfeiture orders it was held that the court was concerned that the appellant had not had a proper opportunity to establish that the court of first instance should not be satisfied that the money related to the offence.

WOOLF, L.J. (at p. 96): "The Court is anxious to make clear that the power to order forfeiture is valuable in drug offences and should be exercised when it is appropriate to do so. Regrettably this is another case on which, no doubt because of the pressure to which Crown Court is now frequently subject, the proper investigations were not made so as to ensure that the court can make a forfeiture order. It would be preferable that a little more time were taken to inquire into these matters to ensure that the provisions of the statute were fulfilled. If that were done it would not be necessary for the Court to interfere with regard to otherwise desirable forfeiture orders."

Order quashed.

12. R. v. Maidstone Crown Court *ex parte* Gill   **11.3.12**
[1987] RTR 35

The applicant's son was charged on indictment with supplying a small quantity of heroin and also supplying one kilogramme of heroin. He pleaded not guilty to the first charge and guilty to the second charge. The pleas were accepted by the Crown and the son was sentenced to four years' imprisonment on the second charge.

After sentencing the son, the trial judge was minded to order the forfeiture of two cars. The son had used a Volvo with regard to the matter for which a plea of not guilty was accepted and he had used a Triumph with regard to the supplying of the kilogramme of heroin. The decision on forfeiture was adjourned as the son was present but the applicant was not.

At the adjourned hearing the trial judge accepted that both cars belonged to the applicant and not to the son and that the applicant had no knowledge that his son was dealing in controlled drugs. The trial judge forfeited both cars on the authority of section 27(1) of the 1971 Act. The applicant sought judicial review by way of an order of *certiorari* to quash the judge's order.

LORD LANE, C.J. (at p. 39): "There are two aspects: one relates to the Volvo motor car alone, and the other aspect relates to both motor cars. From what has already been said, it is plain that the Volvo motor car was not used in the second transaction to which a plea of guilty was entered, namely the November 13 transaction when a kilogramme of heroin was handed over to the sergeant. It was used in the other earlier transaction, namely the allegation that the defendant had handed a small quantity of heroin to the same recipient at the earlier date. In respect of that count the plea of not guilty entered by the defendant Sarjit at the outset of the trial remained unaltered. It is a question therefore whether the words 'anything shown to relate to the offence' in terms of section 27(1) were satisfied in those circumstances. I think that they were not.

Counsel for the prosecution submits to us that the earlier occasion, on November 8, was really all part and parcel of the main transaction. The smaller transaction was simply handing a sample to the proposed purchaser, and therefore it can properly be said that the Volvo motor car was so to speak used or related to the charge to which the plea of guilty was entered. I disagree. I think that the matter was unresolved, namely whether the Volvo motor car had in fact been used for the purpose of the count to which the defendant pleaded guilty. That was a matter which the jury would have had to decide. They did not. So it remains a matter undecided. Accordingly insofar as the Volvo was concerned at any rate, this forfeiture order should not have been made ...

That leaves the Triumph ... It may be that there will be cases where a man who lends a motor car should have been put on notice or on suspicion that the car was going to be used for some illegal purpose, and in those cases it may be perfectly proper for a judge to make orders of forfeiture to mark his disapproval of the failure to take the necessary precautions. But this was not such a case at all, because on the judge's findings this man Dava [the applicant] was under no reason to suppose that the car was going to be used for anything other than legitimate purposes. Both these cars apparently were used as family cars, sometimes for taking children to and fro from school, other times for ordinary family business. There was no reason, on the judge's findings, for Dava to be under any sort of suspicion about what was going on. It certainly would not have prevented the offence if Dava had said 'Son, you must not use this car for illegal purposes.' It certainly would not have helped if he had asked Sarjit 'Are you going to use the car for ferrying heroin?' because the answer would obviously have been 'No.'

It is difficult therefore to follow the judge's reasoning … it is difficult to understand how forfeiture in the circumstances of this case could act as a deterrent to the man convicted or how in the future, by forfeiting cars in these circumstances, anyone would be deterred.

Application allowed, order quashed.

13. R. v. Bowers   11.3.13
[1994] Crim.L.R. 230

B. pleaded guilty to possessing cannabis resin with intent to supply and supplying cannabis. He was stopped by police at a motorway service area. His passenger at his request threw a slab of cannabis resin out of the car. B. admitted buying the cannabis resin for £1,380 for personal consumption and for sale to a small circle of friends; he hoped to make a profit of between £350 and £400.

B. was sentenced to 12 months' imprisonment and an order was made under section 27 of the 1971 Act in respect of his car (worth about £800), and a confiscation order in the amount of £127. He claimed that the order in respect of the car should not have been made, as it had been bought with money provided by his elderly mother and the forfeiture of the car caused hardship as the appellant used it to take his mother to visit his mentally handicapped brother.

Held, section 27 allowed the court to order anything shown to the satisfaction of the court to relate to the offence to be forfeited and destroyed or otherwise dealt with. It was clear that the car related to the offence, as it had been used as the means of transport on the journey in the course of which the appellant was arrested. The car was registered in B.'s name and used by him as his own; the information about the money which was before the court was consistent with the view that the money had been given or lent to B. by his mother. The Court could not say that the court had wrongly exercised its discretion in ordering the forfeiture of the car. The sentence of 12 months' imprisonment was not excessive.

NOTE
    It is not necessary for the thing which is to be the subject of an order under section 27 to belong to the accused. Section 27(2) allowed a person other than the

accused who claims to be the owner of the property or otherwise interested to apply to be heard; if such an application is made, the court must not make an order under section 27 until the person has been given an opportunity to show cause why the order should not be made. No provision is made for the court or prosecution to give notice to anyone who may claim to be interested in the property. In a case where it is apparent that some person other than the accused has an interest in the property, or where the accused asserts that the property concerned belongs to someone else, the rules of natural justice would require that the person concerned be notified that an order affecting the property is under consideration. The fact that a person other than the accused establishes that he is the owner of the property does not mean that the court may not make an order under section 27, if it considers it appropriate to do so, as might be the case where the court considers that the third party was aware of the intended use of the property.

There is an early decision that things which were tangible at the time of arrest could be the subject of a forfeiture: *R. v. Marland* (1985) 82 L.S.Gaz. 3696.

The requirement that the object to be forfeited must be shown to relate to the offence applies equally to money: see *Haggart v. H.M. Advocate*, 1996 G.W.D. 38–2207.

14. Purdie v. Macdonald
1996 G.W.D. 27–1601

P. was convicted of driving a car while unfit to do so because of drugs. He was disqualified for a year and the car was forfeited.

P. was also fined in respect of three contraventions of the 1971 Act.

P. appealed the order for forfeiture on the ground that it was excessive. The sheriff had not raised the possibility of forfeiture during the plea in mitigation.

Held, the forfeiture was not excessive and that penalty was not unfair or unreasonable.

The appeal court observed that the sheriff would be wise to intimate the possibility of a forfeiture order before making it to allow for representation thereon.

Appeal refused.

NOTE

The car seems to have been forfeited on general statutory authority rather than on the specific one under section 27 of the 1971 Act. However, the observation of the appeal court holds good for either approach.

Forfeiture does not seem to depend on any particular value of controlled drugs: in *Payne v. Howdle*, 1997 G.W.D. 7–273, cannabis valued at only £400 resulted in forfeiture of a car. However, in all sentencing matters a sense of proportion is necessary.

CHAPTER TWELVE

Interpretation   **12.1**

Introduction   **12.2**

The Misuse of Drugs Act 1971 provides by section 37 that in that Act, except in so far as the context otherwise requires, certain expressions have statutory meanings assigned to them. Section 37 contains a list of those expressions and some of them, and individual words in the Schedules to the 1971 Act, have been considered judicially.

(i) Cannabis resin   **12.3**

"'[C]annabis resin' means the separated resin, whether crude or purified, obtained from any plant of the genus *Cannabis*."

1. R. v. Thomas   **12.3.1**
[1981] Crim.L.R. 496

T. was tried on a charge of unlawful possession of cannabis resin. The prosecution evidence was that she was in possession of a morphous brown substance which had been produced by compacting the shakings or scrapings of part of a cannabis plant; on microscopic examination the substance was seen to contain intact cannabis-bearing glandular trichomes from which the cannabis had not been removed. A contention that insufficient separation of the resin had occurred for the substance to comply with the definition of cannabis resin was rejected and the appellant was convicted. She appealed against conviction.

Held, that the fact that the substance, which otherwise had all the hallmarks of cannabis resin, was seen on microscopic examination to contain some trichomes, did not prevent the substance from being cannabis resin. It was crude cannabis resin, which had been separated as explained in *D.D.P. v. Goodchild* [1978] 1 W.L.R. 578 at p. 580. The fact that the separated material contained the trichome husks did not prevent sufficient separation from taking place for the morphous mass to constitute cannabis resin within the statutory definition.

Appeal dismissed.

NOTE
The terms "cannabis" and "cannabis resin" are frequently used interchangeably in everyday language although they are separate substances in terms of the 1971 Act: see *Arnott v. MacFarlane*, 1976 S.L.T. (Notes) 39.

12.3.2   **2. Guild v. Ogilvie**
                              1986 S.C.C.R. 67

O. was charged with the unlawful possession of cannabis resin. The Crown evidence included a report from authorised analysts who spoke to the material in question being cannabis resin. At the conclusion of the Crown case it was submitted for the defence that the possibility that the particular drug had been manufactured synthetically had not been excluded. Thus, it was said, there was no case to answer. The sheriff upheld the submission.

On appeal by the Crown, counsel for the respondent conceded that the sheriff had erred in upholding the defence submission. However, in view of the issues which had been raised by the appeal the High Court of Justiciary made certain observations on the matter.

The Court well understood how counsel for the respondent had made the concession. The analyst's report, referred to above, stated explicitly that the material in question was cannabis resin within the meaning of the 1971 Act. Further, there was no evidence led at the summary trial "suggesting even the possibility" that the material was other than cannabis resin or that there was any question of it being synthetically produced.

                              Appeal sustained and remitted to sheriff to
                              proceed as accords.

12.4 *(ii) Preparation*

Schedule 2. Part 1, para. 5.
"5. Any preparation or other product."

12.4.1   **1. R. v. Stevens**
                              [1981] Crim.L.R. 568

S. was found in possession of powdered mushrooms of a type containing psilocybin, a derivation of psilocin. He was charged with unlawful possession of a preparation containing psilocybin. He had made a statement to the effect that the sun had dried out the mushrooms. Expert evidence was that the mushrooms if left alone would rot and that the powder had resulted from their being dried, probably at a low heat.

The jury were directed that the word "preparation" had its natural and ordinary meaning. Following conviction an appeal was taken on the ground that "preparation" in the statutory context had to be a technical pharmaceutical meaning as signifying a distillation of the pure drug, psilocin, with something to make it palatable.

The Court of Appeal *held* that the lack of a technical definition in the interpretation section made it clear that the word was intended to have its ordinary and natural meaning. In order for the mushrooms to be prepared they had to cease to be in their natural growing state and in some way altered by the hand of man to put them into a condition in which they could be used for human consumption. The jury was properly directed.

Appeal dismissed.

NOTE

That "preparation" must be given its ordinary and natural meaning was reasserted in *R. v. Walker* [1987] Crim.L.R. 565.

2. Murray v. MacNaughton   12.4.2
1984 S.C.C.R. 361

M. was charged with the unlawful possession of 3.3 grammes of "dried uncrushed vegetable material containing the drug psilocin." The material was in a condition in which it could be used for human consumption and it was known as "magic mushrooms." There was no evidence as to how the accused had acquired the packet of "magic mushrooms" or in what circumstances the material in the packet had been picked and placed in the packet, or where or by whom it had been picked.

The sheriff convicted on the basis, in effect, that the picking of the drugs and keeping them in a bag without having done anything whatever to them, the accused had converted the "mushrooms" into a "preparation" containing psilocin within the meaning of the Act.

On appeal, the High Court of Justiciary *held* that as the material had not been altered in any way by the hand of man, mere continued possession of it did not make it a preparation.

Conviction quashed.

3. R. v. Cunliffe   12.4.3
[1986] Crim.L.R. 547

C. was found to be in possession of about 100 dried mushrooms. He had told the police that he had picked the psilocybin mushrooms some weeks earlier and had then dried them. Nothing else was done to the mushrooms by way of preparation. He used them in tea. There was evidence that the mushrooms contained psilocybin which was an ester of psilocin. Psilocin is a controlled drug and the police charged C. accordingly.

On conviction, an appeal was taken on the point that the mushrooms had not undergone a change which could properly be called "preparation." The Court of Appeal followed *R. v. Stevens, supra.*, which concerned virtually the same facts and *held* that the process of drying the mushrooms amounted to an act of preparation for future use.

Appeal dismissed.

12.5 *(iii) Substances and products*

> 5. Schedule 2. Part 1.
> "(a) ... substances and products."

12.5.1   **1. R. v. Greensmith**
                    [1983] 3 All E.R. 444

G. was convicted of possessing a controlled drug, namely cocaine, with intent to supply it to another. He appealed on the ground that the trial judge had erred in rejecting the defence submission that as the Crown had failed to establish whether the controlled drug forming the subject matter of the charge was cocaine, or a stereoisomeric form or salt thereof, he ought not to have been convicted.

LAWTON, L.J. (at p. 445): "The point of law turns on the construction of ss. 2 and 5(3) of the Misuse of Drugs Act 1971, and Pt. I of Sch. 2 to that Act. More particularly, the problem is whether the word 'cocaine' when used in para. 1 of that part of the schedule is used in a generic sense so as to include the specific forms, derivatives or preparations of it which come within the wording of paras. 2 to 5 of Pt. 1. If what is referred to in these paragraphs are different substances or products from 'cocaine' as that word is used in para. 1, important analytical and legal consequences follow. The analysis of a substance suspected to be 'cocaine' will have to be more elaborate than it has commonly been in the past and informations and indictments will have to specify whether the controlled drug is 'cocaine' within the meaning of para. 1 or a form, derivative or preparation of it within one of the paras. 2 to 5.

The word 'substance' has a wider meaning than 'product.' Any kind of matter comes within 'substance' whereas 'product' envisages the result of some kind of process ...

'[C]ocaine' can be a natural substance or a substance resulting from a chemical transformation; but both substances are cocaine. In our judgment the word 'cocaine' as used in para. 1 is a generic word which includes within its ambit both the direct extracts of the cocoa leaf, the natural form, and whatever results from a chemical transformation. Paragraphs 2 to 5 of Pt. I of the schedule, in our judgment, deal with the various kinds of substance which can result from chemical transformations. It is significant that in each of these paragraphs what is referred to is a chemical form 'of the substance specified.' What section 2 and 5(3) are dealing with are 'substances or products.' This case is concerned with the substance 'cocaine' which may have a number of forms but they are still cocaine."

                              Appeal dismissed.

2. Heywood v. Macrae
1987 S.C.C.R. 627

12.5.2

M. was charged with unlawful possession of amphetamine. The Crown
evidence was that a test of substance in his possession revealed it to contain
amphetamine. The analyst could not say if it was amphetamine or a salt
of amphetamine. The sheriff acquitted M. The Crown appealed on the
ground that the sheriff had erred in requiring it to prove the particular
form in which the amphetamine found in the accused's possession existed.

THE LORD JUSTICE-CLERK (ROSS) (at p. 630): "In my opinion, Part II of
Schedule 2 to the Act of 1971 must be looked at as a whole. What are listed
are various substances and products. Although the substances and products
listed in paragraph 1 are mutually exclusive, it does not follow that the
form or preparations listed in paragraphs 2 to 4 are separate and distinct
from the substances and products listed in paragraph 1. To the contrary, the
reference in paragraph 2 to 'a substance ... specified in paragraph 1,' and
in paragraph 3 to 'a substance ... specified in paragraph 1 or 2' and the
reference in paragraph 4 to 'a substance or product ... specified in any of
paragraphs 1 to 3' show clearly that paragraphs 2 to 4 are further defining
other chemical forms of the substances or products listed in paragraph 1."
(At p. 631)
"[Paragraphs 2 to 4] should be regarded as amplifying paragraph 1 by
specifying certain forms or preparations of the substances and products
listed in paragraph 1."

LORD McDONALD (at p. 632): "I do not find it necessary to decide whether
or not the word 'amphetamine' as used in paragraph 1 is generic or
otherwise. I consider that the substances described in paragraphs 2 and 3
are definitive of the word amphetamine where it occurs in paragraph 1. In
other words, when Part II is read as a whole, its meaning is that
amphetamine is a Class B controlled drug and it is to be held to include
any stereoisomeric form of it or any salt of it."

LORD WYLIE (at p. 633): "The provisions of paragraphs 2 to 4 are an
amplification of paragraph 1 for the purpose of underlining that the
legislation is striking at the possession of amphetamine in any of its forms."

Appeal allowed and remitted to sheriff to
proceed.

3. Hodder v. D.P.P.
The Independent, December 14, 1989

12.5.3

H. and another had 44 packets of frozen mushrooms which they kept in
the freezer compartment of a fridge. Each packet was labelled and

contained 100 mushrooms which H. and the other had picked and intended to use to hallucinate.

For a charge of unlawful possession the prosecution relied on paragraph 5 of Part 1 of Schedule 2 to the 1971 Act which provides that "any preparation or other product contained in a substance or product" specified in Schedule 2 was a Class A controlled drug.

The justices in the Magistrates Court held that the mushroom contained Psilocin, a Class A drug listed in Schedule 2, and convicted the accused who then appealed.

ROCH, L.J.: "The case made it clear that for a substance to be 'a preparation' within paragraph 5, a natural substance must have been subjected to some process performed by a human being which prepared the natural substance for future use as a drug. The word 'prepare' meant 'to make ready or fit; to bring into a suitable state; to subject to a process of bringing it to a required state.'

The freezing of the magic mushrooms did not convert the frozen mushrooms into a preparation. Freezing was not an act of preparation; it was simply an act of preservation.

However, the mushrooms picked, packaged and frozen did come within the meaning of 'product' or 'other product'. The defendants were producing packages of frozen magic mushrooms in the same way that supermarkets produced packaged and frozen vegetables. The calling of packets of frozen vegetables 'products' was an ordinary and natural use of language."

Appeal refused.

NOTE

The judgment of Roch, L.J. concludes with the observation that it would remove much artificiality from the law if magic mushrooms were added to Schedule 2 of the 1971 Act. For further discussion on the point see [1990] Crim.L.R. 262.

12.6 *(iv) Amphetamine*

Sched. 2. Part II
"amphetamine dexamphetamine"

12.6.1   **1. R. v. Watts**
                                     [1984] 2 All E.R. 380

W. had been in possession of a powder which analysis showed to contain amphetamine. He pleaded not guilty to unlawfully possessing amphetamine with intent to supply. It was not in dispute at the trial that amphetamine usually consisted of a racemic mixture of its two stereoisomers, namely dexamphetamine and levoamphetamine. However it was said by the defence that as there was no evidence that the powder contained dexamphetamine, the possibility that levoamphetamine only was present could not be excluded.

The relevance of the distinction lay in the list of Class B drugs in Part II of Sched. 2 to the 1971 Act. There the list of controlled drugs included "amphetamine" and "dexamphetamine" but not "levoamphetamine." The trial judge directed the jury that if amphetamine in any of its stereoisomeric forms had been present in the powder then W. was in possession of amphetamine. He was convicted and appealed.

The ground of appeal was that levoamphetamine by itself was not a controlled drug because "amphetamine" in Part II of Sched. 2 to the 1971 Act meant "a vacemic mixture of dexamphetamine and levoamphetamine."

Purchase, L.J. (at p. 383): "The construction of the schedule places before the court two alternatives. Parliament, in drafting the categories in Class B, has generally speaking referred to specific chemical names and in para 2 of Pt II of the schedule put in the extra definition, namely: 'Any stereoisomeric form of a substance for the time being specified in paragraph 1 of this Part of the Schedule.' Had the description dexamphetamine not been included in the category of Class B drugs, in our view it would not have been arguable but that levoamphetamine, on the evidence agreed in this case being a stereoisomeric form, together with dexamphetamine would both fall under the generic term 'amphetamine.' But the question raised is whether para 2 is applicable when one of the two stereoisomeric forms is specifically mentioned in para 1."

(At p. 384)

"The fine point of construction therefore is whether in including amphetamine Parliament intended that generic term to embrace both dexamphetamine and levoamphetamine. If this was not the case the inclusion of amphetamine in addition to dexamphetamine was otiose and surplusage in the category of drugs listed in Pt II. To put the question in another way, why did Parliament include dexamphetamine, when that particular stereoiosmeric form of amphetamine was already embraced in the generic term 'amphetamine'?

The court has ... to look at this problem as a pure matter of construction ...

[W]e have come to the conclusion that greater effect will be given to the intention of Parliament, as disclosed by the content and context of the statute, by holding that amphetamine embraces both forms of it. The addition of dexamphetamine was unnecessary, and its inclusion is certainly not sufficiently strong to justify the maxim [of *expressio unius exclusio alterius*] ... which would have the startling effect that one of two stereoisomeric forms of amphetamine would be excluded from the category of drugs, quite apart from the fact that it would raise considerable practical difficulties in analysing the all too frequently small amounts of the drug that is available.

Taking the question of construction in the round we have therefore come to the conclusion that the full generic meaning of the word 'Amphetamine', where it appears in para 1 of Pt II of the schedule, should be given to it."

Appeal dismissed.

12.7 *(v) In the possession of another*

Section 37(3) of the 1971 Act provides that "For the purposes of this Act the things which a person has in his possession shall be taken to include any thing subject to his control which is in the custody of another."

12.7.1   **1. Amato v. Walkingshaw**
                          1989 S.C.C.R. 564

A. was employed as a seaman on a ship travelling between Larne in Northern Ireland and Cairnryan in Scotland. He addressed an envelope to himself at the ship's office in Larne. The envelope arrived there but as A. was not then on duty the pursuer retained it intending to deliver it to A. when he appeared.

The pursuer became suspicious of the contents of the envelope and handed it to the authorities when the ship arrived in Cairnryan. The police opened the envelope and found a substance later proved to be diamorphine. A. was later charged with unlawful possession of that drug and, on being convicted, he appealed. The ground of appeal was that at the relevant time the diamorphine was not in the appellant's possession.

On appeal it was *held* that the appellant must have known what would happen to the envelope and that it was likely to be carried between Larne and Cairnryan while being held by the pursur on his behalf. The elements of knowledge and control necessary to establish possession were made out.

Appeal refused.

12.8 *(vi) Controlled drug*

12.8.1   **R. v. Couzens and Frankel**
                          [1992] Crim.L.R. 822

The appellants had been convicted of offences including producing a Class A controlled drug, methylenedioxymethylamphetamine, known as MDMA or Ecstasy. C.'s defence at the trial was that powder found at his flat, although containing MDMA did not constitute a Class A drug within the meaning of the 1971 Act because it did not fall within paragraph 1(c) of the second schedule of the Act. It was submitted on his behalf that the statutory definition required MDMA to be produced in a particular way and that C. having produced the MDMA by a different route, had not produced the controlled substance as defined by Parliament. That submission having been rejected by the trial judge, C. pleaded guilty and it was argued on appeal for both applicants that the trial judge had been wrong to reject the submission.

The expression "controlled drug" was defined in section 2(1)(a) of the 1971 Act which referred to the substances specified in the second schedule to the Act. The Misuse of Drugs Act 1971 (Modification) Order 1977 had added the following subparagraph to the list of Class A drugs "(c) any compound (not being methoxyphenamine or a compound for the time being specified in sub-paragraph (a) above) structurally derived from phenethylamine, an N-alkylphenethylamine, a-methylphenethylamine, and N-alkyl-a-methylphenethylamine, a-ethylphenethylamine or an N-alkyl-a-ethylphenethylamine by substitution in the ring to any extent with alkyl, alkoxy, alkylenedioxy or halide substituents, whether or not further substituted in the ring by one or more other univalent substituents."

At the trial, the only expert scientific witness was Dr G., who was called by the Crown. His evidence included the following matters: (1) the powder found contained the chemical substance MDMA; (2) MDMA was structurally derived from an N-alkylphenethylamine by substitution in the ring with an alkylene-dioxy substituent; (3) MDMA was not specifically named in the schedule but fell within the generic definition in subparagraph (c); it was one of a group or family of chemicals defined by the particular way in which the molecule of the substance was structured; that group or family could in practice contain thousands of substances and in theory an indefinite number of substances; (4) the structure of a molecule was the way in which the atoms which make up the molecule are joined together; (5) in the case of N-alkylamethylphenethylamine if one or more of the hydrogen atoms in a molecule was replaced by one of alkylenedioxy the result was MDMA, a controlled Class A drug.

Dr G.'s evidence also included the following points: (a) the first two substances named in subparagraph (c) were not controlled drugs whereas all the remainder listed before the words "by substitution" were Class B drugs; (b) MDMA could be made from non-controlled, legal substances which already have the alkylenedioxy substituent in the ring of their molecules; one such being the natural substance isasofrole. To make isasofrole into MDMA, another part of the molecule had to be changed; (c) the procedure said to have been followed by the appellant C. to produce MDMA did not involve a chemical process to achieve a substitution of alkylenedioxy into the ring of the molecule because the alklenedioxy was already present in isasofrole; (d) that he could not say from his analysis what had been the particular starting material; (e) that he as a chemist read the words of subparagraph (c) as words which simply identified the controlled drug and not as a definition which specified that a drug would only be controlled if it was produced from the substances listed by a particular chemical process; it was most unlikely that anyone would try to produce MDMA by starting with the fourth of the six substances listed and by direct chemical substitution of the alkylenedioxy substituent into the ring.

At trial and before the Court of Appeal it was argued for the defence that the phrase "structurally derived from" should be given its ordinary dictionary definition; the Crown argued that it was a term of art and should be given the technical definition given by Dr G. In relation to the phrase, "by substitution in the ring to any extent" the defence argued that this imported a positive human act or intervention and at a stage subsequent to the identification of the first substance. The Crown argued that there was nothing in the subparagraph which required such positive human intervention.

Held, the fundamental principle was that Parliament's intention must be derived from the words used in the statute and words in an Act of Parliament must be given their ordinary and natural meaning. Nevertheless, when a statutory provision was dealing with a technical subject, as was subparagraph (c), the words could not be given their ordinary and natural meaning because anyone other than a trained chemist would be incapable of understanding the subparagraph without the assistance of an expert. The words must therefore be given their ordinary and natural meaning to a person qualified to understand them; the only evidence from such a person was from Dr G. and his evidence was that subparagraph (c) was descriptive of the myriad of hallucinatory substances which could be produced with molecules of a particular type of structure. The words used by Parliament did not and could not be intended to confine the prohibition to hallucinatory substances produced in a particular way from the six substances listed because it was extremely unlikely that the hallucinatory substances could be produced by following literally what was stated in the subparagraph. Parliament must have known of these matters and have intended to classify the whole family of hallucinatory substances, of which MDMA was one, as Class A drugs. The judge was entitled to accept Dr G.'s evidence on the ordinary and natural meaning of this subparagraph to a qualified chemist, that evidence being unchallenged by any other competent evidence. Dr G. had described the subparagraph as a term of art describing the proscribed substances by their molecular structures and not by reference to the chemical processes by which those substances were produced.

This conclusion avoided the absurdity that it would be criminal conduct to produce MDMA manufactured in one way from the six listed substances but no crime would be committed if the same substance had been produced from another feedstock by different chemical processes. Dr G.'s evidence made it clear that the difficulties of establishing what the starting material and the process had been would have been enormous if not insuperable. Where there were two possible constructions, one of which gave a sensible result and one of which produced an absurdity, the Court was entitled, even obliged, to adopt the construction that would avoid the absurd result.

Appeal dismissed.

(vii) Production   **12.9**

1. R. v. Harris and Cox   **12.9.1**
[1996] Crim.L.R. 36

R., the co-defendant, grew cannabis plants from seed, which when harvested weighed some 21 kilogrammes. R. took the plants to C.'s attic where C. and H. stripped them in order to separate out those parts which could be used for smoking from those that could not. R. took some photographs of the activities. When these were sent for processing the cannabis resin plants were recognised and the police were informed. C. and H. were charged with and convicted of being concerned in the production of a Class B controlled drug, namely cannabis. They appealed on the grounds that the cannabis plants, having been grown and harvested, had already been produced before the appellants stripped them and therefore they could not have been concerned in the production of something that had already been produced.

Held, that the definition of "cannabis" covered both the plant and any part of the plant, that the definition of "production" referred specifically to "cultivation, manufacture or any other method", the "other method" here being the preparation of plants to discard those parts which were unusable; that the stripping of the plants was with a view to producing a part of the plant which would be suitable for the purpose of smoking; and that, accordingly, those appellants were indeed producing the part of the plant which amounted to the controlled drug in the circumstances of this case.

Appeal dismissed.

CHAPTER THIRTEEN

13.1 Problems arising from controlled drugs

13.2 *Introduction*

The cases considered below illustrate certain principles or topics relating to controlled drugs but not necessarily the Misuse of Drugs Act 1971.

13.3 *(i) Lawful authority*

13.3.1

1. R. v. Scott

(1921) 86 J.P. 69

S. was seen by policemen to speak with a woman in a London street. He was heard to say, "How many do you want tonight?" The woman was heard to reply, "Four packets — if it is the pure stuff." There was then an exchange of items. S. and the woman parted but the policemen were noticed. The woman threw away something, which on being recovered, was discovered to be two packets containing powder. Nothing was found on S. At trial there was evidence that the powder was cocaine.

At the close of the Crown case, counsel for the accused submitted that there was no evidence that the accused was an unauthorised person. That could have been done, it was said, by calling someone from the Home Office to say that no licence had been issued to the accused. The Court dismissed the submission.

SWIFT, J. (at p. 70): "The onus of proving the fact of possession of a licence or authority was on the defendant. He could do it quite easily if a licence or authority existed. It might be very difficult or impossible for the prosecution satisfactorily to prove that he did not possess any one or other of the qualifications which might entitle him to deal with the drug. But the defendant could prove without the least difficulty that he had authority to do it."

Found Guilty.

NOTE
The same point in relation to dangerous drugs was considered in *R. v. Ewens* [1966] 2 All E.R. 470 with the same result. See also *Wood v. Allan, supra*, at paragraph **5.3.26.**

(ii) Locked receptacle **13.4**

1. Rao v. Wyles **13.4.1**
[1949] 2 All E.R. 685

R. was a registered medical practitioner and thus authorised in law to possess dangerous drugs. He left his car in a park near a cinema. The car was locked but a leather case left inside the car was unlocked. The case contained dangerous drugs. The car was stolen but later recovered. The drugs had been removed. On conviction of failing to keep dangerous drugs in a locked receptacle, R. appealed.

LORD GODDARD, C.J. (at p. 686): "I am deciding this case merely on these facts, and I am not speculating as to what might be the result if different facts had been found, such as that this [leather] case had been locked or if the motor car had contained a locker in which these things were kept. First, I think that the regulation contemplates that drugs of this sort are to be kept regularly in some receptacle, and not that it can be said that at any particular moment because a lock is turned somewhere, that there is a compliance with the regulation. It is impossible to say that a motor car is a receptacle within the meaning of this regulation ... No-one, I think, would call a motor car a receptacle for drugs any more than he would call a house a receptacle for them."

Appeal dismissed.

NOTE
The doctor was convicted of contravening the Dangerous Drugs Regulations 1937, as amended. The report does not disclose the exact drug involved. The security of controlled drugs is now regulated far more precisely by The Misuse of Drugs (Safe Custody) Regulations 1973 (S.I. No. 798).

(iii) Prescription **13.5**

1. R. v. Jagger **13.5.1**
[1967] Crim.L.R. 587

J. had obtained amphetamine tablets in Italy. His defence was that he had mentioned the tablets to his doctor who had said that he could take them in an emergency when under stress but that he was not to take them regularly. This, it was submitted, amounted to the issue of a prescription in terms of the 1964 Act. The trial judge withdrew the defence from the jury. J. was convicted and appealed.

Held, that the trial judge was right in doing so. Without deciding whether a prescription could be oral, it was clear that what took place could not amount to a prescription. The doctor did not know the constituents of the tablets or the dosage and could not have prescribed them if asked to do so as they were not obtainable in England.

Appeal dismissed.

NOTE
The conviction was in terms of the 1964 Act and the meaning of the word "prescription" had to be construed in that context. The nearest that Parliament has come to define the word "prescription" in relation to controlled drugs is in The Misuse of Drugs Regulations 1985 (S.I. No. 2066), regulation 2. There "prescription" means a prescription issued by a doctor for the medical treatment of a single individual, by a dentist for the dental treatment of a single individual or by a veterinary surgeon or a veterinary practitioner for the purposes of animal treatment." The use of the word "issued" suggests written matter but the point is not yet settled.

13.6 *(iv) Expert evidence*

13.6.1

1. R. v. Richards
[1967] Crim.L.R. 589

R. was charged with permitting his house to be used for the purpose of smoking cannabis. Part of the evidence was that a girl who was at a party at his house was "clad only in a wrap" and was "merry and unconcerned." It was the prosecution case that her behaviour was consistent only with having smoked cannabis and a policeman gave evidence of the effects of smoking cannabis.

R.'s defence was that he was unaware that anyone had smoked the drug at his house and he had not given anyone permission to do so. R. was convicted and appealed on the ground that the evidence about the girl was inadmissible, or alternatively that the trial judge should have excluded it in the exercise of his discretion.

Held, the policeman's evidence was based only on textbook knowledge. The trial judge could not be said to have exercised his discretion wrongly. The evidence about the girl was highly prejudicial and the evidence was tenuous. The trial judge ought to have warned the jury that that evidence was tenuous and consequently the conviction was unsafe.

Appeal allowed.

13.6.2

2. White v. H.M. Advocate
1986 S.C.C.R. 224

W. was convicted of possessing lysergide with intent to supply it to another. She appealed on the ground that opinion evidence given by the police officers in the Drugs Squad, as to the dosage a drug user would consume was inadmissible as the officers were not medically qualified.

THE LORD JUSTICE-CLERK (ROSS) (at p. 226): "Police officers who have served for some time with the Drugs Squad do acquire knowledge of such matters as the quantity of drugs which a drugs user would consume in a day or in a week and so forth. Provided such a witness's qualifications as a police officer and his experience in the Drugs Squad are first established, such evidence, in our opinion, is clearly competent. Evidence of this nature is not competent only to medically qualified witnesses. In practice, evidence of this kind is frequently led at trials involving alleged contraventions of the Misuse of Drugs Act 1971 and, in our opinion, such evidence is quite competently led."

Appeal refused.

3. Haq v. H.M. Advocate   13.6.3
1987 S.C.C.R. 433

H. was convicted on indictment of possessing cannabis resin with intent to supply it to another, contrary to section 5(3) of the 1971 Act. It was not disputed that the appellant was in possession of a block of the drug weighing over 91 grammes, and the Crown relied for proof of intent on the size of that block and evidence from one police officer from the Drugs Squad who said that it was too large to be for personal use. H. appealed to the High Court on the ground that there was insufficient evidence of intent to supply.

Held, that there was sufficient evidence to entitle the jury to draw the necessary inference of intent.

THE LORD JUSTICE GENERAL (EMSLIE) (at p. 436): "The appellant is Anwar-ul-Haq, who was convicted after trial of charge (1) and charge (4) [a charge of possessing cannabis resin at a separate locus, to which he pleaded guilty] in the indictment. We are concerned with charge (1) in particular in this appeal because it was a charge of possession of cannabis resin in his shop on 11 June 1986 with intent to supply it to another or others. The facts were that according to the evidence a block of cannabis weighing 91 grammes was found to be in the possession of the appellant in his shop. That was a single block, and according to [counsel], and we accept this, there was no evidence of the finding of the usual dealer's paraphernalia in the house. There was no finding of small quantities made up for evident supply. There was no vast sum of money found in the premises, and [counsel's] submission to us was that it was not open to the jury to draw an inference from the size of the block alone, supported by opinion evidence from one woman police officer of experience, that this was not for Mr Anwar-ul-Haq's own use, but was intended to be supplied to others. We had an interesting discussion about who is and is not an expert, but the substance of the matter is that the opinion evidence given by the police officer provided some guidance for the jury in deciding what inference they themselves ought to draw from the size of the block in question. Without going into the police officer's reasons for expressing the opinion which she did, we are entirely satisfied that the evidence was sufficient to permit the jury to draw the inference which they undoubtedly did, and it has to be said that the appellant himself gave evidence, claiming that the block was for his own use, and it is clear from the verdict of the jury that they disbelieved that explanation. In the whole matter we shall refuse the appeal."

Appeal refused.

13.6.4   **4. Wilson v. H.M. Advocate**
1988 S.C.C.R. 384

W. was charged with being concerned in the supply of cannabis resin in the form of cannabis oil. Evidence was led at the trial from Drugs Squad officers and forensic scientists as to common methods of importing the drug in this form. That evidence was based on information obtained by them at seminars and in discussions with customs officers. Objection was taken to the evidence as hearsay. The trial judge repelled the objection. W. was convicted and he appealed *inter alia* on the basis that the trial judge had erred in admitting the evidence.

THE LORD JUSTICE GENERAL (EMSLIE) (at p. 385): "Drug enforcement knows no police boundaries within the United Kingdom and it is not surprising that those engaged in drug enforcement should be required, in order to perform their duties, to be fully informed about all matters which are relevant to the performance of these duties. Putting the matter shortly, it appears to us that the evidence given by the drugs squad officers and the forensic scientists could be described as simply disclosure of the received wisdom of persons concerned in drug enforcement, wisdom which they were bound to have picked up in various ways in order that they might perform their duties."

Appeal refused.

13.6.5   **5. Bauros and Ferns v. H.M. Advocate**
1991 S.C.C.R. 768

The appellants were each charged with possession of about four ounces of cannabis, with intent to supply it to others, contrary to section 5(3) of the 1971 Act. The Crown relied solely on the quantity of the drugs concerned for proof of the intent to supply. A constable from the Drugs

Squad gave evidence in chief that the quantity was too large for personal use, but stated in cross that it might represent a supply for two months of personal use. The sheriff rejected a submission of no case to answer, and the appellants were convicted. They appealed to the High Court.

Held, that it was for the jury to assess the constable's evidence and decide what they should make of it, taking it as a whole.

THE LORD JUSTICE GENERAL (HOPE) (at p. 771): "The appellants are Rudolph Bauros and Charles Ferns, who were found guilty in the sheriff court at Falkirk on indictment on two separate charges of possession of cannabis with intent to supply it to another, contrary to sections 4(1) and 5(3) of the Misuse of Drugs Act 1971. These were separate charges, in which each of them was separately involved, with separate quantities of cannabis resin in each case. But the issue in both of them was the same, and that is whether the drugs which were found in their possession were for their own use or were there with intent to supply them to another or others, contrary to the relevant subsections. It should be noted that they were charged only with possession with intent to supply, and that there was no alternative charge of simple possession in either case. The jury, by majority, decided to convict them both of the charges as libelled, and they were sentenced to periods of imprisonment. The appeals are taken only against conviction.

It should be mentioned, by way of background, that in the case of the first appellant the amount of cannabis resin which was found in his possession was a single block of 101.2 grammes, or approximately four ounces. In the case of the second appellant there were two pieces, one of which was quite small, 16.8 grammes, but then there was another of 103.2 grammes in a single block. The quantities which were found in their possession were not so large that they plainly could not have been in their possession for their own use. So this was, or can be regarded as, a marginal case. There was no other evidence pointing to drug dealing of any kind, and the whole matter depended upon what was to be made of the quantity found in their possession, together with such evidence as was available from a police officer called Detective Constable Motion, who had many years' experience in dealing with controlled drugs.

When he came to charge the jury on these matters, the sheriff referred to the fact that the Crown had led evidence from Detective Constable Motion to, as he put it, 'help you on the issue as to whether the quantities were in the possession of the accused with intent to supply to others.' He then went on to summarise for the benefit of the jury the evidence which had been given by this police officer. The police officer began by stating in evidence in chief that the quantities which were found in the possession of each of the appellants were such that they were too large for the personal use of either of them, and that they must have been in their possession with intent to supply. Had matters remained there throughout the evidence of this police officer, there would have been no appeal, because it was accepted that the case would then have been on all fours with the case of *Haq* v *H.M. Advocate* [1987 S.C.C.R. 433]. In that case a police officer gave evidence, which was unshaken throughout, to the effect that she was 100 per cent certain that the quantity was such that it was in the possession of the accused with intent to supply to others, and it was held that the evidence was sufficient to permit the jury to draw the necessary inference.

But the matter did not end there because, as the sheriff pointed out in his charge, when the detective constable came to be cross-examined, he changed his evidence. He gave a different version, because he said that it all depended on how much the individual was going to smoke and how much he was going to use. He conceded in his cross-examination that, perhaps, for a heavy user, four ounces of cannabis might represent two months' use. He was then re-examined, and the examination brought the matter back to some degree to the position which he had spoken to in evidence in chief. He said, according to the sheriff's recollection, that it was unlikely that this quantity would be for the personal use of the accused and that his conclusion was that it was probably in their possession for supply. It should be mentioned that the sheriff was careful to point out in his charge, in several places, that the jury were entitled to take one part of a witness's evidence and to reject another part. He made it clear that this was a matter for the jury to assess, and that, as he put it in his charge, 'it's up to you to decide.'

This brings us to the point of criticism which was advanced in support of these appeals by [counsel] for the first appellant and [counsel] for the second appellant. The arguments were very much to the same effect. [Counsel for the first appellant's] approach was this, that what the detective constable was doing was giving evidence as an expert. The jury had therefore to perform a task which, in the result, was one which they could not properly perform, since they had been given two different propositions, one in chief and one in cross-examination. They had two different analyses of the quantity and its effect, and, since this was a matter of expert evidence, they had no proper basis upon which they could select between the two. The sheriff was wrong to leave the matter to the jury, because it was a matter for expert evidence and was outside the general knowledge of members of the public. It was not a matter that could be decided by the jury on a simple assessment of the demeanour of the witness. It required some understanding of the level of expertise of the witness, and since his evidence was contradictory it was not evidence which could properly go before the jury at all.

[Counsel for the second appellant] adopted the same approach. He submitted that this case was one where the evidence of the detective constable was crucial to the case. There being no other evidence to support the Crown case, which depended solely upon the quantity of the drugs found and the conclusions that might be drawn from it, there had to be clear evidence from this police officer on which the jury would be entitled to rely. He referred us to a discussion of the position of the expert witness and an assessment of expert evidence in *Davie* v *Magistrates of Edinburgh* [1953 S.C. 34], where Lord President Cooper said, at p. 40, that expert witnesses cannot usurp the functions of the jury or the judge. 'Their duty is to furnish the Judge or jury with the necessary scientific criteria for testing the accuracy of their conclusions, so as to enable the Judge or jury to form their own independent judgment by the application of their criteria to the facts proved in evidence.'

He added that if conflicting scientific expert evidence is adduced by a party, he cannot complain if on that account alone the whole of it is treated with more than suspicion. [Counsel for the second appellant's] criticism was that the evidence of this police officer, taken as a whole, did not come up to the standard which the Crown had to achieve if it was to be relied on as expert evidence, so it was evidence which could not properly be relied upon by the jury in support of the Crown case. It can be seen that there are perhaps two slightly different approaches adopted by [counsel for the first and counsel for the second appellant]. But both of them depended upon the critical point that the evidence of Detective Constable Motion changed to a significant degree in cross-examination from that given by him initially in evidence in chief.

It is worth reminding ourselves that in *Haq* v *H.M. Advocate*, at p. 436, the Lord Justice-General said that the substance of the matter was that the opinion evidence given by the police officer in that case 'provided some guidance for the jury in deciding what inference they themselves ought to draw from the size of the block in question.' That was a case where the police officer was 100 per cent certain that the size of the block was such that it was in possession of the accused with intent to supply to others. But it is significant that in his approach to the matter the Lord Justice-General regarded this not as something which concluded the matter so far as the jury were concerned, but as evidence which was available to them for their guidance as to what inference they themselves ought to draw. This, as it happens, is precisely in line with the remarks to which our attention was directed in *Davie* at p. 40, and also remarks to the same effect in Lord Russell's opinion at p. 42. The question is that the opinion expressed by an expert witness is evidence which is available for assessment by the judge or jury, but that the expert can never usurp the function of the judge or jury, which, in the end of the day, is to assess the effect of the evidence as a whole.

So it is to the present case. The jury were presented with evidence from the detective constable and it was their function to assess his evidence and to decide what they should make of it, taking it as a whole. We entirely appreciate the point which has been made with care by both counsel about the way in which the evidence changed as it developed under cross-examination. Nevertheless, the more that was said by them by way of criticism of this evidence, the clearer it became to us that the exercise of assessment was essentially one for the jury who heard that evidence. This is not a case where it can be said that the witness did not at any point in his evidence come up to the necessary standard to enable the jury to draw the conclusion that the appellant was guilty of these charges beyond reasonable doubt. It is conceded that evidence to that standard is to be found in his evidence in chief. So the question is whether that evidence was undermined to such an extent by what happened later that no reasonable jury would have been entitled to rely upon any part of his evidence for guidance in deciding what to make of the quantities of cannabis which were found in the possession of the accused. That is a question which cannot be seen as anything other than a jury question, and we think that the sheriff was well founded when he took the view, as he tells us in his note, that he did not consider that the function of assessment was one for him to undertake. As he puts it, he formed the view that this issue should more properly be left to the jury. We agree that he was right to do that and we consider that the directions which he gave were sufficiently full and complete on all the relevant issues to enable the jury to perform their function."

Appeal refused.

NOTE

It has been observed that it is improper to ask an expert witness to express an opinion on an essential fact beyond reasonable doubt, that being an invitation to usurp the function of the jury: *Hendry v. H.M. Advocate*, 1988 S.L.T. 25. For an interesting discussion of this run of cases, see Bovey, "Expert Evidence in Prosecutions" (1995) 40 J.L.S. 355.

13.7 *(v) Entrapment*

13.7.1 **1. H.M. Advocate v. Harper**
1989 S.C.C.R. 472

Policemen had information that controlled drugs were being sold from an ice-cream van of a description that fitted the van being operated by the accused. A policeman approached the van and asked the question, "Have you got a couple of trips?" The accused asked the policeman who had sent him and the latter gave a nickname. The accused then sold the policeman controlled drugs. The accused was charged with supplying a controlled drug to another.

At his trial the accused's solicitor objected to evidence of the supply as having been unfairly obtained by entrapment. The trial judge repelled the objection and ruled that the evidence was admissible. The accused then pleaded guilty.

In the course of a written judgment on the point at issue the trial judge held that there was no defence of entrapment in Scots law and that in the absence of any evidence of deception, pressure or encouragement to commit the crime the evidence was admissible.

SHERIFF SPY (at p. 475): "As Lord Justice-General Clyde noted in the case of *Marsh* v. *Johnston*, [1959 S.L.T. (Notes) 28] it would otherwise be difficult to prove offences of this nature. It seems equally apt to me to go on to say as he did in that case that if evidence of this kind is necessarily to be regarded as incompetent there would be wholesale flouting of the provisions of Acts of Parliament — in this case the provisions of the Misuse of Drugs Act 1971. In any event, as I have said, I cannot hold on the evidence as a matter of law that the police pressed or tricked the accused into committing an offence which he would not otherwise have committed, and it must be borne in mind that the accused did have possession of controlled drugs which is in itself an offence under statute."

Plea of guilty.

NOTE
In *R.* v. *Beaumont* [1987] Crim.L.R. 786 the Court of Appeal (Criminal Division) held that in the circumstances of that case the entrapment aspect provided a substantial mitigating factor and reduced a sentence of imprisonment on that ground.

2. Weir v. Jessop 13.7.2
1992 S.L.T. 533

W. was charged on summary complaint with supplying cannabis resin to a police officer and also with possession with intent to supply. During the trial, evidence was led that police officers in possession of a search warrant had gone to the door of the accused's house and without executing the warrant had asked if they could be supplied with cannabis, pretending to have been sent by the accused's brother. They had been supplied with drugs and thereafter executed the search warrant. The sheriff repelled a defence objection to the leading of the evidence on the grounds that it was unfairly obtained, and convicted the accused, who appealed to the High Court.

Held, (1) that whether or not the evidence was admissible was a question of fairness; (2) that cases such as the present were different from those involving evidence of statements made by suspects to the police after the commission of a crime, where the test of fairness also applied; (3) that there was no unfairness to the accused, he not having been pressurised or induced to commit an offence which he would otherwise never have done.

THE LORD JUSTICE-CLERK (ROSS) (at p. 537): "Where as here a police officer poses as a drugs buyer in order to establish whether the accused is dealing in controlled drugs, there is no question of the Crown being able in effect to make the accused a compellable witness. There is no question of the evidence of the police being used as a substitute for the evidence of the accused. On the contrary, the evidence given by the police officers was merely evidence of investigations which they carried out in order to ascertain whether there was dealing in controlled drugs at this house.

Admittedly, [the detective constable] deceived the accused as to his identity. He gave every appearance of being a member of the public and not a police officer. He also deceived the appellant in another respect. In order to establish his bona fides, he professed to have been sent to the house by the appellant's brother. None the less, apart from representing that he would like to obtain cannabis, he applied no pressure, encouragement or inducement to incite the appellant to commit an offence which he would otherwise not have committed. It might be different if the appellant had appeared reluctant to carry out the transaction and the police officer had pleaded with him to do so. Again it might have been different if the appellant had indicated that he was not in the habit of carrying out such transactions or that he had never sold drugs before in this way. But there was no such suggestion in the evidence and the only reasonable inference from the evidence is that the appellant was prepared to supply controlled drugs to callers, always provided that the callers could offer some colourable explanations for having come to his door for that purpose. There is nothing at all in the findings to suggest that supplying drugs was something which the appellant would never have done but for the approach made to him by the police officer. Accordingly, applying the test of fairness as it was described in *Cook v. Skinner* 1977 S.L.T. (Notes) 11, I am of opinion that the conduct of [the detective constable] did not amount to an unfair trick upon the accused. Moreover, even though there was an element of deception in the two respects already described, I am satisfied on the findings that there was no pressure, encouragement or inducement to commit an offence which would never otherwise have been committed at all."

LORD MORISON (at p. 539): "But although deception as to the policeman's true identity was involved, that deception cannot reasonably be regarded as having induced the commission of the crime of supply, if the supply was one which would in any event have taken place as a result of a request by a genuine customer. The criminality of the appellant's act lay in the fact that he supplied drugs to another, not that he did so to someone who turned out to be a policeman. That essential feature of the crime was not one which resulted from any undue pressure or persuasion on the part of the policeman. It was a purely voluntary act on the part of the appellant. The appellant was not tricked into doing something which he would not ordinarily do. I see no reason in principle to exclude evidence of the act merely because the appellant thought that he was dealing with an authentic customer. His criminal behaviour was induced not by the deception, but by the fact that he was a person willing to supply drugs on request to anybody in whom he had confidence."

LORD CAPLAN (at p. 540): "The position of the police is, however, quite different where the primary objective is not to seek evidence against a person suspected of a particular crime but rather to carry out an investigative function to ascertain whether crime is in fact being committed. In respect of the investigative function of the police it would be quite unrealistic to suppose that a certain amount of covert investigative work requiring a degree of what could be described as deception is not sometimes necessary. This must be particularly so under modern conditions where the police are often faced with requiring to investigate crimes, such as drug dealing, carried out by organised professional criminals who themselves, without hesitation, resort to more than a fair degree of deception. The public have a considerable interest to secure the detection of crime and if a reasonable and necessary degree of undercover operation is necessary to achieve that end then there is justification for tolerating it, provided that the process is not in any respect unfair to the supposed perpetrator of the crime. That, however, is not to say that deception is a desirable technique for the police to employ except in circumstances where it is necessary. However, deception should not in any event be used indiscriminately and certainly not in any way that might unfairly induce a person to commit a crime which he might not otherwise have been prepared to commit. Thus the circumstances under which police carrying out investigations may employ undercover techniques in order to secure information later to be used in evidence against a perpetrator of the crime are also governed by rules of law and the most important of these is that an accused should not be jeopardised by investigative methods which on a balanced view could be described as unfair. Just what investigative procedures may be regarded as fair or unfair will vary with the circumstances."

Appeal refused.

NOTE

For a discussion of this case see Fraser, "Undercover Law Enforcement in Scots Law" 1994 S.L.T. (News) 113, where that writer concludes that the tactics of the police were "unobjectionable in principle" and the decision of the High Court of Justiciary to be correct.

In England there has been more concern about entrapment: it was recognised in *R. v. Beaumont* (1987) 9 Cr.App.R. (S.) 342 that entrapment could be a substantial mitigating factor in sentencing. For an example of substantial mitigation in regard to controlled drugs, see *R. v. Chapman* (1989) 11 Cr.App.R. 222.

In regard to substantive law the worries are frequently directed to the exclusion of evidence obtained in what might be described as doubtful ways, but in the context of the Police and Criminal Evidence Act 1984: see Sharpe, "Covert Police

Operations and the Discretionary Exclusion of Evidence" [1994] Crim.L.R. 793
and Robertson, "Entrapment Evidence" [1994] Crim.L.R. 805.

13.7.3   **3. R. v. Mackey and Shaw**
                             (1993) 14 Cr.App.R. (S.) 53

The appellant Shaw pleaded guilty to being concerned in the supply of a
Class A controlled drug, heroin. S. met an undercover police officer posing
as a possible heroin purchaser. They agreed that S. would arrange a supply
of heroin and then contact the officer, which he did later that day. They
agreed to meet the following day, and a meeting took place between the
officer, the two appellants and a third defendant (C.). The officer tested
the heroin, and then Mackey (M.) and C. brought it out of the house
where the testing had taken place so as to exchange it for the cash which
the officer had in his car. At this point other officers arrested the three
defendants; the third defendant had in his possession almost one
kilogramme of heroin of 61 per cent purity, worth an estimated £150,000.
M. was sentenced to eight years' imprisonment and S. to seven years'
imprisonment. On behalf of S. it was argued that the sentencer had wrongly
treated the alleged entrapment of S. as having no significance in mitigation.

   Held, it was clear from the decisions of the Court that circumstances
such as those put forward by S. in the present case were capable of
affording material for mitigating the sentence from what would otherwise
have been appropriate. The principle was plainly established in *R. v.
Beaumont* (1987) 9 Cr.App.R. (S.) 342, and *R. v. Chapman* (1989) 11
Cr.App.R. (S.) 222. The Court was impressed by the argument that the
sentencer had erred in not reflecting the element of entrapment by way of
mitigation, and would reduce the sentence on S. to six years. M.'s sentence
was not excessive.

FRENCH, J. (at p. 56): "It was urged upon us that in the instant case the
learned judge either did not consider that the element of entrapment was
something which he should bear in mind in mitigation at all, or, at the
very least, had that been his view he should have referred to that in his
sentencing observations. He did not. Alternatively he should, had he taken
the view that it was a matter which could properly be brought into account
in mitigation, have reduced the sentence in the case of Shaw below that
of seven years. In either event, submits [counsel for Shaw], the learned
judge was in error in not reflecting the 'entrapment' element by way of
mitigation.

   We are impressed by that argument. In the judgment of this Court the
proper course for us to take is to quash the sentence of six years and
substitute for it a sentence of five years' imprisonment in order to reflect
the 'entrapment' point, and also to reflect the impressive element of effort
made by this appellant to improve his personal life and his domestic life.

So far as the appeal of Mackey is concerned, we do not accept the argument, advanced attractively though it was by [counsel] for Mackey, to the effect that the previous experience before the Court of his client should not have been reflected in the imposition of an additional year's sentence in his case. We consider that in regarding that earlier sentence for importing drugs as a shot across the bow, and as one which should have been taken as a warning by Mr Mackay, the learned judge was entirely right. Accordingly, no complaint can be made on this score. Nor can we, as we are urged to do, find any ground for reducing what was otherwise conceded to be a proper tariff sentence on the ground of some distinction between the role played by Mackey and the role played by his co-accused.

Accordingly, in the case of Mackey his appeal is dismissed."

Appeals dealt with accordingly.

NOTE

In *Williams v. D.P.P.* (1994) 98 Cr.App.R. 209 the question arose as to whether the police had acted as agent provocateur rendering their evidence inadmissible. However, the Court held, using a helpful phrase, that the police in the relevant circumstances had done nothing "to force, persuade, encourage or coerce' the appellants. Subterfuge is a different matter but even then it does not necessarily lead to evidence being excluded: *R. v. Maclean and Kosten* [1993] Crim.L.R. 687. For discussion on entrapment see *R. v. Pattemore* [1994] Crim.L.R. 836.

4. Bekar v. H.M. Advocate 13.7.4
High Court of Justiciary, unreported, August 11, 1994

B. appealed against a sentence of 12 months' imprisonment for supplying cannabis, valued at £45, from his cafe to newspaper journalists.

THE LORD JUSTICE-CLERK (ROSS): "It appears that a national newspaper was doing a series on drugs in Scotland. As a result of various articles in the newspaper they received telephone calls suggesting that drugs could be acquired quite openly in the [...] which was the cafe of which the appellant was the proprietor in Glasgow. As a result the newspaper dispatched two young reporters to the cafe. They asked the appellant for drugs. They were asked for £45 of money which they paid over. They were told to return the cafe about two hours later and when they did so the appellant gave them a brown paper bag which contained cannabis. The police were informed and it transpired that the bag did indeed contain cannabis sufficient for twenty to fifty reefer-type cigarettes.

The sheriff took the view that this was a serious contravention of the Act because, as he put it, it appeared that the appellant had sold cannabis almost literally across the counter in his cafe to two persons who were strangers and who had come in requesting that they be supplied with drugs.

We agree with the sheriff that the offence was undoubtedly a serious one. [Counsel] has drawn attention to a number of features favourable to the appellant. He is a successful business man. He owns his own cafe. He is a first offender. There is a favourable social enquiry report and in all the circumstances [counsel] has suggested that a non-custodial sentence should be considered. The social worker had taken the view that the appellant, because of his business would be unable to carry out community service but [counsel] assured us that that was not so and that he was willing to carry out community service.

Having regard to the nature of this offence as we have already described it, we are satisfied that the sheriff was fully entitled to impose the sentence which he did. This was, as we see it, a bad case of supplying drugs to members of the public and in these circumstances, although the quantity involved was relatively small, we are quite satisfied that the sheriff was fully entitled to select a period of twelve months' imprisonment in this case. Nothing which [counsel] has said today would persuade us that we would be justified in interfering with the sentence selected by the sheriff."

Appeal refused.

NOTE
A brief report of this appeal is at 1994 G.W.D. 31–1859.

13.7.5   **5. R. v. Latif and Shahzad**
[1996] Crim.L.R. 414

H., a paid informer employed by the United States Drug Enforcement Agency in Pakistan, agreed a plan with the appellant S. in Pakistan to import 20 kilogrammes of heroin into the United Kingdom. S. delivered the heroin to H., who delivered it to a Drugs Enforcement Agency officer. The drugs were then brought to England by a customs officer, who although acting under the orders of his superiors had no licence under section 3 of the 1971 Act to import them. H. then came to England and persuaded S. to follow him and collect the heroin in London. When S. arrived in London he, together with the appellant L., arranged to meet H. to pay for and collect the heroin. A customs officer, purporting to act on H.'s behalf, carrying bags of Horlicks made up to resemble the original bags of heroin, handed the bags to S., who was immediately arrested, as was L. shortly afterwards. Both appellants were tried on an indictment containing two counts, (1) being knowingly concerned in the fraudulent evasion of the prohibition on the importation of a controlled drug (heroin), contrary to section 170(2) of the 1979 Act and (2) with attempting to be knowingly concerned in dealing with goods subject to a prohibition on importation with intent to evade each prohibition, contrary to section 1(1) of the Criminal Attempts Act 1981. The judge ruled against submissions (i) that the proceedings were an abuse of process and should be stayed since S. had been incited to commit the offence by H. and the customs officer who had lured him into the jurisdiction; (ii) that the judge should have excluded the prosecution evidence of H., and the customs officer under section 78 of the Police and Criminal Evidence Act 1984; and (iii) that on the prosecution evidence the appellants were not guilty of the offence charged on count 1. They were convicted on count 1 and the judge discharged the jury from returning a verdict on count 2. Their appeal to the Court of Appeal on the ground that the judge's rulings were erroneous was dismissed and they appealed to the House of Lords.

Held, that (1) in criminal proceedings, weighing countervailing considerations of policy and justice, it was for the trial judge, in the exercise of his discretion, to decide whether there had been an abuse of process, which amounted to an affront to the public conscience and thereby required those proceedings to be stayed. In the instant case, assuming that the customs officer had committed an offence against section 50(3) of the 1979 Act neither his actions nor those of the informer H. in luring the appellants to England amounted to such an abuse of process that the proceedings against the appellants should be stayed.

(2) As the appellants had not been prejudiced in their defence by the admission of the prosecution evidence of H. and the customs officer, and their submissions of abuse of process had failed, the judge had not erred in not excluding that evidence under section 78 of the 1984 Act.

(3) Although S. was not guilty of the full offence against section 170(2) of the 1984 Act, since the importation was carried out by the customs officers, nevertheless, he had committed two attempts against evasion; first, in Pakistan, where S. had delivered the heroin to H. for onward transmission to the United Kingdom, and, secondly, where he tried to collect the heroin from H. in London for distribution in the United Kingdom. Thus, nothing the customs officers did could absolve S. of his criminal conduct. The English courts had jurisdiction over such criminal attempts even where overt acts had taken place abroad. S. had intended to commit the full offence, and was guilty of steps more than merely preparatory to the commission of the full offence and had committed attempts at evasion contrary to section 170(2). As an offence contrary to section 170(2) could be committed in one of two ways, evasion or attempted evasion, S. had been rightly convicted of an offence under section 170(2) of the 1984 Act. Similarly, L.'s conduct in London had been sufficient to found a similar conviction contrary to section 170(2).

Appeal dismissed.

13.8 *(vi) Prisoners*

13.8.1 1. R. v. Board of Visitors at Highpoint Prison, *ex parte* McConkey
The Times, September 23, 1982

McC. was a prisoner who was permitted a good deal of freedom by day and night. He went to a particular room to play cards with certain named prisoners. Prison officers went into that room as they suspected that cannabis was being or had been smoked there. The room was searched and a pipe and some cannabis were found.

The matter concerning McC. was put before the Board of Visitors and on the evidence the Board was satisfied that cannabis had been smoked in the room in the presence of McC. and that he must have been aware of that fact. McC. was found guilty of an offence against discipline, contrary to rule 47(20) of the Prison Rules 1964 and he was ordered to forfeit 90 days' remission of sentence.

McC. applied for an order of *certiori* to quash the finding of guilt and the award of 90 days' loss of remission.

McCULLOUGH, J.: "The special problems of prisons justifies the existence of rules which would be intolerable in the outside world, but they provided no reason to adopt an approach to interpretation which was harshly at odds with the generally accepted notion of criminal responsibility.

No doubt there were circumstances in which presence at a party would be an offence against good order and discipline, for example, where there was in effect an order that prisoners were not wilfully to remain in the presence of others whom they knew to be using drugs; but no such rule was alleged here."

Application granted.

NOTE
The Prison Rules apply only to a particular and limited group of people as do the Army Act 1955, the Air Force Act 1955 and the Naval Discipline Act 1957. McConkey's case serves as a reminder that the general rules of criminal liability continue to apply even though there may be special problems arising from the use of controlled drugs in circumstances where strict discipline is required.

13.8.2   **2. Kerr v. H.M. Advocate**
1991 S.C.C.R. 774

K. was convicted of supplying £7 worth of cannabis resin and nine buprenorphine tablets to a prisoner whom he was visiting. He was sentenced to two years' and 18 months' imprisonment on the respective charges, the sentences to run concurrently. He appealed to the High Court.

Held, that the circumstances made the charges very serious indeed, despite the small quantities involved, and that the sentences were not excessive.

THE LORD JUSTICE GENERAL (HOPE) (at p. 775): "The circumstances in which the supply took place were such that the charges with which we are concerned here are very serious indeed. They amounted to a plain and deliberate contravention of the regulations by which visits to prisoners are permitted. The supply of drugs to prisoners is a well-known evil which requires to be dealt with severely, when it is detected ... When passing sentence the sheriff told the appellant that the courts in Scotland had given repeated warnings that those who engage in the dealing of drugs or supplying of drugs, in any form, are likely to be very severely punished indeed. He added that it was a particularly serious matter to have been supplying drugs to a prisoner, within a prison, because of the well-known problems that the prison authorities encounter as a result of this activity. We agree entirely with what the sheriff said in these comments, and we are quite unable to regard the sentences which he passed on these two charges as in any way excessive."

Appeal refused.

NOTE

Kerr's case is one of a series on the theme of prisons. A clear distinction exists between the supply of controlled drugs by members of the public to prisoners and offences by prisoners. Sentences in regard to the former category have tended to be exemplary, usually immediate imprisonment. Sentences in the latter category are frequently modest because of associated results of the offence such as loss of remission.

For instances in Scotland of the supply to prisoners, see *McAulay v. H.M. Advocate*, 1987 G.W.D. 34–1223; *Humphries v. H.M. Advocate*, 1988 G.W.D. 10–414; *Gordon v. H.M. Advocate*, 1988 G.W.D. 7–276; *Chaplin v. MacPhail*, 1988 G.W.D. 30–1283; *Carr v. H.M. Advocate*, 1990 G.W.D. 12–605; *Dailly v. Docherty*, 1990 G.W.D. 20–1121; *Ogilvie v. H.M. Advocate*, 1991 G.W.D. 37–2249; *McVeigh v. H.M. Advocate*, 1992 G.W.D. 31–1822; *Brown v. H.M. Advocate*, 1993 G.W.D. 33–2125; *Robb v. Douglas*, 1993 G.W.D. 35–2242; *Morrison v. H.M. Advocate*, 1993 G.W.D. 39–2579; *Smith v. Donnelly*, 1994 G.W.D. 8–488; *Oliver v. Howdle*, 1995 G.W.D. 28–1491; *Hamilton v. MacLeod*, 1996 G.W.D. 14–831; *White v. Douglas*, 1996 G.W.D. 25–1430; *Ferguson v. Douglas*, 1996 G.W.D. 28–1673; *Flintoft v. Scott*, 1997 G.W.D. 2–52; and *Watson v. Speirs*, 1997 G.W.D. 8–320.

For instances of prisoners committing offences, see *McGarry v. Wilson*, 1989 G.W.D. 40–1862; *Reilly v. Jessop*, 1990 G.W.D. 30–1742; *Roy v. Docherty*, 1991 G.W.D. 13–777; *Murray v. MacPhail*, 1992 G.W.D. 2–75; *Walker v. MacDougall*, 1993 G.W.D. 5–324; *McDowell v. Douglas*, 1994 G.W.D. 16–1015; *McJimpsey v. H.M. Advocate*, 1995 G.W.D. 14–771; *Glancy v. H.M. Advocate*, 1995 G.W.D. 29–1529; and *Alexander v. Normand*, 1997 G.W.D. 15–672.

13.8.3
3. R. v. Savage
(1993) 14 Cr.App.R. (S.) 409

S. was convicted of supplying cannabis. He visited a prisoner and during the course of the visit handed over a small quantity of cannabis. He was sentenced to six months' imprisonment.

Held, taking drugs into a prison was a serious matter, in view of the trouble that drugs could cause in prison. The sentence imposed was proper for a man of good character.

ROCH, J. (at p. 410): "The taking of drugs into prison is a serious matter, because drugs inside prison have much greater value than they have on the streets. Drugs have become the main currency in prison. The trouble that drugs can cause in prison is obvious: injury to persons, particularly prison staff and damage to property can easily follow from the taking of drugs in a prison setting. Such offences are all too prevalent and require the courts to impose deterrent sentences. These are not sentences for which a nominal period of imprisonment is appropriate, despite the mitigation which may exist for the individual defendant. In most cases the defendant will be a person of good character, and have available other points of mitigation."

Appeal dismissed.

13.8.4
4. R. v. Holloway
(1995) 16 Cr.App.R. (S.) 220

H. pleaded guilty to possessing a Class C drug with intent to supply. H. went to visit a friend who was a prisoner and H. was found to be carrying 86 diazepam tablets. He admitted that he intended to give them to his friend, who could not sleep. H. was sentenced to three months' imprisonment.

Held, smuggling into prison was a serious and frequent offence: the sentence was not manifestly excessive.

TUDOR EVANS, J. (at p. 221): "In our view, smuggling into prison is a serious and nowadays a frequent offence. The potential for harm in this type of offence is obvious: for example, if the drugs had come into the possession of a remand prisoner who was in a state of depression, then the risks of self-harm are clear.

In our view, the judge was right to pass a custodial sentence in this case in order to make it absolutely clear to members of the public who are minded to behave as this appellant did, that such conduct will receive condign punishment.

We have considered whether on the particular facts of this case a sentence of three months was excessive. In our view, it is possible to argue that the sentence was on the high side but we consider that it was by no means manifestly excessive. If the gravity of the offence is to be marked with a custodial sentence, then in this case a sentence of three months was appropriate."

Appeal dismissed.

(vii) Publications **13.9**

1. John Calder (Publications) Ltd v. Powell **13.9.1**
[1965] 1 Q.B. 509

The police seized a large quantity of books from a bookshop in Sheffield and that included copies of Alexander Trocchi's *Cain's Book*. An order was made by the justices for forfeiture, the justices having heard expert evidence and having read the book themselves. They concluded that Trocchi's book was obscene and likely to deprave and corrupt, and that the defence had not proved publication to be justified as being for the public good on the ground that it was in the interests of science, literature or learning or of other objects of general concern in accordance with section 4 of the Obscene Publications Act 1959. The publishers appealed.

LORD PARKER, C.J. (at p. 515): "In my judgment it is perfectly plain that depravity, and, indeed, obscenity (because obscenity is treated as a tendency to deprave) is quite apt to cover what was suggested by the prosecution in this case. This book — the less said about it the better — concerned the life, or imaginary life, of a junkie in New York, and the suggestion of the prosecution was that the book highlighted, as it were, the favourable effects of drug-taking, and, so far from condemning it, advocated it, and that there was a real danger that those into whose hands the book came might be tempted at any rate to experiment with drugs and get the favourable sensations highlighted by the book.

In my judgment there is no reason whatever to confine obscenity and depravity to sex, and there was ample evidence upon which the justices could hold that this book was obscene."

Appeal dismissed.

NOTE
Since 1965 there have been many publications concerned with what might be termed the non-legal aspects of controlled drugs. Few of these publications have been destroyed or where there has been destruction little in the way of reported cases has developed. However, in *R. v. Skirving* [1985] Crim.L.R. 317, the publication involved seemed to have been even more explicit than Trocchi's book. S., the appellant, had for publication for gain, copies of a book or pamphlet entitled *Attention Coke Lovers. Free Base. The Greatest Thing Since Sex.* It was aimed at those who were actual or potential users of cocaine, contained detailed instruction

and recipes for obtaining the maximum effects of the drug and dealt with the principal methods of ingestion. It also explained in detail how to carry out certain chemical operations in order to obtain free base. On conviction, an appeal was taken on the ground that expert witnesses had been used to explain the effects of cocaine. That was held not to usurp the function of the jury and the appeal was dismissed.

13.9.2   **2. R. v. Skirving**
                                   [1985] 1 Q.B. 819

The appellants, who were book distributors, had copies of a book which was aimed at actual and potential abusers of cocaine and described in detail how to prepare the drug into "free-base" for smoking as being the best method of ingestion for enabling the maximum effect to be obtained. The appellants admittedly had the book for publication for gain and were tried on a count of contravening section 2(1) of the Obscene Publications Act 1959 as amended by section 1(1) of the Obscene Publications Act 1964. Expert evidence which was admitted, gave a scientific assessment of the characteristics of cocaine, the physical and mental effect on users and abusers and explained the different effects of the various methods of ingesting the drug. The appellants were convicted and appealed against conviction on the grounds (a) that the judge erred in ruling that expert evidence could be called as to the effects of taking cocaine, (b) that such expert evidence was inadmissible, (c) that it was for the jury to decide unaided whether the book was obscene, and (d) that the verdict was unsafe or unsatisfactory because the admission of such evidence could only have confused the jury causing insufficient regard to be had to the question whether the book itself tended to deprave and corrupt and exclusive or excessive regard to be paid to the question whether the drug tended to deprave and corrupt.

Held, that since the expert evidence was not aimed at establishing that the book had a tendency to deprave and corrupt its likely readers and since the effect of cocaine and the various methods by which it could be ingested were not within the experience of the ordinary person, scientific evidence was essential to ensure that the jury were equipped with the information necessary to enable them to decide whether the book had a tendency to deprave and corrupt.

Appeal dismissed.

13.10 *(viii) Breach of the peace*

13.10.1   **1. Thompson v. MacPhail**
                                  1989 S.C.C.R. 266

T. was seen to enter a cubicle of a toilet in a restaurant. He remained in there for an extended period of time. The manager became suspicious and called the police who forced open the door. The police saw T. inside the cubicle in the act of removing from his arm a needle attached to a syringe and they saw blood on the toilet wall and floor. The policemen were not alarmed by this sight but the manager was concerned for the safety of himself, his staff and his customers when he saw the syringe.

T. was charged with a breach of the peace in that he injected himself with an unknown substance "to the alarm of the lieges." On behalf of T. it was submitted that there was no case to answer in that there was no evidence as to what was in the syringe; that the cubicle concerned was self-contained and could not be looked into and that to see T. one had actually to open the door and open the cubicle. The Crown based its case on the period of time that T. was actually in the cubicle and the presence of blood. On conviction, T. appealed.

Held, that while there might be circumstances in which conduct of the kind alleged would constitute a breach of the peace, the findings in the present case left so much, including the length of time that the appellant was in the toilet, to conjecture that it could not be said that there had been a breach of the peace.

Appeal allowed.

2. Porter v. Jessop   **13.10.2**
1991 G.W.D. 11–647

P. was found guilty after a trial on a charge of breach of the peace. The evidence revealed that the police had stopped to detain two men in a car shortly after midnight. P. repeatedly sounded the horn of the vehicle and shouted, "Run Tam, it's a drugs bust" or similar words. The co-accused struggled with the police officers and ran away. Lights came on in various houses and a number of people emerged as a result of the commotion. The police officers were apprehensive that a serious situation could develop and they were required to summon assistance.

Held, that there was sufficient evidence to entitle the sheriff to find the appellant guilty of the charge.

THE LORD JUSTICE-CLERK (ROSS): "It is well established that where something is done in breach of public order which might reasonably be expected to lead to the citizens being alarmed or upset that may constitute a breach of the peace. There is no limit to the kind of conduct which may do so. It is a matter of fact and circumstances."

Appeal refused.

(ix) Ambiguous indictments   **13.11**

1. R. v. Best   **13.11.1**
(1979) 70 Cr.App.R. 21

B. and others were charged with the unlawful possession of a controlled drug namely cannabis resin. In the course of a trial the Crown was permitted, for tactical reasons, to amend the indictment to read "cannabis or cannabis resin." On conviction, B. and others appealed on the basis that the indictment was "bad for duplicity."

LORD WIDGERY C.J. (at p. 23): "In our judgment cannabis and cannabis resin seen together in that context [*viz.* Part II, Class B, of Schedule 2 to the 1971 Act] can be charged as they were charged in this case without offending the rules against duplicity. What was alleged here was a single act, an act of possessing a particular substance which the evidence has shown to be cannabis or cannabis resin. Being in possession of that substance and none other, it was perfectly fair to proceed as was done here. In effect what the pleader is saying is 'you are in possession of a substance found in an ashtray. That substance is either cannabis or cannabis resin, or part one and part another, we do not know. It matters not, because each comes under the same class and under the same rule in the Act. Indeed they are linked together.'"

Appeal dismissed.

NOTE

In *R. v. Newcastle-under-Lyme Justices, ex parte Hemmings* [1987] Crim.L.R. 416 the point arose again although more as a matter of testing the validity of the English committal proceedings involved in that case. Professor J.C. Smith, Q.C., in his note to *Hemmings'* case asserts that the main point in *R. v. Best* was that the prosecution alleged a single act of possessing one substance, which the evidence showed to be either cannabis or cannabis resin. He says further that it does not necessarily follow that an indictment alleging possession of "cannabis *and* cannabis resin" is good for this seems to allege possession of two distinct substances and two offences. The learned professor appears not to be wholly convinced on the latter point for he continues his note with a submission to the contrary. The form of Schedule 2 to the 1971 Act may suggest that the two substances are to be equated.

Part of the difficulty in this problem arises because of the apparent willingness of prosecuting authorities in England and Wales to commence actions without clear reports from forensic scientists following their examinations of the relevant substances. This practice was referred to by Lord Mackay of Clashfern, L.C. in *R. v. Hunt* [1986] 3 W.L.R. 1115 at p. 1131:

"I consider that this case [*i.e., Hunt's*] emphasises the need for absolute clarity in the terms of the analyst's certificate founded on by the prosecution in cases of this sort and, in my opinion, it would be wise where there is any possibility of this sort and, in my opinion, it would be wise where there is any possibility of one of the descriptions in the relevant Schedule [of the 1971 Act] applying to the substance which is the subject of the certificate that the analyst should state expressly whether or not the substance falls within that description as well as stating whether or not it is a controlled drug within the meaning of the act of 1971."

There seems also to have been a willingness in England and Wales to accept the word of an accused or former co-accused as prima facie evidence that a substance forming the basis of a charge against the accused is a controlled drug:

cf. Bird v. Adams [1972] Crim. L.R. 174. There is even authority that if the substance has been seized and is available for analysis (it was not in *Bird v. Adams*) then the prosecutor should be granted an adjournment to allow an expert to attend and give evidence of the nature of the substance: *Harding v. Hayes* (1974) 118 S.J. 736.

2. Penman v. Crowe   13.11.2
1991 G.W.D. 36–2186

P. was charged on a summary complaint with supplying "lysergic acid diethylamide, a Class A drug." The substance specified in the 1971 Act was "lysergide." The Crown moved for an amendment of the summary complaint and that was allowed. A plea of no case to answer was rejected. P. was convicted and appealed.

LORD MURRAY: "This stated case raises a short, sharp issue arising out of the refusal of the sheriff to uphold a submission of no case to answer in a summary prosecution against the appellant on a charge of supplying a controlled drug described as 'lysergic acid diethylamide, a Class A drug' specified in the 1971 Act. [Counsel], for the appellant, explained that the only issue to be argued for the appellant was whether there could be a case to answer in the absence of evidence that lysergic acid diethylamide, which, it is common ground, is not as such specified in the list of Class A drugs scheduled to the 1971 Act, is in fact lysergide, which is so specified. This argument would have been persuasive had it not been that, in the course of replying to the submission made on behalf of the appellant, the procurator fiscal depute moved to amend the complaint by substituting 'lysergide' for 'lysergic acid diethylamide', which the sheriff allowed him to do. In the course of his reply the procurator fiscal referred to the meaning of the word 'lysergic' in the Oxford Dictionary and 'lysergide' in Martindale's Pharmacopoeia, the latter in particular specifically identifying lysergic acid diethylamide with lysergide. [Counsel] submitted that these references could not make good the absence of testimony as the procurator fiscal was not a witness let alone an expert chemical witness. This was not disputed by the advocate-depute, who submitted that the only point of giving the textual references was to support the prosecution's motion that the complaint should be amended as defective in form, not in substance.

Accordingly, we need not decide to what extent, if at all, reference to a dictionary meaning of a word may assist to meet the challenge to the sufficiency of evidence led on a particular charge where the word appears. In the light of what happened, the issue raised in the stated case thus narrows down to whether the sheriff was entitled to allow the complaint to be amended to substitute the statutory name of the drug for that used in the charge. The advocate-depute pointed out that section 335 of the Criminal Procedure (Scotland) Act 1975 provided that it was competent at any time prior to the determination of a summary prosecution to amend a complaint so as to cure any error or defect therein or to cure any discrepancy or variance between the complaint and the evidence. Curing of a formal discrepancy between complaint and evidence directly covered the present case. It was not disputed that the production of the drug recovered was not objected to nor was the forensic report that it was in fact lsyergide; nor was it disputed that evidence was led that the label production was lysergide. Findings in fact 7, 8 and 9 were not challenged in the stated case. They were to the effect that, after caution that he was suspected of supplying a controlled drug, the appellant said that it was 'blotter', which is a word used for lysergide, as indeed the substance was found to be on chemical analysis. In these circumstances the advocate-depute submitted that there was no merit in the submission that the sheriff was not entitled to allow the complaint to be amended in terms of the prosecution motion. We agree with the advocate-depute. The only other point advanced by counsel for the appellant was that the complaint was a fundamental nullity in that it did not disclose a crime known to the law of Scotland. As an objection on that basis was not taken at the trial, this submission falls foul of section 454 of the 1975 Act and does not assist the appellant. The appeal accordingly fails. The question for the opinion of the court is answered in the negative."

Appeal refused.

NOTE
The Opinion of the Court is set out at 1992 S.C.C.R. 686.

13.11.3   **3. Scott v. Morrison**
1992 S.C.C.R. 682

M. was charged with possession of cannabis. After some evidence had been led that he had been in possession of cannabis resin, the Crown moved to amend on statutory authority the charge by inserting the word "resin", but they withdrew this motion when it was opposed. They renewed the motion at the close of their case. The sheriff refused to allow the amendment on the grounds that it changed the character of the offence and would be unfair to the respondent. The prosecutor appealed to the High Court by stated case.

Held, that it was unnecessary to determine whether the amendment would have had the effect of changing the character of the offence, since the sheriff had a discretion to refuse the amendment, and it could not be said that in the circumstances he was not entitled to conclude that it would be unfair to allow the amendment.

Appeal refused.

4. R. v. Mitchell
[1992] Crim.L.R. 723

It was alleged that M. approached an off-duty police officer and offered to sell him some "nice hash." The officer declined, went away and returned with another plainclothes officer. M. said to him, "You've changed your mind. £20 for the hash." M. was arrested and searched. On him was found a grassy substance which was not a drug. He was charged with offering to supply a controlled drug, namely cannabis. At his trial he denied making any offer. The count was amended by leave of the judge to an offer to supply "cannabis ... or cannabis resin" because prosecution evidence has confirmed that "hash" meant cannabis resin as opposed to herbal cannabis. The judge directed the jury that it did not matter whether M. had any controlled drug in his possession or whether he intended to supply a controlled drug or something bogus, so long as he made an offer. M. was convicted and appealed, submitting that the judge wrongly allowed the prosecution to amend the indictment.

Held, that the court had considered whether the addition of the words "or cannabis resin" made the count bad for duplicity. However, only one offer to supply was alleged, and it had been held that cannabis and cannabis resin were essentially the same substance: *R. v. Best* (1979) 70 Cr.App.R. 21 at p. 23 *per* Lord Widgery C.J. and commentary at [1979] Crim.L.R. 788. The count was therefore (as amended) not duplicitous.

Appeal dismissed.

(x) Evidential matters: general principles. **13.12**

1. Allan v. Taylor **13.12.1**
1986 S.C.C.R 202

T. was charged on a summary complaint with possession of a controlled drug, namely diamorphine, contrary to section 5(3) of the 1971 Act. A report by analysts was served on the accused and as a result, and in accordance with the aim of the statute, there were no forensic scientists at trial to speak to the terms of their report. The defence did not object to the report but the defence solicitor objected to the evidence in the report being admitted. The objection was founded on the suggestion that the terms of the analysts' report were not sufficiently linked to the real evidence which was the item on which a small quantity of a powder was found.

The sheriff took the view that the absence of a timeous objection by the defence meant that it was barred from challenging the facts or conclusions as to fact contained in the report. However, the sheriff nevertheless held that the description of the item examined by the analysts did not sufficiently refer to the real evidence and he thus sustained the defence objection to the report. On the accused being acquitted, the Crown appealed.

Held, that section 26(3) of the Criminal Justice (Scotland) Act 1980 provided for time limits for objection and that as these had not been adhered to the defence was barred from challenging the facts or conclusions as to fact contained in the report. The sufficiency of evidence was another matter and section 26 of the 1980 Act did not bar a challenge such as was made at trial. However, on the facts, there was sufficient coincidence between the expressions used in the label and in the report.

Appeal allowed and case remitted to sheriff to proceed.

13.12.2

2. McMillan v. H.M. Advocate
1988 S.L.T. 211

M. was charged with the unlawful possession of cannabis resin. The Crown evidence included only one forensic scientist who spoke to the terms of a report completed by that scientist and another. That report established that the substance in question was cannabis resin and thus a controlled drug. The second scientist was not called to give evidence. The Crown did not lodge the execution of service of intimation of intention to call only one forensic scientist to speak to the terms of the report. The accused was convicted and he appealed on the ground that there was insufficient evidence that the substance was cannabis resin.

THE LORD JUSTICE-CLERK (ROSS) (at p. 211): "Section 26(1) and (2) is dealing with a situation where the Crown do not intend to lead parole evidence at all on these matters and where the certificate or report itself will constitute sufficient evidence provided that the provisions of section 26(3) and (4) are complied with. Section 26(7) on the other hand dealing with a different situation, namely a situation where one witness will be sufficient to speak to a report such as a forensic science report. If section 26(7) is to be relied on by the Crown, the Crown at the time of lodging the report must intimate to the accused the intention to call one witness to speak to the report. It is to be observed that it is not stated in the section that the intimation requires to be in writing but of course plainly such intimation as is referred to in the subsection may be in writing. If a dispute arises as to whether intimation has been given it will be necessary for the Crown to be in a position to satisfy the court that intimation did take place and if intimation has been in writing it may then be easier for the Crown so to satisfy the court."

Appeal refused.

NOTE
The intimation of the intention of the Crown to lead the evidence of only one witness in accordance with section 26(7) of the 1980 Act is often given with the indictment. The form of wording used is thus: "Joint Report dated … by ABC and DEF, both Forensic Scientists, Forensic Science laboratory (address) and in terms of section 280 of the Criminal Procedure (Scotland) Act 1995, notice is hereby given that it is intended to call only the said ABC to give evidence in respect thereof." Intimation is effected with service.

3. R. v. Martinez-Tobon 13.12.3
[1994] 1 W.L.R. 388

M-T. was tried on a count of being knowingly concerned in the fraudulent evasion of the prohibition on importing cocaine. The prosecution case was that he was deeply involved in arranging a drug run for a man, who later gave prosecution evidence as an accomplice, and that M-T. was to be involved in receipt of the drugs in a packet on the accomplice's arrival. The defence case, denied by the accomplice, was that M-T. had been expecting and had discussed with the accomplice a consignment of emeralds. M-T. did not give evidence. In summing up the judge directed the jury that a defendant was under no obligation to testify, that they should not assume guilt because he had not given evidence and that suggestions by counsel were not evidence; but he went on to comment that, if the appellant had thought the packet was emeralds not drugs, "one might have thought that he would be very anxious to say so."

M-T. appealed against conviction, on the grounds that the conviction was unsafe and unsatisfactory because the judge's comment was a misdirection from which the jury might have inferred guilt.

Held, that where a defendant had failed to testify, the judge should give the jury a conventional direction to the effect that the defendant was under no obligation to testify and that the jury should not assume that he was guilty because he had not given evidence; that, provided those essentials were complied with, stronger comment might be appropriate where the defence case involved alleged facts which were at variance with prosecution evidence or additional to it and exculpatory, and which, if true, had to be within the knowledge of the defendant; that the nature and strength of such comment were for the judge's discretion and would depend on the circumstances of the individual case, but must not contradict or nullify the essentials of the conventional direction; and that, in the circumstances, the judge had been entitled to comment as he had and the jury had been entitled to take into account the fact that there was no evidence from the appellant to support what remained a bare assertion.

Appeal dismissed.

13.12.4 (a) Evidential matters: known drug users

13.12.5   **1. Forsyth v. H.M. Advocate**
                              1992 S.L.T. 189

Two accused persons were charged along with others with being concerned
in the supply of cannabis resin contrary to section 4(3)(b) of the 1971
Act. There was evidence of meetings which both accused had over a period
of time with two persons not named in the Crown list of witnesses nor
referred to in the indictment. In answer to questions from the advocate-
depute, police officers gave evidence that they recognised these two men
from other investigations into misuse of drugs and that they knew that
these men had convictions for drug offences. Objection was taken to this
evidence as being inadmissible but was repelled by the trial judge. The
accused were convicted and appealed contending, *inter alia*, that the
evidence of the character of the associates of the accused was wrongly
admitted.

   Held, (1) that the risk of unfairness by the leading of such evidence
was such that the trial judge should have disallowed questions about the
men's character, no notice having been given of the intention to lead
evidence of the accused's association with them or that evidence of their
records would be given in their absence and the trial judge had misdirected
himself in repelling the objection; (2) that had the jury not heard the
evidence of character (and an inadmissible line of cross-examination by
the Crown which was another successful ground of appeal), they might
well have acquitted the accused and accordingly a miscarriage of justice
had occurred.

                   Appeals allowed and convictions quashed.

13.12.6   **2. Craig v. H.M. Advocate**
                              1992 S.C.C.R 496

The appellants were charged with being concerned in the supply of drugs,
contrary to section 4(3)(b) of the 1971 Act. The Crown produced lists of
names and nicknames which were found in their house. A police officer
gave evidence that he could not say that the names and nicknames on the
list referred to persons he knew but that he could say that he knew persons
who were involved with drugs who had the same names or nicknames.
The evidence was admitted by the sheriff after he had repelled objections
to it on the ground that it was speculative. The appellants were convicted
and appealed to the High Court.

   Held,that having regard to the nature of the evidence, the objection
had been correctly repelled, it being for the jury to say whether they thought
the evidence was significant or that the fact that the names or nicknames
were the same was coincidental; and appeal refused.

NOTE
The difficulty of proof of some offences makes this case important but, as Sheriff Gordon pointed out in his commentary on the case, the "value of speculative evidence that the names on the list might be those of persons involved in drugs can hardly be very high but there is no general rule in Scotland, as there is, I believe, in England, which entitles a court to reject evidence which is technically competent on the ground that its probative value is outweighed by its likely prejudicial effect, the value of the evidence being left, like so many other things in Scotland, to the good senses of the jury.": 1992 S.C.C.R. 500.

3. R. v. Rothwell   13.12.7
(1994) 99 Cr.App.R. 388

R. was convicted of a number of offences of possessing and supplying heroin, a Class A prohibited drug, and of one offence of attempting to possess cocaine with intent to supply. The case against him arose out of police surveillance, during which he was seen to pass small packages or wraps to various people. At the trial, a police officer, who kept observation on R., gave evidence that four of the recipients were known to him as heroin users. Counsel for the defence had submitted unsuccessfully that that evidence should be excluded on the ground that it was hearsay and therefore inadmissible or, alternatively, if it was admissible, that the judge should have exercised his discretion under section 78 of the Police and Criminal Evidence Act 1984 and have excluded it. R. appealed against the judge's ruling on the ground that it was clear that the officer was relying upon information given to him by the others.

Held, that (1) where the Crown wished to adduce evidence that the recipient of a package from a defendant charged with supplying controlled drugs was a known user of the drug supplied, the judge should inquire into the basis of the prosecution witness's evidence and that evidence should only be admitted, subject to the court's discretion to exclude it under section 78 of the Police and Criminal Evidence Act 1984, where it was based on the alleged recipient's convictions for possession of the drug in question, or *e.g.* on the observation by the witness of hypodermic needle marks on the recipient, or on first-hand knowledge of the witness that the recipient was in possession of the drug or had received treatment for addiction to the drug. If the basis for the evidence proves to be statements made to the witness by others, including the recipient, the evidence would be inadmissible as hearsay. (2) In the present case, as the police officer did not have direct personal knowledge which would justify him in concluding that the aforesaid four persons were heroin users, the judge had erred in admitting that part of his evidence. However, notwithstanding that there had been a material irregularity in the trial, the Court was satisfied that there had been no miscarriage of justice, for on the admissible evidence with a correct direction the only reasonable and proper verdicts would have been ones of guilty. Consequently, the proviso to section 2(1) of the Criminal Appeal Act 1968 would be applied.

Appeal dismissed.

13.12.8 (b) Evidential matters: scientific evidence

13.12.9   **1. R. v. Hill**
                        (1993) 96 Cr.App.R. 456

H. was the subject of police surveillance over a period of time, on the suspicion that he was involved in drug dealing. He was observed, on three occasions, to hand over to another for cash something which was described by the witnesses as "small and very dark" "a small dark object" and "a dark substance". He was duly charged, *inter alia*, with supplying cannabis resin. He was convicted and appealed, *inter alia*, on the ground that, even if the jury were entitled to infer from the evidence that drug dealing had taken place, there was no evidence to identify the drug alleged to have been supplied since the prosecution had failed to produce any scientific evidence, such as an analyst's certificate, to prove that the dark substance was cannabis resin.

Held, while scientific evidence was not in every case required to identify a drug, the prosecution must establish the identity of the drug that was the subject matter of a charge with sufficient certainty to achieve the standard of proof required in a criminal case. In the instant case, the descriptions given by police witnesses of what had changed hands was insufficient to justify a certain inference that it was cannabis resin. Thus, the prosecution had failed to prove the charge as laid and the conviction on those three counts would be quashed.

Appeal allowed in part.

NOTE
    In this appeal *R. v. Hunt* (1987) 84 Cr.App.R. 163 was applied. For further discussion of the issues, see Roberts, "Taking the Burden of Proof Seriously" [1995] Crim.L.R. 783, especially at p. 789.

13.12.10   **2. Martin v. H.M. Advocate**
             High Court of Justiciary, unreported January 21, 1994

M. was convicted of certain charges on indictment and sentenced to a period of imprisonment. He appealed conviction, *inter alia,* on charge 4, which was a charge of supplying cannabis to three persons named in that charge.
    Held, that when no challenge was made to the plain evidence in chief of witnesses that they had bought cannabis, it was unnecessary to lead further evidence as to the nature of the substance.

THE LORD JUSTICE-CLERK (ROSS): "The sheriff tells us in his report that there was evidence from these three individuals to the effect that they had been at the cottage in question within the previous month or so and had bought cannabis from the appellant, that was the evidence upon which the Crown relied. [Counsel] maintained that there was insufficient evidence to justify the jury convicting of this charge and that the sheriff ought to have upheld a submission of no case to answer. He pointed out that there was no forensic analysis of the substance which the appellant was alleged to have supplied to the persons named and that is not, perhaps, surprising, as there was no recovery of the substance from the persons. He also observed that there was no evidence from these persons as to the effect which the substance had upon them. He maintained that there was a lack of corroboration as to the nature of the substance and that accordingly the evidence was insufficient. The advocate-depute on the other hand pointed out that the evidence which these witnesses had given had not been challenged and that being so there was no need for any further evidence to be led. If there had been cross-examination as to whether it was indeed cannabis which they had received, then no doubt further evidence would have been led and they might have been asked questions about their familiarity with cannabis and whether what they purchased on this occasion had the effect which they expected it to have, but we are satisfied that there was no need for such evidence to be elicited from these witnesses when no challenge was made of their plain evidence that they had bought cannabis. The fact that they each of them had bought cannabis from the appellant was, of course, corroborated by the evidence of the others. The situation was no different from what it would be if a witness maintained that he had bought a bottle of spirits from a shop. Unless there was challenge that that was what the bottle contained, we are not persuaded that it would be necessary for the witness to be asked questions as to what the contents of the bottle tasted like and what effect, if any, they had upon him. Having regard to the absence of any challenge of the evidence of the witnesses to the effect that they had bought cannabis from the appellant, we are satisfied that there was sufficient evidence to entitle the jury to hold this charge established. The sheriff was, in our view, correct in rejecting the submission of no case to answer."

Appeal refused.

NOTE
A brief report of this case is at 1994 G.W.D. 11–637.

(c) Evidential matters: certificates   **13.12.11**

1. Normand v. Wotherspoon   **13.12.12**
1993 S.C.C.R. 912

W. was charged with possessing a controlled drug with intent to supply it to others, contrary to section 5(3) of the 1971 Act. The Crown produced a certificate signed by the two authorised analysts which stated that the substance in question was examined and found to contain a controlled drug. The certificate did not state that the substance had been examined or analysed by the signatories and, on the grounds that it was accordingly defective and did not conform to the statutory requirements, a submission was made that there was no case to answer. The sheriff upheld the objection and acquitted the respondent. The prosecutor appealed to the High Court.

Held, that in order to be qualified to sign such a certificate the analysts must themselves have been the persons who analysed the substance concerned, that it was necessary for the certificate to narrate *in gremio* that the signatories had themselves analysed the substance and that, in the absence of that narration, the sheriff was right to acquit the respondent.

THE LORD JUSTICE GENERAL (HOPE) (at p. 914): "The respondent is Donald Martin Wotherspoon, who went to trial in the sheriff court at Glasgow charged with having a Class C drug, Triazolam, in his possession with intent to supply it to another, contrary to section 5(3) and section 25 of the Misuse of Drugs Act 1971. The Crown relied upon a certificate purporting to have been lodged in terms of section 26 of and Schedule 1 to the Criminal Justice (Scotland Act) 1980 in order to establish that tablets which were found in the respondent's possession when he was searched contained the Class C drug libelled in the charge. At the end of the Crown case motion was made that there was no case to answer under reference to the terms of that certificate. The motion was sustained by the sheriff, who found the respondent not guilty on the ground that the certificate did not satisfy the requirements of section 26 and Schedule 1 to the 1980 Act and that accordingly the Crown were not entitled to the benefit of the provisions of subsection (1) of section 26. In the note attached to the stated case she has provided the following reason for this decision. 'The requirements of section 26 of Schedule 1 to the 1980 Act are quite clear. They are also quite straightforward. There is no reason why, if the signatories of the report carried out the analysis, they should not state that in the body of the report. They did not do so. Accordingly, it could not be ascertained ex facie the report that it was signed by authorised analysts who had analysed the substance as requires in terms of column 2 of Schedule 1.'

The statutory background to the discussion before the sheriff and the expression of opinion which we have just quoted is to be found in section 26(1) of and in Schedule 1 to the 1980 Act. Section 26(1) provides: 'For the purposes of any proceedings for an offence under any of the enactments specified in column 1 of Schedule 1 to this Act, a certificate purporting to be signed by a person or persons specified in column 2 thereof, and certifying the matter specified in column 3 thereof shall, subject to subsection (3) below, be sufficient evidence of that matter and of qualification or authority of that person or those persons.'

Subsection (3) provides an opportunity for the certificate to be challenged in certain circumstances.

The relevant part of Schedule 1, which contains an entry in column 2 with respect to the enactment entitled 'The Misuse of Drugs Act 1971', is in these terms. 'Two analysts who have analysed the substances and each of whom is either a person possessing the qualifications (qualifying persons for appointment as public analysts) prescribed by regulations made under section 89 of the Food and Drugs Act 1955 (c.16), or section 17 of the Food and Drugs (Scotland) Act 1956 (c.30), or a person authorised by the Secretary of State to make analyses for the purposes of the provisions of the Misuse of Drugs Act 1971 mentioned in column 1.'

"That column, that is to say column 2, is headed by the words 'Persons who may purport to sign certificate.'

The certificate which was lodged in the present case contained a declaration in the first paragraph that the signatories were persons authorised by the Secretary of State for the purposes of section 26(1) and Schedule 1 to the 1980 Act to make analyses for the purposes of the relevant provisions of the Misuse of Drugs Act 1971. But they did not state anywhere in the certificate that it was they themselves who had analysed the tablets in the forensic laboratory. The certificate proceeds by narrating, in the third person, the receipt of an article from Strathclyde Police, its examination in the laboratory and the findings that were then made. It also sets out the conclusion which was reached upon analysis, but that conclusion is not said to have been the conclusion of the two analysts who provided the certificate.

The Lord Advocate submitted that the sheriff had fallen into error by requiring too much of the terms of the certificate. He accepted that only persons who could sign the certificate for the purposes of section 26 were persons who had analysed the substance which is described. But he submitted that it was not necessary for the certificate to state in terms that that was so. That submission was made under reference to the wording of section 26(1) which we have already quoted and, in particular, under reference to the concluding words of that subsection. These declare that, on the conditions set out in it, the certificate is to be sufficient evidence of the matter specified in column 3 and of the qualification or authority of the person or persons as specified in column 2. He pointed out that there was no reference in that subsection to indicate that the certificate was to be sufficient evidence that the persons who provided the certificate had themselves carried out the analysis. The fact that that point, which was stated in column 2 of Schedule 1 as being a requirement, was not referred to in subsection (1) of section 26 indicated that it was not necessary for the certificates to state that fact.

[Counsel] submitted that the sheriff, in her brief but succinct note, had said all that needed to be said on this issue. The conclusion which she reached was well founded, because the only way in which one could find out under this procedure whether the persons who provided the certificate had carried out the analysis themselves was by their stating that fact in terms of the certificate. He made reference to the best evidence rule and, in reliance upon that rule and the terms of column 2 of the Schedule, he submitted that it was essential that the certificate should state that the analysis was carried out by persons giving the certificate. This was not a matter which could be left to implication and, on a proper construction of the statute, an express statement was required.

The point is a short one, although we recognise its importance in practice. In our opinion, the answer to it is provided with complete accuracy by the note which the sheriff has appended to the stated case. We consider that the terms of column 2 of Schedule 1 are perfectly clear as to the conditions which must be satisfied by those who purport to sign certificates for the purposes of section 26(1) in regard to the relevant sections of the Misuse of Drugs Act 1971. In terms of that column, there are two conditions which must be satisfied in order to qualify analysts to sign such a certificate. The first is that they themselves were the persons who analysed the substance described in the certificate. That would seem to be entirely in accordance with the best evidence rule, in order to ensure that these certificates are not prepared on the basis of hearsay, and it is not surprising that it is stated as a requirement in the column. The other is that they must have been authorised by the Secretary of State to make analyses for the purposes of the statute. If these two conditions are stated in terms of the certificate to have been satisfied, it can then be said it is a certificate purporting to have been signed by a person or persons specified in column 2 of the Schedule. The prosecutor will then be entitled to the benefit of the presumption of sufficiency which is set out in section 26(1). But without a complete statement in the certificate of the matters set out in column 2 it cannot be said in terms of section 26(1), that it is a certificate purported to be signed by the person or persons therein specified and the presumption will not be available to the prosecutor.

For these reasons we consider that the sheriff did not err in law in the decision which she took. We consider that it was necessary for the certificate to narrate in gremio that the signatories had themselves analysed the substance which was found to contain the Class C drug and accordingly that she was right to acquit the respondent for the reason that she gave."

Appeal refused.

2. McCrindle v. Walkingshaw
                    1994 S.C.C.R. 299

McC. was charged with possessing cannabis resin, contrary to section 5(2) of the 1971 Act. Evidence was led of his possession of a matchbox containing resinous material. Two police officers spoke to putting the matchbox into a polythene bag which was sealed and labelled with a unique police reference number. One of these officers gave evidence that some months later he had collected the bag from the police station and sent it to the forensic laboratory with a request for analysis.

A forensic scientist gave evidence that he had collected from the laboratory production room an envelope bearing a unique laboratory reference number inside which was a polythene bag with the police reference number spoken to by the constables. He had opened the bag and carried out tests by placing a sample from the bag on a plate and a sample on a slide. Beside each sample he placed the laboratory reference number. He had then prepared a report along with a second scientist. The second scientist had not been present when the material was removed from the bag or put on the plate and slide, but she had seen them on the plate and slide and had seen the laboratory reference number beside them. Both the forensic report and the form containing the police request for analysis bore the police and the laboratory reference numbers.

The sheriff repelled a submission of no case to answer based on an argument that the Crown had failed to prove that the material referred to in the forensic report was the material found in the appellant's possession and convicted McC., who appealed to the High Court by stated case.

Held, (1) that there was material before the sheriff justifying the conclusion that the matchbox collected by the scientist from the laboratory production room was the matchbox which the police took from the appellant's possession; and (2) that there was sufficient material before the sheriff to enable him to conclude that the first scientist's evidence was sufficiently corroborated, the second scientist having checked the laboratory reference number against the plate, the slide and laboratory records.

Appeal refused.

3. O'Brien v. McCreadie 13.12.14
1994 S.C.C.R. 516

The respondent was charged with possessing a controlled drug, contrary to section 5(2) of the 1971 Act. The Crown produced a report signed by two authorised analysts which was headed "Report" and stated that its signatories "hereby report" that the substance in question was analysed and identified as a controlled drug. The report did not state that the substance had been analysed or identified by the signatories, and a submission was made that there was no case to answer on the ground that it was accordingly defective and did not conform to the statutory requirements. The sheriff, relying on *Normand v. Wotherspoon, supra,* which was concerned with a certificate under section 26(1) of the 1980 Act, upheld the objection and acquitted the respondent. The prosecutor appealed to the High Court.

Held, that the document concerned was a report and not a certificate, and that accordingly it fell under section 26(2) and not 26(1) of the Act, and that it fulfilled the requirements of that subsection and was accordingly sufficient evidence of any fact or conclusion as to fact contained in it.

Observed, that a section 26(2) report might well contain information in the nature of hearsay, as may a section 26(1) certificate issued in connection with statutory provisions other than the 1971 Act.

Appeal allowed.

13.12.15   **4. O'Brien v. H.M. Advocate**
1996 S.L.T. 1177

O'B. was tried on indictment for, *inter alia,* a contravention of section 4(3) (b) of the 1971 Act. The Crown lodged a report signed by two forensic scientists relating to the analysis of the controlled drug. The report did not state who had carried out the analysis. O'B. did not require the attendance of the second scientist when the Crown intimated its intention of calling only one of the authors of the report. The scientist gave evidence that the analysis was carried out by the other author of the report but that they both examined the results of the analysis. Objection was taken to the scientist's evidence on the ground that it was hearsay evidence, but the sheriff repelled the objection. O'B. was convicted and appealed.

Held, that section 26(7) of the 1980 Act removed the need for the evidence of the forensic scientist who gave evidence to be corroborated and also implied that the evidence of that witness about the work which was done by the other signatory to the report, which would otherwise be hearsay evidence, was admissible.

Opinion reserved, on the consequence of neither of the signatories being able to speak from his knowledge to a fact contained in the report because the work was done by someone else who had not signed the report.

Appeal refused.

13.12.16   **5. Donnelly v. Schrickel**
1994 S.C.C.R. 640

The respondent, S. was charged with possessing a controlled drug with intent to supply it to others or, alternatively, with possessing it unlawfully, contrary to section 5(3) and section 5(2) respectively of the 1971 Act. The Crown lodged as a production a certificate of analysis issued under section 26(1) of the 1980 Act and signed by two analysts, which stated that the articles in question were amphetamine, a controlled drug, but which did not state that its signatories had analysed the articles. Parties entered into a joint minute agreeing that the production was a joint report which was true and accurate and related to the examination of the articles in question. The sheriff upheld a submission of no case to answer on the ground that the certificate was defective in terms of *Normand v. Wotherspoon, supra,* and that the joint minute could not cure that defect, and acquitted S. The procurator fiscal appealed to the High Court.

Held, that section 26(1) of the 1980 Act provided only one method of proving the necessary facts and that the way in which the parties approached this matter relieved the Crown of the need to rely on section 26(1) and enabled them to rely on the agreement that the findings in the report were true and accurate; and appeal allowed and case remitted to the sheriff to proceed as accords.

Appeal allowed.

6. Dryburgh v. Scott   13.12.17
1995 S.C.C.R. 371

D. and another man, R., were charged on summary complaint with contraventions of the 1971 Act. The Crown led in evidence an analysts' report headed "Case against [R.] + 2" which referred *inter alia* to "24 plastic phials labelled 'Accused's home address'". The report bore the same case number as the labels on the phials produced by the Crown, which had been signed by the analysts. The Crown also led evidence that both accused and a third man were arrested together in a car, that the police had found 24 plastic wraps in D.'s house and had transferred the contents of each into plastic phials and that the items found by the police had been sent to the laboratory on the date given as the date of receipt in the report. D. was convicted and appealed on the ground that there was insufficient evidence to identify the drugs referred to in the report with the material taken from his house.

Held, that there was sufficient coincidence between the labels and the report to justify the sheriff in holding that the report was linked to the appellant.

Observed, (1) that it was undesirable for reports to be in the vague and unspecific form of the report in this case and that steps should be taken to ensure that in future certificates or reports are expressed more clearly and with greater specification; and (2) that the standard of evidence necessary before the link could be inferred is the same whether or not the document is one which has statutory force.

Appeal refused.

7. Allan v. Ingram   13.12.18
1995 S.C.C.R. 390

A. was charged on summary complaint with contraventions of the 1971 Act. Police officers gave evidence of finding a metal tobacco tin containing vegetable material, cigarette papers and seeds, and also a yellow plastic box containing nine "deals", both in the living-room at A.'s address. The police referred to these articles at the trial by reference to their label numbers, but did not give evidence as to what was written on the labels or that the articles had been sent for analysis. The Crown produced an analysts' report under section 26 of the 1980 Act which referred to items of these descriptions "labelled living-room at [A.'s address]" and with the date in question. A. was convicted and appealed on the ground that there was insufficient evidence to identify the drugs referred to in the report with the items taken from his house.

Held, that bearing in mind the particular terms of section 26(2) (*viz.*, that, in the absence of prior objection, a report by authorised scientists shall be sufficient evidence of any fact or conclusion of fact contained in it), the necessary link could be found in the facts and circumstances, and the sheriff was entitled to draw the inference which he did in repelling a submission of no case to answer.

Appeal refused.

13.12.19 **8. L.A.W. Mining Ltd. v. Carmichael**
1996 S.C.C.R. 627

The appellants were charged with a contravention of the Control of Pollution Act 1974. The Crown relied on an analysis of samples which had been carried out by a chemist, F. They relied for corroboration on the evidence of another chemist, D., who was F.'s superior. D. had instructed F. to carry out the analysis, had discussed it with F., had agreed with him the extent to which some of the samples should be diluted and had checked F.'s calculations and compared them with value standards in the laboratory's computer. He had not been present when analysis was carried out. The appellants were convicted and appealed to the High Court on the ground that F.'s evidence was not sufficiently corroborated.

Held, that it was not necessary that every step taken by F. should be corroborated by D. peering over his shoulder, that it was enough that the tests were carried out in accordance with standard laboratory procedures which had been discussed beforehand between the two scientists, and that the results were independently checked by D.

Appeal refused.

13.12.20 (d) Evidential matters: conspicuous wealth.

13.12.21 **1. R. v. Wright**
[1994] Crim.L.R. 55

W. appealed against his conviction for possessing cocaine with intent to supply. Part of the evidence against W. was the search of his flat by customs officers who found concealed there £16,000 in cash and a gold necklace worth about £9,000. W. appealed on the ground, *inter alia*, that that evidence should not have been admitted as it was irrelevant. The finding of the cash and the necklace was argued to be irrelevant because its presence was equally consistent with W.'s story that it was lawfully used for the running of his music promotion business.

Held, the evidence was relevant; the question was whether such a large sum of cash tended to prove that drugs found in a person's possession were for supply to another. There was no doubt that the finding of a large quantity of cash was capable of being relevant to an issue the jury had to consider. The Court rejected the submission that the evidence was inadmissible because irrelevant.

Appeal dismissed.

NOTE

In the commentary to the original report above it was noted that in Wright's case the court relied on the proposition that traders in the clandestine business of drug trafficking require to keep by them large sums of money in cash and so the finding of such a sum at the home of one who has already been found in possession of drugs is capable of giving rise to an inference of dealing. To this it might be objected that the evidence is equally consistent with a variety of innocent explanations, but perhaps the answer is that the court allows itself a little more latitude when the equivocal evidence relates to the accused himself, who is entitled (though not of course bound) to adduce other explanations for it.

It is interesting to note that the court, when hearing appeal against sentence, disagreed with the trial judge's finding that the accused had been involved in "wholesale" dealing. The finding of the cash, it was held, provided no basis for an inference that the accused was a supplier to other drug dealers as opposed to a person supplying directly to members of the public.

2. R. v. Batt
[1994] Crim.L.R. 592

13.12.22

B. was charged with possession of 500 grammes of cannabis resin with intent to supply. Police officers found the drugs in a rabbit hutch in B.'s garden. They also found two grammes of the drug in an egg-cup and a set of scales and weights; there were traces of cannabis resin on the scales. B. said that the cannabis in the egg-cup belonged to her husband and that she knew nothing of the drugs in the garden. The police also discovered £150 in cash in an ornamental kettle in the house. B. appealed against conviction, submitting, *inter alia*, that the judge should not have admitted evidence of the finding of the money.

Held, the possession of the money was not probative of the offence with which B. had been charged because the money found could not have anything to do with intent to supply in future the cannabis that had been found; while it could have a highly prejudicial effect. B. was not charged generally with drug dealing; it may have been a "hallmark" of such dealing as the Crown contended to have a float to assist the trade, but it was also a hallmark of propensity to supply or past or future supplying generally. The jury did not direct the jury as to how to treat the evidence of the money and the conviction was not safe.

Appeal allowed.

NOTE

It is doubtful if this case would be persuasive in Scotland because of the basis of the decision, namely that the conviction was "unsafe". The test in Scotland is whether there has been a miscarriage of justice: section 103(b) of the Criminal Procedure (Scotland) Act 1995.

The basis for the decision is itself very odd because the court does not seem to have questioned the admissibility of the possession of the scales and weights. It is worth recalling that the scales were contaminated.

The intention as to future conduct is essentially an inference drawn from various facts and circumstances. To separate the money from the scales and weights is illogical, as is, with respect, the general observations by the court as to the significance of the money found.

13.12.23   **3. R. v. Gordon**
[1995] 2 Cr.App.R. 61

G. was convicted of possessing a Class A controlled drug, crack cocaine, with intent to supply. He was sentenced to six years' imprisonment. A confiscation order for £16,000 was made.

One of the grounds of appeal related to the question of loose cash found in the appellant's house. £4,200 cash was found in the pockets of various jackets and £2,000 was found under a mattress. The police would not have found it but for the fact that G. told them it was there and showed them where it was.

Held, in order to be admissible, evidence of cash or other property found in the possession of the accused or of financial dealings by him had to be relevant to the intention to supply the particular drugs. To be relevant the evidence had to be logically probative of that intention. Evidence of marginal relevance may and should be excluded if it would lead to a multiplicity of issues.

It was the duty of the trial judge, whether objection were taken or not, to ensure that irrelevant evidence, particularly if it was prejudicial to the defence, was excluded. Should such evidence nevertheless have been received then the judge had the special responsibility of directing the jury either to disregard it or how to treat it, as the circumstances required.

HENRY, L.J. (p. 64): "The principles to be applied seem to us to be clear. They are these:

1. The intention to supply must relate to the parcel of drugs that the appellant was found to be in possession of.
2. In order to be admissible, the evidence would have to be relevant to that intention.
3. To be relevant, that evidence would have to be logically probative of that intention, *i.e.* that evidence made his intention to supply those drugs more or less probable.
4. Evidence of marginal relevance may and should be excluded if it would lead to a multiplicity of subsidiary issues.
5. It is the duty of the judge, whether objection is taken or not, to ensure that irrelevant evidence (particularly when it is prejudicial to the defence) be not received in court. Should such evidence have been received, then the judge has the special responsibility to direct the jury either to disregard it or how to treat it, as the circumstances require.

We turn to the evidence that was admitted in this case. Cases of this kind differ greatly the one from the other, each depends on its own facts, and in this passage of the judgment we merely seek to apply the general principles set out above to the facts in this case ...

The next question relates to the loose cash found in the house. This Court dealt with that problem in *R*. v. *Wright* [[1994] Crim.L.R. 55]. There Beldam L.J. said: 'The question for decision is whether the finding of such a large amount of cash is a fact which, if proved, makes it more probable that a person suspected of dealing in narcotic drugs, and who is found to be in possession of them, is in possession of them for the purposes of supplying them. In other words, does the fact of the possession of a large amount of cash tend to prove or render more probable the other facts the prosecution have to prove? That is, that the drugs were in his possession for the purposes of supplying them to another. It may be that in some cases the finding of a large quantity of cash, or the fact that there is a large quantity of cash available, is of comparatively little relevance. In others it may be a much more significant feature. It was described by [counsel], though not in entirely the correct context, as a question of proximity. There is no doubt that a finding of a large amount of cash is capable of being relevant to an issue the jury had to consider in this case and we reject the submission that this evidence was inadmissible because it was irrelevant.'

There a stock of drugs had been found at a co-defendant's house, and the appellant had links with his co-defendant.

This court reached a different conclusion on the facts of *R*. v. *Batt* [[1994] Crim.L.R. 592]. There enough cannabis to make 3,000 cigarettes was found in a rabbit hutch inside a dog kennel at the bottom of the appellant's garden. A small amount of cannabis was found in the house together with a set of scales and weights and traces of cannabis resin on them. There was also found £150 in notes stuffed in a teapot. Evidence of that was given without any direction being given by the recorder as to how the jury should treat such evidence. The court there referred to *Wright* and sought to distinguish it on the basis that that was a 'drug trading case' as distinct from a case where the charge was possession with intent to supply. Examination of the two cases shows that the ground of distinction was erroneous: they are both cases of possession with intent to supply. The submission of the Crown, which the court rejected, was that loose cash was 'a hallmark of intent to supply, that the supplier has, not only of course, cannabis itself but such things as scales and the like and money by way of float or capital in order to aid and assist this trade'. The court rejected that submission in the context of this case. The court said that the possession of loose cash was: 'A hallmark not of intent to supply the cannabis found, but a hallmark of a propensity to supply generally, or a hallmark of the fact that there has been past supply, or that the money will be used in future to obtain cannabis for future supply. None of those hallmarks applies to the specific charge brought against this appellant. On the contrary, as we have already indicated, it seems to us that there is great force in [counsel's] submission that without any direction by the recorder as to how the jury should treat the evidence of the money, the jury may well have concluded that it demonstrated that the appellant was a dealer or trader in cannabis, and should go down for that reason ... In those circumstances we think it was wrong for the recorder to admit this evidence of the money. It proved nothing with regard to the charge in question, and was unfair and prejudicial to the appellant, in that it raised the suggestion that she was in the business of drug dealing.'

Reconciliation of those two cases is not easy. The court agrees entirely with the way the court in *Wright* dealt generally with the question of cash.

We turn to examine the case of *Batt*. The importance of that case seems to us that there was no direction by the recorder as to how the jury should treat the evidence of that money. The presence of sums of cash in a house is likely to be equivocal, for not only are many legitimate trades cash based, but there are also many innocent explanations for having a large sum of cash at home at a given time. Therefore the jury needs a careful direction on this question. That was lacking in *Batt*. And in *Batt* only a relatively small amount of money was involved. But if the court in *Batt* was expressing a general principle that 'money ... (to be) used in future to obtain cannabis for future supply' is not a hallmark to the specific charge of possession with intent to supply, we respectfully differ. Cash for the acquisition of stock for present active drug dealing must be relevant to a count of possession with intent to supply.

Returning to the facts of this case, in our judgment the evidence of this loose cash was admissible but the jury required a careful direction in relation to it. The judge dealt with the appellant's explanation for the presence of the money (cash trading in motor cars) and then said: 'The

Crown asks you to draw the inference that these not insubstantial sums of money are the proceeds of dealing in drugs.'

If they were the proceeds of past drug dealing, rather than the capital for present active drug dealing, then a pedant would say that inference did not go to the incident charged. For our part, if that point stood on its own, we would not construe this sentence in a summing-up so strictly, but it does not stand on its own.

Both the purchase and the sale of drugs require immediate financial liquidity. The drug dealer buying from his supplier is not going to get credit because he says he can offer his house as security. Therefore, the investigation of the appellant's title to [...] (which he inherited some years before) and the lies contained in his initial denials of having any financial interest in that property, could not be relevant to this charge. As to the presence of active current building society accounts, all opened some years before, counsel for the Crown submits that often the defence in these cases is that the explanation for the large sums of cash found at home is that the accused does not trust banks. It may be that to forestall such a defence the presence of such savings accounts admissible, but what is inadmissible (because irrelevant) is to allow cross-examination as to the past credits and withdrawals which could only found an inference of drug dealing (as opposed to present and active drug dealing). Thus (for instance) the appellant should not have been put in the position where he had to prove that payment into that account of some £800 was a direct payment to him of rent by the housing benefit authorities. The jury were given no help as to how they should approach the savings accounts or the ownership of [the property at ...]. If they looked on them as representing past 'proceeds of dealing in drugs' and convicted the appellant on the inference, then they would have been wrong to do so. Evidence of the use of the savings account and the ownership of [the property] was irrelevant, likely to confuse the real issue, and should not have been admitted.

Lastly, we have the third category of evidence, the alleged ownership of the Vodaphone, and the BMW motor vehicle, each being registered in the name of another. The possession and use of these two items is seen as part of the stereotype of not only drug dealers but also, for example, the young and upwardly mobile. Registration of one's own property in another's name may be standard practice for drug dealers, but it is also standard practice for non-drug dealers who wish to defeat or frustrate their creditors. As there was no evidence of the actual use of the car or the Vodaphone in drug dealing, it seems to us that these matters were, even if possibly relevant, so much on the fringe of this inquiry that the evidence of them should not have been admitted. If evidence went in, then a careful direction was required. Such direction is not to be found in this summing-up.

In our judgment, this was a simple case which got swamped with superfluous, irrelevant and eventually prejudicial issues. Evidence of those issues having been admitted, nothing was done in the summing-up to right the matter or to keep the jury focused on matters that could properly go to proof of possession with intent to supply. In our judgment, at the end of the day there is here a real risk that this jury convicted of intent to supply on the basis of the suspicion of ill-gotten gains arrived at in an investigation of his life style which did not simply concentrate on the intention to supply the drugs found, but extended back into his life, apparently to suggest past drug dealing."

Appeal allowed.

13.12.24   **4. R. v. Morris**
                          [1995] 2 Cr.App.R. 69

After a lengthy surveillance operation M. was arrested at her parents' address. She was said to have dropped a number of bags found to contain over £5,000 and when apprehended in an upstairs toilet M. was searched. Heroin was found concealed in her bra. Further quantities of cash and a notebook containing names and figures were found at the property. She was charged with possession of heroin with intent to supply. The trial judge admitted the evidence concerning the monies and the notebook. In his summing-up the judge gave no indication as to how the jury should evaluate that evidence, which was referred to as "peripheral". M. was convicted, and appealed, contending that the evidence regarding the money and notebook was inadmissible.

Held, the judge did not appear to have grasped the probative significance, if any, of the evidence relating to the cash and the notebook. The jury had not been given proper directions about it and the conviction was thereby rendered unsafe and unsatisfactory.

MORLAND, J. (at p. 74): "The judgment in *R. v. Batt* [*supra*] specifically rejected the Crown's submission in the context of that case and stressed the significance of the recorder's failure to give any direction as to how the jury should treat the evidence of money. But we were told that, in some quarters, the judgement has been understood as laying down a general proposition that evidence of possession of money is never admissible when the charge is possession of a drug with intent to supply. We do not so read the judgment, particularly bearing in mind that the court in *Batt* held to have been rightly admitted the evidence of contaminated scales which, like the possession of money, might equally be thought, depending on the circumstances, to be referable to past rather than future supply.

If, however, we are wrong and the court in *Batt* intended to advance such a general proposition, this would, as it seems to us, be inconsistent with *R. v. Wright* [[1994] Crim.L.R. 55], and we are unable to accept it. Indeed, as is plain from *D.P.P. v. P.* [(1991) 93 Cr.App.R. 267], merely because evidence of possession of money might tend to show the commission of offences other than that charged would not, of itself, render the evidence inadmissible in law. Furthermore, with great respect to the Court in *Batt*, we are unable to see substance in the purported distinction drawn in the judgment on the basis that *Wright* was, but *Batt* was not, a drug trading case."

(And at p. 75)

"Although we do not question the actual decisions in *Batt* or *Wright* on their own particular facts, we find it difficult to accept that different approaches to the principle of admissibility of evidence of monies in the possession of a defendant can be right.

"In our judgment, both cases were drug trading cases despite the international dimension in *Wright* arising from the presence at Heathrow of the car containing cocaine. In *Batt*, whoever was the possessor of the cannabis was in possession as a commercial retailer. The evidence of the amount and nature of the cannabis in the rabbit hutch and the scales in the house established that.

In *Wright*, the evidence of the monies found at the flat which was used by Wright and to which he had the key was inadmissible because it was capable of having probative significance. The inference could be drawn that, as a drug dealer, he went to Heathrow with the hired car knowing it contained cocaine which was there for supply to another.

In our judgment, evidence of large amounts of money in the possession of a defendant or an extravagant life style on his part, prima facie explicable only if derived from drug dealing, is admissible in cases of possession of drugs with intent to supply if it is of probative significance to an issue in the case.

The fact that a defendant gives an explanation for possession of large sums of money does not itself render such evidence inadmissible; the Crown may be required to rebut such an explanation. If the Crown can establish that explanations, such as winnings from the Irish Sweep, cash profits from market trading, the proceeds of bank robbery or the proceeds of dealing in jewellery and stolen clothes are false, the false explanation may be of significance — if a defendant is in control of a house, car or bag in which drugs are found — to prove that the defendant was knowingly in possession of the drugs and had the drugs in his possession for supply.

If a judge decides that such evidence is admissible in law he must then decide whether or not to admit it in his discretion, having regard to its probative value and its prejudicial effect.

If such evidence is admitted, it is incumbent upon the judge to spell out to the jury what its probative significance can be while making it clear to the jury that it is for them to decide whether it has or has not that probative significance.

The judge must then warn the jury that, if they reach the conclusion that the defendant is a drug dealer, this is not of itself either evidence of possession of drugs on a particular occasion or a basis for disbelieving a defendant."

Appeal allowed, conviction quashed and re-trial ordered.

13.12.25

5. R. v. Lucas
[1995] Crim.L.R. 400

L. was convicted of being knowingly concerned in the fraudulent evasion of the prohibition on the importation of cannabis and Ecstasy, and of possession of cannabis with intent to supply. He was said to have been involved in a convoy accompanying the lorry in which cannabis and Ecstasy was imported. His house was searched, and a quantity of cannabis (the subject matter of the count of possession with intent) and money (£44,650) were found. The judge refused an application for the charge of possession with intent to be severed. In his evidence, L. said that the prosecution evidence in respect of the importation was false and gave an innocent explanation of his movements. The cannabis found at his home had, he said, been planted by customs and excise officers and that he had earned the money as a market trader. On appeal, it was argued that the judge's summing-up in respect of the finding of the money was inadequate, in reliance on *R. v. Morris, supra.*

Held, that, taking the materiality of the cash into account, the judge's direction was adequate. He told the jury that the possession with intent count was a separate matter, and that if they concluded he was guilty of that offence, it was not evidence of his guilt in relation to the importation, except in so far as it rebuts what he said about innocent involvement. The court noted that the evidence against L. in respect of the possession with intent was overwhelming.

Appeal dismissed.

13.12.26

6. R. v. Brown
[1995] Crim.L.R. 716

B. appealed against his conviction of possession of cannabis with intent to supply. The issue on appeal was whether the finding of items, including scales and sums of money (totalling £2,075) in B.'s possession was admissible. The Crown submitted that they were relevant to the question of whether an intent to supply was proved as opposed to simple possession. The defence submitted that the evidence went only to the general question of whether B. was a dealer in drugs and was irrelevant to the question as to whether he had an intent to supply the 11.6 grammes of cannabis found in his pocket.

Held, there is no general proposition that evidence which may show that a defendant is a drug dealer is never admissible in any case where the defendant is charged with possession of drugs with intent to supply. The question for the judge to decide is whether or not the evidence is relevant to an issue in the case; that will usually be whether the defendant has the particular drug in his possession with intent to supply it to another or for his own use. Different considerations may apply to items such as scales, as opposed to money, found in the possession of a defendant. Money may not always be relevant; it will depend upon the circumstances. If the evidence is relevant, it is admissible subject to the judge's discretion to exclude it. On the facts of this case the money, scales, 1.78 grammes of cannabis in the refrigerator, plastic bags, mobile phone and the evidence of the appellant's flight, either taken together or in such parts as the jury thought right, were clearly capable of pointing to the inference that the appellant possessed the cannabis with an intent to supply.

Appeal dismissed.

7. R. v. Simms 13.12.27
[1995] Crim.L.R. 304

S. was convicted of possessing cannabis with intent to supply. His house was searched and police officers found three stones of cannabis vegetation wrapped in blocks. Small amounts of cannabis which had been boiled away in a saucepan and dried in a baking tray were also found. The bath was full of greenish water with a sediment. A sum of £8,455 in cash and a set of kitchen scales with weights were seized. In interview, S. said that the cannabis vegetation was his. He denied selling it, but said that he administered the cannabis to himself and others in the form of a drink made like tea. S. said that he bathed in water infused with cannabis. The money was derived from car dealing.

The prosecution case was that S. would have sold to others the cannabis left over from the teas and baths and any other which he chose to sell. The evidence about the money and scales was introduced without objection by defence counsel and the judge gave no particular direction as to how the jury should deal with that evidence. Some time after his conviction, counsel for S. read of the decision in *R. v. Batt, supra*, and concluded that objection should have been raised to the admissibility of the evidence in relation to the money and the scales, and that, if that had failed, the judge should have directed the jury how to approach those items of evidence. S. applied for an extension of time and leave to appeal against conviction.

Held, if objection had been taken to the admissibility of the evidence, the judge would almost certainly have regarded it as relevant and exercised his discretion to admit it. In the light of the authorities, he should have gone on to warn the jury how they should approach that evidence: not simply to treat it as evidence of propensity. In all the circumstances of the case (the massive amount of cannabis resin, no alternative explanation really for the possession of a very substantial sum of money, the appropriateness of the scales for the type of drug), if the warning had been given, the jury would have proceeded in exactly the way it was thought they did, namely to treat the evidence of the existence of the money and the presence of the scales, as evidence of current intended dealing and not simply as evidence of dealing in the past which might lead them to conclude that he ought to be convicted because he was a known drug dealer. Although there was an irregularity, there was no miscarriage of justice.

Applications dismissed.

8. R. v. Nicholas
[1995] Crim.L.R. 942

13.12.28

N. was convicted of possessing crack cocaine with intent to supply (count 1). He was also charged with unlawful possession, because counsel for the Crown was concerned as to whether he could properly adduce, in proof of count 1, evidence of a mobile phone and £600 found on N. One ground of appeal was that, although he was acquitted on count 2, on which the evidence was admissible, there was a risk that the jury could not disregard the evidence when considering count 1 on which it was not admissible.

Held, even if the evidence was inadmissible in proof of count 1, since it was admissible in proof of count 2, it could properly be admitted in a trial on an indictment containing both counts. That would then be subject to a necessary direction that it could only be taken into account by the jury on count 2 and not on count 1. The judge gave that direction in the clearest terms on at least two occasions. Nonetheless, it was submitted that such direction as was given would require intellectual gymnastics of the jury which should be regarded as a defiance of common sense, and there must be good reason to consider that the jury was bound to have taken into account the money and the phone in reaching their verdict on count 2.

The reason the Crown was not content to proceed on count 1 lay in the decision in *R. v. Batt* [1994] Crim.L.R. 592 where it was held that £150 found in an ornamental kettle had nothing properly to do with intent to supply cannabis in the future. It might betoken past dealing in that drug, but not future dealing. Such evidence was no more than a hallmark of a propensity to supply generally and was not proof of intent to supply the cannabis identified in the count. The effect of that decision caused the Crown to seek the leave to add count 2 because it feared that the Court might exclude the evidence of the money and phone if the defence made a submission based on *Batt.*

In *Batt,* the Court purported to distinguish from *R. v. Wright, supra,* which held that evidence of the finding of £16,000 was admissible on a charge of possession with intent to supply. It was difficult, if not impossible, to reconcile *Batt* and *Wright* and the suggestion in *Batt* that they were distinguishable because Wright was a "drug dealing case" was an analysis which offered no satisfactory basis for the suggested distinction. The Court was fortified in that conclusion by the case of *R. v. Morris*, [*supra*], where Morland J., who quoted extensively from *Wright* and *Batt*, was unable to see substance in the purported distinction drawn. It was to be noted that on one view the decision in *Batt* was treated by the Court in *Morris* as turning essentially upon the fact that in *Batt* the recorder failed to direct the jury as to how they could properly use the evidence of the money found in the appellant's possession. If that was so, then the decision in *Batt* was not out of line with the principle expressed in *Wright* and reiterated in *Morris*. Final support was to be found in *R. v. Gordon*, July 28, 1994 where the issue was the admissibility of money in savings accounts, and the Court said that reconciliation of *Batt* and *Wright* was not easy, and agreed with the way the Court in *Wright* dealt with the issue of cash.

The decisions in *Gordon* and *Morris* were subsequent to N.'s trials, but no doubt was entertained that had it been otherwise the Crown would not have been moved to amend the indictment as it had done. Bearing in mind that in *Batt*, contaminated scales were ruled admissible and the Court was impressed by a non-direction as to the relevance of money, it might be possible to conclude that the decision was peculiar to its own circumstances.

Evidence of money was not as a matter of principle inadmissible. Whether it was admissible depended on the circumstances of each case; there was no general rule of exclusion. In those cases where it was ruled admissible — the majority of cases — the judge should direct the jury as to its specific relevance to an issue in the trial so that it did not lend itself to possible misinterpretation of the kind alluded to and identified by the Court in *Batt*. That was the law, and applied here, the evidence of the money, in the form and in the circumstances in which it was found, was admissible in proof of count 1. The judge was at pains to put the phone on the periphery and there was no reason to doubt that the jury did the same.

Appeal dismissed.

9. R. v. Grant   13.12.29
[1995] Crim.L.R. 715

G. was convicted of possession of 28.26 grammes of crack cocaine (enough for about 140 doses) with intent to supply, his plea of guilty to simple possession being unacceptable to the Crown. Following his arrest he was found to have on him 4.86 grammes of the drug (which he said he had bought that day from his own supplier for his own use); another 23.4 grammes of the drug (which he said he had picked up and kept, again for his own use, after the supplier had unwittingly dropped it in the street);

and £912.50 in cash (which he said was for buying a car that, in the event, he decided not to buy). He appealed against his conviction, arguing that the judge had been wrong to admit the evidence of the finding of the money.

Held, (1) the evidence of the money had been rightly admitted. The finding of money in a defendant's possession was capable of being relevant to the issue of whether he had an intent to supply drugs also found in his possession. It was for the jury to decide whether the money was, in all the circumstances, indicative of an ongoing trading in the drugs and therefore of an intent to supply them.

(2) There was, however, a misdirection in the present case in that the judge failed to direct the jury as to how they should approach the question of whether the finding of the money was probative of the necessary intent. In such cases as this it was necessary to direct the jury (a) that they should regard the finding of the money as relevant only if they rejected any innocent explanation for it put forward by the accused; (b) that, if there was any possibility of the money being in the accused's possession for reasons other than drug dealing, the evidence would not be probative; but (c) that if they concluded that the money indicated not merely past dealing but ongoing dealing in drugs, they could take into account the finding of the money, together with the drugs in question, in considering whether the necessary intention had been proved. Nevertheless, the evidence against the appellant was so overwhelming, and his explanation for it so incredible, that it was proper to apply the proviso.

Appeal dismissed.

13.12.30

10. R.v. Okusanya
[1995] Crim.L.R. 941

Following conviction of possession of a controlled drug with intent to supply, the issue was whether evidence of £8,800 in cash found on O., £1,783 found on his wife, which he agreed was his, and of money in their bank accounts should have been admitted in evidence. O. had explained the cash by saying that, as a Nigerian, it was his custom not to put his money in banks. This was found to be untrue when three separate accounts in his name were identified. It was argued that the money was irrelevant as the Crown's case was not that he had supplied in the past, but had intent to do so in the future. Alternatively, if the evidence was properly admitted, no adequate direction as to its probative significance was given. The reason for the application being made 21 months out of time was because the Court of Appeal had quashed the conviction in a case which appeared to be on all fours with this: *R. v. Batt, supra.*

Held, having regard to all the foregoing authorities, *supra,* the judge in this case was correct to rule that evidence of the cash being found was both relevant and admissible, and probative of the case against him.

The evidence of the money in the accounts was also relevant to rebut O's false explanation for having so much cash in the car. *R. v. Batt* should be regarded as a case strictly confined to its own facts, and not one which contained any statement of general principle. In particular, it should be remembered that the £150 in that case was too small and its hiding place too unremarkable to be the hallmark of present and active drug dealing.

As to the second ground, no two cases were the same, and a judge had to tailor his directions to the needs of the case and the particular issues on which the jury had to decide to arrive at a proper verdict, which had been done here.

Extension of time granted. Renewed
application refused.

11. R. v. Smith　　　　　　　**13.12.31**
[1995] Crim.L.R. 940

S. was convicted on a retrial of possession of a Class A drug (Ecstasy) with intent to supply and possession of a Class B drug (amphetamine) with intent to supply. He admitted possession but denied intent to supply. Twenty Ecstasy tablets and 24.82 grammes of amphetamine in powder form, some in wraps, were found in his possession at his uncle's house. S. maintained that all the drugs were for his personal consumption. His bank book revealed that some £9,000 had been deposited in recent months though he was on income support, of that amount £2,100 was unexplained by various legitimate transactions. In his evidence S. said that he bought the drugs the day before his arrest. He had never sold or given away any drugs. Objection was made to the admissibility of documents in his possession which were alleged to contain jottings relating to drugs and prospective purchasers, and to the evidence of the money in his possession. The judge admitted them in evidence. On appeal it was submitted that the judge wrongly admitted evidence of the documents and the money and that the judge misdirected the jury concerning the relevance of the money.

Held, the judge rightly admitted evidence of the documents and of the money in S.'s possession. However as the court in *R. v. Grant, supra,* had made clear, the judge should have directed the jury as to the relevance of the money — *i.e.* as evidence of an ongoing (and not previous) trade in drugs — he merely told the jury what use they could not make of the evidence: *R. v. Wright, supra, per* Beldam L.J. The existence of money was one of the most important features of the case and the failure to direct the jury properly about it made the conviction unsafe.

Appeal allowed.

NOTE

The learned commentator on this case adverted to the amount of trouble which this problem gave the courts: [1995] Crim.L.R. 941. Another view is that the English appellate judges gave themselves the problem by failing or omitting, with respect, to grasp the nettle at the earliest stage and deciding whether cash was relevant and admissible in proving an intent to supply.

The commentator observed that "the question is the simple, basic issue of relevance, but simple questions are sometimes difficult to answer. In the present case the court did not dispute the relevance of the evidence of the issue, but only the adequacy of the direction to the jury.

It has to be said that this is a bit puzzling. If the conviction was unsafe, it was because the jury had taken the challenged evidence into account in deciding the only matter in issue, *i.e.* that S. had the necessary intent to supply the drugs found in his possession. If they had not taken it into account on that issue, no harm was done. But the conviction is quashed because the judge did not tell them that they should consider the relevance of the evidence to that issue. If he had told them that they might do so, and they had, that would have been all right, but because they might have done it without having been instructed to do so, the conviction is quashed. They had been told not to apply for forbidden (though perfectly logical) reasoning — *i.e.* the possession of the money shows that he had been guilty of drug dealing in the past, therefore it was likely that he was going on to deal with these drugs. What did that leave but the permitted reasoning?

Moreover, 'ongoing' must include past as well as future. It would be wholly unrealistic to tell the jury that the possession of money is no evidence that he has done any drug dealing in the past but is evidence that he was about to do so in future. The term 'ongoing' is used with approval in all three of these cases. It seems that the trial judge should tell the jury that if they think that the possession of money is related to drug dealing but that they think it shows nothing more than past dealing, they should ignore it, but if they are satisfied that it shows that the defendant was engaged in an ongoing business of supplying drugs, then that is a fact which they may take into account in deciding whether they are satisfied that he had an intent to supply these drugs."

All this it is arguable, reveals, case law that is running out of control for "ongoing" is a word nowhere to be found in the 1971 Act and "possession with intent to supply" must, looking at it as a phrase of the English language in its ordinary sense, mean possession now with an intention or willingness to supply now or later.

To try to rely now on what may have happened in the past to try to prove the future is needlessly complex and thus risks injustice: prosecutors must at all times be reasonable.

13.12.32   **12. R. v. Halpin**
[1996] Crim.L.R. 112

H. appealed against his conviction of possessing heroin with intent to supply. He was found asleep at an address searched by the police. In addition to cash totalling £6,460 the police found six wraps of heroin. On the same day at the home of H.'s estranged wife, police found 400 grammes of heroin (street value £25,000–£32,000), personal letters and photographic equipment belonging to H.

Two charges of supplying heroin were added to the indictment, despite objection from the defence. One charge related to a specific incident on July 30 when H. was said to supplied the drug to a man and a woman at a public house. The second alleged drug dealing between January and July. The prosecution relied upon evidence of lifestyle — lavish furnishings at his wife's flat, the purchase of a caravan in August 1992 and payment for a holiday in Majorca. H. was acquitted on those counts. Counsel for H. challenged the admissibility of that evidence on the first and second counts.

Held, whether such evidence could be relevant to an issue of intent would be rare. The comments of the Court in *R. v. Morris, supra,* — that evidence of large amounts of money or extravagant lifestyle prima facie explicable only if derived from drug dealing was admissible in cases of possession of drugs with intent to supply if it is of probative significance to an issue in the case — went too far. It was unarguable that such evidence could not afford any probative value where the issue is possession. When such evidence is allowed as part of a case against somebody who is charged with possession with intent to supply it is vitally incumbent on the judge to spell out the restricted use that the jury may make of such evidence — that it is not and cannot be relevant to the issue of whether or not the defendant was in possession of the drug. In the present case there was a grave danger that the jury, even though they acquitted on the added counts, were misled and the whole case was suffused in an unbalanced fashion by the appellant's lifestyle rather than on concentrating on such evidence as went to show whether or not he was in possession of the drugs.

Appeal allowed. Retrial ordered.

NOTE

From the Scots point of view two points should be made. First, charges cannot simply be "added to" the indictment mid-trial. Secondly, the Appeal Court can grant authority for a new trial but cannot "order" one.

13. R. v. Barner-Rasmussen   13.12.33
[1996] Crim.L.R. 497

B. was convicted with others of being knowingly concerned in the importation of cocaine. When the courier arrived at the airport and a search revealed the cocaine, she agreed to assist customs officers. She said that B.'s part in the plan was, having been assured of the safe arrival of the drugs by another of those involved, for him to telephone her at the house of a third member of the group and collect the drugs from her. She went to the house. Customs officers recorded a telephone conversation in which B. said that he understood she had a present for him. She gave him directions to the house and he was arrested when he arrived. When B.'s house was searched, certain items of drug taking paraphernalia were found, on some of which were traces of cocaine. In interview, B. told officers that they would find a small quantity of cannabis in his house, and, later, that he had in the past occasionally smoked small quantities of crack cocaine. In evidence, he denied any knowledge of or involvement in drug smuggling. He said one of the co-accused was a close friend of his, who had told him that the courier had a present for him. The finding of the paraphernalia at the time that he was suspected of drug smuggling was, he said in cross-examination, an unfortunate coincidence.

On appeal, it was argued that (1) the evidence of the paraphernalia and previous drug taking was either irrelevant, or of such marginal relevance that it should not have been admitted by the judge in exercise of his discretion, counsel relying on the original principles in *D.P.P. v. Ball* (1910) 6 Cr.App.R. 31 and *Maxwell v. D.P.P.* (1934) 24 Cr.App.R 152; (2) the prosecution improperly and unfairly concentrated on B.'s past history as a drugs user in cross-examination; (3) the judge failed, in his summing-up, to direct the jury as to the relevance of that evidence or offer them any guidance on their approach to it.

Held, (1) the paraphernalia and admissions were relevant to the disclosed defence of innocent knowledge or involvement, in accordance with *R. v. Peters* [1995] 2 Cr.App.R. 77 and *R. v. Willis* (unreported, January 29, 1979). The judge exercised his discretion to determine whether or not to admit the evidence, and it could not be said that he erred in principle. (2) There was a disproportionate emphasis on previous drug taking in the cross-examination of B., and questions were asked which should not have been. Some went beyond the issue of knowledge or innocent involvement. Although reprehensible, the questioning was not, however, so oppressive or prejudicial as to amount to a material irregularity. (3) There should have been a direction which identified that the purpose for which the evidence was admitted was to rebut the assertion that B. was an innocent dupe. The judge's directions did not do so with adequate emphasis or clarity. Such a direction could have included the following passage: "If you consider that that evidence does assist you on the issue of whether or not this man had knowledge or involvement with these drugs, then you will take it into account. If you consider it does not assist you in that regard, you should disregard it altogether." The failure to give the direction amounted to a material irregularity. The proviso was applied.

Appeal dismissed.

13.12.34   **14. R. v. Scott**
                                      [1996] Crim.L.R. 652

S. appealed against his conviction of two counts of possessing a controlled drug (amphetamine and temazepam) with intent to supply. At his trial, evidence had been adduced that his house had been searched on two occasions, ten days before and the day after his arrest. The police had found items commonly associated with drug dealing, including self-sealing bags and a newspaper wrap containing traces of amphetamine.

S. was arrested when police officers stopped a car in which he was a passenger. His co-accused was sitting in the car with a holdall on his knees, the holdall containing 447 grammes of amphetamine packed in plastic bags. There was also a bin liner in the car, containing self-sealing bags and 284 temazepam capsules and 292 grammes of amphetamine. S. had £311 on him when arrested, his co-accused had 58 pence. A scientist gave evidence that the amphetamine found in the holdall, the bin liner and the newspaper wrap from S.'s house was a very close match, and that there were similarities between the plastic bags found in the holdall, the bin liner and S.'s house.

The only issue at the trial was possession, S. and his co-accused in effect each conducting a cut-throat defence. It was admitted that an intent to supply could readily be inferred from the quantities of drugs found. The question on appeal was whether evidence of S.'s possession of money and drugs paraphernalia should have been admitted.

Held, that following the decision in *R. v. Halpin, supra*, evidence of money, lifestyle or other extraneous matters would in the ordinary way have been irrelevant since the only issue in the case was possession. However, in the present case there were special facts which led to a different conclusion. First, there was a very close match between the amphetamine found in the car and that found in the appellant's house, and secondly there were some links between the plastic bags found in the car and the appellant's house. In the court's judgment that evidence was relevant, and the question then was whether the judge should have excluded it because its prejudicial effect exceeded its probative value. In the opinion of the court it did not matter whether the judge should have excluded the evidence from the prosecution case since counsel for the co-accused was entitled to rely on all the disputed evidence as affecting the appellant's credibility.

Appeal dismissed.

(e) Evidential matters: tracker dogs.   **13.12.35**

R. v. Pieterson and Holloway   **13.12.36**
[1995] Crim.L.R. 402

At the appellants' trial for robbery, one of the issues related to whether the evidence of a tracker dog's following of a trail and finding of a strap matching a holdall belonging to P. was admissible. It was contended that evidence of what the dog had done was analogous to hearsay because there was only its handler's evidence of the actions and reactions of the dog, which could not be cross-examined. Alternatively, such evidence was unreliable; a dog had a will of its own; it might act mischievously or in a way inconsistent with the Pavlovian reaction sought to be induced in it by training. On appeal following conviction it was argued that the judge should not have admitted the evidence.

Held, there was no direct English authority on tracker dogs, but reference was made to the laws of other jurisdictions.

In the present case, the judge had held that, providing the proper foundation was laid for the reliability of the dog in question to be able to follow a scent by reason of its training and experience, the evidence should be admitted. As a matter of principle, the court agreed with that ruling and followed the approach adopted in the cases cited from jurisdictions other than South Africa. If a dog handler could establish that a dog had been properly trained, and that over a period of time its reactions indicated that it was a reliable pointer to the existence of a scent from a particular individual, then that evidence should be properly admitted.

However, it was important to emphasise two safeguards: (i) proper foundations must be laid by detailed evidence establishing the reliability of the dog in question; and (ii) the judge must alert the jury to the care they needed to take and to look with circumspection at the evidence of tracker dogs, having regard to the fact that the dog might not always be reliable and could not be cross-examined.

It was not accepted that the judge gave an inadequate warning to the jury in this case. However, the dog handler's statement supplied by the Crown in support of the dog's reliability was insufficient. It recited the length of time the dog had "been on the books", and gave no account of the nature of its training, nor of its reliability on controlled tests. Accordingly, bearing in mind the scrupulous care which had been said, in the cases cited, to be necessary before such evidence could be properly adduced, it was not considered that the foundation had been properly laid in this case and for that reason the evidence ought not to have been admitted.

As to materiality, it was a peripheral matter in the case, the evidence being sought to establish that the strap found a matter yards from the scene of the crime was from the bag used in it. That was already proven in evidence by the employee at the premises robbed, who was shown it within 15 minutes of the occurrence and who positively identified it as the same strap seen on the bag. It might be that her evidence was open to challenge in cross-examination, but it was positive identifying evidence of the strap as having been involved, with the bag, in the robbery. The dog merely supported that, and was not crucial to the issue, so the lack of proper foundation for admission of the evidence did not amount to a material irregularity and, if it had, looking at the rest of the evidence, it would have been an appropriate case for applying the proviso.

Appeal dismissed.

(xi) Addiction **13.13**

1. R. v. Lawrence **13.13.1**
(1988) 10 Cr.App.R. (S.) 463

L. pleaded guilty to seven charges of burglary in houses, blocks of flats or self-contained rooms. The total value of goods and money stolen was over £6,000 but only about £1,500 worth of goods was recovered. During one of the burglaries L. broke into a house, ransacked it and broke the gas meter. The owner returned to find escaping gas in the house.

On arrest and interview L. admitted the burglaries and said that they were committed to finance his heroin addiction, which was then costing him some £90 per day. On pleading, L. admitted six previous convictions, three of them for dishonesty. He was sentenced to three years' imprisonment and sought leave to appeal.

Leave to appeal was given by the judge expressly "because there seems to be scant authority on the question of whether and to what extent, the fact that the motive for burglary was solely to feed drug addiction, could be a mitigating factor."

SIMON BROWN, J. (at p. 464): "Let this appeal henceforth stand as that authority if in truth it be needed. We cannot make too plain the principle to be followed. It is no mitigation whatever that a crime is committed to feed an addiction, whether that addiction be drugs, drink, gambling, sex, fast cars or anything else. If anyone hitherto has been labouring under misapprehension that it *was* mitigation, then the sooner and more firmly they are disabused of it the better."

Appeal dismissed.

NOTE
Drug addiction as mitigation was expressly rejected in *R. v. Gould* (1983) 5 Cr.App.R. (S.) 72. *R. v. Goldenberg* [1988] Crim.L.R. 678 and *R. v. Crampton* [1991] Crim.L.R. 277 both concern admissions made by drug addicts in interviews at a time when they were said to be suffering from withdrawal symptoms. Scots lawyers should note that both these cases are concerned with the statutory requirements of the Police and Criminal Evidence Act 1984 (c. 60).

2. MacLeod v. Co-operative Insurance Society Ltd **13.13.2**
1988 S.C.L.R. 247

A policy of life insurance contained the following clause, "This policy shall be void if before the expiration of 1 year from the date hereof the life assured shall die at his or her own hand."

The pursuer's son, Mark, entered into a life insurance contract with the defenders on September 7, 1983. He died on March 13, 1984. An inquest held into his death concluded that he had died from "morphine poisoning, drug addiction." The defenders refused to pay out under the policy, arguing that Mark had died at his own hand and in terms of the policy it was open to them to avoid payment. The pursuer, as executrix dative of her son, raised an action for payment of the proceeds of the policy.

Held, that the terms of the policy entitling the defenders to avoid it in the event of the insured dying "at his own hand" must be construed as referring to the death of the insured as a result of suicide, that is, with the deliberate intention of causing his own death, but that the taking of illegal drugs, which he had obtained on the illegal drugs market and were probably contaminated, was not sufficient to suggest that the deceased intended to take his own life.

Decree granted.

13.13.3   **3. R. v. Moore**
(1990) 12 Cr.App.R (S.) 384

M. pleaded guilty to two counts of burglary and asked for three other offences to be considered. The burglaries were carefully planned attacks on substantial houses, involving the theft of property worth over £40,000. M. had been diagnosed in 1986 as HIV positive, and there was a likelihood that he would develop AIDS within about two years. Medical treatment could be carried out in prison, although it would be easier if M. were at liberty.

Held, there was no medical evidence that the appellant's life expectancy would be diminished as a result of his being HIV positive. It was not the function of the Court to base its decisions on possible medical considerations of this sort: the Court did not know what the future might hold with regard to medical expertise. If the time were to come when for practical reasons or reasons of humanity it was no longer possible to hold the appellant in prison because of his medical condition, the Home Office could deal with the problem under established procedures. The sentence was not too long for two well planned and highly sophisticated burglaries.

Appeal dismissed.

13.13.4   **4. R. v. Flatt**
[1996] Crim.L.R. 576

F. was convicted on four counts of possession of drugs with intent. His defence was duress. He was addicted to crack cocaine and owed his supplier £1,500. Some 17 hours before the police searched his flat, the drug dealer told him to look after the drugs found, saying that if he did not, he would shoot F.'s mother, grandmother and girlfriend.

On appeal, it was argued that the judge should have told the jury that, in assessing the response of the hypothetical person of reasonable firmness to the threats, they should have invested that person with the characteristic of being a drug addict.

Held, that drug addiction was a self-induced condition, not a characteristic. There was no evidence that F.'s addiction (or indeed that of anyone else) would have had an effect on a person's ability to withstand a threat from a drugs dealer. It was not enough to adduce psychiatric or other evidence to say that F.'s ability to withstand threats was in any way weakened. It may well be that he felt under some obligation to look after the supplier's drugs.

Appeal dismissed.

NOTE

There are examples of accused taking controlled drugs, not because of addiction, but for relief from pain: see *Dowell v. Adam*, 1996 G.W.D. 16–935; *Crawford v. H.M. Advocate,* 1996 G.W.D. 23–1325; *May v. H.M. Advocate*, 1996 G.W.D. 24–1374; and *Kelly v. Friel*, 1996 G.W.D. 35–2058.

(xii) Aggravation of locus: chemist shop. **13.14**

Brown v. H.M. Advocate **13.14.1**
1987 G.W.D. 10–336

B. and M. pled guilty *inter alia* to a charge of breaking into a chemist's shop and stealing a vast quantity of drugs including Class A drugs — morphine, diamorphine, cocaine and pethidine. The drugs were said to have a street market value of £10–18,000. M. also pled guilty to a charge of breach of the Bail Act. B. and M. were both sentenced to four years' imprisonment and M. to six months' imprisonment on the breach of bail. B. was also sentenced to five years concurrent on a charge of possession with intent to supply. Both appealed against sentence on the basis that the trial judge had taken the view that the purpose of the theft was the resale of the drugs. It was argued that B. and M. had pleaded guilty on the basis that they had stolen the drugs for their own private use and had not been found in possession of the usual paraphernalia associated with supply. M. also argued that he should not have been imprisoned as another, I., who also pled guilty to the first charge had sentence deferred for two years.

Held, having regard to the sheer quantity of drugs obtained it was inconceivable that they were for the private use of B., M. and I.. The quantity alone allowed the trial judge's conclusion as a legitimate inference. The judge's reasons for deferring I.'s sentence (he had no previous convictions and had been led astray) were speculative; B. and

M.'s sentences would not be reduced. M.'s sentence for breach of the Bail Act was quashed and the maximum of three months substituted.

Appeal refused.

NOTE
   Theft by housebreaking where the locus is a chemist's shop, a health centre or a clinic is probably regarded for sentencing purposes as an aggravation either because of the locus or because of the quantity of controlled drugs and medicines stolen.
   For further examples of attacks on chemist's shops, see *Walker v. H.M. Advocate*, 1987 G.W.D. 27–1053; *Gammie v. H.M. Advocate*, 1988 G.W.D. 1–29 (where the High Court of Justiciary observed that such offences were serious and were becoming too common); *Ronald v. H.M. Advocate*, 1988 G.W.D. 14–608; *North v. H.M. Advocate*, 1989 G.W.D. 29–1308; *Robertson v. H.M. Advocate*, 1993 G.W.D. 39–2588; *Smith v. McGlennan*, 1994 G.W.D. 16–1025; and *Hamilton v. Hamilton*, 1995 G.W.D. 9–480.

13.14.2 *Aggravation of locus: places of entertainment*

13.14.3   **1. Donnelly v. H.M. Advocate**
                                         1992 G.W.D. 15–874

On appeal, held that three years' detention for supplying a Class A drug (Ecstasy) in a place of entertainment frequented by young persons, although severe, was not excessive, notwithstanding that D., aged 16 and a first offender, had been taken advantage of by an older youth who had received a sentence of $3^{1}/_{2}$ years.

Appeal refused.

NOTE
   It was said in *Murdoch v. H.M. Advocate*, 1993 G.W.D. 4–258 that "severe sentences were imposed where persons deliberately dealt in drugs at places of entertainment frequented by young people." See also *McDonald v. Normand*, 1993 G.W.D. 14–930; *Glanaghan v. H.M. Advocate*, 1993 G.W.D. 24–1504; *Burns v. H.M. Advocate*, 1993 G.W.D. 35–2240; *Faris v. H.M. Advocate*, 1993 G.W.D. 36–2331; *Richardson v. Hamilton*, 1994 G.W.D. 10–602; *Moyce v. H.M. Advocate*, 1994 G.W.D. 26–1573; *McColl v. O'Brien*, 1994 G.W.D. 40–2369; and *Barr v. H.M. Advocate*, 1995 G.W.D. 9–498.
   In *Mills v. H.M. Advocate*, 1992 G.W.D. 7–368 the appellant was employed as a steward at a night club and he had attempted to take controlled drugs past security at the night club. He was a first offender but he was "clearly in breach of the trust placed in him." Similarly, in *Thomson v. Ruxton*, 1996 G.W.D. 22–1267 the appellant had a special pass which entitled him to enter a rave without being searched. He took in controlled drugs with the intention of handing them back to his friends. On appeal it was held that a custodial sentence was justified.

2. Stephen v. H.M. Advocate
1993 S.C.C.R. 660

13.14.4

S., a 23-year-old first offender, pleaded guilty to possession with intent to supply, being concerned in the supply of and offering to supply to police officers, amphetamine and cannabis resin, contrary to the 1971 Act. He was a student and had brought with him to a folk festival some £370 worth of drugs, packaged for sale. He was sentenced to concurrent periods of twelve months' imprisonment on each charge and appealed to the High Court.

Held, that the court regards it as a serious matter that the appellant was present at a folk festival with drugs packaged into saleable quantities and that the sheriff erred in not imposing a longer sentence; and sentences quashed and concurrent sentences of two years' imprisonment on each charge substituted.

Appeal refused.

(xiii) Assistance to authorities

13.15

1. R. v. Sivan
(1988) 10 Cr.App.R. (S.) 282

13.15.1

The appellants pleaded guilty to being concerned in the importation of cannabis resin. They had been concerned in the importation by sea of a container in which 1,800 kilogrammes of cannabis resin (estimated street value £4$\frac{1}{2}$ million) was concealed. Three appellants were sentenced to 10 years' imprisonment, the other to six years. One appellant had given information relating to matters in which he was not involved, but had received no discount from his sentence in the light of *R. v. Preston and McAleny* (1987) 9 Cr.App.R. (S.) 155.

Held, it was now a well established feature of sentencing practice that credit should be given to a defendant in certain circumstances for assistance or information given to the authorities. There were many difficulties — it was not always easy to discover the true facts, and the defendant himself would not be anxious for his activities to be aired in public, so that any information which he did impart would often have to be conveyed to the court in writing, or in private. It was not always easy for the judge to determine exactly what credit he should give for the information provided: among the matters to which he would pay regard were the nature and effect of the information (did it relate to serious or trivial offences, did it bring to justice persons who would not otherwise have been brought to justice); the degree of assistance provided (was the offender prepared to give evidence if necessary to bring home the information he had provided and assist in the conviction of an offender); and the degree of risk to which the defendant had exposed himself and his family. Within those limits the judge must bring himself to tailor the sentence so as to punish the defendant, but at the same time reward him as far as possible for the help he had given, in order to demonstrate to offenders that it was worth their while to disclose the criminal activities of others for the benefit of the law abiding public in general. In important cases it might be desirable for the court to have a letter from the senior officer of the police force or of the Customs and Excise, unconnected with the case, who examined all the facts and was able to certify that the facts were as reported by the officers conducting the investigation. There should be a statement in writing from the officer in charge of the investigation setting out those facts which would be certified by the senior officer; in the more important cases the officer in charge of the investigation should be available to give evidence if necessary, whether in court or in the judge's chambers as the situation might demand. The shorthand writer should be present to take a note of what transpired in the judge's room.

It was apparent that the object of the exercise was to gain information about criminal activities which would otherwise not be available. It followed that information of that sort would be equally acceptable, whether it was information relating to the crime in respect of which the defendant had been convicted or whether it was related to some other criminal activity which had nothing directly to do with the crime to which the defendant had pleaded guilty. Concern had been expressed about the decision of the Court in *Preston and McAleny* (1987) 9 Cr.App.R. (S.) 155, where it was said that as a matter of principle a defendant should not be given credit for information which did not relate to the offence in which he had been involved. The Court had come to the conclusion that *Preston and McAleny* ought not to be followed. The Court was entitled to take that view as no distinction had been drawn in a whole series of earlier cases between information given about the case in question and information about other cases, and in some cases (for example, *R. v. Henry*, July 26, 1985 [unreported]) discounts were given for information which plainly did not relate to the offence to which the defendant had pleaded guilty; the Court had always been prepared to reconsider its decisions where the amendment operated in favour of the defendant. In the light of these considerations, the sentence on the defendant concerned would be reduced to six and a half years' imprisonment (the sentence on two other appellants who had not given information, and were considered not to have been the organisers of the scheme, were reduced from 10 years to nine).

Appeals allowed and sentences varied.

NOTE

R. v. Sivan was the first detailed decision on discount for co-operation, although the principle had been mentioned earlier: *R. v. Afzal, The Times*, October 14, 1984.

2. Isdale v. Scott
1991 S.C.C.R. 491

13.15.2

I. pleaded guilty to being in possession of 28 grammes of cannabis resin. The sheriff stated that if I. identified to the authorities the persons who had supplied him with the drugs, the disposal would be more lenient. I. did not accept the opportunity offered and instead gave the authorities a fictitious name and address. The sheriff then sentenced him to 60 days' imprisonment. I. appealed to the High Court.

Held, that while the provision of information about a drug supplier can be a mitigating factor, failure to provide that information is not a reason for a custodial sentence.

LORD COWIE (at p. 492): "Of course it is true to say that if somebody is given a chance to give information about a drug supplier and provides that information, that can be a mitigating factor in sentence, but if the person does not give that information or refuses to give that information, we should make it quite clear that we do not consider that a reason for choosing a custodial sentence as opposed to some other form of disposal."

Appeal allowed and sentence varied.

3. R. v. Debbag and Izzet
(1991) 12 Cr.App.R. (S.) 733

13.15.3

The applicants were convicted of being concerned in the importation of heroin and sentenced to 14 years' imprisonment. Confiscation orders were made against each applicant under the 1986 Act. They were concerned in importing 15.9 kilogrammes of 25 per cent heroin, worth about £1.7 million. Following their conviction, while inquiries for the purposes of the 1986 Act were in progress, the applicants indicated that they would assist the police with information about other offenders. They gave certain information to the police after they had been sentenced, but the information was already known to the police. It was submitted that the applicants should receive some reduction in their sentences, which were not otherwise challenged, on account of the help they had given to the police.

Held, considering *R. v. Sivan, supra*, the value to the courts and the public in reflecting assistance by serious offenders is in enabling the authorities speedily to arrest those other offenders and where drugs are involved, to prevent their further distribution. It was a matter to which the court would normally have regard when the person volunteering the information was sentenced; normally such information would be provided when pleas of guilty were entered, and as part of the general remorse of the offender concerned. If the offender were allowed to fight his corner to the last and seek a reduction from the Court of Appeal when faced with the sentence imposed on him, the Court would be faced with great difficulty in assessing the genuineness of the information. There was a clear public policy interest in encouraging the speedy proffering of information as part and parcel of their acceptance of their own responsibility for the matters which they are charged. The Court of Appeal could not readily countenance a system of what would amount to negotiation after conviction and sentence for a reduction in sentence on the strength of lately volunteered information, particularly where the information proved to be of no practical assistance to the authorities. The sentences could not be reduced.

Appeals refused.

13.15.4   **4. R. v. Catterall**
(1993) 14 Cr.App.R. (S.) 724

C. pleaded guilty to supplying a Class A controlled drug, Ecstasy, possessing Ecstasy with intent to supply, possessing LSD with intent to supply, and supplying LSD. C.'s father discovered tablets in C.'s possession and reported him to the police. C. admitted supplying drugs to his friends and other established users. He was sentenced to four years' detention in a young offenders institution.

Held, given the relatively small quantities of drugs involved in this case, the appellant's youth and plea of guilty, a sentence of about three to three and a half years was appropriate: a further discount should be given to reflect the fact that it was the appellant's father who brought the matter to the attention of the police. A sentence of two years' detention would be substituted.

BELDAM, L.J. (at p. 725): "Mr Catterall [having found the drugs in his son's car] then took a most unusual, responsible and praiseworthy course, entirely in the interests of his son. He called the police. Although we have had numerous cases before this Court, this is, as far as we are concerned, the first occasion on which this has happened. It was obviously greatly in the public interest as well as in the interests of his son that Mr Catterall took this course because the damage being done to society today from these dangerous drugs (for dangerous they undoubtedly are) is so serious that society must leave no stone unturned to try to trace the source of them. If a parent, out of consideration for his son or daughter acts in his interests and the public interest, it seems to us that it is right for the Court to tale his action into account when it comes to consider how to deal with offences thus brought to light.

In other similar situations substantial credit is given to a person who is charged with offences of this kind who himself gives assistance in tracing the origins and sources of supply of these drugs. It may be said that it is not so much to the credit of the appellant as to his parents that the matter has come to light in this way. However, the Court is entitled to look at the background to the offences and the way they were discovered, as well as to the background of the offender in deciding upon the sentence which is to be imposed …

There is the additional feature that the appellant's father cares so much about his future that he was prepared to disclose the offences to the police. He and the appellant's mother are likely to support the appellant's attempts to give up this habit and it was to this end that they brought the position to the notice of the police. It seems to us that the Court should take those facts into account by giving a further discount over the sentence which would otherwise have been appropriate. The need to deter this offender, the protection of the public and his own interests all react upon the length of sentence which it is necessary to impose which should not be longer than is necessary in the particular facts of the case.

Therefore, entirely thanks to his father for his responsible actions, the appellant is entitled to a further discount over the sentence which would have been imposed. We think that, in the circumstances of this case, taking everything into account, the sentence imposed by the recorder was too long. It gave insufficient allowance for Mr Catterall's responsible action. We would reduce the sentence to one of two years' imprisonment. We emphasise to the appellant that that reduction is entirely due to his father's actions. We think he should be extremely grateful to him. We hope that in future the appellant will bear that in mind."

Appeal allowed.

5. R. v. X.   **13.15.5**
[1994] Crim.L.R. 469

X. was convicted of participating in a major conspiracy to import cocaine and sentenced to 16 years' imprisonment. Following his conviction and sentence, the appellant gave information to the prosecuting authorities in a foreign country, and gave evidence in that country at the trial of a co-conspirator. This led directly and indirectly to the conviction of other conspirators and the seizure of a substantial quantity of cocaine. The appellant invited the Court to reduce his sentence on account of the assistance he had given since his sentence.

Held, where a defendant had given valuable assistance to the authorities, either in connection with which he was charged or otherwise, the sentencing judge should normally give him some credit. This principle was not confined to assistance given to prosecuting authorities in this country. The question of giving for assistance given after conviction and sentence was considered in *R. v. Debbag and Izett, supra*, the general principle to be extracted from that case was that credit for assistance of this sort should be given only if proffered early enough for it to be potentially useful. The purpose of the credit was to reflect the offender's own attitude and acceptance of guilt and remorse, and to assist in the arrest of others. There was no true remorse if the offender fought his corner and volunteered information only when sentenced. To leave offenders with such an option would be no incentive to them to face up to their guilt at the outset or provide early assistance to the authorities. The applicant had contested his trial, and did not offer any assistance until 15 months after sentence. The assistance, though late, had been of great help in the apprehension of others, but the Court could not countenance a sentencing regime in which an offender might at a time of choosing seek to renegotiate sentence by proffering information which he could have put before the authorities long ago.

NOTE
>This case is reported as *R. v. H., The Times*, March 1, 1994.

13.15.6
6. R. v. Martin
(1994) 15 Cr.App.R. (S.) 613

M. pleaded guilty to supplying amphetamine and possessing psilocybin. Police officers searching a house he rented found a pill-making machine, tablets containing traces of amphetamine, and 86 grammes of psilocybin, a Class A drug. M. admitted that he had purchased the pill-making machine for £7,000 with a view to making pills containing amphetamine, and estimated that he had made over 240,000 pills over a two-month period. He was sentenced to seven years' imprisonment with a confiscation order under the 1986 Act in the amount of £107,000, with two years' imprisonment in default.

Held, considering *R v. Shaw* (1986) 8 Cr.App.R. (S.) 16 and *R. v. King* (1993) 14 Cr.App.R. (S.) 252, the sentencer was right to use as his starting point the top of the scale for similar cases: he had discounted the sentence for a number of matters but could have given greater credit for the appellant's assistance to the police. The sentence would be reduced to six years.

SCOTT BAKER, L.J. (at p. 615): "We do wish to emphasise that, particularly in this type of case, it is of particular importance to give a defendant full credit for assistance with the police, not only in clearing up the particular matter on which he was being interviewed, but generally. We think that the appellant did give the police very considerable assistance and we think that the learned judge could properly have given him rather greater credit for it."

Appeal allowed.

13.15.7
7. Cormack v. H.M. Advocate
1996 S.C.C.R. 53

C. was convicted of a number of contraventions of the Misuse of Drugs Act 1971, a number of contraventions of the Firearms Act 1968, and a charge of assault. He was given a cumulo sentence of eight years on the drugs charges, a cumulo sentence of five years on the firearms offences and a sentence of four years for the assault, these to be consecutive to each other, making 17 years in all. He appealed to the High Court on the ground, *inter alia*, that he had given information to the procurator fiscal in connection with cases involving drugs and was to give evidence for the Crown at a forthcoming trial, a matter not referred to in the trial judge's report.

Held, that, in the special circumstances of the case and having regard to the fact that the investigations related to cases involving drugs, that was a matter which should have been taken into account.

THE LORD JUSTICE-CLERK (ROSS) (at p. 55): "The final matter which the appellant raised was that he informed us that he had given assistance to the procurator fiscal in connection with investigations being made in relation to cases involving controlled drugs and involving police officers and that he is to be an important witness at a forthcoming trial in that connection and he maintained that that should have been taken into account when sentence was being imposed. This is not a matter which has been expressly raised in the grounds of appeal. However, we have from the trial judge a full report explaining how he came to impose the sentences totalling 17 years and he has provided us with a note of what he said when he was imposing sentence. From that note it does not appear that the trial judge did have regard to this aspect of the matter, namely that the appellant was co-operating with the authorities and was going to be giving evidence at a forthcoming trial. In the special circumstances of this case and having regard to the fact that these investigations related to cases involving controlled drugs, we have come to the conclusion that this was a matter which should properly have been taken into account. That being so, we are prepared to give some effect to that circumstance by reducing the cumulo sentence of eight years which the trial judge imposed ... We shall quash that sentence and in substitution for that sentence we shall impose a sentence of six years in cumulo. The other sentences will remain. The result therefore is that the total sentence is now 15 years instead of 17."

Appeal allowed in part.

NOTE

There are no authorities in Scotland that are as explicit as *R. v. Sivan, supra,* and *R. v. Debbag and Izzet, supra,* but it would seem from this case that the approach taken by the judiciary might be the same as in England and Wales. There are certainly other cases in which mitigation has included an assertion of assistance by the appellant: in *McLaughlin v. H.M. Advocate,* 1989 G.W.D. 20–841 the appellant "had repented and assisted the police". In *Sutherland v. H.M. Advocate,* 1996 G.W.D. 14–829 the appellant had "co-operated with the police at some risk to himself". In *Gass v. H.M. Advocate,* 1996 G.W.D. 18–1052 the appellant had "named his supplier to the police", and in *Rollinson v. H.M. Advocate*, 1996 G.W.D. 18–1053 the appellant gave a detailed statement of his involvement and that of the co-accused, but see, in contrast, *Choucha v. H.M. Advocate*, 1997 G.W.D. 1–22.

For an example of the dangers inherent in dealing with controlled drugs, especially where things go wrong, see *R. v. Hall* (1995) 16 Cr.App.R. (S.) 921, a case of kidnapping and assault.

13.16 *(xiv) Observation posts*

13.16.1

1. R. v. Johnson
[1989] 1 All E.R. 121

J. was seen to be selling drugs by police officers watching from private premises which were used by the police as observation points in a known drug-dealing locality. J. was charged with possessing and supplying controlled drugs. At his trial the only evidence that J. had been supplying drugs was that given by the police officers stationed at the observation post and J.'s counsel applied to be permitted to cross-examine the officers on the exact location of the observation posts so that he could test the police evidence by reference to their distance from the alleged transactions, their angle of vision and possible obstructions in their line of sight. The Crown contended that the police officers should not be required to reveal the exact location of the observation posts because it would put at risk occupiers who had permitted their premises to be used by the police as observation posts. The judge ruled that the exact location of the observation posts need not be revealed. J. was convicted and appealed, contending that his defence had been so hampered by the judge's ruling that there had been a miscarriage of justice.

Held, a trial judge could exclude evidence which would reveal the address and identity of occupiers of private premises which were used by the police as observation posts provided that there was a proper evidential basis for the exclusion of such evidence and that he was satisfied that the defendant would nevertheless receive a fair trial and that the desirability of protecting from reprisals those who assisted the police outweighed the principle that there should be full disclosure of all the material facts. In order that the judge should be in a position to make such an evaluation a senior police officer should be able to testify, from visits made by him both before the observation commenced and immediately prior to the trial, as to the attitude of the occupiers towards the possible disclosure of their addresses and identities. Since on the facts the appellant had not received an unfair trial, because the judge had given the jury directions which safeguarded his position in the light of the judge's ruling to exclude evidence of the exact location of the police observation posts, the jury's verdict was not unfair or unsatisfactory.

WATKINS, L.J. (at p. 127): "[The cases cited] show that it has been regarded as part of the exclusionary rule that, provided there is a proper evidential basis for it, a trial judge may on application exclude evidence which, if given, would reveal not only where the police have kept observation from but also, if they have kept the observation at premises, especially dwellings, the identity of the occupiers.

The paramount consideration here is of course whether the appellant had an unfair trial which led to a verdict which is either unsafe or unsatisfactory. Although the conduct of the defence was to some extent affected by the restraints placed on it by the judge's rulings, which were in our view properly made, we are not persuaded that this led to any injustice. The jury were well aware of these restraints and most carefully directed about the very special care they had to give to any disadvantage they may have brought to the defence. It was a summing up which was as a whole, we think, favourable to the defence and which contained safeguarding directions which could have left the jury in no doubt as to the nature of their task.

The judge was not, of course, acquainted with the guidance we are about to give and did not receive evidence which conformed to it before making the rulings complained of. But he heard some evidence going part of the way to meet that guidance and he had knowledge from previous trials conducted by him of the difficulties police encounter in obtaining help from the public in the area where the appellant's offence was found to be committed. He was, we think, in a sound enough position to balance the competing interests between the principle of full disclosure of material facts on the one hand and the need, in the interests of justice, to in some degree conduct a trial without confirming with it. It is risking condescension to say of him that he knew well the legal principles involved. Moreover, we cannot agree that his rulings went too far to meet the needs of the protection sought. We cannot accept that there was unfairness in this trial, or that the verdict was either unsafe or unsatisfactory.

While the judge, who is, as has already been indicated, so very experienced in handling criminal trials, took infinite care to satisfy himself that there was in his opinion a satisfactory evidential basis in the circumstances of this case for ruling that there be non-disclosure by the police of information which could lead to identification of places used for the purpose of observing the suspected comission of criminal offences, we accept that, for the benefit of the police, counsel and judges who will have to face in the future a similar problem to that which confronted this judge, some guidance from this court on basic evidential requirements would be found helpful. The submissions as to that, from counsel for the appellant in particular, we have found valuable in considering what that guidance should be.

Clearly a trial judge must be placed by the Crown, when it seeks to exclude evidence of the identification of places of observation and occupiers of premises, in the best possible position to enable him properly in the interests of justice, which includes of course providing a defendant with a fair trial, to determine whether he will afford to the police the protection sought. At the heart of this problem is the desirability, as far as this can properly be given, of reassuring people who are asked to help the police that their identities will never be disclosed lest they become the victims of reprisals by wrongdoers for performing a public service.

The minimum evidential requirements seem to us to be the following, (a) The police officer in charge of the observations to be conducted, and no-one of lower rank than a sergeant should usually be acceptable for this purpose, must be able to testify that beforehand he visited all observation places to be used and ascertained the attitude of occupiers of premises, not only to the use to be made of them but also to the possible disclosure thereafter of the use made and facts which could lead to the identification of the premises thereafter and of the occupiers. He may, of course, in addition inform the court of difficulties, if any, usually encountered in the particular locality of obtaining assistance from the public. (b) A police officer of no rank lower than a chief inspector must be able to testify that immediately prior to the trial he visited the places used for observation, the results of which it is proposed to give in evidence, and ascertained whether the occupiers are the same as when the observations took place and, whether they are or are not, what the attitude of those occupiers is to the possible disclosure of the use previously made of the premises and of facts which could lead at the trial to identification of premises and occupiers.

Such evidence will of course be given in the absence of the jury when the application to exclude the material is made. The judge should explain to the jury, as this judge did, when summing up or at some appropriate time before that, the effect of his ruling to exclude, if he so rules.

There are trials waiting to be held, where we have to suppose the requirements of (a) cannot be satisfied or wholly satisfied, because the guidance of this judgment was not available at the material time or times. In that event we think a judge may, according to the quality of the evidence before him under (b), and possibly in part satisfaction of (a), be able properly and safely to exclude evidence of facts sought to be protected."

Appeal dismissed.

2. R. v. Hewitt and Davis
(1992) 95 Cr.App.R. 81

The defendants were both in separate operations arrested for supplying prohibited drugs on the basis of information obtained by police in observation posts in various buildings. At trial each defendant alleged false, fabricated or mistaken identification. In both cases the trial judges upheld prosecution applications to exclude evidence that might disclose the whereabouts of these observation posts. The appellants were each convicted and appealed, contending that the trial judge in each case should not have exercised his discretion to exclude examination of police witnesses because (a) the police had not brought themselves within the "minimum evidential requirements" as set out in *R. v. Johnson* [1989] 1 All E.R. 121; and (b) the public policy which denied the defendant disclosure of certain knowledge possessed by the police clashed with the public interest allowing the defendant to present his defence in the best possible way. The anonymity of observation posts was not covered by the doctrine of public interest in the same way as the anonymity of police informers.

Held, that the detection of crime called in appropriate and circumscribed ways for an increase in the anonymity granted to police action. There was no essential difference in that respect between informers and the providers of observation posts; for both in different ways provided the police with indispensable assistance in the detection of crime; provided there was a proper evidential basis for it the exclusionary rule of evidence may apply.

Appeals dismissed.

NOTE

In a commentary on this case Ostin noted that defence lawyers will "from time to time be confronted with this particular problem, namely, that the only evidence against their clients will be police evidence of observations, but the observation posts will not be revealed. The prosecution will maintain their position by calling senior officers to say why the identity of the locations should not be revealed and it will then be a matter for the court to make a decision on submissions. In the event of the competing interest falling in favour of a defendant, it is highly likely that the prosecution will be withdrawn.": see "Police Observation Posts" (1992) 156 J.P. 423. That writer failed to refer to the inherent dangers in such co-operation with the police in providing observation posts: the matter is more than mere non-disclosure.

3. Blake and Austin v. D.P.P.   13.16.3
(1993) 97 Cr.App.R. 169

From an observation post, two police officers watched the activities of the appellants in a churchyard, and subsequently justices convicted them of indecent behaviour in a churchyard, contrary to section 2 of the Ecclesiastical Courts Jurisdiction Acts 1860. The appellants were both of previous good character. They appealed to the Crown Court where it was argued that the prosecution had failed to provide the court with sufficient cogent evidence that the position of the observation post required protection. The police officers gave evidence that if the position of the observation post was disclosed, the occupier, who had given permission for the officers to use it, would be in danger of harassment from such people as the appellants. The judge ruled that the occupiers of the observation post were entitled to protection and dismissed the appeal. On appeal therefrom to the Divisional Court by way of case stated, it was submitted that the judge's ruling was unreasonable because the guidelines in the Court of Appeal [in *R. v. Johnson* [1989] 1 All E.R. 121] required at least an actual threat of violence, if not severe violence, before protection should be offered to an occupier of an observation post.

Held, that there was no logical reason to deny the same protection to those who supplied the police with the facility to gather information as was supplied by police informers; nor was there any reason to suppose that protection from harassment, as opposed to violence, was not contemplated by the Court of Appeal's guidelines. Accordingly, there had been no misdirection in the instant case.

Appeal dismissed.

13.16.4   **4. R. v. Grimes**
                            [1994] Crim.L.R. 213

G. was convicted of two counts of supplying a Class B controlled drug, on the basis of the evidence of police officers who had been keeping watch from an observation post in a building within 100 yards of the public house in the vicinity of which the supply was alleged to have taken place. At trial, the issue was identity, G. maintaining throughout that he was not the man whom the police had observed.

At the start of the trial, the Crown had applied for a ruling entitling police officers to decline to answer questions in cross-examination which might lead to the disclosure of the whereabouts of the observation post. A police inspector gave evidence that he had visited the premises prior to the start of the observation and had spoken to the occupant, who was worried that disclosure of his identity or that of the premises might lead to damage to the property and that he feared for his personal safety. A chief inspector who had visited the premises before the operation began and also spoken to the occupier on the day before the trial, gave similar evidence and confirmed that the occupier was still of the same view.

The trial judge ruled that the guidelines outlined by the Court of Appeal in *R. v. Johnson, supra*, had been complied with, that he was satisfied that if the restrictions sought were imposed there would be no risk of a miscarriage of justice and that the police officers could decline to answer questions which might tend to reveal the identity of the occupants of the observation post or its location beyond the following matters (i) that the observation post was within 100 yards radius from the central point of the public house; (ii) that the observation was carried out from inside a building and (iii) that there was more than one vantage point inside the building from which observations were carried out. It was common ground that the observations were carried out through glass.

On appeal it was argued (1) that the restrictions imposed were so onerous as to lead to the risk of a miscarriage of justice; (2) that the judge had failed to stress to the jury with sufficient care the disadvantages under which the appellant had been placed and to emphasise the dangers of a miscarriage of justice.

Held, (1) In such cases the court had to weigh the public interest in preserving the anonymity of those who assist the authorities in the prevention or detection of crime against the public interest that the defendant should receive a fair trial and that evidence should not be excluded if to do so would lead to the risk of a miscarriage of justice.

(2) The trial judge had pointed out to the jury at the outset of the summing-up that the main question for them to decide was identification. He had explained that he had had to impose restrictions on cross-examination as to the location of the observation post and that this placed an extra burden on them. He had then given a careful direction on identification and the court was satisfied that the jury had been left in no doubt about the disadvantages which the defence had faced and of the care with which they had to examine the identification evidence.

Appeal dismissed.

(xv) Syringes   **13.17**

1. Gemmell v. H.M. Advocate   **13.17.1**
1990 G.W.D. 7–366

G. was about to be searched by a policeman who repeatedly asked if he was in possession of any knives, needles, syringes or other sharp instruments. G. denied that he was in such possession. The policeman searched G. and in doing so a hypodermic needle in G.'s pocket pierced the policeman's finger and exposed him to the risk of infection.

G. was charged with culpably and recklessly denying possession of the items listed. He pleaded guilty and was sentenced to two years' imprisonment. He appealed the sentence and it was held to be excessive, albeit the charge was a serious one, and 12 months was substituted.

Appeal allowed.

NOTE

The relevancy of the charge against Gemmell does not seem to have been doubted. The point was taken at first instance in *Normand v. Morrison*, 1993 S.C.C.R. 207 where it was held that the apparent conduct of Morrison, comparable to that of Gemmell, disclosed a total disregard for the health and safety of the police officer who was acting in the course of his duty.

In *Donaldson v. Normand*, 1997 G.W.D. 15–652, an appeal against conviction of culpable and reckless conduct for failing to inform police during a personal search that he possessed a syringe was refused. The appellant's loss of memory was attributable to self-induced intoxication.

13.17.2   **2. Kimmins v. Normand**
                          1993 S.L.T. 1260

K. was charged on summary complaint with culpable and reckless conduct in respect that having been detained under section 23 of the 1971 Act and advised by a constable that he as to be searched, he falsely denied, when asked if he had any needles, syringes or sharp instruments in his possession, being in possession of any such instruments and permitted the constable to place his hand in the accused's pocket, whereupon a needle entered the constable's hand to his injury and exposing him to the risk of infection. K. objected to the relevancy of the charge but the sheriff repelled the objection. K. appealed, contending that the charge disclosed no crime known to the law of Scotland because no act was performed by the accused and because there was no causal connection between the denial and the injury to the constable.

Held, (1) that by making the denial in the light of the advice he was given as to why he was asked the question, the accused was doing something which could amount to criminal conduct; and (2) that since it must have been clear to the accused why the question was put to him it was a reasonable inference from the denial that his answer would lead to the constable doing what he did.

                                                      Appeal refused.

NOTE
    The possession of a syringe was an aggravation of a breach of the peace: *Taylor v. H.M. Advocate*, 1992 G.W.D. 11–601. However, the appellant threatened a member of the police and at the same time said that he was HIV positive.

13.18 *(xvi) Telephones*

13.18.1   **1. Ludi v. Switzerland**
                          (1993) 15 E.H.R.R. 173

After being released by a German court without trial on a drug trafficking charge, the applicant returned to Switzerland where, pursuant to a preliminary investigation by a court, his telephone was tapped. Although not provided for by Swiss law, the police authorised an undercover agent to interact with him. The applicant offered to obtain drugs for the agent, and was subsequently convicted of several offences linked to drug trafficking. At his trial and on appeal, the agent was not called as a witness. The applicant complained that the telephone tapping interfered with his private life in violation of Article 8 of the Convention and that his inability to examine the agent as a witness violated Article 6(3)(d) of the Convention and deprived him of a fair trial within the meaning of Article 6(1) of the Convention.

Held, (1) unanimously, that the Government's preliminary objection that the applicant was not a victim be dismissed; (2) unanimously, that there had not been a violation of Article 8; (3) by eight votes to one, that there had been a violation of paragraph (1) in conjunction with paragraph (3)(d) of Article 6; (4) unanimously, that the respondent State pay the applicant within three months 15,000 Swiss francs for costs and expenses; (5) unanimously, that the remainder of the claim for just satisfaction be dismissed.

Appeal allowed in part.

NOTE

The relevant parts of Article 6 of the European Convention on Human Rights are:

"1. In the determination of ... any criminal charge against him, everyone is entitled to a fair and public hearing ... by an independent and impartial tribunal ...

3. Everyone charged with a criminal offence has the following minimum rights ...

(d) to examine or have examined witnesses against him and to obtain the attendance and examination of witnesses on his behalf under the same condition as witnesses against him;"

Article 8 of the Convention reads:

"1. Everyone has the right to respect for his private and family life, his home and his correspondence.

2. There shall be no interference by a public authority with the exercise of this right except such as is in accordance with the law and is necessary in a democratic society in the interests of national security, public safety or the economic well-being of the country, for the prevention of disorder or crime, for the protection of health or morals, or for the protection of the rights and freedoms of others."

In *Nazir Chinoy* [1991] C.O.D. 105 it was observed (at p. 107) that "English law had always acknowledged the fact, unpalatable as it might be, that the detection and proof of certain types of criminal activity might necessitate the employment of underhand and even unlawful means."

2. R. v. Kearley
[1992] 2 W.L.R. 656

13.18.2

K. was charged on indictment with, *inter alia*, possession of a controlled drug with intent to supply, contrary to section 5(3) of the 1971 Act. He pleaded not guilty. At the trial, the prosecution sought to call evidence that, following the appellant's arrest and not in his presence or hearing, a number of telephone calls had been made to his house in which the callers requested to speak to him and asked to be supplied with drugs and that a number of persons had called at the house asking to be supplied with drugs. None of those persons was called to give evidence. The trial judge, overruling the appellant's objection, allowed police officers to give evidence recounting the callers' requests. K. was convicted and the Court of Appeal (Criminal Division) dismissed his appeal against conviction. K. then appealed to the House of Lords.

Held, (Lord Griffiths and Lord Browne-Wilkinson dissenting) that, in so far as the callers' requests for drugs merely manifested the callers' state of mind, *viz.* their belief or opinion that the appellant would supply them with drugs, such state of mind was irrelevant and evidence as to it was, accordingly, inadmissible; and that, in so far as the callers' requests could be treated as having impliedly asserted the fact that the appellant was a supplier of drugs, evidence of the requests was excluded by the rule against hearsay, since that rule applied equally to implied as to express assertions, and the fact that a multiplicity of requests for drugs might have greater probative force than a single request was not a ground for disregarding it.

Appeal allowed.

13.18.3

3. R. v. Preston
[1993] 3 W.L.R. 891

Following a surveillance operation mounted by the police, during which a telephone interception warrant had been issued pursuant to section 2(2)(b) of the Interception of Communications Act 1985, the defendants were charged, *inter alia*, with conspiracy to evade the prohibition in force in respect of the importation of cannabis. In addition to evidence of personal contact between the defendants, the prosecution relied on the frequency of calls made on the defendants' telephones. During the trial the question was raised whether there had been a telephone interception. In the absence of the defendants and their solicitors, prosecuting counsel disclosed that a warrant had been issued and indicated that, subject to the prohibition under section 9 of the Act against the giving of any evidence suggesting the existence of a warrant, he would seek advice from the Home Office with a view to disclosing any intercepted material that might assist the defence. He later reported to the court, again in the absence of the defendants and their solicitors, against whom the judge had made rulings restricting what they could be told of the nature of the deliberations in camera, that the Attorney-General had advised that it was not prosecuting counsel's duty to look at any such material as might exist, since it could not in any event be given in evidence without disclosing the existence of the warrant contrary to section 9. It was later disclosed that the material had been destroyed. Pursuant to section 78(1) of the Police and Criminal Evidence Act 1984, defence counsel made an application for the exclusion of all evidence relating to the making of telephone calls upon which the jury was being invited to draw inferences. The judge refused the application and the defendants were convicted. They appealed against conviction on the grounds, *inter alia*, that the prosecution's failure to disclose details of the interceptions, and also the judge's rulings excluding the defendants from attending, or receiving information on, the hearings in camera, amounted to immaterial irregularities. The Court of Appeal dismissed the appeals.

Held, (1) that the prohibition in section 9 of the Act of 1985 against adducing evidence tending to suggest that a warrant for interception had been issued was insufficient reason for an investigating authority to refuse to disclose information which might assist a defendant, since the fact that such information could not be put in evidence did not mean that it was worthless, and prosecuting counsel, in his role as arbiter between the adversarial interests of the prosecution and the broader dictates of justice, could only play his part in the decision as to whether the overall evidence warranted the carrying on with a prosecution if he was fully aware of all information material to the case.

But (2), that the power of the Secretary of State to issue a warrant under section 2(2)(b) of the Act "for the purpose of preventing or detecting serious crime" did not extend to the amassing of evidence with a view to the prosecution of offenders; that the investigating authority were therefore under a duty under section 6 of the Act to destroy all material obtained by means of an interception as soon as its retention was no longer necessary for the prevention or detection of serious crime, and they did not have to retain the material until trial for disclosure to the defence; that although the policy underlying sections 2 and 6 was in contradiction with the duty to give complete disclosure of unused materials, the intent of the Act to keep surveillance secret, and to give the maximum privacy to those whose conversation had been overheard, prevailed; and that, therefore, the destruction of the documents obtained from the interception, and their consequent unavailability for disclosure could not be relied upon by the defendants as a material irregularity in their trial; that, further, the fact that the intercepted material had been destroyed and the contents irretrievably lost did not prevent the adducing in evidence of telephone companies' records as to the defendants' use of telephone equipment; and that, accordingly, the trial judge had correctly exercised his discretion under section 78(1) of the Police and Criminal Evidence Act 1984 to allow the jury to draw inferences from the fact that telephone calls had been made by the defendants.

(3) That it had not been necessary to exclude the defendants and their solicitors from the legal argument concerning the disclosure of the intercepted material, since such argument could not have contained anything detrimental to the public interest or to the safety of an informant; that it had been equally unnecessary for counsel to be prevented from informing their clients as to the nature of those discussions; and that the judge's rulings on those matters amounted to material irregularities in the course of the trial; but that, on application of the proviso to section 2(1) of the Criminal Appeal Act 1968, the irregularities did not cast doubt on the reliability of the jury's verdict and the defendants' convictions would stand.

Appeals dismissed.

13.18.4

4. R. v. Effik
[1994] 3 W.L.R. 583

E. and another were indicted on counts of conspiracy to supply controlled drugs. Part of the evidence against them consisted of telephone conversations between them and one S., which had been intercepted and taped by police officers. The telephone apparatus in S.'s house consisted of an ordinary fixed handset and a cordless telephone. The latter comprised a base unit, connected to the mains electricity and, by means of a wire and jack, to a telephone socket in the house, and a handset, which could be used as a mobile telephone within a limited range of the base unit. When the cordless telephone was used, a radio receiver, operated by police officers in an adjoining flat picked up the radio signals being transmitted between the base unit and the handset and enabled recordings to be made of the conversations.

The appellants at the trial applied to the judge to exclude the evidence of telephone conversations overheard and recorded in that way on the ground that they had been intercepted in the course of transmission by means of a public telecommunication system and were accordingly rendered inadmissible by sections 1 and 9 of the Interception of Communications Act 1985. The judge ruled that the cordless telephone was a privately run system and, although connected to the British Telecommunications system, designated as a public telecommunications system for the purposes of the Act, was not part of it. The appellants were convicted on four counts and two counts respectively of the indictment, and their appeals against conviction were dismissed by the Court of Appeal (Criminal Division): see (1992) 95 Cr.App.R. 427. They appealed to the House of Lords.

Held, that the cordless telephone used by S. was a privately run system not "comprised in" the British Telecommunications public telecommunication system for the purposes of the Interception of Communications Act 1985; that the telephone conversations between the appellants and S. had not been intercepted by the police officers in the course of their transmission "by means of" a public telecommunication system within section 1(1) of the Act of 1985 since they had not at that time been passing through the public system; and that, accordingly, evidence of them had not been excluded by section 9(1) of the Act of 1985.

Appeals dismissed.

NOTE
     R. v. Effik and *R. v. Preston* are the subject of analysis in Nash, "Interception of Communications in the European Union" 1996 J.R. 321.

13.18.5

5. R. v. Khan
[1996] 3 W.L.R. 162

K. visited the house of a man suspected by the police of being involved in the supply of heroin on a large scale. Because of those suspicions, the police had, in accordance with Home Office guidelines of 1984, been authorised to install on the outside of the house, without the knowledge or consent of the owner or occupier, an electronic listening device from which a tape recording was made of a conversation between K. and others in the house during the course of which he said things plainly showing that he had been involved in the importation of heroin with a street value of almost £100,000. K. was charged with being knowingly concerned in the fraudulent evasion of the prohibition on the importation of a Class A drug. The Crown conceded that the installation of the listening device had involved civil trespass to the outside of a private building and the infliction on it of some degree of damage with a consequent intrusion on the privacy of those who believed themselves to be secure from being overheard when they had the crucial conversation. The Crown also accepted that without the tape recording K. had no case to answer and if it were ruled inadmissible no evidence would be offered against him. The trial judge declined to rule the evidence of the recorded conversation inadmissible under section 78 of the Police and Criminal Evidence Act 1984 and K. pleaded guilty and was sentenced. The Court of Appeal dismissed K.'s appeal against conviction and he appealed to the House of Lords.

Held, (1) that it was an established principle of English law that the test of admissibility was relevance; that relevant evidence, even if illegally obtained, was admissible; and that, therefore, the evidence of the tape recorded conversation was admissible.

(2) That in the circumstances, including the facts that the trespass and damage were slight and that the criminal conduct being investigated was of great gravity, albeit the evidence constituted a breach of Article 8 of the European Convention for the Protection of Human Rights and Fundamental Freedoms (1953), the invasion of privacy with the attendant trespass and damage was outweighed by the public interest in the detection of crime, and could not be regarded as having such an adverse effect on the fairness of the proceedings that the judge ought to have excluded the evidence of the conversation in the exercise of his discretion under section 78 of the Police and Criminal Evidence Act 1984.

Appeal dismissed.

NOTE

See also *R. v. Rasool* [1997] Crim.L.R. 448. In *Gillilan v. Miller*, 1997 G.W.D. 6–229, it was observed that mobile phones are something which are commonly used in relation to drug dealing.

(xvii) Television   **13.19**

1. R. v. Rhuddlan Justices *ex parte* HTV Ltd   **13.19.1**
[1986] Crim.L.R. 329

A camera crew employed by the applicants, HTV Ltd, filmed the arrest of a man called S. for drug offences. The film was to be shown as part of a television programme about drug trafficking at a time which closely approximated to the proceedings against S. before the justices. S. pleaded guilty at that hearing. S.'s solicitor, having heard of the applicant's intention to include the film in the programme, invited the justices to make an order under section 4(2) of the Contempt of Court Act 1981. The justices made the order. The applicants sought in the Divisional Court to have the order quashed on the ground that the jurisdiction of a court under section 4(2) of the 1981 Act was confined to the making of an order that publication of a report of proceedings in court (or any part thereof) be postponed for such period as the court thought necessary, and did not extend to the making of an order restraining publication of any matter other than a report of proceedings in court.

Held, that the justices had no jurisdiction to make an order under section 4(2). The words "legal proceedings held in public" meant proceedings which were held in court at a hearing of a charge of a person for a criminal offence. That applied to the provisions of both subsection (1) and (2) of section 4.

In a case where employees of television companies or journalists employed by newspapers sought to report by radio, television or newspaper, matter which might prove to be embarrassing and prejudicial to the forthcoming trial of a person who was, or might be, affected by the material which was published the proper remedy was to seek an injunction in the High Court so that that court could consider the provisions of sections 1 and 2 of the Act.

If the High Court concluded there was a danger of the strict liability rule being breached by a report it would no doubt grant an injunction. That was not the procedure followed in the present case and the justices' order would be quashed.

Appeal allowed.

NOTE
In Scotland the nobile officium also exists to be used where there is more than a minimal risk of prejudice at trial: see *Muir v. BBC*, 1997 S.L.T. 425.

13.19.2
2. R. v. Dye and Williamson
The Times, December 19, 1991

Although, at a proper time co-operation with television programme producers who were endeavouring to show the extent of drug trafficking might be appropriate, it must always be subservient to the overriding requirement to hold a fair trial.

WATKINS, L.J.: "Following an approach by a television company to the Customs and Excise, three witnesses for the Crown were interviewed and filmed as though they were giving evidence-in-chief at the trial.

It was almost like a dress rehearsal of their forthcoming appearances in the witness box. The perils which might result from such conduct were all too plain even where, as in the instant case, the film was not broadcast until the trial was over.

Leading counsel for the Crown was asked for his advice on the request for co-operation. He advised, wrongly the court felt bound to say, that it could properly be provided before the trial.

The court could not envisage any special circumstances which would allow of what happened here and prosecutors should be made acutely aware of the need to forbid it.

That unsatisfactory situation was exacerbated by the fact that counsel for the Crown did not inform defence counsel until after the trial was over that, pre-trial, those three important witnesses for the Crown had rehearsed their testimony before television cameras. That was a serious error.

If defence counsel had known of that at the trial they would have cross-examined those witnesses as to any differences in their filmed evidence and the evidence they gave at trial.

The court had examined those differences but were not persuaded that the defendants were placed at any material disadvantage by not having been made aware of them at the trial.

Although that amounted to a material irregularity it was nevertheless a classic case for the application of the proviso and the appeals were accordingly dismissed."

Appeals dismissed.

NOTE

It has been pointed out that the court considered that the making of the film *and* the failure to tell defence counsel about it constituted a material irregularity: [1992] Crim.L.R. 450. This may be contrasted with *Lilburn v. H.M. Advocate*, 1990 G.W.D. 19–1048 where it was held (not in a drugs case) that the appellant had not been prejudiced by the BBC having interviewed certain witnesses before his trial where the programme was not broadcast until afterwards and no reference to it was made during the trial. It is not apparent from that brief report that the Crown knew of the filmed interviews.

(xviii) Deportation   **13.20**

1. R. v. Secretary of State for the Home Department *ex parte* **13.20.1**
Alavi-Veighoe
[1990] C.O.D. 39

The applicant sought to challenge a decision of the Immigration Appeal Tribunal upholding a deportation order against him.

He was a citizen of Iran who arrived in the United Kingdom with his father in July 1984, having entry clearances issued in Vienna. Both were arrested when they were found to be carrying £600,000 worth of heroin and were convicted of being knowingly concerned in the fraudulent evasion of the prohibition on the importation of a controlled drug. The applicant was sentenced to six years' and his father to nine years' imprisonment. The trial judge did not make a recommendation for deportation. Subsequently, both applied for political asylum and those applications were refused. The Secretary of State then made deportation orders against them under section 3(5)(b) of the Immigration Act 1971 on the grounds that their deportation would be conducive to the public good. Their appeals under section 15 of the 1971 Act were heard by differently constituted Tribunals. The father's appeal was allowed but that of this applicant was dismissed. The father's claim to political asylum was upheld by the Tribunal.

The applicant submitted that he was subject to double jeopardy should he be returned to Iran, on the grounds that the death penalty was in force in Iran for drug traffickers and that he would be subject to prosecution for his religious as well as for his political beliefs since he had converted to Christianity.

He further submitted that the Tribunal had failed to take into account all the relevant compassionate circumstances of this case as required by paragraphs 154 and 159 of the Immigration Rules and the authority of *R. v. Immigration Appeal Tribunal, ex parte Bakhtaur Singh* (1986) Imm.A.R. 352.

Held, the Tribunal had not considered all the relevant factors in deciding the issue. In particular, it had not considered the implications of deportation to a country which imposed the death penalty for drug smuggling, which was capable of being a relevant matter in considering compassionate circumstances.

In addition, the cases of the father and the son were so similar that a fair distinction could not be drawn between their merits.

					Application granted.

13.20.2   2. R. v. Secretary of State for the Home Department *ex parte* Anderson
					[1991] C.O.D. 38

This was a renewed application for leave to apply for judicial review of a decision to the Immigration Appeal Tribunal dismissing an appeal against the Secretary of State's decision to make a deportation order against the applicant on the basis that his deportation would be conducive to the public interest.

The Parole Board had released the applicant on licence in respect of his fifth drug-related conviction. The prison governor, probation officer, the prison chaplain and the education officer had come to the conclusion that the appellant was a changed man who would no longer indulge in drug-related offences. The Tribunal, however, came to the conclusion: "... after having seen the appellant in the witness stand and looking at the evidence as a whole, that he is likely to continue to earn his living by supplying drugs to other persons ..."

The applicant argued that that decision was perverse; further that the fact that the Parole Board had released the applicant on licence was inconsistent with the Tribunal's decision that it was conducive to the public good that he should leave the country.

Held, (1) A court was not an appellate but a review body. There was nothing perverse in attaching importance to the way in which the appellant had given his evidence such that it overrode the weight attached to other matters.

(2) Although both the Tribunal and the Board were concerned in part with the extent to which the applicant was likely to re-offend, it was the duty of the Tribunal to decide on deportation. The Tribunal had taken into account the fact that the applicant had not been recommended for deportation but they had come to the conclusion on the evidence that it was conducive to the public good that he should be deported.

Application refused.

3. H.M. Advocate v. Riganti 13.20.3
1992 S.C.C.R. 891

Section 3(6) of the Immigration Act 1971 provides that where a person who is not patrial is convicted of an offence punishable with imprisonment he may be recommended by the court for deportation.

Article 48 of the Treaty Establishing the European Community, the Treaty of Rome, provides for freedom of movement for workers within the Community which, in terms of Article 49(3), entails the right to remain in any member state after having been employed there. Article 3 of EEC Directive 64/221 provides that measures taken by a member state on grounds of public security shall be based exclusively on the personal conduct of the individual concerned and that previous convictions shall not in themselves constitute grounds for taking such measures.

The accused, who was an Italian national, pleaded guilty to two charges of theft, one of which involved £5,000, and to charges of contravening the 1971 Act, including charges of possessing lysergide and amphetamine with intent to supply to others. He was sentenced to a total of 30 months' imprisonment and the Crown moved the court to make a recommendation for his deportation. He had no previous convictions and had been working in the United Kingdom from 1988 to 1991. He had been a drug addict since before he came to the United Kingdom but was taking steps to resolve his addiction.

Held, that a recommendation could be made in the case of a Community national only where his continued presence in the United Kingdom would be a genuine and sufficiently serious threat affecting one of the fundamental interests of society and that no such threat was manifest, nor did the circumstances demonstrate a propensity to commit acts which set a pattern of personal conduct which was likely to be repeated to the detriment of the community.

LORD CAMERON OF LOCHBROOM (at p. 892): "In considering the question arising from the notice which has been served upon the accused under section 6(2) of the Immigration Act 1971, as amended, I was referred to a number of cases, both in this jurisdiction and in England.

In the case of *Willms* v *Smith* [1982 S.L.T. 163] Lord Justice-Clerk Wheatley specifically accepted the views expressed in the two English cases cited there, *R.* v *Caird* [(1970) 54 Cr.App.R. 499] and *R.* v *Nazari* [(1980) 71 Cr.App.R. 87].

The question is whether the potential detriment to this country of the accused remaining here has been shown to be such as to justify the recommendation, as was stated in *R.* v *Caird*. I refer particularly to the passages which were cited from the earlier case of *Caird* in *R.* v *Nazari* at p. 1372.

In *Caird* the court, after making reference to the question of whether potential detriment has been shown to be such as to justify the recommendation, went on to say this: 'It desires to emphasise that the courts when considering a recommendation for deportation are normally concerned simply with the crime committed and the individual's past record and the question as to what is their effect on the question of potential detriment just mentioned.'

Furthermore, the court in *Nazari* went on to set out certain guidelines and to point out that one of the matters to which attention should be paid was the effect that an order recommending deportation will have upon others who are not before the court and who are innocent persons.

In this case, it is further to be observed that the accused is an Italian national, who came to this country in 1988 and was thereafter employed in the craft of screen printing until he was paid off in December 1991. He is a 'worker' within the meaning of Article 48 of the European Economic Community Treaty. Accordingly, he is entitled to have the protection from deportation afforded thereby, in the light of article 3 of the EEC Directive 64/221.

As was stated by the European Court of Justice in *R.* v *Bouchereau* [(1977) 66 Cr.App.R. 202]: such a recommendation will be justified only if the continued presence of the offender in the United Kingdom would be 'a genuine and sufficiently serious threat affecting one of the fundamental interests of society.'

I am doubtful whether this test is, in effect, any different from that which has been expressed in cases such as *Willms* v *Smith* or the two English cases to which I have already made reference or indeed in the other Scottish cases to which I was referred.

I am in no doubt that the offences committed in this case, particularly those in charge (1) — theft by housebreaking — and in charges (3) and (5) — contraventions of section 5(3) of the Misuse of Drugs Act 1971 — are serious offences.

However, looking at the circumstances — that this accused had employment until immediately before the first offence, notwithstanding information from his counsel that he has been a drug addict since before his coming to the U.K.; that while divorce proceedings were initiated by his wife upon his remand in custody, there has since been a form of reconciliation to the extent that she has visited him in prison while on remand and with their daughter is presently holidaying with his mother in Italy; ... that the accused has indicated an intention to resolve his drug addiction and has taken some steps to that end; and, finally, that he has no previous convictions — I am not satisfied that there is manifest a genuine and sufficiently serious threat affecting one of the fundamental interests of society or, to adapt words used in *Caldewei* v *Jessop* [1991 S.C.C.R. 323], that the whole circumstances demonstrate a propensity to commit acts which set a pattern of personal conduct which is likely to be repeated in the future to the detriment of the community.

In these circumstances, therefore, I shall not make the recommendation which was sought."

Motion refused.

4. R. v. Frank
[1992] Crim.L.R. 378

13.20.4

F. pleaded guilty to being concerned in the fraudulent evasion of the prohibition on the importation of a controlled drug. He was stopped on arriving in England by car ferry. His car was found to contain 19.93 kilogrammes of cannabis, with a street value of £65,000. The sentence under appeal was two years and nine months' imprisonment and a recommendation for deportment.

Held, given *R. v. Aramah* (1992) 4 Cr.App.R. (S.) 407, a sentence of two years would be substituted. The recommendation for deportation had apparently been added as a last-minute afterthought, without any proper inquiry.

The point about deportation had been considered in *R. v. Bouchereau* (1977) 66 Cr.App.R. 202 and in *R. v. Nazari* (1980) 2 Cr.App.R. (S.) 84 and other cases. Both the European Directive and the principles of natural justice required that there should be a full inquiry before a recommendation is made, and reasons should be given for the recommendation. The late addition of that recommendation did not in any way comply with the law and the recommendation would be quashed.

Appeal allowed.

13.20.5 **5. R. v. Secretary of State for the Home Department *ex parte* Marchon**
The Times, February 23, 1993

M., a consultant psychiatrist, was a national of India and Portugal, who worked in England in the national health service. In April 1986 he was convicted of conspiracy to evade the restriction on the importation of a Class A drug, namely diamorphine with a street value of £450,000. His sentence was varied on appeal to 11 years' imprisonment.

Thereafter, the Home Secretary made an order to deport M. on the ground that it would be conducive to the public good to do so. M. applied for judicial review of that decision, but his application was dismissed by a single judge. He then appealed against that decision to the Court of Appeal.

Held, that the Secretary of State for the Home Department was entitled to order the deportation of a person convicted of a serious drug trafficking offence even though he was an E.C. national and had no propensity to commit further offences.

DILLON, L.J.: "The court had to consider the seriousness of the offence and whether that itself merited deportation. The offence in itself was an affront to the requirements of public policy and involved a disregard of the basic fundamental tenets of society."

Appeal dismissed.

13.21 *(xix) Culpable homicide and manslaughter*

13.21.1 **1. Lord Advocate's Reference No. 1 of 1994**
1995 S.L.T. 248

An accused person was charged on indictment with culpable homicide. The evidence disclosed that the accused supplied amphetamine to the deceased at her request in a potentially lethal quantity and that the deceased divided it and selected the dose which she ingested, and that she died as result of consuming the drug. At the close of the Crown case the trial judge held that there was no case for the accused to answer as the chain of causation had been broken by the deceased's actions in the absence of the accused's having mitigated, suggested or encouraged the ingestion of the drug.

The accused was acquitted by the trial judge and the Lord Advocate presented a petition to the High Court in terms of section 263A(1) of the Criminal Procedure (Scotland) Act 1975 to obtain the court's opinion as to whether, on the basis of the evidence that the accused supplied the drug to the deceased for the purpose of abuse, that this purpose was achieved by the deceased's ingesting the drug and that the ingestion caused the deceased's death, the trial judge was entitled to acquit the accused on the basis that it was not open to the jury to conclude that the accused caused the deceased's death.

Held, (1) that the causal link was not broken merely because a voluntary act on the part of the recipient was required in order to produce the injurious consequences; (2) that the accused's conduct was the equivalent of culpable and reckless conduct and the trial judge was accordingly wrong to acquit the accused insofar as the charge contained an allegation of culpable homicide.

Opinion stated.

2. R. v. Clarke and Purvis
(1992) 13 Cr.App.R. (S.) 552

13.21.2

The appellant Clarke pleaded guilty to manslaughter and to supplying a Class A drug, and to possessing a Class A drug. The appellants and the deceased were habitual users of heroin. The appellants had obtained a quantity of heroin, and the appellant Clarke injected the deceased with heroin at his request. The deceased died from heroin poisoning, aggravated by alcohol. The scientific evidence showed that the quantity of heroin which the deceased had taken was within the range of herbal doses, but at the lower end of the range. C. was sentenced to five years' imprisonment for manslaughter, with three years concurrent for supplying a Class A drug.

Held, (considering *R. v. Cato* (1976) 62 Cr.App.R. 41 and *R. v. Dalby* (1982) 74 Cr.App.R. 348) dabbling in the injection of heroin was dabbling in potential death, but insufficient credit had been given for the plea of guilty; the sentence would be reduced to three and a half years.

Appeal allowed.

3. R. v. Wiggins
(1994) 15 Cr.App.R. (S.) 558

13.21.3

W. pleaded guilty to possession of LSD with intent to supply, supplying LSD, and possessing and supplying amphetamine. W. obtained a small supply of LSD and amphetamine and sold them to teenagers at a village hall. A girl aged 18 died of LSD poisoning after using a tab of LSD supplied by W. He was sentenced to a total of three years' detention in a young offenders institution with a confiscation order under the Drug Trafficking Offences Act 1986 in the amount of £70.

Held, (considering *R. v. Clarke and Purvis, supra*), the sentence was excessive. The sentence would be reduced to two and a half years' detention in a young offenders institution.

Appeal allowed.

NOTE

In England, imprisonment has been upheld for causing a noxious thing to be administered or taken with intent when controlled drugs are involved but death has not ensued: see *R. v. Hogan* (1995) 15 Cr.App.R. (S.) 834.

In Scotland it has been held that it is not proper to have regard to a death where there has been no evidence that it was connected with the actings of the accused or appellant: *Main v. H.M. Advocate*, 1987 G.W.D. 26–991.

INDEX

penalties 1.2.25, 1.2.50, 1.7.6
possession of articles for production and administration of drugs 1.2.9A
production and supply 1.2.4
supply of syringes 1.2.9A
Drugs *see* **controlled drugs; drug offences**
Duress, sentencing 13.13.4

Ecstasy
composition 12.8.1
concern in supply 4.4.25
evidence of conspicuous wealth
importation 13.12.25
possession with intent to supply 13.12.31
offers to supply 4.4.10
sentencing
concern in supply 4.6.32
conspiracy to produce 3.4.9
importation 2.5.40–43
possession 5.4.20–21
possession with intent to supply 5.4.55–66
Electronic notepads, whether documents 9.4.12
Electronic surveillance, admissibility of evidence 13.18.5
Entrapment 2.5.33, 4.4.7, 13.7.1–5
test of fairness 13.7.2
Entry powers 1.2.23, 9.3.6
forced entry without request 9.3.10
European Convention on Human rights
electronic surveillance 13.18.5
telephone tapping 13.18.1
Evidence *see also* **admissibility of evidence; analysts' certificates; entry; expert evidence; forensic reports; search powers**
certificates issued by foreign jurisdictions 1.2.36
conspicuous wealth
importation 13.12.25
possession with intent to supply amphetamines 13.12.31
possession with intent to supply cannabis 13.12.22, 13.12.26–27
possession with intent to supply cocaine 13.12.21, 13.12.23, 13.12.28–29
possession with intent to supply ecstasy 13.12.31
possession with intent to supply heroin 13.12.24, 13.12.32
controlled drugs and medicinal products 1.9.1

corroboration
forensic reports 13.12.15, 13.12.19
statutory defences 10.3.8
knowledge
accused not testifying about lack of knowledge 13.12.3
car passengers 2.3.15
nature of substances 13.11.1, 13.12.2, 13.12.9
challenges 13.12.10
objections, time limits 13.12.1
observation posts, addresses 13.16.1–4
parole evidence, intimation 13.12.2
seizure, powers 1.2.23
Exempted drugs 1.3.6, 5.3.24
burden of proof 5.3.26
Expenses
Secretary of State 1.2.35
tribunals 1.2.46
Expert evidence
drug enforcement officers, on importation methods 13.6.4
policemen
on the effect of drugs 13.6.1
on LSD dosage 13.6.2
on quantities for supply 13.6.3, 13.6.5
Exportation
antiques 2.4.1
meaning of 'concerned in' 2.4.1
penalties 1.7.4
sentencing 2.6.2
statutory offences 1.2.3, 1.7.4
time 1.7.2
Extradition *see* **deportation**

False information 1.2.18
Fire precautions, occupiers 7.3.4
Forensic reports *see also* **analysts' certificates**
corroboration 13.12.19
form 13.12.14–15
labelling of items 13.12.17–18
objections 13.12.1
parole evidence 13.12.2, 13.12.15
Forfeiture 1.2.27, 11.2, 11.3.1–14
conspiracy offences 3.3.4
foreign bank accounts 11.3.5
heritable property 11.3.7
money 11.3.1, 11.3.3, 11.3.6, 11.3.8–11
motorcars 11.3.12–14
ownership 11.3.12–13
timing of orders 11.3.4
Forgery, penalties 1.7.3